Public
Financial
Management

PUBLIC ADMINISTRATION AND PUBLIC POLICY

A Comprehensive Publication Program

Executive Editor

JACK RABIN
Professor of Public Administration and Public Policy
School of Public Affairs
The Capital College
The Pennsylvania State University—Harrisburg
Middletown, Pennsylvania

Assistant to the Executive Editor
T. Aaron Wachhaus, Jr.

Available Electronically

Public
Financial
Management

edited by
Howard A. Frank
Florida International University
Miami, Florida

Taylor & Francis
Taylor & Francis Group
Boca Raton London New York

A CRC title, part of the Taylor & Francis imprint, a member of the
Taylor & Francis Group, the academic division of T&F Informa plc.

Published in 2006 by
CRC Press
Taylor & Francis Group
6000 Broken Sound Parkway NW, Suite 300
Boca Raton, FL 33487-2742

Library of Congress Cataloging-in-Publication Data

Catalog record is available from the Library of Congress

Taylor & Francis Group
is the Academic Division of Informa plc.

Visit the Taylor & Francis Web site at
http://www.taylorandfrancis.com

and the CRC Press Web site at
http://www.crcpress.com

Dedication

To Lee Anne and Henry; Jane, Eugene, Julia, Janelle, and Gabrielle.

To Gloria A. Grizzle and William Earle Klay

Foreword

Howard Frank, in *Public Financial Management*, brings to the academic and practice communities a collection of chapters written by both some of the most senior scholars in public financial management but also some of the more accomplished newcomers to the field. This text not only explores broad trends about the context of public financial management but it probes the more technical aspects of the sub-discipline like debt management, financial condition analysis, assessment of public pensions, and the use of performance management.

There are two underlying themes in this volume. The first is that "Results Oriented Management" has become the most widely used paradigm in public administration and public management. In addition to Section V, which includes six separate chapters on performance budgeting, measurement, and management, many of the other articles in the volume also reinforce the need for public organizations to include a "Results Oriented" philosophy in their planning, decision making, and management. Although "Results Oriented Management" has been around for decades, the paradigm really became the dominant one with the publication of David Osborne and Ted Gaebler's book, *Reinventing Government* in 1992. Almost all of the authors recognize this paradigm shift and include the core values of this orientation in their articles. This integration of core values into public financial management has made the field more coherent and oriented toward "best practice."

The second theme in the collection is the necessity and importance of including quantitative analysis as an integral part of public financial management. Whether looking at future ways of financing public services, selecting and managing a public pension system, or working on debt management, quantitative analysis is also at the core of public financial management. Authors in this volume illustrate both the importance but also the utility of including comparative and historical quantitative analysis of financial conditions and practices in their planning and decision making.

Today there are over 300 graduate programs in Public Administration, Public Management, and Policy Analysis. Most programs of any size include a faculty person with expertise in public financial management and almost all of these programs also include a course in public budgeting or public finance. That means that there will be a good audience for this volume that includes the faculty teaching core graduate courses in public budgeting and public finance. Also, junior and senior level courses in public administration, political science, economics, and management at the undergraduate level will find this volume a good supplement to a standard text. Finally, practitioners in the field, especially at the state and local level, will find the topics in this volume relevant to their jobs and illustrative of the critical trends taking place around the country and world at large. It is a "must" read for people trying to keep up with the public financial management field.

Milan J. Dluhy, Ph.D.
Department of Political Science
University of North Carolina
Wilmington, N.C.

Preface

Those familiar with texts in the public budgeting realm will note that they generally come in two "flavors:" comprehensive texts that cover a wide gamut of topics, albeit not with much depth, or anthologies that seem to cover a wide variety of topics but with differing depth or intellectual coherence. This work occupies an intellectual middle ground. Its contents do not cover all that comes under the realm of public financial management, but its five major themes, context, public finance, retirement systems, performance measurement and budgeting, and international perspectives, cover pillars of this emerging sub-discipline within public administration. In my judgment, the sacrifice in comprehensiveness is more than made up for by depth of treatment within critical areas.

Over the past two decades, public budgeting and financial management has evolved and matured. There are three major journals dedicated to the field. Practitioners and academics alike attend the Association for Budgeting and Financial Management's annual conference. Most public administration programs have at least one core course and several electives in financial management. The material in this text reflects the emergence of critical intellectual boundaries within that sub-discipline.

The audience of this text is two-fold. Practitioners seeking "news they can use" in their day-to-day operations would enjoy this work. Upper-division undergraduates or graduates in public administration or public management programs would value this text as a grounding for their own knowledge base development as future professionals or researchers. In an applied discipline such as public administration, this duality is to all parties' benefit, as practitioners turn to academics for guidance in the increasingly fluid environments in which they operate, and academics seek grounding for the validity of their findings.

Some might ask if the text can be read chapter-by-chapter, or would reading from cover-to-cover be preferred? While each chapter stands on its own merits, there is a clear intellectual funnel that emerges when digested from front to back: the increasingly tight fiscal environment in which all governments operate is forcing the recasting of financial management within the context of "reengineered" government. Governments around the world are seeking linkages between resource allocation and "value added" for their citizens and other stakeholders. This trend is driving innovations in operations as well as increased transparency in reporting, not only in the Western democracies, but in emerging states as well. A global economy puts pressures on all governments to manage scarce resources wisely, across all facets of financial management.

I hope that readers enjoy this volume. The contributors have done a wonderful job distilling a vast body of knowledge into eminently readable and relevant chapters. My intent is that you will come away from the book with at least one kernel of thought that can be put to use in practice or be further investigated in the academic setting. If each reader can make that claim, the text will have achieved its end.

Acknowledgments

To outsiders, production of a book is the equivalent of the loneliness of the long distance runner. Part of that image is true but the reality of authorship, particularly in an edited volume such as this, is very much one of a team sport.

My first acknowledgment is to Dr. Jack Rabin, who graciously asked me to take on editorial responsibility for this volume. At first I was reluctant to accept this task. Now that it is complete I can appreciate two things: (a) the final product is one of value to academics and practitioners alike; and (b) editing the work has given me the opportunity to associate with a wonderful set of authors, all of whom are consummate professionals.

My academic family — the Public Administration Program faculty at Florida International University — have been supportive and warm colleagues for nearly two decades. James Carroll, Keith Revell, Fred Becker, Valerie Patterson, Harvey Averch, and Allan Rosenbaum in particular have provided encouragement to maintain a scholarly oeuvre despite heavy administrative and community outreach responsibilities. Their friendship is deeply appreciated.

Dean Ray Thomlison and Executive Dean Ronald Berkman have been similarly supportive and encouraging throughout the years, gently or not-so-gently nudging me to remain a productive scholar. Associate Director Lourdes Rassi has also played a critical role in enabling me to juggle research, teaching, university service, and public outreach.

The Frank Family may reside 1200 miles from South Florida, but its love and moral support are always close by. For this I am most grateful. The same holds for my neighbors and closest friends, Ana Carazo and Guillermo Chaverri, who help keep a smile on my face.

Ms. Claire Miller, Mr. Richard O'Hanley and Ms. Rachael Panthier of Taylor and Francis deserve special thanks for helping me over the late-stage humps associated with publication. They and their staff are remarkable professionals. Ms. Anjana Narayanan and her colleagues at Keyword Group also deserve recognition for producing the text.

Jayesh D'Souza, a doctoral candidate in the Public Administration Program at Florida International University and contributor to this text, assisted with the initial contacting of fellow contributors. He strongly encouraged me to take on the editorial responsibilities after Dr. Rabin's offer. I thank him for his constructive input.

My last and most important acknowledgment is to the contributors. As editor I am an impresario. Ultimately they are the performers. Their expertise, craft, and labor are the backbone of this work. My hat is off to them.

I apologize for any omission of gratitude. Likewise, I accept any responsibility for errors or omissions.

Contributors

William G. Albrecht
William G. Albrecht is Assistant Professor of Political Science and Public Administration at the University of North Carolina at Pembroke. Dr. Albrecht received his B.S. degree in business administration from Ferrum College, M.B.A. degree from Western Carolina University, and his Ph.D. in public policy with a concentration in public finance from the Nelson Mandela School of Public Policy and Urban Affairs at Southern University. He teaches in the areas of public policy, public budgeting and financial management, managerial economics, and municipal government administration. Dr. Albrecht's research has focused on the investment practices of state and local government pension funds.

Liucija Birskyte
Liucija Birskyte is a Ph.D. student at the School of Public and Environmental Affairs, Indiana University, Bloomington. Her research interests include tax compliance, international tax competition and harmonization, tax policy and administration in countries with transitional economies.

Deborah A. Carroll
Deborah A. Carroll is an Assistant Professor in the Department of Political Science at the University of Tennessee-Knoxville. She received her Ph.D. in 2004 from the University of Wisconsin-Milwaukee. Her research interests focus on public financial management and policy issues pertaining to state

and local governments, with an emphasis on taxation, revenue diversification and urban economic development.

Wes Clarke

Dr. Wes Clarke is Director of Research and Policy Analysis at the Carl Vinson Institute of Government at the University of Georgia. In that capacity he directs the work of faculty engaged in policy research, program evaluation, opinion polling, and other survey research. Dr. Clarke's own research interests include government budget processes and capital investment and finance. Prior to joining the Vinson Institute, Dr. Clarke spent nine years on the faculty at the University of North Texas, where he taught graduate courses in budgeting, capital planning, and research methods. While at North Texas, he wrote the study guides and examinations for the certification program of the Government Finance Officers Association of Texas. Dr. Clarke also spent twelve years in private sector management with responsibilities for expense planning and control, and receivables management.

Paul Coates

Paul Coates is Associate Professor of the Public Administration and Policy Program in the Political Science department, Iowa State University, and the Director of the Office of State and Local Government Extension Programs. He has worked with state and local officials, citizen groups, and community organizations in Iowa for more than 20 years and was one of the co-principal investigators of the Iowa "citizen-initiated performance assessment project."

Jerrell D. Coggburn

Jerrell D. Coggburn is Associate Professor and Chair in the Department of Public Administration at the University of Texas at San Antonio. He is a past recipient (1997) of the William and Frederick Mosher Award for the best *Public Administration Review* article written by an academician. His research has appeared in *Public Administration Review, Journal of Public Administration Research and Theory, Public Performance and Management Review, Review of Public Personnel Administration, International Journal of Public Administration, Public Administration Quarterly,* and other scholarly outlets. He received the B.A. degree in political science from Oklahoma State University and the M.P.A. and Ph.D. degrees from the University of South Carolina.

Esteban G. Dalehite

Esteban G. Dalehite is Assistant Professor at Florida International University. His Ph.D. is from Indiana University-Bloomington. Dr. Dalehite's research interests include state and local public finance, school finance, economic development incentives, the role of courts in tax policy, and tax policy in developing countries.

Dwight V. Denison

Dwight V. Denison, Ph.D., recently joined the Martin School of Public Policy and Administration at the University of Kentucky as Associate Professor of Public and Nonprofit Finance. Previously, he was Associate Professor at the Wagner Graduate School of Public Service at New York University. His research interests include tax-exempt bond markets, debt management, and tax administration.

Milan J. Dluhy

Milan J. Dluhy is Professor of Public Administration at the University of North Carolina-Wilmington. He teaches in the M.P.A. Program. He formerly held faculty and administrative positions at Florida International University, American University, and the University of Michigan. He is the author or co-author of eight books and over 60 professional publications. His fields of expertise and interest are results-oriented management, policy analysis, program evaluation, and metropolitan administration governance and planning. Dr. Dluhy received his Master's degree in Government Administration from Southern Illinois University and his Ph.D. in Political Science from the University of Michigan.

Jayesh D'Souza

Jayesh D'Souza is a Research Associate and Doctoral Candidate at Florida International University's Public Administration Program. His research interests are in public finance, public budgeting, and performance measurement. Mr. D'Souza has published in the *International Journal of Public Administration* and has several technical and policy studies to his credit. Prior to commencing his doctoral studies, Mr. D'Souza was a policy analyst with the Government of Ontario with responsibilities in energy, science, and technology.

Howard A. Frank

Dr. Howard A. Frank is Associate Professor of Public Administration and Coordinator of the Doctoral Program. He has published in the areas of public financial management and performance measurement. Professor Frank has held a number of administrative positions at the University and also serves as Research Fellow at FIU's Metropolitan Center in downtown Miami. Throughout his career, Dr. Frank has maintained an active outreach to the world of practice. Dr. Frank earned his M.P.A. from the University of Delaware, and his Ph.D. in Public Administration from the Florida State University. Prior to his academic career, Professor Frank served with the U.S. Department of Housing and Urban Development, the Office of the Comptroller of the Currency, and the Broward County Office of Planning.

J. Edward Gibson

Ed Gibson is a Management Consultant for a federal government contractor, and is a doctoral candidate in Public Administration at Virginia Tech. While consulting for the U.S. Courts and other federal agencies, he has analyzed budgeting and financial management functions, recommended approaches for improving capital asset management, and conducted numerous benefit-cost analyses and similar studies. His research interest is application of qualitative analytic methods to public organizations to balance recent reliance on methods and metrics originated in the private sector. He is the author of articles published in the *International Journal of Public Administration* and *Administration & Society.*

Merl Hackbart

Merl Hackbart, Ph.D., is Professor of Finance and Public Administration at the University of Kentucky. He has previously served as State Budget Director for Kentucky, as a Senior Policy Advisor to the Governor of Kentucky and on the Kentucky Council on Postsecondary Education. He currently serves on the Kentucky Consensus Revenue Forecasting Group, is a member of a GAO Intergovernmental Issues Panel and is a Senior Fellow at the Council of State Governments. His research has focused on state financial management issues, including state budgeting, debt management, transportation finance and state investment policies.

Alfred Ho

Alfred Ho is an Associate Professor at the School of Public and Environmental Affairs, Indiana University-Purdue University at Indianapolis. His research focuses on state and local finance, performance measurement, and e-government development. In 2001–04 he was the co-principal investigator of the Iowa "citizen-initiated performance assessment" project, funded by the Alfred P. Sloan Foundation. Dr. Ho's publications have appeared in the *American Review of Public Administration, the International Journal of Public Administration, the Journal of Public Administration Research and Theory, Public Administration Quarterly, Public Administration Review, Public Performance and Management Review,* and *State and Local Government Review,* among others.

Dr. Yilin Hou

Dr. Yilin Hou is on the faculty of the University of Georgia. He holds an M.A. and Ph.D. in Public Administration from the Maxwell School at Syracuse

University. His current research focuses on counter-cyclical fiscal policy and budgeting reforms.

Aman Khan

Aman Khan is Associate Professor of Political Science and Public Administration at Texas Tech University, where he teaches public budgeting, financial management, and quantitative methods. Trained as an economist and planner, he has an M.A. in economics, an M.Sc. in urban and regional planning, and Ph.D. in public administration. He has previously served as Director of the Graduate Program in Public Administration at Texas Tech and currently serves on the editorial board of several professional public administration journals. Dr. Khan has authored and coauthored several books and contributed works to various edited collections and professional journals.

Steven G. Koven

Steven G. Koven is Professor of Urban and Public Affairs and Director of the Master of Public Administration Program at the University of Louisville. He received degrees from the City College of New York (BBA), Baruch College (MBA) and University of Florida (Ph.D.). Since 1982 he has taught in urban studies, public administration, and political science programs at the University of Mississippi, Troy State University, Iowa State University, and the University of Akron. His research interests are in public finance, American culture, and American economic development.

The Reverend Dr. Thomas D. Lynch

The Reverend Dr. Thomas D. Lynch is Professor of Public Administration at Louisiana State University. He is probably best known for *Public Budgeting in America*, which has been a leading textbook for over 30 years. In 1992–93 he served as President of the American Society for Public Administration. He has written or edited over 10 books and 75 refereed articles and book chapters in his career.

Yun Ma

Yun Ma earned his Ph.D. in Public Administration at the University of Nebraska-Omaha in 2002. Dr. Ma is an Associate Professor at the College of Politics and Public Affairs at Zhongshan University (People's Republic of China), where he also serves as assistant dean of the college and vice director of the Institute of Public Administration Research. His teaching and research interests are in public budgeting and public management. He has published two book chapters with Dr. John Bartle, applying transaction cost theory to public budgeting and financial management. He has also published in *Administrative Theory and Praxis* and the *Journal of Public*

Budgeting, Accounting & Financial Management. Dr. Ma has also published in China, including articles in *Economic Studies*.

Susan A. MacManus

Dr. Susan A. MacManus is the Distinguished University Professor of Public Administration and Political Science in the Department of Government and International Affairs at the University of South Florida, Tampa. She has served as a member of the Governor's Council of Economic Advisors under two Florida governors. She has published numerous articles on public finance in the *Public Administration Review, Public Budgeting & Finance, Government Finance Review, Public Budgeting, Accounting, and Financial Management, Journal of Politics*, and many others.

Justin Marlowe

Justin Marlowe, Ph.D., is Assistant Professor in the Department of Public Administration at the University of Kansas. His research and teaching interests include public financial management, governmental accounting and auditing, municipal management, and research methods.

J. Scott McDonald

J. Scott McDonald, Ph.D., is Professor of Political Science at Valdosta State University, where he teaches budgeting and finance, economic development, and innovation in the Public Administration Program.

Dean Michael Mead

Dean Mead is Project Manager at the Governmental Accounting Standards Board. He is the author of the GASB's seven-volume User Guide Series — non-technical, plain-language introductions to government financial statements, written specifically for non-accountants. He has also authored the plain-language supplements to the GASB's exposure drafts on note disclosures and other post-employment benefits. In addition to coordinating the GASB's outreach efforts to financial statement users, he has led the efforts on net asset reporting and economic condition reporting. Prior to joining GASB, Mr. Mead was the Deputy Research Director at the Citizens Budget Commission in New York City, where he is currently completing his doctorate in Public Administration at New York University.

John L. Mikesell

John L. Mikesell, Ph.D., is Professor of Public Finance and Policy Analysis and Director of the Master of Public Affairs Program at the School of Public and Environmental Affairs at Indiana University. His research in property and sales taxation has appeared in such journals as *National Tax Journal, State and Local Government Review, Southern Economic Journal*, and

Land Economics. He has worked with the U.S. Agency for International Development, the World Bank, and in reform projects in several countries of the former Soviet Union.

Patrick R. Mullen

Patrick R. Mullen is a senior analyst with the U.S. General Accounting Office in Washington, DC., and a doctoral candidate (ABD) in the public administration and policy program at Virginia Polytechnic Institute and State University. He is President of the American Association for Budget and Program Analysis; Secretary of the Board of Directors of Public Financial Publications, Inc., which oversees publication of the journal *Public Budgeting and Finance*; a Certified Government Financial Manager; and a lifetime member of the American Society for Public Administration.

Meili Niu

Meilu Niu is earning her Ph.D. in Public Administration at the University of Nebraska at Omaha. She earned her Master's degree in Economics from Dongbei University of Finance and Economics in China. In addition to her doctoral studies, Ms. Niu has maintained her employment with the Research Institute of Dalian Municipal Public Finance Bureau (P.R. China). Her research is focused on budgetary reform, comparative budgeting, intergovernmental fiscal relations, financial management, and transportation finance.

A. Premchand

A. Premchand, a retired Assistant Director of the Fiscal Affairs Department, International Monetary Fund, is the author/editor of a dozen books, 30 book chapters and 70 papers. Two books, *On the Fringes of Government; A Personal Journey* (UBS Publishers) and *Controlling Government Spending; The Ethos, Ethics, and Economics Of Expenditure Management* (Oxford University Press) were published in early 2005.

Christopher G. Reddick

Christopher G. Reddick is an Assistant Professor of Public Administration at the University of Texas at San Antonio. Dr. Reddick's research interests are in e-government, public budgeting, and employee benefits. Some of his publications can be found in *Public Budgeting & Finance, Government Information Quarterly*, and the *e-Service Journal.*

Alejandro Rodriguez

Alejandro Rodriguez is an Assistant Professor with the School of Urban and Public Affairs at the University of Texas, Arlington. He worked in local governments in New York and Florida for 14 years before completing his doctorate at Florida International University in 1999. His teaching and research interests are public budgeting, government reform, and public administration theory. His work can be found in *Publius: The Journal of Federalism, The International Journal of Public Administration,* and *Public Works Management & Policy.*

Lee Schiffel

Lee Schiffel is Assistant Professor of Accounting at the Jones School of Business at the State University of New York-Genesco. She earned both a B.S. (1992) and an M.Pr.A. (1993) from the University of Utah, and a Ph.D. (2003) from the University of Missouri. Her research interests are information systems and performance measures in government, education, and healthcare. She is a Certified Government Financial Manager (CGFM) and is serving as a reviewer for the AGA's Certificate of Excellence in SEA program. She has experience in school district business services and in internal auditing for the state of Utah.

Benjamin J. Sharbel

Benjamin J. Sharbel received his Master of Public Administration degree in 2005 from the University of Tennessee, Knoxville. He currently works as Project Analyst for the Department of Community Services in the Office of Knox County Mayor.

Ken Smith

Ken Smith is Assistant Professor of Accounting and Information Systems at the Atkinson Graduate School of Management at Willamette University. He earned a B.A. degree (1988) from Anderson University, M.B.A. (1992) from Ball State University and a Ph.D. (2001) from the University of Missouri. His current research interests are performance measurement, benchmarking, and external performance reporting by governments and media. He is a Certified Public Accountant (CPA) and has audited and consulted with government and nonprofit organizations. Dr. Smith has published in *Accounting Horizons, Government Finance Review, Journal of Government Financial Management,* and *International Public Management Journal.*

Stuart C. Strother

Stuart C. Strother, Ph.D., lives in southern California, where he is an Associate Professor in the School of Business and Management at Azusa Pacific University. His research interests include telecommunications policy, economic development, and the emerging market of China.

Contents

Chapter 1

Introduction

HOWARD A. FRANK, Ph.D.
Public Administration Program, Florida International University

1.1 The Lay of the Land

In 1989's inaugural issue of *Public Budgeting and Financial Management*, Jack Rabin challenged us to define the boundaries of the emerging sub-discipline of public budgeting within the broader context of its parent discipline, public administration. This book is written with that challenge in mind. Nearly two decades have passed since the challenge was issued. The reader may ask: have we established the boundaries? This text provides a partial answer. Its content provides an overview and exploration of material that anchors the emerging sub-discipline. The volume's audience is broad-gauged — academics and students seeking foundations for learning and research, and practitioners seeking guidance for informing their critical decisions in managing public finance. Both newcomers to study of the field and those with a deeper knowledge base will find the material informative and stimulating.

In order to establish boundaries and facilitate learning, I have divided this book into six sections:

Section I: The Context of Public Financial Management: These five chapters are a foundation for what follows, with emphasis on historical and financial trends that drive managerial behavior.

Section II: Public Finance: These chapters constitute an overview of critical components of the revenue structure in America, with emphasis on critical issues such as the impact of the internet and nature of tax compliance in a world economy.

Section III: Debt, Working Balances, and Financial Condition Analysis: These five chapters address the critical decisions attendant to maintaining the infrastructure, assurance of sufficient liquidity to maintain operations, and overarching — and increasingly important — the use of ratio analysis to assess the fiscal health of a jurisdiction.

Section IV: Public Pensions: The two chapters in this section cover the basics of pension management, such as defined benefit vs. defined contribution plans, the composition of pension boards, the current status of pension benefits, and the importance of performance benchmarking of investment returns. The chapters also explore the impact of board size and composition on investment strategy and returns.

Section V: Performance Budgeting and Management: These six chapters address what are arguably the most important subjects facing public financial managers in the new millennium — utilizing and presenting performance information that informs allocation of scarce resources while securing public support for collective provision. The five chapters in this section approach the subject from both the strategic and tactical perspectives, showing how implementation of "results-oriented" budget formats comprises technical, administrative, and political aspects that require simultaneous consideration.

Section VI: International Perspectives: The two chapters in the valedictory section, "International Perspectives," examine public financial management through a transnational perspective. These chapters illustrate the permeability of national boundaries when it comes to principles of financial management. They also demonstrate how the United States is both an importer and exporter of expertise and approaches to financial management. Moreover, these chapters serve as an excellent summary by illustrating the universal themes that impact public financial management in all countries.

1.2 The Context of Public Financial Management

Those of us with graying temples may recall that 1974 was the year of Richard Nixon's impeachment and a recession. But, as A. Premchand reminds us in "Public Expenditure Management: Selected Themes and Issues," it was also the year in which the Budget Reform Act was passed in an effort to check ever-increasing dominance of the executive in American budgeting. That watershed also symbolized Congressional recognition that budgetary restraint was going to be a new rule of its operations.

Premchand's magisterial overview of budgeting suggests that all countries, developed and developing, democratic and authoritarian, have come to grips with a constant struggle to face staggering demands for services, while facing equally severe fiscal constraint. This era of constraint has brought with it increased use of third-party governance, performance measurement, private sector accounting models, and other administrative advances in financial management. Nonetheless, as Premchand makes clear, there is no silver bullet, and all nations and sub-national governments struggle to provide effective public services while living within serious budget constraints.

When most of us think of public budgeting and financial management, media images of recent program expansions or terminations come to mind. At first blush, we view budgeting in the present tense. Take a breath and reflect on Athens and the Parthenon, or Philadelphia and Independence Mall, or New York City and Central Park. Instantly you come to recognize that decisions regarding physical plant impact a community for years, decades, and yes — possibly even millennia.

This is one of Wes Clarke's central contentions in "Capital Budgeting and Planning" in which he frames a central question facing public financial managers: Will they bequeath an infrastructure to future generations that is as good as the one they inherited from their forebears? Assessing this condition, and making evaluative decisions regarding capital investment, remain core financial management tasks that must be integrated into discussions of the operating budgets that seem to capture media and public attention.

Anyone involved with public financial management is directly or indirectly an economic development official. Defining economic development may not be easy, but any generally accepted notion connotes or denotes activities intended to bring increased jobs and higher wages to a particular jurisdiction.

J. Scott McDonald's "Financial Management of Economic Development" describes the interplay of the competitive federal model the Founders established over two centuries ago and contemporary financial management. What started with "smokestack" chasing during the Depression has evolved into a profession in both the public and nonprofit sectors, whose members design, implement, and monitor an often bewildering array of incentives designed to attract and retain jobs in their respective communities and states.

Ultimately, the effectiveness of these incentives is a source of concern to financial management professionals and elected officials, who must balance tax levels and quality of community life in an increasingly competitive world economy. Thus, economic development is an integral part of contemporary financial management, and McDonald's chapter provides an important intellectual overview of best practice in that arena.

Effective public financial management entails short- and long-term considerations. Over the short-term, public finance officials must balance budgets, frequently against the backdrop of rapidly changing economic conditions. In many jurisdictions, simply enacting the annual budget is a Herculean task, melding organizational savvy and political consensus building. Nonetheless, public budgeting is also a planning tool. Operating and capital budgets have long-term impacts on their respective jurisdictions, and effective budgeting must be multi-year in perspective.

As Yilin Hou and Yun Ma note in "Annual Budgeting and Long-Range Planning: Is There a Fit? — Lessons from Three Case Studies," the marriage of short- and long-range perspectives in budgeting has not always been pleasant. In China, the heavy-handed five-year plans adopted under traditional centralized planning precepts were too disconnected from ongoing reality to work and they were discarded in the late Seventies. The State of New York was once recognized for its work with Planning Programming and Budgeting Systems (PPBS) in the late Sixties and early-Seventies. But the onerous paperwork associated with planning was crowded out by the exigencies of traditional budgetary execution and control. As such, elements of PPBS remain, but the dream of an integrated budget and financial planning system has not been realized in "The Empire State."

The authors' success story is the city of Sunnyvale, California, which has received many kudos over the last 15 years for its PPBS-style budgeting. Is this success due to the nature of local budgeting, where policy priorities may be clearer than state or federal counterparts? Is this a factor of the expertise of principals involved? Does Sunnyvale's political culture foster a rational-analytic approach to budgeting? Hou and Ma do not address those questions directly, but their work suggests that those seeking to implement rational, output-oriented budget systems need to address those queries prior to implementation.

1.3 Public Finance

Government's lifeblood is taxation collected from individuals and businesses. One of the oldest forms of taxation is that on property, with roots as far back as 12th century England. I began this section of the text with Deborah Carroll and Benjamin Sharbel's "The Property Tax: Past, Present, and Future," because no source of revenue is as controversial. As the authors note, the property tax has declined in importance as a mainstay of local government and public school finance during the past 50 years, having faced a number of constitutional restrictions based on its political unpopularity and horizontal inequity. Yet it remains the primary own-source revenue for both sectors despite these limits. Carroll and Sharbel observe that the property tax is a political lightning rod for the electorate's acceptance of government; at the same time, its increasingly professional administration cements its place as a pillar of local government autonomy.

Assume for a moment that you purchase a new laptop computer at your neighborhood office supply store but forget to buy anti-virus software. Rather than make a return trip, you purchase the software on the web via credit card and download it directly to the computer, saving time, gasoline, and wear-and-tear, while avoiding the local sales tax. Is this unfair competition to the "bricks-and-mortar" retailer that lost your business? Is it fair to the similarly-situated person who might not have a credit card? Will this transaction — and countless thousands like it daily — undermine the fiscal health of state and local governments that rely on consumption taxation for their operations?

In "E-Commerce and the State Tax System," Christopher Reddick and Jerrell Coggburn raise these and other questions related to the burgeoning use of electronic commerce and its potential impact on fiscal federalism in the United States. They remind us that the "E-Commerce" problem is a component of the larger and long-standing dilemma of sales tax losses related to remote (out-of-state) commerce. How governments come to grips with the technical and equity concerns related to sales taxation and e-commerce will be a major issue in the coming decades. Reddick and Coggburn assert that its resolution will ultimately impact the highly decentralized and localized administration of the sales tax.

Governments throughout the developed world are fortunate in that the overwhelming majority of their taxpayers and businesses voluntarily comply with timely payment of tax bills. Nonetheless, as John Mikesell and Liucija Birskyte note in "Lessons of Tax Compliance Research for Lawmakers and Tax Administrators," there is still a gap between taxes collected and taxes levied for all sources of revenue. How big is that gap? What are the drivers of its size? What administrative factors play a role in its mitigation?

Using cross-cultural comparisons, Mikesell and Birskyte explore factors such as tax rates, third-party reporting, vendor (remote vs. onsite), and taxpayer characteristics (age, income, and education) and preparer (self vs. professionally-assisted) and their potential impacts on compliance. With limited funds for increased tax collection staff and technology, these findings may help pinpoint compliance methods with the biggest payoffs. Ultimately the authors point out that compliance may be closely correlated with cultural norms of honesty and "civitas" inculcated early in life, reinforced or extinguished by the perceived fairness of the tax system and efficiency of government operations.

The tourism and hospitality sector employs nearly one in eight workers in Florida. This sector took a serious "hit" in the aftermath of "9/11." State coffers, which are highly dependent on sales tax receipts (Florida has no income tax) also nosedived.

In "The Lottery as an Economic Stimulus Tool: The Case of Florida," Susan MacManus describes an innovative team approach adopted by the tourist industry and the state to use the lottery as an economic incentive tool to visit hard-hit tourist hubs and to spend at tourist-related merchants and restaurants. Lottery winners **and** losers (another unique feature of this program) received discounts at these establishments and other participating retailers, in addition to a myriad of prize packages such as free cruises, hotel nights, and admission passes. Empirical evidence suggests that this public-private partnership played a key role in jump starting Florida's tourism sector after "9/11." As MacManus notes, the lottery is an often maligned revenue source but under these circumstances it provided an interesting and innovative incentive that displayed creative thinking on the part of many actors.

The use of tax incentives to attract and retain businesses and jobs is an accepted practice but one that is fraught with controversy. The empirical evidence regarding the efficacy of tax abatements in the aggregate and the property tax, in particular, do not reveal any "slam dunk" strategies guaranteed to work under all circumstances across all jurisdictions.

In "Promoting Economic Development with Tax Incentives: A Primer on Tax Abatements," Esteban Dalehite helps the reader tease out the various perspectives that inform current research on this subject. He describes the growing use of enterprise zones and the current emphasis on the economics of clustering (i.e., agglomeration of firms within a sector). Ultimately, property tax incentives may play a decisive role in business location within a region, but they may have little impact on inter-regional competition. Moreover, their utility in job retention may be dubious, whereas their deployment in attracting new employers to an area has greater impact.

Dalehite's work is an excellent reminder of the simple social science truth that knowledge is often built over time with small increments, not with one-time breakthroughs. After 30 years, our knowledge in the economic development realm is beginning to accumulate and this chapter helps us comprehend the findings in a critical policy context. Perhaps the most critical of Dalehite's conclusions consistent with the absence of a "slam dunk," is that elected officials should allow economic development professionals considerable leeway in tailoring incentives to different clients and circumstances.

1.4 Debt, Working Balances, and Financial Condition Analysis

The concepts of systems theory and the learning organization are cornerstones of contemporary organization design. Collectively, they suggest that formal organizations must take resources from their ever-changing environments and efficiently and effectively add value if they are to survive and thrive. If, for example, governments fail to adapt to economic downturns, it is unlikely they will default on their outstanding debt. But rating agencies such as Standard & Poor's, Moody's, and Fitch ICBA, will threaten them with downgrades, making future borrowing more expensive and lowering the face value of current bondholders.

In "Rating General Obligation Debt: Implications of Resource Scarcity," Steven Koven and Stuart Strother remind us that the bond rating agencies provide critical signaling behavior to senior management and elected officials alike. These agencies' ratings are a commentary on the financial management and fiscal capacity of jurisdictions, with serious implications for citizens and other stakeholders.

Using the recent fiscal crises in California and Virginia as backdrops, Koven and Strother illustrate how political and administrative stakeholders in these states reacted to credit rating "signals" regarding their General Obligation debt (a downgrade in the former, a threatened downgrade in the latter), as the basis for long overdue fiscal policy changes.

This chapter underscores the critical disciplinary role that these agencies play in contemporary public financial management, one that counterbalances short-term political expedience with technical expertise and concrete benchmarking across jurisdictions.

Comparative assessment of state and local government performance is a relatively new concept. But structured comparison of debt levels across state boundaries is a well-established paradigm. In "State Debt Capacity and Debt Levels," Merl Hackbart and Dwight Denison explore the recent work undertaken by practitioners and academics alike in this critical realm. As debt of all kinds expands, states are increasingly aware of the need to manage its overall level and structure over time. This has been accompanied by increasingly sophisticated peer state comparisons that account for factors such as the level of earmarked funding and growth in personal income.

Different states have different political cultures, and are likely to differ in their placement along the "pay-as-you-use vs. pay-as-you-go" capital funding continuum. Nonetheless, as Hackbart and Denison note, financial managers need to be cognizant of how their jurisdiction's debt service levels stack up relative to peer benchmarks. Development of these comparative tools is a high priority in contemporary financial management, and Hackbart and Denison lay out an excellent framework for understanding how reliable peer comparisons are developed.

Maintaining sufficient liquidity is a principle that individuals, businesses, and governments can all appreciate. It is important to have sufficient cash on hand to facilitate the paying of bills in a timely manner without dipping into savings, while avoiding late fees or obtaining pre-payment discounts wherever possible. For large organizations such as governments, decisions on the appropriate level of working capital take on a more prominent role: keeping too much cash on hand means less potential interest earnings, which can be a significant revenue source for fiscally-strapped governments. Contrariwise, keeping too little means foregone interest or, worse still, negative ramifications for bond rating.

In "Working Capital Management in Government: Basic Concepts and Policy Choices," Aman Khan discusses the "art" and "science" of estimating appropriate working capital balances. Dr. Khan discusses the essentials of balance sheet analysis and walks us through the estimation process with appropriate concern for the matching of short- and long-term liabilities with concomitant revenues. Meanwhile, he reminds us that that is imperative to keep an eye on Federal Reserve interest policy and the yield curve. Professor Khan also notes that some communities may be greater risk takers than others, preferring higher interest bearing instruments and maintaining lower balances than their more conservative counterparts. Thus, the determination of "adequate" balances is in part an objective reality and in part a function of community risk preference.

Private sector observers are often surprised at the large size of general fund balances in state and local governments, particularly the latter. Some have argued that these balances are an appropriate cushion against unmitigated spending pressure, and are particularly important for local governments that are largely reliant on inelastic property taxes as their major revenue source.

In "Fund Balance, Working Capital, and Net Assets," Justin Marlowe examines these balances to ascertain if they really are as large as they appear, given possible legal obligations. He also estimates the size of balances needed given the risks attendant to possible economic downturns. Marlowe notes that not all general fund balances are unreserved; many are earmarked for special purposes, while others may be unofficially designated but informally set aside for possible future obligations.

Marlowe's investigation of Michigan municipalities suggests that many of its local governments have unstated policies regarding the appropriate size of their general fund balances, but only a handful have formal policies; fewer still designate a budget stabilization fund. Fund balances averaged about 25% of annual general fund expenditures, approximately twice the size formal mathematical assessment called for in the event of an economic downturn.

This suggests that, in Michigan, local general fund balances were larger than needed for purely economic reasons. Maintaining the aforementioned cushion against unexpected political pressures to spend outweighs technical considerations of adequate reserves. According to Marlowe, this phenomenon is frequently masked as strategic management by a local bureaucracy that is leery of political spending discipline.

The 1975 New York City fiscal crisis, along with its "sister" events in Cleveland and other Midwestern and Northeastern cities, served as catalysts for the development of fiscal indicators that might give senior managers a "heads up" as to possible fiscal stress. The International City Managers Association, the Government Finance Officers Association, and others, have developed a number of indicators related to debt, expenditures, and socioeconomic characteristics that are intended to provide this distant early warning.

In "A Manageable System of Economic Condition Analysis for Governments," Dean Michael Mead of the Government Accounting Standards Board (GASB) provides readers with a 10 indicator system that has integrated information made available by the implementation of GASB Statement 34. With its heightened emphasis on accrual accounting and fixed asset depreciation, this statement should enable governments to ascertain a more accurate picture of their fiscal health.

In a broader context, Mead's discussion relates to the heightened emphasis contemporary management systems place on "Key Performance Indicators" as a metric for understanding organizational health. Further, Mead shows how careful analysis with peer communities augments the use of the 10 indicator system. It is a robust distillation of several decades of research on financial condition indicators, combining experience with larger sets of indicators with the new information GASB 34 brings to bear.

1.5 Public Pensions

According to Jerrell Coggburn and Christopher Reddick in "The Management of Public Pensions," in 2002 America's 2,700 state and local pensions paid nearly 110 billion dollars in benefits. This staggering sum speaks to the trillions of dollars of plan assets; it is also a reminder that if inadequately managed, recipients, taxpayers, and elected officials will be negatively impacted through a combination of lower benefits, higher taxes, and lower bond ratings. Hence, the sound management of public pensions is of paramount importance.

As the authors note, most plans in the public sector are of the defined benefit variety, promising a level benefit based on experience and income. But a growing number of plans are following the private sector example and either shifting to defined contribution plans or encouraging employees to supplement their defined benefit income with greater reliance on plans requiring at least a modicum of investment knowledge. This leads the authors to conclude that many public employers will have to do a better job educating their workforces regarding retirement issues.

Meanwhile, Coggburn and Reddick suggest that public pension management has become more professionalized in terms of benefit administration and investment decision-making. Nonetheless, the influence of politics through actuarial assumptions and contribution deferral remains ongoing threats to professionalized management and long-term solvency. The authors note that commitment to pension solvency must be long-term; evidence suggests that political decision makers cannot allow short-term market downturns or fiscal crises to obscure sound long-term management practices and time-tested investment practices.

As individuals we often face a bewildering array of investment choices. Examples might be: should we invest overseas and if so, where? Should we purchase old-style mutual funds with active management (i.e., portfolio managers making buy and sell decisions), or purchase exchange-traded funds or index funds that simply buy "bundles" of stocks that comprise a pre-determined universe such as the Standard & Poor's 500 or "Dogs of the Dow?" What mix of stocks, bonds, and cash is appropriate? Can we trust ourselves to make investment decisions, or do we need outside advisors to guide us?

As William Albrecht and Thomas Lynch note in "An Econometric Assessment of State and Local Government Retirement System Governance Practices, Investment Strategies, and Financial Performance," state and local pension plans face these and similar decisions in the course of their operations. Unlike individual investment decisions, however, public pension decision-making is embedded in a political and organizational environment that inhibits and encourages a variety of investment decisions with serious repercussions on investment returns. For example, Albrecht and Lynch explore the potential impacts of the size of investment advisory boards, and whether or not they are elected or appointed, as potential determinants of investment return.

The authors also examine something quite fundamental but often overlooked in this area — do public pension managers compare investment performance relative to traditional benchmarks such as the aforementioned Standard and Poor's 500 — or do they adjust their performance for the risk of their portfolios? While evidence is limited, Albrecht and Lynch's findings suggest that appointed boards' investment returns are higher than those that are elected, the use of funds for economic development within the jurisdiction may lower returns and increase risk, and that relatively unrestricted investment policies are put to good use by pension boards who may not need as "close a leash" as previously thought. This piece is a good example of methodologically sophisticated research being deployed to provide "usable knowledge" for daily practice.

1.6 Performance Budgeting and Management

As I have noted elsewhere (Frank and D'Souza, 2004), much of the academic research in the performance measurement realm is survey driven. Regrettably, the use of Likert scale fixed response questions fails to capture the blood, sweat, and tears required to convert an agency from line-item, control-oriented budgeting to a results-oriented format, in which allocations are made in line with productivity and strategic aims.

In "Toward Financial Freedom: Budgeting Reform in the U.S. Courts," J. Edward Gibson chronicles the multi-year effort of the U.S. Courts to adopt performance budgeting. As the author notes, the U.S. Courts were an unlikely testing ground for budget innovation and the late Chief Justice William Rehnquist was an unlikely advocate for reform. But increasingly stringent budgets and a commitment to change brought a model of performance budgeting into being. The price, however, was steep. Many actors required two budget cycles of training. The 11th Circuit was a "guinea pig" used as a pilot for several years to get the proverbial kinks out of the system. Many actors had to amend their traditional budgetary roles; many of the proponents had to acknowledge that not all their objectives could be met.

In the final analysis, an environment that rewarded commitment to change and a tolerance for the risks attendant to its institutionalization were critical ingredients. This case study provides an excellent overview of institutional factors contributing to the success of performance-based budgeting and shows a keen understanding of the nuances of leadership and trust that facilitate its implementation.

Many have advocated performance-based budgeting and management as a mechanism for demonstrating to citizens that their government can produce high quality services that are consistent with their needs. In "Public Participation in Local Performance Measurement & Budgeting," Alfred Ho and Paul Coates detail the findings of their multi-year Sloan Foundation funded grant in nine Iowa communities that explicitly tested for the ability to link citizen input into the development of performance measures.

From the editor's perspective, the most interesting component of this study is not the development of citizen relevant performance measures.

More important was the re-socialization of both the citizens and the bureaucracy that took place during the research period. The former came to understand the differences between private and public service delivery, and to gain respect for the bureaucracy as a service provider. Similarly, the bureaucracy was sensitized to the fact that citizens could provide them with useful input on what to measure. Further, the bureaucracy learned to appreciate that performance measures were not simply an internal performance improvement tool; they could indeed play a vital role in educating taxpayers. This is an important lesson, one that demonstrates a potentially high payoff to investment in performance-based management mechanisms.

Milan Dluhy's "Enhancing the Utilization of Performance Measures in Local Government: Lesson from Practice," is based on the author's research and experience as Director of the Institute of Government at Florida International University in Miami. Dluhy notes that an unfortunate misstep the bureaucracy often takes in budget reform is failure to consult with the legislative branch prior to implementation. This was the mistake that Lyndon Johnson made in 1966 when he tried to implement Planning, Programming, and Budgeting at the Federal level and as Dluhy notes, it appears that many would-be implementers of performance budgeting at the local level make the same mistake.

Dluhy notes the import of developing SMART measures (e.g., specific, measurable, achievable, relevant, and trackable) with the appropriate "buy-in" from experts and political stakeholders. Institutionalizing performance measures takes time. It also requires an organizational champion who assures it is not simply a paper exercise, but one which is put to use in budget submissions, strategic planning, and employee remuneration. And lastly, Professor Dluhy notes that implementation of performance measurement and budgeting cannot be viewed as a personal political agenda — it must be deployed as a tool for improving jurisdiction well-being.

The notion that local governments should monitor and report performance of their operations is nothing new. Ken Smith and Lee Schiffel note in "The Intersection of Accounting and Local Government Performance Measurement," a young man (and future Nobel laureate) interning with the International City Managers Association, by the name of Herbert Simon, was advocating such measurement in 1938!

Fast forward nearly 70 years and we find many professional organizations, the International City and County Managers Association (ICMA) and the Government Accounting Standards Board (GASB), to name just two — that are advocating for such measurement. But, as Smith and Schiffel detail, these organizations have conflicting ideas about what should be measured and how it should be reported. From the authors' vantage, these unanswered questions inhibit development of a common performance reporting language that would facilitate benchmarking and interjurisdictional comparisons.

Further, as Smith and Schiffel note, the rather spotty participation in the current ICMA effort lends credence to the reality that comparative performance measurement across jurisdictions presents thorny definitional and benefit-cost questions that academic researchers have neglected. Meanwhile, the accounting profession, which advocates mandatory performance reporting, and the general public administration community, which sees performance measurement for internal performance improvement, fight a performance measurement paradigm war that intellectually shortchanges both sides.

This is a sobering and thought-provoking chapter that suggests performance reporting and budgeting are not fads. But the perceived cost-effectiveness of implementation remains uncertain to many practitioners due to the failure to agree upon the parameters of a common reporting model.

Performance measurement, like any other activity, does not take place in a vacuum. Institutional settings and the political climate are drivers of performance. In "Reformed County Government Structures and Service Delivery Performance: An Integrated Study of Florida Counties," Alejandro Rodriguez examines the impact of structure and performance in the area of road maintenance. As the readers probably know, Public Choice adherents believe that smaller, overlapping jurisdictions will perform better than those with less competition. Contrariwise, mainstream public administration adherents see "bigger as better" with the Weberian monocracy yielding better performance for taxpayer dollars. Using both quantitative and qualitative findings, Rodriguez finds that counties that were more reformed — organized with fewer jurisdictions and more direct county authority over road maintenance — had better maintained roads at lower cost.

Would these findings be replicated elsewhere? That is impossible to answer. What is important to note is that however we define performance, it is likely that institutional arrangements and intervening characteristics, such as community income and education levels, may be critical determinants of performance outcomes respective of administrative actions. Stated differently, Rodriguez's findings are a reminder that there may be elements of performance that are beyond direct management control; this is a critical factor that all stakeholders in a performance measurement system must understand at the onset.

The design and development of performance measures for any agency is likely to be a difficult task. As Patrick Mullen notes in "Federal Performance Reporting Requirements: From Financial Management to E-Government," development of these measures at the federal level has been extraordinarily difficult. Many agencies have conflicting goals and objectives and readily available benchmarks or peers may be nonexistent. Furthermore, many stakeholders feel that the Government Performance and Reporting Act (GPRA) of 1993 may eventually go the way of other federal budget reforms such as Planning Program and Budgeting Systems (PPBS) or Zero-Based Budgeting (ZBB). What's more, at the same time that agencies are being required to comply with GPRA they are also facing a plethora of mandates in the realms of accounting and e-government.

This broad-gauged effort at "reengineering," however well-intended, has the potential to overwhelm personnel and to subvert the intended improvements. Nonetheless, a positive unintended outcome of these simultaneous reform efforts is the experimentation taking place in the realm of performance reporting. Agencies are now developing annual reports that comply with GPRA and the other management reforms that have taken place in the federal government in the last 15 years. In essence, federal agencies are now developing reports that have a "balanced scorecard" feel to them, detailing financial management, information technology, and operating performance measures. The "crowded management space" that Mullen describes is the apparent necessity that is fostering innovation in the reporting realm. Mullen's work describes a model that may have application beyond the federal sector.

1.7 International Perspectives

Anyone who thinks that application of the "New Public Management" (NPM) is limited to the United States is sorely mistaken. Indeed, much of the Developed world is embracing the application of "results-oriented" government that links the inputs and resources utilized to project outcomes and larger strategic concerns.

In "Public Finance Reform in Selected British Commonwealth Countries," Jayesh D'Souza recounts recent implementation of the "results-oriented" approaches to central government budgeting in Britain, New Zealand, and Canada. Interestingly, these nations adopted the NPM-type budget approaches nearly a decade before American implementation of GPRA in 1993. Per the United States experience, increasing budget deficits and an embittered, tax-averse public, has prompted these nations to adopt private-sector like approaches to resource allocation.

In Britain, the budget planning and process horizon is now multi-year, with considerable attention paid to intergenerational impacts of deficits. Full accrual accounting has been adopted to assure that all costs of operations are included; SMART performance measures are mandated to be adopted within a balanced scorecard framework. New Zealand and Canada have adopted the same measures, along with stringent limits on deficits as a percentage of gross domestic product. They have also developed annual reporting that details actual performance and programmatic impact.

D'Souza's conclusion, echoed in the United States experience, is that performance measurement is increasingly important throughout the Commonwealth. However, the benefits and costs of implementation, as well as the principal audience of its utilization (the public or the bureaucracy) remain unanswered questions.

The struggle between the executive and legislative branches in government is nothing new. Likewise, debates over the pros and cons of zero-based budgeting, program budgeting, and target-based budgeting would be commonplace to most readers. And as anyone familiar with Schick's **Budget Innovation in the States** (1971) understands, the Federal government has frequently looked to its sub-national units for cutting edge reforms. In-point-of-fact, as Schick notes, the states had executive budgeting led by the governor through a centralized budget bureau long before the Budget Act of 1921 established a presidential budget with its concomitant creation of the Bureau of the Budget.

But "commonplace" is context driven. Many readers would be surprised to note that in the People's Republic of China, legislative-executive budget debates, budget format experimentation, and center-periphery diffusion are being played out in much the same way as in the Western democracies. These points are detailed in Jun Ma and Meili Niu's chapter, "Public Financial Reforms in China." It is fascinating to consider that the People's Congress no longer rubber stamps the Communist Party's Central Committee budget; that China is experimenting with zero-based and target-based budget formats, and it is the local governments that are providing insight to the central government in how to implement these reforms. In addition, China is improving its procurement (faster execution, more competition, less corruption), and has actually implemented the legislative veto in two of its provinces.

In short, China is in many ways emulating our own budgetary development and looks to the United States and other developed countries for solutions to the dilemmas it faces. Coping with scarcity is a universal problem. China's recent budget reforms suggest that even an authoritarian state will borrow ideas from more experienced developed nations in an effort to modernize its budget formulation and execution.

1.8 Some Integrating Themes

Trying to distill the 24 remaining chapters in this book to a small number of integrating themes is daunting. Nonetheless, six critical concepts emerge. None of these conclusions is surprising but in the aggregate they reinforce paths for future administrative behavior and research.

1. *Financial management is a system*: Lennox Moak's (1975) **Concepts and Practices in Local Government Finance** is a classic in the area. One of the work's central tenets is that effective financial management requires that an eye be kept on a number of simultaneous prizes: debt management, economic development, pension solvency, budget balancing, and performance measurement among them. What Moak contended over three decades ago is as true today as it was then.

2. *Globalization extends the competitive federal model*: In the past, civil servants and elected officials may have worried about their neighboring city or state's tax rates and quality-of-life. The realities of globalization broaden the net. International competition leaves no jurisdiction sheltered from the "Wal-Mart" effect of incessant downward pressure on wages and production costs. This in turn results in governments around the world being pressured to "do more with less" and introduce best practice into their daily operations. It also compels them to take economic development more seriously as a means of preserving real wages and their own tax bases.

3. *Customer satisfaction matters*: The "citizen-as-customer" may not always resonate with mainstream public administration, which sees government's regulatory functions as differentiating it from traditional private sector service providers. Nonetheless, most modern governments recognize the symbolic and substantive value of "listening" to citizen desires and preferences in terms of strategic planning and operational effectiveness. This precept also applies to "internal customers" within the agency or jurisdiction.

4. *There is increasing systematic comparison of performance and financial capacity across jurisdictions*: Inter-jurisdictional comparisons have been undertaken for decades, but this practice is becoming more routine and systematic. At present there is no government analog to the **Morningstar** mutual fund rating system, but it appears that a number of jurisdictions and organizations are heading in that direction. Meanwhile, the shibboleth that "our jurisdiction is unique and can't be compared" will have less validity over time.

5. *Liberals, conservatives, and authoritarians alike are forced to confront the size of government and to enhance its efficiency and effectiveness as a service provider*: While Margaret Thatcher may have started the reengineering and privatization of government in Great Britain, Tony Blair's Liberals have expanded upon her efforts. The Government Performance and Results Act (GPRA) was enacted under

Democratic President Clinton and spearheaded by his Vice President, Al Gore. GPRA has recently been reenacted under President Bush and, as our contributors Yun Ma and Meili Nu noted, reengineering is now taking place in China. Government size, scope, and efficacy are universal concerns that obligate financial managers to constantly scrutinize means and ends.

6. *There appears to be a convergence of public and for-profit accounting models:* The simple reality that a government's revenues and expenditures are in balance is no longer sufficient as a reporting model; enumeration of actual resources employed within and between generations is becoming accepted practice. Governments throughout the world are introducing concepts such as accrual accounting, activity-based accounting, and fixed-asset depreciation into their daily operations. Moreover, as Siciliano (2003) notes, all bodies — public and private — are being obligated to heighten the comprehensiveness and transparency of their financial reporting. Finkler's (2001) path breaking financial management text reflects diffusion of this convergence model. Patrick Mullen's chapter suggests that the federal government is already grappling with this trend; the Smith and Schiffel chapter elaborates from a state-local perspective. The revolution in financial reporting has started!

How these trends play out is subject to conjecture. One thing seems certain. The material in this book bears out L.R. Jones (1991) contention that many graduates of typical MPA programs are shortchanged in public financial management training relative to their MBA counterparts. The typical one-semester required course in most public affairs and administration programs is simply insufficient to convey the knowledge that will be needed to operate under the aforementioned "convergence model."

The trends that impact pedagogy will undoubtedly impact research as well. We are already beginning to see studies detailing, for example, the impact of GASB in the realm of municipal forecasting (Frank, Gianakis, and McCue, forthcoming). How accrual and activity-based accounting impact budget decisions, or how increased disclosure of fixed-asset depreciation impacts municipal bond ratings are other subjects that are likely to be on the proverbial front burner.

No text can cover all subjects. Nonetheless, contributors to this volume have done an excellent job in responding to Rabin's (1989) challenge to set disciplinary boundaries while conveying a valuable body of knowledge in the process. Hopefully, readers will continue to meet this challenge in their own efforts crafting the future of public financial management research and practice.

References

Finkler, S.A. (2001). *Financial management for public, health, and not-for-profit organizations.* Upper Saddle River, NJ: Prentice-Hall.

Frank, H.A., and D'Souza, J. (2004). Twelve years into the performance measurement revolution: Where we need to go in implementation research. *International Journal of Public Administration,* 27(8/9): 701–718.

Frank, H.A., Gianakis, G.A., and McCue, C.M. (forthcoming). Forecasting local forecasting post-GASB 34: A preliminary view from the trenches. *Journal of Public Budgeting, Accounting, and Financial Management.*

Jones, L.R. (1991). Public financial management curriculum and course design: A response to the National Task Force report. *Public Budgeting and Financial Management,* 3(1): 171–190.

Moak, L. (1975). *Concepts and practices in local government finance.* Chicago: Municipal Finance Officers Association of the United States and Canada.

Rabin, J. (1989). Editorial Policies. *Public Budgeting and Financial Management,* (1): i–v.

Siciliano, G. (2003). *Finance for non-financial managers.* New York: McGraw-Hill.

Schick, A. (1971). *Budget innovations in the states.* Washington, DC: Brookings.

THE CONTEXT OF PUBLIC
FINANCIAL MANAGEMENT

I

Chapter 2

Public Expenditure Management: Selected Themes and Issues

A. PREMCHAND
International Monetary Fund (Retired)

Public expenditure management has been in existence, in one form or other, for more than two millennia, although the terms of usage, in their present form, came into being only toward the end of the twentieth century, and their usage was extensively promoted by governments and international agencies alike to emphasize the growing importance of public expenditures, their underlying policies, the benefits and the costs that they entail, and their implications for overall financing, as well as their impact on fiscal sustainability. Many of the elements that formed part of the expenditure management systems in ancient monarchical regimes continue to this day, not merely because of reliance on traditions and a reluctance to change them, but because of their enduring and viable contributions to the effectiveness of the system. A cursory examination of the history of the system reveals, however, that it changed over the years, and that it is continuing to change, in scope and in underlying concepts, as well as the purposes to be served. Such a change is an integral part of the evolutionary process of governments. As these changes take place, some deliberately planned and consciously introduced, while some take place more as a reaction, it is necessary to examine whether the changes were in the right direction and whether they have been adequate or whether more radical changes are indicated. This chapter aims at undertaking such a review of, in particular, the more recent reforms attempted during the eighties and nineties, and that continue to be implemented by the developing countries, transition countries and industrial countries. It is appropriate, however, that before undertaking the proposed review the evolution of the expenditure management is considered, albeit briefly, so as to have a perspective on the origins of recent reforms, their relevance for the fiscal policy and systemic issues faced by various countries, and to evaluate the advances made in the process.

2.1 Perspectives on Evolution

Each country has undoubtedly its own history of the development of the administrative system generally and of the expenditure management systems in particular. Despite the inevitable differences among the system, some common features and specified stages of development of the system can be ascertained. While, in some degree, there were contemporaneous developments, in a few cases there was also constant interchange of ideas, and experiments introduced in one country found very soon replicas elsewhere. For purposes of analytical convenience, three major stages in the development of expenditure management system can be discerned.

In ancient regimes, as can be gleaned from the histories of China, India and Greece, the primary function that was sought to be addressed was the establishment of the royal treasury and its maintenance in a manner to prevent defalcation by the civil servants and others. The royal treasury was viewed, as a direct measure of not only the wealth of the royalty, an important consideration in itself, but as an index of the current and potential power of the kingdom. The civil services included accountants, auditors and revenue collectors, but no expenditure controllers. The purposes and tasks associated with the royal treasury were to protect the wealth of the kingdom (which included metals and jewellery), and to engage in their effective use for financing the wars that were almost frequent and common. To maintain the treasury, and to control both inflows and outflows, three steps were built into the administrative systems. In regard to payments from the treasury (which were needed for the payment of wages, maintenance of the royal household, acquisition of equipment for fighting wars, and to engage in relief works during periods of severe drought), these were, respectively: (a) establishment of the claim for payment — that it was valid, and that the decision leading to payment was made by the designated authority; (b) that the claim has been verified arithmetically and in terms of availability of resources (informal borrowing or accumulation of unpaid bills, for want of resources in the treasury came much later — in the 21st century); (c) that the claim has been liquidated after making the appropriate payment. Similar procedures were followed in regard to revenue collection. History shows that in countries as far apart as England and China, common procedures for payment were followed. In both countries there were three clerks, working at tables that were covered with checkered cloth, where these three stages of work were performed diligently. These transactions were then consolidated on a daily basis and were later subjected to regular audit by the court of auditors. These three steps contributed the first steps in organized expenditure management. The major concerns, at this stage, related to the legality and the regularity of payments. The essentiality of these administrative steps is obvious from the fact that, even to this day, regardless of the fact whether the payment systems are organized on a manual or electronic basis, the legality of the claim is verified, and a payment is made only after the legal formalities are satisfied. To this day, payments in the United States are required to be certified by the officials of the Department of the Treasury (now on an electronic basis) before being made. The French treasury system, as is the case with less known systems, resolves around these three stages. Looking back, this way is considered as the first stage in the development of the expenditure management system.

The second stage refers to the gradual emergence of the legislatures as major centers of power. Having acquired the rights about the levy of taxes, legislatures gradually moved to acquire power about expenditure too. After a prolonged struggle, it was agreed that the final control of purse was to be in the hands of the legislature, and that no expenditure could be incurred without explicit authorization from it. As a counterpoint to the legislature, the treasuries within the executive wing of the government were also strengthened, and it was specified as a rule of transactions that no expenditure could be incurred without prior approval from the treasury. These twin pillars of control were expected to assure the community that firm arrangements were in place, both within and outside government, to manage the national finances. In due course further demands came to be made about the content of expenditure management. During the sixteenth and seventeenth centuries, when national debt levels were very high in Great Britain, new demands were made by the Parliament about the adequacy of the accounting system, in particular relating to debt. As a result of this emphasis, three important milestones emerged. First, it was specified that there should be a cadre of officials responsible for the compilation of government accounts. This was the beginning of an accounting cadre in governments. Second, it was agreed that governments would submit annual accounts on how the money was utilized. Third, it was also specified that the annual accounts would be audited by a separate agency, and that the audited accounts would be reviewed by a regular committee of the legislature. These three aspects also instituted for the first time ground rules about fiscal transparency, and institutionalized arrangements for accountability. More significantly they contributed to the emergence of a budget cycle — various phases of operations — that started with the submission of a budget for approval, and concluded with the rendition of annual accounts. In turn, expenditure management came to be exercised as an integral part of the budget cycle.

The functioning of the legislatures has gone through various phases and, in the current situation, three distinct systems of expenditure control by legislatures are in operation. In one system, essentially drawn from the practice of the House of Commons in the United Kingdom, the budget process is dominated by the executive, and the powers of the legislature are limited to approval and, at the end of the year, to a review of accounts. The executive plans for spending are not amendable to change by the legislature. Expenditures proposed cannot be increased; in principle they could be reduced, although such actions, depending on the nature of the reduction proposed by the legislature, could become a confidence issue on the government with potential implications for its stay in power. In a second system, which has its origins in the American approach of a balanced distribution of power among the legislature, executive and judicial wings of government, the budget presented by the President can be revised in any manner deemed appropriate by the legislature, and it's finally approved by the President after a series of checks and balances. As the system developed it revealed two major weaknesses. The members of the legislature could enact any program of expenditure regardless of the availability of the resources. This inevitably led to an accumulation of programs awaiting funding from the government. The system also shows that there was no balance in the roles of the legislature as a budget maker, and as a reviewer of budgetary performance at the end of the year. Both these aspects were rectified through improved procedures of congressional budgeting (introduced in 1974) under which new programs were subjected to be undertaken within congressionally approved aggregate ceilings, and with emphasis on review of performance. This legislative system has proved to be a heavy favorite of east European countries during recent years as they have adopted variants of the system to guide their own affairs. The other type of system refers to passive legislatures, whose role is limited to debating the executive proposals, but is not called upon to vote on them. A variant of this system is to be found in China, where the People's congress approves the budget, usually a quarter after the start of the year, but does not engage in deliberation or approval of individual programs. Together these systems reflect the symbiotic relationship between the executive and the legislature and its impact on expenditure management, which has become a shared responsibility.

The next stage in the evolution of expenditure management refers to the convergence of several forces with an enduring impact on the course and content of the system. In particular, the macroeconomic and the "human face" dimensions of expenditure management came to be prominently recognized during this phase. The Depression during the thirties brought about the use of expenditures as a major tool of counter cyclical fiscal policy. Although there was some discussion about the relative merits of current and investment expenditures in stimulating economic activity, the latter had the advantage in a balance sheet in that assets had the potential of matching the growing financial liabilities. The extensive use of expenditures as a counter cyclical policy instrument also brought with it, in due course, the other side of its usage, in that, during periods of inflation, utmost restraint had to be exercised on the growth of expenditures and on the overall size of the budget deficit. The macroeconomic dimension of expenditure management came to be further enhanced and widened after the Second World War, as the developing countries, which become newly independent, resorted to development programs with special emphasis on public investment planning. In turn, this added two features that came to be part of the permanent arsenal of expenditure management. It was recognized that the achievement of many fiscal policy objectives may not be achieved during a fiscal year, but needed a medium term. Accordingly, expenditure planning came to be undertaken over the medium term; in addition, it was also recognized that decision making on investment projects, could not be merely intuitive, but needed to be subjected to the application of quantitative techniques of investment appraisal. This too became an enduring feature of expenditure management.

As expenditure continued to grow, reflecting the investment needs and other demands for service, the issue of performance and its linkages to the allocation and utilization of resources came to be raised. In effect, this contributed to an explicit recognition of the human aspects of expenditure management, in that it tended to focus on the expenditure benefits created, and their utilization by the various clientele groups of the society. In turn, this required the specification of performance objectives and formulation of performance measurements, both of which continue to dominate the expenditure management reforms.

As a result of the diversified experience, expenditure management acquired a place of prominence in the annual formulation of fiscal policies.

As integral parts of this effort, the rate of growth of expenditure is either sought to be moderated or stepped up depending on the situation. Furthermore, to provide systemic underpinning to public policy in making, expenditures came to be planned over the medium term, and many new proposals came to be subjected to investment appraisal techniques. Moreover, the specification of performance measures contributed to a more intensive examination of the relative merits of different techniques of delivery of services, while also exploring the possibilities of procuring technical efficiency or economies in operation. In day to day management the experience translated itself into three major aspects of expenditure management: (a) linkages between macroeconomic trends and expenditure strategy; (b) linkages between resource allocation and performance or the effective delivery of services; and (c) the search for operation technical efficiency — or delivery of services at a lower cost.

Meanwhile, as these changes are taking place in the objectives of expenditure management, there were also changes in the functioning of governments that posed new, if as yet not completely resolved, issues for expenditure management. As the range of functions undertaken by governments grew in size and complexity, many of the services came to be contracted out and carried out by non-governmental organizations. A cursory glance at many governments in all types of countries, including those in transition, reveals that many of the social services — education, medical facilities — are provided by a network of government agencies, corporate firms, nongovernmental organizations, and private individuals. Regardless of the location of the service provider, and its corporate identity, the services are funded by governments. But the separation of funding from provision of service (the buyer–supplier link) has brought with it several issues of expenditure planning and management into the limelight.

Meanwhile, there has been a general development that tended to transform the operational aspects of expenditure management. This development took place in the area of application of electronic technology to the processing of government operations. Although initially this application contributed, by virtue of dependence on main frames, which was then the technology that was available, to a considerable degree of centralization, the next stage in the development of computer technology, viz, personal computer, eased the problem a good deal. Primarily, the application had a three-fold beneficial impact. It reduced the cost of compilation of data, which also significantly reduced the time spent on the process. It transformed the relationship between central and spending agencies into a partnership by virtue of simultaneous availability of information to both. To that extent, the divide between the controllers and controlees was, in theory, reduced. Finally, this also reduced the hitherto existing great divide between industrial and developing countries, as the latter group also quickly took to the application of computer technology partly on their own initiative and, partly, from the loan facilities provided by the international financial institutions.

2.2   Fiscal Trends and Issues

The expenditure management system, which traditionally had been confronting the problem of inexorable growth of expenditure, began to face a new situation during recent decades that came to be called as a fiscal stress. The revision of the oil prices in the early seventies, and the subsequent periods of high inflation and stagflation contributed to additional fiscal strain; dependence on borrowing, both in domestic markets and the international market, contributed to "crowding out", increase in the interest rates, and to greater shares of expenditure devoted to debt-servicing. Each increase in the interest rates, which the central banks introduced as a part of their anti-inflation campaigns, contributed to further increases in debt servicing. And each such increase reduced, correspondingly, the flexibility available to budgeting in the allocation of resources. Other categories like entitlements also contributed to increasing rigidity and the whole pheno-menon of government expenditures came to be considered, at least for a period, as uncontrollable. This anguish, and the inability to address the problem of expenditure growth in the short-term, together provided a fresh impetus for a search for new approaches that would, somehow, help bring a modicum of control of expenditure growth.

The nature and dimensions of the fiscal stress was such that it became abundantly clear that the traditional methods of nip and tuck, or a cut here or there in the sectoral allocations, would not serve the purpose. Indeed, such approaches were tried in the early stages, but the futility and the total inadequacy of the systemic response was too transparent that efforts had to be devoted in other directions. What was needed, it became clear, was a total revision of the way in which governments carried out their operations, and changes in the underlying political philosophy. Limits were needed on the range of activities undertaken by governments; similarly, changes were also needed, not merely in the expenditure management area, but in the very underlying assumptions, in that the operations had to be subjected to market tests and the application of principles of competition. It was also clear that mere systemic changes would not be adequate and that these had to be combined with deficit reduction packages, primarily comprising a severe reduction in the staff employed and divestment of selected activities to lower levels of government or to be performed by a nongovernmental organizations.

The measures taken in the light of above recognition covered several areas, ranging from policy measures to a variety of improvements in the expenditure management system, including the selective applications of the new management philosophy. These measures, together with their features, are summarized in Table 2.1. To be sure, many of the features of systemic innovations, such as medium term expenditure planning, recognition of performance links, cash management, selected applications of corporate practices, emphasis on improved governance through greater fiscal transparency and enhanced framework of financial and program accountability, were drawn, either in their original form or in a slightly modified form, from the previous practices. The distinction was in the way in which these instruments were packaged with other ingredients, such as greater emphasis on the rule of law (in the event through fiscal responsibility legislation or other similar legally enforceable limits that would, in principle, exercise a major restraining influence on public policy making), emphasis on the application of accrual budgeting and accounting, and reorganization of government though establishment of task-oriented, managerially accountable organizations, and improved budget making through the formulation of centrally devised resource ceilings. As a whole, the new measures were expected to contribute to a moderation in the rate of expenditure growth, to greater efficiency in spending, and to improved accountability in governments.

The expectations may have been, in the event, over pitched. Many of the measures, by their very nature, were such that they had little capability to moderate the growth of expenditures. The real impact in terms of short term reductions in expenditure came from the policy packages, such as reduction in the personnel, reform of pension systems, and reductions in subsidies and defense outlays. Systemic measures had no such immediate direct influence. The fiscal responsibility legislation, as is clear with the implementation of the Maastricht treaty in the European cities, did not, in the event, have much restraining influence. In Latin American countries, particularly in Argentina, it had very little impact, as is evidenced in the fiscal crises experienced in late 1990s. On the other hand, the legislation had a good deal of rigidity in that it did not permit the pursuit of timely counter cyclical policies. Similarly, medium term expenditure planning, which provided greater clarity about the changing profiles of expenditure, did not have any discernible impact on moderating expenditure, as most adjustments were back loaded. The one systematic measure that in theory had a major potential for securing economies was the deployment of fundamental reviews of selected government activities. Very few developing countries adopted this approach. India, which appointed a National expenditure commission, was one of the very few that adopted this approach, but most expenditure reductions were made along established lines, such as

Table 2.1 Changes in Expenditure Management

Area	Changes	Remarks
Resource allocation policy measures	Deficit reduction packages	Comprised several measures that included wage freeze, reduced borrowing, reduced defense spending, etc.
Improved policy planning	(i) Fiscal responsibility legislation	Introduction of legislation aimed at reinforcing restrictive legal mechanisms that would also have a restraining influence of governments in planning future budgets.
	(ii) Preparation of medium term fiscal outlook	This is intended to facilitate fiscal adjustment over the medium term and expected to supplement the annual budget process, while clarifying policy goals.
	(iii) Preparation of medium term rolling expenditure budgets	As an integral part of above, rolling expenditure budgets are prepared for all programs.
	(iv) Formulation of functional or program resource ceilings	In the light of above assessment, ceilings are prescribed within which individual agency demands are formulated.
Annual budget	1. Recognition of risks and associated measures	As a part of annual budget formulation, macroeconomic risks are recognized and contingent measures are contained.
	2. Formulation of priorities and strategies	Priorities determine the categories of expenditures that could be given up in the event of revenue shortfall.
	3. Explicit recognition of performance links	Linkage between resource allocation and expected results outlined.
Search for economies	Fundamental or periodic reviews	Periodic reviews are undertaken to reduce expenditures through abandonment or modification of existing programs.
Explicit recognition of liabilities and costs	Introduction of accrual budgeting and accounting	The accrual system is expected to facilitate an explicit recognition of all liabilities, and the computation of costs through the application of depreciating accounting and capital changes. Balance sheets produced as a result are expected to provide improved information on the overall status of public finances.

(continued)

Table 2.1 Continued

Area	Changes	Remarks
Resource utilization		
Budget releases	Cash management (Treasury management)	Is expected to smooth the process of budget implementation while linking up with debt management.
Exposure to market principles	Most activities are subjected to contracting in which internal agencies also can participate	Greater resort to contracting is expected to lead to a refinement of the buyer–provider nexus and to improved delivery of services.
Expenditure tracking	Introduction of expenditure tracking systems	As the value chain between provider and funding agency expands, it becomes necessary to ensure that the budgeted funds reach the intended destination and that the administrative overheads are held to a minimum.
Payment	Electronic payment system	Traditional methods of payment are being abandoned in favor of cheaper, effective and quick payment systems. Payrolls, pension payments and debt servicing tasks are being privatized even.
Performance	Performance measures are specified to enhance accountability,	In some cases, performances data are provided.
Periodic financial reporting	Data are now periodically provided to facilitate an assessment of the fiscal policy posture	More and more governments are trying to adhere to international guidelines on reporting.
Resource-use accounting		
Annual accounts	Where accrual accounting is introduced. Balance sheets and other statements are proposed	This change from routine appropriation accounts is expected to facilitate a better assessment of the fiscal situation.
Establishment of cost and responsibility centers	To shore up fiscal discipline and as a part of the overall design, these centers are also organized	

Supporting administrative infrastructure

Corporate practices	• Creation of task organized agencies • Provision of managerial autonomy • Performance contract • Client orientation	In several countries, supporting administrative infrastructure arrangements have been made, mostly drawn from the new management philosophy and from selected corporate practices.
Improved governance	• Fiscal transparency • Enhanced accountability • Ethical practices	International guidelines have been formulated in this area. Emphasized: no guidelines are provided. Emphasized: Attention limited to the establishment of anti-corruption bureaus.

reduction in personnel and scaling down of subsidies, while controversial and unproductive programs were left generally untouched.

The emphasis on performance in the delivery of services was an important and much needed improvement. By its very nature, the specification of a desired level of performance also implied that necessary resources had to be allotted for this purposes. Thus, it was also a basis of allocation of resources and, as such, it had a greater potential for ratcheting up the level of expenditures from time to time rather than moderating the growth rate of expenditures. More or less the same could be stated about the impact of the introduction of new management philosophy. The introduction of centrally managed ceilings on the allocated resources generated the false feeling that, as a result, the expenditure growth rate may have been somewhat moderated. A deeper examination shows that the formulation of ceilings, while restraining the urges of spending agencies to periodically seek additional allocations, may have made them far more conscious of the need for pitching their initial needs with a higher built-in slack to accommodate the later needs. In the process the central agencies lost a valuable opportunity to review the operations of the spending agencies in detail. The convenience associated with the determination of individual ceilings came with a price tag — loss of detailed control which hitherto was the main vehicle of control of central agencies.

The emphasis on the proper compilation of national assets and liabilities, including contingent liabilities was, again, an important step. Many countries, both at the national and sub national levels, enacted new legislation governing the provision of guarantees and the arrangements for risk sharing. As a result, an annual review, generally as a part of the budget making process, of the contingent liabilities is being undertaken. But the general introduction of accrual budgeting and accounting has not gained much acceptance even in the industrial world, except for four countries. In the United States the application of accrual basis is limited to accounts. Some governments continue to contend that application of accrual accounting, with depreciation accounting and capital charges, makes more sense where commercial transactions, with profit motive, are undertaken. There is also little evidence to suggest that publication of balance assets would be helpful in making governments, and the public, debt averse. Indeed, the experience of the last four years suggests that the trend is on the opposite side, in that many governments have opted for the soft constraint of debt, rather than engage in the mobilization of additional revenue measures. In any event, the experience with the introduction of accrual budgeting and accounting is so limited that it does not provide a reasonable basis for optimism.

The emphasis on the virtues of competition, and therefore on contracting, is in a way continuation of an old theme, but with the difference that, as a part of the reform package, contracts were extended to the service area and to personnel management. As the range of services provided by governments expanded, there was recognition that, instead of expanding government agencies, it might be more advantageous to rely on other sources such as non-governmental organizations, where the buyer-seller contractual arrangements could be made an effective tool for the delivery of services. Experience shows that, traditionally, contracting has proved to be an Achilles heel for governments, as they have always found it difficult to overcome the wily strategies of the contractors. It appeared that they always had a way of taking advantage of governments, and the built-in advantage of the biggest buyer was not always effectively exploited. In that context, extending contractual arrangements to other areas, particularly to organizations which did not have viable legal administrative infrastructures, did not prove to be a welcome departure from the practice with a potential for saving money. It was also doubtful whether the non-governmental organizations were more effective in the provision of services. It also became clear that many of the developing countries did not have the traditions or laws that contribute to the smooth implementation of contractual agreements. In the circumstances, reliance on this technique brought a whole new slew of problems without solving any of the existing issues.

The above discussion should not, however, lead to the misleading conclusion that no improvement had taken place. Available evidence, primarily in the form of reports issued by the international financial institutions, shows that major improvements took place in the transition companies which opted for many of the legislative controls found in the western democracies. Their efforts concentrated on endowing more powers in the legislatures and their committees, in approving and modifying the budget proposals, and in having a continuing oversight on budget implementation. In addition, many developing and transition countries have also introduced multi-year rolling expenditure planning as a part of an effort to improve policy planning. Among the industrial countries, France, which hitherto did not choose multi-year estimates, began to produce them. In the United States reliance continued to be placed on expenditure projections although, at the level of congressional appropriation committees, more data were made available on the medium term profile of experience.

In sum, the attempts yielded minor results in term of moderating the expenditure growth. As a result of wage and grade freeze, and reduction in force, the rate of growth of expenditure decelerated in the OECD countries during the early 90s but, like a catapult held on high leash, the previous path of expenditure growth continued during more recent years, contributing in turn to greater budget deficits. The lack of success in the central objective of expenditure management is attributable in part to the very nature of systemic improvement sought and in part to the changing economic climate. Emphasis on performance based approaches was not compatible with the approaches to moderate expenditure growth or with concerns of macroeconomic stability. Meanwhile, to contend with the changing climate, and to reckon with frequent revenue shortfalls, many governments relied on underfunding as a way out of fiscal problems. But underfunding contributed to greater discontent over the delivery of sources, and raised even more questions about the credibility of governments and the adequacy of their expenditure management systems.

2.3   Next Steps

The situation, as one looks ahead from this point of time, is far from satisfactory. Years of dedicated effort at improvement have not yielded the desired results. The rate of growth of expenditure, in most cases, continues unabated. In addition there are numerous policy commitments already made which threaten the viability and sustainability of government finances. Notwithstanding the steady erosion in the credibility of governments and their management systems, new demands are being made for enhanced levels of service or for new services. The existing commitments relating to the modernization of national security systems, including enhanced capacity to deal with the problem of cross border terrorism (indeed, no borders seem to exist for terrorist operations), imperative need to enhance the technical and economic infrastructure, and the urgency to improve the delivery of services while addressing the issues of waste and fraud inherent in third-party payment systems, are all aspects that would require higher outlays. Further, the deep holes in the funding of pension liabilities would also claim more resources to be allocated. From a systematic point of view, the expenditure management system is now first required to aim at a restoration of its severely damaged creditability; it also has the task of reducing uncertainty felt by the spending agencies in the provision of resources, and it has the more fundamental task of improving the delivery of services, while being economical in that endeavor. Efforts at securing technical efficiency must be realistic and should have enduring results. In short, it means that the basic tasks associated with expenditure management would be better served through resorting to improved techniques, where possible, through a reconciliation of macroeconomic compulsions with microeconomic requirements and through the pursuit of a coherent and viable strategy of improvement. It is clear that resorting to ambiguous and umbrella themes like transparency and accountability have very little impact on the more immediate concerns of expenditure management, nor do they address the broader issue of the functioning of an expenditure management system in a democratic system.

In addressing the large variety of issues, attention has to be devoted to both the technical and the larger issues of expenditure management in a changing context of growing hopes and diminishing results. Admittedly, not all issues can be considered, given space limitations, here; rather, the approach is selective and four major areas are considered in a broad way, not to provide a coherent strategy, which anyway is not the attempt here, but to furnish a foretaste of what is to come.

2.3.1 *Expenditure Management in a Democratic Society*

Notwithstanding the differences in the forms and varying content of democracies, it is generally accepted that the primary responsibility for decision-making relating to the determination of expenditures at an aggregate and at detailed levels, is that of an elected legislature. While there are some legislatures which have no deliberative power in this regard, in either type, the final power of the purse rests with the legislature. In both executive and legislature dominated systems, there are adequate checks and balances between the various pillars of democratic society. From the point of expenditure management, two major issues have cropped up during recent years that need to be addressed immediately.

In both systems, it is now recognized that there has been a massive shift in decision making from the legislature to the executive. In the management of finances, a major portion of the budgetary outlays is governed by the existing legislation and, increasingly, the share that is brought within the ambit of annual control is becoming smaller and smaller. Furthermore, governments appear to have, prior to the Maastricht treaty and the introduction of fiscal responsibility legislation, practically unlimited powers to borrow routinely from international financial institution without getting prior or later approval from the legislature. With the increasing and inevitable movement toward greater globalization it is even suggested that governments need more power to act quickly and decisively to stop capital flight or to attract foreign direct investment. From these points of view, legislatures are viewed as obstacles to proper and judicious economic management and therefore the shift of decision making power to the executive is both necessary and justified. It is also suggested that when legislatures decide to act they assume adversarial and inquisitorial roles rather than engage in constructive dialogue with the executive. Moreover, the constraints they impose are rather too soft and not hard enough to have any major restraining influence on governments. The legislation enacted is incoherent, long and may occasionally be self-contradictory, with the inevitable result that the judiciary is brought into the picture. Therefore, the argument goes that there is much that the legislatures have to do in reforming themselves and in improving their operating systems. The legislatures argue, on the other hand, that much of the blame is to be allotted to the people too, in that their preferences are far from clear, that they often underestimate the future financial implications of many of the policy initiatives they support, and that on many issues dominant interests manage to get decisions in their favor, leading to large scale patronage and cronyism. The capture and management of the voter's preferences becomes even easier in a context of growing apathy and lack of participation in matters and on issues when their involvement counts. The voter remains largely uneducated or fully informed about the multiple dimensions of proposed expenditure policies, as the bureaucracy is generally reluctant to share information with the community. The veil of secrecy is too pervasive and firmly imbedded into the system that vigorous efforts are needed to reduce its spread.

These and related systems have received considerable efforts during recent years and many proposals have been advanced with a view to addressing the problems. Broadly, the proposals are of two types — those that aim at taking the legislator to the people and improving the voter–representative relationship and those that aim at the improvement of legislative involvement in expenditure management matters. The first type includes proposals relating to fixed terms for the legislators, introduction of more ballot initiatives, greater transfer of tasks and responsibilities, with attached funding power, to the local levels, and formation of citizen panels. Some progress has already been made in terms of transferring more tasks to the local levels. But this transfer has also become problematic, in that requisite financial powers were not transferred but continue to be exercised by central governments. Similarly, formation of citizen panels has selectively been done at the local level, providing opportunities to the users or potential beneficiaries to have a voice in the implementation of programs. Ballot initiatives are, on the other hand, viewed with some concern, in that they tend to be costly, indeterminate in results, and may have the impact of interrupting legislative business.

The second type of proposals deal specifically with expenditure management, in that they advocate specific legislation rather than resort to omnibus legislation, more avenues for ensuring accountability and the introduction of a two-year budget cycle. While the first proposal is to be welcomed, the progress in ensuring more channels of accountability has been confined to introduction of performance orientation to the allocation of resources and to greater post-budget oversight. In some cases, the establishment of websites is deemed to be a major step in ensuring accountability. In reality, these measures have little bite in them, and have had, as yet, little impact on the expenditure management culture and associated mindsets. The introduction of a two year budget has little inherent capacity to resolve the basic problems that have weakened the role of the legislature. On the other hand, it could contribute to greater acceleration on what is admittedly a downhill journey.

The major issue that is waiting to be resolved relates to the involvement of the legislatures in the making of fiscal policy and restoring its legitimate role. It has often been suggested that there should be a balance in the relative functioning of the legislature and the executive, but the exact nature of this balance or its location at a point of time has never been specified; rather, it has been a convenient abstraction that receives instantaneous approval from all. What are the functions and tasks to be performed if the role of legislature is to be restricted to the approval of budgets and oversight of macro policies? Notionally, they already have power (where it is so endowed) to approve the budget, to approve policies, to approve specific staff levels, to approve funding and limits on programs and projects, and to approve the borrowing levels, and even to approve, in unusual circumstances, the periodic funding of programs. It is true, however, that the allocation of respective powers in these areas differs very widely among countries. It is necessary to review each country's experience in these areas and to endow greater powers in the legislatures where needed. From this point of view, the greatest need for improvement is felt in the British Commonwealth type of systems, where a government, once elected, can function, with a party whip, in a semi autocratic way for the next five years. It would also be prudent to restrict the possibilities of excessive interference by congressional type systems, and to provide selected opportunities during a fiscal year for congressional intervention.

Another issue that needs to be addressed relates to the role of the community in fiscal decision making. Once the representatives are elected, the community has little role to play, except in critical periods when it galvanizes its efforts to either oppose or to approve legislation that is then under consideration. Entrusting it with a greater power of oversight may be equivalent to an expression of lack of faith in the effectiveness of the legislative institutions. Should powers be given to the community to replace the existing system or to supplement the existing system? In most cases the efforts are related to the latter objective and revolve around the provision of more information to the electorate to make up its mind and to express its preferences. It is pointed out that the community is generally informed after a decision has been taken, after a policy has been formulated, or at a stage when it is too late to make its presence felt and its voice heard. In this regard, notwithstanding all the recent emphasis on fiscal transparency, there is a good deal that remains to be done. The issues raised here suggest that expenditure management continues to be a work in progress and there are several gaps in its functioning in a democratic society that need to be addressed.

2.3.2 Institutional Development and Expenditure Management

During the last two decades considerable emphasis has been laid by the international financial institutions (and more financial resources devoted) on the development of institutions and related administrative capacity, to serve the needs of improved governance. To some extent this emphasis is very well deserved. In regard to expenditure management, the issue is not one of creating new institutions (except in transition countries, which offer a different set of issues), but one of addressing the hurdles or the factors that have been contributing to their relative lackluster performance. Most developing countries have already in place an inherited framework of institutions, which include a budget office with separate identity or as a part of finance ministry, a central accounting office responsible for the collection and consolidation of government finance data, and an established and well functioning audit system with significant independence in the choice of its work program. In addition, several countries have a planning organization responsible for the provision of policy guidance, and an evaluation office responsible for carrying economic evaluation of completed programs and projects. To that extent, it could be argued that there is an adequate nucleus of institutions. But the major question is: why are they not effective?

In addressing this question, three strands of thought have emerged over the years. The first addressed the issue of technological underpinning needed for the efficient functioning of the expenditure management system. Although the usual quota of technological glitches continues to affect the systems in a few cases, this has been an area that witnessed significant progress in a short duration. The second strand deals with the structure of relationships between central and spending agencies. International financial institutions tend to take the view that strong central agencies are essential for the successful pursuit of macroeconomic policies. The approach is based more on assertions than on empirical evidence. In fact, if anything, the problem seems to be the highly powerful finance ministries that tend to interfere and that dominate the day to day working of spending agencies. Many finance ministries tend to argue that there is no financial conscience in the spending agencies, and as such all the tasks devolve on the central agencies. The reality, however, is one where governments have grown so big that no single agency, however powerful it is, is in a position to ensure a government-wide adherence by locating the responsibility for day to day management in itself. The impact of these approaches may not be felt on the overall growth of the economy, which is determined by several other factors. But it is generally known that, while the results of centralization of power cannot be statistically proven, it is a malaise that is common and ubiquitous and with a general adverse impact on the way in which government organizations are expected to work. Centralization leads to accumulation of power, and to the potential arbitrary use of power. Resource use is of common concern to all agencies and should therefore be internalized into decision making of every agency. This requires greater decentralization of power from the finance ministries to the spending agencies. There is a need for an urgent review of the complex web of relationships between the central and spending agencies and to remove the many irritants now felt.

Yet another issue reflects on the adoption of best practices in the improvement of expenditure management system. The international financial institutions have been urging the countries for more than a decade on the need for adopting best practices. The United Nations and others, who have been aiding the New Partnership for African Development (NEPAD), have advocated the use of best practices for the development of sub-Sahara African countries. Experience shows, however, that practices found to be best in some countries may not lend themselves for replication elsewhere. The implementation of performance budgeting and its variants in many developing countries during the late sixties and early seventies shows that, in the absence of compliance of preconditions, innovations grafted from abroad would not work and, in the event, despite an urgent need to move away from the conventional budgeting system, the imported ideas did not develop roots in the countries. This aspect has been recognized by the World Bank, which has shifted its advocacy from best practices to best fits or the importance of identifying the local needs first and then tailoring the remedy to suit the local situation.

Institutional improvement is too important a matter to be left to the specialization of International Financial institutions. It requires the joint efforts of the country authorities and the international institutions and in each case the ground realities need to be ascertained first. Umbrella themes advocated by the international financial institutions need to be translated into specific action packages to deal with identified problems which differ from one country to another.

2.3.3 Fiscal Policy and Expenditure Management

The experience of the last three decades has conclusively illustrated the linkages between fiscal policy and expenditure management and how the latter moved from what was considered as a marginal factor to the heart of national economic management. The primary goal of expenditure management is now to secure macroeconomic stability and to effectively buttress the pursuit of fiscal policy in all possible ways. But there are significant differences between countries of the industrial world and the developing world in the way in which fiscal policy is formulated and implemented. An important dimension of fiscal policy is to evolve a countercyclical strategy when needed. In the industrial world, this task is considerably facilitated by the development of automatic stabilizers. In the developing world, there are as yet very few automatic stabilizers and all actions tend to be discretionary in nature. The formulation and implementation of discretionary policy packages takes time, and by the time they are brought into force the developments in the economy may have changed and the policy packages may have lost their relevance. Yet another distinction relates to the state of capital markets. These are well developed in the industrial countries and governments have an advantage in tapping them. In the developing worlds there are very few that have a well developed capital market and, as such, resort has to be made to external borrowing that takes considerable time and, more significantly, provides a prominent voice in policy making to external creditors, and a corresponding loss of economic sovereignty and independence in policy making. A third feature that separates the developing countries, requiring in turn a more cautious approach to policy making and greater resort to risk management approaches, relates to the high level of economic vulnerabilities and their impact on economic stability. Capital inflows and outflows have their own logic and associated uncertainties. A quick and large outflow of capital may require, in several cases, substantial revisions in the fiscal policies and change of directions. The sudden reversals are often difficult in developing countries and as a consequence they tend to be more crisis-prone. These differences illustrate the additional built-in difficulties encountered in developing countries.

In both types of countries the major problem during recent years has been perceived to be the inexorable growth of expenditure and the consequent widening budget deficits. Both types have been engaged in the prolonged fight against this tendency and, in the process, the expenditure management system has been given new tasks and new instruments to tackle them. But their effects have been too short-lived and, as noted before, there are several factors contributing to demands for additional expenditure. More specifically there are three factors that merit recognition. First, the normal demands for additional expenditures have been repressed too long and cannot afford to be kept on a short leash any longer, except at considerable cost to economic growth. Second, there have been steady changes in the demographic factors that have been contributing, in turn, to steady growth in old age pensions and medical care of the elderly. Third, greater reliance on borrowing has contributed to an increase in gross expenditure. Such reliance leads to short-term comforts and additional mobilization of resources is unavoidable in the medium term. These factors place additional stress on the expenditure management machinery that needs to be addressed with other problems that have surfaced during years.

The experience of governments with fiscal stress in both industrial and developing countries shows that the expenditure machinery had little capacity to anticipate the coming fiscal crises, and to prepare itself for dealing with it. Now, however, there are all sorts of indexes that are available to governments to monitor so as to be ready to anticipate the crises. It is important, however, that this aspect is internalized into the management practices and a capacity developed to deal with contingencies. The experience also shows that the austerity management was far from successful, primarily because it lacked a balanced strategy. Far too heavy a reliance was placed on compression of investment outlays and across-the-board cuts that had unanticipated adverse impact on the delivery of essential services. The system also overlooked the emergence of steady leakages and resorted to escape mechanisms that were working counter to the policy intent. In several cases the restrictions on manpower were compensated through resort to the hiring of consultants; where purchase of machinery was denied, there was a growing resort to leasing of machinery. Where the budget disciplines tended to be restrictive, extra budgetary accounts were created outside the normal process of control. These factors, which vary in incidence from one country to another, need to be identified, and the management system strengthened to deal with them. Moreover, the experiences also show that, in aiming at a moderation of the rate of expenditure growth, emphasis was placed on ad hoc approaches that essentially missed the contributory factors. In most cases annual increases in expenditure are caused by grade inflation (more positions than necessary), pay revision in anticipation of future cost increases, higher cost of selected categories of equipment, particularly in defense and medical services, and greater resort to domestic borrowing as a means of financing, with the inevitable effect of an increase in program costs. In this context, across-the-board cuts or prolonged suppression of investment outlays are unlikely to have any enduring effect on the growth of expenditures. Rather, the approaches of expenditure management should place more emphasis on fundamental reviews and on reduced borrowing, The experience shows that, as more reliance is placed on public–private partnerships to provide services, and as the third party payments grow relentlessly, the public sector is also losing the battle on the control of payments, because of the growing distance between funding and service provision, on the one hand, and arrangements for the risk sharing, on the other.

If expenditure management is to serve the goals of fiscal policy, it is imperative then that reliance on outmoded instruments is reduced, and greater emphasis placed on the development of new tools aimed at dealing with the new problems.

2.3.4 *Anchor of Expenditure Management*

Every management system has either an intended or perceived anchor which is well recognized by both the central and spending agencies. Traditionally, such an anchor was perceived to be the special attention to the creation of personnel positions in the agencies. Such an emphasis was justified on the consideration that the size of manpower was the most important component of government expenditure and the argument was that, once the level of manpower was determined, there was an assured control on a major section of expenditures. But this battle against the growth of manpower was lost a long time ago, as most of the requirements were determined with reference to supply-driven formulas that had little to do with the availability of resources or with the demand for services. As governments assumed several new functions it became inevitable that the formula based determination of manpower would contribute to growing expenditures, and the futility of expenditure control approaches became too apparent to be continued. As a consequence, reliance on manpower has yielded place, over the years, to the formulation of overall resource ceilings for agencies. In several industrial countries, the determination of manpower requirements is now delegated as a management task to the agency heads for so long as it is assured that their operations would be carried out within the individual allotted ceilings of resources.

In developing countries the anchor shifted, at least for a period, from manpower determination to control of investment projects. Toward this end, investment appraisals were adopted, and emphasis was placed on scrupulous adherence to the golden principle. As the share of investment outlays declined, so also the importance of this anchor declined. In this flux of time there was recognition that the base of the anchor should be far wider and broad-based in scope. In due course, the concept of "running cost" — all outlays on a program or a project became the notional anchor of expenditure management. In theory, this concept should have given a comprehensive tool to review the cost components of every program. In practice, however, it proved less than successful, as computation of costs in government is, as yet, an art that is invoked only at infrequent intervals and there is no system that spews out data on costs regularly. To some extent, this handicap is inherent in a cash based system. Also, the annual budget determination for the running costs became an automatic affair, as it was based on supply driven formulas, or were permitted to grow at the same rate as the projected rate of growth of G.D.P. In the event, this automatically contributed to regular increases in expenditures, and had no moderating influence on the rate of growth of expenditure. What was expected to become a new tool of control became a problem that was worse than the malady. New anchors remain to be developed.

Looking forward, it is to be hoped that the technique of activity-based costing would provide the much needed anchor. This technique, which is widely used in the corporate sector, permits a computation of costs for each activity of an agency, and therefore an analysis of cost drivers and the reasons contributing to cost growth. In governments, these reasons could be extremely diverse in view of the large range and varied nature of the work. But the technique permits an identification of the growth-contributing factors, each in its own setting. Cost computation does not always need as a condition precedent the introduction of accrual accounting. Every activity need not be costed, and the inquiry could be limited to those areas where a considerable growth is being experienced. In those cases, cost can be computed through ad hoc efforts.

The absence of a reliable anchor implies that the system is becoming vapid and arbitrary. It is therefore of utmost importance that an anchor is developed at the earliest. Past experience shows that management systems have adequate, if always a step behind the needs, resilience and adaptability. It should now be made forward looking, and endowed with a capacity to rapidly adjust to the changing requirements.

Chapter 3

Capital Budgeting and Planning

WES CLARKE, Ph.D.
Institute of Government, University of Georgia

Capital budgeting is the process by which entities acquire facilities, infrastructure, and many other costly items needed for their activities. State and local governments use a variety of processes to identify and select capital items; they also finance these acquisitions in a number of ways, but primarily with debt in the form of municipal bonds. Regardless of the specific manner in which an entity produces its capital budget, capital items are generally defined as those things that produce benefits beyond the current year. Unlike operating expenditures, such as personal services and office supplies that provide benefits only in the year they are purchased, capital items typically provide benefits for much longer periods. The Golden Gate Bridge, for example, has been in use since 1937. Though it has been in use for nearly 70 years it is being consumed as surely as any office supply item. With proper maintenance it will last for many more decades. Without proper maintenance it would deteriorate very rapidly. Capital budgeting, then, consists not only of acquiring the infrastructure needed to provide services but also maintaining those items in order to achieve their longest possible use.

Capital planning is critical to the well being of a jurisdiction and its citizens. The cost and permanent nature of most capital items means that mistakes made in selecting and evaluating projects can have negative consequences for many years. At least two stages of project evaluation are often required before a project gains approval. The initial screening activities ensure that only those projects that make sense within the goals of the entity's strategic plan are considered for the capital budget. In subsequent phases, the projects that survive this initial screening are evaluated in terms of their feasibility, both practical and economic.

The high cost of capital items means that relatively large shares of a jurisdiction's resources must be committed. If the central supply unit of a municipal government purchases boxes of ink pens that do not work well, there is no great loss, but if the city builds a government building in the wrong place, or with the wrong floor plan to serve the intended purpose, the problem is much more difficult to address. The economic concept of opportunity cost is important in evaluating individual projects and in deciding between competing projects. Commitment of resources for one project means foregoing some other project or activity.

The process used to produce an entity's operating budget is not appropriate for the capital budget for other reasons as well. Capital items are generally designed to meet the community's needs for several years. No jurisdiction wants to build a new capital facility that will be obsolete in a year. Capital items are also complex. While the city manager's office may be able to forecast its operating needs in terms of personal services and office supplies, a new city hall will likely serve a number of different and separate operations (city manger, finance department, municipal clerk, planning and zoning, etc.) whose needs for office and storage space, and equipment, must be coordinated in the design and construction of the facility. Also, the process for evaluating the construction of a new municipal facility will be nothing like the appropriate process for deciding where to locate a school or public park, or purchase new police vehicles. Because the items under consideration vary from year to year, the routine used for producing an operating budget is simply not appropriate.

Capital spending is cyclical. Entities experience tremendous variation in the amount of capital that is acquired each year. Buchanan (1965) compared this cyclical characteristic of capital budgeting to a club that builds facilities as its membership reaches certain plateaus, both in numbers and diverse preferences. An entity that constructed a particular type of facility, say a new jail, in one year, might not need to construct another one for a decade or more. He also noted that it is quite likely that, as certain population plateaus are achieved, several new facilities (jail, police station, water plant, etc.) would be needed at once. These aspects further suggest that capital planning and budgeting require special processes.

Capital items are expensive, making funding difficult. Two major approaches to funding capital items are pay-as-you-go and pay-as-you-use. In the former, capital purchases are funded with current resources, those received this year or saved from previous years. In the latter, debt in the form of municipal bonds is sold in the market with the proceeds used to purchase the capital item. Over time the debt is repaid with current resources. There are two major types of debt available depending on the nature of the project to be financed. If the capital item produces an identifiable revenue stream, such as water system infrastructure or a toll road, that revenue can be pledged for repayment. This type is called a revenue bond. For capital items that have general benefits and do not produce direct revenue streams, such as a city hall or most parks, general obligation debt is used. This type is backed by the ability of the jurisdiction to extract resources in the form of taxes, often called the full faith and credit of the issuing government. The pay-as-you-go and the pay-as-you-use approaches each have their benefits and limitations, which will be discussed in a later section.

3.1 Process

3.1.1 Project Identification

For entities that do not currently use a separate capital budget process, the first step in implementation is to produce an inventory of capital items. Many entities have recently undertaken this activity following the issuance of GASB Statement 34 from the Governmental Accounting Standards Board that requires reporting the fair value of capital assets in their Comprehensive Annual Financial Statements (for a discussion, see Martin and West, 2003, chapter 5; Ruppel, 2002, chapter 12). Using the knowledge gained from such an exercise, officials should have a general understanding of the condition of existing infrastructure, and have a context within which to evaluate projects that are proposed for the future.

Once the inventory is produced, officials should solicit proposals for new projects. Most needs, especially those for maintenance of existing facilities, will be identified by employees working in those facilities. The so-called hidden infrastructure, such as water and sewer lines and the mechanical systems in public buildings, are best assessed by individuals who are trained to work with those systems. In some cases, engineers or consultants may be needed to perform a condition assessment and determine the available and unused capacity of systems. Capacity assessment is especially important when growth is experienced or anticipated.

While employees identify most of the critical needs of the jurisdiction, projects will be proposed from many other persons both inside and outside government. Elected officials will propose projects, especially in their districts in the case of members of a council or commission. Mayors, city managers, and other executives may propose projects to fulfill a campaign promise, advance a personal goal or vision, or to satisfy demands from particular citizens or groups. Citizens' preferences for capital projects will vary a great deal. One citizen or group may want more park space, while another wants a project that produces economic activity, growth, and jobs.

3.1.2 Prioritization of Needs

The first goal in evaluating proposed projects is to screen out those that are not feasible or that do not fit well with the strategic plan for the jurisdiction. The two, sometimes competing, interests in evaluating the projects that make this first cut are political considerations and economics (Bland and Clarke, 1999). Neither necessarily trumps the other with most decisions taking both into consideration. Nunn (1991) describes the process in terms of the formal process that includes procedures for proposing and evaluating projects, and the informal process that takes place in every jurisdiction. The formal process specifies how projects are proposed and evaluated. Evaluation usually consists of feasibility and, in the case of projects that are expected to produce revenue, some type of cost-benefit analysis or cost efficiency analysis.

The informal process consists of deals between public officials, between officials and developers, or between state and local officials. In some instances, projects are moved ahead of others due to public safety or health concerns, a short window of opportunity, or because the plans of another agency or entity make it expedient. The classic example of the public works department repaving a street, only to have the water department tear it up a month later to install a new water main, has been told about numerous entities.

There are a number of critieria that should guide the prioritization of capital projects within the larger political and economic considerations. Assuming there does not exist a total lack of resources, the first criteria is public safety or health. Projects that are needed to address major safety and health risks should have priority. Items that have a critical safety function, such as a traffic control device, levy, or dam that is damaged, must be repaired immediately even if other projects must be delayed. Beyond prioritizing the project, though, economic considerations may determine how best to achieve the desired outcome. It may make economic sense to replace a wooden bridge that becomes unsafe with some other type of span. The economic analysis and the availability of resources will guide the choice of how best to replace the structure.

Table 3.1 Suggested Evaluation Criteria

1. Fiscal impacts (on costs and revenues)
2. Health and safety issues
3. Community economic effects
4. Environmental, aesthetic, and social effects
5. Amount of disruption and inconvenience caused by the project
6. Distributional effects — who is affected and how
7. Feasibility, including public support and project readiness
8. Implications of deferring the project
9. Amount of uncertainty and risk
10. Effects on interjurisdictional relationships
11. Advantages accruing from relationship to other capital proposals

Beyond public safety, there are a number of ways to develop a general priority of projects. Hatry, Millar, and Evans (1984) suggest the criteria in Table 3.1 as appropriate. These criteria should be considered in a holistic sense, especially when evaluating disparate projects. It is one thing to consider the long-term maintenance costs of two types of bridges that are being considered. It is quite another to compare the operating budget impacts of a new building and a park. The importance of each item in Table 3.1 will depend on the particular projects under consideration.

Another scheme for ranking projects is presented in Table 3.2. Under this rubric, projects are evaluated taking existing capital into consideration. Projects that improve the utilization of existing infrastructure, or that expand an existing facility to meet increased need, are given priority over new construction. After ranking projects according to the criteria in item one, decision makers should consider the issues in item two. What will be the consequences of waiting another year? Is there new technology (or a

Table 3.2 Project Evaluation Strategy

1. Criteria for evaluation
   a. Safety issues
   b. Facilitate utilization of existing facilities (renovation)
   c. Expanding facilities to meet increased demand
   d. New facilities for new programs
2. Other major considerations
   a. Can the project wait another year?
   b. How sensitive is the plan to changes in population, technology, etc?
   c. Is the projected cost comparable to experience with other projects?
   d. Are more cost effective options available? (Remodelling, renovation etc.)

price decrease) likely in the near future that would warrant waiting? Does the project make sense in terms of its costs and feasibility?

Henry Thomassen (1990) warns that we too often focus on capital acquisition, usually in the form of new construction, rather than the issue of capital consumption. All capital is consumed, even the Golden Gate Bridge, as noted above. Thomassen suggests that we should consider the value of the capital stock and the change from year to year in that figure rather than on the amount spent on new projects. Our goal should be to leave the capital stock in better condition at the end of the year than it was at the beginning. Only by focusing on maintenance and cost-effective use of new spending can this be accomplished.

Up to this point, projects that have been proposed have been subject to an intial screening and a general prioritization. At least two other issues in the prioritization should take place at this point. First, projects of an elective nature (the way a face lift is elective compared to an appendectomy) should be prioritized along district lines. Members of a city council or county commission that represent a single geographic district will compete for capital dollars since projects are the electoral coin of the realm. Decision makers should be careful that elected officials' affinity for new, flashy projects does not undermine the critieria in Tables 3.1 and 3.2. Thomassen (1990) suggests that this is a real danger in planning capital projects. There is nothing about a new roof and air conditioning system for city hall that can be turned into votes. A ribbon cutting at a new branch library is much more useful for the purpose. It is important to make sure that capital spending is equitably distributed to all areas and districts in the jurisdiction.

In 1971 the Fifth Circuit Court of Appeals ruled in *Hawkins versus Town of Shaw, Mississippi* (437 F.2d 1286) that the town's ad hoc approach to capital improvements over a period dating back to the 1930s, while seemingly justifiable on economic development grounds, had favored white neighborhoods to a much greater extent than African-American ones. (For a discussion of *Hawkins versus Town of Shaw*, see Rosenbloom, Carroll, and Carroll, 2000.) It is interesting to note that capital construction (paving, street lights, water improvements, etc.) had proceeded without a master plan. Indeed, the author of the Court's decision notes that, while there is no evidence that the town intended to discriminate, the cumulative disparate impact of decisions over time violated the equal protection clause of the U.S. Constitution. Using a master plan and determining how proposed projects fit within the plan, and paying attention to the distribution of spending across districts, can prevent problems like those found in Shaw.

The second consideration following a general prioritization is to ensure that projects are reasonably distributed across functions. Too much spending on roads and bridges to the neglect of buildings and parks will create problems in the future and may favor one segment of the population over another.

3.1.3   The Capital Improvement Plan

Projects that survive the initial screening and are prioritized become part of the capital improvement plan (CIP). The CIP is a list of capital projects that the city intends to complete over a five- to seven-year period. Again, decision makers should view the CIP as an extension of the city's master plan. In some jurisdictions the two are part of a single document, but projects contained in the CIP should be viewed as tools to advance the broader goals stated in the plan.

The formal process used in most jurisdictions calls for projects to be added to the out year (year five or seven) and work their way up until they become part of the capital budget. Although many projects can be traced through the process in the prescribed manner, some projects will be fast-tracked through the process either for health and safety concerns, or due to elements of the informal process discussed earlier. Also, some projects will drop off the CIP after one or more years because the need no longer exists or the project becomes unfeasible. What may seem like a good idea at one time may not make sense two years later. This may be especially true for projects that involve technology purchases.

Figure 3.1 contains a page from the CIP for the city of Anderson, South Carolina. This detail presents a basic description of the item to be built, its estimated cost and the year that it will be constructed. The page also includes a statement of the impact the project will have on the operating budget. In this case the impact is rather small. There may be some inspection and maintenance activities, but those may be absorbed under the current budget for the department with this responsibility. In some instances, especially when infrastructure is replaced or upgraded, the maintenance costs in terms of personal services and other resources may actually be reduced.

Figures 3.2 and 3.3 contain pages from the city of Plano, Texas' CIP. The summary page in Figure 3.2 presents a total of all municipal facilities projects that are included in Plano's plan. Note that not all of these projects will be built in the current year since the CIP is a five-year plan. Plano's CIP contains a detail page on each project like the one for the Animal Shelter Expansion in Figure 3.3. This page presents information on the project to be built, a map showing the location of the facility, the time frame for construction and completion, the funding source (in this case bonds), and the impact the expansion of this facility will have on the operating budget beginning in 2007–08.

City of Anderson
CIP project
Planning and Transportation
FY 2004 – 2008

Project: **Bicycle/Pedestrian Pathway**

Divisions: **Planning & Transportation**

Description:
Based on the Bicycle/Pedestrian Pathway Plan, engineering for the first three phases of the project can proceed. These phases include the greenway along Cox's Creek and linkages to the Sports Complex from the greenway. After the engineering phase is complete, construction can begin on those phases, utilizing enhancement funding.

Financing plan

Facility/ equipment	Type of improvement	Estimated cost	Year needed
Phase I, II, III of Bicycle Pedestrian Pathway	Construction	600,000	2004
		$ 600,000	
Financing sources:			
	Enhancement	$ 480,000	
	funds shortfall	$ 120,000	
		$ 600,000	

Assessment of operating impact:
There are negligible increased operating costs associated with this project.
Assessment of financing issues:
None

Figure 3.1 CIP item from Anderson, SC.

3.2 Methods of Evaluating Projects

The cost estimates for a particular project, such as the facility expansion project in Figure 3.3, may be of the ball park variety when the project is initially proposed and even after it is included in the CIP. At some point, however, the city will need to prepare an accurate projection of the project's costs. This estimate will need to take into consideration increases in materials and labor costs that may have occurred since the initial proposal

Municipal Facilities Projects

Project	Prior years	Re-est	2004-05	2005-06	2006-07	2007-08	2008-09	Future	Total
Police facilities									
93105 Criminal justice expansion	3,906,000	9,000	0	0	0	0	0	0	3,915,000
93106 Police parking expansion	470,000	30,000	0	0	0	0	0	0	500,000
93107 Tri-city academy expansion	0	2,389,000	1,210,000	0	0	0	0	0	3,599,000
25-P02 Court/jail expansion	0	0	0	0	0	0	0	5,500,000	5,500,000
	4,376,000	2,428,000	1,210,000	0	0	0	0	5,500,000	13,514,000
Fire facilities									
10105 Fire station reconfiguration	1,923,000	18,000	0	0	250,000	2,750,000	0	0	4,941,000
10211 Fire station 12	2,000	0	2,300,000	3,425,000	0	0	0	0	5,727,000
10212 Fire station 11	0	237,000	3,100,000	0	0	0	0	0	3,337,000
10213 Fire station 13	656,000	0	0	0	250,000	3,350,000	0	0	4,256,000
10214 Fire station 4 expansion	0	0	0	0	150,000	1,950,000	0	0	2,100,000
28-P01 Emergency operations center	0	0	0	250,000	4,250,000	0	0	0	4,500,000
28-P02 Storage/warehouse space	0	0	0	150,000	1,350,000	0	0	0	1,500,000
28-P03 Security enhancement	0	0	0	2,000,000	0	0	0	0	2,000,000
28-P05 Engine	0	0	0	0	400,000	0	0	0	400,000
	2,581,000	255,000	5,400,000	5,825,000	6,650,000	8,050,000	0	0	28,761,000
Library facilities									
17107 Haggard library expansion & parking lot	253,000	210,000	3,500,000	180,000	0	0	0	0	4,143,000
27-P01 Library improvements	0	0	100,000	1,250,000	1,400,000	0	0	0	2,750,000
27-P02 Library #6	0	0	0	0	0	750,000	5,050,000	0	5,800,000
	253,000	210,000	3,600,000	1,430,000	1,400,000	750,000	5,050,000	0	12,693,000
Parking facilities									
19001 Municipal center parking expansion	709,000	50,000	91,000	0	0	0	0	0	850,000
19002 Downtown parking expansion	599,000	150,000	51,000	0	0	0	0	0	800,000
	1,308,000	200,000	142,000	0	0	0	0	0	1,650,000
Other facilities									
56532 Collin County cultural arts district	70,000	696,000	0	0	0	0	0	0	766,000
57541 Animal shelter expansion	2,250,000	149,967	0	200,000	1,155,000	0	0	0	3,754,967
59591 Service center site improvements	1,024,000	19,000	0	0	0	0	0	0	1,043,000
61100 Joint use facility	3,394,000	606,000	0	0	0	0	0	0	4,000,000
31-P01 Environmental education building	0	0	0	280,000	720,000	0	0	0	1,000,000
31-P02 Radio system infrastructure replacement	0	0	0	0	0	15,000,000	0	0	15,000,000
	6,738,000	1,470,967	0	480,000	1,875,000	15,000,000	0	0	25,563,967
Total municipal facilities	15,256,000	4,563,967	10,352,000	7,735,000	9,925,000	23,800,000	5,050,000	5,500,000	82,181,000

Figure 3.2   Facilities summary page — CIP, City of Plano, TX.

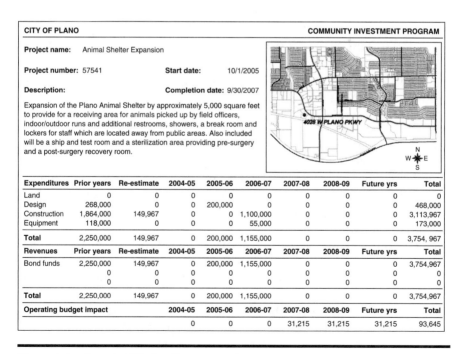

Figure 3.3   Sample CIP detail page — Plano, TX.

was accepted. If these figures vary greatly, however, officials should explore the reasons, to make sure that the project has not been modified in any material way and that its feasibility and intended use still fit with the overall plan for the jurisdiction.

Many projects, such as an animal control facility, are not optional. Jurisdictions are expected to provide certain services that are capital intensive. However, some economic development projects are proposed because we believe they will attract new businesses, tourists, jobs, or other development. In these cases, an economic analysis is appropriate to provide confidence that the benefits are likely to materialize and often so that competing projects can be evaluated based on the benefits they are likely to produce.

3.2.1 Cost Benefit Analysis

The use of cost benefit analysis (CBA) is appropriate when a project produces primarily economic benefits. It is less appropriate when the benefits of a project are largely aesthetic or otherwise intangible. That is not to say that intangible benefits cannot be valued. CBA is used in many instances where monetary values are placed on intangible benefits and concepts like beauty and human life. If CBA were the sole form of analysis used to evaluate public projects, we would proceed with those where the ratio of benefits to costs is greater than one, and eliminate from consideration those that fail to achieve at least a one-to-one ratio. In practice, CBA is only one tool that we use to evaluate projects. Decision makers should use CBA where appropriate as part of the process, but politics and personal preferences will play a role as well.

Four essential steps make up the CBA procedure (Nas, 1996, 60: (1) identify all the relevant costs and benefits, (2) measurement of costs and benefits, (3) comparison of cost benefit streams accruing during the lifetime of the project, and (4) project selection.

In the first step, the costs and benefits related to the project are identified and justified. In every analysis there will be winners and losers. Someone will benefit from the project and someone will pay, usually in the form of taxes, but also with land exactions, and opportunity costs of the resources. Sunk costs should be ignored in determining whether to proceed or eliminate a project from consideration. For example, the original cost to build a municipal office building should not be included in the analysis to decide whether to renovate or replace the structure.

The process of identifying benefits includes determining which benefits to count in the analysis. Some that may seem appropriate may not be. For example, a municipality that decides to build a new golf course may expect an increase in property values in the area because of the new facility and additional economic development that will occur. The increase in property values accrues to individuals, not society as a whole, and should not be counted in the benefit column. These benefits are said to be pecuniary rather than real output effects. To the extent that property or sales tax revenue are expected to increase, society benefits and those benefits should be included.

In step three, the costs and benefits are measured. Most costs associated with capital projects at the local level are fairly easily estimated. A number of estimation techniques may be used, including pricing out of materials specified in the plans from competitive markets sources, and estimating the cost per square foot based on similar projects. If the goal is to get an analysis done quickly and easily, the latter may have to suffice. In cases where more uncertainty exists, the more detailed method may be necessary.

Some benefits associated with a project may be easily identified. The expansion of a convention center or other venue may produce additional revenue that can be estimated with surprising accuracy based on surveys of potential users. The municipal golf course example is a good one. Many consulting firms specialize in this and other types of public facilities and are very adept at determining the viability of such a project. Of course, it is not uncommon for a municipality to proceed with a project like a golf course even after the analysis indicates that it is a bad idea.

Intangible costs and benefits cannot be ignored even though they are difficult to value. A road project that is expected to cut the commute times of 20,000 persons by 11 minutes has produced a benefit to society. This benefit, though it accrues to individuals, is not pecuniary since the benefit accrues to such a large number. Other benefits that may accrue from this project are improved air quality from fewer cars idling in bumper-to-bumper traffic, and less wear and tear on pavement if more traffic lanes are now carrying the load. As difficult as these benefits are to value, the most difficult is human life. Many road improvement projects are designed to reduce the frequency and severity of accidents, reducing loss of life. Several methods of valuing human life have been used, including the expected lifetime earnings of persons and interviewing persons to determine how much a person would pay to reduce the probability of his or her death (Nas, 1996, 108). Other intangible benefits include the aesthetic value of green space, individual enjoyment of parks and other public spaces, and civic pride. This last item is often used to justify investment in sports venues when teams threaten to leave a city.

The benefits and costs that are expected over the lifetime of the project must be converted to a net present value. That is, a dollar of benefit that is not expected for a year is worth something less than one dollar to society today. Because costs and benfits are experienced at different times and at different rates, the selection of a discount rate is critical. Often the analyst will perform the analysis using several discount rates to determine its sensitivity to the rate. Among other things, the discount rate must take into consideration the cost of money, risk and uncertainty, opportunity costs of investment in the project, and the likelihood that future generations' preferences will change.

Project selection using cost benefit analysis is appropriate when the considerations are primarily economic as noted above. Many agencies, such as the North Texas Tollway Authority in the Dallas-Fort Worth metroplex, use a fairly straightfoward economic analysis in deciding which projects are built and which are not. The expected revenues in the form of tolls must be sufficient to meet the debt service on the bonds required to construct the road, bridge, or tunnel. For many special districts that provide capital intensive services such as toll roads, CBA may be the only decision calculus. For municipal and county governments that provide a broad array of services and facilities it should be used where appropriate to help inform the decision.

3.2.2   Other Evaluation Standards

Cost effectiveness analysis (CEA) and return on investment (ROI) are two other rules for evaluation that may be appropriate in some cases. Cost effectiveness analysis is used to evaluate competing projects, either in terms of their cost to produce a given benefit, or in terms of the benefit each would produce at a specified cost level. In either case, the analysis technique is similar to the one described in the preceding section. Often, when the primary benefit is intangible and difficult to measure, CEA provides an easier means of evaluating the relative advantages of two or more alternative projects.

Return on investment is used extensively in business where the decision is between competing investments. Its use in the evaluation of public facilities is limited, but can provide additional information when other things are equal. The ROI is calculated as the discount rate that produces a net present value of zero. Most spreadsheet programs can perform this function easily given a stream of net revenues (revenues less expenditures in each year). Two excellent and detailed treatments of the CBA process are Nas (1996) and Gramlich (1990b).

3.3   Funding the Capital Budget

Officials ideally should fund about 20 percent of their CIP projects in terms of the number of projects or the total dollar volume of projects that have been approved for the CIP. Failure to fund projects at an acceptable rate may mean that too many projects that have been proposed and accepted will languish in the CIP for longer than five years. This may be indicative of poor planning and could cause political turmoil among supporters of those projects. The projects that have moved to the top of the CIP, either over a period of years, or due to their urgency, become the capital budget. The exact number of projects that are funded will be determined by the amount of resources that can be dedicated to capital acquisition. It is not uncommon that one or two projects slated for construction, having moved up the CIP over the five-year period, will have to wait another year.

As mentioned earlier, capital items may be funded in two basic ways. Current resources, either cash on hand or revenue that will be received during the course of the fiscal year, is often used to fund small capital items, or when fund balances are higher than needed for prudent financial management. Another advantage to using current resources when funds are available is that voter approval for such expenditures is not needed, as it typically is for issuing general obligation debt. The cost of conducting a special bond referendum when an emergency need arises simply may not be a wise expenditure when the project must be undertaken to correct a dangerous situation.

There are other benefits to using current resources. It avoids interest expense and preserves the debt issuance capacity of the jurisdiction (for a discussion see Hackbart and Ramsey, 1993). It may also limit profligate spending by a city council or county commission. Requiring that certain types of projects or items be funded from current resources may limit the bells-and-whistles mentality that often accompanies debt financing. Finally, capital acquisition that does not increase the debt total of the entity improves the debt to assets ratio that bond rating companies use as one factor in establishing general obligation debt ratings.

Funding with debt has pros and cons as well. Using debt links the cost of capital facilities with users. Building a fund balance in its general fund sufficient to construct a major facility, say a library, might take several years in even a large entity. Each year is a different generation of taxpayers. Some move away and others move in each year. Some who contributed nothing or very little will have use of the facility while some who contributed quite a bit move and receive no benefit. This intergenerational inequity is resolved through the use of debt for major capital acquisitions, especially those with very long useful lives.

Some projects simply cost too much ever to be built with current resources. One of the trends in the use of capital construction for economic development are massive projects such as airports, rail transit systems, central city highway projects like the so-called Big Dig in Boston. The funding strategies for projects like the one in Boston are so complex that federal, state, and local officials must work closely with one another (Altshuler and Luberoff, 2003), unlike a century ago when major projects could be bartered by well connected individuals (see Doig, 1995).

The use of debt also allows governments to purchase what they need, when they need it, and build a greater variety of projects. As noted earlier, the cyclical nature of capital acquisition makes it fiscally impossible to pay for even most capital purchases with current revenue. The use of debt allows entities to maintain stable tax rates. The property tax, relied on heavily by most local governments, needs to remain fairly level from year to year so that taxpayers, both homeowners and businesses, can plan their budgets.

3.3.1   Setting the Capital Budget

The amount of resources available for funding capital projects is determined by the current resources that can be devoted to purchases and debt service. Debt is typically repaid over two to twenty years, sometimes longer. In any given year old debt is retired, allowing the jurisdiction to issue a similar amount of new debt without increasing the budget for debt service. Debt service is commonly structured so that payments of principal and interest are equal over a period of time. The maturity period when debt is fully retired should be no longer than the life expectancy of the capital item funded. Many jurisdictions limit the maturity on debt to 80 percent of the expected life, a more conservative policy. Other debt policy considerations are discussed in another section.

3.3.2   Types of Debt and Method of Sale

3.3.2.1   GO Bonds

General obligation, or GO bonds, are backed by the full faith and credit of the issuing government, the ad valorem taxing power. In most states, GO bonds require a special election and are approved for specific purposes. For example, the proceeds from the sales of bonds approved for street projects cannot be used to fund a public building. GO bonds are viewed by the municipal bond market as the most secure type of debt and therefore sell at the lowest interest rates for municipal bond debt. In most, but not all states, GO bonds must be sold by sealed competitive bid. This means that underwriters responding to the offer to issue such debt propose an interest rate the issuing government pays, with the issue being sold to the lowest competent bidder.

In some states, local governments, including school districts, are authorized to issue general obligation debt that does not require voter approval. Often called a certificate of obligation or general obligation certificate, these instruments are usually issued for small or emergency needs. In some cases, however, they are used to fund large projects that have been mandated by higher levels of government when voter refusal to approve the debt would not affect the jurisdiction's responsibility to construct the project. Requirements for certain minimum size and quality facilities have been imposed on local governments in several areas, but primarily schools, jails, and hospitals.

3.3.2.2 Revenue Bonds

Revenue bonds are backed by a dedicated stream of revenue produced by the capital facility funded by the debt. Utilities are most often funded with such debt and repaid with revenue from utility customers. Revenue debt does not usually require voter approval; it is sold by approval of the legislative body and sells in the market at rates slightly higher than for GO debt. The interest cost differential is typically 25 basis points (0.25%) for comparably rated issues.

Revenue bonds are often sold by sealed competitive bid, but in many cases the complexity of the project may dictate that issuers work with a single underwriter and negotiate the interest cost. The amount of time and resources an underwriter expends to prepare a bid on a GO issue is very small. However, the amount of resources needed to gain an understanding of a complex issue may be prohibitive, especially when the underwriter is not guaranteed the business. For this reason, the negotiated sale is some times preferable.

The choice of whether to issue debt through a competitive bid process or a negotiated sale is dictated either by state constitution or statute, or by local ordinance, policy, or preference. Issuing governments are advised to obtain the services of a financial advisor (FA) when considering the issuance of debt. The FA is a finance professional who follows the municipal bond market closely and understands how to structure the issue and time the market. Finance directors, even in large cities, simply do not have time to acquire the knowledge needed to bring an issue to the market. Part of the FA's services will include advising on the type of sale that is most appropriate, obtaining the services of adequate bond counsel, and helping to market the issue.

3.3.2.3 Certificates of Participation

Certificates of participation (COP) are used to fund leased property. In such an arrangement, the government entity sets up an agency to serve as the lessor so that investors work with a single agency rather than each of the agencies that may occupy the building or other facility. There is also a trustee, often a bank or other financial institution, who represents the interests of the investors, receiving and holding bond proceeds, and receiving and disbursing lease payments once the project is completed.

The lessor agency issues the COPs and works with the trustee that sells the obligations. In some instances, the trustee may simply maintain the COP as part of its own portfolio. Once the project is complete, lease payments from the issuing government are sent to the trustee for distribution to the individual investors. Upon retirement of the debt the leased facility becomes the property of the government. This is often called a lease-purchase agreement.

The primary benefit of this type of debt is that, technically, it is revenue debt. That is, the lease payments are pledged by the lessor agency as the stream of revenue that secures the debt. This means that the debt may sell at a slightly higher interest rate, but the bonds do not require voter approval and may not count against a constitutional or statutory debt limit.

3.3.2.4 Tax Increment Bonds

Tax increment bonds are generally associated with a geographic area called a tax increment financing district (TIF). Pioneered in Illinois, the TIF district was conceptualized as a means of spurring economic development in blighted areas where it would not likely occur otherwise. The basic idea is to identify improvements that will produce economic development causing property values to rise. The debt used to fund the improvemnts is secured by the ad valorem property tax increase (see Paetsch and Dahlstrom, 1990).

The first step in establishing a TIF is to determine the boundaries of the district. In some states the TIF is still limited to blighted areas, but more and more local governments are using the tactic as a way to accelerate growth in thriving areas. Once the boundaries are set, each of the overlapping jurisdictions that have taxing power are enlisted to participate in the TIF. This is critical for success and, in most instances, an absolute requirement. For tax levy purposes, each jurisdiction freezes the assessed value of each parcel within the district and continues to bill the property owner based on that value for a specified period of time, typically five or ten years but possibly longer.

The TIF district proceeds with improvements that may include streets, sidewalks, street lighting, water and sewer lines. The agency may also demolish abandoned structures or sell abandoned property to developers at bargain prices. Once development occurs, property values are reassessed. The incremental ad valorem property tax revenue is paid to the TIF district to retire the debt. After the specified period, the TIF district is dissolved and each overlapping district uses the new property values for its levy.

3.3.2.5 Other Types of Debt

A number of other types of debt are used in many states, including short-term instruments like anticipation notes. These are often used to fund preliminary expenses on projects such as the services of a surveyor, architect, or designer. Once permanent funding for the project is secured, the short-term obligation is retired. Anticipation notes can normally be secured by pledge of any revenue source, including ad valorem property tax, sales tax, or the proceeds of a bond sale.

3.3.2.6 Development Impact Fees

The use of development impact fees has become widespread over the past quarter century. These fees, first used in Florida, California, and Colorado to help manage and limit growth, transfer part of the cost of new infrastructure to the private sector by charging developers a fee for items such as water and sewer connections, street and sidewalk projects, and parks. Abuses in the use of fees led to lawsuits from developers, who charged that jurisdictions were using the fees to stop growth by charging fees many times the actual cost of the infrastructure involved. The case law established across the country in the 1980s and 1990s produced the rational nexus standard contained in Table 3.3. This standard links the fee with the actual cost of the infrastructure and requires the jurisdiction to use the funds in a timely manner for the intended purpose. For a discussion see National League of Cities (1987); Clarke and Evans (1999); and Nicholas, Nelson, and Juergensmeyer (1991).

Table 3.3 Rational Nexus Standard for Development Impact Fees

1. Each exaction must be well-designed to meet service needs directly attributable to the project bearing the cost.
2. Where facilities are to serve more than a single development, costs must be allocated in proportion to services rendered.
3. Such facilities must be elements of a comprehensive local plan for service improvements.
4. Where facilities are to be financed by a combination of tax and impact fee revenues, special care must be taken to ensure that project occupants, who pay taxes like everyone else, are not double-billed. The impact fee calculation, in other words, must be net of anticipated tax contributions.
5. Impact fee revenues must be segregated until used and must be expended in a timely fashion (generally, within five to six years for the purpose originally designated).

3.4 Capital Planning and Debt Policies

With few exceptions (and none come to mind) written, formal fiscal policies should guide the management of a jurisdiction's financial resources. These should be adopted by the governing body to provide consistency in the management of finances and to ensure that employees understand the importance of following the policies. The purpose of adopting policies formally should not be viewed as a means of binding future councils or commissions; policies can be changed, but change should be well reasoned, and adopted policies are more likely to be changed from reasoned consideration than on a whim.

In the area of capital budgeting, two main areas of policy are important: process and debt management. Policies that guide the capital budget process ensure that the actions taken in the heat of political battle, or in pursuit of a minor goal, do not work at cross purposes to the strategic or master plan. Before policy processes are established, however, the jurisdiction should define what will be considered capital and what will be considered an operating expense. Most local governments established a floor value that an item or project must cost in order to be funded in the capital budget. In a small municipal government that may be $2,000. For very large cities and states it is often in the $100,000 range. Establishing this guideline will prevent the capital budget from becoming a means of funding what is really an operating expense.

The process used to identify, prioritize, and select projects for inclusion in the CIP and capital budget should be adopted. Often, officials will solicit suggestions from department and agency officials, but having a scheduled meeting or workshop, where members of the public are given a chance to present their ideas and preferences, should be included in the calendar. A committee that includes agency and elected officials, the city manager or other executive officer, and members of the public, should be established to screen and review proposed projects. Information such as the purpose and estimated cost of projects may be all that is needed at this stage.

Evaluation of projects that are approved for the CIP should be evaluated in a consistent manner. If cost benefit analysis is used in some cases, it should probably be used in all cases unless officials can explain why it was inappropriate. In some cases, projects must be built to meet state and federal guidelines. Even in such cases cost efficiency analysis may be useful if there are several options to achieve the desired purpose. The important issue here is to be consistent. One project should not be subjected to less or greater scrutiny unless there is a compelling reason.

As discussed previously, the selection of projects from the CIP to be included in the capital budget is a function of available resources.

Since most large capital items are funded with bonded debt, formal debt policies should be adopted. The debt policies for the city of Dallas contained in Table 3.4 help the city achieve a number of goals. Policy number one, already mentioned in this chapter, should be the first item in any jurisdiction's adopted policies. Next, there are a couple of policies that limit the amount of debt the city may issue. GO debt is limited to 4 percent of the city's assessed valuation, and total debt plus overlapping debt, which is the

Table 3.4   Debt Policy — City of Dallas, TX

1. Any capital projects financed through the issuance of bonds shall be financed for a period not to exceed the expected useful life of the project.
2. The Net General Obligation (GO) Debt of Dallas will not exceed 4% of the true market valuation of the taxable property of Dallas.
3. Total direct plus overlapping debt shall be managed so as not to exceed 8% of market valuation of taxable property of Dallas. All debt which causes total direct plus overlapping debt to exceed 6% of market valuation shall be carefully planned and coordinated with all overlapping jurisdictions.
4. Interest, operating, and/or maintenance expenses will be capitalized only for facilities of enterprise activities and will be strictly limited to those expenses incurred prior to actual operation of the facilities.
5. Average (weighted) General Obligation bond maturities shall be kept at or below 10 years.
6. Annual General Obligation debt service (contribution), including certificates of obligation debt for risk management funding, shall not exceed 20% of the total locally generated, non-enterprise, operating revenue.
7. Per Capita General Obligation Debt, including Certificates of Obligation, equipment acquisition notes and General Obligation Bonds, will be managed not to exceed 10% of the latest authoritative computation of Dallas' per capita annual personal income.
8. Debt may be used to finance betterments intended to extend service life of original permanent capital improvements under the following conditions:
   a. the original improvement is at or near the end of its expected service life.
   b. the betterment extends the life of the original improvement by at least one-third of the original service life.
   c. the life of the financing is less than the life of the betterment
   d. the betterment is financed through either COs or GOs.
9. A letter certifying that the use of interest earnings does not adversely impact the completion of Council-authorized projects will be submitted with the City Manager's proposed budget each year.
10. Certificates of Obligation should be used only to fund tax-supported projects previously approved by the voters; or for risk management funding as authorized by the City Council; or non-tax, revenue-supported projects approved by the City Council.

(Continued)

Table 3.4 Continued

11. Certificates of Obligation Debt, including that for risk management funding supported by an ad valorem tax pledge, should not exceed 15% of total authorized and issued General Obligation (GO) Debt. All COs issued in lieu of revenue bonds should not exceed 10% of outstanding GO Debt.
12. Certificates of Obligation will be limited to projects consistent with Financial Management Performance Criteria for debt issuance.
13. Certificates of Obligation for an enterprise system will be limited to only those projects which can demonstrate the capability to support the certificate debt, either through its own revenues or another pledged source other than ad valorem taxes.
14. Certificates of Obligation authorization will remain in effect for no more than five years from the date of approval by the City Council.
15. Certificates of Obligation authorized for risk management funding shall be issued for a term not to exceed 20 years.
16. Tax Increment Financing zones should be established where revenues will recover the public cost of debt with adequate safety margin.
17. No more than 10% of the property (i.e. parcels) in a Tax Increment Financing zone, excluding property dedicated for public use, may be used for residential purposes. "Residential purposes" includes property occupied by a house which has less than five living units.
18. No more than 5% of the City's tax base will be in Tax Increment Financing zones.

debt of other taxing jurisdictions, cannot exceed 8 percent of market value. This policy takes into consideration the operations of entities such as the Dallas Independent School District, several other special purpose governments, and Dallas County.

Debt policy number five limits the total amount of debt service to 20 percent of own-source, non-enterprise revenue, which is primarily the general fund; policy number seven uses a computation of the city's per capita annual personal income. These policies are designed to limit the burden placed on these two measures (one governmental and one drawn from the population) of capacity to service debt.

Other policies contained in this list provide guidelines for the use of debt by enterprise funds; the use of non-voter approved general obligation debt; and guidelines for maintaining an acceptable average maturity for all city debt. Non-voter approved purposes are limited to risk management projects and those that produce an identifiable stream of revenue. Finally, the city limits the use of tax increment financing by establishing a ceiling for the proportion of the tax base that can be included within a TIF district.

Among the items considered by the Government Finance Officers Association to award its Distinguished Budget Presentation Awards Program are the presentation of information on capital projects, a description of the planning process used to select those projects, and the policies used to manage bonded debt (see Powdar 1999). As a matter of policy, state local governments should require that the budget document meet these and other GFOA Distinguished Budget Presentation Award criteria. Establishing a process for the identification and selection of capital projects that allows for citizen input, and that clearly conveys information about the projects to be built, is critical in meeting the public sector goals of transparency and accountability.

References and Additional Resources

Altshuler, Alan and David Luberoff. 2003. *Mega-Projects: The Changing Politics of Urban Public Investment*. Washington, DC: Brookings Institution Press.

Blakely, Edward J. and Mary Gail Snyder. 1999. *Fortress America: Gated Communities in the United States*. Washington, DC: Brookings Institution Press.

Bland, Robert L. and Wes Clarke. 1999. "Budgeting for Capital Improvements," in Meyers, Roy, ed., *Handbook of Government Budgeting*. San Francisco: Jossey-Bass Publishers.

Bland, Robert L. and Samuel Nunn. 1992. The Impact of Capital Spending on Municipal Operating Budgets. *Public Budgeting and Finance* 12(2): 32–47.

Buchanan, James. 1965. "An Economic Theory of Clubs." *Economica* 32(125): 1–14.

Clarke, Wes and Jennifer Evans. 1999. Impact Development Fees and the Acquisition of Infrastructure. *Journal of Urban Affairs* 23(3): 281–288.

Doig, Jameson. 1995. "Politics and the Engineering Mind: O.H. Ammann and the Hidden Story of the George Washington Bridge." Chapter in Perry, David C., ed., *Building the Public City: The Politics, Governance, and Finance of Pubic Infrastructure*. Thousand Oaks, CA: Sage Publications.

Fortune, Peter. 1995. "Debt Capacity, Tax Exemption, and the Municipal Cost of Capital: A Reassessment of the New View." Working Paper Series of the Federal Reserve Bank of Boston. Boston: Federal Reserve Bank.

Gramlich, Edward M. 1990a. "How Should Public Infrastructure Be Financed?" From Munnell, Alicia H., ed., *Is There a Shortfall in Public Capital Investment?* Boston: Federal Reserve Bank of Boston.

Gramlich, Edward M. 1990b. *A Guide to Benefit-Cost Analysis*. Prospect Heights, IL: Waveland Press.

Hackbart, Merl and James R. Ramsey. 1993. "Debt Management and Debt Capacity." Chapter in Lamb, Robert, James Leigland, and Stephen Rappaport, eds., *The Handbook of Municipal Bonds and Public Finance*. New York: New York Institute of Finance.

Hatry, Harry, Annie P. Millar, and James H. Evans. 1984. *Guide to Setting Priorities for Capital Investment.* Washington, DC: The Urban Institute Press.

Leigland, James. 1995. "Public Infrastructure and Special Purpose Governments: Who Pays and How?" In Perry, David C., ed., *Building the Public City: The Politics, Governance, and Finance of Pubic Infrastructure.* Thousand Oaks, California: Sage Publications.

Martin, Susan W. and Ellen N. West. 2003. *Today's Essentials of Governmental and Not-For-Profit Accounting & Reporting.* Mason, Ohio: Thomson South-Western.

Morgan, David R. and Robert E. England. 1999. *Managing Urban America,* 5th edition. New York: Chatham House Publishers.

Nas, Tevfik. 1996. *Cost-Benefit Analysis: Theory and Application.* Thousand Oaks, CA: Sage Publications.

National League of Cities. 1987. *Financing Infrastructure: Innovations at the Local Level.* Washington, DC: National League of Cities.

Nicholas, James C., Arthur C. Nelson, and Julian Conrad Juergensmeyer. 1991. *A Practitioner's Guide to Development Impact Fees.* Chicago: American Planning Association.

Nunn, Samuel. 1991. "Formal and Informal Processes in Infrastructure Policy-Making." *Journal of the American Planning Association* 57(3): 273–287.

Paetsch, James R. and Roger K. Dahlstrom. 1990. "Tax Increment Financing: What It Is and How It Works." From Binham, Richard D., Edward W. Hill and Sammis B. White, eds., *Financing Economic Development: An Institutional Response.* Newbury Park, California: Sage Publications.

Powdar, Juliet Carol. 1999. *Budget Awards Program: Illustrations and Examples of Program Criteria.* Chicago: GFOA.

Rosenbloom, David H., James D. Carroll, and Jonathan D. Carroll. 2000. *Constitutional Competence for Public Managers: Cases and Commentary.* Itasca, IL: F.E. Peacock Publishers, Inc.

Ruppel, Warren. 2002. *GAAP for Governments 2002.* New York: John Wiley & Sons, Inc.

Snyder, Thomas P., and Michael A. Stegner. 1989. *Paying for Growth: Using Development Fees to Finance Infrastructure.* Washington, DC: Urban Land Institute.

Steiss, Alan W. 1998. New Financing Instruments for State and Local Capital Facilities. *Public Budgeting & Finance* 18(3): 24–41

Temel, Judy Wesalo. 2001. *The Fundamentals of Municipal Bonds,* 5th ed. New York: John Wiley & Sons.

Thomassen, Henry. 1990. "Capital Budgeting for a State." *Public Budgeting & Finance* 10(4): 72–86.

Vogt, A. John. 2004. *Capital Budgeting and Finance: A Guide for Local Governments.* Washington, DC: ICMA, and Chapel Hill: The Institute of Government, University of North Carolina.

Chapter 4

Financial Management of Economic Development

J. SCOTT McDONALD, Ph.D.
Department of Political Science, Valdosta State University

4.1 Overview and Definitions

This chapter explores financial management issues surrounding economic development. The intent is to construct a comprehensive overview of how community values impact financial management choices, which in turn shape a region's economic development efforts. Attention is focused on how communities select and apply financial instruments in various situations. The chapter is organized into seven sections and each section approaches the financial management of economic development from a different perspective. Readers will develop an understanding of diverse economic development finance issues and demands placed on management structures and functions. This first section focuses on key definitions and the difficulty of delineating between economic development finance and other areas of public and private finance. It includes a discussion of the relationships between public finance, economic development, community development, planning, strategic planning, and government intervention. The second section employs a historical perspective to demonstrate how economic development policy and related financial instruments evolved. Section three looks at the "localness" of economic development, using a geographic perspective to review diversity of local financial management tools. Institutional perspectives of public sector, private sector, and not for profit sector roles are the focus of Section four. Section five focuses on federalism and how the availability and appropriateness of financial tools is impacted by the U.S. federal system. The sixth section uses an instrumental perspective to review financial instruments employed by economic developers. While not exhaustive, numerous financial tools and organizing principles are discussed. Finally, Section seven gives an overview of future opportunities and pitfalls that impact the financial management of economic development.

4.1.1 Economic Development

Economic development has been variously defined. Practitioners and scholars have produced nearly countless case studies and meta-studies of the role of economic development in a community and recipes for success. One issue is clear from this plethora of study; there is no single, widely accepted definition. Definitions tend to fall into two categories, narrow and broad. The narrow definition focuses exclusively on economic impacts, most commonly job generation. The broad definition shares focus between purely economic measures and social measures such as community ambiance and quality of life. Unfortunately, the term economic development is used to convey both narrow and broad concepts. However, the broader concept is more accurately referred to as community development. It is not uncommon for two highly knowledgeable professionals, either academics or practitioners, to suffer confusion regarding definition.

Simply stated, economic development focuses on growth, i.e., is the economy growing? Community development is focused on both growth and change, economic growth in the economy and positive change in non-economic, socially important factors, e.g., quality of life, diversity, improved physical environment.

The prior narrow definition warrants more attention. Ordinarily, most communities, i.e., states, regional organizations, cities, and counties define economic development as changes in employment. Numbers of jobs created or retained in a community are the primary measures. Secondary measures are quality of jobs, primarily measured in terms of wages. For both ease of measurement and political reasons, discussed below, communities seldom look beyond these measures of economic development.

A broader definition of economic development starts with economic growth, and incorporates one or more additional measures associated with a community's social and environmental capital. Social capital may be narrow or far reaching, including such items as recreation options, youth programs, educational infrastructures and programs, public safety, and health care options. Environmental capital likewise may be narrowly or broadly defined to include such items as open space; air, surface and ground water qualities; and brownfields (abandoned industrial sites), to name a few.

Unless otherwise noted, this chapter will employ the broad definition of economic development, i.e., the incorporation of social and environmental capital, along with economic capital. The rationale behind this decision is straightforward; the profession and much of the scholarly focus have moved or are moving toward a broader definition. This is a critical matter, as increasingly communities find themselves competing on such matters as educational opportunities and quality of life, as will be displayed in the final section of this chapter.

4.1.2 Financial Management Implications of a Broad Definition of Economic Development

The financial management implications of employing a broad definition of economic development are substantial. Under the broad definition almost any public investment and wide arrays of not-for-profit and private invest-ment might fall under the domain of economic development finance. Of course this would result in considerable overlap with other topics covered in this book, e.g., debt, pension funds, capital budgets, tax policies, among others. Additionally, the entire realm of education finance, including primary, secondary and higher education would be included. This chapter will make every effort to avoid redundancy with other chapters in this book or with the extensive literatures on the finance of education and general fund finance. However, this chapter will endeavor to identify critical impacts of other finance issues as they impact economic development.

4.1.3 Perspectives on Economic Development and Its Finance

To understand the financial management of economic development one must have in hand a solid grasp of the field of economic development and variations of practice within the field.

4.1.3.1 A Brief Overview of the American Experience in Economic Development

Economic development is nothing new to the U.S. experience. The early immigrants to the New World had a variety of goals; some fled religious persecution, others sought adventure, but almost all were in search of a good life, one that provided more opportunity than in the Old World. In America land was limitless, the forests beyond description, and the opportunities for success were without peer in the rest of the world. With the founding of the U.S., government sought to create a good business environment (Wright, 2002). An early example was the 1791 incorporation of Alexander Hamilton's private company, the Society for Establishing Useful Manufacturers, as a vehicle for industrial development (Eisinger, 1988). The company was awarded tax exempt status. Companies like Hamilton's were evident in many states. Turnpikes, canals, and railroads were constructed and justified on the grounds of economic growth, generally involving one or more state governments, local government and/or the national government. Whether governments were floating or securing bonds or offering tracts of land, it was clear that government was active in the finance of economic development.

Local economic development in a more modern sense finds its roots in the "smokestack chasing" efforts of southern states beginning in the 1930s. These states offered inducements to attract northern firms to relocate a portion of their manufacturing processes to the South. Firms were offered tax abatements, land, and infrastructures (Fitzgerald and Leigh, 2002). Most states eventually followed suit. Like it or not, today we find American communities pitted against competitors half-way around the world seeking the same types of investment. All fifty states and most cities and counties have an economic development function located somewhere in their bureaucracies.

4.1.3.2   Economic Development Practice

Economic development and finance are inseparable concepts. Most of the tools communities employ to attract and retain industries involve incentives, most frequently involving adjustments to costs: taxes, land, infrastructures, and labor. Financial mechanisms are fundamentally important to economic development practitioners, scholars, and politicians. One factor driving the professionalizing of economic development practice is the importance of and complexity of financial matters. For example, the Economic Development Masters Degree at University of Southern Mississippi, for a time the only such program in the U.S., has two of its 11 recommended courses: Economic Development Finance and Accounting for Decision Makers, focused on finance, while several of the other courses devote at least some attention to this issue (University of Southern Mississippi, n.d). A search of the worldwide web turns up university courses such as Accessing Capital for Community Development (Apgar, 2003), Capital Markets and Economic Development Finance (Gershberg, 2003), and Economic Development Planning and Finance (Brice, 2002).

Robert Reich summed up the delicate economic development balance. He observed, "The old job of leadership was to make decisions. The new job of leadership is to attract (and keep) money and talent." (2000, p. 207). Reich argues that this explains shifts in taxation policy away from higher income earners to lower income earners paying a greater share of the cost of government services (2000).

Economic development, finance, and the management skills to effectively direct financial tools that maximize community returns are inseparable if communities are to succeed in efforts to expand and improve. This is the essence of financial management of economic development. To better understand the critical interrelationships among these three elements: economic development, finance, and management, the majority of this chapter will explore six essential perspectives.

4.1.3.3 Essential Perspectives

How governments manage the finance of economic development is both a function and a causal factor impacting a wide variety of environmental factors. Most critical among these factors are the following.

- *Historical* — the evolution of government's role in the economy and the evolution of financial instruments.
- *Geographical* — conditions, needs, resources and appropriateness of financial instruments vary according to region and rural-urban differences.
- *Institutional* — public sector, private sector, and not-for-profit organizations (NPOs) affect the economic development finance roles and potentials. How a community allocates responsibility for economic development impacts the choice of financial instruments and ultimately how community economic development efforts proceed.
- *Federalism* — federal, state, and local governments; not-for-profit corporations; and private sector firms bring unique financial instruments to the table.
- *Instrumental* — each of the many major economic development finance instruments has a niche where it is most likely to generate success. Often this niche is a function of the industrial life cycle of a firm or an entire industry. As a firm or industry matures the appropriateness of each financial instrument will vary.
- *Futuring* — as the economy and communities change, economic development practice and financial management will likewise need to evolve.

Each of these perspectives represents a different layer; as we peel them back we can further understand the complex relationships between management, finance, and economic development. The remainder of this chapter explores the various perspectives to better understand managing economic development finance.

4.2 Historical Perspective

The historical perspective is important because it provides a framework for understanding economic development and finance through time. As economic development practice, thought, and finance progressed though time, new practices took foot and grew. New practices seldom resulted in wholesale replacement of old practices; rather they added another layer to an increasingly complex issue.

4.2.1 Before 1900

The roots of American economic development can be traced back to the earliest European settlers. With the birth of the U.S., the Founders put structures in place to facilitate economic expansion. Charles Beard noted the founders were, among other things, "hard-fisted conservatives," protecting business interests (as cited in Diamond, Fisk, and Garfinkel, 1970). Early construction of turnpikes and canals, clearly intended for economic development, was generally assisted by state governments. With the westward expansion into territories and less populous states, Federal assistance was necessary. Soon railroad construction supplanted canals and pikes, with most finance coming from the Federal government. The predominant methods of finance were direct cash outlays by the Federal government for each mile of line constructed and massive land grants for railroad construction. Eventually, land grants were used for railroad construction in 20 of 22 states west of the Mississippi (Texas and Oklahoma were exceptions), and in seven states east of the River: Indiana, Illinois, Michigan, Wisconsin, Mississippi, Alabama, and Florida. Four of five transcontinental railroads were built with land grant assistance. Without this U.S. government assistance, railroad construction would have been greatly curtailed as private banks were unwilling to loan the capital necessary to undertake these massive ventures (Library of Congress, n.d.). Land grant financing was a massive subsidy that greatly expedited the settlement of the west.

4.2.2 After 1900

The modern era of economic development practice and finance has roots in the Great Depression of the 1930s. Every state (except Delaware) established comprehensive planning units incorporating economic development as a condition to receive federal public works funds. In 1936 Mississippi was the first state to use tax-exempt bonds (general obligation) for private industry (Eisinger, 1988).

Scholars have variously categorized eras or phases of economic development, beginning with events in the 1930s. For brevity, this discussion relies upon Joan Fitzgerald and Nancy Leigh's efforts that identify five phases of economic development practice.

4.2.2.1 Phase 1: Industrial Recruitment

Individual states worked to attract industry in the 1930s. States employed tax abatements, loan packaging, infrastructure, and land development to create a good business climate. The overarching principle during this phase was using public finance to grease the skids (Fitzgerald and Leigh, 2002).

4.2.2.2 Phase 2: Political Critiques of Economic Development Activity

Inner-city decline, manufacturing exodus from city to suburb and from Rustbelt to Sunbelt, failure of redevelopment efforts, and civil disturbances led to wholesale questioning of the efficacy and distributional characteristics of economic development practice. Between the 1960s and early 1990s focus, like in the 1930s, remained on job creation, but scholars and practitioners questioned the use of incentives (Fitzgerald and Leigh, 2002, p. 11).

4.2.2.3 Phase 3: Entrepreneurial and Equity Strategies

A fundamental shift between supply-side industrial attraction focus to a more entrepreneurial focus occurred in both state and local economic development practice (Eisinger, 1988; Fitzgerald and Leigh, 2002). Local governments and states began investing in new initiatives such as R&D facilities, international trade promotion, venture capital funds, small business development, and other programs to promote entrepreneurialism. In addition to growth, new values such as equity became more important in economic development thought and practice.

4.2.2.4 Phase 4: Sustainability with Justice

Fitzgerald and Leigh noted that, in addition to equity, there were increased calls for environmentally responsive economic development over the last two decades. Over time, economic development has increasingly been driven by three values: economic growth and efficiency, social justice (economic opportunity and income equality) and environmental protection.

4.2.2.5 Phase 5: Privatization and Interdependence

Beginning in the late 1980s through to the present, economic development thought and practice has been dominated by a market-driven approach. Government continues to facilitate and finance private investment, notably public–private partnerships and integrate minority firms into mainstream markets. Federal, state, and local empowerment zones (EZs), designed to promote economic revitalization of impoverished areas, is the prototypical example of privatization and interdependence (Fitzgerald and Leigh, 2002).

4.2.3 Economic Development Phases, Values, and Financial Implementations

The five phases described above were each value-driven, i.e., the reflected social and administrative values regarding economic development, public finance, social well-being, and the physical environment. Additionally, most often one phase did not exist independent from other phases. That is to say, one phase was not abandoned by a move to another phase. For example, the State of Wisconsin, like most states, offers financial assistance that falls within each of the five categories. Wisconsin Department of Development (WDOD) has several programs to provide incentives for industrial recruitment (Phase 1), e.g., tax incremental financing (TIF) and industrial revenue bonds (IRBs) (State of Wisconsin, n.d.). The State also has several programs intended to assist underrepresented groups (Phase 2: political critiques of economic development activity). The Wisconsin Women's Business Initiative Corporation is targeted at growing women owned and managed firms. The state also operates the Bureau of Minority Business, providing services to aid in minority business development.

Wisconsin is active with a venture capital fund and the University of Wisconsin at Madison operates a business park for high tech start-ups. Each of these programs falls in Fitzgerald and Leigh's entrepreneurial and equity strategies (Phase 3) (2002). Most notable among the State's sustainability and justice (Phase 4) efforts are brownfields and state sponsored recycling efforts. Both efforts are intended to convert economic, social, and environmental liabilities into assets. Finally, the State also exhibits programs displaying privatization and interdependence (Phase 5). Most notable here are three programs: Agricultural Development Zone, Community Development Zone, and Enterprise Development Zone, each intended to stimulate job growth in targeted areas (zones).

4.2.4 Summary

Three lessons emerge from reviewing the history of economic development finance. First, American governments have been involved in financing economic development since the Founding. Second, financing economic development has progressed from exclusive dependence on direct assistance (land grants) to multiple programs and instruments. Third, since the 1930s, economic development programs and their finance have expanded greatly, an expansion driven largely by social values.

4.3 Geographic Perspective

Westward rail expansion was expedited by generous land grants to railroad companies. Such a program was not needed in the East where populations were dense, but in the West, with vast expanses of low population densities, the enormous investments for railroad infrastructure needed some sort of direct government support (subsidy).

Clearly one size does not fit all with regard to economic development, or its finance. Communities have varied needs and abilities to create and implement finance programs. This section highlights important program variations and financial mechanism as they vary geographically. These variations include:

- Jurisdiction
- Topography
- Transportation
- Labor
- Housing
- Poverty
- Environmental contamination
- Clustering

4.3.1 Jurisdiction

For anyone interested in policy, jurisdiction plays a highly significant role. Two jurisdictions separated by a border, often nothing more than an arbitrary line, a historical remnant, a political relic, may have significantly differing policies, programs, and procedures. This is often evident in metro areas where different communities will exhibit variations in public policy. In terms of economic development and finance, a clear example shows communities that pay for infrastructures (water, sewer, roads, parks, and/or schools) with impact fees, are at a clear disadvantage compared to communities that employ another finance mechanism. Suburbs that have benefited from white flight, in the experience of this author, are less likely to offer the same minority business programs as the central city they surround. Differences in programs are not the only impact of borders; they also can lead to bidding wars between jurisdictions attempting to attract the same facility. For example, New York provided the New York Stock Exchange with a $720 million package of tax breaks and subsidies for the Exchange to construct a sixty-story office tower across the street from the present site. The New York bid beat out New Jersey, which had tried to lure the Exchange out of the City. Another example is the gaming (gambling) industry. Travel across state lines to buy lottery tickets, play the ponies, or feed the slots is a multibillion dollar industry providing thousands of jobs in places like Las Vegas, Atlantic City, and Tunica, Mississippi, while siphoning dollars from other communities.

4.3.2   Topography

Clearly topography — the physical features of a landscape — impacts local economic development and its finance. An example helps to clarify. The Ohio River, itself a significant topographic feature, is the boundary between Kentucky to the south and Ohio, Indiana, and Illinois to the north. Both Indiana and Illinois permit riverboat gambling while it is not permitted in Kentucky. Unfortunately for its northern neighbors, Kentucky inherited from Virginia jurisdiction over the entire Ohio River, jurisdiction that it defends vigorously (Sublett and Walk, 1994). This impacts gambling boat operations that only move a few feet into the river, for fear of trespassing into Kentucky and being subject to its laws and taxes (Rose, 2002). In a tongue and cheek effort to stem the cash drain (estimated at $500 million between Kentucky and Indiana casinos) the Kentucky legislature proposed a unique solution; the State of Kentucky would purchase the USS Louisville, a US Navy atomic submarine, to patrol and intercept interloping casino boats (Mikkelson and Mikkelson, 2002).

There are numerous other examples where topography impacts economic development and finance. Drainage basins often place limitations on sewer systems. To extend beyond the divide between basins often is cost prohibitive due to the need for pumps. On a grander scale are natural valleys that, when combined with local climate, result in high levels of air pollution, resulting in US Environmental Protection Agency non-attainment restrictions on new development. Wetlands, floodways, steep escarpments, and natural vistas are additional natural features that often limit or otherwise impact on development.

4.3.3 Transportation

As with real estate, some economic development professionals identify the three most important economic development factors as location, location, and location. This fact makes transportation exceedingly important to economic development. Depending on the industry, location near high quality roads, rail, airports, and/or a port/harbor is essential. Grants, loans, forgivable loans, and credits are frequently applied to enhance a site with regard to transportation. For example, most heavy and many medium industries require rail and/or waterborne transportation. Almost every industry requires good roads, usually implying proximity to a four lane divided, ideally Interstate quality highway. Firms manufacturing products that are high value and low volume, or that are time-sensitive, e.g., catalog sales, want proximity to an airport with FedEx or UPS type service. Communities, states, and the Federal government are constantly adding to or adjusting transportation infrastructures to make a locality more attractive/competitive. Natural gas and electricity also fit this mode, in that proximity to high tension electricity lines or high volume gas lines is required by operations consuming high amounts of energy or needing highly reliable service.

4.3.4 Labor

Labor is unevenly distributed in terms of number of workers available, quality of workers, specialized skills, and wages. For many high tech and service firms, labor is the most important location factor. If large numbers of workers are required, a location in a metropolitan area is almost a certainty. Since the North American Free Trade Agreement (NAFTA) and the opening of China, low skill manufacturing employment in the U.S. has plummeted. The loss of blue collar employment was shrugged off by many investors, academics, and politicians. Now, with many white collar industries under assault by foreign competition, e.g., micro chip engineering and call centers relocating to India and Malaysia, new concern is growing over job losses. Communities, states, and the Federal government each provide grants and loans for skill development so that a community, especially a disadvantaged community, can be more competitive. Technical colleges, universities, and even primary educational systems have served as economic development assets. The most important basic research institutions in the U.S. are 200 universities that receive Federal, state, and private sector funding to conduct research in such cutting edge areas as theoretical physics, advanced materials, and molecular biology. These institutions often pay great dividends to their communities.

For example, there are more than 1,000 MIT-related companies in Massachusetts with global sales of $53 billion (1998) (Committee for Economic Development, 1998).

4.3.5 *Housing*

Of course, housing is not evenly distributed; urban areas obviously have more housing than do rural areas. But, of more concern to policy makers and economic development officials is the quality of housing, and any concentration of low quality housing in particular geographic areas. Most notable in this context are inner city neighborhoods, but older suburbs and rural areas such as the Mississippi Delta are growing concerns. Neighborhood development and housing are the focus of numerous programs. This concern is typified by the U.S. Department of Housing and Urban Development where housing and urban development are combined into a single department, indicating how these issues are inseparable. Federal, most states, and countless communities actively seek to improve housing conditions. For example, communities can use state monies to match Federal grants to refurbish sewer and water infrastructure to prepare sites for housing, with the housing developed by a not-for-profit organization such as Habitat for Humanity. This sort of creative financing is not unusual as communities struggle with complex community development issues by melding Federal, state, local, and not-for-profit monies, with volunteer labor and sweat equity. Federal programs that insure mortgages and secure mortgage interest write-offs constitute the largest housing program in the country.

4.3.6 *Poverty*

Poverty and wealth tend to be concentrated in specific localities. Economic development programs often target areas where low income households are concentrated, most notably the Federal empowerment communities (ECs) and enterprise zones (EZs). Numerous states and localities have developed programs to parallel Federal efforts, thereby creating multiple layers of development programming. Areas of concentrated poverty are defined employing U.S. Census data. Once an area is certified as an EZ or EC (discussed below), it becomes eligible for a wide range of economic development programs, ranging from HUD monies for repairing and replacing infrastructure, housing programs, and other investments; tax credits on a range of economic development activities including hiring from within the community, investment in the community, training employees; among others. One of the major drivers of economic development finance is eradication of highly concentrated pockets of poverty.

4.3.7   *Environmental Contamination*

We all suffer the effects of some environmental contamination. Ozone depletion, surface testing of nuclear weapons in the 1950s, and increased atmospheric levels of various gases and solids have contributed to our personal risk of cancer and other maladies. But, it is equally clear that contamination is greatly concentrated in specific locations. While the U.S. has not suffered a Chernobyl, Ukraine or Bhopal, India, we have our Three Mile Island and Love Canal, each of which had significant economic development impacts. But, herein we limit our discussion to a single issue, that of contaminated industrial sites. Historically, it has been less expensive to develop a business site on undeveloped land, a greenfield site, named after the characteristics of the agricultural land use to be supplanted. This left as un-developable large tracts of land abandoned by former operators. Found largely in the inner city and older suburbs, these parcels contributed to the difficulties faced by citizens, planners, and economic developers. This was especially the case when contamination or threat of contamination entered into the calculus of facility location.

Superfund and other programs were established to clean up contaminated sites. But Superfund has a waiting list of several thousand sites and the purpose of Superfund was to address the worst sites. If a community must await Superfund cleanup, the site will likely continue as blight on a community for the foreseeable future.

This situation is exacerbated by Federal and many state laws that assign clean up responsibility to any name that has appeared on the title of the property or that has operated the facility. It would be irrational for any firm to assume the risk of redeveloping an existing site while a greenfield site presents no such risk. Federal, state, and local governments have acted to put remediation programs in place to overcome this serious impediment to economic development. Under the moniker of brownfield redevelopment, governments have acted to: (a) reduce the liability of the new operator, (b) provide some technical assistance for cleaning up a site, and (c) employed a wide range of financial tools to facilitate and stimulate redevelopment of the site.

Some of the more important financial implementations available for brownfield redevelopment include grants, loans, and tax credits for remediation and redevelopment. Far and away the most important financial tool has been tax credits: Federal, state, and local. The urgency of brown field redevelopment is that brownfields often fall in communities with high concentrations of poverty.

4.3.8 Clustering

The last geographic factor discussed herein is the concept of clustering. A cluster is a geographically proximate group of interconnected and associated institutions in a particular field, linked by commonalities and complementarities. The geographic scope of a cluster relates to the distance over which informational, transactional, incentive, and other efficiencies occur (Porter, 2000). Depending on the industry, clusters may be quite small or large. A typical example of a small cluster is the service businesses located around a rural Interstate highway on-off ramp. Surrounding a ramp are the ubiquitous gas, food, and lodging franchises. A classic example is Hollywood, where the climate was the initial draw and then access to talent, technology, and finance reinforced this cluster. On grander scales are the petrochemical developments around the Houston Ship Canal and the Mississippi River from New Orleans to Baton Rouge. Silicon Valley, the MIT area, and the North Carolina Research Triangle are three localities where high-tech firms have clustered. Clustering is a "natural" economic and geographic phenomenon. The net result of clustering is to amplify a region's advantage at the expense of other areas. Governments invest to stimulate development of a new cluster or to reinforce an existing cluster.

4.3.9 Summary

Economic development is not evenly spread across space, nor are the community issues that motivate government action and/or impede successful development. Since these matters are not evenly spread, it comes as no surprise that the appropriate application of economic development financial instruments varies across space. What is important is that government, as investor and stimulator of non-governmental investment, recognizes when and where various instruments are and are not appropriate.

4.4 Institutional Perspective

This section discusses the roles of the three basic economic sectors: public, not-for-profit, and private sector. Within each sector, key actors are identified. Key actors within the private sector are identified and discussed regarding their impact on economic development finance. The public sector is viewed within a federalism framework: the financial roles of local, state, and national actors are detailed. Local and national not-for-profits are discussed as they impact on financing of economic development.

Economic development within the U.S. framework involves each of the three economic sectors. Relationships within and between the sectors are diverse, shifting, and complex. Successful economic development requires an alignment of at least two of the sectors. However, the primacy of the private sector is fundamental; government and not-for-profit roles are to encourage and subsidize the investment of private capital (Eisinger, 1988). Public and not-for-profit sectors often have a goal of job generation, but it is only through private sector action that these goals can be realized. The public and not-for-profit sectors seek private sector actors to produce public good.

4.4.1   Private Sector Role

The private sector is the principal actor and overwhelmingly its most important goal is profit. A rational model adequately describes private sector goals and actions — private sector actors assess risk and then seek to maximize return. A higher level of risk makes a project less appealing and as risk is reduced the willingness to invest increases. Generally, despite government financial contributions to economic development projects, the vast portion of financing comes from the private sector.

First and foremost, a private sector actor is not interested in economic development; their goal is profit *via* some investment. Any location decision is highly complex and first involves a query — expand at one of the firm's current locations or open a new facility elsewhere. If the response is elsewhere then there are multiple stages to identify a continent (remember, it's a global economy), a country, a region, a state, and then, finally, a specific site. Ultimately, when a site is selected, it is a "best-fit" based on key concerns, including availability or raw materials, access to markets, production costs, and start-up costs (including time — time is money). Friar (1999) found, in his meta-review of four studies, that labor, infrastructure (particularly transportation), and quality of life were among the most important location factors (in the top five or six). See Table 4.1.

In addition to these factors and their associated costs, time is a key factor. The adage "time is money" has a literal translation in economic development efforts. Construction and start up-costs are immediately out of pocket expenses that cannot be offset until a facility generates revenue. Therefore firms make extra efforts to limit up-front costs.

Table 4.1 Key Location Factors in Order of Importance: Summary of Four Studies

Importance	McKay	Tatum	Bergeron	McKay
1.	Labor	Labor quality	Labor	Real estate Availability and cost
2.	Physical infrastructure (including transporta- tion)	Business costs (including taxes)	Transportation	Labor
3.	Business infrastructure	Infrastructure	Finance	Transportation/ access
4.	Site issues	Access	Business factors	Regulatory environment
5.	Financial issues (including incentives)	Quality of life	Quality of life	Quality of life
6.	Quality of life			Tax issues

Source: Friar, J. (1999). Economic development incentives: A review and recommenda- tions. *Economic Development Review,* 16, 3–7.

4.4.2 Public Sector

While the private sector is the primary mover of economic investment, the public sector attracts, stimulates, and encourages private sector economic development efforts. Using finance and management tools, the public sector influences private sector decision making. Public sector influence is often classified into two approaches — supply-side and demand-side. While some financial instruments might fit into either approach, and the ultimate goal of both is job generation (under the narrow definition), demand-side imple- mentations are much more likely to look beyond job generation to other measures of economic development.

Both supply-side and demand-side approaches seek to attract new private sector investment into a community. However, each approaches economic development and investment from a substantially different perspective.

4.4.2.1 Supply-Side Approach

This approach to economic development uses traditional incentives to attract economic activity to an area (Wolman and Spitzley, 1966).

Some common ones are: tax abatements, debt financing schemes, infrastructure investment, regulatory policy, tax increment financing (TIF) arrangements, enterprise zones (EZ), and land and site development (discussed below) (Reese, 1992). The force driving this approach is to create a comparative cost advantage for a site/firm by altering a site's comparative advantage.

The literature has not been kind to supply-side economic development programs. Eisinger described the research on the efficacy of supply-side inducements as divided (1988). Kotler, Haider, and Rein noted that disappointed expectations, failed deals, and poor bargaining on the part of public officials soured the public on incentives (1992, pp. 244–245). It is safe to say that early enthusiasm for supply-side incentives was partly misplaced. However, criticism of supply-side in the late 1970s and later was overzealous. Economists recognize both supply and demand are necessary for production; therefore; neither the supply-side or the demand-side approach can be totally rejected (Blair, 1995).

4.4.2.2 Demand-Side

The demand-side approach requires government to play an entrepreneurial role, a role normally reserved for the private sector. Government is motivated to act entrepreneurial, not out of a drive for profit but rather to generate jobs. Demand-side economic development practice and finance requires managers to anticipate the economic development market, i.e., prepare their communities in anticipation of demand. Any entrepreneurial strategy implies risk, something with which many public sector managers, appointed or elected, are not comfortable. In supply-side economic development, a community responds to opportunities. In demand-side, the community seeks to create opportunities (Eisinger, 1988). Demand-side management may imply longer lead times for implementations. For example, developing human capital usually requires developing educational infrastructures and programs. Assuming a supply-side approach requires private sector entrepreneurs to exploit the opportunities created by public investment.

The policy, investment, and financial implications of a demand-side approach are many. An additional factor complicates the situation; seldom does a demand-side approach totally replace supply-side efforts, rather a community operates with dual approaches. But demand-side management presents the opportunity for longer-term, more sustainable (environmental and other) development. Communities that invest in anticipation of demand, i.e., developing infrastructures attractive to entrepreneurs, seek to meet the traditional (demand-side) needs of business and also look to create new opportunities for business to exploit. Demand-side policy engages government in technical innovation and efforts to assist firms to move these innovations to the marketplace. In addition to human capital investments, communities generate new ideas (basic research and R&D), provide technical assistance to new and expanding firms, assist in financing start-up and rapidly expanding firms (venture capital), and help to develop new markets (e.g., marketing and export promotion) (Eisinger, 1988).

Today, governments have more on their economic development plates than at any time in the past. And the stakes are higher as competition grows more intense and the gap between winning and losing communities grows wider. Enter a third actor, one that bridges public and private sectors, and provides additional options and opportunities.

4.4.2.3 Not-for-Profit Sector

Not-for-profit organizations (NPOs) exist to serve a wide array of functions, including religious, health care, social welfare, issue advocacy, and capacity-building, to name a few. While any NPO can serve multiple functions, this discussion will highlight those NPOs focused on capacity building.

With regard to economic development finance, two types of NPO activities warrant particular attention, project/program finance and management. NPOs provide a small but important role in financing economic development. Seldom do NPOs provide sustained financial backing for a program, rather NPOs most often serve as "angels" who assist in program start-up or as mediators working between public and private sectors. NPOs have been particularly effective in demand-side efforts targeted at enhancing human capital (most often education), developing local entrepreneurial skills, and community planning.

More interesting are those NPOs that have built substantial, usually local, sometimes state, capacity in economic development finance. Most notable among this group are public–private partnerships (PPPs) that lead and manage economic development programs and projects. PPPs can be narrow or broad, involving just one government and one firm or involving large numbers of governments and firms. A PPP may be a single shot project effort or an on-going endeavor with multiple projects and programs. The National Association of State Development Agencies lists 83 statewide public–private partnership economic development organizations (n.d.). While no numbers are available for the number of local PPPs, they total in the thousands. Often a PPP will execute all or a major portion of a community's economic development efforts. PPPs are ideally suited to meld public and private resources, and to manage the finance economic development efforts. Partnerships have proved effective at every level of government.

4.5   Federalism Perspective

The U.S. federal structure has three principal layers of government. Each level has unique yet overlapping responsibilities regarding economic development and its finance. In the U.S. there are 87,576 units of government (2002): 1 national, 50 states, 3,034 counties, 19,429 municipalities, 16,504 townships, 35,052 special district governments, and 13,506 school districts (U.S. Census Bureau, 2003). Employing the broad definition of economic development, most of these have a role in economic development and its finance. The remainder of this subsection looks at the typical economic development finance roles of the federal government, state governments, and local governments.

4.5.1   Federal Government

Economic development finance at the Federal level is extensive and stretches from macro level responsibility for maintaining an economic system to individual pork barrel projects. The Federal role of economic system maintenance is fundamental to all economic development finance.

4.5.1.1   The Prime (Lending) Rate

The Constitution gave the national government primacy in maintaining a strong national economy. This ranges from issuing patents and copyrights to managing currency and commerce. Without the Federal government maintaining a healthy free market environment where intellectual property is protected, little economic development would be possible. More than any other factor, the Federal Reserve prime rate impacts the likelihood of a project being undertaken and the cost of financing said project. Between December, 1980 and June, 1982 when the Prime Rate soared to all time highs (between 12.0 and 14.0 percent), firms hesitated to invest in new facilities, the cost of money was simply too high. This contrasts with the good years of President Clinton's first term when the Prime Rate hit a 30 year low of three percent and hovered there for 21 months. Beyond the Prime Rate, the Federal government greatly impacts economic development finance in several other ways.

4.5.1.2   Tax Law and Regulations

While the Prime Rate impacts all interest rates regardless of the instrument, Internal Revenue Service policies and tax law impact the relative attractiveness of financial instruments. For example, the appeal of tax exempt bonds for local projects is clear. Purchasers of tax exempt bonds accept lower interest payments, thereby saving the issuing government money. The tax exemption is, in effect, a subsidy by the Federal government and any other government honoring the exemption. In short, the Federal government foregoes tax revenue on this investment. Changing Federal regulations on these bonds impacts their attractiveness. For example, in 1968 the government more carefully delineated the purposes for which these bonds would be issued. In 1978 the Carter Administration doubled the permitted size of issuance, resulting in an immediate doubling of total issuance between 1978 and 1979. In 1982, 1984, 1986, and 1988 regulations were tightened so that much of the tax exemption was lost by 1988 (Eisinger, 1988, p. 160).

4.5.1.3 Federal Purchases

The Federal government is the largest customer in the world and this directly and indirectly influences private sector investment patterns. For example, recycled paper manufacturers had struggled for more than a decade but, with President Clinton's signature on Executive Order 12873 in 1993, the Federal bureaucracy and any business doing Federal work were mandated to use recycled paper products. This instantly created new economies of scale and new comparative advantages, and shifted invest-ment patterns almost overnight (Clinton, 1993). Today, all 50 states have some type of legislation or executive order in place encouraging, or requiring, the use of recycled paper. The demand for recycled paper is so high that most products today meet the Federal standard (Recycled Paper Coalition, 2000).

4.5.1.4 Federal Investment in Infrastructure

While most infrastructure spending takes place at the state, local, or private sector level, the Federal government exerts considerable influence on what infrastructures are built. There are four ways that Federal spending influences infrastructure development. First, the Federal government acquires and maintains an enormous amount of assets such as office buildings, dams and flood control systems, military installations, and wea-pon systems, among others. Second, the Federal government indirectly supports infrastructure operated by other governments through grants, loans, and loan guarantees. The funds must be applied to specific purposes as specified in legislation. For example, the Federal share of capital funding for highways is about 45 percent (FY1995), for transit about 54 percent (FY1997), and for airports about 20 percent (FY1996). Third, *via* tax incentives, the Federal government guides infrastructure investments by others, e.g., the Low-Income Housing Tax Credit. Finally, Federal legislation and regulation impacts the way infrastructure is designed and built. For example, standards for highways, safe water, waste disposal, and worker safety, to name a few, impact the construction of a wide variety of local and state infrastructures.

Federal infrastructure investment has declined each fiscal year from 1987 to 1998 from $174 billion to $118 billion (computed in 1998 dollars). This decline is attributed to decreased investment in military infrastructure which peaked in 1987 at $121 billion and declined to about $54 billion in FY 1997 and FY 1998. Since 1995, spending in non-defense infrastructure showed a slight increase (USGAO, 2000).

4.5.1.5 Federal Law and Regulation

State and local economic development efforts are impacted by Federal law and regulation in ways much more far reaching than the construction of infrastructure. Federal mandates, both funded and unfunded, shape state efforts in diverse policy arenas such as education, water, sanitation, public safety, transportation, transit, and recreation, to name a few. For example, sewer systems in 772 communities need to be overhauled to meet a Federal mandate to separate storm and sanitary sewer systems. This will require $3 billion for Atlanta, $1 billion for Indianapolis, $700 million for Providence, and $1.3 billion for the Cleveland area, to name a few. Unfortunately for these communities, the Federal share of this investment is only about five percent (Copeland, 2003).

4.5.1.6 Financing Federal Economic Development Investment

The Federal government has huge impact on economic development finance, although Federal investment in economic development generally is channeled through other actors. Certainly the Federal government's greatest impact on economic development is Federal Reserve monetary policy, most specifically the prime rate. More than any other factor in the economy, this one policy instrument determines the degree of economic expansion (or contraction) and, therefore, is the primary driver of economic development investment. Thus, the most significant impact the Federal government has on economic development has negligible cost and does not present a financial management issue.

Most Federal economic development investment is through the general fund, i.e., financed annually by taxes and debt financing. A few federal economic development investments are from trust fund monies generated by special taxes. Most notable here are highway and airport monies that are generated by special taxes on users.

Behind the prime rate, the Federal government's most significant impact on economic development lies in the unfunded mandates foisted upon state and local governments. These mandates set local spending priorities and force local governments to forego other opportunities. Despite considerable rhetoric in Washington, mandates continue and contribute to the weak fiscal positions of state and local governments. In 2003 (April 16), the National Conference of State Legislatures identified a sample of four Federal programs that were unfunded or under-funded national mandates/expectations: IDEA — Special Education, No Child Left Behind, Election Reform, and Homeland Security. These four programs require state and local governments to pony up an initial $23.5 billion with lifetime costs of $82.5 billion (2003). These are monies communities might have spent on programs and projects more relevant to local economic development needs.

Federal tax laws greatly impact the relative attractiveness of specific financial instruments, various investments, and of certain localities. The degree to which specific financial instruments are tax deductible impacts the interest rates that a government must pay to borrow money. As rates go up, borrowing capacity is decreased, thereby limiting the numbers and/or sizes of projects. Also, tax deductibility, e.g., individual housing and low interest housing, impacts what gets built.

In summary, Federal investment in economic development is largely funded by the general fund, sale of treasury securities, and passing expenses to state and local governments. The issue of temporal equity regarding economic development investment warrants further analysis. However, since economic development is intended to produce benefits into the future, there may not be as much temporal inequity as with other Federal spending (or borrowing).

4.5.2 States

States serve four significant roles in economic development — they (1) maintain a local political system conducive to economic development, (2) conceive and implement their own policies and programs, (3) respond to mandates in various ways — one avenue is to pass a mandate down the line to local governments, and (4) initiate their own mandates impacting local governments. Regarding finance, (a) states fund a large number of economic development activities, (b) serve as pass-through for much Federal funding, and (c) create mandates, usually under- or unfunded, requiring local government responses.

Like the Federal government, states serve the essential function of maintaining the local economic system. While the state role of system maintenance is not as significant as that played by the Federal government, it is nonetheless an essential role. States must ensure that laws, policies, and regulations are in place to support local economic activity and economic development. State tax law, like Federal tax law, can impact the relative attractiveness of investments, though to a lesser extent.

State governments are major consumers and purchasers, potentially impacting the local economy. State governments inject money into a local economy, especially for communities surrounding state facilities. This is most evident in and around a state capital with thousands of salaried bureaucrats, around public universities, prisons, and other state facilities where state investment greatly impacts and potentially shapes the local economy. Like the Federal government, states invest in infrastructures from parks to universities, to research stations, to highways. Some states own other infrastructures such as rail lines or convention centers, but this varies greatly state to state.

States are key economic development actors as all states have a state office devoted to attract, develop, and retain industry. Each state employs incentives and other inducements to attract and retain business. While economic development functions vary widely between states, there are general commonalities. The remainder of this subsection focuses on commonalities of program offerings and economic development finance.

Considerable research has been devoted to better understanding of state economic development policies and programs. Fundamental to any local economic development program is state law regarding taxing and bonding authority for economic development purposes. State governments also place debt limitations on local governments, thereby controlling how much bonding a local government can undertake. States also serve a pass-through function with regard to Federal monies which assist local governments with economic development activities.

Additionally, states are directly involved in their own economic development pursuits. Each state employs some combination of tax, grants, loans, and other programs to attract and retain business. Most of these programs are financed *via* combinations of general fund (annual appropriations) and special bond issues.

4.5.2.1   Tax Policies

Four state level tax policies impact economic development: general tax policy, targeted tax incentives (company-specific), general tax incentives, and tax increment financing.

4.5.2.1.1   General Tax Policy

States are frequently compared in terms of their business climates. Government impact on business climate is significant as public services, taxation, and regulation create the context within which governments operate. Yet, the term "business climate" has become almost synonymous with the pressure to cut taxes, reduce services, and decrease regulation (Dabson and Rist, 1996). At one time or another, most states have pursued a policy of cutting taxes, particularly business taxes, in the name of improving business climate. The efficacy of state efforts to impact business climate is uncertain. Carroll and Wasylenko found that the effects of state and local fiscal policy on employment growth and personal income were substantial in the 1970s but these impacts had waned by the 1980s (1994). Bartik reviewed 57 studies and concluded that state taxes have a large impact on business activity (1991). Likewise, Hodge, Moody, and Warcholik argue that tax decisions by states impact business climate which, in turn, impacts the relative attractiveness of a state compared to its neighbors (2003). So, regarding academic literature, the jury is out as to whether or not state taxes have significant impact on economic development. What is clear is that state policy leaders act as though they believe state taxes have a significant impact on economic development.

Former Labor Secretary in the Clinton Administration, Robert Reich, observed state efforts to be more attractive to firms. According to Reich, states have methodically reduced business taxes and taxes on upper income households, those most likely to make business location decisions. Reich cites a two-fold impact: (1) tax burden was shifted to lower income households with less ability to pay, and (2) social services and education were reduced. Reich argues that this is a very shortsighted approach (2000).

4.5.2.1.2 Targeted Tax Incentives

Targeted tax incentives are deal-specific, as opposed to general tax incentives that apply to an entire industry or class of business operations. Targeted tax incentives are the most widely recognized of all state business activities because of their frequent high profile. It's a cliché to say that U.S. communities compete in a global market, but that is clearly the case with targeted incentives. Nowhere is this more obvious than in the location of automobile manufacturing and assembly plants. With few large-scale facilities in play, the bidding for automobile plants is fierce. State officials seek these facilities for jobs, externalities (other facilities locate nearby and create additional employment), prestige, and the political well-being this generates in the home state. Competition in the U.S. for such facilities is almost mind-boggling, as every state, county, and city has entered the fray. States offer major firms incentive packages of $100 million, $200 million, $300 million, and more. And companies are getting very savvy at this game. Most large U.S. companies employ incentive specialists or consultants, who search for the maximum tax breaks and grants from communities. The stakes are high as states try to outbid one another while not putting themselves in the red. Alabama competed, won the bidding war, and "landed" four major auto plants in recent years: DaimlerChrysler, Honda, Toyota, and Hyundai. Together, the State expended close to $700 million in incentives (Brooks, 2002). To land the Hyundai deal, Alabama had to pony up $76.7 million in tax breaks, $61.8 million in training grants, and $34 million in land purchase assistance. (Labyrinth, 2002). The stakes are clear — offer too little and a state loses the project, too much and the state pays more than it would get back in taxes and employment benefits, thereby requiring taxpayers to essentially subsidize a facility.

States enter into the economic development "wars" seeking jobs. In 1978, Pennsylvania gave incentives totaling $3,550 per job to attract a new Volkswagen assembly plant. In 1980, Tennessee paid Nissan $11,000 per employee (Labyrinth, 2002). The Hyundai and DaimlerChrysler deals cost Alabama $117,317 (Cason, 2002) and $150,000 per job (Labyrinth, 2002). This type of spending prompted Greg Le Roy, founder of Good Jobs First, a Washington, D.C. think tank specializing in investment incentives, to note, "since the mid-1990s (economic development organizations) have been on a spending binge like drunken sailors." (Labyrinth, 2002) While no definitive numbers exist, total annual business incentives by U.S. states likely exceed $50 billion per year (Labyrinth, 2002).

Let's examine one deal, the $252.8 million dollar Hyundai package that the state of Alabama put up. The private sector (mostly utilities) is investing $18.2 million in the project. The remaining $234.6 is public investment, divided between the state government, local governments, and the state employee retirement systems (Carson, 2002). The local share of this package is about $25 million (Cason, Hendrick, and Dugan, 2002), from at least 16 governments (Sherman, 2003) leaving the state to foot approximately $210 million.

4.5.2.1.3 General Tax Incentives

While targeted tax incentives are deal-specific, general tax incentives apply to an entire class of economic development activity. General incentives tend to fall into four categories: tax abatements, tax exemptions (tax is not owed), tax credits, and tax increment financing.

i **Tax Abatements** Tax abatement is a reduction in a tax, usually a property tax, for given piece of real estate for a specified period of time. Although abatements usually apply to a property tax, ordinarily impacting the locality more than the state, they are considered a state incentive as they require state (enabling) legislation and are often granted at the state level. The period of abatement usually ranges from 5 to 25 years in most cases.

Emerging in the South during the depression, this device was quickly adopted elsewhere and is today widespread. One major reason for this is that an abatement is program politically appealing. An abatement has little current cost, the real costs are in future taxes foregone. Abatements also have a symbolic value, i.e., an abatement signals a community's willingness to work with the private sector (Eisinger, 1988). Operationally, abatements tend to favor larger projects and larger firms. The literature generally reflects that abatements seldom work (Levy, 1990).

ii **Tax Exemptions** Tax exemptions are exclusions from the tax code, i.e., specific property that is not taxed. Many homeowners are familiar with a homestead exemption that reduces the taxable value of a primary residence, resulting in a lower property tax bill. Like abatements, exemptions are state enabled programs that impact local government and are often implemented at the local level. Exemptions are one way a state can encourage a particular type of development. Two of the more common tax exemptions are: (1) the freeport exemption which exempts property in transit, that property imported from out-of-state and destined for export, and (2) the inventory exemption. It is not unusual for a state to offer prospective businesses multiple exemptions with particular exemptions targeted at different types of property. For example, Wisconsin exempts or partially exempts four classes of business property from property taxes: machinery and equipment used in manufacturing, merchants' and manufacturers' inventories, pollution abatement equipment, and computer equipment. Additionally, Wisconsin exempts manufacturing machinery and equipment from sales tax (Wisconsin Public Service, n.d.).

iii **Tax Credits** A tax credit applies a credit to a percentage of money recently expended for business purposes, usually applied to the corporate income tax. Tax credits are intended to reduce the cost of investments. Most commonly, tax credits reduce the cost of capital investments, training, or social goods such as pollution reduction or job creation. The most common tax credits seem to be for investment, job creation, and job training. Many states offer some sort of offset for capital investment. For example, New York State manufacturers can offset 5% of their first $350 million of investment and 4% on any additional investment against their tax bill. Job creation tax credits are available in every state. In Pennsylvania a job creation tax credit gives companies $1,000 for every "leading-edge technology" job created, as long as 25 jobs are created within 3 years (Labyrinth, 2002). Related to job creation are credits for enhancing job skills. Most states have such programs however, what is and is not covered varies a good deal. Some states exclude on-the-job training while others offer preference for these types of experiences.

iv Tax Increment Financing Tax increment finance (TIF) is a creative application of tax law that diverts tax proceeds (usually property taxes) for a specified period to fund capital improvements within the TIF district. TIFs are state enabled and locally applied. TIF assists local governments to undertake public projects that stimulate (re)development otherwise not likely to occur. The increment is equal to the difference between the taxes collected on the improved parcel less the taxes that would have been collected had the parcel remained unimproved. Proceeds from the increment usually are used to pay off government investment (most often bonds) used to improve the parcel. TIFs are used throughout the country, most heavily in the Midwest, especially the Upper Midwest. TIFs are politically appealing because the increment is intended to pay for the improvements, and the community gains with little or no pain. But, should the increment fall short of being self-sustaining, the local government is liable to make up the difference. TIF districts may be detrimental to taxing authorities who are brought into the scheme involuntarily. For example, if a school tax is included in a TIF project, and the district attracts new employees to the community, schools will be negatively impacted as enrollments climb without new revenue.

v Other Incentives States employ a wide array of additional incentives that tend to fall into one or more of three categories: targeted, business cycle, and pragmatic. Targeted incentives are those that seek firms in a specific industry, e.g., tourism, or firms willing to locate in a particular area, e.g., an inner-city. Enterprise zone and economic community efforts (discussed below), aimed at low income areas, also fit into targeted programming. Business cycle incentives assist firms to overcome impediments they may face at a particular point in their business cycle, e.g., start-up, expansion, or modernization. Venture capital programs and entrepreneurship programs are two of the many types of business cycle programs governments may offer. Pragmatic type incentives are simply those programs that are neither targeted or business cycle based. Sometimes, a specific program may fall into more than one category. For example, a technical assistance program for local governments assisting business start-ups in high poverty areas would cross over all three categories.

Business cycle programming provides support for a firm's specific needs. As a firm evolves through its business cycle, from youth to growth, to maturity, to old age, its needs change. As a firm passes through these stages, its needs will vary. Business cycle programming exists to facilitate business development tailored to the evolving needs of a firm. A business cycle approach will focus extra support on start-ups and youth stages of development as these are points when firms are particularly in need of assistance. Most governments have an array of programming to decrease the capital costs to businesses at these stages.

All economic development programming tends to be pragmatic, i.e., looking to address existing problems; pragmatic, as employed herein, refers to programs that are neither targeted nor life-cycle based, but provide competitive services (compared to other states) and protect the state's investment. Funding mechanisms for several of these programs is discussed in later sections. Local governments often have programs that parallel state programs.

4.5.3 Local

Local economic development refers to efforts undertaken by the vast majority of governments located at a sub-state level. This level includes full-service governments — counties and cities, and an array of special service units of governments. Often overlooked in this group is the most numerous unit of government — school districts. This subsection focuses on county and city governments, herein referred to as local government(s).

4.5.3.1 Local Means Politics

The late great Speaker of the U.S. House of Representatives, Tip O'Neill said, "All politics are local." In this same vein, all economic development is local. And, since taxes drive most local political agendas, we encounter the stress of local economic development: communities need to invest today for tomorrow. While politics impacts economic development at all levels, it is at the local level where the intersection of politics, public finance, and economic development grows most stressed.

Layoffs, plant closings, unemployment, and underemployment are felt most directly at the local level. Citizens see and feel the pain daily. Local leaders are expected to care for the community, to create jobs and to preserve their community as a good place to live and to work. Local officials are under pressure to make things right for the community, yet the most important factors impacting the community's development rest outside their control: the national economy and mandates. All the while these governments are in competition with communities down the road, across the state, or half-way around the globe. Political survival at the local level has grown more complex and difficult.

Most Federal and state economic development assistance is channeled through local governments. Two important management skills have rapidly gained in importance: grant writing and grant management. Successful grantsmanship helps a community to obtain leverage, and creatively maximize return on its investment.

Poverty is most keenly felt at the local level, and where most programs to address this and other social ills are implemented. At the other end of the policy spectrum, local Chambers of Commerce and other business associations are powerful actors in many communities, lobbying for local government action to create a better business climate. While definitions vary, a "better business climate" often equates with (1) low taxes and (2) high quality business services and infrastructures. With these pressures, it is amazing that anybody wants to hold public office in local government!

Despite increased professionalization, economic development and especially local economic development are focused on job creation. Ordinarily, elected leaders and economic development professionals are judged by the numbers of jobs created. Politics are a matter of, "what have you done for me lately?" A stunning success has very short legs; it will not carry a politician or an economic development official very far. They are faced with continuous pressure to produce new projects, new jobs.

Local leaders need to produce and demonstrate visible output. This creates an unfortunate and often unproductive bias toward the creation of new jobs at the expense of maintaining existing jobs. While this syndrome occurs at all levels, it is particularly acute at the local level. The need to display success in job creation is a reason behind many grand ribbon-cutting ceremonies, where local dignitaries show the masses "look at the great job we're doing."[1] Unfortunately, job creation is considerably more expensive than job retention, but it is easier to define and to display. This explains why it is not unusual to see 90% of a local economic development organization's resources focused on job creation *versus* the more efficacious job retention.

4.5.3.2 Shifts in Federal–Local Funding for Infrastructure

A major U.S. General Accounting Office report found substantial differences in infrastructure investment patterns between Federal and state and local governments (2000). The study found two-thirds of Federal infrastructure spending went for acquisition and construction while two-thirds of state and local government spending was for improvements and maintenance. The study also found Federal funding for many infrastructures declined in real dollars, shifting actual fiscal responsibility to state and local governments. In the period FY 1956 to 1977 the Federal share of transportation and water resources expenditures expanded 17%. However, since the 1980s, state and local governments have contributed approximately 75% of public infrastructure spending in these areas. Since the 1950s Federal infrastructure spending has been dominated by spending on highway development. During the 1970s federal spending focused more on wastewater treatment and mass transit but, in the 1980s through the 1990s, focus shifted back to highways and aviation. Since the 1970s state spending focused most on highways (USGAO, 2000). Highways are seen as a fundamental element in any state economic development program. Federal highway investments have been tied to suburbanization, the decline of central cities, and urban sprawl (USGAO, 1999).

4.5.3.3 Impacts and Implications of Local Programming

Other than infrastructure spending, Federal and state decisions greatly affect local economic development programming. Federal and state mandates, both unfunded and under-funded, have enormous impact on how local governments pursue economic development. Additionally, state and Federal economic development related initiatives influence the types of projects undertaken by local governments.

As noted above, most Federal dollars for economic development are spent locally. For rural areas and small cities much of these dollars are administered on a pass-through basis by state government. For larger entitlement cities, much of these resources pass directly from Federal to local government, bypassing state government. Localities are either entitled to these resources because they meet some pre-established criteria (e.g., percentage of population below the poverty level) or must compete for monies *via* a grant process.

The nature of state incentives often determines whether or not a community can compete for certain types of development. For example, it is less likely that a distribution facility would locate in a community without freeport and inventory tax exemptions than in a community with these exemptions.

Many state economic development incentives cost local governments considerably more revenue than state governments. For example, most abatements come off the property tax, and hit local governments particularly hard. There is a degree of volunteerism to most abatements, since local government, city or county, grants them. In some jurisdictions, school taxes are also abated at the same time, creating a difficult situation for a local school district that was not party to the abatement negotiations. Fortunately, in a growing number of states, school tax abatement is prohibited or considered as a separate matter.

4.5.4 Institutional Perspective Summarized

All three levels of government recognize their role in economic development is to facilitate private sector projects. Even though economic development is essentially local, state and Federal governments play essential roles. However, most of the specifics of project development and packaging of incentives falls directly on local level administrators.

The Federal government's most significant roles in financing economic development are: (1) provide appropriate legal and institutional framework to facilitate private sector development, (2) maintain a healthy investment climate, most importantly low and stable interest rates and (3) provide financial assistance to states and communities.

States also contribute to the legal and policy environment in which economic development takes place. State laws and policies need to be conducive to positive development. States have been increasingly important actors sculpting the business climate. Often this translates into seeking an "ideal" mix of tax policy (low business taxes) coupled with high quality services. States provide technical assistance and financial support, especially in the form of incentives, for economic development.

Local governments are the key actors in spurring economic development. Job creation and job retention efforts are site specific and key factors such as land availability and zoning, utilities, education, public safety, and quality of life are in the domain of local government. It is at the local level where "the rubber meets the road," and where citizens are most aware of public finance, i.e., tax issues. Property taxes and jobs are local political hot buttons. Additionally local governments are caught in the pincer grips of a citizenry acutely aware of tax rates and superior governments passing down unfunded and under-funded mandates. Local governments are becoming increasingly sophisticated at leveraging Federal, state, and local government dollars with private sector dollars to generate local economic development.

4.6 Instrumental Perspective

This section reviews several key economic development finance instruments in terms of the specific niche(s) they serve. There is a plethora of instruments available to assist governments, depending on the goals and objectives they seek to achieve. The instruments range from macro to micro-economic and include generic as well as environmental specific policy implementations. Table 4.2 displays a sample of some of the more common economic development finance instruments. There exist a large

Table 4.2   Economic Development Finance Instruments

Instruments	Discussion
Self-financing	Private sector executes project (development) with no financial support from government. Far and away the most frequent circumstance.
Incentive	An inducement by government to get private sector investors to respond in a way desired by government.
Tax	Employing provisions in the tax code to make a locality more attractive.
Other	Public sector underwrites a portion of development costs.
Tax abatement	A reduction in a tax, usually a property tax, for given piece of real estate for a specified period of time.
Tax credit	Applies a credit to a percentage of money recently expended for business purposes, usually applied to the corporate income tax.
Loan	A government provides money for a private sector project with the expectation that the money will be repaid within a specified time, with or without interest, depending on the conditions of the loan.
Guarantee	A government insures repayment of all or a portion of a firm's guarantee, thereby serving to increase credit worthiness.
Grant	A government provides money for a private sector project with no condition of repayment. Grants are usually awarded contingent on a firm producing some measurable output, e.g., hiring a specific number of employees. A grant might or might not be secured against performance, i.e., firm is forced to repay if grant conditions are not met.
Bond	The primary way governments issue debt.
General obligation	Secured by the full faith, credit, and taxing powers of the issuing government.
Revenue	Secured by revenues generated by a specified enterprise or project.
Tax exempt	Interest income on bond is exempt from federal income taxes. Many states also exempt interest on certain bonds.
Microcredit	Small loans (a few $1,000s) available to very small businesses.
Venture capital	High risk loans provided to businesses are their early stages of development and involving long-term equity investment.
Interest rate reduction	Loans made at rates below the market rate.

(Continued)

Table 4.2   Continued

Instruments	Discussion
Second mortgage	A long-term lien on a property that is riskier than a first mortgage. In the event of a default, the claims of the first mortgage are settled prior to a second.
Subordinate debenture	A bond backed by the credit of a corporation rather than by asset(s) that is subordinate to other debt instruments in the case of dissolution. A relatively high risk loan that, should the firm go broke, is settled only after other loans.
Depository selectivity	A government can direct its short-term deposits to a preferred institution.
Secondary position loan	Secondary to a first loan with regards to claiming capital in case of default.
Equity injection and equity kicker	Government purchase of ownership shares of a firm's stock.
Indirect equity injector	Government induces an intermediary to purchase shares of a firm's stock.
Direct subsidy	A grant of money paid to a firm with no expectation of repayment.
User charge	A fee for service. User charges can be reduced as an incentive.
Procurement program	A program whereby a local government provides educational and/or technical assistance to help local businesses sell to state and/or Federal governments.
Foreign trade zone	A place is legally considered outside of the territory of an entity with regards to one or more taxes. A foreign trade zone is treated legally, for the purposes of duties, to be outside the U.S.
Tax reinvestment	Taxes paid by an entity, usually a firm, are reinvested back into an investment that creates a positive environment for the firm.
Clawback	A clause in agreement between firm and government that allows government to retrieve some of its investment should the firm fail to meet the stipulations of the agreement.

number of economic development incentives to assist firms as discussed by Eisinger (1988), Levy (1990), Kottler, Haider, and Rein (1993), Lyons and Hamlin (2001), and a multitude of case studies.

Most economic development is self-financed, that is a firm pays all expansion costs. Governments can facilitate firm activities by administrative streamlining, regulation simplification, and educational or technical assistance programming. However, the primary role of government participation in economic development is *via* incentives. Incentives fall into two broad categories, tax incentives and other incentives designed to directly underwrite a portion of the costs of development.

4.6.1 Packaging Incentives

Governments often offer a prospective firm a (sometimes complex) package of incentives. For example, Hyundai agreed to construct a $1 billion dollar plant employing approximately 2,000 in Montgomery, Alabama after being offered incentives valued at $252.8 million: $76.7 million in tax incentives, $157.9 million in other incentives, and $18.2 million in private incentives (electricity, telecommunication, natural gas, and local services) (Hyundai won over ..., 2002). In addition to the State contribution, 16 local governments also put up incentives (Sherman, 2003) and the state employees' retirement system chipped in $10 million. The non-tax incentives included housing rebates for employees, a $7 million training facility, $54.8 million worth of training equipment, $34 million in land acquisition and site improvements, $29 million in road/highway improvements, $21 million in water and sewer improvements, and $10 million for advertising among others (Cason, 2002). The State put out a $118 million bond issue to cover a portion of its share (Hyundai won over..., 2002).

4.6.2 Lowering Interest Rates

States can also assist firms by lowering the cost of borrowing. For example, a grant might cover a portion of land development costs, thereby helping a firm to avoid some borrowing. In cases where borrowing is necessary, governments can decrease the interest rates that a firm must pay. Governments do this either by becoming a lender or by guaranteeing a loan. All state governments and many local governments have one or more lending programs designed to attract firms and facilitate growth of existing firms. As a lender, governments can charge below market rates. Rate reduction can be a matter of subsidization, with the government making up the subsidized share or government acts as an intermediary.

As an intermediary, a government becomes a re-lender. As a rule, governments are considered to be better credit risks than their private sector counterparts, especially counterparts needing to borrow money. Additionally, government borrowing may have an additional advantage of tax-free interest payments. Governments can therefore borrow at a substantially lower interest rate than firms. Governments can re-lend all or a portion of the money at slightly higher rates and break even, while the firm enjoys a substantially reduced interest rate.

An especially large project might result in a firm borrowing from multiple sources for many purposes. Various government programs permit grants and loans for specific applications. Additionally, commercial lenders do not loan beyond the life expectancy of an asset and prefer to loan for shorter periods on most commercial assets. A firm starting up a new complex facility may find itself with multiple loans, each with differing terms. A blended interest rate is the weighted average of the rates on all borrowed monies.

4.6.3 Life Cycle of a Firm

Firms and industries are often described in terms of life cycle. Parallel to the stages of a human life, firms and industries are described in terms of birth, youth (growth), maturity, old age, and death. A firm's need for government assistance evolves over time, with much assistance needed in the early stages. The traditional methods of raising financial resources: bank loans, stocks, and bonds were inadequate to meet the needs of these firms. With the growth of private sector venture capital investors, the need was partially met, but a significant role has been left for government. Increasingly governments find that investments into micro-credit and venture capital schemes lead to win–win situations.

4.6.3.1 Micro-Credit

At inception, a firm generally consists of one person, working part-time in a basement, garage, or spare room. At this early stage a firm is highly vulnerable to collapse. The step from after hours in the garage to becoming an individual's primary source of employment is a large transition for any firm. Small loans can facilitate this step, since generally only a few thousand dollars are needed. With few assets, the fledgling business person is too great a risk for a conventional bank loan and is certainly not ready for larger scale equity financing. While risks from micro-credit lending to fledgling firms are substantial, the pay-offs for lenders and communities can be ample. Governments increasingly find themselves making small-scale loans, especially in locales where social need is great, e.g., areas of concentrated poverty and areas with high levels of minority and/or female under/unemployment.

4.6.3.2 Venture Capital (Equity Investment)

Once a firm begins to show promise, its need for capital grows as the firm tries to move its concepts/products toward marketplace. This is most seen in cutting-edge technologies with high development costs and substantial failure risks. Traditional debt financing is inappropriate since the loans come due before an ability to pay is developed. The most appropriate method of finance is equity financing, i.e., venture capital, whereby investors gain partial ownership in the firm. Since the risk of failure is high and the salvage value of the firm is usually low, a wise investor performs substantial due diligence and spreads risk by investing in several small firms.

In areas such as Silicon Valley with substantial venture capital infrastructure, there is little or no need for government intervention. Likewise there is little need for government intervention in the high-tech corridors around Boston, Chicago, and Madison, Wisconsin. However, most communities lack venture capital infrastructure, thereby forcing innovators to leave the community or suppress their creative endeavors. This situation provides government an opportunity to play an important role as venture capitalist. Typically, private sector venture capitalists provide management services to protect their equity/investment; however governments have been reluctant to undertake that important function.

4.6.3.3 Foreign Trade Zones

For tax purposes, foreign trade zones are considered to be outside the U.S. Firms may import and export goods duty and quota free for an unlimited period of time. Within the zone, goods may be stored, mixed with other materials, used in manufacturing process, or exhibited for sale. Imported goods used in manufacturing within the zone may be subject to a lower or no duty. Unsold goods may be destroyed. Any good that is re-exported is considered to never have entered the U.S. (Fitzgerald, n.d.; Kansas City Area Development Corporation, 2004; North Carolina Department of Commerce, 2004). In essence, foreign trade zones permit a community to benefit by assisting firms to avoid federal (import and export) taxes.

4.6.3.4 Special Development Zones

Special development zones are geographic areas designated by one or more governments that warrant special consideration for economic development initiatives. The Federal government specifies three such areas: Renewal Communities (RC), Empowerment Zones (EZ), and Enterprise Communities (EC). State and local governments generally follow Federal lead, creating zones with multiple layers of programmatic benefits. The Federal government offers tax and other incentives to entice businesses to locate or expand in one of 178 designated EZs, ECs, or RCs, or to hire employees who reside in one of the zones (USHUD, 2003). These incentives include:

- Wage Credits
- Empowerment Zone Employment Credit
- Renewal Community Employment Credit
- Work Opportunity Tax Credit

- Welfare to Work Credit
- Indian Employment Tax Credit
- Deductions
- Increased Section 179 Expensing
- Commercial Revitalization Deduction
- Environmental Cleanup Cost Deduction
- Depreciation of Property Used on Indian Reservations
- Bond Financing
- Enterprise Zone Facility Bonds
- Qualified Zone Academy Bonds
- Capital Gains
- Zero Percent Capital Gains Rate for RC Assets and DC Enterprise Zone Assets
- Non-recognition of Gain on Sale of Empowerment Zone Assets.
- Partial Exclusion of Gain from Sale of Empowerment Zone Stock.
- Other Incentives
- New Markets Tax Credit
- Low-Income Housing Tax Credit (U.S. HUD, 2003)

U.S. HUD contracted an intensive evaluation of six EZs to determine program impacts after five years. The study found overall positive impacts, especially in communities that had established organizational infrastructure prior to implementing an EZ. Five of six study areas developed at rates faster than areas outside the program. The study indicated that incentives, combined and applied intensively within a distressed area, can positively assist both job and wealth creation. However, the capacity for some communities to sustain development after program incentives end was in doubt (Herbert, Vidal, Mills, James, and Gruenstein, 2001).

4.6.3.5 Clawbacks

In the competition to attract economic development, states and local governments offer firms incentive pages based on limited knowledge of a firm's intentions. For major projects, a firm's actions (job creation) are projected for several years based on preliminary data. Environmental or internal changes within the firm may greatly alter the original plan, resulting in less job creation than expected. Kottler, Haider, and Rein describe the expanding place "war" of escalating bids (incentives) to attract firms that took place through the 1960s, 1970s and 1980s:

> ... corporations and their negotiators were taking advantage of the public. Places were being played off against one another over jobs and being whipsawed on concessions ... .

A public reaction began to take place against politicians who offered excessive inventive packages ... . Elected officials could stiffen their resistance to corporate blackmail ... . Public officials became better place bargainers. They developed more consistent policies on subsidies as opposed to ad hoc, case-by-case actions. They developed analytical capability ... and learned in many cases to negotiate with businesses as equal partners ... . Finally, they learned how to protect themselves and public investments through legally binding contracts that included cancellation of agreements for nonperformance and recovery of subsidy expenditures, penalties, and adjustments for renegotiation of agreements and nonperformance (1993, pp. 245–246).

Clawbacks are money-back guarantees that tie incentives to performance. With a clawback clause, a government can reduce or recover a subsidy if a firm fails to deliver. A clawback may be prorated, pegging consequences to a firm's performance. Less often, a clawback might include one or more financial penalty clauses. Clawbacks are highly advisable and are rapidly becoming standard for a growing number of states and communities. In 2002, 17 states had clawback provisions, up from 9 a decade earlier. Additionally, 37 states had some provision for the quality of jobs created, up from 8 just a decade prior (Peirce, 2002).

4.6.4 Summary

Economic development practitioners today have more options available to them than ever before. There is a growing sophistication in the use of economic development finance tools and increased pressures for accountability of government and firms receiving incentives. More states and communities have normalized their incentives programs, moving from an *ad hoc* case-by-case approach to a level of standardization. Yet, there is much room for improvement and, in an increasingly unpredictable environment, incentive programs will become more scrutinized and competitive.

4.7   The Future of Economic Development Finance

This section addresses the future of economic development finance from two perspectives: (1) current shortcomings in practice or knowledge, and (2) issues facing communities involved with economic development finance.

4.7.1 Shortcomings in Practice and Knowledge

Two interrelated trends will continue to impact economic development finance and practice into the future: (1) the field will continue to evolve and become more professional, and (2) intensified public scrutiny on economic development, economic development finance, and rational economic development practices. These trends will likely lead to experimentation in business–government relations, expanded intergovernmental relations, and greater use of performance evaluation.

4.7.1.1 Professionalizing the Practice in Economic Development Finance

Education and training of economic development professionals has progressed considerably in recent years. Most states tout some sort of professional development for economic development practitioners and/or local elected officials. Ordinarily, a portion of this training focuses on financial issues. Economic development education leaders devote a substantial proportion of their curricula to financial issues. For example, the International Economic Development Council offers a professional development series with five core courses, two of which are finance courses (IEDC, n.d.). ACCRA (not an acronym), teamed with the University of Southern Mississippi, offers an Executive Masters Degree in Economic Development that focuses three of nine courses on finance (University of Southern Mississippi and ACCRA, 2003). The National Association of Development Organizations offers a certificate program in Small Business Loan Fund Management (NADO, n.d.). Undoubtedly this trend will intensify as state and local budgets grow more constrained and development deals and incentive packages become more complex.

4.7.1.2 Higher Levels of Public Scrutiny and Increasingly Rational Practices

Public dissatisfaction with overly generous incentives packages will grow more acute. As public awareness and scrutiny expand, elected and appointed officials may be less willing to over-subsidize development projects. Public advocacy efforts are now adding "deliverables," "risk assessment," and "accountability" components to the incentives equation. This new development is exemplified by the recent founding of Good Jobs First (GFJ), an organization whose mission is to "help grassroot groups and policy-makers ensure that economic development subsidies are accountable and effective (Good Jobs First, 2004). GJF's publications list, with titles such as *No More Secret Candy Store: A Grass Roots Guide to Investigating Development Subsidies* (Good Jobs First, 2002) and *Minding the Candy Store: State Audits of Economic Development* (Hinkley and Hsu, 2000) reads something like a manifesto to hone accountability.

Tight budgets, increased professionalism, intensified public scrutiny, and growing reluctance by public officials to overspend on subsidies, will move incentive programs to be more rational, productive, effective, and marketable.

4.7.1.3   Expanded Application of Evaluation

Evaluation is a key component of rational public policy making. To date, evaluation of economic development has been meager. Part of this stems from the political imperative elected officials feel, i.e., they must appear to be active regarding the local economy. The act of doing something may be more important than being effective or efficient. If an evaluation indicated actions approved by an official were not effective, this could make her/his political life more difficult.

Reese and Fasenfest observe that evaluation requires identification of values, and that this is seldom the case in economic development. Rarely does a community ask itself what it is trying to achieve with economic development, i.e., to specify community values (1997). In a way this may fly in the face of the pragmatic history of economic development discussed in a prior section.

State economic development programs have rarely been evaluated. And when they are evaluated, the results are often much less positive than hoped (LeRoy and Slocum, 1999; Hinkley and Hsu, 2000). Politicians may view evaluation as an unnecessary political liability, leading them to avoid evaluation when possible.

Even in the best of situations, measuring economic development program outcomes is a challenge. Any basic text in program evaluation warns that assessing programs wholly in terms of inputs is inadequate, but economic development outcomes are considerably more difficult to measure than inputs. In the economic development arena we have difficulty measuring outputs, especially secondary outputs created by multipliers (Reese and Fasenfest, 1999; Felsenstein and Persky, 1999).

Evaluation is an essential component if economic development and economic development financing are to be more rational. And the trend is clear. Through the first 50 years of economic development (1930s to the 1980s), evaluation was seldom mentioned in the literature. Since 1990, evaluation has become a prominent issue in the literature, as exemplified by John Blair's *Local Economic Development: Analysis and Practice* (1995) and Lyons and Hamlin's, *Creating an Economic Development Action Plan*

(2001). Proactive states, like Minnesota, with the first subsidy disclosure law in the nation, create a more suitable environment for evaluation (LeRoy and Slocum, 1999). It seems safe to conclude that evaluation will garner more attention in a field increasingly long on demand and short on resources.

4.7.1.4   Expanded Firm–Government Relations and Intergovernmental Relations

Escalating global and local competition will require governments to inno-vate, coordinate, and leverage their relationships with other organizations.

Globally, the trend has been for national governments to decrease their equity shares in both public and private sector firms. The national sell-offs of state-owned enterprises in the last 25 years was dazzling: the sale of Conrail in the US; liquidation of national coal and steel assets in Britain; elimination of subsidies across Europe; privatization of huge national assets in Russia, other former Soviet states, and Eastern Europe; and the pri-vatization of public assets such as phone and utility companies in much of Latin America, Africa, and Asia.

During this same period, local governments in the U.S. became more experimental in their relationships with private sector firms. The most extra-ordinary examples of this experimentation are local governments taking equity stakes in start-up firms. Business incubators (Lyons and Hamlin, 2001) and government developed shell buildings into which firms can grow (Stucki, 1998), are two additional examples of more complex relationships between government and private sector firms.

Intergovernmental relations will continue to expand. With increased pressures from global competition and from a citizenry more closely scrutinizing incentive deals, local governments able to capture larger shares of externalities can offer more lucrative incentive packages. A key to cap-turing externalities will be to involve more local governments. While this trend is not new, especially to urban areas, it can be expected to intensify and to further penetrate rural areas. Increased rationalization of economic development practices will make it easier for local, state, and Federal governments to cooperate on a more normalized basis rather than on the project by project basis seen currently in most places.

4.7.2   Potential Issues Facing Communities Involved in Economic Development Finance

The world of economic development finance, like everything else, will grow increasingly complex in the next decade. Competition will grow fiercer, the public will continue to expect more for its money, and time horizons will shorten. The global market of communities seeking economic development will result in places offering nearly identical products. These factors appear to indicate a more chaotic world. However, in circumstances such as these, intangible differences may be what separate winners from losers. Increasingly communities will need to broadly define economic development, and include a wide array of quality of life and other aspects of a community.

4.7.2.1 Preparing for Increasing Rapid Change

It is almost cliché to speak of increasingly rapid change in society and technology. However, communities must accept this cliché and prepare to compete in this new environment. These preparations will encompass the development of sensory, communication, and action skills. Communities must build the sensory organs to be alert to environmental change. However, sensory organs alone will not permit timely and successful responses. Organizations that can process information promptly and accurately to identify opportunity, and then act quickly will enjoy comparative advantage. Sound like the private sector? Absolutely!!! Community economic development efforts, already the most entrepreneurial side of government, will need to become even more skilled.

4.7.2.1.1 Improved sensory skills

Economic development organizations, and governments in general, will need to become better at sensing the environment. Organizations, like nature, can do this is a number of ways: more eyes and ears — a "herd" model; better eyes and ears — the hawk/rabbit model; and better placed eyes and ears — the lookout model. Communities will need to be effective with all three models. Networking in professional associations, geographic associations, and other opportunities such as trade shows will enable communication between a greater number of eyes and ears. "Better eyes and ears," while not sufficient in themselves, will help a good deal, i.e., communities will need to do better with the tools they have. For example, it is amazing to this author the large proportion of city and county governments that lack subscriptions to the *New York Times* or *Wall Street Journal,* two superb avenues to "better eyes and ears." Communities seldom draw on the large numbers of lookouts from within, e.g., company officers and others who are highly attuned to developments in their industry. A first step toward future success will be for communities to better utilize the available sensory resources.

4.7.2.1.2 Better Processing

All the sensory data in the world will not help unless an organization can cull important information from environmental noise and convert the information to meaningful action. According to Wurman, Sume, and Leifer, organizations and individuals seldom suffer from a scarcity of information; more often than not, they have too much information available. In actuality it is not the amount of information, it is an inability to process the information. Just like "more eyes and ears" help, additional processors help, as long as communication networks are effective. Multiple processors can specialize and squeeze more value (meaning) from the information. The easiest way to gain more and better processors is for an organization to develop the reasoning skills of its members and to reward them for using these skills. Additionally, organizations need to network with each other and use consulting firms as avenues to increase their processing power.

4.7.2.1.3 Acting on information

Sensing and processing does an animal little good if it freezes in its tracks. The same can be said of economic development organizations. Streamlined decision making, as long as it does not detract from organizational sensory and processing skills, will be key to survival. Economic development organizations need to aim for a swift, empowered, multifunctional, decision making structure. Economic development organizations with slow reaction times will suffer the same fate that their private sector counterparts suffered in the 1980s, 1990s, and 2000s. If you snooze you lose!

4.7.2.2 *Leaner and Meaner Options for Managing Economic Development Finance*

Public–private partnerships (PPPs) are the product of decades of evolution. They came into their own in the 1980s, largely as a response to Federal cuts in urban redevelopment monies (Lyons and Hamlin, 2001). This final subsection identifies PPPs as the best suited structure for rapid and effective economic development and finance decision making.

Management of economic development finance requires organizations that exhibit:

- Greatly reduced reaction times.
- Higher levels of diverse sources of information.
- Ability to adapt and compete with continuously improving competition.

- Skills in adapting to a rapidly changing environment.
- Capacity to capture greater proportions of externalities.

Only PPPs exhibit the most potential to rapidly develop and meet these five requirements for economic development finance in the near future. PPPs, by involving public and private sector organizations, have the potential to draw on a much broader information base than either governments or the private sector. Additionally, PPPs have rapid access to decision makers in both sectors, thereby cutting information cycle times. PPPs can be comprised of several governments and businesses, serving as the nexus between public finance and private finance, and offering the best of both worlds.

Inevitably, more information, faster change, and rapid reaction will result in more mistakes. Mistakes, as any entrepreneur recognizes, are simply a cost of doing business. Governments are generally very unforgiving of mistakes. They get stuck avoiding mistakes at the expense of using mistakes as learning opportunities. This explains why bureaucracies are conservative. Additionally, political systems penalize mistakes, often grossly out of proportion to their severity. Politicians therefore learn to avoid mistakes, cover them up, or to scapegoat them, certainly not what is needed for a learning organization trying to organize and finance deals at an ever increasing pace. As one step removed from government, a PPP management is in a more survivable situation, enabling the organization to take greater risk.

To decrease the negative impacts associated with risk and failure, entrepreneurs seek to spread risk. There are two viable risk spreading options for communities involved in economic development. First, the community can "broaden its portfolio," i.e., more deals make the risk from any single deal proportionately smaller. Second, bring in more investors, i.e., share an investment with other communities/PPPs. PPPs are well suited to reduce risk in both of these manners. An economic development PPP, unlike a general purpose government, focuses on one key aspect of a community. It is therefore in a stronger position to work many deals at any one time. PPPs are also well suited to spread risk among more parties. They are not bound by the geographic limitations of governments; they can expand territory as needed and work across municipal, county, and even state boundaries. Additionally, they have more ready access to the private sector.

By bringing together public and private sectors, PPPs are in superior position to negotiate deals than would be either sector. Since economic development deals often blend public and private sector monies, the PPP is ideally situated. Additionally, since PPPs are outside of government, they can negotiate outside the public arena, i.e., they can negotiate in secret, which is far more difficult or impossible, depending on the government.

4.7.2.3 One Final Comment on Environmental Change

Finally, it is fitting for this discussion of the financial management of economic development to come full circle and to revisit the questions posed early in this chapter — what is economic development and how can economic development finance be managed to produce the most positive results? The environmental changes discussed above bring these questions back to the forefront as it becomes clear that, to be successful, communities will need to change they way they did business in the past.

Firms and their operations are increasingly footloose, i.e., their location is less and less determined by some scarce combination of resources. Capital is free to migrate from community to community, from country to country. Two examples serve to make this point. The classic example is the auto industry. Detroit suffered when the Big Three auto makers lost market share to the Japanese and European firms, as Americans purchased cars built in Japan and Germany. These "Japanese" and "German" cars are increasingly built in the U.S., but not in Detroit, rather in Kentucky, South Carolina, Alabama, and Mississippi. For another example, open any CPU and one is likely to find components manufactured in several countries and assembled in yet another country. This machine may be delivered direct from a foreign factory to our doorstep without ever being touched by any of the vendor's U.S. based personnel. At a grander scale, corporate investment timelines and payback periods are all shortened. Business guru Tom Peters argues against any sort of corporate long range planning and encourages firms to own as few assets as possible (2003). What does this mean for communities striving to be successful in economic development finance? The simple answer and the most honest answer — we don't know yet.

One thing seems certain; the large incentive packages may grow less important. Other factors impacting a firm's location choices may grow more significant, e.g., community aspects like ambiance, safety and, above all, education. If the name of the game in the 21st Century is value-added, then education is what will separate the superstar communities from the also-rans. World class education systems will likely be at the heart of successful economic development. Developing environments where well-educated, highly mobile workers want to live will also be a key. Thus, when we revisit questions of "what is economic development and how to best manage the finance of it?" we come full circle and arrive back to the broad, holistic definition of economic development.

Note

1. This drive for job creation may lead to accepting creation of jobs at any wage. Creation of excessive numbers of low wage jobs can lead to downward wage spiral, substitution of low wage labor for capital investment, and a long-term decline in economic competitiveness and community well-being.

References

Apgar, W. (2003). *Accessing Capital for Community Development.* Retrieved February 2, 2004 from http://www.harvardred.com/gsd5483m4.pdf

Bartik, T. (1991). *Who Benefits from State and Local Economic Development Policies?* Kalamazoo: W. E. Upjohn Institute for Employment Research.

Brooks, R. (2002). Big incentives won Alabama a piece of the auto industry. *Wall Street Journal,* April 3.

Blair, J. (1995). *Local Economic Development: Theory and Practice.* Thousand Oaks: Sage.

Brice, K. (2002). *Economic Development Planning and Finance.* Retrieved February 2, 2004 from http://www.gsu.edu/~wwwpsp/academics/courses/syllabi/paus4451_fall2002_brice.htm

Carroll, R. and Wasykenko, M. (1994). Do state business climates still matter?—Evidence of a structural change. *National Tax Journal* 47, 19–37.

Cason, M. (2002). Hyundai incentives cost $252.8 million. *Montgomery Advertiser,* April 5. Retrieved January 3, 2004 from http://www.nasvf.org/web/allpress.nsf/0/4ce6b8a86f63153a86256b9200467e5?OpenDoc...

Cason, M., Hendrick, D., and Dugan, K. (2002). Hyundai picks Montgomery: City gets $1B plant. *Montgomery Advertiser,* April 2. Retrieved January 3, 2004 from http://www.nasvf.org/web/allpress.nsf/pages/4384

Clinton, W. (1993). *Executive Order 12873: Federal Acquisition, Recycling, and Waste Prevention, October 20.* Retrieved 3 January 2004 from https://www.denix.osd.mil/denix/Public/Legislation/EO/note17.html

Committee for Economic Development (1998). *America's Basic Research: Prosperity through Discovery, a Policy Statement by the Research and Policy Committee.* New York: Committee for Economic Development.

Copeland, L. (2003). Sewer overhauls drive fee hikes. *USA Today,* October 26. Retrieved January 28, 2004 from http://www.usatoday.com/news/nation/2003-10-26-sewer-upgrades_x.htm

Dabson, B. and Rist, C. (1996). Business climate and the role of development incentives. *Region (Federal Reserve Bank of Minneapolis).* June. Retrieved January 8, 2004 from http://minneapolisfed.org/pubs/retion/96-06/dabson.cfm

Diamond, M., Fisk, W., and Garfinkel, M. (1970). *The Democratic Republic: An Introduction to American National Government (2nd edition).* Chicago: Rand McNally.

Felsenstein, D. and Persky, J. (1999). When is a cost really a benefit? Local welfare effects and employment creation in the evaluation of economic development programs. *Economic Development Quarterly,* 13, 46–54.

Eisinger, P. (1988). *The Rise of the Entrepreneurial State: State and Local Economic Development Policy in the United States.* Madison: University of Wisconsin Press.

Fitzgerald, J. and Leigh, N. (2002). *Economic Revitalization: Cases and Strategies for City and Suburb.* Thousand Oaks: Sage.

Fitzgerald, S. (n.d.). Foreign trade zones. *Bizsites.com.* Retrieved February 21, 2004 from http://www.bizsites.com/stateads/FTZ/index.asp

Friar, J. (1999). Economic development incentives: A review and recommendations. *Economic Development Review,* 16, 3–7.

Gershberg, A. (2003). *Capital Markets and Development Finance.* Retrieved February 2, 2004 from http://www.newschool.edu/milano/course/sp04/4319/oldsyllabus.pdf

Good Jobs First (2002). *No More Secret Candy Store: A Grassroots Guide to Investigating Development Subsidies.* Washington, D.C.

Good Jobs First (2004). *Good Jobs First: Promoting Accountable Development.* Retrieved January 30, 2004 from http://www.goodjobsfirst.org

Herbert, S., Vidal, A., Mills, G., James, F., and Gruenstein, D. (2001). *Interim Assessment of the Empowerment Zones and Enterprise Communities (EZ/EC) Program.* Washington, D.C.: U.S. HUD.

Hinkley, S. and Hsu, F. (2000). *Minding the Candy Store: State Audits of Economic Development.* Washington, D.C.: Good Jobs First.

Hodge, S., Moody, J., and Warcholik, W. (2003). *State Business Tax Climate Index (Background Paper).* Washington, D.C.: Tax Foundation.

Hyundai won over by Alabama's southern charm (2002). *FDI (Foreign Direct Investment).* April 2. Retrieved January 6, 2004 from http://fdimagazine.com/news/printpage.php/aid/107/Hyundai_won_over_by_Alamam

International Economic Development Council (n.d.). *The IEDC Professional Development Series.* Retrieved January 5, 2004 from http://wwwiedconline.org/prodev_course_desc.html

Kansas City Area Development Council (2004). *Foreign Trade Zones.* Retrieved March 15, 2004 from http://www.smartkc.com/3_locating/3e_tax_profile/3e14_foreign.htm

Kottler, P., Haider, D., and Rein, I. (1993). *Marketing Places: Attracting Investment, Industry, and Tourism to Cities, States, and Nations.* New York: Free Press.

Labyrinth of incentives (2002). *Foreign Direct Investment.* Retrieved January 3, 2004 from http://www.fdimagazine.com/news/printpage.php/aid/187/Labyrinth_of_incentivesUnited_

LeRoy, G. and Slocum, T. (1999). *Economic Development in Minnesota: High Subsidies, Low Wages, Absent Standards.* Washington, D.C.: Good Jobs First.

Levy, J. (1990). *Economic Development Programs for Cities, Counties and Towns (2nd edition)*. New York: Praeger.

Lyons, T. and Hamlin, R. (2001). *Creating an Economic Development Action Plan: A Guide for Development Professionals* (revised and updated edition). Westport: Praeger.

Mikkelson, B. and Mikkelson, D. (2002). *Hello Submarine*. Retrieved March 2, 2004 from www.snopes.com./legal/kentucky.htm

Library of Congress (n.d.). *Rise of Industrial America, 1876–1900: Railroads in the Late 19th Century*. Retrieved February 2, 2004, from http://memory.loc.gov/learn/features/timeline/riseind/railroad/grants.html

National Association of Development Organizations (n.d.). *EDFA*. Retrieved March 1, 2004 from http://www.nado.org/edfs/index.html

National Association of State Development Agencies (n.d.) *Statewide Public-Private Partnership Economic Development Organizations*. Retrieved February 25, 2004 from http://www.nasda.com/statewide_public_private_partner.htm

National Conference of State Legislatures (2003). *State Economic Development*. Retrieved January 15, 2003 from www.ncsl.org/programs/econ/topics.htm

National Conference of State Legislatures, Budget and Revenue Committee (2003). *Unfunded Mandates Imposed—As of April 16, 2003*. Retrieved March 3, 2004 from http://www.ncsl.org/standcomm/scbudg/budgmandates03.htm

North Carolina Department of Commerce (2004). *What Are the Economic Benefits to Zone Users?* Retrieved March 1, 2004 from http://www.exportnc.com/ftz/benefits.sap

Peirce, N. (2002). Corporate handouts: A call for accountability. *Seattle Times*. August 19, 2002.

Peters, T. (2003). *Re-imagine!: Business Excellence in a Disruptive Age*. New York: DK.

Porter, M. (2000). Location, competition, and economic development: Local clusters in a global economy. *Economic Development Quarterly*, 14, 15–34.

Recycled Paper Coalition (2000). *Buy Recycled: Recycled Paper*. Retrieved January 8, 2004 from http://www.papercoalition.org/PaperFactSheet.pdf

Reese, L. (1992). Local economic development in Michigan: A reliance on the supply-side. *Economic Development Quarterly*, 6, 383–393.

Reese, L. and Fasenfest, D. (1999). Critical perspectives on local economic development policy evaluation. *Economic Development Quarterly*, 13, 3–7.

Reese, L. and Fasenfest, D. (1997). What works best?: Values and the evaluation of local economic development policy. *Economic Development Quarterly*, 11, 195–207.

Reich, R. (2000). *The Future of Success: Working and Living in the New Economy*. New York: Vintage Books.

Rose, I. (2002). *Status of Gambling Laws — Part 2: Georgia — Maine.* Retrieved January 21, 2004 from http://rose.asinocitytimes.come/articles/980.html

Sherman, M. (2003). State calls in Hyundai pledges. *Montgomery Advertiser,* July 26. Retrieved January 4, 2004 from http://www.montgomeryadvertiser.com/specialreports/hyundai/StoryLocalincent26w.htm

Stucki, H. (1998). Shell buildings as development tools. *Economic Development Review,* 16, 55–56.

Sublett, M. and Walk, F. (1994). *Location.* Retrieved February 11, 2004 from http://www.lib.niu.edu/ipo/iht19402.html

University of Southern Mississippi (n.d.). *Master's Program in Economic Development.* Retrieved February 18, 2004, from http://www.usm.edu/ecodev/pages/masters.htm

University of Southern Mississippi and ACCRA (2003). *Economic Development for the New Economy.* Retrieved January 5, 2004 from http://www.usm.edu/growingbusiness/execmasters/

U.S. Census Bureau (2003). *Federal, State, and Local Governments: Governments Integrated Directory.* Retrieved February 2, 2004 from http://www.census.gov/govs/www/gid2002.html

U.S. General Accounting Office (1999). *Community Development: Extent of Federal Influence on Urban Sprawl Is Unclear.* Washington, D.C.

U.S. General Accounting Office (2000). *U.S. Infrastructure: Funding Trends and Opportunities to Improve Investment Decisions.* Washington, D.C.

U.S. Department of Housing and Urban Development (2003). *Tax Incentive Guide for Businesses in the Renewal Communities, Empowerment Zones, and Enterprise Communities.* Washington, D.C.

Wisconsin Public Service Corporation (n.d.). *Tax Incentives and Benefits.* Retrieved January 28, 2004 from http://www.wisconsinpublicservice.com/business/bcd_tax_incentive.asp

Wisconsin, State of (n.d.). *Wisconsin Business Incentives.* Retrieved 4 February 2004 from http://www.wisconsin.gov/state/core/wisconsin_business_incentives.html

Wolman, H. and Spitzley, D. (1996). The politics of local economic development. *Economic Development Quarterly,* 10, 115–150.

Wright, R. (2002). *Hamilton Unbound: Finance and the Creation of the American Republic.* Westport: Greenwood Press.

Wurman, R., Sume, D., and Leifer, L. (2000). *Information Anxiety 2.* New York: Que.

Chapter 5

Annual Budgeting and Long-Range Planning: Is There a Fit? — Lessons from Three Case Studies

YILIN HOU, Ph.D.
Department of Political Science, University of Georgia

JUN MA, Ph.D.
College of Politics & Public Affairs, Zhongsan University,
People's Republic of China

Public budgeting is concerned with the allocation of financial resources. As such, it is technical but heavily loaded with politics. Of this technical-political bi-partite structure, politics has often drawn more academic attention because it is very complicated, and thus more interesting and holding more explanatory power of the budgeting process. Aaron Wildavsky's work is a good example among the vast amount of literature on the politics of the budgetary process. Any study of the technical side has to refer to the political side also because one simply " ... cannot take politics out of budgeting" (Donohue, 1982, 62). Nonetheless, the technical side is also fascinating and sophisticated, deserving due examination. This chapter focuses on one aspect in the technical side — the relationship between budgeting and planning. As Allen Schick put it, the format of budgeting is "more a product of bureaucratic than of political influences" (1971, 195).

Planning is one of the three basic functions of public budgeting (Schick, 1966, 1998) but in the vast budgeting literature (which is mostly of and about developed countries) it is mentioned much less frequently than the other two functions. In the American budgeting literature, planning is studied much more in the period from WWII to the Great Society (mid- to late-1960s) and the early 1970s. Since the late 1970s, planning is more referred to as strategic planning. Even when planning is mentioned, the tone is sometimes more negative than positive, as a "communist approach" to national economic planning (Richard Brown, 1978).

In developing and transitional countries, however, planning has been noticed to be much more important, though not successful in implementation. (Caiden and Wildavsky, 1974). In fact, even in developed countries, limitations of the annual budget cycle have drawn some attention to multi-year perspectives (Caiden, 1981; Forrester, 1991; Guajardo, 2000; Boex, Martinez-Vazquez and McNac, 2000; and Hou, forthcoming), which is closely linked to planning. There have been famous experiments in the U.S. in the 1960s with the Planning-Programming-Budgeting System (PPBS); more recently some European countries paid more attention than before to planning; the World Bank has been promoting the Mid-Term Expenditure Framework (MTEF). This chapter examines the relationship between budgeting and planning, assuming that well balancing this relation and incorporating planning into budgeting, or vice versa, is very significant because budgeting as an administrative instrument plays an indispensable role in improving governance capacity for all types of countries.

A detailed study of the relationship between annual budgeting and medium- and long-term financial planning carries great potential in making a theoretical contribution to existing literature, and practical contribution to improving policy implementation in developed and developing, as well as transitional, countries. This chapter starts with a general framework for analysis of this relationship. The next three sections examine three cases that represent three models of the interaction between budgeting and planning. From each case, the chapter tries to draw lessons and merits. The conclusion offers further discussion and policy recommendations.

The three cases for analysis in this chapter are China, the state of New York, and the City of Sunnyvale, California. To some readers, this choice may seem odd: they are not at the same level and are far off from each other in their respective size of population and economy. The choice, however, can seem reasonable if we consider the (un)availability of "good and fit" examples. The choice may appear even rational once we take into account their respective features. China used to be under the old regime of typical central economic planning (1949–78) before its adoption of the market economy system. As the most populous country in the world, and now still in transition into a fully-fledged market economy, it has been, since the 1980s, exceptionally successful in economic development in comparison with transitional countries in Eastern Europe.

New York State experimented with the Planning-Programming-Budgeting System (PPBS) in the 1960s. Among the (5-5-5) pilot governments in the State and Local Finances Project, New York made many systematic explorations in theory, practice and institution building. Though it never fully implemented PPBS and abandoned it in 1970, its experience is worth careful re-examination. As a subnational government, New York is similar to a province in China; but under China's high degree of institutional uniformity, each province would have been very much like a country on a smaller scale. In this sense, a comparison between China and New York is not out of scale.

Sunnyvale, a small municipality in the Silicon Valley, California, is no comparison at all to the other two entities. However, it has been successful in conducting long-term forecasting and planning, and in incorporating budgeting into planning. It placed annual budgeting in the framework of long-term financial planning and has kept and maintained the system since the mid-1970s. Its success forms a striking contrast to the failure of the other two. It is for this purpose that this chapter examines Sunnyvale.

5.1   Budgeting and Planning: an Analytical Framework

Budgeting and planning are both administrative instruments for efficiency and effectiveness in policy development and implementation. They are expected to go in harmony; but the annularity of budgeting often collides with the long-range nature of planning, resulting in conflicts. In America, modern public budgeting was established to control public expenditure and to increase accountability of public officials. The idea of "planning" was somewhat avoided. It was the case from 1921 to the late 1940s. The first wave of performance budgeting in the 1950s and the PPBS in the 1960s were attempts to change the control-only orientation by adding elements of planning and management; but both reforms went off without much success. Since the 1980s the scene has changed quite a bit: some U.S. state governments changed the name of their budget office into an "office of (strategic) planning and budget," indicating that a change of perception had occurred and this trend is to spread further.

5.1.1 Rationalist versus Empiricist Norms for Budgeting

In fact, planning is very significant because "even in a market economy, the budget presents the basic national economic plan" (Mikesell, 2003, 80). The debate over planning in budgeting goes as far back as the history of executive budgeting in the United States — the planning perspective was one of the three fundamental conceptions underlying the executive budget (Schick, 1971, 15). Nearly a century ago, Frederick Cleveland, one of the three founding fathers of public budgeting in the U.S., noted that

> "careful, understandable, responsible planning ... has been conspicuously lacking in our federal, state and municipal government ... The lack of planning has been an incident of 'invisible' or 'irresponsible' government, [because] the budget is a financial plan." (1915, 17)

It was in fact an intended omission in the anti-(executive branch) government sentiment prevailing from the colonial days till the turn of the 20th century. To argue for the executive budget, Cleveland stated that "the only person is the chief executive ... [who] can think in terms of the institution as a whole, who can be made responsible for leadership" (ibid.). Cleveland carried the issue to the representative character of democratic government,

> "The constitutional or institutional purpose of a budget is to make the executive responsible and responsive to the people through their representatives and through the electorate ... No plan can serve this purpose which comes from individual representatives any more than it could if it came from individual electors." (1915, 18)

In the process of the executive budget movement, the planning orientation receded to the control orientation because the latter was more in accord with the then urgent demand to reduce public spending and curb corruption (Schick, 1971, 17). After about 20 years of the executive budget into actual use, V.O. Key redrew academic attention to the fundamental issue of resource allocation, thereby indirectly back to planning:

> "[Though] planning agencies and professional planners have been more interested in the abstract problem of ascertaining the relative utility of public outlays than has any other group, they have not succeeded in formulating any convincing principles,

either descriptive or normative, concerning the allocation of public funds … Perhaps the approach toward the practical working out of the issue lies in the canalizing of decisions through the governmental machinery so as to place alternatives in juxtaposition and compel consideration of relative values." (1940, 1138–42)

The rationalist approach to budgeting was presented more explicitly and comprehensively later by Verne Lewis (1952) and especially by Arthur Smithies (1955): public policies should be made clear and explicit, presented together with explicit alternative means on how to achieve those objectives. For this purpose, good coordination between revenue and expenditure should be made, with deliberate benefits and costs analysis for each outlay. In this regard, the whole policy-making should be unified and comprehensive.

Empiricists, however, opposed. To them, though the budget process with no planning is "fragmented" and "seemingly uncoordinated," it is far better in allocating resources because it is less likely to neglect important political interests and thus easier technically and politically (Braybrooke and Lindblom, 1963; Wildavsky, 1964; Lindblom, 1965). Aaron Wildavsky had been blunt in pointing out that any search for a rational basis of such decision-making would be fruitless because such a task "is impossible to fulfill." Reviewing literature since Key's paper to 1960, Wildavsky summarized that "no progress has been made" (1961, 183). Allen Schick tackled the dilemma from the budget cycle. While budgeting must have neatly-cut start-and-end points for the fiscal year, planning cannot. Planning must operate on a "multi-year frame … to consider alternatives to the present course of action" (Schick, 1971, 209).

When the Planning-Programming-Budgeting reform was staged in the early 1960s, Allen Schick identified "strategic planning" along with "management control" and "operational control" as the three functions (alternatively "orientations") of budgeting. Schick defines "strategic planning" as

"the process of deciding on objectives of the organization, on changes in these objectives, on the resources used to attain these objectives, and on the policies that are to govern the acquisition, use, and disposition of these resources." (1966, 244)

The tri-partite classification of budgetary roles later by Schick (1998) into aggregate control, allocative efficiency and operational efficiency also implicitly includes planning under allocative efficiency. The Bank's more recent Medium-Term Expenditure Framework (MTEF) becomes more explicit about the importance of planning by extending the timeline from single year into the mid-term future.

Thus, it can be summarized that, despite theoretical differences that remain to be solved, the planning perspective has been almost universally recognized in government practice. In contrast to the United States, European countries have not been shy of endorsing the planning idea. There have been many experiments with economic planning: Germany used economic regulation and rationing during the First World War (Tarschys, 2002, 85). Sweden and other northern European countries used national planning in recent decades. In poor developing countries, resource scarcity had always made it imperative to plan carefully the use of limited revenue and international aids (Caiden and Wildavsky, 1974).

5.1.2 Power Relationship in Resource Allocation

Since budgeting is to allocate limited resources between policy alternatives, we need to view the planning-budgeting relationship as the search for a fit between the two functions among key players in the allocation process. First, planning comes in different types by its context of occurrence. Caiden and Wildavsky (1974) notice the striking gap between developing and developed countries. In resource-scarce and resource-rich environments, planning is done quite differently. In a poor country, planning is primarily *for resource mobilization* so that the limited resources can be fully exploited for utmost effectiveness (Tarschys, 2002, 85). This is especially so when a government is targeting quick policy impacts. Naomi and Wildavsky pointed out that "political leaders would be motivated to press harder for growth if they were more confident of reward for their sacrifices" (1974, vi). Because it is to gather scarce resources for concentrated use, such planning is to deprive some sectors of the society of their due share. These sectors have to self-sacrifice in the process of development. Even in a country where people are disciplined and determined, resource mobilization often is done with coercion rather than voluntarily. The policy quickly generates impact, which, however, may not last long.

In a resource-rich environment, planning is more *for coordination of priorities*. Planning itself is comprehensive and done centrally, but without coercion. Often it is implemented through regulation or tax incentives for policy impacts on the economy. The expectation is that the policy will take some time to materialize; the effect is indirect but lasts long. Of the three cases in this chapter, China is of the first type, New York the second. Sunnyvale is of a sub-type in the second, where planning is to link resources to programs, to bridge service demands to finances. It is long-term *financial planning* or, in the terminology of PPBS, *programming.*

Second, given that both planning and budgeting are necessary for allocative and technical efficiency in the use of resources, how to connect the two becomes the key issue. In the classic or conventional view, the budget is also a plan (although it is limited to the coming year only). The planning function of the budget in this sense is the short-term financial plan (Schick, 1966). In this regard, budgeting is financial planning. The two are indistinguishable. Issues emerge when planning is extended into the far future: as the plan extends beyond the boundary of the fiscal year (budget cycle), the link is broken between budgeting and planning. This disconnection involves power distribution at decision as well as administration levels.

At the decision level, power struggle occurs between the executive and the legislative branches. By the rationalist approach, planning is best done by the chief executive for comprehensiveness (against legislative pork barreling) and consistency over time, but the annual legislative review grants legislators the opportunity for constituency interests. When the two sides go into conflict, annual budgeting does not fit into the planning framework. Power distribution at the administrative level occurs between the budget office and the planning agency. Resource allocation is the traditional turf of the budget office; any encroachment may trigger reaction from budgeters. Planners, knowing that without jurisdiction over resource allocation, their plans will merely stay on the paper, will try to exert their influence onto allocation. This is how strife occurs between the two offices.

There are also technical issues between the two sides. First, planners tend to ignore the annual budget process. To them, the one-year span of the budget is negligible as a plan for future action (Walker, 1944, 97–8). Budgeters may brush off any plan that goes too far because, once extending beyond the budget cycle, a plan serves little practical purpose, with revenue and expenditure forecasts being guesstimates at best, useless calculation exercise at worst. Second, annual budgets provide details that are closely linked to the next year that managers can feel and touch, things that no one can afford to ignore. In contrast, long-range plans seem to offer nothing concrete but visions and prospects that are detached from the current situation. No manager will feel any pain from oversight of a plan. Therefore, when the budget office asks agencies for next year's estimates, the request will be handled carefully. When the data request comes from the planning agency for the coming ten years, agencies will complain because it grinds on their staff time and resources. Exhibit 1 displays in summary form some of the major differences in perspective between the two functions, some of which are also causes of non-cooperation by line agencies.

Exhibit 1   Factors leading to non-cooperation between budgeting and planning

	Planning	*Budgeting*
Staff	Planners	More accountants
Emphasis	Broad purposes and administrative problems of the programs being financed	Forms, procedures, accounts
Vision	Forward-looking, 10–20 years	Next year or two years only
Substance	Vague, detached from reality	Detailed, specific
Tempo	No time pressure to meet deadlines	Under deadlines in preparing annual budget
Reputation	Planners and planning agencies are "impractical" and "aloof from … politics and administration."	• View appropriations estimates restrictively, not in terms of desirable public policy. • "Obstructionists not facilitators" to policy makers and planners.

5.1.3   Centralization-Decentralization Continuum

Planning as a comprehensive, long-range, global activity is best done top-down, in a centralized fashion, because the top executive has the best panoramic idea while agencies may have better ideas on efficiency. This brings in an additional dimension to the planning-budgeting relationship. Centralization is a natural phenomenon, a management principle, always present to a greater or lesser extent (Fayol, 1916; Frederickson, 1980). It is positively correlated with hierarchy, which is a function of the size and structural complexity of organizations. The more hierarchical an organization is in structure, the more centralized its power-control mechanism tends to be. Thus, centralization is a phenomenon of degrees varying from case to case. Later scholars notice, as Fayol and other classical theorists did, that centralization as a method of management and administration should not be judged good or bad by itself, nor can it be adopted or discarded at the whim of managers or circumstances.

The core of centralization is power. Any useful analysis of centralization is necessarily an examination of the allocation of decision-making power in the organization and the methods of influence employed by the higher levels to affect the decisions at the lower levels (Simon, 1946). The objective to pursue is the optimum utilization of all faculties of the human factor in organizations (Fayol, 1916). The same pursuit of optimum utilization of the human factor in organizations gives rise to decentralization — dispersion of decision-making power, which is also a natural phenomenon, automatically assuming momentum with the increase of layers in the hierarchy of the organization. In other words, the bigger and the more complex an organization is, the greater the need for, and momentum of, decentralization.

Centralization and decentralization do not necessarily mean a contradiction but can be expressed as two ends of a scale, a continuum. It is a question of proportion, a matter of finding the optimum degree for the particular concern. The degree may vary constantly because the organization is changing over time in size and structure; and both the absolute and relative values of leaders and employees are also changing. The balance is to be sought according to circumstances, to the best satisfaction of the organizational goal, as well as the personal interests of leaders and public servants. This issue of optimum degree presents a challenge not only to top leaders, but also to managers at all levels. As a matter of optimum degree, centralization of proper powers is operable only by decentralizing some other powers, whereas decentralized powers must be under central oversight (Hoover Commission Report, 1949) to ensure proper understanding and implementation of uniform policies and goals, so as not to turn out as anarchy or chaos. Scholars such as Power (1998) call this phenomenon an "irony" hidden in devolution: "the greater the amount of policy-making power being decentralized, the greater the accretion of centralized regulatory power is likely to be." In our perspective, this so-called irony is nothing but truth directly stated. Donald Kettl, in his appraisal of the National Performance Review, also points out that oversight capacity must be strengthened (1994). To decentralize is to fix responsibility and maintain means of accountability. It is an element in most policy questions. As Paul Appleby says, "Whatever the decision is, adequate decentralization of responsibility for performance of the function agreed upon at the level agreed upon is essential to popular control" (1949, 162).

5.1.4 Analytical Framework

To summarize, long-range planning, as advocated by the rationalists, holds its position in public budgeting in both resource-rich and resource-scarce environments. The fit in the planning-budgeting relationship depends on several factors emphasized by the empiricists. An agreement between policy makers is the political basis to ensure long-range goals are established and accepted by both branches of government. Cooperation between the budget and planning offices is the administrative foundation for smooth operation of the fit. An optimum combination of centralized planning and oversight with decentralized managerial discretion and accountability structure will trigger initiative and enthusiasm of line agencies and managers into the integrated planning-budgeting process. The analysis of the three cases follows this analytical framework.

Case 1: Annual Budgeting Under Central Economic Planning 1949–78

Fiscal administration in China from 1949 to 1978 presents a typical case of central economic planning. Targeting quick industrialization, China took planned economy and centralized management systems as natural options (Hou, 2003). In this context, annual budgets were subordinate to annual economic plans. Budgeting was used to the extreme for channeling all possible resources into capital construction. Reoccurring delays in budget formulation and frequent random changes to revenues and expenditures rendered budgets useless. Under centralized "frenzy" economic planning, budgeting lost its financial planning function. Absence of fiscal/budgetary discipline left officials and government with no control over expenditure. Budgeting was a handy tool when it fitted needs for capital. When budgetary restraints blocked the way for large-scale construction, the concept of budgeting was ignored. In sum, planning and budgeting did not serve China well in this period. Had they been used properly, planning and budgeting could have helped China tremendously in improving effectiveness of its governance, efficiency of its economic development, and accountability of officials and government entities.

5.1.5 Why Central Economic Planning?

Fiscal administration in China followed the Soviet-style central economic planning, with national medium-term five-year construction plans under a long-range development program. It all started from a national dream for prosperity. When the Communist Party of China (CPC) won over the country in 1949, the CPC targeted quick industrialization, despite eminent difficulties of runaway inflation, absence of modern industries, lack of economic and financial expertise, unavailability of foreign aid and hard currency. Top leader Mao Zedong assumed that "national economy should not be more difficult to manage than military affairs" (Gu, 1993, entry for August, 1958). To implement large scale construction in such an environment, central planning seemed to be the best choice because the Soviet-style planning for mobilizing resources suited China's need. After a few years of preparation and intensive learning from Soviet experts, the first five-year plan started in 1953.[1]

Chinese economy was run on a market-based fashion in the first three years, with free markets for all farm produce and private enterprises being subject to no central planning except limited regulatory "guidance." Only state-owned enterprises were fully subject to central plans. In late 1953, when food supply fell into unexpected trouble in cities, threatening the implementation of the on-going five-year plan, nationwide ration provision of daily necessities, obligatory sale of harvest by farmers to the government, and segregation of rural from urban residents (tight control of citizen mobility) became the only policy option. This was copied from the Soviet Union.[2] Within a few years, all private enterprises were "merged" into state ownership and the whole national economy was placed under rigid central plans.

5.1.6 Central Economic Planning and Annual Budgeting

Under its one-party rule system, China had no problem in achieving unanimous agreement on national policies. The annual policy-making process starts with the Party Central Committee's economic development policies and guidelines, which then become the economic development plan and the annual budget. The economic plan and budget are deliberated at the CPC Central Economic Conference, then consulted with democratic parties, and finally submitted to the National People's Congress for approval (Figure 5.1).

The real challenge was in administration. A central planning system was set up in 1952, with detailed rules on the structure, procedures, units of planning, and rules regarding the compilation and review of economic plans.[3] A powerful State Planning Commission (SPC) was created as a super-ministry in charge of all economic planning activities, with its most important task being compiling the annual plan for national economic development. The central budget agency is the Ministry of Finance, lower in rank than the SPC. A formal budgeting process was created and approved in 1951 as the "interim rules on budgets and final accounts" (Figure 5.2). Under this construct, the annual [national and local] budget and the budgeting process was merely the policy tool to implement the economic plan (Figure 5.3).

The complex nature of economic planning and the fact that the CPC was not at all familiar with managing economic activities often delayed in-time completion of plans. In the extreme case of 1963, "it took a whole year to finish the annual plan."[4] Whenever the budgeting procedures conflicted with economic planning, the resulting budget would be

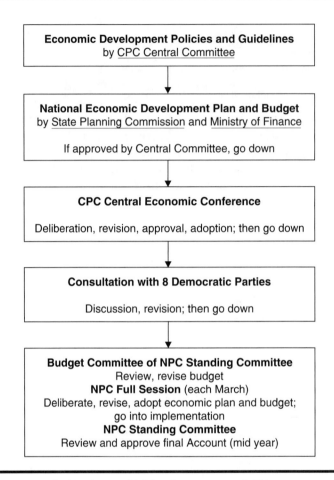

Figure 5.1 Annual planning and budgeting process of China.

unpredictable, subject to frequent changes by following the belated development plan. In this sense, the budgeting procedures never really worked. Mid- and late-year budgeting and multiple budgeting were common in those years. The budget utilizes also monetary instruments. The Central Bank was a secondary tool for implementing the economic plans. The annual currency issuance and working capital addition was part of, and included in, the annual budget.

Frequent, long delays in compiling the annual economic plan and budget caused serious consequences to fiscal administration. Long delays and frequent changes in the development plan led to widespread uncertainty. No one at the central or local levels knew how much they would have for the next year, which was a huge disincentive for local economic development. Budgets could not serve as usable guide for operations; huge wastes

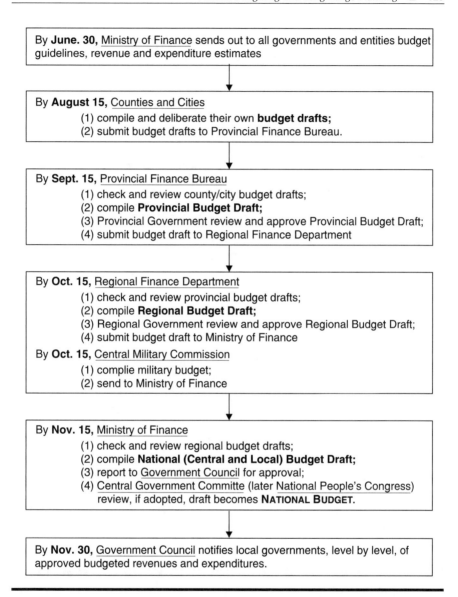

By **June. 30,** <u>Ministry of Finance</u> sends out to all governments and entities budget guidelines, revenue and expenditure estimates

By **August 15,** <u>Counties and Cities</u>
    (1) compile and deliberate their own **budget drafts;**
    (2) submit budget drafts to Provincial Finance Bureau.

By **Sept. 15,** <u>Provincial Finance Bureau</u>
    (1) check and review county/city budget drafts;
    (2) compile **Provincial Budget Draft;**
    (3) Provincial Government review and approve Provincial Budget Draft;
    (4) submit budget draft to Regional Finance Department

By **Oct. 15,** <u>Regional Finance Department</u>
    (1) check and review provincial budget drafts;
    (2) compile **Regional Budget Draft;**
    (3) Regional Government review and approve Regional Budget Draft;
    (4) submit budget draft to Ministry of Finance
By **Oct. 15,** <u>Central Military Commission</u>
    (1) complie military budget;
    (2) send to Ministry of Finance

By **Nov. 15,** <u>Ministry of Finance</u>
    (1) check and review regional budget drafts;
    (2) compile **National (Central and Local) Budget Draft;**
    (3) report to <u>Government Council</u> for approval;
    (4) <u>Central Government Committe</u> (later <u>National People's Congress</u>) review, if adopted, draft becomes **NATIONAL BUDGET.**

By **Nov. 30,** <u>Government Council</u> notifies local governments, level by level, of approved budgeted revenues and expenditures.

Figure 5.2   China's annual budgetary process as prescribed by the "Interim rules on budgets and final accounts" (Government Council, July 1951).

were common and unavoidable. The budget also lost its function as an oversight instrument to hold officials and agencies accountable because the highly centralized process did not allow much participation at lower levels. Absence of managerial discretion and performance incentive resulted in disinterest and irresponsibility. After China started its reform program, this centralized planning-budgeting system went into disuse.

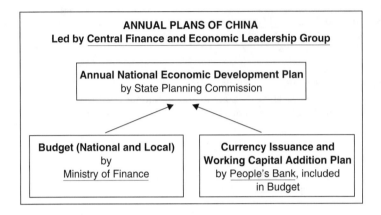

Figure 5.3   Annual economic and finance plans of China.

5.1.7   Two Lessons

The China case bears two lessons in the planning-budgeting relationship. First, planning and budgeting are complementary equals. Subordination of one to the other destroys the fit between the two functions. China's long-range economic planning did not provide a natural link to annual budgeting. It was divorced from the budgeting process, done regardless of how budgeting went. When conflicts occurred between the two, it was always budgeting that conceded. In so doing budgeting did not serve as well as it could have done to economic operation. Second, a highly centralized system does not provide adequate room for active agency initiative, nor does it provide incentives for agencies, inducing no cooperation or responsibility. In this case, agencies merely muddled through, contributing little if anything to performance or accountability.

Case 2:   Frustrating Experiment of PPBS in New York 1964–70

The State of New York started executive budget in 1926. It was done through a constitutional amendment that was approved in late 1927. A Division of Budget (DoB) was created, its head reporting to the governor (NY Division of the Budget, 1981). Under this system, the governor is charged with the annual revenue and expenditure plan. From the 1930s to the 1960s, New York State experienced substantial growth in population and urban development, along with its economy and personal wealth, which gave rise not only to extra resources but also rising expectations for new public services. For example, under pressure of increasing disparity, "low-income groups organized to cry for state help in areas that were previously the exclusive responsibility of local governments" (Budget Guidelines, 1966, 5). As a response to the various needs, Nelson A. Rockefeller (Governor 1959–73) proposed "the responsible state" and initiated numerous new programs in transportation, housing, education, environmental protection and public health (Kerker, 1994, 169). The ambitious governor wanted to interpret the gubernatorial role in an "expansive" fashion and serve as a model for governors in other states as well (Connery, 1974, 14). This was very much similar to the mentality of leaders in developing countries and very much like the situation in China in the 1950s.

At the national level, expansion was the fashion. Fiscal surpluses in the early 1960s from the mass personal income tax during WWII made it possible to expand public services on an unprecedented scale, which coincided with the presidency of John Kennedy to result in overwhelming confidence in government's ability to change everything. The numerous new programs demanded coordination. Thus, in New York, as in many other states, top-down, comprehensive, long-range regional development planning went hot (Kerker, 1994, 168; Schick, 1971, 119) with which grew a chasm between planning and budgeting (State-Local Finances Project, 1969a).

5.1.8   Start of Planning in New York State

To meet the needs of massive expansion, Governor Rockefeller in 1961 established the Office for Regional Development (ORD) as the state planning agency. The need was recognized for "a carefully conceived planning process ... to deal with the needs in a more effective fashion" (Budget Guidelines, 1967, 5). The New York State Joint Legislative Committee on State-Local Fiscal Relations made clear that the reasons for planning are:

> "Annual legislative battles over local budgets and taxes prevent local governments from engaging in long-range planning to solve their mounting problems. Such battles also prevent the Legislative and Executive branches of the state government from engaging in such planning." (1966, 46)

The ORD consisted of a small staff but was assigned four "global," principal functions: (a) to help coordinate the planning and development activities of all state departments; (b) to help coordinate state planning and development activities with those of the local and federal governments; (c) to encourage comprehensive planning on a regional basis; and (d) to facilitate, by state action, local planning and development activity (NY ORD, 1964, 152). The 1964 report by this office was an ambitious document describing a 60-year (1960–2020) land use and development outlook for the whole State. They designed 15 basic steps for action on the future role of planning. Among its recommendations, two are worth more attention. One is preparing long-term *comprehensive* regional plans:

> "These plans would be prepared by the State with the cooperation of local governments and with the help and advice of the Regional Councils. They would provide significant information for the preparation of the State capital construction budget, and would be reviewed and updated periodically by the State and Regional Councils." (ORD, 1964, 143, No. 3)

The other is annual update of the plans:

> "Annual preparation of and submission by the Budget Director to the Governor, as a part of the proposed Executive Budget, of a specific physical program and a financial program." (ORD, 1964, 143, No. 6)

Given the scale of program expansion and manual style of budget work at that time, the required planning and annual updates meant a daunting amount of work to agencies, as can be seen from Figure 5.4 "the required program plan reports."

Since 1964 New York had been "attempting to cope more effectively with the increasing complexities of government through the development of a 'planning-programming-budgeting system (PPBS) that systematically relates the expenditure of funds to the accomplishment of planned goals,'" (New York OPC and DoB, 1967, 5). This new tool was devised for three main reasons. First, it takes the government operating structure as an "integrated system directed toward the fulfillment of a great variety of goals" (ibid.). Second, it can provide policy makers with "a more objective basis for making policy decisions" by furnishing "information and analyses on both immediate and future consequences of program and budget decisions" (ibid 5–6). Finally, it was designed

> "with full recognition of the continuing need for expenditure controls, management control, and management improvement to assure that specific activities are carried out effectively and efficiently, ... for a carefully conceived balance among all administrative functions." (ibid 6)

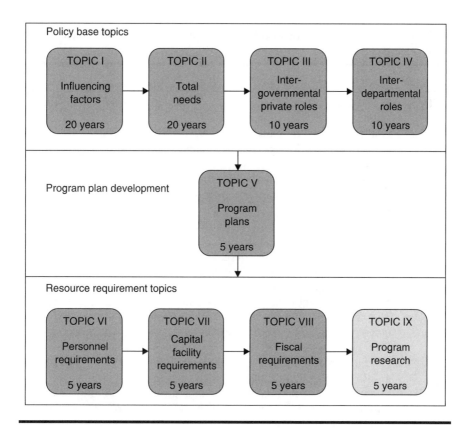

Figure 5.4   Program plan reports, New York State.
Source: Guidelines for Integrated Planning, Programming, Budgeting 1967, (page 18) by the State of New York Office of Planning Coordination and the Division of the Budget.

Since start of modern executive budget in the 1920s, PPBS "was the first budget system *designed* to accommodate the multiple functions of budgeting" (Schick, 1966, 244). Table 5.1 provides timeline of major events on planning and budgeting in New York State.

When the Division of Budget maintained its usual focus on control, which was out of tune with the governor's expansionist vision and development priority, the Governor turned to the Office of the Secretary to the Governor. That office, with a 100-person staff (most were "program associates" assigned to specific functions) became the center for policy making and program formulation (Schick, 1971, 118–9). This office was more powerful in expansion years than in years when the governor was more fiscally conservative. And its relation with the Budget Division thus varied (Schick, 1971, 119, note 3). Planning and budgeting staff often held quite different perspectives on the same issues. The planners often were skeptical of the

Table 5.1   Timeline of Major Events on Planning and Budgeting in New York State

Year	Event
1958	Legislative staff report: responsibilities of DoB not compatible with planning
59–60	DoB lost ground on planning
1961	DoB strengthened long-range planning capability as an adjunct to its Research Unit
1961	October, Hurd appointed Marshall Deputy Budget Director to oversee Budget's role in capital construction
1961	• Office for Regional Development established • Planning Coordination Board created, an interagency body chaired by Commissioner of Commerce
1964	Within the Division of the Budget • Budget examination units reorganized "along program lines to allow greater staff attention to long-range impact of programs ..." • A new Budget Planning & Development Unit attached to Director's Office
1964	Governor appointed Hurd chairman of Interdepartmental Management Improvement Council
1964	Planning-Programming-Budgeting System initiated
1965	• May 6 meeting of IMIC, Marshall acknowledged problems of interagency coordination, overlapping responsibilities of DoB and ORD, and need to define purpose and scope of long-range planning effort more precisely; • May 11, Governor announced DoB to concentrate on fiscal and financial planning; ORD to undertake massive statewide comprehensive planning • Governor instructed DoB and ORD to coordinate any future demands on agencies for planning data
1965	August, President Johnson adopted PPBS in the federal government
1966	ORP changed to Office of Planning Coordination (OPC); PPB is termed as "Integrated PPB" in *Guidelines*
1966	Dec., Hurd asked for Governor approval to conduct management study of DoB by consulting firm McKinsey and Co. Report came out in May 1967
1967	PPBS gained national reputation; in NY it was divorced from planning
1967	Oct. Lanigan memo to Marshall protesting McKinsey recommendations
1969	May, IMIC session: "defining and measuring effectiveness continue to be major stumbling blocks in PPBS"
1969	PPBS stopped
1970	Program Analysis and Review (PAR) replaced PPBS
1971	June, PPBS stopped at federal level

negative attitude of budgeters toward new programs; while the budget examiners as often questioned the spending attitude of planners (ibid).

With the publication in 1964 of the 60-year plan for urban land use and infrastructure construction by ORD (1964), the Division of Budget felt a threat to its leadership role in capital programming and financial management. DoB claimed it wrong to split resource planning from the annual budget, while the ORD rebutted that this type of planning was not covered in the budget process. Governor Rockefeller resolved this jurisdictional fight by granting ORD and Budget joint responsibility. Thus was born the hybrid of "planning-programming-budgeting" (Schick, 1971, 119). The New York PPBS required three conditions: (a) each agency should have permanent, specialized staffs to conduct continuing, in-depth analyses of agency objectives and the various needs to meet these objectives; (b) there should be a multi-year planning and programming process to incorporate an information system and to present data in a way so as to facilitate decision-making by the leaders; and (c) the budgeting system and process can translate broad program decisions into the annual budgetary context (Novick, 1965). These are true at the federal and also state levels (NY Joint Committee, 1966). None of the components of PPBS was new at that time, but integrating them into one system for effective policy making was a demanding task; any success would rely heavily on the cooperative and coordinated efforts, based on the willingness of elected officials, planners, budgeters, and program managers.

5.1.9   PPBS in New York

New York's seven-year experiment with PPBS can be roughly divided into two phases. In the first phase (1965–67), PPBS was mainly planning with a little budgeting. In the second phase (1968–70), PPBS became mainly budgeting with some program reporting (Schick, 1971).

5.1.9.1   Phase 1: Planning with Some Budgeting

A system of long-range, comprehensive planning was instituted in 1965. The annual budget guidelines, called "Integrated PPB", were issued jointly by the Office of Planning Coordination and the Division of the Budget (the OPC was listed first). The emphasis was on planning rather than budgeting. The Guidelines asked each department for program projections on policy-based topics and resource requirement topics, both for five to 20 years. This document pointed towards preparing "comprehensive state policies" in urbanization, transportation, public facilities, and economic and social development (1966 Budget Guidelines, 8–9).

The dominant feature in these three years was comprehensiveness of planning: PPBS was "conceived as a planning process with budgeting as just one of its many components" (Schick, 1971, 121). Among the multiple stages in a full PPBS cycle, as indicated in Figures 5.5 and 5.6, five were on preparing long-range projections; and most time in budget preparation, January to September, was on making projections. PPBS was successful in this period in drawing more of decision makers' attention onto program objectives. Their attention, however, was not on "delineation of program structure, policy analysis, or program effectiveness" (SLFP, 1969, 24–5). It became almost a game of future-for-future's sake.

5.1.9.2 Phase 2: Budgeting with Some Program Reporting

Soon budgeters were tired of the game; program managers did not like to spend time on anything impractical. Once detached from the annual needs of line departments, PPBS shifted gear from its original "planning" to more "budgeting." Budgeters and managers went back to their daily routines; but planners were less interested in the daily operations; thus, OPC shifted its attention to long-term development plans and distanced

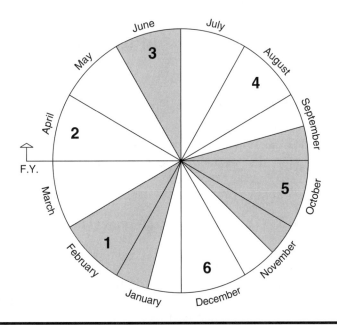

Figure 5.5   Annual planning-programming-budgeting cycle in New York State. *Source: Guidelines for Integrated Planning, Programming, Budgeting 1967* (page 8) by the State of New York Office of Planning Coordination and the Division of the Budget.

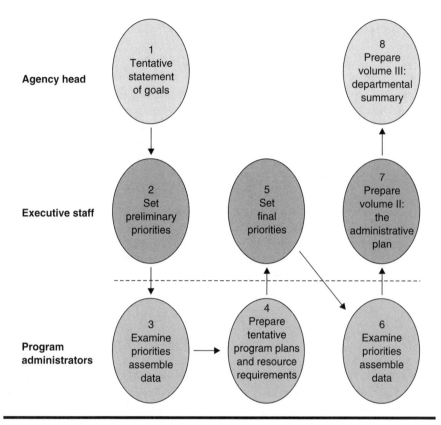

Figure 5.6 Basic stages in preparing program planning reports, New York State.
Source: Guidelines for Integrated Planning, Programming, Budgeting 1967 (page 12) by the State of New York Office of Planning Coordination and the Division of the Budget.

itself from budgeting (Schick, 1971, 123–4). These changes were clearly reflected in the 1968 Budget Guidelines where the Budget Division was listed in front of the OPC and the word "integrated" was dropped. The document explicitly stated that an "extensive re-evaluation of PPBS in New York [in 1967] introduced changes in the system to make it more *useful* for executive decision making" (1968 Guidelines, 7). Statewide comprehensive planning "will be realistic only if the strategic decision makers participate in their development," and OPC would focus on a statewide development strategy. Furthermore, "only issues requiring policy action by the governor in 1968–69 will be considered" (Ibid, 8). Even the reporting system was "refined": only a "shorter and more succinct report is requested from each agency … to review their existing program structure, to develop measures of effectiveness for their programs, and to analyze alternatives" (Ibid, 9).

5.1.10 Why PPBS Did Not Succeed?

Almost at the very beginning, the state legislature had expressed serious concerns about the "considerable confusion surrounding efforts at budgetary reform" because "budgeting is on the verge of a fundamental change" (NYS Joint Legislative Committee, 1966, 10). Out of disillusionment, New York, again not surprisingly, became the first state to abandon PPBS in 1970. The 1970 Budget Guidelines were less than 10 pages, the aim being "to emphasize elements of the system whose value has been proved, and revise or eliminate features whose immediate benefits have been less worthwhile."

> "The revised system recognizes the difficulty in applying any single budgeting or planning system to all problems in every agency. Selectivity is a keystone of the new approach, with increased cooperation between staff and operating agencies to arrive at mutual decisions on problems requiring special attention." (Budget Guidelines, 1970)

This is the Program Analysis Review (PAR) and the review committee was chaired by the Division of the Budget. The Office of Planning Coordination was thrown out.

Possible causes can be easily identified for the failure of PPBS in New York. On the political side, from the very beginning, it was the governor's initiative; the legislature was skeptical about the overhaul of the existing system. The Division of the Budget was very defensive of its turf on resource allocation. It never fully cooperated with the Office of Planning Coordination. There were also institutional/personnel reasons. Except for four years during the Harriman administration (1955–59), the Budget Division was headed by the same person from 1950–70, which may have contributed to the resistance of new ideas. In the same period, the examinations section of the Budget was also led by the same person (Schick, 1971, 118). On the technical side, the system was far too burdensome for agency managers and budgeters and almost useless to budget examiners in the annual budgeting process. Besides, the system did not have room for agency initiatives or provide incentives for agency performance. Agencies did not think it helped them. To "correct" the wrongs of PPBS, Program Analysis Review was selective, agency-oriented. It was not to reform the old process but only to inject analysis.

Although PPBS as a reform effort to change the state's budget traditions was not successful, it did not disappear without leaving a trace. The experiment was a reflection of, and made budgeters recognize, the inadequacies of the line-item, control-oriented budget process. Even the Program Analysis and Review Committee headed by the Budget Division, after abandoning PPBS, identified five obvious areas in the previous budgeting system that needed improvement. These are: (a) effective treatment of inter-departmental issues; (b) multi-year implications of current choices; (c) consideration of alternative proposals; (d) pre-crisis identification of potential problems; and (e) effective use of analysis tools (PARC, 1970). The Joint Legislative Committee on Legislative Fiscal Analysis and Review listed in its report a recommendation, among others, that "the budget should present . . . a long-range view of the state's construction program" (1970, 39–41). Most important, PPBS became a heritage to be taken over by subsequent reform efforts like the one in Sunnyvale.

5.1.11   *China versus New York: Similarities and Differences*

China and New York both failed in linking their annual budgeting process to that of long-range planning. The two operated under different political and economic systems: China was under public ownership with centrally planned economy; New York was an open market economy. Obviously, the success or failure had little to do with their political or economic system. Planning occurred against a similar background in both cases. Central planning in China was to promote industrialization; New York's regional planning went for rapid growth. Both were large-scale, coordinated, comprehensive, and long-range plans.

On the technical side, the two share as many apparent similarities as striking differences. Planning and budgeting were the responsibility of two separate bodies; but the two bodies carried different weight in the two cases and the weight changed over time. In China, it was primarily planning. The planning agency, State Planning Commission, dominated the annual procedures; the budget agency, Ministry of Finance, was a subordinate in comparison. When the two processes collided, it was always budgeting that gave in. In New York, the planning agency (ORD and later OPC) was parallel with the Budget Division. Even when ORD was at its peak, it could not (and did not care to) take over the "boring, routine" budgeting functions. The two agencies worked "together" (not smoothly though) for a few years; after several years of power struggle, the whole thing fell apart. It was after all still budgeting. For China, planning was a noble enterprise; for New York, planning was an information-collection exercise at best.

As the nature of the business demanded, central planning in both cases was top-down. To feed the monster requirement of comprehensiveness, the annual planning-budgeting cycle demanded a huge amount of data collection and reporting from agencies that involved far too much time and paper work, a lot of which did not directly improve resource allocation.

Because the exercise of data gathering and forms filling did not generate benefits in efficiency or effectiveness of program operations, planning became a game and thus a subject of ridicule. New York chose to give up the game to restore budgetary order. China, under rigid political control, went along to muddle in the black box of planning for nearly three decades, where waste and inefficiency was rampant due to inadequate care for a sound budgeting system. In these two cases, there was not a fit between the annual budgeting and long-range planning processes.

Case 3: Annual Budgeting Within Long-term Framework

Though the State-Local Finances Project to promote the PPB system in the mid-1960s and early 1970s did not generate expected achievements, the reform initiative to improve the then prevalent system was not completely given up. In fact, the General Accounting Office (GAO) spearheaded an effort in the 1970s to develop a better budgeting and accounting system in the state and local sector. The City of Sunnyvale, California, started their reform as a response to the GAO initiative. Then, in the late 1970s, Sunnyvale began to integrate long-range planning, resource allocation, and pay for performance for management employees (CBO, 1993, 16). In this sense, the city has used performance-based budgeting (PBB) for over twenty years; while in most other parts of the U.S. PBB was revived only after the early 1990s.

The core of Sunnyvale's current budgetary system is the "Planning and Management System (PAMS)," which, some scholar observes, is a combination of strategic planning, performance-based budgeting, and pay for performance (Joyce, 1999, 604). Long-term (20-year) financial planning is comprehensive, covering all funds. The plan includes capital needs over the 20-year period. The City's General Plan lays out the vision for the community over the long term, including land use. The fully integrated PAMS framework includes eight key elements (see Exhibit 2). An on-site examination of the system by an OMB and GAO joint team in 1991 confirmed the list of key elements and concluded that PAMS is "among the most sophisticated in the country," and "perhaps the best-known system for measuring the performance of local government" (CBO, 1993, 13–7).

The city states that, regarding planning, this framework has over time granted the city capability "to accomplish [its] long-range strategic goals;" in terms of cyclical fiscal stability, PAMS has "assisted in maintaining, and even expanding, services during times of numerous federal/ state mandates and revenue restrictions or reductions." More important,

Exhibit 2   Key Elements in the Sunnyvale Integrated PAMS Framework

Key element	Explanation
1. Long-range strategic planning	Divided into general plan elements and sub-elements
2. Long-term financial planning	Resource allocation plan including 20-year projections
3. Short-term allocation of resources	Two-year action budget
4. Outcome measurement of service delivery	
5. Council Study Issues process	
6. Performance "contracts" for management	
7. Annual performance reporting and evaluation	
8. Performance audits based on risk assessment	

Source: Tabulated by author from Sunnyvale's *Comprehensive Annual Financial Report for Fiscal Year 2004*, available on line at www.sunnyvale.state.us.

the framework has also "served as a valuable tool in producing and capturing remarkable gains in efficiency and productivity" (Sunnyvale, 2004, CAFR, vi).

The long-term perspective has generated huge benefits in cyclical fiscal stability. By the city's General Plan, the City Manager must propose each year a budget that is not only balanced for the current fiscal year but also balanced for the 10-year resource allocation plan. In fact, the City Council has adopted since FY1994 a financial plan balanced to the 20th year. This practice has made it effective that policy decisions of today must guarantee availability of "resources to provide quality services in the out years as well"; and the 10-year resource allocation plan prevents "wild swings in service levels during the upturns and downturns of economic cycles" (ibid).

5.1.12   Where is the Fit?

Contributors to the success of the Sunnyvale PAMS system, according to the joint investigative team of OMB and GAO, include its adoption of full cost-accounting, its focus on output, outcome-oriented goals and performance measures, its emphasis on early warning, as well as monetary incentives for outstanding performance (see Exhibit 3).

Exhibit 3 Contributors to Success of Sunnyvale's PAMS

Factor	Explanation
Accounting system	Operating on a full cost-accounting basis enables the city to identify true cost of services
Budget focus	Output, not spending. City Council approves program goals (when the level resource needed to meet the goals implicit) but does not vote on the budget in the traditional line-item sense
Outcome-oriented objectives and performance measures	Exhaustive list covers all municipal functions
Emphasis	Early warning and long-range planning
Incentives for city employees	Pay-for-performance system ties explicitly individual with organizational performance

5.1.12.1 Incorporation of Planning into Budgeting

The city's form of government is no small factor. The council-manager form nullifies any possible friction between the executive and legislative branches. The Council as the sole policy-making body directs its hired manager to operate the municipal government. Once the city as a whole decides to adopt long-range planning and build its annual budget on the plan, city agencies under the manager's leadership only implement the policies.

The lean government structure at the municipal level does not allow impractical entities. Long-range planning for infrastructure construction is the business of a citizen's planning board, which then goes through referendum for adoption, and is ultimately translated into policy by the council. The city's finance department, without competitors for power and influence before the council and city manager, is concerned only with the technical mechanisms for fitting the annual financial plan — the budget — into the long-range framework.

The budget format matters tremendously. Shifting from the traditional line-item to program goals, the city council puts its emphasis on output and outcome instead of spending. What it approves is the level of resources needed to meet the goals. "Underwriting" this choice of format is the city's wealth. Located in the Silicon Valley with extremely high values of industrial property, the city enjoys a tax base that expands excellently with the economy.

By giving up the line items, a fair amount of discretion is granted to managers, which alleviates any contention between the finance department (budget agency) and line agencies that is common in jurisdictions under fiscal stress. Control, however, is not sacrificed; but it follows in a different, more rational manner. The full-cost accounting system guarantees identification of true costs of public services whether it is personnel or materials. Program objectives and performance measure that target outcome link every program and manager (with their salary) to specific benchmarks, thus holding every manager accountable for their costs. Those meeting the measures will win and those failing will lose.

The long-range plan is not used to determine exactly how much to spend in a particular future year, but to identify trends in revenues and expenditures and to understand when there may be structural imbalances. This practice generates special benefits, in that any major deviance from the long-term financial plan will be under scrutiny for causes and solutions, which better serves cyclical fiscal capacity. Besides, Sunnyvale budgets only confirmed revenues. Intergovernmental grants, which are subject to swings of fluctuation, are budgeted only one year for what they know they are going to receive, not what is anticipated. This practice also helps towards budgetary stability.

5.2 Conclusion

Though planning and budgeting are among the three original basic orientations of public budgeting since the beginning of the executive budget movement, the relationship between the two has not been handled as well as expected; often it was bumpy and full of conflicts. The root of the problem is the contradiction between the annularity of budgeting and the long-range nature of planning, plus the related issues of separate agencies (power struggle) and control versus managerial discretion. Policy makers have not been particularly happy about the control orientation that tends to bind their ambition for more and bigger programs; but budget offices seem to have held resistance to any change that threatens their conventional turf. At the same time, however, reform efforts have never stopped completely. Performance budgeting in the 1950s and PPBS in the 1960s are two good examples; even after these failed, new initiatives kept emerging.

This chapter has been exploring the fit between planning and budgeting. Can there be a fit at all between the two? Have there been success stories of the relationship? The three case studies offer some lessons to draw from. First, budgeting can go along with planning. The annual process of budget preparation can fit well into the long-term framework of planning. By nature, the two are not against each other. One does not have to be achieved at the cost of the other. In the China case, budgeting was given up because the then Chinese government took central planning as the supreme policy and subjected budgeting to the mercy of planning. When the two are not equal, one becomes the cost of the other. In the case of New York, budgeting had a long tradition and deep root in the bureaucracy system while planning was new. Two separate organs competed for influence and power over resource allocation. Though the governor favored planning for policy reasons, the impractical, tedious data collection and the detachedness of planning from annual operations ultimately sent planning out of the budgeting system. In Sunnyvale, planning and budgeting find the fit through one integrated planning-budgeting system, with just one agency in charge.

Second, being two complementary functions of the budgeting process, planning and budgeting can promote and facilitate each other. As Walker (1944) pointed out, planning can contribute to annual budgeting by providing a framework for more smooth operations; likewise, budgeting is also a plan on an annual basis. As such, the annual budgeting process can also contribute to long-range plans with regular revisions for more exact vision and forecasts. In the China case, this relationship did not come true, because the medium-range and annual economic plans were often delayed too long, which disrupted the annual budgeting process. Consequently, planning became bondage instead of framework; it could by no means facilitate budgeting but only damaged it. In New York's PPBS, the annual planning process became much a chore of useless data and numerous forms, most of which were not linked to financial operation. In Sunnyvale, the two became real complements under an integrated budgeting system. The long-term financial plan provides policy makers and managers more information for decision making and management; in return, the annual process contributes to correction of deviances, which builds into long-term budgetary stability.

Third, it seems that to maintain a complementary planning-budgeting relationship demands some prerequisites, about which, however, this chapter offers only some hints but cannot yet be conclusive. Why planning and budgeting did not fit in the China and New York cases but did fit in Sunnyvale? Was it because of the single agency structure and level of wealth in Sunnyvale or something else? Is there just one model or multiple models? Reflecting on the failure of PPBS in the American states, Allen Schick observed that

> "There is no need for forcibly transplanting *the* PPBS onto alien political soil. A government can design its PPBS to suit its political conditions. In the states, a variety of different PPBS experiences are emerging, with each state shaping PPBS to its particular circumstances." (1971, 194)

It may well be true that there will be more models for the fit between planning and budgeting. The annularity-long range link may come in different formats at different levels of the government structure in different countries. But for sure, the two can fit nicely into each other. Alongside budget reforms, advances in technology have played a significant role: analyses of multi-year program demands into the future were extremely burdensome in the 1960s in New York; now in Sunnyvale it is an automated fast process that no one takes as extra work.

Finally, the Sunnyvale case is in fact not only about planning and budgeting. It is also closely involved with the management of budgeting — outcome orientation, performance measures, incentives for managers and employees, etc., — which is beyond the scope of this chapter. Those details will be the topic of future research.

Acknowledgment

The authors express sincere thanks to Ms. Grace Kim, finance manager for budget, Finance Department of the City of Sunnyvale, California, who provided detailed information about the Sunnyvale budgeting system; to New York State Division of the Budget for providing information about the history of budgeting in New York State.

Notes

1.   There has been no authoritative source for the origin of "five-year" plans. Some say Joseph Stalin was inspired by the input-output matrices of Russian economists (Tarschys, 2002, 85).

2.   The Supreme Soviet spiritual leader Vladimir Lenin got his inspiration mostly from the German experience in economic regulation and rationing during WWI (Tarschys, 2002, 85).

3.   See the "Interim rules on the compilation of national economic plans," issued by the Central Finance and Economic Committee.

4.   Chen Yun, China's economic tsar in the 1950s, made this comment at a conference in the 1980s.

References

Appleby, Paul H. 1949. *Policy and Administration.* University, Alabama: University of Alabama Press.

Bo, Yibo. 1991. *Major Decisions and Events: a Retrospect.* Beijing: CPC Party School Press.

Boex, L.F. Jameson, Jorge Martinez-Vazquez and Robert M. McNac. 2000. "Multi-year budgeting: A Review of international practices and lessons for developing and transitional economies." *Public Budgeting and Finance,* (20)2: 91–112.

Braybrooke, David and Lindblom, Charles E. 1963. *A Strategy of Decision: Policy Evaluation as a Social Process.* New York: Free Press.

Brown, Richard. 1978. "Toward a communalist approach to national development planning," *Public Administration Review,* Vol. 38, No. 3 (May): 262–267.

Caiden, Naomi. 1981. "Public budgeting amidst uncertainty and instability." *Public Budgeting and Finance,* (1), Spring.

Caiden, Naomi, and Wildavsky, Aaron. 1974. *Planning and Budgeting in Poor Countries.* New York: Wiley and Sons.

City of Sunnyvale. *Comprehensive Annual Financial Report 2004.* available online at http://sunnyvale.ca.gov/Departments/Finance/Accounting/CAFR+Home.htm

Cleveland, Frederick A. 1915."Evolution of the budget idea in the United States," *Annals of the American Academy of Political and Social Science,* Vol. 62: 15–35.

Congressional Budget Office. 1993. *Using Performance Measures in the Federal Budget Process.* Washington, D.C.: Government Printing Office.

Connery, Robert H. 1974. "Nelson A. Rockefeller as governor," in *Governing New York State: the Rockefeller Years,* edited by Peter W. Colby. Albany, NY: the State University of New York Press, 2nd edition, 14–15.

Contemporary China Finance Editorial Office. 1990. *Reference Materials to the Finance History of the People's Republic of China 1949-1985.* Beijing: China Finance and Economics Press.

Donohue, Leo. 1982. "You can't take politics out of budgeting." *Public Budgeting and Finance,* Vol. 2, No. 2 (Summer): 62–72.

Fayol, Henri. 1916. *General Principles of Management.*

Forrester, John P. 1991. "Multi-year forecasting and municipal budgeting." *Public Budgeting and Finance,* (11)2: 47–61.

Frederickson, George H. 1980. *New Public Administration.* University, Alabama. University of Alabama Press.

General Planning Department of the Ministry of Finance, China. 1982. (ed). *Financial Management System (1950-1980), Part I of Historical Documents of the Finances of the People's Republic of China.* Beijing: China Finance and Economics Press.

Government Council, China. 1951. "Interim Rules on Budgets and Final Accounts." Beijing.

Gu, Longsheng. 1993. *Economic Choronical of Mao Zedong.* Beijing: CPC Party School Press.

Guajardo, Salomon A. 2000. *An Elected Official's Guide to Multi-Year Budgeting.* Chicago: Government Finance Officers' Association.

Hoover Commission Report on Organization of the Executive Branch of Government. 1949. New York: McGraw-Hill.

Hou, Yilin. 2003. "In search of budgeting: China 1949-78." Paper presented at the annual conference of the Association for Budgeting and Financial Management (ABFM), September 18–20, Washington, D.C.

Hou, Yilin. 2006. "Budgeting for fiscal stability over the business cycle." Forthcoming in *Public Administration Review*, 2006.

Joyce, Philip. 1999. "Performance-Based Budgeting," chapter 24 in Roy Meyers (ed.) *Handbook of Government Budgeting*. San Francisco: Jossey-Bass, 597–619.

Kettl, D.F. 1994. *Inside the Reinvention Machine*. Washington, D.C.: Brookings Institution.

Kerker, Robert P. 1981. *Executive budget in New York State: a half-century perspective*. Albany, NY: New York State Division of the Budget.

Kerker, Robert P. 1994. "The state of the executive budget," in *Governing New York State,* edited by Jeffrey M. Stonecash, John Kenneth White, and Peter W. Colby. Albany, NY: The State University of New York Press, 3rd edition, 165–77.

Key, V. O. 1940. "The lack of a budgetary theory," *The American Political Science Review*, Vol. 34, No. 6. (Dec): 1137–1144.

Lewis, Verne B. 1952. "Toward a Theory of Budgeting," *Public Administration Review*, Vol. 12, No. 1. (Winter).

Lindblom, Charles, E. 1965. *The Intelligence of Democracy*. The Free Press.

Mikesell, John L. 2003. *Fiscal Administration: Analysis and Applications for the Public Sector*. Sixth edition. Wadsworth Publishing.

Mosher, Frederick C. 1954. Program budgeting: theory and practice, with particular reference to the U.S. Department of the Army. Chicago, IL.: Public Administration Service.

National Bureau of Statistics, China. *China Statistical Yearbook* series. Beijing: China Statistics Press.

Novick, David. 1965. Program budgeting: program analysis and federal budget. Cambridge, Mass.: Harvard University Press.

Power, John. 1998. "Decentralization". *The Internation Encyclopedia of Public Policy and Administration*. Boulder: Westview Press.

Shick, Allen. 1966. "The road to PPB: the stages of budget reform" *Public Administration Review,* Vol. 26, No. 4 (December): 243–258.

Schick, Allen. 1971. *Budget Innovation in the States*. Washington, D.C.: The Brookings Institution Press.

Schick, Allen. 1998. A Contemporary Approach to Public Expenditure Management. World Bank Institute.

Simon, Herbert A. 1946. The Proverbs of Administration. *Public Administration Review*, 6: 53–67.

Smithes, Arthur. 1955. *The Budgetary Process in the United States*. New York: McGraw-Hill.

State of New York Division of the Budget. 1981. *The Executive Budget in New York State: a Half-Century Perspective*. Albany, NY.

State of New York Joint Legislative Committee on State-Local Fiscal Relations. 1966. *Foundations of the Fiscal system*. Albany, NY: March 31.

State of New York Office for Regional Development. 1964. *Change/Challenge/Response*. Albany, NY.

State of New York Office for Regional Development and Division of the Budget. 1966, 1997. *Guidelines for Integrated Planning, Programming, Budgeting*.

State of New York, Division of the Budget and Office for Regional Development. 1968. *Guidelines for Planning, Programming, Budgeting*.

State-Local Finances Project. 1969a. *Implementing PPB in State, City and County*. Washington, D.C.: The George Washington University Press.

State-Local Finances Project. 1969b. *PPB Pilot Project Reports, "The State of New York."* Washington, D.C.

State of New York, Division of the Budget and Office of Planning Coordination. 1970. *Guidelines for Program Analysis and Review*.

State of New York. 1970. Report of the Joint Legislative Committee on Fiscal Analysis and Review. Albany, NY: March 31.

Stonecash, Jeffrey M. (ed.) 2001. Governing New York State. Albany, NY.: Albany State University of New York Press.

Tarschys, Daniel. 2002. "Time horizons in budgeting," *OECD Journal on Budgeting*, Vol. 2, No. 2, 85.

Walker, Robert A. 1944. "The relation of budgeting to program planning," *Public Administration Review*, Vol. 4, No. 2 (Spring 1944): 97–107.

Wildavsky, Aaron. 1961. "Political implications of budgetary reform," *Public Administration Review*, Vol. 21, No. 4. (Autumn): 183–190.

Wildavsky, Aaron. 1964. *The Politics of the Budgetary Process*. Boston: Little Brown.

Zhu, Jiamu and Liu, Shukai (eds). 2000. *Chronicles of Chen Yun*, in 3 volumes. Beijing: CPC Archives Press.

PUBLIC FINANCE

II

Chapter 6

The Property Tax: Past, Present and Future

DEBORAH A. CARROLL, Ph.D.
Department of Political Science, University of
Tennessee, Knoxville

BENJAMIN J. SHARBEL, M.P.A.
Knox County Mayor's Office, Knoxville, Tennessee

The property tax can perhaps be considered the oldest form of taxation for modern government. Dating back to medieval times, property taxation was instituted as an obligation for the use of land that was not owned but rather supplied through royal favors (Hale, 1985). This form of taxation was based upon a person's status or class within society, rather than upon any determination of the land's value. The first secular property tax was instituted in England in 1194, in which local subjects, acting on behalf of the king, estimated the wealth of each resident to determine their tax liability (Hale, 1985). While the modern form of property taxation has changed significantly since these first examples, the concept of a tariff or duty imposed upon individuals who use real estate has remained largely the same. This chapter highlights the evolution of the property tax by discussing property taxation in the past, present and future.

6.1 Property Taxation in the Past

6.1.1 Property Tax Origin and Structure

The American version of the property tax can be traced back to the original colonies. The American colonies developed a system of taxation that was independent of the British tax system and included a variety of revenue sources (Fisher, 1997). During this time, revenue was generated through poll taxes, faculty taxes imposed on the ability to earn income from certain trades or skills, imposts on goods imported or exported, excise taxes on consumption goods, and property taxes (Fisher, 1997) to raise local revenue for common activities like defense (Institute of Property Taxation, 1993). In the colonies, during the 18th Century, these property taxes accounted for about two-thirds of all tax revenue (Council of State Governments, 1978). During the Revolutionary Period, emerging corruption in some of the colonies by the controlling elite, which placed greater tax burdens on the poor, led to the first instances of resistance and calls for tax reforms seen in this country (Fisher, 1997). During this time, property taxation was largely justified as a means to help finance the Revolutionary War as well as other local services (Institute of Property Taxation, 1993), despite the fact that taxation was a major cause of the war (Renne, 2003). However, it was at this time that the concepts of equality and uniformity began to be incorporated into the basis of property taxation (Institute of Property Taxation, 1993). Those who believed that the current system of using specific property tax rates discriminated against them began to advocate an ad valorem basis of taxation as an attempt to create uniformity and greater fairness in the tax system (Fisher, 1997). In the post-Revolutionary Period, the adoption of the United States Constitution not only gave the federal government the power to levy taxes and duties, but also stipulated that direct taxes like the property tax had to be apportioned among the states by population (Fisher, 1997).

6.1.2 Valuing Property For Taxation

The call for uniformity in taxation that began during the Revolutionary War Period led some states to begin to levy property taxes according to the value of assets held by taxpayers. Subsequent to this time, uniformity in taxation became a major constitutional issue with thirty-one states adopting constitutional uniformity clauses between 1834 and 1896 (Fisher, 1997). With little definitive legal meaning prior to its appearance in state constitutions (Fisher, 1997), uniformity continues to serve as the basis for property taxation throughout this country. Market or cash value of property is defined as "the price at which a property will sell from a willing seller to a willing buyer, both cognizant of all pertinent facts and neither being under duress"

(Institute of Property Taxation, 1993, 95). The three approaches currently used to determine the market value of property include: the cost approach, the income approach, and the sales comparison approach.

In the cost approach, the land is first valued as if it were vacant (Youngman, 1994) using sales comparison, capitalization of ground rent, or the land residual techniques for valuation (Institute of Property Taxation, 1993). Then the improvements to the land are valued using either the reproduction or the replacement cost approaches. The reproduction cost approach values the improvements as the cost to construct an exact duplicate or replica at current market prices using the same materials, construction standards, and design that the building was originally constructed with, while also considering all the deficiencies, super-adequacies and obsolescence of the structure (Institute of Property Taxation, 1993). Functional obsolescence is a form of depreciation that results in a loss of value due to a lack of utility or desirability inherent in the design of the property, while economic obsolescence is depreciation related to impairment in value that has resulted from industry or economic factors external to the property. The replacement cost approach values the improvements based on the cost to construct a building of equivalent utility at current market prices using modern materials and current standards and design. In general, the building cost estimate should include both direct costs like labor and materials and indirect costs such as professional fees, financing costs, and taxes (Institute of Property Taxation, 1993). Once the value of the improvements has been determined, physical depreciation and functional and/or economic obsolescence of the building is assessed and subtracted from the building value. Finally, the land value is added for the total valuation of the property. A caveat, however, is that for this approach to be equitable, current market information must be used in developing the depreciation schedules and land values (Renne, 2003).

The income approach values property based on the future stream of income an owner could expect, which is converted into present value through capitalization (Youngman, 1994). This approach bases the value of the property on its ability to produce net rental income. The approach first measures the expected rental stream generated from leasing the facility, which includes assumptions about the type of leases and expenses included in the lease agreements. The valuation must include reasonable estimates for potential gross rental income, adjusted for occupancy and rental trends, and expenses such as taxes and insurance (Youngman, 1994). Next, a capitalization rate is determined based upon the "prudent investor" standard. The assumption is that the normal goals of an investor are a return on investment and a return of investment. As such, the capitalization rate includes the three elements of income (I), rate (R), and value (V) — such that I/RV (Institute of

Property Taxation, 1993). The capitalization rate is then divided into the net income stream to determine the current value of the property.

The sales comparison approach analyzes the sales of similar properties and then determines a value for the subject property through comparison (Youngman, 1994). For this approach there must be a sufficient number of reliable market transactions from which comparisons may be made. For example, comparable properties must have similar attributes such as square footage, number of bedrooms, and total acreage. Sources of information for comparable sales include appraisers' files, public records, commercial and industrial realtors and lenders, published data banks, and market surveys (Institute of Property Taxation, 1993). Because this approach concerns market behavior, it may be used to provide information on market conditions to the taxpayer (Renne, 2003). Finally, this valuation approach requires adjustments to be made to account for fluctuations in the normal real estate market resulting from time of sale, location, size, land-to-building ratios, physical and income characteristics, and terms of financing (Institute of Property Taxation, 1993). After these adjustments have been made, a valuation per square footage is determined for the property based on the above comparisons and adjustments. The total property value is then determined by multiplying the derived value by the total square footage of the property (Institute of Property Taxation, 1993).

6.1.3   Classifying Property For Taxation

Throughout the 19th century, an increased need for public services and transportation improvements resulted in an expansion of public expenditures, which subsequently led to a broadening of the property tax to cover additional quantities and types of property (Institute of Property Taxation, 1993). However, it was also at this time that states began to recognize difficulties in (1) applying a tax so that all forms of wealth were taxed equally and (2) finding and assessing tangible and intangible personal property (Fisher, 1997). As a result, property slowly came to be divided into classifications and taxed at different rates (Institute of Property Taxation, 1993). The most notable distinction that has developed over time is between properties classified as real versus personal property. This distinction, which is based on common law concepts, involves the degree of attachment, the intent of the owner, and its adaptation to use (Institute of Property Taxation, 1993). Real property is generally considered to be real estate, realty or land and is immovable. Buildings and fixtures are also examples of real property (Youngman, 1994). If the removal of the property would cause irreparable damage to the structure it is attached to, the property is considered real estate. Personal property constitutes everything that is the subject of ownership that is not real property and not permanently affixed to real property (Institute of Property Taxation, 1993). Personal property is movable and includes items such as machinery, equipment, and household items (Youngman, 1994). If the attachment can be easily removed with no damage, it is generally considered to be personal property. Second, if the intent of the owner when making the annexation of the property was to permanently affix the property, then it is considered real estate. However, if the intention were only a temporary affixation that would eventually be removed, the property would likely be considered personal property. Finally, if the property is intimately intertwined with the use of the land or was an integral and indispensable part of a building adapted for a particular use, the property would be considered real estate.

The development of a distinction between real property and personal property has been extremely important for property taxation. Real property is taxed on the basis of the perceived intangible rights and benefits of owning physical real estate, including the right to live in, sell, or lease the property (Appraisal Institute, 1992). For purposes of taxation, real property is assessed at fair market value using the valuation approaches previously discussed. On the other hand, personal property is assessed for taxation at depreciated historical cost rather than the market valuation technique used for real property. In addition, personal property is often exempt from property taxation because of the inherent difficulties in valuing and reporting these assets, which can be both tangible and intangible. Thus, the development of a distinction between real and personal property has been important for determining taxpayer liability with respect to property taxation.

6.1.4 Exempting Property From Taxation

The Great Depression Years saw a sharp rise in expenditure needs and property tax delinquencies (Fisher, 1997). In response, states began to adopt both sales and income taxes to reduce or replace their dependence on the property tax (Fisher, 1997). These taxes are often preferable because they fluctuate with income and consumption and are not all paid by the taxpayer at once (Council of State Governments, 1978). As a result of the development of both the income tax and the sales tax, states became less dependent on revenue generated through property taxation, while local governments remained heavily dependent on this revenue source (Institute of Property Taxation, 1993). Within a few years after the Great Depression, the property tax became a local tax and was primarily used to finance education and municipal services (Fisher, 1997). Up until World War II, the property tax dominated local government revenue, representing the only major tax for local governments (Cantrell, 1954). For example, the property tax accounted for 94% of all local revenue for the 1938 fiscal year (Institute of Property

Taxation, 1993). Due to the many social and economic programs that were created and expanded after World War II, property tax rates continued to rise into the early 1980s. For example, the estimated effective tax rate applied to single family residential properties had increased from 1.42% in 1958 to 2.13% in 1971 (Institute of Property Taxation, 1993). In addition, the aggregate amount of state and local tax revenue generated through property taxation increased from $6.1 billion in 1948 to $37.9 billion in 1971 to $89.1 billion in 1983 (Institute of Property Taxation, 1993). During this time, local governments were so dependent on the property tax that the scope of their services was largely determined by their tax base (Cantrell, 1954). As a result, property tax relief measures became popular and states enacted many exemptions on personal property, particularly on household belongings, livestock, and machinery (Institute of Property Taxation, 1993).

Over time there have been a number of exemptions established with respect to property taxation for both real and personal property. These exemptions are based either on ownership or the specific purpose for which the property is used, including educational, religious, charitable, and non-profit uses (Sexton, 2003).

Publicly owned property is generally not subject to taxation on the basis of interference by one public taxing entity with the sovereignty of another public entity and on the general uselessness of exchanging money between governmental entities. For example, property owned by foreign governments for non-commercial purposes (i.e. foreign embassies) and property owned by state and local governments are usually exempt from property taxation (Council of State Governments, 1978). In addition, state and local governments do not have the authority to tax property belonging to the Federal Government due to the Supremacy Clause in the U.S. Constitution (Council of State Governments, 1978).

Privately owned property might be exempted from property taxation because of the financial circumstances of the property owner or to encourage certain types of activities (Sexton, 2003). For example, exemptions may be provided as economic development incentives. Local governments trying to encourage economic growth may provide an exemption to a business to persuade it to re-locate into the community. Certain groups, such as veterans or the elderly, may also be exempt from taxation upon all or a portion of the assessed value of their property, which decreases their tax liability (Institute of Property Taxation, 1993). Such exemptions are usually for low-income property owners or for individuals who have performed a significant service to the community, such as served in the military (Institute of Property Taxation, 1993). Finally, a number of exemptions are provided to individuals based on their profession or income level. For example, development property and parts of farmland may be exempt in some cases (Reeves, 1983). Homestead exemptions, where a limited portion of a person's home is exempt, have also increased in popularity (Roemer, 1983). Finally, circuit-breaker programs, where homeowners receive a credit or refund based on their income, have also become common (Roemer, 1983).

Property tax exemptions are also provided on the basis of the specific purpose for which the property is used. For example, property owned by religious organizations is often exempt from taxation because of the philanthropic and educational nature of the services provided, which serve a public purpose and might otherwise have to be provided by the government. These exemptions vary from state to state depending on how states define religious groups and beliefs (Institute of Property Taxation, 1993). However, these exemptions generally apply to the land, parking, and equipment used for worship. Property used for educational purposes is also often exempt from property taxation. In fact, all fifty states and the District of Columbia exempt public school property (Sexton, 2003) from property taxes. Privately owned property used for benevolent or educational purposes have also been exempted on the basis that the services performed provide relief to the government of the public burden of providing such services. However, several private and for profit schools are not exempt in some states (Institute of Property Taxation, 1993). The determination of exemption is generally based on the benefit that the organization provides to the public. Certain non-profit and charitable organizations are exempt from paying property taxes as well. Property used for other public purposes follows the historical practice of providing exemptions to reimburse organizations supplying a public service that would otherwise have to be provided by the government. However, it is generally the responsibility of the organization itself to prove that its property is used for charitable and non-profit purposes to receive the tax exemption.

6.1.5   The Tax Revolts

With a consistent rise in property tax rates after World War II, property tax relief became a major concern. In some instances, small tax relief measures succeeded in keeping taxpayer opposition to a minimum (Institute of Property Taxation, 1993). However, local citizen revolts in several states forced limits to be placed on the growth of the property tax for both state and local purposes (Howard, 1989). Though many limitations have origins dating as far back as the Great Depression (Mikesell, 2003), a notable onset of these limitations came about in the late 1970s and early 1980s, an era characterized largely by citizen distrust and disapproval of government, due in part to Watergate and the Vietnam War (Kirlin, 1982). In addition, the significant inflation that occurred during this time period increased individuals' tax burdens by pushing them into higher federal income tax brackets (Kirlin, 1982) and skyrocketing the price of real estate and property taxes concomitantly (Sears and Citrin, 1982). For example, in the 1977–78 biennium just prior to the passage of Proposition 13, property taxes in California peaked at 52 percent above the national average (Sears and Citrin, 1982). Although the primary target of the tax revolts had been the local property tax, limitations were also directed specifically at state governments (Joyce and Mullins, 1991). Many of the tax revolt movements were instigated by citizen initiatives; however, most of the resulting tax and expenditure limitation measures were enacted by state legislatures rather than through referenda. Some have suggested that the anti-tax sentiment throughout the country had become so strong that legislators voted for tax and expenditure limitations from fear of losing their bids for re-election (Howard, 1989).

While it is difficult to pinpoint a single direct cause of the tax revolts, a number of explanations have been offered. Some explanations have proposed that many people believed government had grown beyond the preferences of voters (Joyce and Mullins, 1991), while others thought that taxes were simply too high. Some have suggested that the tax revolts represented citizen demands for smaller and more efficient government that did not compete with private sector interests (Swartz, 1987). Others propose that Proposition 13 centered on citizen demands for smaller residential property tax burdens without a corresponding reduction in public service provision (Shapiro, Puryear and Ross, 1979). In fact, a recent study shows that increases in property taxation and local revenues relative to state revenues will increase the likelihood that tax and expenditure limitations are approved in state elections (Alm and Skidmore, 1999). In addition to the high level of taxation, citizens at the time believed the level of public service provision was too low compared to what they paid in taxes, thereby leading to a desire to limit government growth (Sigelman, Lowery and Smith, 1983). Figure 6.1 illustrates the increasing trend of state tax revenue collections during the time period 1965–1980 in constant dollars.[1] As can be seen from Figure 6.1, the total amount of tax revenue generated by state governments increased almost every year during the time period, with the height of tax revenue collections occurring in 1978. This trend represented a doubling of state taxation during the 15-year time period with a 109% increase in tax revenue generated between 1965 and 1978. Other citizens believed that the property tax was inequitable and that individuals paid more than their fair share in taxes (Lowery and Sigelman, 1981). Others simply could not afford to keep paying an increasing level of taxes, particularly during periods of recession and inflation (Lowery and Sigelman, 1981). Finally, an increasing conservative political ideology, a declining confidence in government, and a simple lack of information or ignorance towards government might help to further explain the tax revolts (Lowery and Sigelman, 1981).

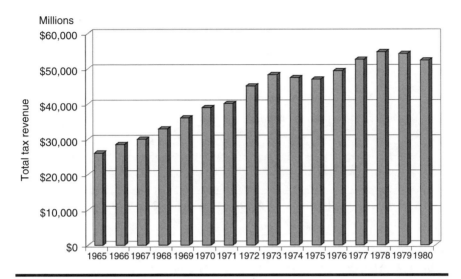

Figure 6.1   State tax revenue collections 1965–1980. *Data Source*: World Tax Database, University of Michigan Business School, Office of Tax Policy Research.

While the influence of the tax revolts has been widespread, citizen revolts did not occur in every state (Sigelman, Lowery and Smith, 1983). In particular, states in the western region of the United States were most affected and subsequently enacted the majority of the tax and expenditure limits (Howard, 1989). Perhaps the two most famous tax revolts are California's Proposition 13 and Massachusetts 2½. Proposition 13 in California represented the start of the tax revolts across the country (Institute of Property Taxation, 1993). Passed in 1978 by an almost two-thirds majority (Galles and Sexton, 1998), the initiative produced several changes in the California constitution regarding the property tax. Proposition 13 diminished property tax assessments to their 1975 level, limited increases in assessments on properties that did not change ownership or undergo substantial improvements to a maximum of 2% per year, prohibited property assessments that exceeded a property's full market value, required that two-thirds of a jurisdiction's voters approve all local tax increases, and stipulated a two-thirds majority in both houses of the California legislature to increase state taxes (Galles and Sexton, 1998). Finally, Proposition 13 prohibited state and local governments from "imposing any other property taxes, sales taxes, or transaction taxes on real property" (Sexton, Sheffrin and O'Sullivan, 1999, 99).

There are believed to be several factors that led to the passage of Proposition 13 in California. However, the most significant influence was perhaps the trend of dramatically increasing property values in California in the early to mid 1970s, which resulted in significant increases in annual property tax burdens for residents. For example, the homeowners' share

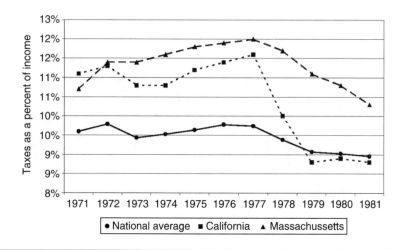

Figure 6.2 State-local tax burden 1971–1981. *Data Source*: The Tax Foundation.

of property taxes in California increased by ten percent from thirty-four percent in 1974 to forty-four percent in 1978, while the tax rate remained stable (Sexton, Sheffrin and O'Sullivan, 1999). Figure 6.2 illustrates the state-local tax burden during the time period 1971–1981 for California and Massachusetts compared to the national average.[2] As can be seen from Figure 6.2, the tax burden for both California and Massachusetts is considerably higher than the national average throughout most of the time period. While the national average state-local tax burden only reaches a high of 9.786% during the time period, California and Massachusetts exhibit maximum tax burdens of 11.6% and 12%, respectively. In fact, some have projected that, without Proposition 13, California would have accumulated a surplus of around ten billion dollars (Sexton, Sheffrin and O'Sullivan, 1999). However, since legislators did not take action to lower taxes during this time, California citizens took matters into their own hands and the tax revolt emerged (Sexton, Sheffrin and O'Sullivan, 1999).

In 1980, voters in Massachusetts approved a property tax limitation measure known as Proposition 2½ with fifty-nine percent of the vote (Rothenberg and Smoke, 1982). The purpose of this measure was to lower the property tax burden and halt the rate of local government spending in Massachusetts. High property taxes in Massachusetts were largely due to the fact that local governments in Massachusetts were more dependent upon the property tax compared to other states (Rothenberg and Smoke, 1982). This dependence had resulted from lower levels of aid from the state government and minimal use of user charges and fees by local governments (Rothenberg and Smoke, 1982). For example, in the year that Proposition 2½ passed, municipalities within the state collected almost three hundred dollars more per capita in property taxes than the national average (Rothenberg and Smoke, 1982). At that time, property taxes in Massachusetts as a proportion of personal income also accounted for almost three percent more compared to the national average (Rothenberg and Smoke, 1982).

The main provision of Proposition 2½ placed a cap on the effective property tax rate at 2.5% and limited the nominal annual growth in property tax revenues to 2.5%, unless residents approved a referendum allowing for a greater growth rate (Bradbury, Mayer and Case, 2001). Municipalities that already exceeded the 2.5% limit needed to reduce their levies by fifteen percent each year until the limit was met (Rothenberg and Smoke, 1982). As a result of Proposition 2½, local governments in the state of Massachusetts were faced with the options of cutting expenditures, seeking new sources of revenue, or increasing debt. In general, Proposition 2½ resulted in revenue losses for Massachusetts municipalities, the extent of which was largely dependent upon the size and wealth of the community. Smaller, wealthier communities experienced insignificant losses and other adverse effects compared to larger, poorer communities (Rothenberg and Smoke, 1982).

While California's Proposition 13 and Massachusetts 2½ represent the most well-known and influential examples of the tax revolts, many other states were also adversely affected by the revolts and followed suit in passing some version of tax and expenditure limits (Institute of Property Taxation, 1993). Thus, the primary implication of the tax revolts has been the emergence of tax and expenditure limits throughout the country, which consist of a variety of forms. There are currently 30 states with some type of tax and expenditure limitation in place (Rafool, 1996). The most prominent form of a state limitation on a government's ability to tax is a limitation on the property tax rate (Preston and Ichniowski, 1991). These limits, which vary significantly by state and among classes of property, consist of a limitation on the tax rate applied to assessed property valuation that is imposed by cities, counties, special districts, and other local governments (Preston and Ichniowski, 1991). Some of these tax rate limitations only apply to those taxes used for financing the operating budget, while others apply to a government's entire budget.

The second major form of tax and expenditure limit imposed by states is a limitation on the amount a property assessment can increase. This limit prevents increases in the assessment valuation of property from being automatically translated into higher tax bills for property owners receiving increased assessments (Mikesell, 2003). This type of limitation has been implemented in states such as Arizona, Idaho, and California. However, some have argued that this type of limitation more severely affects governments' abilities to raise revenue through property taxation because it caps the "growth in total property tax levies" (Preston and Ichniowski, 1991, 124). While some states imposing this type of limitation do not allow for any increase in their property tax levies, other states have allowed relatively high growth rates in the total tax levy collected. In such cases, the rate increase may be constant or it can vary depending upon population changes or measures of inflation. Finally, a number of states limit the growth of revenue and expenditure categories. These limits are designed more broadly than property tax limitations and usually include exemptions to intergovernmental revenues and services financed through user charges (Preston and Ichniowski, 1991). New Jersey and California, for example, place limitations on total expenditures with exemptions for intergovernmental revenue and services financed by user charges (Preston and Ichniowski, 1991). Nebraska limits a municipality's total expenditures with an exemption on certain capital expenditures (Preston and Ichniowski, 1991). In other states, tax limits are tied to personal income, which allows state governments to grow correspondingly to increases in state population and wealth. Thus, the implications of the tax revolt movement were rather visible for states and localities throughout the country.

Aside from the imposition of various tax and expenditure limits throughout the country, which often adversely affected state and local government finances, the tax revolts can also be attributed to the positive implication of producing greater equity in property taxation. Horizontal equity in taxation refers to equal treatment of taxpayers who are equivalent in all relevant aspects (Mikesell, 2003). Typically, horizontal equity is achieved by frequent and uniform assessment practices that maintain an estimated taxable value of property that is equivalent to its market value. This ensures that the distribution of the tax burden most closely resembles taxpayers' ability to pay the property tax, as measured by the value of property. During the time of the tax revolts, several state courts and legislatures focused enforcement efforts toward full-value assessment standards required by state law in response to taxpayer dissatisfaction with inequities in property assessments (Bland and Laosirirat, 1997). For example, in 1979, the Texas state legislature created 254 central appraisal districts, which were politically independent of the county governments, for the single purpose of appraising property at its full market value (Bland and Laosirirat, 1997). In addition, the increasing role of state governments in public school finance placed an added emphasis on the importance of equitable assessment practices. In particular, state aid formulas intended to offset resource disparities between local public school districts were developed to utilize the local property tax base for determining funding levels (Mikesell, 2003). As a result of these pressures, accurate and uniform property assessments became somewhat of an obligation for local governments following the tax revolts.

6.2 Property Taxation in the Present

6.2.1 Continued Reliance on Property Tax Revenue

Property tax revenue is the single largest source of local government tax revenue throughout the United States (Petersen and Strachota, 1997). "Thus, while local revenue systems now are rather diversified, the property tax still accounts for three-fourths of all local taxes, and nearly half of all locally raised general revenues" (Petersen and Strachota, 1997). The property tax is the only tax to be levied in all fifty states and Washington D.C. (Brunori, 2003). As an ad valorem tax, property taxes are based on the estimated value of the property (Petersen and Strachota, 1997). The dollar amount generated by the property tax is a product of the tax rate and the tax base. With a constant assessment ratio, it is assumed that the tax base increases in direct proportion to the growth in market values. In such a case, a constant property tax rate generates a stable revenue stream (Petersen and Strachota, 1997), which makes this revenue source attractive for local government financing.

Figure 6.3 illustrates the proportion of total local government tax revenue that was generated through property taxation during the time period 1988–2003 using census data.[3] As can be seen from Figure 6.3, a significant proportion of total tax revenue for local governments is generated through the property tax, ranging from 72.74% to 77.9% of total tax revenue. On average, local governments throughout the United States generated

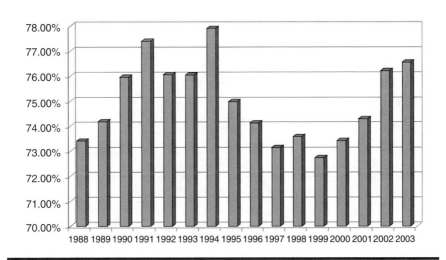

Figure 6.3 Local property tax revenue as a proportion of total tax revenue 1988–2003. *Data Source*: U.S. Census Bureau.

three-fourths of their total tax revenue from property taxation during the time period. In addition, this trend in property tax reliance was generally increasing between 1988 and 1994, at which point property taxation peaked and subsequently declined. Figure 6.3 shows a substantial decline in property tax revenue during the latter half of the 1990s followed by a subsequent increase in property tax reliance again in the year 2000. This decreasing trend seems to correspond closely with the economic boom of the 1990s, which led to surpluses in many states followed by various tax relief measures. However, as the recession set in at the end of 2001, the proportion of total local government tax revenue generated from the property tax — which is considered the most stable revenue source during recessionary times — again increased rather substantially. Between 2001 and 2002 the proportion of tax revenue generated through property taxation increased by almost 2% in a single year. Thus, it is evident that local governments continue to rely on property taxation for a significant portion of their total tax revenue.

Although property tax rates for state and local governments have grown only marginally over time, property tax revenues have grown consistently due to the appreciation of real property value (Brunori, 2003). Figure 6.4 illustrates the amount of state and local revenue generated through property taxation during the time period 1988 to 2003 in constant dollars. As can be seen from Figure 6.4, the differential between state and local governments in terms of the aggregate amount of property tax revenue collected is rather substantial. This shows that local governments are much more

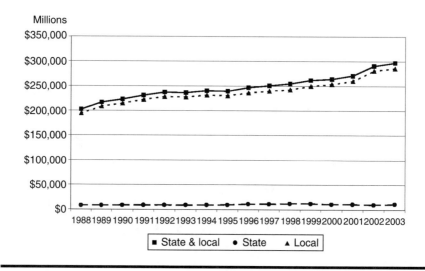

Figure 6.4 State and local government property tax revenue 1988–2003. *Data Source*: U.S. Census Bureau.

reliant on property taxation as a revenue source than state governments, which are typically more dependent upon the sales and income tax to generate revenue. Figure 6.4 also shows the consistent upward trend in total revenue generated from property taxation by local governments, which grew by over 47% during the time period.

This continued reliance on the property tax has been somewhat dependent on the type of local government. Large cities and special districts generally rely on property taxation the least, because of greater diversity in their revenue structures and utilization of user charges and fees, respectively. On the other hand, independent school districts and counties typically rely more heavily on property tax revenue. Figure 6.5 illustrates the proportion of local government property tax revenue that was collected by each type of government for the 2001–2002 fiscal year. As can be seen from Figure 6.5, the largest proportion of property tax revenue for the fiscal year was generated by local school districts with 44% of all property tax revenue collected by that type of governmental unit. The type of government generating the second largest proportion of total property tax revenue for the fiscal year was counties, followed closely by municipalities, with 23% and 22%, respectively, collected by those types of governmental units. Figure 6.5 also shows that special districts collected the lowest proportion of property tax revenue for the 2001–2002 fiscal year, with only 4% of total property tax revenue generated by that type of governmental unit.

Figure 6.6 provides data on the proportions of own-source revenue and total tax revenue generated from property taxation by type of government for the 2001–2002 fiscal year, which provides a greater indication of each type of governmental unit's reliance on property taxation. The first data series illustrates the proportion of total tax revenue that is

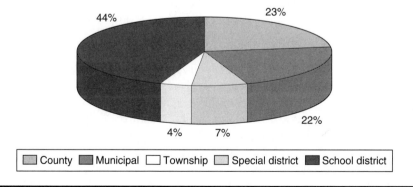

Figure 6.5 Proportion of total local government tax revenue collected by government type 2001–2002. *Data Source*: U.S. Census Bureau.

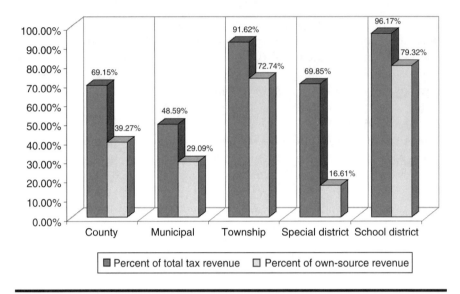

Figure 6.6   Proportion of government revenue generated from property taxation by government type 2001–2002. *Data Source*: U.S. Census Bureau.

generated through property taxation for each government type. The second data series portrays the proportion of total own-source revenue that is attributable to property taxation for each type of government. As can be seen from Figure 6.6, school districts generated the single largest portion of their total own-source revenue through property taxation with 79.32%, while special districts generated the least with only 16.61% of total own-source revenue generated from property taxes. These findings are consistent with the data provided in Figure 6.5. In addition, over 96% of total tax revenue generated by school districts for the fiscal year was through property taxation. While special districts generate the least amount of own-source revenue from property taxation, the proportion of total tax revenue generated by the property tax is much higher at almost 70%. Also highly dependent on property taxation are townships followed by counties. For the 2001–2002 fiscal year, townships generated over 72% of total own-source revenue and over 91% of total tax revenue through property taxation. Some have suggested that this reliance on property taxation is due to the fact that townships do not receive much intergovernmental funding compared to other types of governmental units (Brunori, 2003). Thus, reliance on the property tax as a source of revenue is partially associated with the type of local government generating the revenue.

Reliance on property tax revenue has also shown to vary by regions throughout the country. In general, local governments in the South and

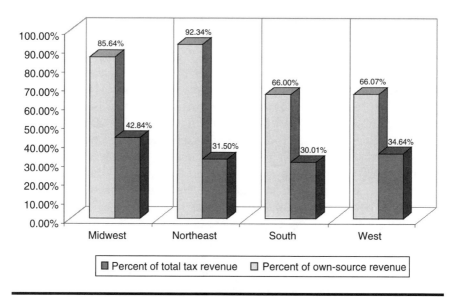

Figure 6.7   Proportion of government revenue generated from property taxation by U.S. region 2001–2002. *Data Source*: U.S. Census Bureau.

West typically rely less on property taxes than governments in the Northeast and Midwest (Brunori, 2003). For example, Alabama and Hawaii collected the least in property taxes as a proportion of personal income in 1999, while Connecticut and some of its neighbors collected the greatest proportion (Brunori, 2003). Figure 6.7 illustrates the proportion of government revenue generated from property taxation by U.S. region for the 2001–2002 fiscal year.[4] As can be seen from Figure 6.7, the proportion of total tax revenue generated from the property tax during the 2001–2002 fiscal year was significantly greater for the Midwest and Northeast regions, with property tax revenue comprising 85.64% and 92.34%, respectively. In the South and West regions only 66% of total tax revenue for each region was generated through property taxation during the same time period. In addition, the Midwest region generated the single largest proportion of own-source revenue through property taxation, with almost 43% of total own-source revenue for the region attributed to property taxation. The other three regions, however, are relatively similar with respect to the proportion of total own-source revenue generated through property taxation, ranging from 30.01% in the South to 34.64% in the West. Thus, regional differences are more apparent when examining the property tax's contribution to total tax revenue, rather than the property tax's relationship to own-source revenue. Nonetheless, it is evident that the property tax still represents a significant portion of local government finance.

6.2.2 Continued Influence of the Tax Revolts

While the property tax remains a significant and persistent component of local government revenue, there have been some noticeable changes in government reliance on property taxation resulting from the tax revolts of the late 1970s early 1980s. Most notably, the property tax as a percentage of total revenue has declined as a result of the tax revolts (Brunori, 2003). After Proposition 13 passed in California, aggregate property tax revenue was almost cut in half from $10.3 billion in 1977 to $5.6 billion in 1978 (O'Sullivan, 2001). Although actual revenue rose to $19.5 billion in 1995, property tax revenue in that year was twenty-five percent below the level it had been in 1977 (O'Sullivan, 2001). Similarly, Proposition 2½ in Massachusetts led to an eighteen percent decrease in property tax revenue (O'Sullivan, 2001).

It appears that the long-term decline in local government revenue collections from the property tax reached its pinnacle right after the tax revolts in 1980 (Duncombe and Yinger, 2001). Much of this decline is attributable to the shift in focus of limitations in the 1970s toward greater restrictions on growth in the tax levy or government expenditures, measures known as truth-in-taxation or full disclosure laws. Developed by the U.S. Advisory Commission on Intergovernmental Relations (ACIR) in 1962, truth in taxation seeks to make public officials more accountable for tax increases (Bland and Laosirirat, 1997). In the absence of full disclosure requirements, "frequent reappraisal of property provides lawmakers with a politically attractive opportunity to hold rates constant while tax yields increase" (Bland and Laosirirat, 1997, 46). In such cases, it is typically the assessor rather than the elected official that is criticized and bears the political repercussions for higher taxes (Bland and Laosirirat, 1997). On the other hand, truth in taxation requires a rollback of statutory tax rates when property is reassessed and the assessment base increases, so there is no corresponding increase in total tax collections (Mikesell, 2003). Only through a formally approved provision can the government realize higher property tax collections, thus subjecting the property tax budget to greater public scrutiny (Mikesell, 2003).

The apparent decline in aggregate property tax revenue collections, however, is somewhat misleading with respect to local governments' dependence on this inexorable revenue source. In 1950 the property tax comprised almost 75% of total local government own-source revenue (Duncombe and Yinger, 2001). In 1996 the proportion of own-source revenue generated through property taxation had dropped to less than 50% (Duncombe and Yinger, 2001). This shift away from the property tax, however, was largely offset by an increase in the cost and level of local government service provision (Duncombe and Yinger, 2001). As a result, the property tax revolts had much less of an impact on the property tax burden than is apparent by examining aggregate tax collections. Despite a small decrease between 1975 and 1980, real property tax burden per capita increased from $578 to $789 between 1965 and 1996 (Duncombe and Yinger, 2001). However, the proportion of property taxes to personal income decreased during this same time period, which might have been the result of the influence of the tax revolts. Between 1965 and 1980, the percentage of property taxes to personal income dropped from 4.1% to 3.0% (Duncombe and Yinger, 2001). In 1996, although the trend had apparently reversed, the percentage was still lower than the 1965 level at 3.8% (Duncombe and Yinger, 2001). Thus, one of the most significant implications of the tax revolts is that the property tax burden had somewhat declined over the past few decades. However, this trend has visibly reversed itself as of late. Recent trends now show the property tax burden with respect to income actually approaching the level seen prior to the tax revolts (Duncombe and Yinger, 2001). This suggests that the decades-old influence of the tax revolts in terms of moving away from property taxation as a primary source of revenue might be waning.

Aside from the direct influence over government reliance on property tax revenue, the tax revolts have had other implications in terms of the quality of public service provision, governmental efficiency, and the overall size of government. However, there has been much disagreement in these areas with respect to the influence left behind by the tax revolts. Some have suggested that the movement away from property taxation has resulted in a lower quality of public service provision, particularly in the area of education, while others claim that the tax revolts have had no impact on education or the quality of public services (Duncombe and Yinger, 2001). Others have suggested that tax and expenditure limits have resulted in decreased local government responsiveness and accommodations to the needs of dependent population (Mullins and Joyce, 1996). Similarly, contradictory studies have both shown that tax limits reduce the wage premium received by public workers, thereby suggesting increased efficiency in government service provision, and that the tax revolts encouraged local governments to increase fees and the use of tax increment financing, resulting in greater inefficiency (Duncombe and Yinger, 2001). Finally, the influence of the tax revolts in terms of the size of government is also questionable. Some have argued that tax and expenditure limitations have decreased both the level and growth of expenditures, revenues, and property taxes (Shadbegian, 1998). In addition, the tax revolts have been shown to reduce property tax burdens in states that have passed tax limitation measures (De Tray and Fernandez, 1986). However, others have shown only expenditure limitations to be effective and revenue limitations to be ineffective in reducing the growth of revenue in states

(Elder, 1992). Thus, the continued influence of the tax revolts has been and continues to be disputed.

6.2.3 Reliance on Other Revenue Sources

With a decreasing reliance on property tax revenue immediately following the tax revolts and no corresponding cuts in expenditures, intergovernmental grants, user fees and charges, and miscellaneous revenue have become increasingly important sources of revenue for local governments (O'Sullivan, 2001). Intergovernmental funds have become a major source of local finance as the federal government collects much of its revenue through income and payroll taxes and then transfers a portion to state and local governments (Kahan, 2003). In 1999 intergovernmental revenue among state and local governments rose to approximately twenty-five percent of total revenue, which has primarily been used to finance education (Kahan, 2003). More importantly, however, has been the increasing use among state and local governments of user charges and fees and other tax revenue sources. Local governments are increasingly more reliant on local option sales and income taxes as major sources of revenue. This is due in large part to the increasing property tax limits for municipalities, counties, and school districts as well as the increased use of user charges and fees by special districts (McGuire, 2001).

After the property tax, the second largest source of local government revenue consists of other tax revenues, particularly the local-option sales tax (Brunori, 2003). Thirty-three of the forty-five states that have sales taxes allow local governments a local option (Brunori, 2003). Twenty-three states even allow both cities and counties to levy a sales tax locally (Brunori, 2003). Around the year 2000, sales tax revenues had significantly increased to a level higher than both income and property tax revenue (O'Conner, 2003). These taxes are usually implemented in addition to similar taxes already collected by states by adding a local rate onto the state rate, which is subsequently collected as part of the state tax (Brunori, 2003). In this type of system, vendors typically collect the aggregate sales tax from consumers and remit it to the state. The state subsequently remits the local portion of the collected sales tax to the local government corresponding to where the purchase or transaction was made. Thus, the administrative burdens associated with collecting these taxes fall largely upon the merchants remitting the tax and the state collecting the tax; therefore, local governments spend little money on collecting the taxes. Because of the convenience to both taxpayers and local governments, the local option sales tax has become rather popular for state and local government finance.

There are both advantages and disadvantages to the increased use of other tax revenues, including sales, income and excise taxes. Although more regressive than the property tax, consumers have a tendency to favor sales and excise taxes because they only pay taxes on what they consume (Brunori, 2003). In addition, state governments often implement these taxes and absorb the administrative costs, while local governments must absorb the administrative costs for property tax implementation (O'Conner, 2003). Finally, these taxes are generally more responsive to economic growth than the property tax (O'Conner, 2003). A disadvantage, however, is that these other taxes are already heavily used by state and federal governments making the combined rates very high (McGuire, 2001). In addition, local-option sales and excise taxes are not as reliable as the property tax for producing a stable revenue stream (Brunori, 2003). They are less stable than the property tax, because they fluctuate with the economy. This is one reason that state and local governments suffered from the recession around the beginning of the 21st century (O'Conner, 2003). Moreover, many goods, particularly groceries, medicine, and utilities are exempt from these taxes (Brunori, 2003). Finally, as a result of the shifting economy from a basis of tangible property and manufacturing to one based on services and intangible property, the sales tax base has subsequently reduced (Brunori, 2003).

Despite the lesser reliability of these taxes, however, their importance for state and local finance has increased considerably. Much of this increasing dependence on other sources of tax revenue was brought about by the tax revolts. As of 1977, $5.4 billion in revenue was generated from local-option sales and excise taxes, which was approximately 7% of total tax revenue (Brunori, 2003). In 1999 these figures had increased to 11% of total tax revenue for a total of $36 billion (Brunori, 2003). However, these taxes continue to comprise a greater proportion of state tax revenue than local revenue (O'Conner, 2003). As a percentage of total local revenue, these taxes have remained at about 3% for many years (Brunori, 2003). While the aggregate amount of revenue generated from other tax sources has grown, local governments rely more heavily on user fees and intergovernmental aid to replace their lost property tax revenue (Brunori, 2003).

User charges and fees are also common alternatives to the property tax and are primarily used to finance utilities and sanitation services (McGuire, 2001). Almost all governments around the country impose user fees and charges upon the users of many government services such as parks, sanitation, sewage, airport services, parking, and others (Brunori, 2003). Between 1973 and 1991, user charges increased 112 percent while the property tax only increased 12 percent (Downing and Bierhanzl, 1996).

In 1999 user fees made up approximately 20% of total local revenue or $195 billion, which was an increase from 1992 of 8% and over $60 billion (Brunori, 2003). The increase in user fees and charges is largely the result of the ability of local governments to consistently secure and increase other revenue sources (Brunori, 2003). In addition, user fees and charges are regarded as economically efficient because they are limited in their distribution, usually to the services for which they are collected (Brunori, 2003). Ultimately, they are efficient in that only those who use the service pay the fee (Brunori, 2003).

The limitations to user charges and fees are inherent in the design of this financing mechanism. There are a limited number of services that can be financed through user charges and fees, namely those services to which government can deny access. User charges and fees function similarly to a private market pricing system, in that supply of the public good or service is only allocated to those who value it most, which is determined by their willingness to pay (Downing and Bierhanzl, 1996). Public goods that are nonexclusionary, or exclusion from which would be harmful for the community at large, are not suitable for financing through user charges and fees. Thus, services like providing police and fire protection and clean air are generally not available for user fees (McGuire, 2001). In addition, user charges and fees utilize pricing principles based on marginal cost of production and distribution and consumer demand (Downing and Bierhanzl, 1996). Marginal costs and demand for public goods vary considerably among communities, which directly affects the price charged for the service (i.e. the user fee), the number of individuals who are able and willing to pay the fee, and subsequently the provision level of public goods financed through user charges and fees. "Like prices, user charges should reflect the cost of providing additional units of the publicly provided good, a cost that often varies by location" (Downing and Bierhanzl, 1996, 263). Finally, there is only so much local governments can charge for a service before the public will stop using it (Brunori, 2003). However, if the price charged for a good or service does not reflect the actual costs of providing it, there is an incentive for consumers to overuse the service, and the quantity demanded will not necessarily reflect consumers' willingness to pay the full cost of providing the service (Downing and Bierhanzl, 1996). For these reasons, the amount of revenue generated from user charges and fees is less able to grow continually or increase drastically. As a result of these limitations it is expected that revenue generated from user charges and fees will level off or decline slightly at some point in the future (Brunori, 2003). Nonetheless, user charges and fees will likely continue to remain a significant amount and important component of local government revenue (Brunori, 2003).

6.3   Property Taxation in the Future

The property tax has been an enduring component of government finance since the origin of this country. However, historical events like the Great Depression and the tax revolts initiated by California's Proposition 13 have had profound effects on state and local governments' reliance on tax revenue generated from property taxes. State governments have undoubtedly developed tax revenue structures that generate very little revenue from the property tax. For example, in 2003 national totals of state government tax revenue amounted to the income tax (both corporate and personal) and the general sales and gross receipts tax, contributing 38.33% and 34.66%, respectively, to total tax revenue (U.S. Census Bureau). In addition, the combination of excise tax revenue generated from motor fuel sales, tobacco product sales and alcoholic beverage sales contributed to 8.74% of total state tax revenue (U.S. Census Bureau). However, property taxes only contributed to 2% of total tax revenue generated by state governments in 2003, which represents the average contribution that the property tax has made to overall state tax revenue since 1988 (U.S. Census Bureau). Thus, the movement of states away from the property tax that occurred after the Great Depression and resulted in the property tax becoming a local government revenue source has steadfastly continued into the present era and will likely continue well into the future.

The past and present state of property taxation have also illustrated a somewhat decreasing reliance on property tax revenue from local governments coinciding with a strengthening of other revenue sources, including intergovernmental revenue, user charges and fees, and other tax revenue. For example, in the 2001–2002 fiscal year, local governments throughout the United States generated 38.11% of their total own-source revenue from charges and other miscellaneous revenue (U.S. Census Bureau). During that same time period, tax revenue derived from sources other than the property tax constituted almost 17% of total own-source revenue for local governments (U.S. Census Bureau). In addition, local governments throughout the country received 40% of their general revenue from federal and state intergovernmental aid during the 2001–2002 fiscal year, while at the same time generated only 37% of their total general revenue through taxation (U.S. Census Bureau). Thus, it is apparent that the property tax has waned somewhat in its importance as a revenue source for local governments. However, aside from intergovernmental revenue, alternatives to the property tax still comprise a relatively small portion of local governments' own-source revenues and in some cases have even declined over time.

Figure 6.8 illustrates the proportion of total tax revenue for local governments generated from motor fuel sales, tobacco product sales and

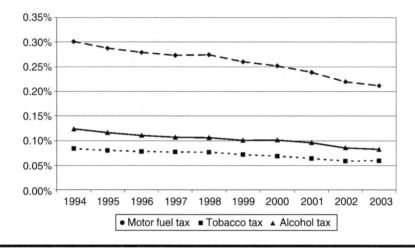

Figure 6.8   Local excise tax revenue as a proportion of total tax revenue 1994–2003. *Source*: U.S. Census Bureau.

alcoholic beverage sales during the time period 1994–2003. As can be seen from Figure 6.8, the proportion of local government tax revenue that is generated from each individual excise tax source amounts to less than one percent for all three sources. These small contributions to local government financing cannot be considered viable alternatives to the property tax. In addition, Figure 6.8 shows that all three of these excise tax revenue sources have been declining in their contribution to the overall tax revenue generated by local governments. The proportion of total tax revenue generated from motor fuel sales declined from 0.30% to 0.21% during the time period. The contribution that taxes on tobacco product sales made to overall local tax revenue declined from 0.08% to 0.06%. Finally, the proportion of total tax revenue derived from alcoholic beverage sales declined from 0.12% to 0.08% during the time period.

Aside from the contributions to tax revenue made by excise taxes, the proportion of total tax revenue generated by local governments from the income tax (both corporate and personal) also declined between 1994 and 2003 from 5.16% to 4.46% (U.S. Census Bureau). While the proportion of total local tax revenue generated from the general sales and gross receipts tax did increase by almost 5% over the time period, this revenue source only contributed to 12.7% of total local tax revenue in 2003 (U.S. Census Bureau). At the same time, the property tax still amounted to 76.55% of total local tax revenue generated in 2003 (U.S. Census Bureau). These findings overwhelmingly suggest that local governments have not yet found a replacement for the property tax. Local governments have continued to depend heavily on property taxation as a means to finance public service provision. Property taxes endure "because they produce reliable, stable, independent revenue for the governments closest to the people and there is no clearly superior alternative for providing fiscal autonomy" (Mikesell, 2003). Thus, the picture for the future seems to be that the property tax will continue as a fundamental source of local government revenue for many years to come.

Notes

1. Data is reported in 1980 constant dollars using the Consumer Price Index. Data amounts refer to the tax revenues collected by state governments alone. As defined by the U.S. Census Bureau, total tax revenue collections comprise gross amounts collected (including interest and penalties) minus amounts paid under protest and amounts refunded during the same period. These amounts also consist of all taxes imposed by a government, whether the government collects the taxes itself or relies on another government to act as its collection agent (http://www.census.gov/govs/www/class_ch7.html#S7.21).
2. State–local tax burden is calculated as total state–local taxes as a percentage of income.
3. Data for Figures 6.3 through 6.8 was obtained from the U.S. Census Bureau, which defines general property tax revenue as relating to property as a whole, which is taxed at a single rate or at classified rates according to the class of property. Property is defined as both real property and personal property, which can be tangible or intangible. These amounts also include: special property taxes levied on selected types of property and subject to rates not directly related to general property tax rates, taxes based on income produced by property as a measure of its value on the assessment date, penalties and interest on delinquent property taxes, proceeds of tax sales and tax redemptions (up to the amount of taxes due plus penalties and interest), and any commissions, fees, or other items representing collection expenses retained from tax proceeds for governments collecting taxes as agents for another (http://www.census.gov/govs/www/qtaxtechdoc.html). Local tax revenue was calculated as the difference between recorded state tax revenue and recorded state and local combined tax revenue. Where appropriate, data is presented in constant dollars using the Consumer Price Index. Property tax revenue that is defined and calculated differently might portray trends unlike those presented in this chapter.
4. The Midwest region includes the following states: Illinois, Indiana, Iowa, Kansas, Michigan, Minnesota, Missouri, Nebraska, North Dakota,

Ohio, South Dakota, and Wisconsin. The Northeast region includes: Connecticut, Maine, Massachusetts, New Hampshire, New Jersey, New York, Pennsylvania, Rhode Island, and Vermont. The West region includes: Alaska, Arizona, California, Colorado, Hawaii, Idaho, Montana, Nevada, New Mexico, Oregon, Utah, Washington, and Wyoming. The South region includes: Alabama, Arkansas, Delaware, Florida, Georgia, Kentucky, Louisiana, Maryland, Mississippi, North Carolina, Oklahoma, South Carolina, Tennessee, Texas, Virginia, and West Virginia.

References

Alm, James and Mark Skidmore. "Why Do Tax and Expenditure Limitations Pass in State Elections?" *Public Finance Review.* Vol. 27, No. 5 (1999): 481–510.

Appraisal Institute. *The Appraisal of Real Estate, 10th edition.* Chicago: Appraisal Institute, 1992.

Bland, Robert L. and Phanit Laosirirat. "Tax Limitations to Reduce Municipal Property Taxes: Truth in Taxation in Texas." *Journal of Urban Affairs.* Vol. 19, No. 1 (1997): 45–58.

Bradbury, Katharine L., Christopher J. Mayer and Karl E. Case. "Property Tax Limits, Local Fiscal Behavior, and Property Values: Evidence from Massachusetts under Proposition 2½." *Journal of Public Economics.* Vol. 80, No. 2 (2001): 287–311.

Brunori, David. *Local Tax Policy.* Washington D.C.: The Urban Institute Press, 2003.

Cantrell, Lang. "Some Basic Modifications of American Property." *The Journal of Finance.* Vol. 9, No. 4 (1954): 427–428.

Council of State Governments. *The Property Tax: A Primer.* Lexington, KY: The Council of State Governments, 1978.

De Tray, Dennis and Judith Fernandez. "Distributional Impacts of the Property Tax Revolt." *National Tax Journal.* Vol. 39, No. 4 (1986): 435–451.

Downing, Paul B. and Edward J. Bierhanzl. "User Charges and Special Districts." *Management Policies in Local Government Finance, Fourth Edition.* Ed. J. Richard Aronson. International City/County Management Association, 1996.

Duncombe, William and John Yinger. "Alternative Paths to Property Tax Relief." *Property Taxation and Local Government Finance.* Ed. Wallace E. Oates. Cambridge, MA: Lincoln Institute of Land Policy, 2001: 243–290.

Elder, Harold W. "Exploring the Tax Revolt: An Analysis of the Effects of State Tax and Expenditure Limitation Laws." *Public Finance Quarterly.* Vol. 20, No. 1 (1992): 47–64.

Elkins, David and Elaine Sharp. "Living with the Tax Revolt: Adaptations to Fiscal Limitation." *Public Administration Quarterly.* Vol. 15, No. 3 (1991): 272–287.

Fisher, Glenn W. "Some Lessons From the History of the Property Tax." *Assessment Journal.* Vol. 4, No. 3 (1997): 40–47.

Galles, Gary M. and Robert L. Sexton. "A Tale of Two Tax Jurisdictions: The Surprising Effects of California's Proposition 13 and Massachusetts' Proposition 2½." *American Journal of Economics and Sociology.* Vol. 57, No. 2 (1998): 123–34.

Hale, Dennis. "The Evolution of the Property Tax: A Study of the Relation between Public Finance and Political Theory." *The Journal of Politics.* Vol. 47, No. 2 (1985): 382–404.

Howard, Marcia. "State Tax and Expenditure Limits: There Is No Story." *Public Budgeting and Finance.* Vol. 9, No. 2 (1989): 83–91.

Institute of Property Taxation. *Property Taxation, 2nd ed.* Ed. Jerrold Janata. Washington D.C.: Institute of Property Taxation, 1993.

Joyce, Philip G. and Daniel R. Mullins. "The Changing Fiscal Structure of the State and Local Public." *Public Administration Review.* Vol. 51, No. 3 (1991): 240.

Kahan, Paul. "An Integrated Tax Structure: Property Taxes Linked to other Business Taxes." *Journal of Property Valuation and Taxation.* Vol. 14, No. 3 (2003): 38–45.

Kirlin, John J. *The Political Economy of Fiscal Limits.* Lexington, Massachusetts: D.C. Heath and Company, 1982.

Lowery, David and Lee Sigelman. "Understanding the Tax Revolt: Eight Explanations." *The American Political Science Review.* Vol. 75, No. 4 (1981): 963–974.

McGuire, Therese. "Alternatives to Property Taxation for Local Government." *Property Taxation and Local Government Finance.* Ed. Wallace E. Oates. Cambridge, MA: Lincoln Institute of Land Policy, 2001: 301–313.

Mikesell, John L. *Fiscal Administration: Analysis and Applications for the Public Sector.* Belmont, California: Thomson Learning, Inc., 2003.

Mullins, Daniel R. and Philip G. Joyce. "Tax and Expenditure Limitations and State and Local Fiscal Structure: An Empirical Assessment." *Public Budgeting & Finance.* Vol. 16, No. 1 (1996): 75–102.

O'Conner, Patrick. "State and Local Government Finances, Property Tax Emphasis." *Assessment Journal.* Vol. 10, No. 4 (2003): 75–97.

O'Sullivan, Arthur. "Limits on Local Property Taxation: The United States Experience." *Property Taxation and Local Government Finance.* Ed. Wallace E. Oates. Cambridge, MA: Lincoln Institute of Land Policy, 2001: 177–198.

Petersen, John E. and Dennis R. Strachota (1997). *Local Government Finance.* Chicago, Illinois: Government Finance Officers Association.

Pomp, Richard D. and Oliver Oldman. *State and Local Taxation, 4th edition.* Richard D. Pomp Publisher, 2001.

Preston, Anne and Casey Ichniowski. "A National Perspective on the Nature and Effects of the Local Property Tax Revolt, 1976–1986." *National Tax Journal.* Vol. 44, No. 2 (1991): 123–146.

Rafool, Mandy. "State Tax and Expenditure Limits: Appendix C." *National Conference of State Legislatures.* November 1996. www.ncsl.org/programs/fiscal/lfp104c.htm

Reeves, H. Clyde. "Leadership for Change." *The Property Tax and Local Finance.* Ed. C Lowell Harris. New York: The Academy of Political Science, 1983: 1–13.

Renne, J. Scott. "Valuation Methodologies for the Assessment Function, Current and Past Practices." *Assessment Journal.* Vol. 10, No. 4 (2003): 103–109.

Roemer, Arthur C. "Classification of Property." *The Property Tax and Local Finance.* Ed. C. Lowell Harris. New York: The Academy of Political Science, 1983: 108–122.

Rothenberg, Jerome and Paul Smoke. "Early Impacts of Proposition 2½ on the Massachusetts State-Local Public Sector." *Public Budgeting and Finance.* Vol. 2, No. 4 (1982): 90–110.

Sears, David O. and Jack Citrin. *Tax Revolt: Something For Nothing in California.* Cambridge, Massachusetts: Harvard University Press, 1982.

Sexton, Terri A. "The Property Tax Base In The United States: Exemptions, Incentives, and Relief." *Assessment Journal.* Vol. 10, No. 4 (2003): 5–34.

Sexton, Terri, Steven Sheffron and Arthur O'Sullivan. "Proposition 13: Unintended Effects and Feasible Reforms." *National Tax Journal.* Vol. 52, No. 1 (1999): 99–112.

Shadbegian, Ronald J. "Do Tax and Expenditure Limitations Affect Local Government Budgets? Evidence From Panel Data." *Public Finance Review.* Vol. 26, No. 2 (1998): 118–136.

Shapiro, Perry, David Puryear and John Ross. "Tax and Expenditure Limitation in Retrospect and Prospect." *National Tax Journal.* Vol. 32, No. 2 (1979): 1.

Sheffrin, Steven. "Commentary." *Property Taxation and Local Government Finance.* Ed. Wallace E. Oates. Cambridge, MA: Lincoln Institute of Land Policy, 2001: 315–319.

Sigelman, Lee, David Lowry and Roland Smith. "The Tax Revolt: A Comparative State Analysis." *The Western Political Quarterly.* Vol. 36, No. 1 (1983): 30–51.

Swartz, Thomas R. "A New Urban Crisis in the Making." *Challenge.* Vol. 30, No. 4 (1987): 34–42.

U.S. Census Bureau, Census of Governments, *State and Local Government Finances.* http://www.census.gov/govs/www/qtaxtechdoc.html.

Youngman, Joan. *Legal Issues in Property Valuation and Taxation: Cases and Materials.* Chicago: The International Association of Assessing Officers, 1994.

Chapter 7

E-commerce and the Future of the State Sales Tax System

CHRISTOPHER G. REDDICK and
JERRELL D. COGGBURN, Ph.D.
Department of Public Administration, University of Texas,
San Antonio

7.1   Introduction

This chapter examines one of the most pressing tax policy issues that state governments face in the 21st century — the taxing of electronic commerce. The sales tax has not been able to keep up with technological advances, especially with the advent of the Internet. This issue is important given the narrowing of the sales tax base because of exemptions, and the inability to collect taxes on all remote sales. In a practical sense, the leakage of revenue from electronic commerce means that states have to recoup these revenues, either by raising sales tax rates, or exploring other options such as collecting more taxes on remote sales. The former option is not as attractive given the antitax sentiment in the U.S. However, political pressure is mounting on state government political leaders to try to find a solution. This chapter outlines the issues surrounding the taxing of electronic commerce and some possible solutions to this contentious issue.

The chapter outlines the scope of the debate surrounding the taxing of electronic commerce. The second and third sections discusses how the sales tax has evolved and its fundamental difference to the use tax. The fourth section discusses the narrowing of the sales tax base as an issue that faces state governments when dealing with taxing Internet sales. The fifth section provides arguments for and against having a sales tax as a revenue source for state governments. The sixth section outlines important Court decisions and their impact on taxing electronic commerce. The seventh and eighth sections outline the arguments for and against taxing electronic commerce. The ninth section presents the estimated state economic losses resulting from not taxing Internet sales. The tenth through twelfth sections discuss the major reforms that have been attempted to address this issue. The last section provides a conclusion, with recommendations on the future possibilities for the taxing of Internet sales.

7.2   Background

The *Internet Tax Freedom Act* of 1998 defines electronic commerce as any transaction conducted over the Internet or through Internet access, comprising the sale, lease, license, offer or delivery of property, goods, services, or information, whether or not for consideration, and includes the provision of Internet access. The Internet is also defined in this act as collectively the myriad of computer and telecommunications facilities, including equipment and operating software, which comprise the interconnected world-wide network of networks that employ the transmission control protocol/Internet protocol, or any predecessor or successor protocols to this protocol, to communicate information of all kinds by wire or radio.

There is an essential difference between sales and use taxes. Generally, states require that in-state sellers collect sales tax on the goods and services they sell at the time of sale, based on the price or value of the goods or services sold. States require out-of-state remote sellers to collect a use tax on the sale of goods and services if the sellers have a substantial presence, or nexus, with the state (to be discussed later). The use tax, which complements the sales tax, is imposed on the purchaser for the privilege of use, ownership, or possession of taxable goods or services. If the out-of-state remote seller does not collect the use tax, the purchaser is required to remit the tax.

There are three types of electronic commerce as outlined by Hellerstein (1998): (1) commerce in tangible products such as books, computers, and wine; (2) commerce in digitalized content downloaded from the Internet such as software, music, games, and videos; and (3) taxing Internet access. Remote sales are transactions that cross state or national boundaries and thus raise questions of the constitutional taxing powers of the states. Traditional remote commerce means mail order. Electronic commerce is a non-traditional form of remote sales.

The history of the proliferation of the Internet and its impact on electronic commerce can be traced back to the 1996 passage of the *Telecommunications Act* (Zorn, 1999). The passage of this act removed unnecessary regulatory barriers such as restrictions on cross-ownership of telephone and cable companies. This opened up the market to competitors. In addition, the Act recognized convergence was occurring in the telecommunications industry as technological developments made it possible for cable companies and other communication and non-communication companies (such as gas and electric utilities) to offer telecommunication services. This change in market structure poses distinct challenges for those responsible for developing and administering tax policy (Zorn, 1999).

There are some key issues in taxing electronic commerce. The underlying economic issue is not whether sales over the Internet (or by mail or telephone) are to be subject to tax because they already are taxed. The issue is rather the cost of collecting such taxes, which will be discussed in detail later in this chapter.

There is also the important issue of taxing tangible versus intangible goods and services (CBO, 2003). For tangible goods, the goods must be shipped to a location, which is a reasonable approximation of where they will be used, and the opportunities for businesses and consumers to behave in ways that minimize their taxes being not that onerous. Digital goods, by contrast, are not subject to similar constraints. For example, Apple's iTunes Music Store does not collect use tax on its online sales of digitalized music. Even if the sellers of such goods decided to collect it, buyers (particularly consumers, whose purchases are more difficult to track than businesses' purchases) could conceivably have the digital product shipped to a computer location and pay for the product with a credit card whose billing address listed a state without a sales tax. The anonymity of Internet transactions seriously complicates both tax administration and tax compliance if taxes are based on the destination of sales or the source of income. However, unlike tangible products, digital content does not stop at a physical location such as a post office. Moreover, since digital content can be reproduced without cost and is not warehoused, it is not possible to check production records or inventories to see how much has been sold (McLure, 2000).

The scope of the discussion on taxing electronic commerce lies in several areas. Some would limit the discussion to electronic commerce in digital content and Internet access, taking the present taxing system of sales by local merchants and of remote sales of tangible products as given. Others argue that it is unrealistic to limit the debate in this way, since: (a) digital content downloaded from the Internet substitutes for tangible products in many applications; (b) electronic commerce in tangible products and other remote sales are often in direct competition; and (c) Internet access and telecommunications are becoming increasingly intertwined and indistinguishable. Many would expand the discussion to include taxation of all remote vendors and/or telecommunications, but not the taxation of traditional commerce. Still others believe that it is an opportunity to rationalize the state sales and use tax by exempting all sales to businesses, expanding the tax base to include most services and intangible products sold to households, which are now largely exempt, and eliminating special taxes on telecommunications (McLure, 2000). In this chapter we explore these different dimensions of the argument for and against taxing electronic commerce and provide some policy recommendations.

The following section discusses the evolution and scope of the state sales and use taxes.

7.3   Sales and Use Taxes

The sales tax was initially a desperation measure. It was borne out of the inability of states in the depression years of the 1930s to finance basic functions from existing sources and the pressure on the states to transfer the property tax to the local governments (Due and Mikesell, 1994). Prior to the 1930s, states had relied on property taxes, some excises, various business taxes and, in some states, income taxes. According to Due and Mikesell, when the state of Mississippi converted its low-rate business tax into a two percent sales tax in 1932, it introduced a new era of state taxation and a new form of tax.

Currently, there are forty-five states and the District of Columbia that have general sales tax programs under which they administer the sales and use tax provisions. GAO (2000) reports that states' reliance on general sales taxes, whether measured as a percentage of tax revenues, own-source revenues, or total revenues, varies considerably across states. Neither state nor local government collects such taxes in the states of Delaware, Montana, New Hampshire, and Oregon. In contrast, state governments in Florida, Nevada, South Dakota, Tennessee, Texas, and Washington obtain over 50 percent of their tax revenues from general sales taxes. On average, general sales taxes account for 33 percent of state tax revenues (GAO, 2000).

Local government use of sales taxes indicates that there are about 7,600 local jurisdictions that have general sales tax programs authorized by 34 states. Generally, state governments administer the state and local sales taxes. This wide range of jurisdictions makes it extremely complicated when collecting the sales and use taxes, especially when it involves electronic commerce.

What are the compliance levels for sales and use taxes? GAO (2000) reports that state officials believe that compliance is highest for in-store sales, next highest for remote sales with nexus (or physical presence to be discussed later), and lowest for remote sales without nexus (Figure 7.1). Their belief rests on three facts. First, in-store sellers are more visible to the states than remote sellers, leaving the states better positioned to enforce compliance through audits and other actions. Second, the states have legal authority to enforce sales and use tax collection by in-store sellers and remote sellers with nexus. Third, because of enforcement costs, the states generally rely on purchasers to voluntarily comply with the use tax when there is no nexus. Differences in compliance costs depend on whether the sale is in-store or remote and for remote sales on whether the remote seller has physical presence or nexus.

McLure (2002a) questions if the sales tax meets the criteria for ideal tax. He argues that the focus of the current sales tax debate is on simplification and an expanded duty to collect the use tax. Use taxes are the legal liability of purchasers with two exceptions; the first for automobiles and other products that must be registered to be used in the state and the second for purchases by business that can be audited. In both these cases taxes are likely to be paid. McLure believes that the existing sales and use taxes satisfy none of the following four criteria for an ideal sales tax: (1) sales to businesses, including sales of capital goods, should not be taxed; (2) taxes

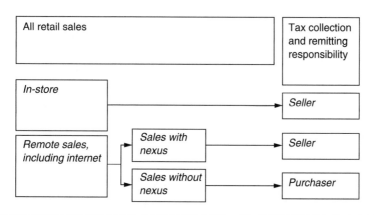

Figure 7.1   Responsibility for sales and use tax collection and remittance.

should apply equally to all sales to consumers; (3) taxes should apply equally to sales made by local merchants and remote vendors; and (4) taxation should be as simple as possible, consistent with other objectives of sound tax policy (McLure, 2002b).

The existing literature demonstrates that the sales tax of the 20th century should be brought into the 21st century, especially because of the increased importance of remote sales. The issue of collecting use taxes is an even more critical concern for states with the narrowing of the sales tax base.

7.4   Narrowing of the Sales Tax Base

Not all states rely to the same extent on the sales tax and not all states have structured their sales taxes to apply to the same transactions (Mikesell, 2001). States make considerably different choices as to what transactions will be taxed, what will be exempt, and in what manner their taxes will be collected. Variations appear in: (1) the extent to which services are in the tax base; (2) the exemption of household purchases of certain goods such as groceries; (3) utilities; (4) taxability of purchases and sales by charitable organizations; and (5) exclusion of purchases of business inputs.

A good gauge of the coverage is the ratio of the estimated sales tax base to state personal income as demonstrated in Table 7.1. States with broad coverage will have a greater ratio than states with narrow coverage. In some states, local governments administer their own taxes, creating a second administrative layer for vendors to deal with as they comply with the tax. In addition, some states do not require their local governments to levy a sales tax using the same base as the state. That creates another order of complexity for vendors.

For the average sales-taxing state, the tax base equaled 51.4 percent of a state's personal income in 1979, but has fallen to 42 percent in 2000 (Bruce and Fox, 2001b). The narrowing of sales tax bases is attributed to three major factors. The first is the expansion in recent years of remote sales, including e-commerce, cataloging and telephone sales, and cross-state shopping. The second factor is the shift in consumption patterns towards greater consumption of services and less consumption of goods. Third, continued legislative exemptions have narrowed the base in essentially every state. States have responded to the narrowing tax bases by raising tax rates. The median state sales tax rate increased from 3.25 percent in 1970 to 4 percent in 1980 to 5 percent in 1990 (Bruce and Fox, 2001b). In 2003 the state average rate was 5.3 percent.

In 1998 the implicit sales tax base to personal income demonstrated that states with the broadest coverage — Hawaii, New Mexico, Wyoming, South Dakota, and Oklahoma — were taxed on average 80.4 percent of

Table 7.1   Sales Tax Base as a Percentage of Personal Income

State	1996	2011
Alabama	39.9	35.8
Arizona	47.8	42.7
Arkansas	64.9	58.5
California	39.6	35.4
Colorado	45.1	40.7
Connecticut	36.7	32.8
Florida	55.4	49.3
Georgia	56.7	50.6
Hawaii	109.2	96.7
Idaho	51.3	46.2
Illinois	32.2	29.1
Indiana	44.3	39.9
Iowa	46.4	42.4
Kansas	48.7	44
Kentucky	46.5	41.9
Louisiana	64.7	58.9
Maine	42.3	37.7
Maryland	35.8	31.9
Massachusetts	29	26
Michigan	47.8	43.1
Minnesota	46.6	41.9
Mississippi	55.5	50.1
Missouri	48.1	43.3
Nebraska	43.1	39
Nevada	58.4	52
New Jersey	29.1	26
New Mexico	86.2	77.4
New York	34.4	30.8
North Carolina	45.8	40.9
North Dakota	51.9	47.6
Ohio	38.8	35
Oklahoma	67.2	61.4
Pennsylvania	32.2	29
Rhode Island	27.6	24.7
South Carolina	52.6	47
South Dakota	65.9	59.5
Tennessee	51	45.6
Texas	48.7	43.9
Utah	61.8	55.6
Vermont	41.6	37.1
Virginia	42.8	38.1
Washington	49.9	44.6
West Virginia	48	43.7
Wisconsin	45.5	41
Wyoming	71.5	65.9
Average	**49.5**	**44.5**

Source: Bruce and Fox (2001b).

state personal income. In contrast, those with the narrowest coverage — Rhode Island, New Jersey, Massachusetts, Illinois, and Pennsylvania — were taxed an average of 30.1 percent of personal income (Mikesell, 2000). Since the tax base the state chooses reflects political will, it is apparent that trying to reach a single uniform base would be extremely difficult.

The following section discusses the arguments in favor and opposed to the sales tax. This information is important to know in order to appreciate the policy issues surrounding taxing electronic commerce.

7.5 Arguments in Favor and Opposed to the Sales Tax

Some of the most pressing issues in sales tax debate are presented by Brunori (2001) in his book entitled *State Tax Policy*. This author observes that the federal government has relied predominately on income taxes, states have relied most heavily on consumption taxes such as sales taxes, and local governments have counted on real property taxes to fund public services. In 1998, for the first time, the personal income tax surpassed the sales tax as the leading source of revenue for the states. In 1998 the personal income tax accounted for almost 34 percent of state tax revenue, while the sales tax accounted for just below 33 percent. Public finance scholars generally believe that personal income tax revenue will continue to grow as a percentage of state tax revenue, while sales tax revenue will continue to decline, which is especially important given the growth in electronic commerce (Mikesell, 2001; Bruce and Fox, 2001b; Brunori, 2001).

There are several reasons the sales tax is a reliable and stable source of revenue for state governments. First, thanks to wide public acceptance because of its established place, the sales tax complies with two notions thought to be necessary for a sound tax system: stability and predictability. Second, with low rates and many exemptions the tax burden is less noticeable than the income tax to consumers because it is spread out over many purchases. Third, consumers in virtually all states pay the sales tax at the time of purchase, making for ease of administration and compliance. However, compliance with the sales tax law is more costly for vendors than for consumers. The vendor must determine the amount of tax owned, collect the tax, keep records of the transactions, file returns, and make payments to the state. Fourth, the sales tax falls under the benefits received principle of taxation that is generally accepted by the public. The sales tax assigns costs according to the spending of the individual. The level of consumption is a barometer for measuring the benefits received by the consumer. Finally, sales taxes are transparent; both liability and burden of payment are usually clear (Brunori, 2001).

Brunori (2001) argues that some of the problems with the sales tax are first that the tax base is riddled with exemptions. Excessive exemptions force the state either to raise the sales tax rates or to forego revenue. Widespread exemptions have the consequence of higher rates on products and services subject to the tax. Second, there is the issue of complexity. Multiple exemptions can also create confusion. Few individuals know exactly what products and services are or are not subject to tax. Therefore, the benefits of transparency are essentially lost with the sales tax. Third, taxing remote sales can be a real problem. By failing to tax remote sales the states create horizontal inequities between traditional in-store purchases and transactions conducted by mail order or the Internet. Fourth, there is the issue of the sales tax being an unfair levy: since the sales tax is regressive, poorer citizens spend a greater share of their incomes on taxable purchases and thus pay a far larger percentage of their income in sales tax than do middle or higher income individuals. Fifth, there is the exclusion of services in today's economy: this results in considerable revenue loss for states. Since 1979, services have risen from 47.4 percent to 57.5 percent of personal consumption. Taxing services will likely make the sales tax less regressive. Wealthier people tend to spend a greater percentage of their income on services. Unlike products, many services do not leave a record of production and inventory, making tracking the quantity and value of services a daunting task. This becomes especially problematic with electronic commerce.

The primary objection of the sales tax has been the argument that the taxes are regressive, taking a larger share of the incomes of lower-income groups than of those with higher incomes. Empirical evidence consistently shows regressivity with the sales tax. Second, the sales tax can be an interstate problem. States lack adequate power to require out of state vendors to collect and remit sales tax and, except for a few registered items such as motor vehicles, it is not possible to collect from the consumer. Third, the sales tax is a source of nuisance and cost to firms selling at retail, particularly when a tax is introduced or significantly changed. Compliance costs of taxes due are estimated in the range of two percent to over four percent of total sales tax collected. Finally, in recent years resistance to sales taxes and a rate increase has been aggravated by the antitax attitude (Due and Mikesell, 1994).

Some scholars propose abolishing the sales tax in favor of an income tax. Beginning in 1997, state and local governments, concerned that consumer migration to the Internet would drastically reduce their available tax base, began pressuring lawmakers to introduce Internet tax legislation (Wiseman, 2000). One possibility would be to eliminate state and local sales taxes altogether in favor of a revenue-equivalent increase in income tax or the establishment of a consumption tax. Although the idea of abolishing sales taxes might seem implausible, recent political developments lend support to the argument. For instance, two bills were introduced into the Virginia legislature in 2000 aimed at abolishing the state's 4.5 percent sales tax. Those in favor of the legislation felt that it was an appropriate way to level the playing field between traditional merchants and online firms. It was thought at that time the lost revenues from sales tax would be more than recouped from the boom in the state's income tax revenue (Wiseman, 2000). However, the economic downturn in early 2000 makes this argument less appealing.

There also is the issue of nexus (or the physical presence of a vendor) to determine if he/she must collect a use tax and this important issue is discussed in the following section.

7.6 The Nexus Issue

As mail-order businesses have expanded, states have sought ways to maintain their revenue base in the face of a growing volume of out-of-jurisdiction purchases. States have tested their authority to require remote sellers to collect the use tax applicable in the customer's state. However, the Supreme Court invalidated those statutes as unconstitutional constraints on interstate commerce in cases in which the remote sellers had an insufficient connection to the taxing states.

For instance, in 1967, in *National Bellas Hess, Incorporated, v. Department of Revenue for the State of Illinois* (1967), the Court struck down an Illinois statute that required remote sellers to collect use taxes on their sales to Illinois customers. National Bellas Hess was a Missouri mail-order business whose only connection with customers in the state of Illinois was through the U.S. Postal Service (a common carrier). The Court held that, under the Constitution's commerce and due process clauses, the firm lacked the requisite physical presence in Illinois or "nexus" with the state either to justify the burden that the statute imposed on interstate commerce. The Court used the firm's costs for complying with such statutes to illustrate the burden that the Illinois statute imposed on interstate commerce. It concluded that if the Illinois statute was upheld, the decision could potentially subject National Bellas Hess's interstate business to the tax rates, exemptions, and record keeping requirements of every potential jurisdiction in the U.S. According to the Court, this would entangle National's interstate business to an unfair burden.

In a more recent case, the Court provided its view of where resolution of the issue of remote sales taxation might be pursued. In *Quill Corporation v. North Dakota* (1992). The Court was again faced with a state statute that required remote sellers to collect use taxes on their sales to out-of-state customers. The Quill Corporation, a Delaware-based remote seller, was connected to customers in North Dakota only by the mail. The Court found that Quill's "minimum contacts" with the state satisfied the requirements of due process but that the firm nevertheless lacked a "substantial nexus" with the state as required under the commerce clause. The Court therefore upheld the standard it had expressed in *National Bellas Hess* and concluded that Quill lacked the requisite physical presence in North Dakota to justify the burden that the state statute imposed on interstate commerce. The Court, however, noted that the underlying issue of taxing remote sales was not only one that Congress might be better qualified to resolve, but also one that Congress had the ultimate power under the Constitution to resolve.

As determined by court decisions, whether a remote retailer is legally required to collect a sales tax depends on whether the retailer has substantial presence or nexus with the taxing jurisdiction. As defined by case law, remote sellers generally meet the nexus standard if they have an office or other place of business, property, or agent in the taxing state. Remote sellers, including Internet sellers that have nexus with a taxing state, are responsible for collecting the use tax from purchasers at the time of sale and remitting the tax to the taxing jurisdiction. Remote sellers with nexus have the same tax collection and remittance responsibilities for in-store, Internet, and remote sellers.

Based on case law interpreting the constitutional requirements, out of state remote sellers generally meet the nexus standards if they have an office or place of business, agent, or property in the taxing state. Nexus is not established if the seller's property is insignificant. The Supreme Court has ruled that contact with in-state purchases by mail or common carrier only does not constitute nexus. Although a business can establish dual entity operations to minimize tax liabilities, the extent to which Internet and in-store operations may interact and retain their distinction has not been resolved.

Court decisions interpreting the provisions of the commerce and due process clauses of the Constitution prevent the states from requiring a remote seller without nexus to collect the use tax. If the remote seller does not collect a use tax, then purchasers are responsible for paying the tax to the taxing state where they use, consume, or store the purchased goods or services.

For example, nexus can be applied if a buyer in New Jersey purchases a pair of shoes from Macy's Website. In this case, Macy's are required to collect sales tax from the buyer because Macy's have a store in New Jersey. Macy's have nexus with New Jersey (Yang and Poon, 2001). If, however, this buyer purchases a pair of shoes from the Website of Saks Fifth Avenue, this store is not required to collect sales tax from the buyer because it does not have a store in New Jersey. Saks Fifth

Avenue has no nexus with New Jersey. Instead, the buyer must remit use tax to New Jersey.

Physical presence rules were further clarified through the *Internet Tax Freedom Act* (ITFA) of 1998. Since nexus (or physical presence) is the key to the taxation of Internet commerce, ITFA required the Advisory Commission on Electronic Commerce (ACEC) to recommend solutions to the nexus problem (Yang and Poon, 2001). The ACEC provided some detailed guidelines about the requirements for nexus. The guidelines clarify that the following factors would not in and of themselves establish a seller's physical presence in a state for purposes of determining whether a seller has sufficient nexus with that state to impose collection obligations:

- a seller's use of an Internet service provider that has physical presence in a state;
- the placement of a seller's digital data on a server located in that particular state;
- a seller's use of telecommunication's service provided by a telecommunication's provider that has physical presence in that state;
- a seller's ownership of intangible property that is used or is present in that state;
- the presence of a seller's customers in a state;
- a seller's affiliation with another taxpayer that has physical presence in that state;
- the performance of repair or warranty services with respect to property sold by a seller that does not otherwise have physical presence in that state;
- a contractual relationship between a seller and another party located within that state that permits goods or products purchased through the seller's Website or catalog to be returned to the other party's physical location within that state; and
- the advertisement of a seller's business location, telephone number, and Website address.

As a result of these clarifications, the Internet merchant is not required to collect sales tax from the buyer even if the Internet seller resides in the same state as the buyer, unless the Internet merchant has a physical store in that state. Furthermore, if the Internet merchant employs another company to handle returns of merchandise or warranties, this arrangement cannot be used to establish state of residency (Yang and Poon, 2001).

The question for public policy: Is the nexus standard still relevant in the 21st century? The traditional nexus principles are based upon concepts of territoriality and the physical presence of the taxpayer in the state. However, such an approach makes little sense with the Internet. The characteristic of the Internet is the irrelevance of geographical borders. The location of tangible and intangible contacts often bear little resemblance to the location of the essential economic activity that electronic commerce comprises (Hellerstein, 1998).

The following section outlines the major arguments for taxing electronic commerce.

7.7   Arguments for Taxing Electronic Commerce

Some of the arguments for taxing e-commerce are also outlined by Fox and Murray (1997). They argue that the key goal in sales tax policy must be to tax all consumption at the same level, and to tax functionally equivalent activities in similar ways. The argument that electronic commerce should remain untaxed because it is a developing industry is a re-statement of the "infant industry" argument that has been rejected by economists. What is happening is that the sales tax would remain the levy on tangible goods as it has traditionally been, and the tax base as a share of consumption will slowly decline with growth in electronic commerce. Horizontal equity and neutrality will be further compromised and the ways that businesses operate will be significantly distorted. Finally, exclusion of electronic commerce from the base distorts interstate commerce, since this offers the opportunity to make transactions that are untaxed when offered in one electronic form and taxed in another physical form.

Some of the arguments for taxing electronic commerce are based on equity, economic neutrality, revenue (or lower tax rates), and simplicity of compliance and administration. There are several strands of equity argument for taxing e-commerce. It is unfair to exempt remote sellers, including those involved in e-commerce, from the duty to collect a tax that local merchants must collect. In addition, it is unfair to exempt e-commerce purchase, which are made disproportionately by the relatively affluent, while taxing purchases from local vendors, made disproportionately by the less affluent. Two aspects of the additional distortions that would be created by exempting all e-commerce are, first, many products can be delivered in either tangible or an intangible digitalized form. Exempting the intangible products would tilt choices toward that form of delivery. Furthermore, exempting sales made by remote vendors would aggravate distortions of location decisions. Given the complexity of the present system, the simplicity of compliance and administration is often cited as an advantage of taxing e-commerce (McClure, 2002a).

McLure (2002b) argues that the existing state sales taxes violate all the principles of economic neutrality and are extremely complex. First, the taxes do not apply to all consumption; most services are exempt, as are a variety of tangible products (with the exemptions varying from state to state). Second, the taxes apply to a wide range of sales to business. It has been estimated that, depending on the state, as much as 20 to 70 percent of taxable sales are not made to consumers. Third, there is essentially no uniformity in any aspect of state sales taxes. Fourth, there are thousands of local jurisdictions who levy sales taxes, not all of which conform to the tax base or other provisions of the state tax of the state where they are located. Moreover, some states administer their own taxes. States generally provide few vendor discounts to offset compliance costs, especially true for small vendors. Because of this complexity, a state cannot compel a vendor to collect its use tax unless the vendor has physical presence in the taxing state (McLure, 2002b).

There is also the issue of the tax wedge which may affect location decisions of businesses that face paying use taxes (Bruce et al., 2003). The tax wedge between local and remote purchases occurs when citizens can buy locally and pay sales tax, or they can buy remotely and more often than not avoid paying sales or use tax on the purchase. The tax differential can amount to a discount of up to 10 percent. Sales taxes encourage firms to locate back office facilities in small population states or even outside the United States to limit the number of people for whom they must collect and remit sales and use taxes. For example, Amazon.com has admitted that one of the reasons for its location in Washington is to limit the percentage of sales on which it must collect taxes. Even in cases where the cost savings from locating warehouses and other production facilities nearer population areas overcome tax considerations. The facilities can be situated in the smallest population state near large population centers.

The predictions of tax losses from electronic commerce may be over exaggerated since, only a few years ago, state and local government officials were warning that their tax base would diminish because of e-commerce. These fears have not been realized because: (1) remote sales to business represent a large fraction of e-commerce — some of these are exempt, and tax on much of the remaining can be collected directly from the buyer; (2) some e-commerce transactions would not be taxable in any event, because products are exempt (e.g., food in many states and services in most); and (3) some e-commerce sales represent a shift from traditional remote transactions that would effectively go untaxed because of the physical-presence rule.

There are also various arguments against taxing e-commerce, which are mentioned in the following section.

7.8 Arguments Against Taxing Electronic Commerce

Some of the arguments against taxing electronic commerce are outlined by McClure (2002a). As mentioned previously, e-commerce might be characterized as an "infant industry," therefore it should experience a period of tax exemption in order to allow it to become established. The second argument is that of the digital divide. Internet access in particular should be tax exempt in order to avoid burdening low-income families. Internet access for their children may represent an important way out of poverty. Third, advocates of exempting e-commerce make the argument that remote vendors should not be required to collect tax because they do not benefit from services provided by the states where their customers are located. Fourth, some cite the threat of competition from foreign vendors as a reason to exempt electronic commerce. Fifth, another argument against taxing e-commerce is holding Main Street merchants hostage in order to gain lower taxes. The reasoning is that, if e-commerce is not taxed, representatives from Main Street will pressure state governments to lower taxes, so that they will not be at such a great a competitive disadvantage (McClure, 2002a).

According to Goolsbee and Zittrain (1999), there are several costs associated with the taxing of e-commerce. First, because of the limited size relative to Main Street retail and because of the type of products being purchased, aggressive enforcement of taxes on Internet commerce would raise only a small amount of revenue over the next several years. Second, Internet commerce does not seem to be primarily fueled by diversion from retail sales tax because there is also business-to-business electronic commerce as well to consider. Third, not enforcing taxes on the Internet does disproportionately benefit higher income and highly educated people, but this effect has lessened substantially with over 60 percent of the US population having Internet access. Fourth, there is evidence of short-term spillovers and information problems that should be considered costs of applying taxes. Goolsbee and Zittrain (1999) believe that, given that the costs of maintaining the status quo are small and the benefits of nurturing the Internet seem to be somewhat concentrated in the short run, a natural compromise position might be a moratorium on enforcement of Internet sales taxes in the short run followed by equal treatment once conditions change in the near future.

Another important argument against taxing e-commerce is the question of fiscal autonomy. Granting authority to collect use taxes on remote sales in exchange for simplifying sales tax regimes would limit states that have sales taxes in tailoring their tax to their citizens' preferences. For example, a consumer might choose to purchase books over the Internet for

$100 inclusive of the shipping cost, pay no sales tax, and fail to comply with the use tax rather than purchase the same books at a local bookstore for $102 inclusive of a local $5 sales tax. The real resource cost of the books (including profit) purchased from the Internet seller is $100. That is the market values of the resources that are used to produce and deliver those books at $100. The real resource cost of the same book (including profit) available for sale from the local bookstore is $97; the portion of the book's cost that is sales tax ($5) is a transfer from the consumer to the government and uses no resources. Therefore, the tax differential that results from the consumer's noncompliance with the use tax causes this consumer to make a choice that increases the production cost of books by $3. That money represents a loss of economic welfare to society because those $3 worth of resources could have been used to produce $3 worth of other goods or services.

Empirical studies have shown that retail prices rise when a sales tax is imposed (CBO, 2003). Research also indicates that differences in sales tax rates along state borders cause consumers to switch their purchases from the higher tax to the lower tax jurisdiction. Some evidence even suggests that taxing tangible goods but not services may have contributed to growth in the consumption of services relative to goods.

Destination-based taxes imposes tax on the basis of the location or destination of the purchased item. In this tax system, if the purchaser resides in the state, the tax is incurred. By contrast, in the origin-based system, the tax is levied at the source or origin of the item being sold. Therefore, if the seller is in the state, the tax is incurred. Thus, under an origin-based sales and use tax system, the difficulty of collecting taxes on remote sales does not arise because remote sales are not taxable. A jurisdiction would lose the revenue from remote sales to its residents but gain the revenue from sales by its merchants to out of state buyers. As a result, implementing an origin-based system could increase interstate tax competition. Lower-tax states would have some advantage in attracting retailers who marketed their goods and services in other, higher taxed states (CBO, 2003).

The rationale for destination taxes is to develop a tax that is levied on consumption rather than on production and to avoid the economic efficiency losses and tax avoidance possibilities associated with origin-based taxes (Fox, 1998). A significant advantage of destination taxes is that they limit tax competition between states because the tax burden is identical regardless of where goods or services are produced. Therefore, firms are not advantaged by producing in low sales tax jurisdictions.

Fox (1998) believes that the argument of the nexus standard for the future must be based on an economic exploitation concept, which means that nexus should be defined to exist whenever a firm exploits a state's market. The basic argument is straightforward. The state that provides the final market for a product is the appropriate site for a destination-based tax, regardless of how the sale is completed (Fox, 1998).

There are also those economists who suggest that e-commerce is an example of networked externalities. Opponents have argued that effectively exempting Internet purchases from sales taxes is a means of inducing more people to use the Internet to stimulate the growth of e-commerce (CBO, 2003). The growth of Internet use is desirable because the Internet exhibits network externalities, implying a person's joining the network benefits not only himself or herself but also other participants. This is accomplished by adding to the total number of participants in the network. Too few people use the Internet when those external benefits are not reflected in the price of access to it. Providing a subsidy would thus increase use of the Internet and benefit society. However, it is difficult to justify incentives for a network such as the Internet, which is used by over half of the US population.

There are also many estimates of the potential loss from e-commerce, which are mentioned in the following section.

7.9 Estimated Economic Losses from not Taxing Electronic Commerce

Cline and Neubig (1999) found revenue losses in 1998 from the failure to tax electronic commerce to be only one-tenth of one percent of total sales tax revenue. Goolsbee and Zittrain (1999) estimated that revenue losses in 1998 were less than one-quarter of one percent of sales tax revenue and that in 2003 losses would be less than two percent of total sales tax revenue. Bruce and Fox (2001b) estimated losses in 2003 to be about 1.5 percent of total state and local tax revenue. The GAO (2000) estimated that revenue losses for 2000 would be less than two percent of total sales tax revenue.

The most significant ongoing effort to quantify the economic losses from e-commerce has been provided by Bruce and Fox (2001a, 2001b). They believe e-commerce is likely to cause total state and local government revenue loss of $13.3 billion. They estimate that by 2006 the loss will be more than triple to $45.2 billion and in 2011 the loss will be $54.8 billion (Table 7.2). Part of the loss would have occurred anyway even without e-commerce on sales, for example, which might have otherwise been made by purchasers using the telephone and catalog sales. In 2011 states will lose anywhere from 2.6 percent to 9.92 percent of their total state tax collections to e-commerce losses. In 2011 rates will have to rise between 0.83 to 1.72 percentage points to replace the total electronic commerce losses (Bruce and Fox, 2001b).

Table 7.2   Projected State and Local Revenue Losses from E-Commerce Activity (Millions of Dollars)

State	2001	2006	2011
Alabama	$177.40	$604.30	$734.40
Arkansas	$143.80	$488.00	$590.90
Arizona	$231.10	$799.20	$982.50
California	$1,750.00	$5,952.00	$7,225.00
Colorado	$200.70	$686.40	$836.20
Connecticut	$190.50	$648.90	$788.20
Florida	$932.20	$3,214.00	$3,944.40
Georgia	$439.00	$1,517.80	$1,865.60
Hawaii	$105.10	$359.20	$438.30
Iowa	$111.80	$372.30	$443.70
Idaho	$44.40	$151.50	$184.60
Illinois	$532.90	$1,795.30	$2,161.70
Indiana	$215.50	$728.50	$879.80
Kansas	$134.40	$451.50	$542.20
Kentucky	$158.70	$535.50	$645.80
Louisiana	$302.60	$1,008.10	$1,202.50
Massachusetts	$200.60	$683.00	$828.60
Maryland	$194.40	$664.30	$809.20
Maine	$43.10	$146.40	$177.50
Michigan	$502.90	$1,696.20	$2,043.60
Minnesota	$270.60	$920.60	$1,117.20
Missouri	$261.60	$884.10	$1,066.70
Mississippi	$136.50	$462.80	$560.00
North Carolina	$293.40	$1,010.90	$1,239.40
North Dakota	$26.40	$87.60	$103.90
Nebraska	$70.90	$238.70	$287.30
New Jersey	$337.80	$1,150.00	$1,396.10
New Mexico	$129.10	$440.20	$535.40
Nevada	$126.30	$441.70	$549.00
New York	$1,052.90	$3,569.20	$4,318.40
Ohio	$446.70	$1,502.20	$1,805.90
Oklahoma	$202.80	$670.60	$794.50
Pennsylvania	$446.40	$1,503.40	$1,811.00
Rhode Island	$36.80	$124.50	$150.40
South Carolina	$153.40	$525.00	$640.50
South Dakota	$39.40	$133.40	$161.30
Tennessee	$362.30	$1,242.80	$1,518.70
Texas	$1,162.10	$3,957.00	$4,805.60
Utah	$104.50	$359.00	$439.20
Virginia	$238.50	$817.00	$997.20
Vermont	$21.00	$71.70	$87.20
Washington	$416.50	$1,427.30	$1,745.30
Wisconsin	$213.50	$721.50	$871.00
West Virginia	$70.10	$232.40	$276.20
Wyoming	$26.10	$85.20	$100.00
Total	**$13,293.10**	**$45,204.30**	**$54,849.50**

Source: Bruce and Fox (2001b).

A recent estimate by the Congressional Budget Office (2003) indicates that estimates of uncollected use taxes from all remote sales in 2003 range from $2.5 billion to $20.4 billion. Projections for 2011 of uncollected taxes from Internet commerce also vary widely, ranging from $4.5 billion to $54.8 billion.

Evidence suggests that the cost of complying with that multiplicity of tax systems, particularly for smaller firms, will exceed compliance costs for local sellers dealing with a single sales tax system. In addition, requiring remote sellers to collect and remit use taxes would have unclear effects on social costs: distortions would probably be reduced, but compliance costs would probably rise. The decision by policy makers to either grant or withhold from states the authority to collect use taxes on remote sales involves a trade-off between those two costs.

In terms of the revenue at stake an estimated 80 percent of sales in electronic commerce are from one business to another; many of these transactions are explicitly exempt, and use tax is currently being collected on the remainder. Second, a substantial share of electronic commerce to households involves services, intangibles, or goods that are not subject to sales and use taxes. Finally, some electronic commerce involves sales to households diverted from other remote vendors that lack a duty to collect use tax. In short, failure to tax electronic commerce may not be as critical because a substantial amount of revenue comes from sales to businesses, which would be taxed and most services would not be taxed. For example, suppose that households in New York order furniture from stores in New Jersey and vice versa for delivery by common carrier on "big ticket" items, the savings from evading the tax would be significant. Both states would be deprived of the revenue they would receive if the sales were made by local merchants. Therefore, there would be a lot of unproductive cross hauling across states (McLure, 2000).

A critical issue that has potentially important consequences for state and local revenues concerns the propensity for tangible goods to be converted into digitalized goods. In some states, sales of certain tangible property are taxable but sales of digital counterpart are not. The revenue loss estimates are overstated to the extent that this shift reduces the tax base, but most states could be expected to react quickly to such base erosion and redefine the base to include many digitalized sales. State and local governments will be confronted with several choices in the face of these revenue losses: they must either cut expenditures, increase existing sales tax rates, or shift to another tax source, such as the income tax (Bruce and Fox, 2001).

Controlling for a variety of conventional demographic characteristics such as income, education, and age, Goolsbee (2000) found that the probability of buying something online grows as the local sales tax rate rises. This author found that the coefficient on local tax rate is positive and significant, which implies that the higher the local sales tax rate, the greater the amount of money the average consumer spends online. Applying existing tax rates to the Internet, Goolsbee concluded that this would reduce the number of buyers online from 20 to 25 percent and reduce total sales from 25 to 30 percent. Furthermore, when controlling for demographic similarities across generations, his results suggest that, as consumers become more aware of the tax code, they become more experienced with the Internet and hence become more sensitive to local sales taxes in their purchase decisions. There seems to be a tax sensitivity on the part of consumers that could have a negative impact on electronic commerce were sales taxes to be instituted.

Several important reforms have impacted the future of taxing e-commerce. These reforms are discussed in the following section.

7.10   Internet Tax Freedom Act

The history of taxing electronic commerce in the United States can be traced back to the Clinton proposal in July 1997 in a report entitled "A Framework for Global Electronic Commerce." It articulated the administration's view that governments should adopt a non-regulatory market oriented approach to policy development of electronic commerce.

The Clinton proposal set forth five principles for facilitating the growth of commerce on the Internet: (1) the private sector should lead; (2) governments should avoid undue restrictions on electronic commerce; (3) where governmental involvement is needed, its aim should be to support and enforce a predictable, minimalist, consistent and simple legal environment for commerce; (4) governments should recognize the unique qualities of the Internet; and (5) electronic commerce over the Internet should be facilitated on an international basis (Horn, 2003). This Clinton proposal set the tone for the passage of the *Internet Tax Freedom Act*.

Following the Clinton proposal was the *Internet Tax Freedom Act* of 1998. This act was concerned with the negative effect of taxation by local governments on the growth in online sales. Therefore, the US Congress, with Clinton Administration backing and the support of Senator John McCain, attempted to make the Internet a tax free zone. This legislation established a three year moratorium on the state and local taxation of Internet access and multiple or discriminatory taxes on electronic commerce. The ITFA major provisions were: (1) a ban until October 1, 2001 (and extended until 2003) on any new taxes on Internet commerce or access charges; (2) grandfathering of existing taxes; and (3) creation of an Advisory Commission on Electronic Commerce.

7.11   Advisory Commission on Electronic Commerce

The Advisory Commission on Electronic Commerce (ACEC) assembled pursuant to the ITFA and consisted of three members from the federal government, eight from state and local governments, and eight from the electronic commerce industry. It is not a surprise that the ACEC, comprised of members with vastly different perspectives, was unable to attain supermajority approval of any proposed plan to submit to Congress as an official recommendation. As a result of the commissioners not being able to attain a supermajority vote, the final proposal concerning sales and use taxes submitted to Congress was not an official recommendation. However, simple majority approval was attained on one proposal and that proposal was submitted to Congress.

The majority proposal of the ACEC contains three basic suggestions that are relevant: (1) extend the moratorium that bars multiple and discriminatory taxation of e-commerce; (2) clarify that certain factors will not, considered alone, provide a sufficient nexus for the purposes of sales collection under the *Quill* decision; and (3) encourage state and local governments to create a simplified version of the sales and use tax (Brown, 2001).

The Streamlined Sales Tax Project, which began in early 2000, is a reform with a goal of simplifying the sales tax system in order for states to override the nexus rules of the *Quill* decision. This reform will be discussed in detail since it frames the current debate on taxing Internet sales.

7.12   Streamlined Sales Tax Project

McLure (2002a) argues that in response to the projected growth of e-commerce most of the states are participating in the Streamlining Sales Tax Project (SSTP). This project is intended to simplify and modernize sales and use tax collection and administration. State and local governments favor a legislative proposal that would in effect override *Quill* for states that adopt the recommendations of the SSTP.

Several states are engaged in the SSTP to simplify their sales and use tax system in order to reduce the burden of collection for all sellers and create a collection system for remote sellers. One hope among SSTP proponents is that a simplified system will result in remote vendors voluntarily collecting the sales tax. Cornia et al. (2004) conducted a quantitative analysis suggesting that voluntary compliance under certain conditions may occur with some frequency.

The SSTPs main goal is to provide a sales and use tax system that has the following characteristics: (1) neutrality — taxability should be independent of the method of commerce used in a transaction; (2) efficiency — administrative costs should be minimized for both business and government; (3) certainty and simplicity — tax rules should be clear and simple; (4) effectiveness and fairness — taxation system should minimize the possibility of evasion; and (5) flexibility — taxation systems should keep pace with changes in the economy (Horn, 2003).

The SSTP envisages that each sales tax state would adopt the model "Uniform Sales and Use Tax Administration Act." The Uniform Act would authorize the taxing authority of the state to enter into the *Streamlined Sales and Use Tax Agreement* with one or more states to simplify and modernize sales and use tax administration in order to substantially reduce the burden of tax compliance for all sellers and for all types of commerce. The Agreement contains all the details of simplification and uniformity and would constitute a "contract" between signatory states regarding what standards must be attained and how the states will act in unison with one another. By 2003, 20 states had adopted the *Streamlined Sales Tax Agreement.*

An important feature of simplification would be the establishment of standards for certified service providers and certified automated systems, and establishment of performance standards for multi-state sellers (McClure, 2002a). This would allow for an information technology solution for many of the problems of complexity in the sales tax system. There would be modern information technology used to further simplify compliance and a proposal that states provide monetary incentives intended to encourage adoption of such technology and voluntary registration of vendors who do not have a duty to collect use tax.

Certified automated system software is at the heart of the technology based solution to the sales and use tax problem. This system would calculate the tax imposed by each jurisdiction, determine the tax to remit to the appropriate state, and maintain a record of the transaction. It would incorporate "look-up" tables mapping addresses to the taxing jurisdictions, indicating the tax treatment of each defined product in each state and the tax rate to be applied to taxable transactions in each jurisdiction. In addition, it would calculate the amount of tax due, attribute it to the proper jurisdiction, and prepare the documents necessary for compliance (McClure, 2002a).

Another mechanism of the SSTP is the creation of Trusted Third Parties (TTP) to collect the use tax for vendors (Mikesell, 2000). Participating states and local governments would pay a TTP to handle compliance for all participating vendors. Participating vendors would then transmit necessary customer order information to the TTP. The TTP would do the appropriate sales or use tax calculations for that order. The TTP would arrange with the appropriate credit card company to add the appropriate tax to the bill.

The TTP would arrange that remittance went to the proper government or governments. The problem with this solution is that there is no inducement for participation even if the state paid for the TTP compliance costs. Mikesell (2000) asks, why would a remote vendor with no physical presence participate in the system?

There are some problems identified in the implementation of the SSTP. Cornia et al. (2001) argue that a recent examination of in-state vendors' costs associated with collecting and remitting the retail sales tax confirms that the costs to businesses are significant. A subsequent study reports that the compliance costs of sales tax collection for multistate firms are much higher than they are for firms operating in a single state.

In the current environment, adoption of a single rate would generally be difficult (Cornia et al., 2001). There are essentially three reasons for this conclusion. First, the loss of local fiscal autonomy would be a difficult obstacle for many states. In states like New York, Colorado, Pennsylvania, California, and Alabama, local governments have significant control over setting the tax rate. In many states, property tax limitations have reduced or eliminated local fiscal control over the property tax rate. Therefore, in these states adoption of a uniform sales tax rate would require state government to play a much greater role in financing local governments. Second, it is likely that the only politically acceptable approach to instituting a uniform sales tax rate is for the rate to be revenue neutral. These constraints mean that a uniform rate is not feasible in most states. Programs that transfer sales tax revenue from current low-rate jurisdictions to current high-rate jurisdictions will be opposed by localities that are unwilling to share the windfall from higher rates with other jurisdictions in the state. Third, there are complexities to local sales taxes beyond those associated with rates. Many local sales taxes are earmarked for special districts that have no other source of tax revenue, or for special purposes or needs that are temporary.

There are three major challenges facing the simplification effort. First, states must find ways to simplify and harmonize the administration of 45 separate and distinct sales and use tax systems (Cornia et al., 2004). Second, states will likely need to make concessions with respect to sales and use tax bases. The goal is for everyone to use similar definitions for goods and services, but not necessarily to have uniform tax bases. Finally, states need to find a way to deal with the thousands of different state and local sales and use tax rates that a national business must understand in order to comply.

While there has been considerable success in getting states to agree on what a simplified system should be, there remain serious obstacles that must be overcome if the proposed changes are to be implemented by states (Cornia et al., 2004). Politics, revenue importance, and technology may undermine the simplification process. On the political front, state and local governments often openly compete with each other for new and old business by offering a variety of tax and fiscal incentives, such as general sales tax holidays and industry or firm specific sales tax exemptions. Second, many states and local governments would oppose policy changes that would force them to give up the autonomy. Third, some groups and individuals who have opposed the tax suggested that the compliance technology would be an invasion of privacy.

The benefits to the firm for collecting the tax are difficult to identify. The remote vendor cannot point to better police or fire services provided by the revenues from the collected tax because remote vendors are unlikely to benefit directly from any expenditure. Also, vendors will not be able to identify lower overall tax rates as a result of collecting and remitting the use tax. In addition, it is uncommon for candidates who run for office to propose increased taxes. However, some larger firms would like a simplified tax system. For example, Wal-Mart, Inc. in 2002 had more than 3,300 retail facilities in the United States, including 3,172 outlets in locations that impose a sales tax. With the differences in tax base definitions and potentially 377 different sales tax rates, it seems clear that the cost of compliance is substantial for firms such as Wal-Mart (Cornia et al., 2004).

In principle, the United States Congress, acting under the power granted by the Constitution to regulate interstate commerce, could enact legislation to override the *Quill* decision, substituting a less demanding test for the physical presence test of nexus. This would be difficult because of the political power of the direct marketing industry (McLure, 2000). Essentially, there is no political constituency for such a reform, but substantial opposition to it (McLure, 2002a).

States that attempt to force remote vendors to collect use taxes have not enacted realistic rules that would exempt small remote vendors in the state from collecting the duty. In addition, vendor discounts fall short of costs of compliance for small firms and would be especially inadequate for remote vendors, who would encounter particularly high costs of compliance. The burden of compliance would be much worse for small firms engaged in electronic commerce. Large firms might be able to deal with the multitude of state and local use taxes, small firms would need substantial simplification and could find interstate sales uneconomical if the duty to collect use tax were expanded.

There are also the political concerns when attempting to implement the SSTP. Mikesell (2001) argues that if successful the SSTP would break two centuries of the American federalist tradition and negotiate a simplified unified sales tax structure for use by all states. Although Congress might seek to simplify compliance by specifying a single uniform sales tax structure for all states to use, this approach would violate the American approach to federalism in which states have responsibility for their own revenue systems. Of much greater practical significance, however, is the reality that Congress has absolutely no experience with the design and implementation of general consumption taxation (Mikesell, 2001). Indeed, the US is one of the few countries without a national sales tax.

The following section provides conclusions and recommendations on possibilities for reform to the existing state sales tax system.

7.13   Conclusion and Recommendations

This chapter has presented the debates surrounding the taxing of electronic commerce. State governments have attempted to address this issue through the SSTP, but politically it is very difficult for states to reach uniformity in tax bases given that tax policy is ultimately determined in a political process. There are numerous debates surrounding taxing electronic commerce, such as those arguing for it on equity grounds, and those against it believing the Internet creates a positive externality and should not be taxed. According to Court decisions, the compliance costs for vendors without a physical presence in a state is too burdensome for them to collect use taxes on remote sales. Therefore, states are attempting to move toward simplification of the sales tax system to override the *Quill* decision. However, any attempt to interfere with the fiscal autonomy of state governments is politically very difficult. Information technology could simplify the existing sales tax system, and third party collection agencies, working on behalf of the state, could decrease compliance costs in the future. However, many tax policy scholars have noted that reform is determined in a political process where it is easier to cobble together decisions than propose systematic reform, thus the tendency to create incremental policies that do not address the underlying issue. The idea behind the SSTP seems noble, but the reality is that systematic reform is required.

There are some solutions to the taxing of e-commerce that should be mentioned as recommendations. Litan and Rivlin (2001) argue the most straightforward would be a federal mandate imposed on all merchants to collect use taxes on goods purchased by out-of-state consumers. First, even if the courts found no violation of the due process requirements of the Constitution, such a mandate would impose considerable burden on merchants, unless a software package were available to track the various sales tax regimes in different jurisdictions on a timely basis and forward the tax proceeds to the jurisdiction. If states and localities could be induced or required to harmonize their taxes, the software would be easier to develop, but the burden on merchants for collecting the tax and getting it to the right place could still be formidable. Second, a variation of a federal mandate would be for the federal government to approve one or more interstate compacts, under which like-minded states would agree on a common sales tax regime of the same base and rate. Moreover, the states in the compact could agree to have merchants send the taxes to a central collection authority. This would act as a clearinghouse and the net amount due would be forwarded to each state treasury at the end of each accounting period. Third, another way of solving the mounting problem of lost sales tax proceeds from e-commerce transactions is for state and local governments that now depend on sales tax revenues to substitute other taxes, such as the income taxes for sales taxes. If the decline in the sales tax base accelerates because of a rapid increase in e-commerce sales, some or many jurisdictions may be tempted to act on their own, replacing the revenue with other sources. Fourth, shifting the reliance of state and local governments from sales to income taxation might strengthen the case of those who like to see the federal government reduce its income tax in favor of a national sales tax or value added tax. Since the federal government can tax sales wherever they occur, a federal sales or value added tax would automatically solve the problem of treating e-commerce and other remote sales equally. However, a national sales tax seems unlikely to pass given the general antitax sentiment of the US.

References

Brown, D.T. (2001). No Easy Solutions in the Sales Tax on E-Commerce Debate: Lessons from the Advisory Commission on Electronic Commerce Report to Congress. *Journal of Contemporary Law* 27 (1), 117–131.

Bruce, D., and Fox, W.F. (2001a). E-Commerce and Local Finance: Estimates of Direct and Indirect Sales Tax Losses. *Municipal Finance Journal* 22 (3), 24–47.

Bruce, D., and Fox, W.F. (2001b). *State and Local Sales Tax Revenue Losses from E-Commerce: Updated Estimates.* Knoxville, Tennessee: Center for Business and Economic Research.

Bruce, D., Fox, W.F., and Murray, M. (2003). To Tax or Not to Tax? The Case of Electronic Commerce. *Contemporary Economic Policy* 21 (1), 25–40.

Brunori, D. (2001). *State Tax Policy: A Political Perspective.* Washington, DC: The Urban Institute Press.

Cline, R.J., and Neubig, T.S. (1999). *Masters of Complexity and Bearers of Great Burden: The Sales Tax System and Compliance Costs for Multistate Retailers.* Technical Report, Ernst and Young Economics Consulting and Quantitative Analysis.

Congressional Budget Office. (2003). *Economic Issues in Taxing Internet and Mail-Order Sales*. Washington, DC: Congress of the United States Congressional Budget Office.

Cornia, G., Edmiston, K., Sheffrin, S., Sexton, T., Sjoquist, D., and Zorn, K. 2001. E-Commerce and the Single-Rate Sales Tax Proposal. *Municipal Finance Journal* 22 (3): 1–23.

Cornia, G.C., Sjoquist, D.L., and Walters, L.C. (2004). Sales and Use Tax Simplification and Voluntary Compliance. *Public Budgeting & Finance* 24(1), 1–31.

Due, J.F., and Mikesell, J.L. (1994). *Sales Taxation: State and Local Structure and Administration*. Second Edition. Washington, DC: Urban Institute Press.

Fox, W.F. (1998). Can the State Sales Tax Survive a Future like its Past? In D. Brunori (ed), *The Future of State Taxation*, pp. 33–48. Washington, DC: The Urban Institute Press.

Fox, W.F., and Murray, M. (1997). The Sales Tax and Electronic Commerce: So What's New? *National Tax Journal* 50 (3), 573–592.

General Accounting Office. (2000). *Sales Taxes: Electronic Commerce Growth Presents Challenges; Revenue Losses are Uncertain*. Washington, DC: United States General Accounting Office.

Goolsbee, A. (2000). In a World without Borders: The Impact of Taxes on Internet Commerce. *Quarterly Journal of Economics* 115 (2), 561–576.

Goolsbee, A., and Zittrain, J. (1999). Evaluating the Costs and Benefits of Taxing Internet Commerce. *National Tax Journal* 52 (3), 413–428.

Hellerstein, W. (1998). Electronic Commerce and the Future of State Taxation. In D. Brunori (ed), *The Future of State Taxation*, pp. 207–222. Washington, DC: The Urban Institute Press.

Horn, S.P. (2003). Taxation of E-Commerce. *Journal of American Academy of Business* 2 (2), 329–338.

Litan, R.E., and Rivlin, A.M. (2001). *Beyond the Dot.coms: The Economic Promise of the Internet*. Washington, DC: Brookings Institution Press.

McLure, C.E. (2000). The Taxation of Electronic Commerce: Background and Proposal, In N. Imparato (ed), *Public Policy and the Internet: Privacy, Taxes, and Contract*, pp. 49–113. Stanford: Hoover Institution Press.

McLure, C.E. (2002a). Sales and Use Taxes on Electronic Commerce: Legal, Economic, Administrative, and Political Issues. *The Urban Lawyer* 34 (2), 487–520.

McLure, C.E. (2002b). Thinking Straight About the Taxation of Electronic Commerce: Tax Principles, Compliance Problems, and Nexus. *NBER/Tax Policy & the Economy* 16 (1), 115–140.

Mikesell, J.L. (2000). Remote Vendors and American Sales and Use Taxation: The Balance between Fixing the Problem and Fixing the Tax. *National Tax Journal* 53 (4), 1273–1285.

Mikesell, J.L. (2001). The Threat to State Sales Taxes from E-Commerce: A Review of the Principal Issues. *Municipal Finance Journal* 22 (3), 48–60.

National Bellas Hess, Incorporated, v. Department of Revenue for the State of Illinois (1967), 386 U.S. 753.

Quill Corp. v. North Dakota (1992), 504 U.S. 298.

Wiseman, A.E. (2000). *The Internet Economy: Access, Taxes, and Market Structure*. Washington, DC: The Urban Institute Press.

Yang, J., and Poon, W. (2001). Taxable Base of Internet Commerce. *Municipal Finance Journal* 22 (3), 70–80.

Zorn, C.K. (1999). Taxation of Telecommunications and Electronic Commerce. In W.B. Hildreth and J.A. Richardson (eds), *Handbook of Taxation*, pp. 703–724. New York: Dekker.

Chapter 8

Lessons of Tax Compliance Research for Lawmakers and Tax Administrators: Getting Best Returns from Limited Resources

JOHN L. MIKESELL and LIUCIJA BIRSKYTE
School of Public and Environmental Affairs,
Indiana University, Bloomington

Tax systems in the United States and other industrialized democracies rely heavily on taxpayer active frameworks for the collection of revenue.[1] While the systems do have serious administrative agencies, it is nevertheless the case that the vast majority of tax revenue is received without any direct enforcement action by these authorities. The revenue rules are voluntarily complied with and taxpayers report and pay the tax that they believe they owe. For instance, of the $1,902 billion collected by the Internal Revenue

Service for the United States government in 2001, only $32 billion (1.69 percent) came from direct enforcement actions — audit, delinquency pursuit, forced collections, etc., (*Transactional Records Access Clearinghouse*, 2004a) And taxpayer active taxes — taxes on personal and corporate income, payroll, retail sales, and selective excises — constitute the overwhelming majority of all taxes collected by federal, state, and local governments in the United States — 87.9 percent of the total in fiscal 1999. (*Bureau of the Census, Governments Division*, 2004). The taxes levied on real property by state and local governments represent the most significant tax collected through heavy administrative action relative to taxpayer effort. In large measure, the revenue system relies on voluntary compliance, not direct enforcement, to generate revenue according to the distribution of that revenue that was envisioned in the tax law.

The sections that follow will (i) review what is known about the nature of tax compliance (or non-compliance), (ii) outline what we know about the likely extent of that non-compliance and why it is important to measure that non-compliance, and (iii) identify several important lessons for tax administrators from tax compliance research. Evasion cannot and should not be totally eliminated because the resource cost required would not be worth the gain in benefits from having the extra revenue for public use. But substantial evasion cannot be tolerated because it is necessary to preserve the revenue base, to protect honest taxpayers, and to keep the actual tax burden distribution consistent with what the law intended.

8.1 Why People Pay Taxes

For a nation relying so heavily on voluntary compliance for tax collection, we know substantially less than might be expected about what induces compliance. There are two broad views about what induces taxpayer compliance — (i) the compliance lottery view and (ii) the responsible taxpayer view. They are not mutually exclusive, although they each offer independent insights and suggest different emphases by the tax administration.

The traditional view is that of the compliance lottery. In this view, the taxpayer is seen to be making a rational calculation that weighs the gains from successful non-compliance (the tax obligation that is kept for personal use) against the expected loss for being caught. As the probability of being caught by tax examiners rises, the expected gain from non-compliance falls and as the severity of fines and other consequences from being caught increases, the expected gain from non-compliance falls. By adjusting the audit rate and the penalties, the tax authorities should be able to control tax non-compliance to whatever level it chooses. The authorities can keep the expected loss below the gain for most taxpayers and can maintain the desired level of overall taxpayer compliance. Enforcement strategy builds the desired compliance rate by a mixture of audit rates and severity of penalties.

There is an important problem with this view of taxpayer behavior. In general, compliance in most developed democracies, including the United States, is considerably higher than the traditional view would lead us to expect. Audit rates are extremely low and financial penalties are reasonably modest. In particular, low and falling audit rates seem to have had no meaningful impact on compliance in recent history. IRS audit rates (including service center audits) of business and non-business returns has declined from 1.57 percent in FY 1988 to 0.57 in FY 2002, while the tax gap remains static at about 17 percent since the IRS first gave an estimate of the gap in 1973. (GAO, 1995; *Transactional Records Access Clearinghouse*, 2004b) The gains from non-compliance should be considerable for many taxpayers, yet non-compliance appears to be neither rampant nor dramatically expanding and most people are in substantial compliance with the tax law.[2] People and businesses appear not to be participating in the compliance lottery in the expected fashion. Some forces beyond simple calculation of expected return from non-compliance, as based on audit rates and penalties, must be involved.

The responsible taxpayer model provides an alternative view to the compliance lottery. This conception holds that people will pay their taxes (i) when they are motivated to do so, (ii) when they understand clearly what their taxpaying obligations are, and (iii) when payment of those obligations is made convenient. Rather than inducing rational economic behavior that leads to taxpayer compliance, the responsible taxpayer model implies a softer approach that encourages compliance and makes compliance easier, an approach that relies more heavily on taxpayer education than it does on enforcement actions against taxpayers. This view, although not fully tested, has been significant for the development of many initiatives instituted in the past decade or so. Its influence is, for instance, clearly visible in the Internal Revenue Mission statement so prominently displayed on its literature since its unveiling in 1998: The IRS mission is to "provide America's taxpayers top quality service by helping them understand and meet their tax responsibilities and by applying the tax law with integrity and fairness to all" (IRS, 1998).

One significant insight from the alternative view of non-compliance is the distinction between intentional and unintentional non-compliance (McKerchar, 2001). Compliance behavior is complex. There are certainly many taxpayers who have only the best intentions in regard to their tax liability but, because they do not know or understand the requirements of the tax law, do not comply with that law. Some of this ignorance may be somewhat self-serving but certainly not all of it; taxpayers have many uses of their time and studying tax law ranks as pleasant use of that time for only a select few. Unless compliance information is conveniently provided, few taxpayers for a complex tax are likely to have considerable knowledge about compliance requirements. That virtually guarantees unintentional non-compliance. Furthermore, if such non-compliance is prevalent, then the policy tools associated with the compliance lottery are considerably less effective. Those lottery tools influence the balancing of expected net gain from non-compliance and will not have leverage against unintentional non-compliance. To deal with unintentional non-compliance, a set of administrative weapons — notably convenience, assistance, and education — considerably removed from audit rates and evasion penalties are necessary.

8.2   Measuring Non-Compliance

One significant contribution from compliance research is in the area of non-compliance measurement. Tax administrators have three critical needs for understanding the rate of non-compliance with the taxes they are responsible for. First, measuring non-compliance is to measure the performance of the administrative agency. While the agency is in the business of collecting revenue to finance government projects, actual collections or even actual collections relative to official forecast, are not acceptable, the former because of the influence of economic activity on collections in any year and the latter because of the well-known notorious inaccuracy of such forecasts. It is actual collection performance against full application of the tax structure — or the compliance gap — that defines the success of the agency in collecting taxpayer active taxes. Tax agencies need compliance measurement to gauge their performance from year to year and legislatures want tax agencies to report on performance as an element of their budget presentations. While monitoring of operating data — like number of tax returns filed, number of audits completed, delinquency rates, and so on — assists the internal management of the agency, the agency *outcome or results* must be measured in terms of the difference between taxes collected by the agency and taxes actually owed. For instance, the Spending Review performance objective of the United Kingdom's HM Customs and Excise states intent to "collect the right revenue at the right time from indirect taxes ..." (*HM Treasury Spending Review*, 2004). In other words, the objective is to produce taxpayer compliance.

Second, the tax administrators need to know the patterns of non-compliance so that they can reach informed decisions as to how agency resources can best be allocated. The agency will not have sufficient resources to support all possible enforcement and taxpayer assistance possibilities and must choose among those available options. An understanding of non-compliance patterns — where the non-compliance occurs and to what extent — can inform the agency as to how those resources may best be deployed.

And finally, non-compliance measurement provides a guide for the direction of taxpayer services. To the extent that the responsive taxpayer view is correct, the pattern of non-compliance provides the exact template for delivery of taxpayer education and assistance. If the tax authorities will direct the appropriate resources to those problem areas, the non-compliance issue will be eliminated. Therefore, measurement of non-compliance is critical to reducing non-compliance.

For these reasons, there is considerable need for reasonable estimates of the amount and distribution of non-compliance for lawmakers and the compliance community. Unfortunately, obtaining estimates of tax compliance is not an easy task, even though the significance of such measures is clear. First, tax evaders generally prefer to keep their behavior quiet. They are not eager to report their successful non-compliance because such reporting could lead to enforcement action specifically against them or to general actions to close profitable evasion opportunities. Tax authorities cannot simply inquire whether particular individuals or businesses have paid all tax owed; no rational entity would self-report such criminal activity and it doesn't require application of the rational compliance lottery model to reach that conclusion! Of course, there are also unintentionally non-compliant taxpayers. These individuals and businesses have no non-compliance plan, but are still non-compliant. Direct inquiries to them would be as uninformative as inquiries to intentional evaders, not because of a desire to keep quiet, but because they do not know that they are non-compliant. Therefore, efforts at direct measurement of non-compliance are doomed to failure. Compliance rates will need to be gauged by indirect means.

Second, compliance measurement requires time, effort, and expertise in the tax administrative agency that could be used elsewhere in enforcement to yield revenue for the government. Agencies are reluctant to divert these resources *to* an activity that can best be classified as research *from* work that is in the direct production flow of the agency. The best compliance measures come from random sample tax audits of economic entities which might have tax obligations. The findings from these research audits are then expanded to the entire population to estimate the overall filing and compliance rate for each reviewed tax. Of course, the regular audit work of the administrative agency involves review of taxpayer returns to identify compliance errors. However, on the assumption that procedures used to select taxpayers for audit are effective, this group of taxpayers will be a biased sample — the returns being audited will be those substantially more likely to reflect non-compliance than will be the typical return. For example, sales tax administrators have found, over the years, substantial compliance problems with certain types of businesses, particularly convenience stores, used car dealers, and bars, and characteristically allocate a disproportionate share of audit resources to these businesses. Thus, the audit sample is biased toward these businesses that are a priori suspected. Assuming the audit administrators are generally correct in their suspicions, expanding the findings from such audits to the full taxpayer population will produce an inflated estimate of non-compliance. And the better the administrative agency is able to target its audit selection, the more exaggerated would be an overall non-compliance estimate based on these audit findings. Furthermore, the work can irritate taxpayers and that irritation can then be transmitted to the administrative agency's legislative masters. That can create problems for the agency as it proposes its budget and other programs for legislative approval.

In spite of these analytic difficulties, there is some evidence about the degree of non-compliance for major federal and state taxes in the United States and some information from other countries.

8.2.1 Federal Evidence

The most extensive analysis comes from the U.S. Internal Revenue Service studies of the tax compliance gap, defined to equal the difference between tax voluntarily paid and tax actually owed (the gross compliance gap) and the difference between total tax collected (including both the amounts voluntarily paid and collected from enforcement) and tax actually owed (the net compliance gap). These studies, done as part of the Taxpayer Compliance Measurement Program (TCMP), used random sample audits to estimate the gap and its component parts. They were used to learn what might create non-compliance, and to establish the criteria to be used in the selection of accounts for audit. The studies thus were conducted to provide the compliance information needed to gauge performance and to inform direction of agency resources. They were for research, not direct revenue.

Table 8.1 presents evidence for 1992, as based on TCMP audits in 1988, the last year of that program. Several significant points appear in these data. The first is the power of withholding. Because a third-party, the taxpayer's employer, withholds and remits taxes from wage and salary income through the year and reports those payments at the end of the year, reporting for this income is almost perfect. Withholding can be a powerful incentive for bringing in taxpayer returns; in 2001 there were more than four times as many federal individual income tax returns with overpayments than there were returns with tax due.

Table 8.1   Federal Individual Income Tax Underreporting and Tax Gap, 1992 Estimates

	Percent of total gap	Reporting percentage
Underreported income	**80.2%**	
Non-business income	25.4%	97.5%
Wage income	4.3%	99.1%
Interest income	1.3%	97.8%
Dividends	1.8%	92.4%
State tax refunds	0.0%	20.0%
Alimony income	0.1%	87.0%
Pensions and annuities	2.4%	96.1%
Unemployment compensation	0.4%	93.3%
Social security benefits	0.3%	95.9%
Capital gains	3.4%	93.1%
Form 4797 income (sales of business property)	1.0%	72.9%
Other income	10.4%	75.9%
Business income	54.8%	
Nonfarm proprietor income	23.0%	68.7%
Informal supplier income	17.3%	18.6%
Farm income	4.6%	68.7%
Rents and royalties	5.0%	83.4%
Partnership and SBC income	4.9%	92.8%
Offsets to Income	**11.2%**	
Adjustments	0.3%	98.1%
Deductions	7.0%	95.7%
Exemptions	3.9%	95.6%
Tax credits	**8.4%**	**61.1%**
Net math errors	**0.1%**	
Total underreporting gap	**100.0%**	

Source: Internal Revenue Service, Federal Tax Compliance Research: Individual Income Tax Gap *Estimates for 1985, 1988, and 1992*, Publication 1415 (Rev. 4-96) Washington, DC.: IRS, 1996, Table 3. Low estimates used in table.

A second significant point is the power of third-party reporting. Reporting for interest payments, dividends, capital gains, and pensions and annuities all exceed ninety percent and all are reported to the IRS by the entity making the payment, a third-party to the relationship between the taxpayer and the tax collector. Because the tax authority has independent evidence of amounts paid, it is not surprising that taxpayers are generally reliable in their reporting of this income. The IRS has the information necessary to verify what the taxpayer has reported and this appears to provide a considerable motivation for reporting, even though not all information reports are actually used in verification.

A third point is the extent to which non-compliance varies across types of business. Sole proprietors are the most difficult group for compliance, but not all business are equal. The highest non-compliance rates were for retail sales (fixed location), 39 percent less than fully compliant; transportation, 36 percent less; retail sales (no fixed location), 31; and production (including construction), 24 percent. The lowest non-compliance rates were for the wholesale trade, 19 percent and finance/insurance/real estate, 16 percent (GAO, 1990).

A final point is the extent to which compliance deteriorates when there is neither withholding nor third party reporting. The reporting rate is only 68.7 percent for farm income, only 68.7 percent for sole proprietors outside the informal sector, and only 18.6 percent for informal suppliers. In other words, when the compliance is truly voluntary, when there is no withholding and no third-party reporting system for checking on honest reporting, the rate of non-compliance rises dramatically. This pattern presents a distinct challenge to the equity of the individual income tax and questions its viability in any economic setting with many informal suppliers, heavy reliance on small agriculture, and many sole proprietors. In sum, the system fares well when administration is easy but does not perform so well when taxpayers face a real compliance choice. As compliance must be more voluntary, non-compliance rates rise.[3]

However, TCMP audits have limitations. They exclude large corporations, non-income taxes (excise and employment), and illegal economic activities. But these were not the primary objections to the audits. The IRS stopped doing TCMP audits because of their reputation as "audits from hell." Complaints about the invasive nature of these audits caused Congress to prevent an extension of this research audit program. The last TCMP for individuals was based on tax returns filed for tax year 1988. The last partnership TCMP was conducted in 1981, the last one for S corporations in 1984, and the last corporate one was in 1987 (Guttman, 2000).

In response to the need to update systemic IRS measures to score tax returns and target audit resources, a new compliance research effort began in 2003 to produce first results in 2005 (GAO, 2002b). The new IRS National Research Program (NRP) is designed to be less intrusive and burdensome to taxpayers than previous tax compliance audits. Instead of 54,000 taxpayers who were required to participate in face-to-face audits in the earlier programs (Guttman, 2002), the NRP will select only 30,000 returns for limited in-person audit and about 2,000 returns would be subject to so-called calibration audits when each line is examined and supporting documentation is required from a taxpayer. The sample will be selected mainly from the returns for tax year 2001. The auditors will rely more on the data already available to IRS, like third-party information, to validate information on returns. Therefore, the NRP audits will take two to three times less to conduct than the previous compliance measurement audits (Hamilton, 2002).

8.2.2 Washington State

The state of Washington has conducted periodic studies of tax compliance, the most recent completed in 2004 (Gutmann and Williams, 2004). These studies, prepared from random sample audits of registered taxpayers, are particularly informative because the state levies neither individual nor corporate income taxes, so the compliance results are purely the result of state efforts and because the evidence is for taxes outside the revenue portfolio of the federal government.

Table 8.2 shows the principal findings from the 2004 study. Several points are particularly noteworthy. First, the estimated non-compliance rate is 2.2 percent, a rate remarkably low, both in absolute level and relative to performance of the federal system. Of course, the tax systems are distinctly different; the compliance potential for the Washington gross receipts taxes, levied as indirect taxes, is likely higher than for the income taxes levied by the federal government. The comparison ought not necessarily be taken as proof of comparative capability of the administrative agencies.

Second, non-compliance rates for the two gross sales taxes — the retail sales tax and the business and occupation tax — are extremely low, only 1.1 and 2.6 percent, respectively. The retailer legally acts as a conduit of tax to the purchaser for the former and, hence, could be considered something of a third party to the transaction between the consumer who

Table 8.2 Registered Taxpayers Non-Compliance in Washington, 2004

Tax	Non-compliance rate (%)
Sales	1.1
Business and occupation	2.6
Use	19.5
Public utility	0.3
Hazardous substance	9.9
Other	-0.3
Overall	2.2

Source: Research Division, Washington Department of Revenue, *Department of Revenue Compliance Study,* Research Report 2004-4. Olympia, Washington: Department of Revenue, December 20, 2004.

bears the tax and the government. The business and occupation tax, although similar in that the base is gross receipts from sales, has no provision for easily adding tax to purchase prices. However, the non-compliance rate for it is low as well, though slightly higher than found in the 2002 study (1.5 percent) (*Department of Revenue Compliance Study*, 2002, 2003).

Third, the non-compliance rate is high for the use tax — 19.5 percent. The use tax serves to compensate for the sales tax that has not been paid because of the constitutional prohibition to levy a sales tax on a purchase made in interstate commerce. The destination state may impose the use tax to prevent out-of-state vendors able to sell without having to apply the sales tax from having an overall price advantage over in-state vendors who must apply the tax. Low compliance rates are not surprising — it is difficult to collect a transaction-based tax from purchasers, as opposed to sellers. However, even this is an understatement of overall use tax non-compliance because the survey was limited to registered firms. A considerable amount of use tax would be owed by individual purchasers, shopping through the internet, from catalogs from out-of-state merchants, etc., and these purchasers, not being registered, would have been outside the survey. The actual level of use tax non-compliance would certainly be even higher than the level found in the study.

Finally, non-compliance rate for hazardous substance excise is higher than for the major taxes, but considerably lower than for the use tax.[4] The total amount of non-compliance is, however, comparatively modest, amounting to about four percent of total non-compliance in the state. In addition, although the rate is still high it has decreased from 14 percent found in the 2002 study and is far from being the most consequential of compliance problems faced by the tax administrators.

The 2002 study kept track of the cause of underreporting in an effort to better understand the causes of non-compliance. Their categorization showed the following: 56 percent of non-compliance came from accounting errors of omission or computation or from a lack of records, 22 percent originated from taxpayer ignorance of tax requirements, 16 percent originated from taxpayer disagreement with interpretation of the tax law, and only 6 percent emerged from negligence or fraud and implied intentional taxpayer evasion. The year 2004 study found that mid-size firms hold much lower rates of noncompliance then the smallest and the largest firms. Also, older businesses tend to pay taxes better than the younger ones (less than two years old). These patterns of non-compliance provide considerable support for the responsible taxpayer model of compliance/non-compliance: with appropriate attention to compliance support and assistance, almost all the underreporting would have been corrected without administrative action and compliance gets better with experience and size. Most of the non-compliance would not have been directly influenced by manipulating the variables in the compliance lottery because the causes of non-compliance were not driven by conscious intention. Education promises greater return than enforcement in these instances.

8.2.3   Idaho Compliance Gap Study

The Idaho legislature prepared tax gap estimates for taxes levied by that state in the mid-1990s. The income tax estimates were based on federal TCMP data, adjusted for the distribution of taxpayers in that state, and sales tax estimates were based on "run-of operations" audits. Hence, there are significant limitations to the strength of their findings but they do provide some calibration of the gaps. Table 8.3 presents these findings.

The individual income tax is the highest yielding tax in the state, producing 39.6 percent of revenue in fiscal 1995, the year of the compliance estimates. Using an approach based on the federal individual income tax compliance data, the evaluation estimates the gross individual income tax gap to be 18.5 percent or $111.2 million. That would have amounted to 7.3 percent of revenue collected by the state in fiscal 1995. Tax Commission efforts were believed to have generated $14.4 million in direct enforcement collections, so the net compliance gap was estimated to be $96.8 million or 16.1 percent.

The gap for the corporate income tax, producer of 8.7 percent of Idaho revenue, was estimated from audit findings and was estimated as an annual average for 1992–1994. The evidence indicated a gross compliance gap of 10.2 percent or 5.5 percent of the total gap estimated for all taxes. However, it was estimated that enforcement efforts would reduce the net gap to only 3.4 percent and that efforts to further reduce the gap were unlikely to be productive.

The sales and use tax, producer of 37.8 percent of state tax revenue, was estimated to generate 49 percent of the gross tax gap and was estimated to have the highest gross non-compliance rate, 20.9 percent.[5]

Table 8.3   Idaho Tax Gap Study Results

Tax	Gross gap (%)	Net gap (%)
Individual income	18.5	16.1
Retail sales	20.9	19.5
Corporate income	10.2	3.4

Source: Office of Performance Evaluations, *Estimating and Reducing the Tax Gap in Idaho*. Report 96-06. Boise, Idaho: State of Idaho Office of Performance Evaluations, 1996.

Abuse or misuse of resale certificates constituted 21.9 percent of the gross tax gap. The study estimated the net sales and use tax gap to be 19.5 percent. The evidence indicates considerably higher non-compliance for sales and use taxes than for the two income taxes. However, before much should be made of this, it should be understood that the sales tax estimate is from regular audit work, meaning that this error measure is likely to be badly biased. Because operational audit results come from an intentionally biased sample of firms, those results cannot be trusted to provide evidence about compliance levels in the full business population. It is even somewhat surprising that the non-compliance rate measured here was not higher. And it should also be noted that the income taxes have the work of both state and federal governments contributing toward enforcement while the sales tax has only the efforts of the state.

8.2.4 Minnesota Sales Tax Gap Analysis

Another significant contribution to measuring and understanding the compliance gap at the state level is the sales tax gap analysis done for the state of Minnesota. The approach in this investigation was, in general, to estimate the amount of sales and use tax revenue that the state economy should have generated and then to compare with actual revenues to measure the gap amount. Identifying the hypothetical total with any confidence is a task that few tax economists would undertake, but the results coming from the analysis are not radically different from those found through other means and they serve to reinforce this entire body of evidence.

Table 8.4 summarizes the evidence from the Minnesota study. Overall sales and use tax compliance is high, almost 90 percent. The bulk of non-compliance — 64.2 percent of the total — comes from underreporting, not from those who are not filing. Of the non-filer total, 77 percent comes from remote vendors (internet, catalog, and similar sellers). However, the combined compliance record disguises a dramatic difference between the sales tax and its use tax companion. For the sales tax, the compliance rate is 95.1 percent. That compares with the 53.1 percent compliance rate for the use tax. This comparison gives further evidence of the great utility from using indirect collection of these taxes on transactions, as compared with attempting administration of the tax on a direct basis. Vendors are quite effective conduits of the sales tax. They function roughly like third parties to the consumer–tax authority relationship and, furthermore, there are many fewer of them for the tax authorities to deal with than there are individual purchasers at retail. Collection indirectly through vendors is an efficient way of collecting the taxes on retail transactions; collection directly from the purchasers is grossly inefficient and, indeed,

Table 8.4 Estimates of the Sales Tax Gap in Minnesota, 2000

Sales and use tax	Total in $ millions	Percent of total owed
Collected	3,792	89.4
Underreported	288	6.8
Nonfilers	163	3.8
Remote vendor nonfilers	125	2.9
Sales tax		
Compliant	3485	95.1
Non-Compliant	180	4.9
Use tax		
Compliant	307	53.1
Non-compliant	271	46.9

Source: American Economics Group. Minnesota Sales and Use Tax Gap Project: Final Report. Prepared for Department of Revenue, State of Minnesota. Washington, DC.: American Economics Group, 2002.

ineffective. When the vendor can be used as the collector of the tax, the compliance gap for the tax is relatively small — much smaller than the Internal Revenue Service has proven able to achieve for the individual income tax.

8.2.5 Some Miscellaneous Compliance Evidence

A number of other studies have developed estimates of compliance rates, although not so broad-ranging as those mentioned earlier. A brief summary of several of these are provided here.

8.2.5.1 United Kingdom

Her Majesty's Customs and Excise estimates the United Kingdom value added tax gap to be 15.7 percent (2002–2003) and has set as its performance goal to reduce it to 12 percent by 2005–2006. Unfortunately, the gap percentage has been generally rising since 1990–1991 when it was 9.9 percent[6] (*Analysis Division, HM Customs and Excise*, 2003). This gap is considerably higher than studies have usually found for the American retail sales taxes, even though the taxes are alternative administrative approaches to taxing general consumption spending. Of course, the statutory tax rate levied in the UK value added tax — 17.5 percent for most purchases — is much higher than for the typical American retail sales tax and higher rates are likely to make non-compliance a larger problem, regardless of the tax.

8.2.6 Tennessee

Tennessee is one of the few states not levying a broad based individual income tax and, therefore, its general sales tax is critically important for the finances of the state. In fiscal 2002, it collected 60 percent of its tax revenue from that source and many local governments rely heavily on their supplements to the state tax as well. The state focuses much of its administrative attention to the proper administration of the tax. Its revenue department has estimated the sales tax voluntary compliance rate, measured as the percentage of tax voluntarily reported compared with total tax liability, at 95.5 percent (Adams and Johnson, 1989). Unfortunately, there has been no recent re-estimation of the results.

8.2.7 New Zealand

There are many studies of the size of underground, hidden, shadow, or black economies in countries around the world. Because this economic activity is informal or even illegal, most if not all of the potential tax base represented by it is outside the normal reach of the tax authorities. Recent data on the shadow economy as a share of official gross domestic product among countries of the Organization for Economic Cooperation and Development show a range from eight percent in Switzerland and nine percent in the United States and Austria to twenty-seven percent in Italy (Heller, 2003). But seldom is there an effort to track these shadow data into the compliance gap. It is not a simple translation because measuring shadow activity does not directly transfer to non-compliance; not all income in shadow activity is taxable. One effort to track shadow activity to tax non-compliance comes from New Zealand. It has been estimated that the tax gap there ranges from 6.4 percent to 10.2 percent of total tax liability (Giles, 1999). About half of the gap was estimated to represent hard-core criminal evasion. Evidence also indicates that a shift toward indirect taxation, away from personal income taxation, can reduce both shadow activity and the tax gap.

Other New Zealand evidence from business tax audits shows large firms to be more compliant than small firms, more efficient firms to be more compliant than less efficient ones, compliance to be higher when firms use standard tax avoidance instruments, and a positive relationship between a firm's effective tax rate and compliance (Giles, 1998).

8.2.8 Canada

Estimates of income tax non-compliance by self-employed individuals in Canada have been prepared by analysis of consumption patterns that compares reported behavior of the self-employed with that of wage and salary earners, for whom third-party reporting affords little opportunity to conceal income. An analysis by Schuetze of data from 1969 to 1992 showed non-compliance by households receiving 30 percent or more of household income from self-employment to range from 11 to 23 percent of household income (Schuetze, 2002). Non-compliance was highest in industries like construction and services, where pay is frequently in cash, making underreporting particularly easy. This range of non-compliance is consistent with estimates by Mirus, Smith, and Karoleff of the size of the Canadian underground economy, measured as 14.6 to 21.6 percent of total economic activity, depending on the estimation method. (Mirus, Smith, and Karoleff, 1994).

8.2.9   U.S. Earned Income Tax Credit

The Internal Revenue Service has conducted special studies of compliance for the Earned Income Tax Credit (EITC), a fully-refundable income tax credit available for certain low and moderate income working families. The program is an income support scheme delivered through the tax system, rather than being delivered by social service agencies, and provides an incentive for work rather than welfare for low wage workers. Compliance estimates have been made on the basis of random audits, information from claims disallowed during return processing, and data from returns subjected to enforcement actions. The analysis for tax year 1999 estimated that, of the $31.3 billion EITC claims made, between $8.5 and $9.9 billion (27.0 to 31.7 percent) should not have been paid (IRS, 2002). The largest component of overclaims involved claiming a child who was not a qualifying dependent child, usually because of residency requirements. The analysis did not, however, make any allowance for EITC not claimed by those otherwise eligible.

8.2.10   State Cigarette Taxes

High selective excise tax rates create a strong incentive for tax evasion. Because the state tax component of cigarette prices is so high — $1 or more per pack in fifteen states plus the District of Columbia — in many states, but quite low in others — below $0.25 per pack in nine states — and available without tax at all on Native American reservations, potential gains from evasion are high. Cigarette consumers do have liability for tax on cigarettes they possess in a state, but states cannot afford to pursue tax on these individual purchases. They can economically collect tax through in-state distributors, but lack legal authority to pursue those from outside the state. Therefore, the low tax vendor, whether operating in a low tax state or on a no tax reservation, has an evasion advantage by selling through the mail.

A federal law, the Jenkins Act (5 U.S.C. 375–378) of 1955, requires any person who sells cigarettes across a state line to a buyer who is not a licensed distributor to report the sale to the tobacco tax administrator of the destination state. That would permit the destination state to collect the appropriate tax from the buyer at modest cost. However, violation of the act is only a misdemeanor and the Federal Bureau of Investigation, the agency charged with administering the act, places minimal priority on its enforcement. The General Accounting Office's analysis of compliance among Internet vendors, both on and off Native American reservations, found a non-compliance rate of 78 percent (GAO, 2002a). However, a few states have found some vendors to be willing to provide customer lists when requested, but the process is far from automatic and not enforced by federal authorities. Overall, compliance is low.

8.2.11 American Sales Tax and Remote Vendors

A continuing compliance problem for state sales tax administrators is collection of tax on purchases made from remote vendors. Interpretation of the United States Constitution prevents states from applying their sales taxes to sales conducted in interstate commerce. However, the state may levy a compensating tax on the use of such purchases. The problem is in the collection of these use taxes. It is extremely difficult to collect transaction taxes *directly* from purchasers; it is much easier to collect the tax *indirectly* through vendors, in the same manner as the sales tax is collected. Unfortunately for the states, a Supreme Court ruling, *Quill v. North Dakota* (504 U.S. 298 (1992), limits required use tax registration to vendors with physical presence in the state.[7] That creates a major compliance loophole: firms selling in a state only via the Internet, catalogs, telemarketing, etc., with no physical presence in the state, may not be required to collect use tax. Because of the great difficulty of collecting the tax directly, a compliance gap appears. Bruce and Fox estimate the Internet loss by 2011 to be from 2.6 to 9.92 percent of total state tax collections (Bruce and Fox, 2001). This creates a considerable equity imbalance between local and remote vendors and the loss of considerable revenue. However, the overall non-compliance rate, even at its highest, falls substantially below that estimated for the federal individual income tax.

8.3 Ten Lessons for Legislators and Administrators from Compliance Research

There have been many studies of the influences on tax compliance/non-compliance using audit and compliance experience in different environments. Most have been conducted on federal taxes, particularly the individual and corporate income taxes, but some have been done on major state taxes, particularly the retail sales tax. A review of these studies provides a dozen useful conclusions that can be used in the formulation of tax policy and especially on its administration.

First, as predicted by the compliance lottery view of non-compliance, a higher tax audit rate does improve the rate of compliance. This has been demonstrated in both sales and income tax studies. However, the relationship between audit coverage and compliance is not linear; that is, the return from extra coverage does eventually decline as that coverage gets higher and the impact is not uniform for all taxpayers. The deterrent impact of auditing of individual income tax payments depends upon the income level. Studies have shown that impact is greater for low and middle income class taxpayers (Beron, Tauchen, and Witte, 1992; Dubin and Wilde, 1988). Similarly, the threat of an audit has a positive impact on the compliance behavior of low and middle income class taxpayers but engenders a "perverse" reaction by high-income taxpayers, as found in a compliance strategy experiment in Minnesota (Slemrod, Blumenthal and Christian, 2001). Whether the experience of a prior audit changes the reporting behavior of the individual and induces him to report the true amount of income also depends upon how large the assessment of the previous audit has been. The larger assessments translate into more substantial improvements in compliance (Erard, 1992). However, other characteristics of the taxpayer, like age, level of income and type of the return required to file, blurs the positive effects of prior audit on subsequent reporting behavior. Compliance rates among small-business owners depend largely on the perceived risk of getting audited (Beron et al., 1992; Witte and Woodbury, 1985). The analyses based on aggregated data consistently confirm that higher audit rates improve compliance significantly, except non-filing (Dubin, Graetz and Wilde, 1990; Plumley, 2002).

Though research on the effects of audits on other taxes is scarce, it also supports results reached in income tax area. Mikesell estimated the impact of audit coverage on the sales tax base per capita. The results indicated that an increase in audit coverage of one percent would lead to a tax base higher by 0.07 percent (Mikesell, 1985). Because Mikesell subtracted direct audit recovery in his analysis, the impact is entirely from induced compliance. On the other hand, research on sales tax compliance in Tennessee and New Mexico finds non-compliance to be driven by the opportunity for evasion (complexity) and not by audit coverage itself (Blackwell, Alm and McKee, 2001; Murray, 1995).

Second, again as predicted by the compliance lottery view, higher penalties do yield improved compliance rates. However, the impact is relatively modest. In terms of relative impact, the effect of audit rates is considerably greater than the impact of increased penalties. First, governments face obvious political and social constraints in setting penalties high (Andreoni, Erard and Feinstein, 1998). Second, for the penalties to be credible the changes in penalty level should be accompanied by higher probability of detection. If the probability of detection is small, large responses to changes in the fine rate would require extreme degrees of risk aversion, following the lottery view of compliance. When audit rates and penalty rates are set close to those that are observed in reality, their effects on compliance are not large (Alm, Jackson and McKee, 1992). With high rates of detection even mild penalties can be an effective deterrent (Hessing, Elfers Robben, and Webley, 1992). The strength of the relationship between the severity of sanctions and compliance depends also upon the audit class. For certain groups of taxpayers — those who have high incomes and are self-employed — the effects of penalties on compliance are significant (Witte and Woodbury, 1985). On the other hand, both higher audit rates and higher penalties may simply induce tax payers to conceal the true income in harder to detect ways (Cowell, 1990; Long and Swingen, 1991).

Third, the indirect revenue effects (deterrence, changed attitudes, etc.,) of audit and other enforcement activities is considerably greater than the direct effect (the collections directly from the action). The latest study done by IRS using state-level aggregate data over a ten year time period (tax years 1982–1991) found that the average indirect effect of audits started in 1991 was about 11.7 times as large as the average adjustment directly proposed by audits closed that year (Plumley, 2002). This means that resource allocation decisions — audit selection, nonfiler discovery, delinquency pursuit, etc., — based on direct collections from the activity may well not be consistent with the objective of achieving best compliance. For example, certain types of business operate in areas of great tax complexity and, as a result, are likely to generate substantial audit discoveries. However, audit of these businesses, while rich in audit findings, provides no deterrence or changed attitudes for similar businesses or even for the audited business; the nature of the business will create tax issues, even if the business intends to be compliant. Audits elsewhere, although less rich in audit findings, are likely to have considerably greater indirect revenue effect and to make a greater contribution to the overall compliance objective. Focusing of direct enforcement revenue can hinder achievement of desired tax compliance.

Analysts often speculate on whether a standard for optimal level of tax enforcement should be based on the idea "that a government should increase spending until the marginal dollar of expenditure produces just over a dollar of additional revenue" (Wetzler, 1991). But the direct revenue generated by properly designed enforcement activities like audit should be dwarfed by the indirect voluntary compliance impacts from that work. Narrow analysis of fiscal impacts — like comparing the costs of putting an extra auditor in the field with the audit recovery from that auditor — provides little helpful guidance about appropriate staffing or other resource allocation. For taxpayer active taxes, the real yield will always be in induced voluntary compliance, not direct short-term revenue recovery.

Because so much of the total effect of audit is through the indirect deterrence effect, it is crucial that tax administrations publicize their audit activities and make the public aware of programs to increase audit activity, whether through hiring new auditors or through redeployment of the existing audit force. It is the potential of audit, not the audit itself, that brings the greatest overall tax compliance and that potential must be broadcast well beyond the taxpayers who are actually selected for audit.

Fourth, though the impact of the marginal rate on the reported income is ambiguous in the basic economic model of compliance, higher tax rates generally reduce compliance. The simple explanation is that a higher tax rate increases the incentive to evade tax. The effects of the tax rate on compliance vary by the audit class, based on the level and source of income. The elasticities of underreporting with respect to marginal rates vary from 0.515 for non-farm businesses to 0.844 for non-business returns. This means that, for a taxpayer with a combined federal and state income tax marginal rate of 0.40, which is sample average, 10 percent decline in tax rate to 0.36 would result in an expected 5 percent to 8 percent decline in underreported income (Clotfelter 1983: 368). Later studies also point out that a higher rate is associated with lower compliance. In an experimental study, Alm, Jackson and McKee (1992) find that underreported income increases with higher marginal rates with a tax rate elasticity of 0.5, roughly confirming Clotfelter's result. Higher rates induce more individuals to move into sectors where detection is more difficult or even to the shadow economy, thus aggravating overall evasion problem (Jung, Snow, and Trandel, 1994). Agha and Haughton estimate that a revenue-maximizing VAT rate should not exceed 24.7 percent, given the initial compliance rate of 100 percent. However, with a more realistic initial compliance of 70 percent, the revenue-maximizing VAT is just 19.6 percent (Agha and Haughton, 1996).

There is a strong positive correlation between income and tax rates, and independent effects of tax rates and income are not easy to disentangle in empirical analysis when both these variables are included. However, both higher income and higher tax rates generally are associated with tax evasion. The effects of marginal tax rate at $15,000 taxable income on the net income reported is positive, while the effect of tax rate at the income level of $57,000 and higher is negative (Plumley, 2002). This seems to support the rational actor framework of tax compliance. As tax rate goes up, the rewards for tax evasion goes up, while the penalty of getting caught stays unchanged. This is also consistent with empirical evidence that income is positively correlated with evasion (Forest and Sheffrin, 2002). The elasticity of expected underreporting to income varies by the source of income, from 0.292 for non-business returns to 0.656 for farm income returns (Clotfelter, 1983). However, reducing tax rates will not necessarily induce greater compliance because, once taxpayers have fallen into a pattern of non-compliance, it is difficult to stop. Paying no tax is even more profitable than paying low tax.

Fifth, complexity reduces compliance. There is a general consensus that American income tax preparation is burdensome and even overwhelming. "A law that can be understood (if at all) only by a tiny priesthood of lawyers and accountants is subject to popular suspicion. By undermining popular support, complexity undermines the self-assessment on which economical compliance depends" (Long and Swingen, 1991, p. 640). In support of this complexity claim is the fact that about half of all individual tax returns are made out by paid preparers, and as many as two-thirds of the long 1040 forms are filed with assistance of paid preparers (Erard, 1993).

There can be several causal directions from complexity to non-compliance. Slemrod (1989) hypothesized that complexity increases cost of compliance and therefore increases noncompliance. The research conducted by Tax Foundation estimates that it costs individuals and businesses $125 billion annually to comply with the federal income tax. This converts into 12 cents per dollar collected (Guttman, 2000). Presumably, the less burdensome and costly compliance is, the more likely a taxpayer is to comply with the tax laws.

Complexity can also frustrate taxpayers in their efforts to comply with tax laws and create a sense of unfairness. Technical complexity and the demands for legal completeness produce significant alienation of taxpayers leading to lower tax morale and consequently evasion (Vogel, 1974). Even if taxpayers do not necessarily view a complex tax system as unfair, the requirement to file a long tax form creates opportunities to evade and negatively effect compliance rates of the taxpayers facing such an obligation (Forest and Sheffrin, 2002).

There is a great variety of instruments for law designers to choose from that contribute to tax complexity. One of them is an option between having a single tax rate or multiple tax rates applied depending upon a transaction. Multiple rates are often justified on the equity grounds. However, it has been found that an additional tax rate in a VAT law increases tax evasion by 7 percent, undermining the equity goals (Agha and Haughton, 1996).

Higher reliance on paid preparers reduces compliance. On the one hand, tax practitioners help alleviate the compliance burden by providing specialized information and computational skills. The use of paid help to file the tax return reduces time and anxiety costs, and uncertainty related with compliance (Erard, 1993). On the other hand, this expertise may be used to exploit gray areas in tax rules to the detriment of compliance with negative consequences for tax equity and efficiency. Klepper, Mark and Nagin have found that where there is no ambiguity in tax code the use of tax preparers promotes tax compliance, however higher ambiguity is related to greater non-compliance (Klepper, Mark and Nagin, 1991).

Tax practitioners are not a homogenous group. Impact of their services on tax compliance depends upon the kinds of services tax preparers provide and upon their characteristics. Some argue that the constraints put on tax preparers by increasingly stringent legislation regulating their profession, and the threat of a potential liability brought upon them by taxpayers for inadequate advice, put some preparers of income tax returns in the position "of acting as gatekeepers for compliance"(Dellinger, 1995). If some tax preparers exercise a cautious approach in their counsel others are less scrupulous. The estimates show that noncompliance is 4.5 times larger when tax returns are prepared with the help of a Certified Public Accountant (CPA) or lawyer than it would be if the returns were self-prepared. Noncompliance on returns prepared by other types of tax practitioners is 15 percent larger than on self-prepared returns. This confirms the survey results that CPAs and lawyers are more aggressive in their practice of tax return preparation than other types of paid preparers.[8] For each mode of tax preparation the frequency of noncompliance rises with income and the complexity of the return. The level of noncompliance though is highest for the returns prepared by CPAs and lawyers (Erard, 1993).

As to the characteristics of the taxpayers who choose to hire tax practitioners, it has been determined that income, age, marriage, self-employment and return complexity are among the factors positively related to the decision to hire a tax expert. Also higher marginal rates and higher audit and penalty rates lead to a more frequent use of tax professionals (Erard, 1993). It is the source of income rather than level of income that determines the use of CPA, lawyer or another practitioner over self-preparation. Hiring a CPA or lawyer is attractive to taxpayers with particular complex returns and high marginal tax rates. Plumley (2002) also finds significant negative relationship between the use of tax preparers and compliance using aggregate data.

Sixth, compliance improves when taxpayers believe the tax system is fair, when they receive something valuable for their payments and when society shows no tolerance for tax evasion. This finding is explained by a broad concept of "the tax culture." Because the compliance as lottery does not account well for the level of actual reporting, researchers have proposed prevailing social norms as an important determinant of overall compliance behavior (Alm, 2001; Andreoni et al., 1998). According to Nerre "tax culture emerges from the tradition of taxation (e.g., an accentuation of [in-] direct taxes) on the one hand and by the interaction of the actors and the cultural values like honesty, justice, or sense of duty on the other hand" (Nerre, 2001, p. 288). Major actors forming tax culture are the government (legislature), tax authority, taxpayers, academics (experts). Tax culture is embedded in national culture and is evolutionary, although it is difficult to model and test. There are attempts to include the "social norm" into the basic economic model of tax compliance (Alm and Martinez-Vazquez, 2003) and to adopt game theory approach for the analysis of the evolutionary nature of the interaction between tax officials and taxpayers (Nerre, 2002). The majority of the research on tax culture is based on surveys and experiments.

Attitudes about the effectiveness of tax administration and by extension "the government" play an important role in compliance behavior (Alm and Martinez-Vazquez, 2003). The convention to demonize IRS by the politicians running an election campaign further augments such perceptions. In the recent debates over tax simplification, advocates of the "flat tax" such as Senator Robert Dole or candidate Steve Forbes claimed that it would eliminate the IRS as Americans currently know it (Alvarez and Brehm, 1998). Though taxpayers often do not distinguish between the fairness of tax system and the "procedural fairness" of the IRS, both perceptions form attitudes that translate into taxpaying behavior. Comparative analysis of different tax cultures indicates that increased enforcement efforts are less effective where the tax regime is viewed as unfair. The motivation for that kind of evasion is the need to compensate for the psychological loss in expected income because of — from a tax cultural view — "excessive" tax payments (Nerre, 2002; Vogel, 1974). Additionally, Forest and Sheffrin (2002) find that taxpayers who believe that they do not receive adequate public goods for their tax payments deem the system to be unfair and are more likely to evade taxes. Brosio and Cassone (1999) find that tax evasion is higher in those Italian regions where the quality of provided public services is lower.

Tolerance for tax evasion breeds more evasion. A high level of evasion puts a pressure on otherwise "law-abiding citizens" to compensate for the additional burden of taxes, creating a tendency to tax evasion even among honest taxpayers (Vogel, 1974). People living in areas where a large number of taxpayers willfully and sometimes successfully ignore efforts of the collecting agency, e.g., delinquent account notices, tend to be less compliant than those living in areas where response to tax administration efforts is quick and positive (Witte and Woodbury, 1985). Higher compliance is associated with low social standing of evaders, viewing tax evasion as "immoral" by an individual, and a stronger sense of social cohesion (Alm and Martinez-Vazquez, 2003).

Direct democracy arguably improves the dialog between the taxpayer and the government through a greater participation in decision process, leading to a fairer tax system and less evasion as found in a research based on the U.S. and Switzerland data (Torgler, 2002). Rising income inequality contributes to the taxpayer stress through financial strain on the lower end of the spectrum and through reduced visibility of transactions, as the wage income declines as a percentage of total income, on the higher end of the spectrum. As a result, the dissatisfaction with the tax system grows and tax compliance deteriorates as an analysis of the U.S. wage and salary data for the period 1947–1999 indicates (Bloomquist, 2003).

However, direct appeals to taxpayer social duty have only limited positive effects on compliance. An appeal that the correct payment of taxes is essential for the provision of valuable public services had a positive effect only on one taxpayer group, namely homeowners (Blumenthal, Charles and Slemrod, 2001). Overall results of the research suggest the policies are more successful if they are designed to target specific taxpayer groups. Notices sent out to taxpayers with delinquent accounts are associated with higher levels of compliance, with elasticities ranging from 0.02 for both small proprietors and upper income self-employed individuals to 0.01 for middle income wage and salary workers (Witte and Woodbury, 1985). Quite a few state revenue departments have made the list of delinquent taxpayers public on the Internet. Such programs should have an effect of reinforcing social norms of tax compliance by exposing the deviant behavior. Whether such compliance strategies are effective deterrents has not been empirically evaluated yet.

So-called "internal norms" that define how an individual understands what is a proper, acceptable or moral behavior are probably harder to influence than the "external norms," like perceptions about the fairness of the tax burden, government's performance in such areas as tax collection and provision of services (Alm and Martinez-Vazquez, 2003). Taxpayers who regard tax evasion as immoral are less likely to evade taxes regardless whether tax rates are low or high, and whether they get a refund or have to pay taxes (Reckers, Sanders and Roark, 1994).

Seventh, federal–state information exchange is an effective enforcement mechanism. Because federal and state audit selection criteria differ, information sharing effectively produces broader audit coverage for each tax. There are productive exchanges outside the income tax as well. For example, a number of states obtain customs declaration data from entry points in their jurisdictions and bill their residents for use tax on high price purchases declared by them (Due and Mikesell, 1994). Even though there may be no voluntary compliance spillover impact from these billings, the direct revenue from these contacts far exceeds the cost of the program.

Eighth, where federal income tax audit rates are higher, state compliance rates are higher. Since state income taxes often mirror federal taxes, state tax authorities can rely on the efforts of the federal government in enforcing their taxes. Out of 41 states levying a broad based individual income tax, 36 states use federal adjusted gross income or taxable income as a starting point for computing state tax liability. This close linkage between the federal and state individual income tax structures allows state revenue administrations to make use of the IRS auditing results to enforce state taxes. Cooperation is facilitated by the exchange of otherwise confidential tax return and audit information. However, apart from direct benefits of cooperation, it has been determined that federal audits have indirect–deterrent–effects on state income tax compliance. Research based on pooled state-level data for the period 1997–2001 indicates that a one percentage point increase in federal audit rates yields 2.15 dollars more per return collected by states (Birskyte, 2003). The finding that federal audits have an impact that spills over to state income tax compliance reinforces the opinion that audits remain one of the most effective tools available to tax authorities.

Ninth, treating taxpayers more like customers rather than suspects can improve compliance. Providing taxpayers with payment options, easy filing, and assistance can reduce unintentional non-compliance. Experimental and survey results suggest compliance behavior is closely related to societal institutions, therefore the presence of effective but service-oriented tax administration is crucial for improving tax compliance (Alm and Martinez-Vazquez, 2003).

There is consensus that consumer friendly services from the IRS have indirect effects on tax compliance (Plumley, 2002). The magnitude of the effect depends upon the type of taxpayers.[9] For example, toll-free telephone assistance for wage and investment taxpayers is evaluated at the score of 54 (on a scale from 0 to 100) relative to other IRS activities, while the same assistance to small businesses and self-employed taxpayers receives the score of 27.3. Taxpayer education as well as walk–in assistance is more effective for small businesses and self-employed (scores of 42.2 and 27.3, respectively) than for wage and investment taxpayers (scores 24 and 19, respectively) relative to other activities and services offered by the IRS.

Tenth, third party cooperation, even collection, dramatically improves compliance rates. This effect is clear in TCMP compliance estimates across types of income. Compliance on income subject to third party withholding is almost total and compliance for income payments subject to third party reporting is almost as high. Having such a disinterested third party intermediary in the transaction between taxpayer and tax authorities dramatically improves compliance. This relationship is also important with retail sales taxes. Compliance for the sales tax — collected from the vendor under the assumption that the vendor will pass the tax to the purchaser — is remarkably high but compliance with the compensating use tax is low — collection directly from the purchaser without a vendor intermediary. These third party collectors provide a critical service to the tax authorities. That does not mean that third-party collection philosophy renders compliance perfect for sales taxes. In business sectors characterized by small size firms, close relationships with customers, and informal records, sales tax compliance is still a problem, although still not as great as for other elements of the tax system. Furthermore, because there are fewer of these third parties than there are of ultimate taxpayers, enforcement is simpler — the tax authorities can direct their attention not to the thousands of ultimate taxpayers but rather to the hundreds of vendors, employers, etc., at great saving of administrative cost.

8.4   Concluding Observations

Non-compliance is an issue for all tax structures that rely on active tax-payer participation in the process of revenue collection. That includes all broad-based taxes in the United States except the state and local taxes on real property and most similar broad-based taxes in other industrialized countries around the world. The evidence is that compliance is far from perfect, even with tax systems employing great technological sophistication in tax administration.

Evidence is clear that voluntary compliance is not a free-will offering by taxpayers. When there is either third-party reporting or collection, compliance is higher than when the taxpaying relationship involves only the taxpayer and the tax authorities. This is particularly apparent in the TCMP data and in comparisons between the extremely low rates of non-compliance for state retail sales taxes and much higher non-compliance rates for individual and corporate income taxes. The results of research have produced several suggestions for tax administrators how to improve tax compliance but the complexity of the taxpaying behavior and the dynamic character of this problem leaves us in the position of chasing a moving target.

Notes

1. There are approaches to collecting these taxes, including the individual income tax, that require substantially less direct taxpayer effort. For an investigation of some of these by the Department of Treasury, as well as consideration of the changes necessary to move to such a system for the federal individual income tax, see U.S. Department of Treasury (2003).

2. Legal tax avoidance, on the other hand, seems rampant (Johnson, 2003).

3. Rather surprisingly, the non-compliance rates for adjustments, deductions, and exemptions — all self-reported without third party verification — are found to be very low. There is no immediately apparent explanation for this pattern.

4. The hazardous substance tax, a privilege tax on first possession of items within the state, applies at a rate of 0.7 percent to the wholesale value of certain substances (petroleum products, pesticides, and certain chemicals) which statute defines as hazardous or are determined to threaten human health or the environment by the Department of Ecology. Proceeds constituted 0.19 percent of state tax revenue in 2003. The public utility tax applies at rates ranging from 0.642 to 5.029 percent on gross income of public and privately owned utilities providing transportation, communications, energy, and water. They yielded 2.2 percent of state tax revenue in 2003.

5. The estimates were for a period before the great expansion of economic activity via the Internet and the non-compliance associated with such business.

6. Their theoretical VAT liability is constructed from national income accounts sources which are independent of the VAT administrative system and that liability is compared with VAT receipts.

7. For a complete review of the problem, see Mikesell (2000).

8. Internal Revenue Service, 1987, Survey of Tax Practitioners and Advisors. Washington, D.C., cited in Erard, 1993.

9. These magnitudes also reflect the indirect revenue-to-cost ratios of different enforcement and non-enforcement programs.

References

Adams, V. N. and Johnson, K. L. (1989). *Estimating the Sales Tax Gap.* Nashville, Tennessee: Tennessee Department of Revenue.

Agha, A. and Haughton, J. (1996). Designing VAT Systems: Some Efficiency Considerations. *Review of Economics and Statistics, 78*(2), 303–308.

Alm, J. (2001). *Tax Evasion.* Retrieved 9/6/2001, 2001, from File:// E:\alm.html

Alm, J., Jackson, B. and McKcc, M. (1992). Estimating the Determinants of Taxpayer Compliance with Experimental Data. *National Tax Journal, XLV*(1), 107–114.

Alm, J. and Martinez-Vazquez, J. (2003). Institutions, paradigms, and tax evasion in developing and transition countries. In J. Martinez-Vazquez and J. Alm (Eds.), *Public Finance in Developing and Transitional Countries. Essays in Honor of Richard Bird* (1st ed., pp. 146–178). Northampton, Ma: Edward Elgar.

Alvarez, M. R. and Brehm, J. (1998). Speaking in Two Voices: American Equivocation about the Internal Revenue Service. *American Journal of Political Science, 42*(2), 418–452.

Analysis Division, HM Customs and Excise. (2003). Retrieved February 26, 2004, from http://www.ash.org.uk/html/smuggling/pdfs/ meas-ind-tax-loss-03.pdf

Andreoni, J., Erard, B. and Feinstein, J. (1998). Tax Compliance. *Journal of Economic Literature, 36,* 818–860.

Beron, K. J., Tauchen, H. V. and Witte, A. D. (1992). The Effects of Audits and Socioeconomic Variables on Compliance. In J. Slemrod (Ed.), *Why People Pay Taxes* (pp. 67–90). Ann Arbor: The University of Michigan Press.

Birskyte, L. (2003). *The Effects of IRS Audit Rates on State Income Tax Compliance.* Unpublished manuscript, Bloomington, IN.

Blackwell, C., Alm, J. and McKee, M. (2001). *Broad Based Sales Taxes: Audit Selection and Compliance.* Unpublished manuscript.

Bloomquist, K. M. (2003). U.S. Income Inequality and Tax Evasion: A Synthesis. *Tax Notes International, 31*(347).

Blumenthal, M., Charles, C. and Slemrod, J. (2001). Do Normative Appeals Affect Tax Compliance? Evidence from a Controlled Experiment in Minnesota. *National Tax Journal, LIV*(1), 125–138.

Brossio, G. and Cassone, A. (1999). Tax evasion across Italy: rational noncompliance or inadequate civil concern? Paper read at the 92nd Annual Conference on Taxation, October 24–26, 1999, at Atlanta, Georgia.

Bruce, D. and Fox, W. F. (2001). *State and Local Sales Tax Revenue Losses from E-Commerce: Updated Estimates.* Knoxville, Tennessee: Center for Business and Economic Research, University of Tennessee.

Bureau of the Census, Governments Division. (2004). Retrieved February 4, 2004, from http://www.census.gov/govs/www/index.html

Clotfelter, C. T. (1983). Tax evasion and tax rates: an analysis of individual returns. *The Review of Economics and Statistics* LXV (3), 363–373.

Cowell, F. A. (1990). *Cheating the Government: The Economics of Evasion.* Cambridge, Ma: MIT Press.

Dellinger, K. (1995). The Problem is Not the Declining 'Real Audit Rate'. *Tax Notes, 66*(275).

Department of Revenue Compliance Study, 2002. (No. 2003-1)(2003). Olympia, Washington: Department of Revenue.

Dubin, J. A., Graetz, M. J. and Wilde, L. L. (1990). The Effect of Audit Rates on the Federal Individual Income Tax, 1977–1986. *National Tax Journal, 43*(4), 395–409.

Dubin, J. A. and Wilde, L. L. (1988). An Empirical Analysis of Federal Income Tax Auditing and Compliance. *National Tax Journal, XLI*(1), 61–73.

Due, J. F., and Mikesell, J. L. (1994). *Sales Taxation, State and Local Structure and Administration* (2nd ed.). Washington, D.C.: Urban Institute Press.

Erard, B. (1992). The Influence of Tax Audits on Reporting Behavior. In J. Slemrod (Ed.), *Why People Pay Taxes* (pp. 95–115). Ann Arbor: The University of Michigan Press.

Erard, B. (1993). Taxation with Representation: An Analysis of the Role of Tax Practitioners in Tax Compliance. *Journal of Public Economics, 52*(2), 163–197.

Forest, A. and Sheffrin, S. M. (2002). Complexity and Compliance: An Empirical Investigation. *National Tax Journal, LV*(1), 75–88.

GAO. (1990). *Tax Administration: Profiles of Major Components of the Tax Gap* (No. GGD-90-53BR). Washington, D.C.: U.S. General Accounting Office.

GAO. (1995). GAO Reports on Tax Gap Symposium. *Tax Notes, 67*(1492).

GAO. (2002a). Internet Cigarette Sales: Giving ATF Investigative Authority May Improve Reporting and Enforcement (No. GAO-02-743). Washington, D.C.: U.S. General Accounting Office.

GAO. (2002b). Tax Administration: New Compliance Research Effort is on Track, But Important Work Remains (No. GAO-02-769). Washington, D.C.: GAO.

Giles, D. E. A. (1998). *Modelling the Tax Compliance Profiles of New Zealand Firms: Evidence from Audit Records.* Retrieved March 23, 2004, from http://web.uvic.ca/econ/wp9803.pdf

Giles, D. E. A. (1999). Modelling the Hidden Economy and the Tax-Gap in New Zealand. *Empirical Economics, 24.*

Gutmann, D. and Williams, J. (2004). *Department of Revenue Compliance Study.* Retrieved January 14, 2005, from http://dor.wa.gov/

Guttman, G. (2000). Measuring the Effectiveness of Internal Revenue Service. *Tax Notes*(89), 1102.

Guttman, G. (2002). IRS National Research Program on Track Despite Training Delays. *Tax Notes, 97,* 331–336.

Hamilton, A. (2002). IRS Vets New Compliance Measurement Proposal. *Tax Notes*(94), 278–281.

Heller, P. S. (2003). *Who Will Pay?* Washington, D.C.: International Monetary Fund.

Hessing, D. J., Elfers, H., Robben, H. S. J. and Webley, P. (1992). Does Deterrence Deter? Measuring the Effect of Deterrence on Tax Compliance in Field Studies and Experimental Studies. In J. Slemrod (Ed.), *Why People Pay Taxes* (pp. 291–305). Ann Arbor: The University of Michigan Press.

HM Treasury Spending Review. (2004). Retrieved February 26, 2004, from http://www.hm-treasury.gov.uk/Spending_Review/spend_sr02/psa/spend_sr02_psace.cfm

IRS. (1998). IRS News Release. New IRS Mission Statement Emphasizes Taxpayer Service (No. IR-98-59).

IRS. (2002). Compliance Estimates for Earned Income Tax Credit Claimed on 1999 Returns. Washington, D.C.: Department of Treasury.

Johnson, D. C. (2003). *Perfectly Legal.* New York: Portfolio.

Jung, Y. H. Snow, A. and Trandel, G. A. (1994). Tax Evasion and the Size of the Underground Economy. *Journal of Public Economics, 54,* 391–402.

Klepper, S., Mark, M., and Nagin, D. (1991). Expert Intermediaries and Legal Compliance: The Case of Tax Preparers. *Journal of Law and Economics, 34*(1), 205–299.

Long, S. B. and Swingen, J. A. (1991). Taxpayer Compliance: Setting New Agendas for Research. *Law and Society Review, 25*(3), 637–683.

McKerchar, M. (2001). The Study of Income Tax Complexity and Unintentional Noncompliance: Research Method and Preliminary Findings. Sydney: University of Sydney (Australia).

Mikesell, J. L. (1985). Audits and The Tax Base: Evidence on Induced Sales Tax Compliance. *Western Tax Review, 6*(2), 86–114.

Mikesell, J. L. (2000). Remote vendors and American sales and use taxation: the balance between fixing the problem and fixing the tax. *National Tax Journal* LIII (4), 1273–1285.

Mirus, R., Smith, R. S. and Karoleff, V. (1994). Canada's Underground Economy Revisited: Update and Critique. *Canadian Public Policy — Analyse de Politiques, XX*(3).

Murray, M. (1995). Sales Tax Compliance and Audit Selection. *National Tax Journal, 48,* 525–530.

Nerre, B. (2001, November 8–10, 2001). *The Concept of Tax Culture.* Paper presented at the 94th Annual Conference on Taxation, Baltimore, Maryland.

Nerre, B. (2002, November 14–16, 2002). *Modeling Tax Culture — a First Approach.* Paper presented at the 95th Annual Conference on Taxation, Orlando, Florida.

Plumley, A. H. (2002, November 14–16, 2002). *The Impact of the IRS on Voluntary Tax Compliance: Preliminary Empirical Results.* Paper presented at the National Tax Association 95th Annual Conference on Taxation, Orlando, Florida.

Reckers, P., Sanders, D. and Roark, S. J. (1994). The Influence of Ethical Attitudes on Taxpayers Compliance. *National Tax Journal, XLVII* (4), 825–836.

Schuetze, H. J. (2002). Profiles of Tax Non-compliance Among the Self-Employed in Canada: 1969 to 1992. *Canadian Public Policy—Analyse de Politiques, XXVIII* (2).

Slemrod, J. (1989). The Return to Tax Simplification: An Econometric Analysis. *Public Finance Quarterly, 17*(1), 3–28.

Slemrod, J., Blumenthal, M. and Christian, C. (2001). Taxpayer Response to an Increased Probability of Audit: Evidence from a Controlled Experiment in Minnesota. *Journal of Public Economics, 79*(3), 455–483.

Torgler, B. (November 14–16, 2002). *Direct Democracy Matters: Tax Morale and Political Participation*. Paper presented at the 95th Annual Conference on Taxation, Orlando, Florida.

Transactional Records Access Clearinghouse. (2004a). Retrieved February 24, 2004, from http://trac.syr.edu/tracirs/findings/national/collpct.html

Transactional Records Access Clearinghouse. (2004b). Retrieved March 12, 2004, from http://trac.syr.edu/tracirs/trends/current/ratesTab3.html

Vogel, J. (1974). Taxation and Public Opinion in Sweden: An Interpretation of Recent Survey Data. *National Tax Journal, 27*(4), 499 – 513.

Wetzler, J. W. (1991). Economic Analysis of Tax Enforcement. *Tax Notes Today, 91–94.*

Witte, A. D. and Woodbury, D. (1985). The Effect of Tax Laws and Tax Administration on Tax Compliance: The Case of the U.S. Individual Income Tax. *National Tax Journal, XXXVIII* (No.1), 1–13.

Chapter 9

The Lottery as an Economic Stimulus Tool: The Case of Florida

SUSAN A. MACMANUS, Ph.D.
Department of Government and International Affairs,
University of South Florida

Q: What was the common thread tying together the Florida Lottery, the tourism sector, state and local tax revenues, and public–private partnerships in the months following the 9/11 catastrophe?

A: The Florida Lottery's "Play FLA USA" scratch-off game.

Q: Did the game make a difference?

A: The general impression is that it did. After Florida launched its "PLAY FLA USA" game in January 2002, the number of visitors increased as did state and local sales tax collections. Maryland immediately followed suit with its lottery, along with several other states. And in the fall of 2003, Florida is again turning to a similar game — "Vacation Cash."

Q: What made it so successful?

A: A large *coordinated* advertising-based campaign crafted via a public–private partnership — one that targeted a vital sector of Florida's economy.

9.1 Introduction: Tourism Plunges after 9/11

In the days following 9/11, Florida faced a projected $7 billion loss in tourism spending with an expected accompanying loss of $434 million in state sales tax revenue (VISIT FLORIDA[TM], 2001, December 14). Both the private and public sectors were suffering. Thus, it was fitting that help came via several coordinated public–private partnerships — one, a rather unusual one involving Florida's lottery. It was one of the nation's first uses of a state lottery as an economic stimulus tool.

9.1.1 Tourism: A Big Sector of the State's Economy

Florida's fiscal health is heavily dependent on the vitality of its tourism industry. Travel-related industries employ over 12% of the state's non-agricultural workers but spark employment in other sectors. Over one-fifth (21%) of 500 Floridians surveyed in October 2001 acknowledged that the slowdown in the state's tourism had "negatively affected their job or business"[1] (VISIT FLORIDA[TM], 2001, November 16).

Tourism accounts for almost $3 billion in state sales tax revenue annually, making the Tourism and Recreation category[2] the third largest single component of Florida's sales tax revenues (approximately 20%).[3] Florida's sales tax is the largest single tax out of 36 taxes and fees administered by the Florida Department of Revenue (2002:6) — generating 62.1% of the total.

Tourism also feeds the sales tax coffers of many local governments who generate considerable portions of their revenue from local option taxes specifically tied to tourism.[4] These taxes generated some $345+ million in the counties where they were in place in 2001 (Florida House of Representatives, 2003).

As predicted, in the months immediately following 9/11, Florida's "tourist economy suffered a significant downturn" (DOR, 2002:12). Tourism-related industries suffered as did state and local governments whose tax intakes plummeted (see Figure 9.1). Action was needed.

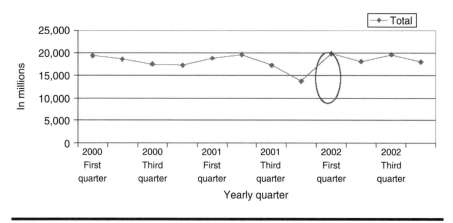

Figure 9.1 Estimates of visitors to Florida, 2000–2002. *Source:* VISIT FLORIDA™.

9.1.2 Fiscal Adversity Prompts Innovation

When state leaders sat down to devise a road map to recovery, one path they took was to develop a highly publicized state lottery scratch-off game designed to encourage Floridians to play the game *and* vacation in their home state in 2002 (the "Stay Here, Play Here" theme).

The press release announcing the game made it clear that the game was intended to boost revenues in both the private and public sectors:

> "Featuring more than **$10 million** in cash prizes and **90 vacation packages**, the Florida Lottery's new Scratch-Off game, **PLAY FLA USA**, leverages the Lottery's strength in the retail marketplace in an effort to boost the Sunshine State's vital tourism industry."
>
> The game was an example of a successful public–private partnership between various tourist attractions, VISIT FLORIDA™ (a nonprofit agency officially tasked with promoting Florida tourism),[5] and the Florida Lottery (see Table 9.1).

9.2 Research Lacking on Link Between Lottery and Private Sector

Traditionally, the literature on state lottery revenues has primarily focused on forecasting (Lockwood, 1999; Przybylski and Littlepage, 1997), yield (Popp and Stehwien, 2002; Elliott, 2002; Mikesell, 2001; Lockwood, 1999; Clynch and Rivenbark, 1999), or regressivity and redistribution (Rubinstein

Table 9.1 The Major Partners and Their Responsibilities

The Department of the Lottery (State agency)	*VISIT FLORIDA™ (Nonprofit corporation officially responsible for marketing Florida tourism)*	*Florida Merchants (Private sector)*
• Produce and distribute scratch-off game with approximately 10,000,000 tickets. • Obtain vacation prize packages from Florida attractions (sponsors). • Advertise: Provide sales support to game by creating, producing, and distributing: — 1 60-second generic TV ad — 1 60-second TV ad of which 15 seconds devoted to *each of* 5 sponsors — 1 60-second radio ad — Various Point-of-Sale (POS) materials promoting the game and sponsor attractions at approximately 11,500 Florida lottery retail locations by Jan. 21, 2002. — Videos and Internet promotionals • Offer double commissions to retailers promoting the game. • Approve participating discount program establishments.	• Waive customary licensing fees and extend limited rights for use of VISIT FLORIDA™ and FLA USA name, logos, and proprietary materials in game, radio, TV, POS, and support elements specific to Play FLA USA game. • Solicit its members to participate in discount programs (Jan. 22–Dec. 31, 2002). • Provide list of discount program participating establishments to lottery — name, type of business, discount offered, and any reasonable restrictions. • Provide (at no cost to Lottery) official graphics, artwork, and video materials to use in game advertising. • Document that each establishment has waived licensing fees for the use of its name, logos, and proprietary materials.	*Sponsors:* (for winning ticket holders) • Structure and redeem Vacation Prize Packages (Retail value — all packages: $233,842) *Participating VISIT FLA merchants* (for non-winning tickets) • Offer free or discounted attractions or added value services • Waive licensing fee for use of name, logos, and proprietary materials. *Advertising firms* • Contracts to produce TV, radio spots, in English and Spanish

Source: Florida Department of the Lottery letters of agreement.

and Scafidi, 2002; Price and Novak, 2000, 1999; Mergenhagen, 1996; Pirog-Good and Mikesell, 1995).

Only recently has lottery research begun to look at ties between the lottery and non-gaming portions of the private sector (Miller and Morey, 2003). Few studies have viewed lotteries as public–private partnerships. In fact, state lotteries are rarely, if ever, viewed as economic stimulus tools. That is what makes Florida's approach so unusual (and the fact that the big prizes were contributed by the private sector).[6] It lends credence to the notion that out of adversity comes innovation.

9.3 Quick to the Draw: The VISIT FLORIDA™ Economic Stimulus Package and The Lottery's Play FLA USA: A Powerful One-Two Punch

Tourism dropped nearly 19% in the months following 9/11 (see Figures 9.1 and 9.2). In December 2001, the Florida Legislature, at the request of the Governor, reacted quickly with a $20 million emergency appropriation for tourism advertising (the Economic Stimulus Package).[7] This was in addition to a $4 million domestic advertising buy begun by VISIT FLORIDA in October 2001.[8] In January, the Lottery launched the "Play FLA USA" game. Coordination of the two entities' advertising campaigns was crucial to the success of the promotional effort in stimulating the tourism sector.

9.3.1 Visit Florida™ $20 Million Advertising Blitz

The $20 million legislative appropriation required a dollar-for-dollar match from the tourism industry. The appropriation was matched "by more than $25 million in cooperative advertising from the various participating tourism industry partners to create the largest tourism recovery campaign in Florida history"[9] (VISIT FLORIDA™, 2002, December 12). Eighty-nine organizations

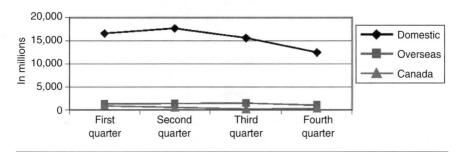

Figure 9.2 Estimates of visitors to Florida, 2001. *Source:* VISIT FLORIDA™.

from every geographic region of the state participated as partners in this effort that began in December 2001 and ran through October 2002.

The Fahlgren Benito Advertising firm of Tampa, Florida (the VISIT FLORIDA^{TM} ad agency of record) handled the advertising campaign aimed at increasing tourist traffic as fast as possible. The goal was "to stimulate enough additional visitation by Florida residents and the 'near-drive' market to help make up for the current downturn in the domestic and international air markets" (VISIT FLORIDA^{TM}, 2001, October 9). The best bet in the short term was to focus on the domestic market (92% of the advertising dollars). Within the domestic market, the natural targets were Florida and neighboring states within driving distance. Air travel had practically come to a standstill, making appeals to international and domestic air (fly-in) markets less viable.[10]

The bulk of the domestic advertising dollars (83.5%) were spent outside of Florida, mostly in the southeastern regional market (71.6%).[11] (see Figure 9.3 for a breakdown of domestic and international advertising expenditures). The message? "Florida is a familiar, friendly and affordable destination" (VISIT FLORIDA^{TM}, 2001, December 14).

9.3.2 The Lottery's "Play FLA USA" Scratch-Off Game

Enter the Florida Lottery's Play FLA USA game with its $5 million advertising campaign exclusively targeted *inside* Florida. It, along with the VISIT FLORIDA^{TM} advertising blitz outside the state, afforded the perfect 1-2 punch in the state's fight to reinvigorate a badly battered sector of the economy.

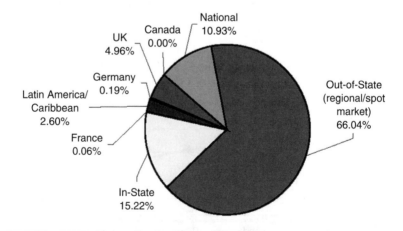

Figure 9.3 Visit Florida $20 million Economic Stimulus Recovery Program advertising: total spending. *Source:* Fahlgren Benito Advertising for VISIT FLORIDA.

Why a scratch-off game? For two primary reasons. First, such a format produces an instant winner. Second, the games have gained in popularity across all states with lotteries — both with the public and with government officials looking for more revenue (Miller and Morey, 2003:121).

9.3.2.1 Timing

The Lottery created the Play FLA USA $2 scratch-off game which ran from January 22 to March 22, 2002. January is generally a good launch date for new games. Residents are likely to pay attention to new ads after being inundated with repetitive sales ads during the Christmas/New Year holiday season. Consequently, new scratch-off sales historically spurt in February and March when advertising takes off ... and more seasonal visitors arrive and play. (Lottery research shows that 29% of Florida's seasonal residents play scratch-off games, just slightly fewer than 31% of year-round residents.[12] There is no breakdown for the proportion of tourists that play).

9.3.2.2 Structure

At the time the game was designed (Fall 2001 after 9/11), the number of tourists visiting Florida had plummeted and it was unclear as to how many seasonal residents would return to Florida. The hardest hit segments of the tourism sector were attractions and lodging (down 40%).[13] Thus, prize packages featuring attractions and lodging made a lot of sense.

It was obvious that any attempt to use a tourist attraction/resort-based prize-based game would have to be structured in a way that: (1) targeted year-round Florida residents to play, (2) prompted winners to redeem their prizes quickly, and (3) enticed non-winners to take advantage of discounts at tourism-related establishments that are VISIT FLORIDA™ partners. Previous marketing and focus-group research had shown that a number of factors prompt individuals to play scratch-off games, including the size of the top prize, colorful and fun graphics, ease of play, newness of game, cost of a ticket, theme, perceived playing time, money images, second chance drawings, and past scratch-off experiences.[14]

9.3.2.3 Player Profile

Available tracking surveys by Ipsos-Reid revealed some differences in the profile of scratch-off and other lottery game players in Florida:[15]

- *Age:* Scratch-off players are slightly younger, with a median age in the 35–44 year range and the highest proportion of players aged 18–34 years.

- *Gender:* A majority (57%) of scratch-off game players are female.
- *Income:* Scratch-off game players have the second highest proportion of annual incomes over $50,000 and the second lowest proportion of players earning under $30,000 annually.
- *Educational attainment:* Scratch-off games have the second most educated playership (behind Lotto).
- *Employment status:* Scratch-off games have the highest percentage of full-time employee players of any game (47%) and the lowest percentage of retiree players (20%).

Approximately 30% of instant game players play once a week or more. Instant games generate nearly one-third of all lottery revenue.[16]

9.3.2.4   Attitudes Toward Tourism in Florida

Research by VISIT FLORIDA™ tracking resident attitudes towards the tourism industry has consistently shown strong support for the tourism industry. In 2001 a high proportion (94%) agreed that "tourism is a good thing for Florida."[17] And nearly one-third (30.6%) attributed some of their household income to tourism.[18]

9.3.2.5   Pleasure Trips Inside Florida

Research has also shown that among the households reporting having taken a pleasure-related trip in a given year, over 40% take one *inside* Florida (Verhine, 2002:3). The most common destinations are to theme/amusement parks, the beach, sightseeing in big cities, and smaller, more rural spots outside large metropolitan areas (eco-tourism, camping, fishing, boating, sports events).

These attitudes and trip patterns were a solid base upon which to build a tourism-based game.

9.3.2.6   Prize Structure and Rationale

The game featured more than $10 million in cash prizes[19] and 90 vacation packages via 5 partners:[20]

- 30 Seven-night cruises for two on Carnival Cruise Lines.[21]
- 20 Dolphin Adventure vacation prize packages for four at Miami Seaquarium.[22]
- 20 Vacation packages for up to four at Universal Studios, Islands of Adventure, Sea World Adventure Park, Orlando.[23]

- 10 Vacation packages for four at Kennedy Space Center.[24]
- 10 Seven-day/six-night vacation packages for four at one of the Panhandle's Emerald Coast Resorts.[25]

These partners were strategically chosen to reach the entire state and include the areas hit hardest by plunging tourism. Clearly, tourism suffered most "in markets most reliant on international visitors and air travel: Orlando and South Florida" (Albright, 2002). Orlando was ranked "second only to Las Vegas among the nation's cities devastated the most economically by the Sept. 11 tragedies" by the *New York Times* (*Orlando Business Journal*, October 12, 2001). Arrivals at the Miami International Airport fell 26% (Frank, 2002).[26]

In addition, all *non-winning* "Play FLA USA" tickets could be presented for discounts on goods and services at more than 270 participating merchants throughout Florida.[27] Adding a "non-winner" dimension to a scratch-off game is done infrequently, usually no more than twice a year. The fact that it was done on this game proves three things: (1) its high priority; (2) its urgency; and (3) belief that Floridians would "cash" in these non-winning ticket discounts at participating tourist-related establishments.

9.3.2.7 Advertising

Advertising is critically important to a game's success. States have learned that the introduction of "new and exciting" games that will capture the public's attention is a key to lottery scratch-off ticket sales (Miller and Morey, 2003; *La Fleur's* Magazine, 2002). Florida research, as previously noted, has confirmed it.

The Lottery expended nearly 1/7 of its entire annual advertising budget on the "Play FLA USA" game. The $5 million advertising budget was spent on: point-of-sale materials (posters, play station centerfolds, brochures), television and radio advertising, and an Internet promotion. Materials were developed in English (Cooper and Hayes) and Spanish[28] (Sanchez and Levitan). The latter was particularly important because previous research had shown that awareness of scratch-off games was significantly lower among the Hispanic population — the fastest growing segment of Florida's population.

The television ad series initially featured the Lottery Department Director informing viewers of the seriousness of the drop off in out of state tourists, while encouraging them to help Florida out by playing the game and playing at various tourist locations. It was the first time that the Secretary of the Lottery had been used in a TV commercial. The ads also featured "real people" excited about winning wonderful trips in Florida instead of animated characters, movie themes, etc. A 60-second ad featuring all five

Table 9.2   Florida Lottery Ad Scripts

"Play FLA USA"

Series 1
Base ad script:

We're lucky to live in Florida. Visitors come from all over to enjoy the backyard we take for granted. To encourage all of us to stay here and play here, the Florida Lottery has teamed up with Visit Florida to introduce Play FLA/USA, the Lottery's newest scratch-off game.

We've got to play! When we play FLA/USA we can win up to 10 grand! And we can win Carnival cruises, vacations to Universal/Orlando, and Sea World, Kennedy Space Center (ooh, astronauts). And Miami Seaquarium! Even golf and fishing trips at Emerald Coast! Plus, all the other tickets are good for discounts at some of Florida's best hotels, restaurants, cruises, tours and attractions! So every ticket's a winner!

And, as always, a portion of every lottery dollar goes to the Educational Enhancement Trust Fund. So, when you stay here and play here, we all win.

Special add-on clips:

****

Play FLA/USA and you could win a fabulous 7-day cruise for 2 on a Carnival Fun Ship right from Miami, Tampa, or Port Canaveral. Plus, all other tickets are also good for an extra $50 off of a 3 to 5-day cruise, or $100 off a 7-day or longer cruise.

Play FLA/USA from the Florida Lottery. When you stay here and play here, we all win.

****

Play FLA/USA and you could win a VIP Vacation to Universal Studios, Islands of Adventure, and Sea World Adventure Park, including 3-nights at the Hard Rock Hotel. Or, show your non-winning ticket and get 3 days admission to all three parks for only $89.95, plus tax.

Play FLA/USA from the Florida Lottery. When you stay here and play here, we all win.

****

Play FLA/USA and you could win one of 20 vacation packages for 4 to Miami Seaquarium. Winners get to swim with dolphins, behind the scenes tours, and 2 nights at Sonesta Beach Resort. Plus, all other tickets are good for half-price admission with a regular-price admission to Miami Seaquarium.

Play FLA/USA from the Florida Lottery. When you stay here and play here, we all win.

****

Play FLA/USA and you could win one of 10 week-long trips for 4 to the white sands and shimmering waters of Florida's Emerald Coast. Each winner receives free golf, sailing, deep sea fishing, jet skiing, para-sailing, ocean view accommodations, car rental, and air fare allowance.

Play FLA/USA from the Florida Lottery. When you stay here and play here, we all win.

****

Table 9.2   Continued

Play FLA/USA and you could win one of 10 vacation packages for 4 at Kennedy Space Center Visitor Complex. Winners get 4 season passes, beachfront lodging, shuttle launch viewing, special tours, and $1000 shopping spree. Plus, all other tickets are good for 40% off regular price admission.

Play FLA/USA from the Florida Lottery. When you stay here and play here, we all win.
****

Series 2
Base ad script:
Honey, come with me. You know that vacation we've been wanting? Well, we are in luck! When we play FLA/USA we can win up to 10 grand!
It's Play FLA/USA, the newest scratch-off game from the Florida Lottery.

And we can win Carnival cruises, vacations to Universal/Orlando, and Sea World, Kennedy Space Center! And Miami Seaquarium! Even golf and fishing trips at the Emerald Coast! All the other tickets are good for discounts at some of Florida's best hotels, restaurants, cruises, tours and attractions! So every ticket's a winner!

Special add-on clips
Play FLA/USA and you could win a fabulous 7-day cruise for 2 on a Carnival Fun Ship right from Miami, Tampa, or Port Canaveral. Imagine: pampering service, fabulous meals, exotic destinations. No wonder Carnival is the most popular cruise line in the world. Plus, all other tickets save you an extra $50 off a 3 to 5-day cruise or $100 off a 7-day or longer cruise.

You scratch! I'll pack! So Play FLA/USA. Because when you stay here and play here, we all win.
****
Play FLA/USA and you could win a VIP Vacation for 4 to Universal Studios, Islands of Adventure, and Sea World Adventure Park. Package includes 3 nights at the Hard Rock Hotel, VIP tours to all 3 parks and much, much more. Or, show your non-winning ticket and get 3 days admission to all 3 parks for only $89.95, plus tax.

You scratch! I'll pack! So Play FLA/USA. Because when you stay here and play here, we all win.
****
Play FLA/USA and you could win one of 20 vacation packages for 4 to Miami Seaquarium. Winners get to swim with dolphins, behind the scenes tours, and 2 nights at Sonesta Beach Resort on Key Biscayne. The perfect place to kick back and relax. Plus, all other tickets are good for half-price admission with a regular-price admission to Miami Seaquarium.

(Continued)

Table 9.2   Continued

You scratch! I'll pack! So Play FLA/USA. Because when you stay here and play here, we all win.

****

Play FLA/USA and you could win one of 10 week-long trips for 4 to the white sands and shimmering waters of Florida's Emerald Coast. Each winner receives free golf, sailing, deep sea fishing, jet skiing, para-sailing, ocean view accommodations, car rental and air fare allowance.
You scratch! I'll pack! So Play FLA/USA. Because when you stay here and play here, we all win.

****

Play FLA/USA and you could win one of 10 vacation packages for 4 at the Kennedy Space Center Visitor Complex. Winners will stay in a beachfront hotel, view a shuttle launch, get special tours, 4 season passes, and $1000 shopping spree in the world's largest space shop. Plus, all other tickets are good for 40% off regular price admission.

You scratch! I'll pack! So Play FLA/USA. Because when you stay here and play here, we all win.

****

Special ad:
We're lucky to live in Florida. Visitors come from all over to enjoy the backyard we take for granted. To encourage all of us to stay here and play here the Florida Lottery has teamed up with Visit Florida to introduce Play FLA/USA, the Lottery's newest scratch-off game.

We've got to play! When we play FLA/USA we can win up to 10 grand! And we can win Carnival cruises, vacations to Universal/Orlando and Sea World, Kennedy Space Center (ooh, astronauts). And Miami Seaquarium! Even golf and fishing trips at Emerald Coast! Plus, all the other tickets are good for discounts at some of Florida's best hotels, restaurants, cruises, tours, and attractions! So every ticket's a winner!

And, as always, a portion of every lottery dollar goes to the Educational Enhancement Trust Fund. So, when you stay here and play here, we all win.

Source: The Florida Lottery.

partners led off the blitz, followed by five 60-second ads, 15 seconds of which featured each of the sponsors (see Table 9.2 for the ad script.) The benefit to these sponsors for their large prize packages was clear: $5 million in free advertising for a several thousand-dollar contribution.[29]

An incentive program was implemented, offering the 11,500 lottery participant retailers *double* commissions (10% or 20¢) on the retail value of each book (full or partial) of Instant Game Number 423 ("Play FLA USA") tickets sold (the commission pool totaled $2 million). Lottery sales representatives were instructed to select five *high traffic/sales volume* retailers to entice participation.[30]

9.3.3 Yield

The game netted $12 million in sales — 93% of the projected revenue (see Table 9.3).

The "play" pattern for the game was consistent with that of other scratch-off games — purchases typically peak in the third and fourth weeks following a launch (see Figure 9.4).

Among the 22 scratch-off games available for play in 2002, "Play FLA USA" ranked 10th in total sales (see Table 9.4). The Department of the Lottery in its annual report (2002:6) declared the game a success for all involved:

> ... the Lottery was able to leverage the buying power of its customer base in an extremely successful promotion that benefited not only education, but also players and the tourism industry. The Play FLA USA Scratch-Off game concept encouraged the Lottery's customer base to frequent Florida's many businesses and tourist attractions, and generated excitement about the magnificent places to visit within the state."

Table 9.3   Sales: Play FLA USA

Length			Sold Out
8 weeks	Gross sales	$8,056,256	54%
	Net sales	$6,982,357	
12 weeks	Gross sales	$9,909,398	66%
	Net sales	$8,588,475	
16 weeks	Gross sales	$11,688,428	78%
	Net sales	$10,130,360	
20 weeks	Gross sales	$12,742,058	85%
	Net sales	$11,043,542	
24 weeks	Gross sales	$13,484,624	90%
	Net sales	$11,687,123	
28 weeks	Gross sales	$13,949,068	93%
	Net sales	$12,089,650	
Total	Gross sales	$13,943,070	93%
	Net sales	$12,084,459	

Source: The Florida Lottery.

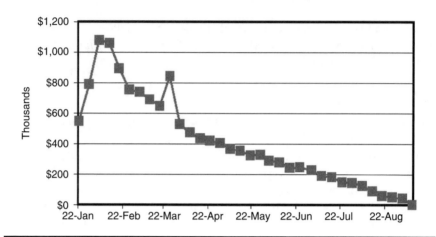

Figure 9.4 Monthly sales pattern, Play FLA USA revenues by month, 2002.
Source: The Florida Lottery.

Table 9.4 Play FLA USA Ranks 10th in 2002 Sales

	Lottery Scratch-Off Rankings	
Rank	*Game*	*Total Sales*
1	Monopoly	$54,476,624
2	Super Wild 7's	$22,352,378
3	24K	$20,344,172
4	Crazy 7's	$18,689,484
5	Harley-Davidson	$15,986,140
6	Yearly Divide	$15,688,194
7	Solid Gold	$15,102,236
8	Monthly Bonus	$14,499,306
9	Holiday Cash	$14,159,988
10	Play FLA USA	$13,991,746
11	High Roller	$13,472,558
12	Poker Party	$13,438,488
13	Holiday Bingo	$12,762,930
14	Fast New Year's Cash	$10,298,796
15	Key West	$10,251,450
16	One-Eyed Jack	$10,041,981
17	Year End Bonus	$9,993,952
18	Royal Riches	$9,978,128
19	Let Freedom Ring	$8,740,324
20	Universal Rules	$8,466,494
21	Fast Springtime Cash	$8,421,434
22	Elvis	$8,388,362

Source: The Florida Lottery.

VISIT FLORIDA™ was awarded a Travel Industry of America Odyssey Award (Travel Marketing–Domestic) for its 2001–2002 Tourism Recovery Campaign funded with the $20 million state economic stimulus appropriation from the Legislature. "The campaign included varied cooperative advertising to important drive-markets, a public service campaign and sales mission led by Florida Governor Jeb Bush, and various partnerships with the public and private sectors,"[31] including the "Play FLA USA" partnership with the Florida Lottery and private sector merchants.

9.4   State Taxable Sales: Tourism and Recreation

The Economic Recovery/Stimulus Package and the "Play FLA USA" advertising campaigns were designed to boost the private sector and, in turn, benefit the public sector, particularly one heavily reliant upon sales taxes.

Florida's Department of Revenue routinely collects tourism-related taxable sales statistics. Its Tourism and Recreation category includes taxable sales figures for restaurants, bars, hotels, and admissions.[32] In the post 9/11 period, hotel taxable revenue fell 25.36% while bar taxable revenues fell 3.6%, admissions −3.5%, and restaurants −1.8% (see Figure 9.5. See Figure 9.6 for graphs of individual source taxable revenue). Overall, taxable sales for 2001 totaled $49.7 billion, down one-half-of-one percent from 2000, most of the drop occurring in the post 9/11 quarter (VISIT FLORIDA™, 2002, February 22).

By October 2002 hotel sales had increased by 15.7%, restaurant sales 6.2%, bar sales 3.5%, and admissions by 1.2%. The third quarter of 2002 was the first quarter since 9/11 that the number of visitors to the state actually exceeded previous year figures (VISIT FLORIDA™, 2002, November 15). A majority (52.5%) of the visitors coming to Florida did not arrive via air.

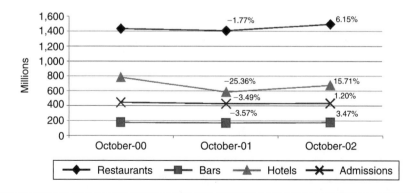

Figure 9.5 Growth percentage October 2000 through October 2002.
Source: Florida Department of Revenue.

By the end of 2002 the number of domestic visitors to Florida rose an estimated 10% over 2001. Overseas visitations for 2002 were off 4%, Canadian visitors down 15%.

Despite the rise in the number of visitors, Tourism and Recreation Taxable Sales for the year were $51.1 billion, up just seven-tenths of a percent from 2001 (VISIT FLORIDA™, 2003, April 2). Part of the explanation for the flatness lies with spending patterns of in-state and drive-in visitors versus international and fly-in visitors. Floridians are more likely to take day-trips and drive-in visitors are more likely to stay with family and friends, rather than in commercial lodging (VISIT FLORIDA™, 2001, December 5). Another part of the explanation is that in Florida, as elsewhere, the tourism industry responded to the tragedies of 9/11 with heavy discounts, thereby reducing sales volume (and sales tax intake).

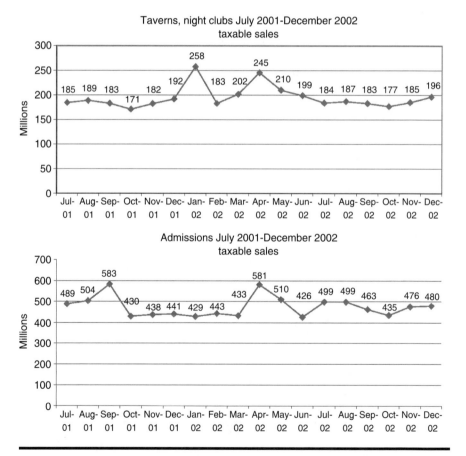

Figure 9.6 Taxable sales: individual taxes. *Source:* The Florida Department of Revenue.

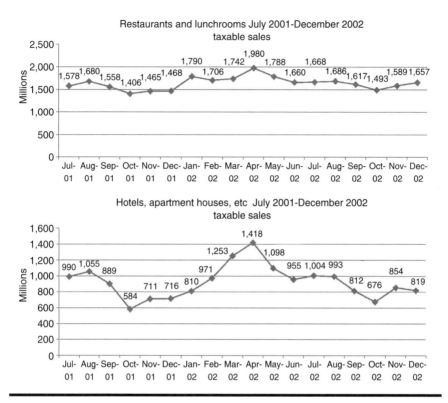

Figure 9.6   Continued.

9.5   Local Government Local Option Taxes

The Florida Legislature has authorized a number of local option taxes. These include: local discretionary sales surtaxes,[33] local option food and beverage taxes, local option fuel taxes, municipal resort tax, tourist development taxes,[34] tourist impact tax, convention development tax, consolidated county convention development tax, additional professional sports franchise tax, consolidated county convention development tax, charter county convention development tax, and special district, special, and subcounty convention development taxes (see www.myflorida.com/dor/taxes/taxtypes.html.) Not all counties impose each type of local option tax. But many of these taxes are greatly impacted by visitor volume.

It is clear that the promotional efforts of the Florida Lottery and VISIT FLORIDA™ stimulated local government local option tax receipts (see Figure 9.7).

The pattern was somewhat similar in the five counties with prize sponsors featured in the "Play FLA USA" ads (see Figure 9.8.)

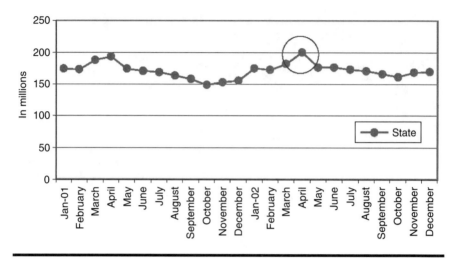

Figure 9.7 Local option tax receipts: state total (Florida's 67 counties). *Source:* Florida Department of Revenue.

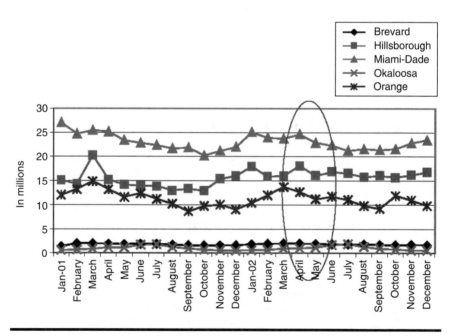

Figure 9.8 Local option tax receipts: counties in which Play FLA USA sponsor is located. *Source:* Florida Department of Revenue.

9.6 Local Tourist Development Tax Revenues

In 2001 48 of Florida's 67 counties levied at least one of the five legislatively authorized tourist development taxes on transient rental transactions (48 — the 1 or 2% tax;[35] 25 — the additional 1% tax; 14 — the professional sports franchise facility tax (up to 1%); 3 — the additional professional sports franchise facility tax (up to 1%); and 2 — the high tourism impact tax (1%) (Florida Legislative Committee on Intergovernmental Relations, 2002: 282–283).

Across the 48 counties, the tourist development tax collection pattern follows that of all local option tax collections — revenues went up after the tourism based promotional blitzes (see Figure 9.9). The pattern in each of the five counties in which a "Play FLA USA" sponsor is located is similar,[36] with the greatest deviation in Miami-Dade County (see Figure 9.10).

Thus, the public and private sectors were both winners of the advertising game partnership between the Florida Lottery, VISIT FLORIDA, and 273 participating Florida merchants, in addition to the five sponsors of the featured prize packages.

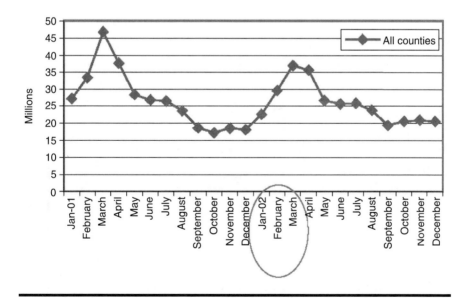

Figure 9.9 Tourist development tax collections: all 48 counties levying, 2001–2002. *Source:* The Florida Department of Revenue.

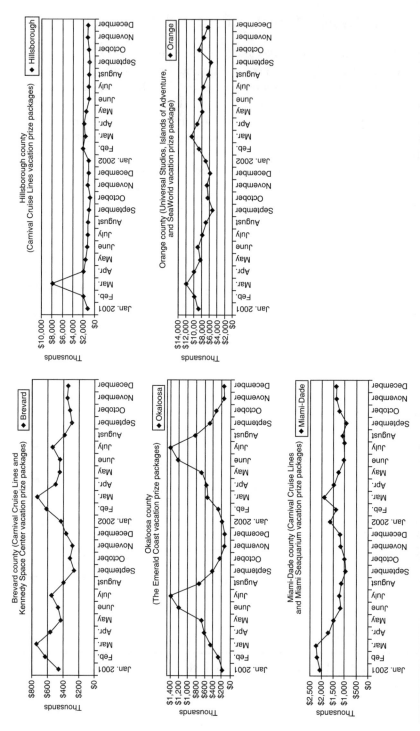

Figure 9.10 Florida local government tourist development tax monthly collections, 2001–2002. (counties in which "Play FLA USA" sponsors are located). *Source:* Monthly tourist development tax collections, Florida Department of Revenue.

9.7 Conclusion

Out of adversity comes innovation. So it was in Florida after 9/11 had such a devastating impact on tourism — the state's most vital industry. Figures from the last three months of 2001 showing a 19% decline in the number of Florida visitors alarmed officials in both the public and private sectors and prompted them to craft creative, quick response plans.

This study of a public–private partnership, involving The Florida Department of the Lottery, VISIT FLORIDA™, and hundreds of businesses across all parts of the state, has shown that successful economic recovery efforts following a catastrophic event are often contingent upon:

1. Planning involving both the public and the private sectors.
2. Targeting a vital industry that is located across the entire state.
3. Advertising to change consumer behavior — advertising based on sound market research *before* a catastrophe hits.
4. Creative and bold actions of *public* administrators — a willingness of top-level officials to think outside the box in how public resources can be redirected and coordinated with private sector resources to "get more bang for the buck."
5. Commitment from elected officials in both the executive and legislative branches to redirect already-budgeted public funds to *private* economic development partners.
6. Pressure and support from local government officials whose own revenue streams suffer when the economy in a sales tax-driven state declines.

While no one would argue that the "Play FLA USA" game was in and of itself the *sole* factor jump-starting the tourism sector, sales and tax receipts clearly show it had some impact in combination with the large-scale VISIT FLORIDA advertising campaign. The lesson here? Public and private advertising campaigns targeting the same population work best when they coordinate their messages and themes. The broader lesson? State lottery games can be important economic stimulus tools.

Acknowledgment

The author wishes to thank The Florida Department of the Lottery, The Florida Department of Revenue, the Governor's Office of Tourism, Trade and Economic Development, VISIT FLORIDA™, and Fahlgren Benito Advertising (Tampa, Florida) for providing invaluable information. The author is solely responsible for the interpretation of the data. Thanks are also due to Brittany Penberthy, USF student, for construction of the tables and graphs.

Notes

1.   A monthly Florida resident survey is conducted by the University of Florida's Bureau of Business and Economic Research.

2.   The tourism and recreation-related sales tax categories are: restaurants and lunchrooms; taverns and night clubs; jewelry, leather, sporting goods; cigar stands, tobacco shops; photographers, photo supplies; gift, card and novelty shops; news stands; admissions; holiday season vendors; rental of tangible property; parking lots, boat docking and storage; hotels, apartment houses, etc.

3.   The largest was nondurables (31%), followed by autos (19.5%), and tourism & recreation (18.6%). Florida Department of Revenue.

4.   There are four types of local option tourist-related taxes: municipal resort tax, tourist impact tax, local option tourist development tax, and the convention development tax (Florida House of Representatives, Committee on Commerce, 2003: 6).

5.   In 1996 the Florida Legislature created the Florida Commission on Tourism and VISIT FLORIDA^{TM} as the state's official tourism bodies. "VISIT FLORIDA^{TM} is the operating company of the Florida Commission on Tourism, which is a private/public partnership made up of top state government officials and representatives of the Florida tourism industry" (www.flausa.com/tools/flausa.php, accessed September 4, 2003). VISIT FLORIDA^{TM} directs statewide tourism advertising, research, promotions, public relations and sales initiatives, and operates the state's five Official Florida Welcome Centers (Governor's Office, May 20, 2003). VISIT FLORIDA^{TM} receives part of its funding from the public sector via a 15.75% share of the state's $2.00 per day Rental Car Surcharge. The rest of its funding comes from the private sector.

6.   Missouri had previously tied tourism and the lottery but the prizes contributed by the private sector were small in scale relative to those contributed in Florida.

7.   The law required that the entire appropriation be used exclusively for advertising. Governor Bush initially released his Economic Recovery request in October (*Orlando Business Journal*, 2001). He suggested the Legislature "speed up transportation and school construction and renovation projects to generate more than 30,000 jobs; temporarily take funds from the aviation fuel tax for airport security and operations; **authorize an extra $20 million to promote Florida tourism**;

expand the existing capital investment tax credit program; give additional capital investment projects fast-track permitting; temporarily suspend sanctions for companies in Qualified Targeted Incentive and Qualified Defense Contractor programs; extend the Qualified Defense Contractor program to general and commercial aviation; and expand housing assistance from the Florida Housing Finance Corp."

8.   The VISIT FLORIDA^{TM} Board of Directors executive committee approved dedicating its $2 million Economic Risk Response Fund to the effort. The advertising campaign begun in October was scheduled to run through February, 2002. The kickoff ad was a TV and radio public service announcement featuring Governor Jeb Bush appealing to Florida residents to "Explore Our Own State" by taking more in-state leisure trips (VISIT FLORIDA^{TM}, October 9, 2001). The announcement was produced in English and Spanish. The overall advertising campaign featured print, broadcast, and Internet ads as well as stepped-up public relations, promotions, sales, and research efforts by VISIT FLORIDA^{TM}. These efforts were targeted to Floridians and to "near-drive" Southeastern states (VISIT FLORIDA^{TM}, October 29, 2001).

9.   The legislation required a dollar-for-dollar match with private support from the Florida tourism industry (VISIT FLORIDA^{TM}).

10.   Data from the state's 14 largest airports for September 2001 showed a statewide drop in enplanements of more than 27% as compared to September 2000 (VISIT FLORIDA^{TM}, 2001, November 16). In 2000 55% of the state's visitors arrived via air (VISIT FLORIDA^{TM}, 2001, October 29).

11.   Figures provided by Fahlgren Benito Advertising.

12.   Florida Lottery Quarter 4 Tracking Table 65. Survey respondents are asked: "In the past 12 months have you spent any money on scratch-off games?" A seasonal resident is defined as one who lives in Florida at least one month of the year.

13.   Figures released in October found that 9/11 had little impact on the state's RV parks and campgrounds (VISIT FLORIDA^{TM}, October 29, 2001).

14.   Office of Research and Policy Analysis, Compilation of Scratch-Off Game Research (2000–2002), Draft, May 14, 2002, p. 4.

15.   Ibid. p. 1.

16.   Statistic provided by The Florida Lottery ("Lottery Players' Purchase Behavior"), no date.

17.   Calculated from statistics presented in Santos (2003). The data for these annual reports are generated from questions that VISIT FLORIDA^{TM} inserts into the Consumer Attitude Survey conducted by the Bureau of Economic and Business Research at the University of Florida.

18.   Ibid.

19.   Each $2 ticket offered a player 10 chances to win up to $10,000 in cash, or one of five outstanding Florida vacation packages.

20.   Three of these partners (Carnival Cruise Lines, Universal Orlando, Miami Seaquarium) had participated in previous games but two had not (Emerald Coast, Kennedy Space Center).

21.   Seven-night cruise on the winner's choice of: Carnival Pride (Port Canaveral), Sensation/Inspiration (Tampa), Smoke-Free Paradise (Miami), Carnival Triumph (Miami), or Carnival Victory (Miami). The cruise was for two guests in an ocean-view stateroom and included non-commission fare (port charges) and government fees/taxes. Air and ground transportation, gratuities and personal expenses aboard the cruise were not included.

22.   Packages were for four people and consisted of: two rooms for two nights at Sonesta Beach Resort, Key Biscayne; breakfast for two days at the Sonesta Beach Resort, lunch at Miami Seaquarium each day of the two-day vacation, "swim with the dolphins" session, set of three digital photos for each person with the dolphins; behind-the-scenes tour of Miami Seaquarium's animal attractions; and four $25 gift certificates to the Miami Seaquarium Gift Shop.

23.   Packages were for up to four people and consisted of: three nights' hotel accommodations in two rooms of the Hard Rock Hotel (not including meals, incidentals, tips, telephone calls, or any other personal expenses), non-exclusive VIP tours to Islands of Adventure and Universal Studios, three Universal Studio parking passes, $100 Universal Orlando Scrip to be used at Universal Orlando, four CityWalk party passes and a movie, Universal Orlando merchandise packages for four people, SeaWorld Adventure Park Florida admission passes, VIP behind-the-scenes tour at SeaWorld, free parking pass at SeaWorld, $50 in Shamu Fun Money to spend at SeaWorld.

24.   Packages were for four people and consisted of: three nights' beachfront hotel accommodations (room and sales and local taxes only); opportunity to view a shuttle launch, depending upon launch schedule; private, escorted behind-the-scenes tour of Kennedy Space Center; private dinner with an astronaut, prepared by the Kennedy Space Center Visitor Complex Executive Chef; four complimentary photos from the Kodak Shooting Stars Booth; four autographed books from Apollo Astronaut Gene Cernan; $1,000 shopping spree in the World's Largest Space Shop; and a $100 gift certificate from Ron Jon Surf Shop.

25.   Packages were for four people and consisted of: seven-day/six-night Gulf-view condominium accommodations (room and sales and local taxes only) provided by Abbott Resorts and located in Destin, Fort

Walton Beach or Okaloosa Island, $200 per person airfare allowance, car rental for one week (not to exceed $250), seven $20 gift certificates and seven $30 gift certificates to local restaurants, round of golf at the Regatta Bay Country Club, Dolphin encounter at the Gulfarium, one day-sailing ticket and one evening-sailing ticket per person, deep-sea fishing, jet-skiing, and parasailing.

26.   South Florida tourism was also affected by economic troubles in Latin American countries. Traditionally, those countries are the biggest source of international visitors to Miami.

27.   Hotels, restaurants, resorts, rental agencies, adventure tours, attractions, museums, etc.

28.   Tracking polls in Florida show that the Hispanic population is significantly more likely to learn about new scratch-off games from TV and radio than other racial/ethnic groups (Ipsos-Reid 3rd Quarter 00-01 Tracking Roll-Up), Office of Research and Policy Analysis, Compilation of Scratch-Off Game Research (2000–2002), Draft, May 14, 2002, p. 2.

29.   The value of the individual prize packages offered ranged from $2,250 to $7,300. The total retail value for all donated vacation packages equaled $233,842. *Source:* The Florida Lottery.

30.   Sales reps used a presentation manual that included four pieces of Point of Sale (POS) materials: a thank you poster displaying all participating merchants; a Florida Vacation Hot Deals poster with website information; a Stay Here, Play Here poster; and voided/oversize tickets. The sales rep was instructed to set up the retailer's lottery Play Station with these POS materials. *Source:* "Draft: Play F-L-A U-S-A Hot Five Promotional Sell-In Tips," no date.

31.   The TIA Odyssey awards are the travel industry's premier recognition program. www.tia.org/Program/natAwardsPhotos02.asp, accessed September 4, 2003.

32.   This is not a comprehensive list of all the taxable sales sources related to tourism, but it does capture those most directly linked to tourism.

33.   Charter County Transit System Surtax, Local Government Infrastructure Surtax, Small County Surtax, Indigent Care and Trauma Center Surtax, County Public Hospital Surtax, School Capital Outlay Surtax, and Voter Approved Indigent Care Surtax. *Source:* Florida Department of Revenue: www.myflorida.com/dor/taxes.taxtypes.html, accessed September 1, 2003.

34.   1 or 2 Percent Tax; Additional 1 Percent Tax; High Tourism Impact Tax; Professional Sports Franchise Facility Tax; Additional Professional Sports Franchise Tax. *Source:* Florida Department of Revenue: www. myflorida.com/dor/taxes.taxtypes.html, accessed September 1, 2003.

35.   By November 2002 the number increased to 53 counties (Florida House of Representatives Commerce Committee, 2003).

36.   All five counties levy the original tax (2% rate) and the professional sports franchise tax (1%). Four levy the additional 1% tax (all but Miami-Dade). Hillsborough County levies the additional professional sports franchise facility tax and Orange County levies the high tourism impact tax.

References

Albright, Mark (2002). "Terror Only One Blow to Tourism," *St. Petersburg Times*, September 7.

Anonymous (2001). "Bush Debuts Economic Stimulus Package," *Orlando Business Journal*, October 12.

Branom, Mike (2002). "Tourism Recovering Since Sept. 11, But Still Below Normal," *Naples Daily News*, March 22.

Clynch, E.J. and W.C. Rivenbark (1999). "Need Money? Roll the Dice," *International Journal of Public Administration* 22: 1681–1703.

Elliott, D.S. (2002). "Has Riverboat Gambling Reduced State Lottery Revenue?", *Public Finance Review 30*(3): 235–246.

Florida Department of Revenue (2002). *DOR: 2002 Annual Report.* Tallahassee: Florida Department of Revenue.

Florida Department of the Lottery (2001). Letter of Agreement With Florida Tourism Industry Marketing Corporation, Inc. (VISIT FLORIDA™), December 20.

Florida Department of the Lottery (2002). "Florida Lottery Teams Up With VISIT FLORIDA™ and Private Partners to Boost Tourism, Economy," January 22.

Florida Department of the Lottery (2002). *Reflections: Florida Lottery Annual Report 2001–2002.* Tallahassee: DOL.

Florida House of Representatives, Commerce Committee (2003). *2003 Report on Florida's Tourist-Related Taxes.* Tallahassee: January.

Florida Legislative Committee on Intergovernmental Relations (2002). *Local Government Financial Handbook 2001 Edition.* Tallahassee: Florida Legislature with the assistance of the Florida Department of Revenue.

Florida Office of Research and Policy Analysis (2002). "Draft: Compilation of Scratch-Off Game Research (2000–02)," May 14.

Florida Senate (2001). *2001 Report on Florida's Tourist-Related Taxes.* Tallahassee: The Florida Senate.

Frank, Mitch (2002). "What Jeb Envies About George," *Time*, January 25.

Governor's Office (2003). "Governor Bush Announces Florida Tourism Increases During First Quarter of 2003," May 20.

La Fleur's Magazine (2002). "After 9ll: Lottery Tourism Tickets," May: 33–34.

Lockwood, Andrew (1999). "Estimating Michigan Lottery Revenue When New Casinos Open," *Proceedings of the 92nd Conference of the National Tax Association*: 191–197.

Mergenhagen, Paula (1996). "Zipping Up Lottery Sales," *American Demographics* 18 (April): 13–14.

Mikesell, John L. (2001). "Lotteries in State Revenue Systems: Gauging a Popular Revenue Source After 35 Years," *State and Local Government Review* 33(2): 86–100.

Miller, James D. and Matthew R. Morey (2003). "Power Markets: Transferring Systematic Risk to Lottery Players," *Public Budgeting & Finance* 23 (Summer): 118–133.

Orlando Business Journal, October 12, 2001.

Pierce, Patrick A. and Donald E. Miller (1999). "Variations in the Diffusion of State Lottery Adoptions: How Revenue Dedication Changes Morality Politics," *Policy Studies Journal* 27(4): 696–706.

Pirog-Good, Maureen and John L. Mikesell (1995). "Longitudinal Evidence of the Changing Socio-Economic Profile of a State Lottery Market," *Policy Studies Journal* 23 (1995).

Popp, Anthony V. and Charles Stehwien (2002). "Indian Casino Gambling and State Revenue: Some Further Evidence," *Public Finance Review* 30(4): 320–330.

Price, Donald I. and E. Shawn Novak (1999). "The Tax Incidence of Three Texas Lottery Games: Regressively, Race, and Education," *National Tax Journal*, LII (December): 741–751.

Price, Donald I. and E. Shawn Novak (2000). "The Income Redistributional Effects of Texas State Lottery Games," *Public Finance Review* 28 (January): 82–92.

Przybylski, Michael and Laura Littlepage (1997). "Estimating the Market for Limited Site Casino Gaming in Northern Indiana and Northeastern Illinois," *Journal of Urban Affairs* 19(3): 319–334.

Rubinstein, Ross and Benjamin Scafidi (2002). "Who Pays and Who Benefits: Examining the Distributional Consequences of the Georgia Lottery for Education," *National Tax Journal*, LV(2): 223–238.

Santos, Nuria (2003). "Pleasure Travel Patterns and Tourism Attitudes of Floridians: January–December 2002," Research Report, Tallahassee: FLAUSA VISIT FLORIDA™, February.

Veiga, Alex (2002). "Florida's Tourism Industry Making an Uneven Recovery," *Chicago Sun Times*, September 8.

Verhine, Vicki (2002). "Pleasure Travel Patterns of Florida Residents: January–December 2001," Research Report, Tallahassee: FLAUSA VISIT FLORIDA™, February 2002.

VISIT FLORIDA™ (2000). "Florida Residents Positive Towards Tourism," June 29.

VISIT FLORIDA™ (2001). "VISIT FLORIDA™ Releases First Quarter Domestic Visitor Estimates," May 21.

VISIT FLORIDA™ (2001). "VISIT FLORIDA™ Releases Second Quarter Visitor Estimates," August 17.

VISIT FLORIDA™ (2001). "VISIT FLORIDA™ Launches Multi-Million Dollar Advertising Program," October 9.

VISIT FLORIDA™ (2001). "VISIT FLORIDA™ Releases First Tourism Industry Barometer," October 29.

VISIT FLORIDA™ (2001). "Third Quarter Sees Drop in Florida Visitors," November 13.

VISIT FLORIDA™ (2001). "Tourism Surveys Released," November 16.

VISIT FLORIDA™ (2001). "Mixed Results in Latest Tourism Surveys," December 5.

VISIT FLORIDA™ (2001). "Florida Tourism Recovery Investment Produced Big Return," December 12.

VISIT FLORIDA™ (2001). "VISIT FLORIDA™ Receives $20 Million for Tourism Recovery Plan," December 14.

VISIT FLORIDA™ (2002). "Florida Tourism Continues Gradual Recovery," January 10.

VISIT FLORIDA™ (2002). "New Florida Lottery Game Helps Promote Tourism," January 22.

VISIT FLORIDA™ (2002). "Florida Tourism Declined in 2001," February 22.

VISIT FLORIDA™ (2002). "Florida Tourism Recovered Significantly in First Quarter 2002," May 17.

VISIT FLORIDA™ (2002). "Florida Tourism Recovery Continued in Second Quarter 2002," August 14.

VISIT FLORIDA™ (2002). "35th Governor's Conference on Tourism Largest Ever," August 14.

VISIT FLORIDA™ (2002). "Florida Tourism Topped Year-Ago Levels in Third Quarter 2002," November 15.

VISIT FLORIDA™ (2003). "2002 A Record Year for Florida Tourism," February 19.

VISIT FLORIDA™ (2003). "Opportunity Florida," April 2.

VISIT FLORIDA™ (2003). "Governor Bush Announces Florida Tourism Increases During First Quarter of 2003," May 20.

VISIT FLORIDA™ (2003). "Governor Bush Announces Another Increase in Number of Visitors Coming to Florida," August 22.

VISIT FLORIDA™ (2003). *2001 Florida Visitor Study.* Tallahassee: Research Office.

Chapter 10

Promoting Economic Development with Tax Incentives: A Primer on Property Tax Abatements

ESTEBAN G. DALEHITE, Ph.D.
Public Administration Program, Florida International University

The purpose of this chapter is to present a primer on property tax abatements (PTAs), one of the most popular tools used by state and local governments to promote economic development. It is expected to be of value to practitioners who are pursuing the design, redesign or evaluation of abatement programs and also to students and scholars in search of an updated and comprehensive account of the state of the literature. The structure of the chapter is organized around the following questions: What are property tax abatements? What types of abatements exist? What do we know about them? And, given what we know, how should they best be designed?

10.1   Definition and Typology

PTAs can de defined as an agreement between government and business where the latter assumes the commitment to invest in a given jurisdiction in exchange for a reduction in the property tax liability on that investment over a determinate period of time. Thus PTAs can be distinguished from pure property tax relief in the form of deductions, exemptions or credits that are permanent or require nothing from the beneficiary. Abatements typically take the form of a deduction from the tax base but a variety of ways are used by states and local governments to achieve the same end (Dalehite, Mikesell, and Zorn, 2005).

There are different types of property tax abatements. First, a distinction can be made between programmatic and ad-hoc abatements. Programmatic abatements refer to specific policies or programs established in statute where states allow local bodies or themselves the right to award a temporary reduction in property taxes pursuant to the procedure and requirements established in legislation. Abatements are thus awarded by local or state bodies applying uniform and previously established rules.

Ad-hoc abatements can take any shape or form that local or state bodies negotiate with potential investors. The most prominent ad-hoc abatements are awarded in highly publicized "bidding wars" between states or local entities to attract new plants from large national or international manufacturers. These can also be referred to as "one-shot, firm-specific" abatements. They will frequently require special legislation to legitimize a specific bundle of pre-negotiated benefits. PTAs are often the main feature in these agreements. A second variety of ad hoc abatements is not as widely publicized and is often considered undesirable. These are the informal, often off-the-record abatements granted by local bodies to business. In fact, programmatic abatements are a means of bringing local abatements into the light and creating a set of common rules.

Second, a distinction between targeted and untargeted abatements can also be made. Targeted abatements can be classified into firm-specific, industry-specific, or area-specific, depending on whether a single firm, entire industry, or a geographic area is targeted. The relevance of this distinction will be apparent below as some will argue that targeting enhances the efficiency and effectiveness of abatements. Third, another distinction can be made between a pure or stand-alone property tax abatement program, and abatements that are part of a bundle of diverse tax and non-tax incentives offered to business. The distinction or overlap between PTA and enterprise zone (EZ) programs is related. Enterprise zones can include PTAs as part of a bundle of diverse incentives (e.g. Indiana's EZ program), they can feature PTAs as the main or only incentive (e.g. Michigan's EZ program), or they can be devoid of PTAs (e.g. South Carolina's EZ program). Also, states may have incentive programs that solely or partly include PTAs that do not appear under the enterprise zone label (e.g. the Indiana Economic Revitalization Area Program). The point is that the particular label used by a state does not define the nature of the incentive program. The distinction helps to clarify terminology but may be valuable for research purposes as well. For example, if one were interested in solely testing the efficacy of PTAs, a stand-alone program, or at least one where PTAs are the main ingredient, should be sought. Also, evaluating the effectiveness of enterprise zones, given the wide variety of benefits that can come under this label, may be an imprecise undertaking.

10.2   Origins of Property Tax Abatements

The birth and expansion of PTAs in America can be tied to several traditions. They initially arose in the Great Depression when low revenues and increasing demand for services led Southern states to establish retail sales taxes, and devise incentives to recruit industry from the Midwest and Northeast (Mikesell, 1999; R. H. Wilson, 1993). The first pure property tax abatement program was established by Louisiana in 1936, the same year that Mississippi established the much cited Balance Agriculture With Industry (BAWI) program which included abatements as part of a bundle of diverse benefits.

The propagation of PTAs and other incentives during the second half of the 20th century has been attributed to diverse factors that increased fiscal stress and made states and local governments take economic development into their own hands: (1) The retreat of the federal government from its previous leadership role in promoting economic development; (2) devolution of spending responsibilities to states; (3) reduction of trade barriers; (4) transition from traditional manufacturing to a service and high technology economy; and (5) greater competition between states over revenue sources and employers (R. H. Wilson, 1993).

As PTAs and other incentives expanded they also experienced a gradual change in orientation, from smokestack chasing to increased focus on expansion of existing plants, small company starts, targeting, and job creation (Hansen, 1991). This new orientation of PTAs and other new policies are known as second wave, new wave or demand-side economic development policies. A distinct influence on the orientation and expansion of PTA programs was the importation and Americanization of the British enterprise zone (Butler, 1991). After the concept was introduced in 1979, the Executive and Congress during the early Reagan years raised expectations about federal matching incentives for investment in poor neighborhoods per incentives offered by states. In response, states began establishing enterprise zones to take advantage of federal matching incentives that never came through (Butler, 1991). The obvious consequence was the further expansion of state and local incentive programs under the EZ label, including PTA programs, but with a new understanding of incentives as tools "to resuscitate specific poor neighborhoods, creating jobs primarily for local people" (Butler, 1991, p. 32).

The number of states offering property tax abatements has gone from 15 in 1964 (Alyea, 1969) to 35 (Dalehite et al., 2005). According to Wolkoff (1983) PTAs are an attractive and popular alternative for the following reasons: (1) they can be applied to all applicant firms; (2) it is one of the few, though small, components of the firm's cost function that local governments can manipulate; (3) their availability in one jurisdiction pressures other jurisdictions into adoption of abatement programs; and (4) the implementation of abatements, much like most tax expenditures, is quite easy, given that there is no visible diversion of funds from any other program or group currently being supported.

10.3 Determinants of PTAs

Researchers have advanced several hypotheses to explain why localities offer incentives. Wolman and Spitzley (1996) provided a review of ideas on the subject. One position is that cities are interested in the well being of citizens and engage in competition to attract mobile capital; maintain or improve their competitive position; and deliver quality services at reasonable tax levels (Peterson, 1981; Swamstrom, 1985). Two separate testable hypotheses can be postulated. One is the fiscal stress hypothesis. According to this hypothesis, cities offer incentives in response to deteriorating fiscal conditions and an imbalance between revenue capacity and service demands (Bowman and Pagano, 1992; Pagano and Bowman, 1995). This hypothesis is consistent with the origins of PTAs explained above.

In contrast, the fiscal health hypothesis posits that it is fiscally healthy cities that are more likely to engage in economic development policies due to leadership vision and city image (Pagano and Bowman, 1995), or quite simply because they are more attractive to potential investors and require a smaller incentive to influence investors' location decisions (Greenstone and Moretti, 2003b; Reese, 1991).

In a recent survey of the literature on the economics of incentives, Glaeser (2001) summarized several additional rationales for awarding incentives. Two of these, similar to Peterson (1981), assume that the objective function of government is to maximize the welfare of their constituency. Under the first, governments offer incentives to attract firms with the purpose of increasing employment and the local supply of goods. This translates into welfare gains for consumers facing downward sloping demand curves and workers facing upward sloping labor demand curves. The hypothesis would be corroborated if governments sought to attract labor intensive firms that supplied local markets.

In a similar vein, Garcia-Mila and McGuire (2001) propose that governments offer incentives to attract firms with the goal of inducing or facilitating the positive spillovers derived from agglomeration economies. A brief introduction to agglomeration economies is in order. There are two main views that try to explain the concentration or agglomeration of economic activity, one that relies on external economies of scale, and the other on internal economies of scale (Hanson, 2000). The first view, attributed to Marshall (1920) and developed by Henderson (1974) and others, posits that positive externalities or spillovers, in the form of mutual learning and exchange of ideas between industry-specific firms and workers, raises the productivity of all and leads to clustering (Hanson, 2000). This view, for instance, seeks to explain the clustering of, say, the film industry in Los Angeles, California. The second view, developed by Krugman (1991), Venables (1996), and others, states that fixed costs (economies of scale over large volumes of production) and transportation costs draw firms to large consumer markets that can be served from a single plant at low transportation costs. In addition, interindustry demand linkages between firms up and down different production chains, serve as a driving force for industry concentration because firms benefit from specialized inputs at low transportation costs (Hanson, 2000). This hypothesis would be corroborated if governments sought to attract firms that either belonged to the same industry as preexisting firms, represented an important link or fit in preexisting production–distribution chains or skill sets, or are considered magnets for other firms. However, it must be noted that the benefits from agglomeration can only go so far before congestion, limited supply of housing, or the simple move to a preferred location after a period of learning, lead to slowing, reversal or shifts in clustering patterns (Hanson, 2000; McCall and Pascal, 1979).

In contrast to welfare maximizing pursuits, Glaeser (2001) and Schneider (1989) suggest that governments may be interested in maximizing revenues to minimize service/tax ratios or other pursuits. This can be done by offering large incentives in exchange for future tax payments from large firms that cannot easily move out upon eventual tax rate increases. This hypothesis would be corroborated if governments sought to attract immobile firms with inelastic demands for land and local labor (Glaeser, 2001). Another way of maximizing revenues would be to impose higher taxes on (i.e. offer less incentives to) firms that have greater need for a particular location (Glaeser, 2001). Beck (1985; 1993) provided theoretical models to suggest that PTAs can be used to increase revenues, assuming that they are only granted to businesses which, in the absence of abatements, would not have made new investments.

In the fiscal zoning tradition, Fischel (1975), White (1975) and Wassmer (1989; 1991; 1992) suggest that communities compete to attract new firms and households but only if they are able to exact fiscal benefits in the form of lower tax prices for old residents. These benefits must, at least, compensate for the loss of environmental quality, public service costs incurred, and incentives offered. As before, PTAs function as tools to bid for firms by lowering their individual tax rate. A very important corollary of this view is that high income communities, given income-elastic demand for environmental quality, will be unwilling to offer incentives and simply zone business out.

Lastly, scholars have suggested that mimicry (McHone, 1987), corruption and influence (Glaeser, 2001), or serving the interests of property developers (Logan and Molotch, 1987; Molotch, 1976; Stone, 1989) as alternative determinants of granting property tax abatements.

Several of these hypotheses have been empirically tested by researchers. Findings for the fiscal stress hypothesis, or for its reverse, the fiscal health hypothesis, have been inconsistent. On one hand, Man and Rosentraub (1998) found that decreases in state aid increase the likelihood of adopting a tax increment finance program, and Wassmer (1992) found that communities with higher local property taxes offer greater property tax abatements. These findings appear to support the fiscal stress hypothesis. Presumably, if the fiscal stress hypothesis holds, revenue–expenditure imbalances would be reflected in higher tax rates or tax prices and communities with higher levels of these would be more likely to adopt abatements, all else being equal.

On the other hand, Anderson and Wassmer (1995) found that communities with higher public service property tax prices are better able to resist the pressure to adopt PTAs when neighboring or competing communities do so. This finding is consistent with Man's (1999) finding regarding the likelihood of tax increment financing adoption. The explanation given by Anderson and Wassmer (1995) and Man (1999) is that overburdened citizens believe that PTAs are unnecessary, or that they will actually result in a tax burden increase, and this leads them to oppose the awarding of PTAs. Nevertheless, these findings are consistent with the fiscal health hypothesis. Communities in a state of fiscal health as measured by low tax rates or tax prices are more likely to offer incentives to attract firms. They are simply taking advantage of their attractive fiscal situation to maintain or improve their relative position in a competitive environment. Laura Reese (1992) found that growing economies, measured by total dollars of new development, had a positive association with the amount of abated dollars in the case of industrial property, and offered this as support for the hypothesis that well-off communities offer greater PTAs. More research is required in this area to resolve theoretical or empirical inconsistencies.

In contrast, a steady finding in the literature is the influence of income and negative community characteristics on the adoption and magnitude of property tax abatements. Anderson and Wassmer (1995) found that communities with higher median income are better able to resist the pressure to adopt PTAs. Wassmer (1992) found that communities with higher crime per capita offer greater property tax abatements. Chang (2001) found that greater unemployment rates, greater non-white population, and older buildings increase the likelihood of offering PTAs. These findings are consistent with the fiscal zoning hypothesis and with blight-area targeting recommended by the literature and included in many state programs.

Anderson and Wassmer (1995) also found evidence to support the copy-cat hypothesis. Lastly, Byrnes, Marvel and Sridhar (1999) examined the abatement offers made by cities under the Ohio Enterprise Zone Program and found that more generous abatements were awarded to firms which offer to create jobs compared to those firms that only offer to retain jobs. This finding could be offered in support of the hypothesis that the objective function of government when offering incentives is to maximize citizen welfare by attracting firms that increase local employment. However, additional rationales could probably be given.

10.4 Effectiveness of Property Tax Abatements

The previous section made reference to the decision of governments to offer incentives. By contrast, this section refers to the decision made by firms to locate in particular areas, and why abatements might influence this decision. The traditional explanations are found in standard production and location theories.

10.4.1 Theoretical Arguments

According to production theory, a reduction in the price of capital (in this case, the PTA) will trigger two effects. The first is an increase in output, a parallel drop in price of the good produced by beneficiary firms, and an increase in demand for both capital and labor. The second effect is a substitution of capital (the factor made relatively cheaper) for labor. The output and substitution effects work in the same direction for capital. Thus, demand for capital will invariably increase and put upward pressure on the price of capital. However, in the case of labor, the output and substitution effects work in opposite directions. If the substitution effect prevails, demand for, and the price of labor, could actually decrease.

The magnitude of the increase in capital investment and assessed value depends on the price elasticity of demand for the goods produced by beneficiary firms. The greater the price elasticity of demand, the greater the expected effect on capital investment and assessed value. According to Ihlanfeldt (1999), the price elasticity of demand is likely to be high for manufacturing industries that compete in the national or international market, because of opportunities for expansion, and low for locally marketed products. Along the same lines, James and Leslie Papke (1984) argue that investment tax incentives increase liquidity and influence the timing of capital acquisition, which encourages firms to retire and replace their plant and equipment more rapidly.

In addition to the standard supply-side, production theory rationale, a well-developed branch of the economic literature, known as location theory, has argued that profit-maximizing firms will choose the location that minimizes costs and thereby increases profits. PTAs and other incentives influence a firm's cost function and its decision to locate within the jurisdiction of the awarding government.

According to Nelson (1993), minimization of basic cost factors (transportation, access to markets, access to material inputs, and availability and cost of labor) was a good predictor of location in studies prior to 1960. In the period thereafter transportation costs decreased and innovations in technology added complexity to the economy. As a result, businesses gradually became "footloose." James and Leslie Papke (1984) define footloose enterprises as those that are

> not bound to particular locations because of resource and/or market availability. These are primarily manufacturers in production facilities for which they can obtain their raw materials and other supplies from a number of different locations and from which they can serve a broad market area. Moreover, they are primarily firms with multi-plant, multi-site operations whose products are sold in multi-state, national or international markets. (p. 65)

With these changes in the economy, other factors such as technical competence of the labor market, state and local taxes and expenditures, regional business climates, quality of life factors, inertia, agglomeration economies, coevolutionary development, serendipity and others became equally important (Nelson, 1993). All of these factors are considered to reduce firm costs in one way or another.

Businesses make location decisions in three stages (Schmenner, 1982). In the first stage the decision to invest is made, and taxes are not considered to be an important factor. Next, the decision to locate in a region or state is taken (market stage), and in this stage taxes are expected to have a greater role, although inferior to variables that weigh more heavily in the firm's cost function, such as labor cost differentials. Lastly, the decision to locate in a specific site is made (site stage) where it is considered that all other factors are relatively equal and hence tax incentives or tax differentials will have the greatest effect. In addition to taxes, government services enter into the equation, either because public spending substitutes for spending that private entrepreneurs would incur in the absence of public spending, because it enhances factor productivity, or because firms may not mind paying higher taxes as long as they receive valued services in exchange (Fox and Murray, 1990). Education is a good example.

Scholars debate whether taxes or tax incentives can play the role attributed by production and location theories. Some argue that taxes are a small fraction of business costs (2–3%) and should not be expected to have much impact (Lynch, 1996), especially if a jurisdiction is not competitive in uncontrollable factors such as transportation, labor and energy costs (Rubin and Zorn, 1985). However, others counter that, though small, they can amount to a significant part of total profits (J. A. Papke and Papke, 1984). According to Oakland (1974), property tax rates often differ by as much as a factor of two and this implies cost differentials of approximately 10 percent of profits. Bartik (1991) is likewise not persuaded by the cost argument and affirms that, even if small, tax differentials may influence location decisions when all other factors are equal, i.e. in intraregional location decisions. Hall and Jorgenson (1991) equally stress going beyond assessing the effect of tax policy on costs to measuring empirically the effect on investment behavior. Finally, some argue that tax incentives may also contribute to economic development because of their positive impact on business climate (J. A. Papke and Papke, 1984).

10.4.2 *Empirical Literature*

The empirical literature on location, taxation and economic development can be segmented according to different criteria. Several literature reviews divide studies according to the methodology employed, namely econometric, survey, case study, or hypothetical firm (P. S. Fisher and Peters, 1997; J. A. Papke and Papke, 1984). Another common approach distinguishes between interstate, intermetropolitan, intrastate and intrametropolitan studies (Bartik, 1991; Wasylenko, 1997). A third way of segmenting is to differentiate between taxation and incentives, depending on whether the treatment or policy variable is an average measure of the level of taxation, such as the effective tax rate, or incentives such as PTAs and tax increment finance districts (P. S. Fisher and Peters, 1997; Wasylenko, 1997). Finally, further distinction draws the line between incentive packages, such as those that may be offered in an enterprise zone, and individual incentives such as tax increment financing or PTAs (P. S. Fisher and Peters, 1997). Most of the research has focused on the effects of taxation — as opposed to incentives — on economic development, and on interstate and intermetropolitan location decisions. Intrastate, interlocal or intrametropolitan studies, as well as research on individual incentives or incentive packages, are in the minority.

Following a period in which empirical research suggested that taxes or incentives were relatively unimportant location factors, recent reviews presented by Greenhut (1956), Bartik (1991) and Wasylenko (1997) have provided encouraging summaries of the effects of taxation on economic development in both interregional and intraregional studies. However, voices continue to expressed caution (Lynch, 1996) and concern over the time dependency and irreplicability of results (McGuire, 1992), and recent evidence has suggested that states may actually be converging and making their tax systems similar (Annala, 2003). Fisher and Peters (1997) have presented a summary of the literature on incentive packages and enterprise zones, and likewise presented a mixed picture.

In the specific area of PTAs, the earliest attempt at verifying whether abatements induce investment was done by Ross (1953) who applied the survey approach to firms receiving abatements in Louisiana and concluded that abatements were ineffective, given that only 7% of investments would not have been made without the abatements. Similarly, Morse and Farmer (1986) used a survey approach on firms receiving abatements in Ohio and found that the percentage of investment influenced was 25%. Royse (1994) also used a survey approach and found that actual jobs and investment created generally exceeded those promised by companies. The problems with the survey approach (biased answers, etc.) are well known and will not be elaborated upon here.

Other approaches have been used. Morgan and Hackbart (1974) concluded that if abatements account for 5 to 10 percent of the increase in property value, a positive net present value can be achieved. Coffin (1982) found evidence that abatements slow the exodus or relocation of firms from the inner city. Wolkoff (1985) estimated that full abatement could decrease the price of capital by 4%, assuming a tax rate of $80 per $1,000 and an assessment ratio of 0.5. However, this percentage fell considerably short of the 75% reduction required to increase the probability of investment from 0.23 to 0.39. Severn (1992) demonstrated that abatements approximate permanent reductions of tax rates on buildings as the abatement period increases.

Leslie Papke (1991; L. E. Papke, 1993) conducted an evaluation of the Indiana Enterprise Zone Program, which exempts inventories from property taxation for a period of 10 years, using three different specifications to control for selection bias. Findings included an 8% increase in the value of inventories in the zones relative to what it would have been without the program, and a decline in unemployment claims by about 19%.

Chang (2001), using similar methodology on the Indiana Economic Revitalization Area program, determined that the effect of PTAs on job creation varies by sector. Abatements given to the service sector are more effective at creating jobs than those given to the industrial sector due to the higher capital/labor ratios of the latter. Finally, the most recent peer reviewed study indicates that industrial abatements are only effective at increasing the tax base in the first years of the program; industrial abatements given at a later stage and commercial abatements are found to decrease the tax base of local jurisdictions (Wassmer and Anderson, 2001).

Although not in the specific area of PTAs, a recent study using a novel research design found encouraging results concerning the effects of successfully bidding for plants. Greenstone and Moretti (2003a) use articles from the journal Site Selection reporting on the winning and runner-up counties from a competition over some large plant. These authors used the runner-ups as the revealed (by profit maximizing firms) counterfactual for what would have happened in the winner counties in the absence of the plant opening. They found that a plant opening is associated with a 1.5% trend break in labor earnings in the new plant's industry in winning counties (relative to losing ones). They also found a relative trend break of 1.1% in property values and considered this as evidence that the net effect on welfare was positive.

10.4.3 Methodological Lessons from Previous Empirical Research

The literature review provides a mixed picture and begs the question of why some studies produce significant results while others do not? One answer to this question is time, i.e., recent studies are more successful at finding significant effects. This has been attributed generally to increased methodological sophistication. Scholars have derived lessons from previous research in the area of taxation and economic development that take the form of design recommendations for future research. One of these recommendations is the need to perform natural experiments (Bartik, 1997). A second is the necessity to control for unobserved variables (Bartik, 1991; R. C. Fisher, 1997; Phillips and Goss, 1995). A third recommendation is the inclusion of public service controls, in addition to tax variables

(Bartik, 1991; R. C. Fisher, 1997; Phillips and Goss, 1995). This third recommendation has evolved over time. Earlier studies that relied on public expenditure data as proxies for public services recommended that the fullest range of expenditures by function be utilized, including public welfare expenditures that may not directly benefit enterprises (Helms, 1985; Mofidi and Stone, 1990). More recently it has been recognized that expenditure data are poor measures of public service quality, and that both revenue and expenditure data are directly and immediately endogenous relative to local economic development (Bartik, 1997). Thus the recommendation subsists but in the sense of including quality measures of public services that matter to business location decisions. A fourth suggestion is to account for the possible endogeneity of independent variables (Bartik, 1991) and jointly model the behavior of firms and host communities (Oakland, 1974).

10.5   The Zero-sum Game Question

Even if property tax abatements are effective, i.e., even if a jurisdiction manages to entice investment into its jurisdiction, there are several important questions that remain. The first question is whether benefits will exceed costs for that jurisdiction. The concern is with local bodies that offer overgenerous abatements and simply fail to consider the cost of increases in demand for public services due to the relocating firm and its ripple (Rubin and Zorn, 1985).

The second question is, again, even if incentives are effective, whether there will be a net gain for the nation or system as a whole. Rubin and Zorn reason that the benefit to one jurisdiction may be the loss to another and that, in net, the nation or system has neither won nor lost despite incentives (1985). The tax competition literature has long envisioned a race to the bottom where tax competition leads to inefficiently low levels of taxes and expenditures, making society as a whole worse off (Oates, 1972).

To put matters in perspective, John D. Wilson (1999) performed a comprehensive review of the tax competition literature and found that the results of theoretical models are highly dependent on assumptions. Tiebout-type models find that tax competition plays an efficiency-enhancing role because they assume that government competition is similar to what occurs between firms in private markets. In contrast, tax competition models find that society becomes worse off because they assume the existence of interregional externalities, where the actions of one government to increase the welfare of its residents lead to the reduction in the welfare of the residents of other regions. A third perspective, that of the Leviathan-type models, finds that tax competition is also efficiency enhancing because it contributes to reduce the size of a bloated government. Interestingly, bidding-for-firms type models, which may be more applicable to the case of property tax abatements, have found that competition for capital lumps (big firms) can also be efficiency enhancing. Wilson's review suggests, at the very least, that the last word on this subject has not yet been said. Lastly, Bartik (1991) argues that, as long as abatements and economic development policies in general encourage productivity and are targeted at distressed, high-unemployment areas where additional jobs are valued the most, economic development policies may not be a zero sum game.

10.6 Conclusions and Design Recommendations

This chapter has provided a comprehensive review of the definition, types, origins, and main research questions concerning property tax abatements and other economic development tools: Why do governments offer them? Are they effective? Even if effective, will jurisdiction or society be better off? The specific empirical literature on property tax abatements is scarce and provides mixed answers to the questions posed. However, two results deserve emphasis. One is that communities with negative characteristics (low-income, high-unemployment, high-crime) are more likely to offer abatements. This should be interpreted as a good sign given that jobs in these areas are more valued and the prospect of increasing net welfare for the community or the nation is enhanced (Bartik, 1991). The other conclusion is that it is uncertain whether PTAs are effective at inducing investment, although more recent, sophisticated studies, have provided evidence that property tax abatements are effective at increasing inventories or jobs (Chang, 2001; L. E. Papke, 1991, 1993), and the manufacturing property tax base in the first years of the program (Wassmer and Anderson, 2001). These findings are not an unqualified endorsement of PTAs. For this reason, this chapter concludes with several rules to guide practitioners in the design or redesign of PTA programs.

The design of a PTA program depends on the objectives of policy makers. Assuming that the objective is to stimulate investment and achieve net benefits to a community, net welfare increases to society, or at least minimize losses, several rules can be derived from the literature. First, abatement programs should strive to influence marginal decisions made by investors. This means awarding abatements only on new investment (Stiglitz, 2003). From the perspective of the property tax, this would exclude abatements on land, preexisting facilities, used equipment, and replacement investment. If this is not done, abatements may turn into windfall earnings for business. Second, abatement programs should be temporary. The purpose of this suggestion is to induce investment within a desired window of time. If the possibility of receiving abatements is permanent there is no added incentive to invest today as opposed to investing in the future (Stiglitz, 2003). This can be achieved through sunset provisions or periodic public referenda on the renewal of programs.

Third, area targeting, specifically targeting blighted or distressed areas is recommended on several grounds: (1) additional jobs will be valued most; (2) existing infrastructure can be used at less cost than, say, building infrastructure from scratch in a greenfield site; and (3) abatements may compensate for negative community characteristics that discourage investment when real estate markets are not working efficiently (Bartik, 1991, 1994; Hansen, 1991; Wassmer and Anderson, 2001).

Fourth, firm targeting is also recommended but from different perspectives and without disagreement. Some have argued for offering abatements to large firms because they are more likely to be footloose, to think strategically, to have alternative location options, and to have a greater price elasticity of demand for their products and thus greater return per abatements offered (Ihlanfeldt, 1999; Ross, 1953; Wolkoff, 1981). Large firm targeting can be of the "ad hoc, one shot, bidding wars" type, or also of the programmatic type. A typical way of establishing large firm targeting is through threshold amounts of new investment or jobs that trigger the abatement award or its relative magnitude. Others counter that state and local governments do not have information or knowledge to maximize rates of return, and that large-firm targeting may be perceived as inequitable, expensive, or as creating an unlevel playing field (Ihlanfeldt, 1999). Additionally, proponents of new wave policies argue that abatements to small, local firms have the greatest job creation potential (Eisinger, 1988; Vaughan, Pollard, and Dyer, 1985). As suggested by Glaeser (2001) above, the type of firm that is targeted may depend on the objective function of the awarding body. For example, if the awarding body is interested in maximizing the welfare of its citizens, then targeting labor intensive firms that supply goods consumed by the local market may be the preferred choice. Productivity-enhancing options may include the targeting of firms that will develop synergies with existing firms (Garcia-Mila and McGuire, 2001), or the offering of abatements on research and development investment.

Fifth, industry targeting is equally recommended as an initial screening process. That is, state and localities should make an assessment about their competitiveness relative to their peers by different types of industries. The purpose is to offer abatement only in those cases in which an industry would be indifferent between locating in alternative areas. If the industry is sure to locate in a given area, offering PTAs is unnecessary. Rubin and Zorn (1985), for example, offered a methodology to determine competitiveness in uncontrollable factors such as transportation, energy, and labor costs. A recent discussion on firm targeting can be found in Buss (1999), Finkle (1999) and Wievel (1999).

Establishing a framework that is conducive to the achievement of positive net benefits for awarding communities is also important. A first step is to provide statutory flexibility to tailor awards depending on benefits received. In this regard, discretionary award processes should be preferred over as-of-right processes, and flexibility regarding duration and amount of abatement is necessary. Empirical research on programmatic abatement programs has found that, even if flexibility is given, local bodies offer abatements to the maximum allowable degree (Wolkoff, 1983). Clearly finding ways of facilitating or inducing tailoring by local bodies is required. Wolkoff (1983) recommends establishing an abatement budget, having local bodies assume the full cost of the abatement, and other rules that might induce local bodies to distinguish between high payoff projects and those that require no incentives. Another important suggestion is for states and local bodies to establish and enforce claw-back provisions. The purpose of such clauses is to collect abated taxes *ex post*, and even impose penalties, when a firm does not follow through with its part of the bargain under the abatement agreement.

Lastly, states should give due consideration to evaluation of PTA programs. All too often evaluation is performed after program design and implementation, under data limitations and circumstances that put the validity of the results in doubt. To avoid this problem, evaluation should be considered prior to program design, redesign, and implementation. In this way, the program can be designed, redesigned, and implemented in a way that maximizes the validity of the eventual impact assessment. Following these seven rules may increase program effectiveness and net benefits to the awarding community and society as a whole.

Acknowledgment

The author gratefully acknowledges support for this research from the Lincoln Institute for Land Policy.

References

Alyea, P. E. (1969). Property-tax inducements to attract industry. In R. W. Lindblom (ed), *Property Taxation USA* (pp. 139–158). Madison: University of Wisconsin Press.

Anderson, J. E., and Wassmer, R. W. (1995). The Decision to "Bid for Business:" Municipal Behavior in Granting Property Tax Abatements. *Regional Science and Urban Economics, 25,* 739–757.

Annala, C. N. (2003). Have state and local fiscal policies become more alike? Evidence of beta convergence among fiscal policy variables. *Public Finance Review, 31,* 144–165.

Bartik, T. J. (1991). *Who benefits from state and local economic development policies?* Kalamazoo, Michigan: W. E. Upjohn Institute for Employment Research.

Bartik, T. J. (1994). Jobs, productivity and local economic development. What implications does ecomomic research have for the role of government? *National Tax Journal, 47*(4), 847–861.

Bartik, T. J. (1997). Discussion (of Ronald C. Fisher's The effect of state and local public services and economic development, same issue). *New England Economic Review* (March/April), 67–71.

Beck, J. H. (1985). Government Shortsightedness and Discretionary Tax Abatement: Local Tax Rates and Business Investment. In J. M. Quigley (Ed.), *Perspectives on Local Public Finance and Public Policy* (Vol. 2, pp. 203–214). Greenwich, CT: JAI Press.

Beck, J. H. (1993). Tax abatement and tax rates in a system of overlapping revenue-maximizing governments. *Regional Science and Urban Economics, 23*, 645–665.

Bowman, A., and Pagano, M. (1992). An analysis of the public capitalization process. *Urban Affairs Quarterly, 27*, 356–374.

Buss, T. F. (1999). The case against targeted industry strategies. *Economic Development Quarterly, 13*(4), 339–356.

Butler, S. M. (1991). The conceptual evolution of enterprise zones. In R. E. Green (Ed.), *Enterprise zones: New direction in economic development* (pp. 27–40). Newbury Park, CA: Sage Publications, Inc.

Byrnes, P., Marvel, M. K., and Sridhar, K. (1999). An equilibrium model of Tax Abatement — City and Firm Characteristics as Determinants of Abatement Generosity. *Urban Affairs Review, 34*(6), 805–819.

Chang, Y.-C. (2001). Evaluating the structural effects of property tax abatements on economic development across industries. Unpublished PhD dissertation, Indiana University, Bloomington.

Coffin, D. A. (1982). Property Tax Abatement and Economic Development in Indianapolis. *Growth and Change, 13*(2), 18–23.

Dalehite, E. G., Mikesell, J. L., and Zorn, C. K. (forthcoming). Variation in property tax abatement programs among states. *Economic Development Quarterly, 19*(2), 157–193.

Eisinger, P. K. (1988). *The rise of the entrepreneurial state.* Madison: University of Wisconsin Press.

Finkle, J. A. (1999). The case against targeting might have been more ... targeted. *Economic Development Quarterly, 13*(4), 361–364.

Fischel, W. A. (1975). Fiscal and environmental considerations in the location of firms in suburban communities. In E. S. Mills and W. E. Oates (Eds.), *Fiscal zoning and land use controls* (pp. 119–168). Lexington, MA: D.C. Heath and Company.

Fisher, P. S., and Peters, A. H. (1997). Tax and spending incentives and enterprise zones. *New England Economic Review* (March/April), 109–130.

Fisher, R. C. (1997). The effect of state and local public services and economic development. *New England Economic Review* (March/April), 53–67.

Fox, W. F., and Murray, M. N. (1990). Local public policies and interregional business development. *Southern Economic Journal, 57*(2), 413–427.

Garcia-Mila, T., and McGuire, T. (2001). *Tax incentives and the city.* Unpublished manuscript.

Glaeser, E. L. (2001). *The economics of location-based tax incentives.* Retrieved December 20, 2004, from http://post.economics.harvard.edu/hier/2001papers/2001list.html

Greenhut, M. L. (1956). *Plant location in theory and in practice.* Chapel Hill, NC: The University of North Carolina Press.

Greenstone, M., and Moretti, E. (2003a). *Bidding for industrial plants: Does winning a 'million dollar plant' increase welfare?* Retrieved December 20, 2004, from http://www.nber.org/papers/w9844

Greenstone, M., and Moretti, E. (2003b). Bidding for industrial plants: Does winning a 'million dollar plant' increase welfare? Cambridge, MA: NBER (working paper 9844).

Hansen, S. B. (1991). Comparing enterprise zones to other economic development techniques. In R. E. Green (Ed.), *Enterprise zones: New direction in economic development* (pp. 7–26). Newbury Park, CA: Sage Publications, Inc.

Hanson, G. H. (2000). *Scale economies and the geographic concentration of industry.* Cambridge, MA: NBER (working paper 8013).

Helms, L. J. (1985). State and local taxes and economic growth. *The Review of Economics and Statistics, 67* (Nov.), 574–582.

Henderson, J. V. (1974). The sizes and types of cities. *American Economic Review, 64,* 640–656.

Ihlanfeldt, K. R. (1999). Ten principles for state tax incentives. In J. P. Blair and L. A. Reese (Eds.), *Approaches to economic development readings from Economic Development Quarterly* (pp. 68–84). Thousand Oaks, California: SAGE Publications, Inc.

Krugman, P. (1991). Increasing returns to economic geography. *Journal of Political Economy, 99,* 483–499.

Logan, V. R., and Molotch, H. L. (1987). *Urban fortunes: The political economy of place.* Berkeley, CA: University of California Press.

Lynch, R. G. (1996). *Do state and local tax incentives work?* Washington, DC: Economic Policy Institute.

Man, J. Y. (1999). Fiscal pressure, tax competition and the adoption of tax increment financing. *Urban Studies, 36*(7), 1151–1167.

Man, J. Y., and Rosentraub, M. S. (1998). Tax increment financing: Municipal adoption and effects on property value growth. *Public Finance Review, 26*(6), 523–547.

Marshall, A. (1920). *Principles of Economics.* New York, NY: McMillan.

McCall, J. J., and Pascal, A. H. (1979). *Agglomeration economies, search costs and industrial location.* Santa Monica, CA: The Rand Corporation (Rand paper series, P-6348).

McGuire, T. (1992). Review of Bartik's "Who benefits from state and local economic development policies." *National Tax Journal, 45*, 457–459.

McHone, W. W. (1987). Factors in the adoption of industrial development incentives by states. *Applied Economics, 23*, 17–29.

Mikesell, J. L. (1999). Sales and use taxation. In W. B. Hildreth and J. A. Richardson (Eds.), *Handbook on taxation* (pp. 1–22). New York, NY: Marcel Dekker, Inc.

Mofidi, A., and Stone, J. A. (1990). Do state and local taxes affect economic growth. *The Review of Economics and Statistics, 72*(4), 686–691.

Molotch, H. L. (1976). The city as a growth machine. *American Journal of Sociology, 2*, 302–330.

Morgan, W. E., and Hackbart, M. M. (1974). An analysis of state and local industrial tax exemption programs. *Southern Economic Journal, 41*(2), 200–205.

Morse, G. W., and Farmer, M. C. (1986). Location and investment effects of a tax abatement program. *National Tax Journal, 39*(2), 229–236.

Nelson, A. C. (1993). Theories of regional development. In R. D. Bingham and R. Mier (Eds.), *Theories of local economic development perspectives from across the disciplines* (pp. 27–57). Newbury Park, California: SAGE Publications, Inc.

Oakland, W. H. (1974). Local taxes and intraurban industrial location: A survey. In G. F. Break (Ed.), *Metropolitan financing and growth management policies*. Madison, WI: The University of Wisconsin Press.

Oates, W. E. (1972). *Fiscal federalism*. New York, NY: Harcourt Brace Yovanovich.

Pagano, M. A., and Bowman, A. (1995). *Cityscapes and capital*. Baltimore, MD: Johns Hopkins University Press.

Papke, J. A., and Papke, L. E. (1984). State tax incentives and investment location decisions: microanalytic simulations. In J. A. Papke (Ed.), *Indiana's revenue structure: Major components and issues Part II* (pp. 60–114). West Lafayette, Indiana: Purdue University, Center for Tax Policy Studies.

Papke, L. E. (1991). Tax policy and urban development: Evidence from an enterprise zone program. Unpublished manuscript. Cambridge, MA: NBER.

Papke, L. E. (1993). *What do we know about Enterprise Zones?* Retrieved December 20, 2004, from http://www.nber.org

Peterson, P. E. (1981). *City limits*. Chicago, IL: University of Chicago Press.

Phillips, J. M., and Goss, E. P. (1995). The effect of state and local taxes on economic development. *Southern Economic Journal, 62*(2), 320–333.

Reese, L. A. (1991). Municipal fiscal health and tax abatement policy. *Economic Development Quarterly, 5*(1), 23–32.

Reese, L. A. (1992). Local economic development in Michigan: A reliance on the supply-side. *Economic Development Quarterly, 6*, 383–393.

Ross, W. D. (1953). Louisiana's Industrial Tax exemption Program. *Louisiana Business Bulletin, 15*(2).

Royse, M. (1994). Evaluating an Economic development Program: The Case of Tax Abatement in Allen County. *Economic Development Review, 12*(4), 61–64.

Rubin, B. M., and Zorn, C. K. (1985). Sensible state and local economic development. *Public Administration Review, 35*(2), 333–339.

Schmenner, R. W. (1982). *Making business location decisions.* Englewood Cliffs, NJ: Prentice Hall.

Schneider, M. (1989). *The competitive city.* Pittsburgh, PA: The University of Pittsburgh Press.

Severn, A. K. (1992). Building tax abatements: An approximation to land value taxation. *American Journal of Economics and Sociology, 51,* 237–246.

Stiglitz, J. E. (2003). *The roaring nineties.* New York, NY: W. W. Norton & Company.

Stone, C. N. (1989). *Regime politics: Governing Atlanta.* Lawrence, KS: University Press of Kansas.

Swamstrom, T. (1985). *The crisis of growth politics: Cleveland, Kucinich, and the challenge of urban populism.* Philadelphia, PA: Temple University Press.

Vaughan, R. J., Pollard, R., and Dyer, B. (1985). *The wealth of 'states: Policies for a dynamic economy.* Washington, DC: Council of State Planning Agencies.

Venables, A. J. (1996). Equilibrium locations of vertically linkes industries. *International Economic Review, 37,* 341–360.

Wassmer, R. W. (1989). *Taxes, property tax abatement, expenditure, and the composition of the property tax base in communities within a metropolitan area.* Unpublished PhD Dissertation, Michigan State University.

Wassmer, R. W. (1991). Taxes, property tax abatement, expenditure, and the composition of the property base in communities within a metropolitan area. In *1990 Proceedings of the Eighty-Third Annual Conference on Taxation* (pp. 132–140). Columbus, Ohio: National Tax Association-Tax Institute of America.

Wassmer, R. W. (1992). Property tax abatement and the simultaneous determination of local fiscal variables in a metropolitan area. *Land Economics, 68*(3), 263–282.

Wassmer, R. W., and Anderson, J. E. (2001). Bidding for business: new evidence on the effect of locally offered economic development incentives in a metropolitan area. *Economic Development Quarterly, 15*(2), 132–148.

Wasylenko, M. (1997). Taxation and economic development: The state of the economic literature. *New England Economic Review* (March/April), 37–52.

White, M. J. (1975). Fiscal zoning in fragmented metropolitan areas. In E. S. Mills and W. E. Oates (Eds.), *Fiscal zoning and land use controls* (pp. 31–100). Lexington, MA: D.C. Heath and Company.

Wievel, W. (1999). Policy research in an imperfect world: Response to Terry F. Buss, "The case against targeted industry strategies". *Economic Development Quarterly, 13*(4), 357–360.

Wilson, J. D. (1999). Theories of tax competition. *National Tax Journal, 52*(2), 269–304.

Wilson, R. H. (1993). *States and the economy-policymaking and decentralization.* Westport, CT: Praeger.

Wolkoff, M. J. (1981). *Analysis of the use of tax abatement policy to stimulate urban economic development.* University of Michigan, Ann Arbor.

Wolkoff, M. J. (1983). The nature of property tax abatement awards. *Journal of the American Planning Association, 49*(1), 77–84.

Wolkoff, M. J. (1985). Chasing a dream: The use of tax abatements to spur urban economic development. *Urban Studies, 22*, 305–315.

Wolman, H., and Spitzley, D. (1996). The politics of local economic development. *Economic Development Quarterly, 10*(2), 115–148.

III

DEBT, WORKING BALANCES, AND FINANCIAL CONDITION ANALYSIS

Chapter 11

Rating General Obligation Debt: Implications of Resource Scarcity

STEVEN G. KOVEN, Ph.D.
Department of Urban and Public Affairs, University of Louisville

STUART G. STROTHER
School of Business and Management, Azusa Pacific University

> Grant I may never prove so fond
> To trust man on his oath or bond
> —William Shakespeare, *Timon of Athens*, I, ii, 64

11.1 Introduction

Accurate assessment of debt obligation is an essential feature of all societies. Since the beginning of time, certain individuals owe allegiance, promises, and/or money to others. In modern, non-coercive, contract-based societies, willingness of lenders to provide money to others is based upon the probability of repayment. The ability of borrowers to secure capital is based upon an assessment of the risk to the lender. Past history of nonpayment increases the difficulty that borrowers face, whether they are an individual or a collective society. Lenders must have good information about ability of borrowers to repay debt in order to freely make investment decisions. Political leaders must have external checks on their ability to raise money. It is beneficial to fiscal management if they are cognizant of outside perceptions about their future solvency.

In theory, debt benefits numerous actors. It matches an investor's desire for a safe return on capital with the goal of borrowers to acquire assets. Government officials need to secure debt financing for long-term projects such as government buildings, schools, colleges, jails, roads, libraries, cultural centers and parks. These projects benefit the entire community and enhance the public standing of leaders who build them. "Ribbon cutting" mayors seek to put their imprimatur on communities through major projects that can only be built through long-term debt financing. "Brick and mortar" projects not only serve as a testament to government leaders but also indicate faith in the future, in the future value of the project and the future ability of investors to recoup their outlays.

A basic review of general obligation bonds, methods of rating bonds, as well as responses to budget scarcity are described in this chapter. The recent situations of budget scarcity in California and Virginia are reviewed in order to more fully understand the range of uses for debt. These case studies seem to indicate that outside evaluation of debt has the positive impact of motivating elected leaders to correct structural budget imbalances. In both California and Virginia elected leaders took proactive steps to alleviate pressing fiscal problems.

It is hoped that this chapter can both provide an understanding of general obligation bonds as well as insight into the political choices that leaders face in times of resource scarcity. In such times, elected leaders still must manage their communities, provide essential services, and work to ensure future prosperity. They must accomplish these goals in environments where demand for public services is rising due to personal hardship of constituents, and readily available revenue is falling due to a slowdown or decrease in taxable economic activity. In these resource environments government officials seek both traditional debt financing and other methods to address their fiscal needs. Prior to describing how California and Virginia chose to address their fiscal needs, background information about general obligation debt, methodologies for rating bonds, and the value of ratings are described.

11.2   General Obligation Debt

11.2.1   Defining General Obligation Debt

General obligation (GO) bonds represent a type of bond where the principal and interest of the bond are secured by the "full faith and credit" of issuing governments. General obligation bonds are issued by states, counties, special districts, cities, towns, and school districts. These bonds are secured by the issuer's general taxing powers as well as investor faith that the issuer will not renege on the obligation. The phrase "full-faith-and credit" means that all available revenues and resources of the issuer, including taxes, stand behind the bonds. Property taxes are normally dedicated to repaying general obligation bonds.

To be a true GO bond, the taxing power on property must be unlimited where neither state nor local law can limit the ability of the issuing local government to levy and raise property taxes to make payments on debt. A state government's GO bonds are typically secured by a full-faith-and credit pledge, which includes all available revenue sources, especially a state's power to levy income and sales taxes. Only revenues that were earmarked prior to the issuance of GO bonds would be exempt from the GO full-faith-and-credit pledge. In 2001, GO bonds accounted for about one-third of the long-term (more than one year) debt issued by state and local governments (Vogt, 2004, 178–179).

For small jurisdictions, such as school districts and towns, property taxes often represent the only unlimited source of tax revenue. For larger jurisdictions such as states and big cities, other tax revenue sources exist. General obligation bonds issued by states can also be supported by appropriations from state legislatures. In the event of default, holders of unlimited general obligation bonds have the right to compel a tax levy or legislative appropriation to secure payment.

Many states have constitutional and/or statutory caps on general obligation debt. Caps limit the amount of GO debt but do not limit the security pledged to repay the debt. Most states that cap GO debt define the limit as a percentage of property tax valuation. Some states have chosen to limit GO debt to a percentage of a jurisdiction's annual revenue. For example, Hawaii limits the amount of GO bonds the state can issue to no more than 18.5 percent of state's average of general fund revenues in the three years preceding the issuance of bonds (Fukumoto, 2002). In contrast, a more fiscally conservative posture is taken by the state of Texas. Texas statutory law requires that additional tax-supported debt may not be authorized if the maximum annual debt service from general revenues exceeds five percent of the average annual general fund revenues for the preceding three years (General Obligation Bonds, 2004).

Limitations are also put on localities. The Iowa constitution limits the amount of debt that local governments in the state may incur to five per cent on the value of taxable property. Cities in Virginia require voter approval for GO debt if it exceeds ten percent of the assessed property value. In Arizona, local governments need voter authorization for GO bonds in excess of six percent of property value (Vogt, 2004, p. 180–181).

Some general obligation bonds are secured not only by the issuer's taxing powers but also from specific fees, grants, and special charges. These additional sources of revenue supplement the general tax revenue and are used in the event that taxing powers are insufficient to make debt payments. Bonds that are backed by these revenues in addition to the general taxing power are referred to as double-barreled bonds. The double barrel refers to the dual nature of revenue sources that back the bond (Fabozzi, Fabozzi, and Feldstein, 1995, 17).

11.2.2 Advantages and Disadvantages of General Obligation Debt

Numerous advantages and disadvantages are cited in regard to general obligation debt. From the perspective of the individual investor, a major advantage of general obligation bond income is its exemption from federal taxation. In some cases, bond income is also exempt from state and local taxes. In addition to the tax advantages, general obligation bonds are viewed as highly secure. GO bonds typically have higher bond ratings than revenue bonds and rate with U.S. Treasury securities for investor confidence. Furthermore, since general obligation bonds are actively traded in a secondary market, owners of GO debt can recoup their investment prior to the bond's maturity.

The high degree of confidence associated with GO bonds seems to be justified. Since first used by New York around 1812, many have regarded GO bonds backed by property taxes as the safest possible investment next to U.S. Treasury bonds. The default rate on municipal bonds between 1940 and the early 1990s averaged less than one percent. Most of the 4,770 municipal defaults between 1929 and 1933 were cured by the 1940s. This was considered an "enviable record" compared to banks and corporations (Standard & Poor's, 1996, 349–350).

Traditionally, GO bonds were considered extremely safe because they are backed by the entire amount of taxable property within a community, and subject to an unlimited tax rate. Homeowners unable to pay property taxes forfeit their house. Furthermore, in cases of default on a mortgage, payment of taxes takes priority over other obligations.

From the perspective of government units, general obligation bonds enable governmental units to borrow money at favorable rates of interest. A favorable rate of interest is secured because of two major factors: (1) the high degree of security associated with general obligation bonds and (2) its tax free status. In addition, administrative costs of general obligation bonds are usually lower than those of revenue bonds.

The necessity of a vote for approval of a general obligation bond can be viewed as an advantage since it confirms popular support for the project in question. Similarly, a rejection of a bond referendum assures that unwanted projects are not foisted upon the populace, who would be required to pay for the project. The expression of popular support as well as voter rejection of unwanted projects is consistent with principles of accountability and responsiveness that is valued by advocates of more direct democracy. Voters can be empowered and feel more connected with their leaders when they are given the opportunity to participate in community decisions.

The need for voter referendum associated with general obligation bonds, however, can also be viewed as a disadvantage. Disadvantages relate to the possible inability of government leaders to raise money to implement programs that they believe are in the best interests of citizens. Important projects can be postponed or categorically rejected. This can be a source of great frustration to government leaders who are convinced of the value of projects and the need to fund those projects regardless of the views of voters.

Another disadvantage of long-term general obligation debt is that benefits from projects might not be aligned with payments. "Pay-as-you-use" financing allows present and future generations of facility users to share the cost. If long-term debt is incurred for yearly expenses an inequitable situation arises since a tax burden is shifted to future generations and benefits are received by the present generation. This violates a fundamental principle of debt financing, namely that debt should not be issued for a maturity longer than the financed projects' useful life (Mikesell, 2003, 555).

Most GO bond issues have repayment terms of about twenty years. In general, jurisdictions are advised to strike a balance between "pay-as-you-go" (finance projects from current revenue) methods and "pay-as-you-use" debt financing. Jurisdictions that rely on "pay-as-you-go" strategies may have insufficient resources to undertake major projects. Jurisdictions that rely predominantly on debt financing run the risk of building up fixed debt and lease charges that can crowd out operating budget spending (Vogt, 2004, 124). Table 11.1 summarizes advantages and disadvantages of general obligation bonds.

Table 11.1   Advantages and Disadvantages of GO Bonds

Advantages	
For jurisdictions	*For investors*
1. Low rate of interest	1. Very low risk
2. Low administrative costs	2. Can sell on secondary market
3. Confirms voter support	3. Tax free status
Disadvantages	
For jurisdictions	*For citizens*
1. Vote may delay or deny projects	1. Increases exposure to taxes
2. Debt may be limited by law	2. May burden future generations

Source: Vogt, John A. *Capital Budgeting and Finance: A Guide for Local Governments*, pp. 228–232; General Obligation Bonds, 2004.

11.3   Assessing Debt Risk

11.3.1   *Historical Overview of Debt Risk in the United States*

Debt is rated because of the need to instruct investors about risk associated with loans. Often, holders of government bonds assume that their payment is guaranteed; however, this has not always been the case. In 1978, Cleveland became the first major U.S. city since 1933 to fall into default (Beck, 1982, 207–216). In 1975, New York City nearly went in default on a total of nearly $7 billion in debt (Columbia University, 2003). The 1984 default of the Washington Public Power Supply System (WPPSS) on payment of $2.25 billion served as a further reminder that all debt associated with governments is not fail safe. The Washington default was largely attributed to construction costs overruns, incorrect estimations of electricity demand, the public mood to walk away from the debt, and unlawful contracts signed by public utility district representatives (Lamb and Rappaport, 1987, 255). Bridgeport, Connecticut's 1991 invocation of Chapter 9 bankruptcy (although it was not permitted by the courts) was a further reminder of uncertainty that exists even in relatively secure forms of debt. The bankruptcy of Orange County, California, in 1994 led to an increased regulatory role for the Security and Exchange Commission in monitoring government investments (Lee, Johnson, and Joyce, 2004).

As might be expected, the data indicate that defaults are most often related to periods of deep economic decline. For example, approximately 75 percent of the total number of all municipal defaults are traced to the depression years of the 1930s. Most of these defaults, however, were related to revenue bonds that were tied to specific sources of revenue and not to general obligation bonds that were backed by property and other taxes (Lamb and Rappaport, 1987, 252).

It is well recognized that factors other than economic decline can contribute to default. For example, the willingness of a sovereign to repay a debt is of paramount concern. Such willingness is often categorized under the concept "good faith" and is viewed as related, yet independent from, other factors such as general prosperity and legal guidelines (Chamberlain and Edwards, 1927, 255). For example, the importance of attitudinal factors were apparent in the 1770s as the debt of the American Revolutionary War remained unpaid under the Articles of Confederation. The repudiation of debt was subsequently reversed when the U.S. Constitution replaced the Articles as the governing document for the nation. In 1790, under the leadership of Secretary of Treasury Alexander Hamilton, a plan for refunding all debt of State Assemblies and the Continental Congress was adopted by Congress. Under the new plan, the war debt was quickly repaid by the issuance of new loans received from abroad (Chamberlain and Edwards, 1927, 137).

In general, the strong currency philosophy of Hamilton has guided U.S. policy since the founding of the republic. Nonpayment of government debt remains rare, however, not unheard of, particularly in periods of severe fiscal hardship. Defaults occurred during the depression era of 1837–45. The major contraction in the South following the Civil War resulted in debt repudiation of seven states (Pennsylvania, Maryland, Indiana, Illinois, Michigan, Florida and Mississippi). Of the four Northern states, only Michigan did not fully reimburse all creditors. Both Maryland and Pennsylvania stopped payment on debt interest in 1842. Of these states, Pennsylvania paid off its debt in 1845, Maryland by 1848. Of the seven defaulting states, only Mississippi and Florida were perceived to be guilty of deliberate repudiation, in contrast to nonpayment attributed purely to fiscal constraint. Both states raised the issue of invalidity (legitimacy of the bond issue in terms of methods of authorization, flotation and the purpose of the issue) in repudiating their debts (Chamberlain and Edwards, 1927, 156).

During the reconstruction period of 1870–1884, nine states from the South (Virginia, North Carolina, South Carolina, Georgia, Florida, Alabama and Louisiana) sought relief from their debts by repudiation. Debt incurred by the Confederate States of America and the respective states that seceded from the union (debt for war purposes) was voided by the Fourteenth Amendment to the U.S. Constitution. Severe financial decline also accounted for many municipal defaults. The war's economic blow to Southern states should not be minimized. It was estimated that between

1860 and 1870 the liabilities of the nine defaulting states doubled and their resources were halved (Chamberlain and Edwards, 1927, 161).

The greatest proportion of municipal delinquencies occurred in or near the Mississippi valley, from Duluth, Minnesota to Mobile, Alabama. It is estimated that more than one-third of the more than three hundred municipalities in Illinois refused to make payment on their bonds, while nine-tenths of the approximately one hundred counties, townships, and cities issuing bonds in Missouri defaulted. All of the bonded communities in Arkansas attempted repudiation (Chamberlain and Edwards, 1927, 194). In general, rural counties were viewed as more likely to default than municipal counties due to their often eccentric and weak administrations (Chamberlain and Edwards, 1927, 197).

The overview presented here affirms the notion that, while government debt is deserving of its reputation for high levels of safety, no debt is one-hundred percent guaranteed. Default and repudiation are part of American history and lenders must always carefully assess their risks when making loans. Since the time of Alexander Hamilton, assessment of risk has grown into somewhat of a science. Various bond rating organizations have been created in the twentieth century for the purpose of condensing the complexity of rating risk into a few simple letters or numbers. Methodologies employed by these organizations are described below.

11.3.2 Bond Rating Organizations

Three commercial rating companies, Moody's Investors Services (Moody's), Standard and Poor's Corporation (S&P), and Fitch IBCA (Fitch) assess risk on general obligation and other government bonds. Moody's has been rating bonds since 1909, Standard and Poor's since 1940 and Fitch since 1913; however, Fitch was not active in rating municipal debt until 1989. Since 1989, Fitch's role in rating municipal debt has grown dramatically and, in 1994, it rated 24 percent of the dollar amount of new municipal debt. In 2002, Fitch rated 70 percent of the municipal debt issued (Vogt, 2004, 221).

Two of the three ratings companies are part of large, growth oriented conglomerates and typically charge fees for their services. Moody's is a unit of Dun & Bradstreet Companies while Standard & Poor's is a part of McGraw-Hill Inc. The objective of each of the companies is to provide good information to potential lenders so they can accurately assess their risk exposure. Ratings agencies can identify gradations of risk based upon various sets of indicators. In the past, however, ratings agencies have not been accurate in the face of major economic decline. For example, data from the Great Depression indicate for all the rated bonds that plunged into default in the 1930s, 48 percent had been rated Aaa by Moody's in 1929 while 78 percent had been rated either Aaa or Aa. In dollar terms, more than 90 percent of the widely-known municipal bonds were rated either Aaa or Aa in 1929 (Twentieth Century Fund Task Force, 1974, 51).

For the most part, there is agreement in terms of risk associated with debt, but slight differences exist between the ratings organizations. Moody's grades municipal bonds according to nine ratings symbols ranging from Aaa to C. Standard & Poor's uses a 10 symbol system ranging from AAA to D and Fitch uses twelve categories that also range from AAA to D. Moody's considers municipal bonds in its top four categories (Aaa, Aa, A, and Baa) as investment grade quality. Slight distinctions within grades are also identified by Moody's. Bonds in the Aa through B categories that Moody's considers stronger are designated by the symbols Aa1, A1, and Baa1, Ba1, and B1. Standard & Poor's also considers bonds within its top four ratings (AAA, AA, A, and BBB) to be investment grade quality. In contrast to Moody's use of numbers, Standard & Poor's uses a plus (+) or minus (−) system to show relative strength within rating categories. The highest four ratings of Fitch (AAA, AA, A, and BBB) are considered investment grade quality (Fabozzi, Fabozzi, and Feldstein, 1995, 179–189). Table 11.2 shows rating differences between the three companies.

Differences exist in terms of how organizations rate debt. For example, Standard & Poor's requires the bond issuer's financial reports to be prepared in accordance with generally accepted accounting principles (GAAP). This is not required by Moody's. Standard & Poor's places more emphasis on the use of state aid to pay local government debt while Moody's places more emphasis on credit factors of the bond issuers. These credit factors include the underlying budget, economic characteristics of the jurisdiction and debt. Moody's applies the same standards to evaluating both state and local bonds when it assumes that states will stand behind the fiscal integrity of localities. Standard & Poor's views state general

Table 11.2 Bond Ratings, Moody's, Standard & Poor's, Fitch

Quality of Bond	Moody's	Standard & Poor's	Fitch
Investment grade	Aaa, Aa, A, Baa	AAA, AA, A, BBB	AAA, AA, A, BBB
Speculative or highly speculative	Ba, B, Caa, Ca	BB, B, CCC, CC	BB, B, CCC
Default probable or in default	C	C, D	CC, C, DDD, DD, D

Source: Fabozzi, Fabozzi, and Feldstein, *Municipal Bond Portfolio Management*, pp. 180–188.

obligation bonds as being in a significantly stronger position than lower level jurisdictions. This position is attributed to a state's broader legal powers in the areas of taxation, broader revenue bases, and more diversified economy (Fabozzi, Fabozzi, and Feldstein, 1995, 185–188).

Slight differences in outlook produced some differences in ratings. Of the 40 states rated by both Standard & Poor's and Moody's in 1994, Standard & Poor's gave a rating of AA or better to 35 states while Moody's gave of rating of Aa or better to 33 states. Moody's as the "tougher grader" assigned ratings that were lower than A to several state GO bonds. For example, between 1975 and 1978 Moody's downgraded Delaware's GO bonds from Aa to Baa1. In May of 1982 Moody's downgraded the state of Michigan's general obligation bonds from A to Baa1. Prior to 1974, Moody's set a rating of Baa1 for Alaska. In the cases of Delaware and Michigan, corrective action was taken following notice of the lower rating. By 1986 the bond rating for Delaware was Aa and the rating for Michigan was A-1 (Fabozzi, Fabozzi, and Feldstein, 1995, 185). In a sense, this demonstrates that "the system works" not only in regard to providing cues to investors but in motivating jurisdictions to act within the normal boundaries of fiscal prudence.

11.4 Key Factors In Rating Debt

Rating bonds is fairly complex and takes into consideration numerous factors, such as financial competence, validity of securities, and good faith. Financial competence is generally viewed as the most relevant factor; however, other issues should not be ignored. Bonds have been repudiated in the past over issues of validity, a concept that includes: (1) the authority of the issue, (2) the purpose of the issue, (3) the process, and (4) debt and tax restrictions.

Proper authority must be followed in issuing bonds. Such authority resides in legislatures, statutes or state constitutions. Voter approval may be necessary in issuing a bond and irregularities that are discovered in balloting may be a reason to invalidate issues. Legitimacy of the purpose of debt must be verified. For example, the purpose of municipal obligations must be public and in keeping with the demands of the jurisdiction. Proper processes (such as advertisement of an issue) should be strictly followed. Finally, many jurisdictions place restrictions on obligations. As described above with reference to Hawaii and Texas, these restrictions usually refer to debt above a specific proportion of property tax value or general fund revenues.

Questions of validity are most often addressed in legal opinions. Since bondholders may have to go to court to enforce security rights, the integrity and competence of the lawyers who review documents and write the legal opinions that are stated in the official documents are very important. Lawyers should determine if issuers are legally able to issue bonds, if the issuer has enacted ordinances, resolutions and trusts without violating laws, and if security safeguards for bondholders are supported by federal, state, and local government laws (Fabozzi, Fabozzi, and Feldstein, 1995, 1996). Good faith refers to the willingness of a borrower to repay a lender. Past behavior of jurisdictions can influence bond ratings and ability to borrow funds. The ability of San Francisco to sell bonds after its earthquake was attributed to both investor confidence in its future and its past history of never repudiating any of its obligations (Chamberlain and Edwards, 1927, 245–256). The exceptionally low interest rates paid on U.S. Treasury bonds, in part, reflects the high level of good faith associated with those obligations.

While concepts such as validity and good faith are relevant, most contemporary public finance texts cite the following factors in rating general obligation debt: economic base, financial factors, debt factors, governance factors and political mood (Lynch, 1995; Mikesell, 2003; Standard & Poor's, 1996; Temel, 2001; Vogt, 2004).

11.4.1 Economic Base

The economic base refers to the local or regional economy. This is often seen as the most critical element in determining an issuer's rating. It incorporates both local and national economic factors. Economic base has been measured by factors such as employment, demographics, tax base, economic diversity, economic stability, local infrastructure, and local policies.

The economic base of a jurisdiction is linked to the importance of exports from the local economy. Sales to buyers outside of the local economy generate labor and business income. Good measures of total economic activity (export and import) include: (1) the dollar value of all goods and services produced, (2) quantities of goods and services produced, and (3) employment. Because employment data are more readily available than dollar or production statistics, the size of a local area's economic base is often measured by employment in various sectors or standard industrial classification (SIC) categories (Galambos and Schreiber, 1996, 80).

In regard to demographics, a jurisdiction's population base can be profiled in terms of age, education, labor skills, wealth, and income levels. Demographic analysis should consider whether a population is becoming more dependent upon government services or is likely to contribute to future growth. Typically, indicators of wealth include changes in wealth over time, per capita personal income, and median family income.

If data does not exist for the jurisdiction issuing the debt, statistics can be obtained from the county or standard metropolitan statistical area.

Tax base refers to all sources that are identified as being taxed. Local governments may choose to include salaries and wages in their income taxes but may exclude income from rents and stock investments. The federal government includes wages in income calculations but excludes employee benefits. A local tax base can be assessed by measures such as property tax valuation, the value of building permits issued, and retail sales.

Diversification considerations refer to the composition of employment (manufacturing, trade, construction, services, government, and agriculture), degree of concentration in major employers, employer commitment to the community, and employment trends. Concentration is viewed as a negative in rating bonds, particularly if the concentration is in a declining sector. For example, Standard & Poor's uses multiple indicators to assess the financial health of farm-based jurisdictions. Credit ratings of farm-based economies have taken into consideration commodity prices for an area's major cash crop, government subsidies, farm debt/equity ratios, foreclosure rates, land values, and local bank failures (Standard & Poor's, 1996, p. 353).

Relevant measures of economic stability include the local unemployment rate. The quality of local infrastructure in terms of transportation systems, utilities, schools, housing, health care facilities, and cultural and recreational amenities has become increasingly important to bond ratings. Finally, a jurisdiction's creditworthiness is also influenced by policies to support development and growth (Vogt, 2004).

11.4.2 Financial Factors

Financial factors refer to a jurisdiction's current, past, and prospective situation with regard to revenues, expenditures, and fund balances. Accounting methods, analysis of revenues and expenditures, balance sheet analysis, and the management of long-term financial obligations are important considerations for rating bonds.

11.4.3 Accounting

Standard & Poor's (1996, p. 354) notes that the first important variable in judging financial performance of jurisdictions is the method of accounting and financial reporting. The use of Generally Accepted Accounting Principles (GAAP) is considered a strength for the jurisdiction, as is the ability to meet the Government Finance Officers Association's (GFOA) Certificate of Conformance requirements. Standard & Poor's state:

> Issuers are expected to supply adequate and timely financial reports. Financial reports prepared by an independent certified

public accountant are preferred. Lack of an audited financial report prepared according to GAAP could have a negative impact on an issuer's rating since the quality of financial reporting may be considered suspect (Standard & Poor's, 1996, p. 354).

11.4.4 Revenues, Expenditures and Balance Sheet Analysis

Standard & Poor's examines revenue sources such as property taxes, sales taxes, income taxes, user charges, intergovernmental aid, and investment income over a three to five year period. They review unusual patterns that could lead to problems in financial performance in the future. Large expenditure patterns are identified to determine if continued growth could endanger existing services or require additional taxation. Typical indicators of spending that can be examined include numbers of full-time workers and spending per capita for salaries. Comparisons for these indicators can be made with spending in similar jurisdictions.

Analysis of balance sheets focus on liquidity, fund balance positions, and the composition of assets and liabilities. Deficits in any of the funds used by municipalities are causes of concern. Whether the deficits are temporary and easily remedied or chronic and longer term should be identified. Deficits or surpluses should be analyzed in light of a municipality's past operations. Healthy levels of working capital as well as liquid current assets are considered beneficial. Reserves for items such as uncollected taxes should be considered (Temel, 2001, p. 180).

A comprehensive analysis of municipal financial performance also considers revenue transfers between funds, short-term finances, and the management of pension funds. Transfers of revenue from other funds to the general fund may be a sign of fiscal stress. Short-term borrowing may indicate a weakening financial position as was the case of New York City in the 1970s and California in the early 1990s. Standard & Poor's asserts that the growth of unfunded pension liabilities must be avoided since it endangers the government's ability to meet its long-term debt obligations.

11.4.5 Debt Factors

A local government's outstanding and authorized debt affects its ability to borrow. Lee, Johnson, and Joyce (2004, p. 464) contend that determining the reasonableness of a state's or municipality's debt level is a subjective judgment. The main factors in making such a judgment are the financial burden on individual taxpayers, the size of the economy, and the perceived value of the goods and services purchased by the debt. Some states such as New York rank high in both per capita income and per capita debt. Others such as Connecticut have high income but low debt levels.

Standard & Poor's measures a jurisdiction's debt burden against the community's ability to repay. Three key indicators of ability to pay are the tax base, the wealth and income of the community, and total budget resources. Standard & Poor's contends that, in general, a debt burden is viewed as high when debt service payments comprise 15 to 20 percent of the total expenditures, including both operating expenses and debt service. Other good indicators of debt burdens exist such as net debt per capita, net debt as a percent of market valuation, net debt as a percent of personal family income, pay down pace on long term debt, and net debt of overlapping jurisdictions.

Standard & Poor's note that debt can be used to cover up underlying fiscal weaknesses, stating the following:

> In difficult fiscal situations where jurisdictions face operating deficits, some entities choose long-term financing of accumulated deficits as a solution. S&P believes the "bonding out" of financial problems is not a permanent cure and may complicate the ultimate resolution of the crisis (1996, p. 356).

As we see from the case of California, jurisdictions use their ability to borrow in order to address their fiscal problems. This is politically expedient; however, according to Standard & Poor's it should be avoided. As demonstrated in New York City's fiscal crisis and numerous other examples, overuse of long-term debt that is used to paper over structural imbalances between expenditures and collections will destroy a jurisdiction's ability to borrow. Operating budget imbalances must be corrected by raising taxes (see Virginia case below) or cutting expenditures. The general rule of debt financing, as stated above, still holds; long-term debt should be used to pay for capital improvements that have a long life span. Payments for such projects should be spaced out so that those who receive the benefits also make the payments.

11.4.6 Governance and Administrative Factors

As described above, criteria for assessing a local government's economic base, financial conditions and debt burden are well established. Numerous quantitative indicators have been developed to assess these factors. Evaluation of governance and administrative factors, however, is more subjective. Vogt (2004, p. 231) states that the following governance factors are important for rating GO bonds.

- Coherence of Government Structure
- Cooperative Nature of the Governing Board

- Degree of Professionalism
- Multiyear Planning Process

Ratings organizations have increasingly recognized the importance of governance issues. Local governance structures are established under state statutes or local charters. A coherent government structure should produce clear assignment of responsibility, good policy making processes, and effective implementation of policies. Local government is also enhanced by members of a governing board that work well together. In general, ratings agencies feel that a strong mayor or council-manager form of government will be able to control finances better than a weak mayor system. Better governance is also associated with multiyear approaches found in capital improvements plans, multiyear forecasting, and strategic planning.

11.4.7 Political Mood

Analysts recognize that changes in the political mood of taxpayers can be as important for the value of bonds as the issuer's financial ability to pay (Temel, 2001, p. 172). This is directly observed in the actions of the first Secretary of Treasury, Alexander Hamilton. Hamilton's declaration to repay Revolutionary War debt signaled a clear change in mood from that of repudiation to that of fiscal responsibility. Such action was not lost on future investors and helped the United States establish the type of credit status it enjoys today.

The Orange County, California, bankruptcy of 1994 presents an alternative example, where a wealthy jurisdiction chose to walk away from its financial losses. Citizen repulsion with what many considered to be inappropriate speculation on the part of civil servants, no doubt, contributed to the county's default. At its height, Orange County was investing its own funds and the funds for almost 200 other local government units in risky securities such as derivatives or financial instruments that based its value on the interest rates of other investments. The aftermath of Orange County caused prices of other California bonds to drop dramatically (Lee, Johnson and Joyce, 2004, p. 466).

Throughout history, willingness to pay has been a critical element is assessing the likelihood of repayment on debt. Perhaps the most infamous example of unwillingness to pay debt is traced to the Treaty of Versailles that ended World War I. The people of Germany were outraged by the amount of reparations they were obligated to pay under the conditions of the treaty. Nationalist politicians such as Adolf Hitler claimed that if they gained power they would stop paying reparations. The 1932 Lausanne Conference attempted to reduce German reparation debt; however, by this time Germany was not making payment, and the Nazi government repudiated what it termed "interest slavery." In 1932 European nations such as Britain and France also ended debt payments on the approximately $7.25 billion in loans made to them by the United States (Blatt, 2001).

Table 11.3 summarizes economic base, financial, debt, and governance factors as well as political mood. As previously stated, these criteria must be considered in assessing the credit worthiness of general obligation debt.

Table 11.3   Criteria for Rating General Obligation Debt

Economic base	
Population	Economic stability
Wealth	Local infrastructure
Local tax base	Local policies
Economic diversity	

Financial factors	
Major revenue sources	Budgeting practices
Number of full-time equivalent positions	Accounting practices
Spending per capita	Revenue administration
General fund balances	Investment practices

Debt factors	
Net debt per capita	Debt service as a percent of general fund spending
Net debt as percent of market valuation	Debt pay down pace
Net debt as percent of personal family income	Debt of overlapping jurisdictions

Governance	
Coherent structure of governance	Professional management
Cooperative governing board	Multiyear planning processes

Political mood	
Willingness to Pay	

Source: Vogt, John A. Capital Budgeting and Finance: A Guide for Local Governments, pp. 228–232; Temel, The Fundamentals of Municipal Bonds, p. 172.

11.5 Value of Bond Ratings

Rating bonds is a valuable exercise for numerous stakeholders. For government issuers of debt, bond ratings can enhance the marketability of bonds and lower borrowing costs. Without nationally recognized rating organizations, the cost of marketing bonds would be greater and individual investors as well as underwriters would have to devote more time and energy to collecting relevant information. With nationally accepted bond ratings, the act of borrowing is an efficient process. Transaction costs and information costs are greatly reduced.

Aside from the issue of improving sales, ratings also help in overall governance. Bond downgrades indicate that borrowing costs of jurisdictions will increase due to a deterioration of perceived creditworthiness and the perception of increased risk. Such information should be interpreted as negative feedback requiring some type of corrective measure. In the view of Katz and Kahn (1966), information feedback of a negative kind enables systems to correct its deviations from course. Information is fed back to some central mechanism which acts on the information to keep the system on target. As with a thermostat that controls temperature, under an open systems perspective, government leaders confronting ratings declines should act to maintain the steady state of creditworthiness. The California and Virginia cases below illustrate the influence of bond raters on the actions of elected officials.

Actions in what Katz and Kahn (1966) refer to as a homeostatic process may include various responses such as less borrowing or changes to key factors that were described above. For example, a deterioration of a jurisdiction's economic base can lead to proactive initiatives on the part of the government leaders to protect their economies. Such proactive initiatives may include financial incentives (such as grants, loans or equity financing), tax incentives (such as abatements, credits, exemptions, or deferrals), and non-financial assistance (such as site development, construction of industrial parks, and relief from government regulations) (Koven and Lyons, 2003, p. 27–46).

From the perspective of investors, bond ratings clearly provide information about distinctions in credit quality. Small institutional or individual investors do not have the expertise, resources, or inclination to make accurate credit judgments. They therefore must rely on the assessments of major rating organizations such as Moody's, Standard & Poor's and Fitch. Because the mission of ratings organizations is to inform and protect both subscribers and investor customers rather than to sell securities, the typical investor is inclined to respect their judgments (Twentieth Century Fund Task Force, 1974, p. 63).

11.6   State Responses to Scarcity

The recent situations of budget scarcity in California and Virginia show how outside evaluation of debt can have the positive impact of motivating elected leaders to correct structural budget imbalances. In both California and Virginia, elected leaders made tough political decisions to resolve an immediate crisis and to proactively alleviate anticipated future fiscal problems. The outside ratings of the states' bonds were instrumental in state leaders' decisions to correct their budget problems. The recent California and Virginia cases are described below.

11.6.1   California

If California were a separate country it would boast the world's fifth largest economy. But if the state were a developing country, the severity of the recent fiscal crisis would qualify California for emergency relief from the International Monetary Fund. This case study notes the causes of the fiscal crisis, explains the relationship between the fiscal crisis and California's bond ratings, and describes the fiscal recovery plan led by Governor Schwarzenegger.

11.6.1.1   California's Fiscal Crisis

In January 2003, California's Department of Finance forecast a smaller than expected economic recovery resulting in a projected $38 billion budget deficit over the next two years. For the remaining eight months of the 2002–03 fiscal year, a $10 billion shortfall was predicted and the following year's shortfall was forecast at $28 billion. The state's tax revenues simply could not meet the amount of the state's planned expenditures. The state's revenue would not be as high as the initial forecasts, and political pressures inhibited elected leaders from reducing expenditures. California's inability to collect enough tax money to pay for its programs and an unwillingness to reduce spending put the state into a major fiscal crisis.

In 2002–03 in California, 96% of General Fund revenue was derived from taxes. Because taxes are levied on economic activity, states face resource scarcity during times of economic recession. In California, the revenue forecasts were too optimistic. The state's economy did not grow as much as expected. In addition to the sluggish economy, other changes resulted in reduced revenues, such as for California's lower than expected tax revenues include reduced sales taxes, changes in corporate taxation, and the progressive nature of the state's tax structure (Spilberg and Alexander, 2003, pp. 557–564).

Sales taxes are levied on tangible goods, but as the overall economy shifts from manufacturing to services, a smaller amount of overall consumption is taxable. Revenues from corporation taxes have also declined due to a "gradual shift to pass-through entities" (Spillberg and Alexander, 2003, p. 562). Corporation taxes are levied based on income but, since the 1980s, over 25% of corporations have become S corporations which are not taxed as single entities. Their income, losses and tax liability are passed on to individual shareholders. Because individuals tend to shield their tax liability better than corporations, states collect fewer taxes. Corporation taxes are also lower because of a rise in the number of tax credits claimed by corporations and an undocumentable rise in the use of abusive tax shelters. About 35% of general fund revenues come from corporate income taxes.

The progressive nature of California's tax structure is perhaps most to blame for the revenue shortfall. California's personal income tax is progressive — with rates from 1 percent up to 9.3 percent. In 2001, the top 1 percent of taxpayers paid almost 40 percent of the personal income tax (PIT), while the bottom 40 percent paid less than 1 percent. Unlike earlier years, by the 1990s California was deriving more than 50% of its General Fund revenue from the PIT. But "incomes at the highest level tend to be more volatile, especially capital gains," resulting in a more volatile tax system (Spillberg and Alexander, 2003, p. 561). The overall decline of the stock market resulted in fewer capital gains and less PIT taxes for California to collect. One could say California's plan to rely heavily on taxing the rich had backfired. The progressive nature of California's tax structure exposes the state to risk and puts the state's revenues at the mercy of the fluctuations of the economy.

In addition to reduced tax revenues, California's escalating expenditures also contributed to the recent fiscal crisis. In the late 1990s the stock market boomed and individual capital gains increased. Consequently, state revenues increased, and so expenditures rose accordingly, as shown in Figure 11.1. From 1998–99 to 2002–03 expenditures grew by 46%. Most of that went to education, medical benefits, and transportation infrastructure (Spillberg and Alexander, 2003, p. 564). After the tech bubble burst in the late 1990s and the stock market declined, political pressures still inhibited elected officials from reducing expenditures down to levels that could be paid for with the newly reduced revenue level. When revenues are rising, politicians eagerly raise expenditures accordingly, but when revenues drop it is difficult to apply the brakes on the already increased expenditures.

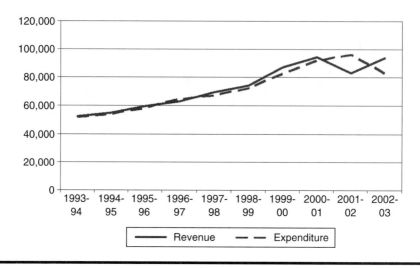

Figure 11.1 California's revenue and expenditures in millions, 1993–94 to 2002–03. *Source*: Spillberg and Alexander, 2003.

11.6.1.2 Bond Ratings and the Fiscal Crisis

Since Moody's began rating California's General Obligation bonds in 1938, the state has enjoyed investment grade ratings with the risk noted as "highest quality," "high quality," or "strong." That is, until the current fiscal crisis began worrying investors. During the fiscal crisis of 2002 to 2004, California's bonds were downgraded two times to near junk-bond status and only after the governor submitted a tighten-the-belt fiscal plan were the bonds upgraded one notch. Figure 11.2 shows the rise and fall of California's GO bond ratings by Moody's.

The first bond downgrade came after Governor Gray Davis announced in December 2002 that the state was facing a $34.8 billion deficit over the next two fiscal years. Fitch and Standard and Poor's both downgraded California's GO bonds from A+ to A. The ratings agencies cited California's lack of proposed corrective action as a major reason to downgrade the bonds (Rosenberg, 2002, p. C12). After the governor sent his budget to the legislature in January, 2003, Moody's also downgraded California's GO bonds, from A1 to A2. An official statement from Moody's noted, "an expectation the state will not be able to sufficiently address the imbalance in the upcoming fiscal year" ("Moody's Cuts Bond Rating," p. A25). Through these downgrades the ratings agencies had sent a firm message to investors that California's investments were growing more risky.

The second downgrade of California's GO bonds came in July 2003, after the state sold $11.6 billion worth of short-term bonds designed to keep

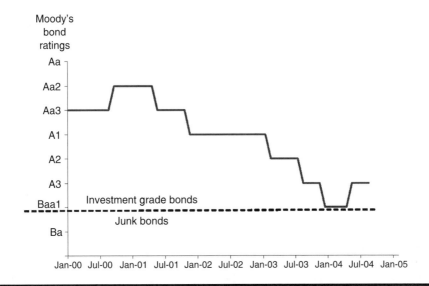

Figure 11.2 Moody's ratings of California General Obligation Bonds from 2000 to 2005. *Source*: E*Trade Financial, 2004.

the state solvent for the next three months — the final three months of fiscal year 2002–03 (Halper, 2003). Throughout the summer of 2003, Democrat and Republican lawmakers were engaged in a bitter budget stalemate. Democrats refused to cut expenditures and Republicans refused to raise taxes. This political strife, coupled with the movement to recall governor Davis, further shook investors' confidence in the state's ability to clean up its fiscal mess. Standard and Poor's, who usually move only one or two notches at a time, downgraded the GO bonds three notches from A to BBB. Only during the Massachusetts fiscal crisis from 1989 to 1992 has a state had lower ratings. The Standard and Poor's analyst responsible for the downgrade explained, "The downgrade is the product of the budget process for fiscal 2004, and the inability of the Legislature to resolve a terrific problem" (Jurgens, 2003, p. 1). A month later, in August 2003, Moody's downgraded California's GO bonds from A2 to A3, and kept them on a watch list for further possible downgrades. These downgrades added additional negative effects to an already dismal fiscal situation.

When the GO bond ratings were dropped, California had to immediately pay $33.6 million in penalties to those banks that had purchased most of the $11.6 billion in short term bonds. A far worse effect is the impact bond downgrades have on investor confidence. When ratings are low, investors are wary of the risk. So the bond issuer must offer higher interest than other states to entice investors to purchase the bonds. This results in higher expenses for the state. To compete with states that have the highest

AAA bond rating such as Delaware, Georgia, and Utah, California's GO bonds had to offer about three quarter percent higher return. The state treasurer's office estimated the higher interest rates due to the bond downgrades cost the state over $980 million (Sylvester, 2003, p. 1). The compounding nature of California's fiscal hardships created enough pressure for elected leaders to set aside their political differences and work together to terminate the crisis.

11.6.1.3   Terminating the Budget Crisis

In December 2003, Governor Schwarzenegger invoked emergency powers and declared a fiscal emergency in the state. He took control of the state's finances away from the legislature, immediately imposed certain short-term spending cuts, and laid out a plan to balance California's budget. The governor's plan included Proposition 57, a measure to issue $15 billion worth of new economic recovery bonds (ERBs) to cover the state's current operating expenses, and Proposition 58, a measure that requires future state budgets to be balanced and also outlaws future short-term borrowing. Voters overwhelmingly approved both measures in March 2004, and the deficit reduction bonds went on sale two months later. Moody's rated the economic recovery bonds at Aa3, well above the ratings of the GO bonds (Saskal, 2004, p. 1).

In May 2004 both the ERB and GO bonds were "oversubscribed," which means demand was greater than supply for the bonds (Kelleher, 2004, p. 1). Investors were optimistic that Schwarzenegger's plan to terminate the budget crisis would be effective. Moody's noted an improving economy in California and cited the state's budget balancing efforts as reasons to upgrade California's GO bond rating from Baa1 to A3. The efforts of the outside rating agencies demonstrated a direct causal effect on resolving California's fiscal crisis.

11.6.2   Virginia

Virginia's fiscal crisis bears many similarities to the California experience. An unexpected downturn in the economy resulted in reduced tax revenue collected by the state. Expenditure levels were based on previous optimistic forecasts but, with the downturn in the economy, there was no way the state could meet these obligations with the reduced revenues. A bitter political battle broke out between the governor and state legislators. During the crisis, the state's bond ratings were not adjusted, but the threat of a downgrade by Moody's and other ratings agencies provided enough outside pressure to encourage the elected officials to resolve the crisis.

Seventeen Republican lawmakers broke ranks from their conservative party and joined the tax-raising Democrats to resolve the crisis.

11.6.2.1   Virginia's Fiscal Crisis

The causes of Virginia's fiscal crisis are essentially the same as for California — overly optimistic revenue forecasts. During the technology boom of the late 1990s, the state enjoyed higher revenues based on growth in Virginia's large technology sector. The optimism continued over the next years, but by the time the state was operating in its 2002–04 fiscal budget it was discovered that actual revenues would fall short of the expected revenues. The previous administration had overestimated revenues by $1.5 billion and the shortfall put the state's finances in a precarious position.

Some critics have blamed Virginia's problems not on declining revenues, but on inflated expenditures. In a press release, the Fairfax County Taxpayers Alliance (2002) labeled the budget situation a "bogus crisis," and noted that revenues have increased every year, and it is only pork barrel programs that have caused expenditures to outpace revenues. For these critics, reining in expenditures, rather than raising taxes, is a preferred way to resolve the crisis.

11.6.2.2   Resolving the Budget Crisis

To resolve the budget crisis, Governor Mark R. Warner did three things: certain administrative functions were streamlined; budget cuts were proposed; and a tax raise was proposed. Warner, a former telecommunications executive, consolidated all of the state's information technology functions into a single agency and similarly reformed procurement procedures. In addition to these innovative cost reduction strategies, the governor also enacted budget cuts that affected each state agency and individual lawmakers. They were all asked to reduce their individual budgets. Governor Warner, a Democrat who campaigned with the promise of no new taxes, also proposed additional taxes that were expected to increase revenues by about $1 billion.

In a surprise move, the Senate, led by Republicans, who also campaigned on the promise of no new taxes, rejected the governor's plan and proposed a budget that raised taxes by $4 billion. The Republican plan called for higher cigarette, gas and sales taxes, and higher income taxes for the wealthy. Taxes on food and lower incomes would be reduced under the plan (Dao, 2004).

A bitter political battle ensued with the Governor, the Senate, and the House fighting against each other. Democrats and Republicans fought against each other, and factions within the political parties bitterly argued about the best way to resolve Virginia's resource scarcity problems. Two former governors, George Allen and Douglas Wilder, joined the debate and argued that the voters should decide through a referendum whether tax hikes should be enacted (Lessig, 2004). Governor Warner did not want the referendum because he feared that the voters did not have the will to make tough decisions regarding tax hikes and budget cuts. The referendum was ultimately rejected and it was up to the elected officials to resolve the crisis.

Unlike California, Virginia's state budget is written biennially. Every two years the legislature has 30 days to agree on a budget that is sent to the governor. Due to the political wrangling in early 2004, a budget was not produced by the mandated March 13 deadline. Fearing a government shutdown if a budget was not passed by July 1, lawmakers agreed to continue to meet to work on the budget.

Because the legislators did not reach agreement on the 2004–2006 biennium budget by the deadline, the state risked losing its coveted Aaa bond rating. Moody's had already put Virginia on the "watch list" for a possible downgrade in 2003, based on the budget crisis. If the state's bond ratings dropped, the state would be forced to pay higher interest rates on its general obligation bonds and perhaps scare off additional business investment because of the perceived instability of the state's finances. During this time, state lawmakers had authorized the sale of $159.3 million in GO bonds designated to upgrade the state police communications system. A drop in the bond ratings would result in the state having to pay higher interest on the police bonds and other future bond offerings. State leaders repeatedly cited the threat of the bond downgrade as a major concern and a good reason to quickly resolve the fiscal crisis.

In addition to the governor's plan to raise $1 billion in new taxes, and the Republican-led Senate's $4 billion plan, the Republican-led House also proposed a plan to boost revenues by $520 million. The Democratic governor found himself in the unusual position of mediator between two Republican groups.

After debating the budget for 115 days, the legislature finally approved a $60 billion budget that has been called "the most extensive rewrite of the Virginia tax code in decades" (Shear and Jenkins, 2004, p. A01). In the new budget all state agencies receive higher spending. Sales taxes and cigarette taxes were raised, while income taxes and grocery taxes were also decreased. Certain corporate tax breaks also were ended. Passage of the budget was only possible when seventeen Republican lawmakers in the House defied their senior party leaders and voted with the Democrats to pass the budget. Shortly after the budget was passed, Moody's took Virginia off its watch list for possible bond downgrades. The threat of the bond downgrade had given elected officials the political will to make the tough decisions required to resolve the crisis.

11.7 Conclusions

A review of history indicates that sovereigns have either borrowed or taken resources from their citizens in order to do what they pleased. In modern democratic societies, jurisdictions typically have assumed long-term debt (backed by their taxing power) in order to finance major projects. Assessing risk on such debt is critical for the free flow of capital to these projects.

This chapter has reviewed basic features of general obligation debts. The cases of two jurisdictions affected by scarcity were discussed in detail. These jurisdictions were influenced by the need to maintain sound credit ratings as well as the need to provide public services. While creditworthiness of borrowers is the fundamental issue in bonding, the cases of Virginia and California suggest that broader issues are involved.

Rating general obligation bonds at least indirectly addresses the issues of the role of government, the need for fiscal solvency, and the need to sustain economic prosperity. The level of public sector spending needed to support future growth is subject to debate as well as the level of necessary borrowing. Jurisdictions cannot borrow themselves into prosperity; however, they must borrow in order to ensure the future development and continuity of their communities. Rating debt obligation serves an important function in that it provides clues to public policy decision makers and outside investors. Policy makers must balance their responsibilities to citizens to support valuable projects with the dictates of the financial community to engage in fiscally responsible behavior. The process of rating, loaning, and borrowing helps jurisdictions to achieve balance between the competing demands for higher spending and fiscal prudence.

References

Beck, J. (1982). "Is Cleveland Another New York?" *Urban Affairs Quarterly,* 18(2), 207–216.

Blatt, D. (2001). Descent into the depths (1930): Rebound from the great depression crash of '29. *Futurecasts Magazine, 3*(3). Retrieved May 19, 2004, from http://www.futurecasts.com/Depression_descent-beginning-'30.htm

Chamberlain, L., and Edwards, G. W. (1927). *The Principles of bond investing.* (Rev. ed.). New York, NY: Henry Holt and Company.

Dao, J. (2004, April 14). Republicans in Virginia help advance tax increase. *New York Times,* p. A24.

E*Trade Financial. (2004, June 24). Bonds. Retrieved June 24, 2004, from https://us.etrade.com/e/t/invest/bonds?traxui=F_FN

Fabozzi, F., Fabozzi, T. D., and Feldstein, S. G. (1995). *Municipal bond portfolio management.* New York: Irwin Professional Publishing.

Fairfax County Taxpayers Alliance Press Release. (2002, October). *Virginia's bogus budget crisis: taxation by misrepresentation.* Fairfax, VA.

Fukumoto, K. (2002). *General obligation bonds.* (Report No. 02-04). Honolulu, HA: Legislative Reference Bureau, State of Hawaii.

Galambos, E., and Schreiber, A. (1996). Economic base: What our jobs are tied to. In J. Rabin, W. B. Hildreth, and G. Miller (Eds.), *Budgeting formulation and execution,* pp. 79–90. Athens, GA: Carl Vinson Institute of Government.

Halper, E. (2003, June 12). State sells bonds to stay solvent. [Electronic version] *Los Angeles Times.* Retrieved July 25, 2003 from http://www.latimes.com/news/politics/la-me-budget12-jun12,1,7396442.story?coll=la-util-news-local

Jurgens, R. (2003, July 25). Credit-rating agency assigns California its lowest bond rating ever. *Knight Ridder Tribune Business News,* p. 1.

Katz, D., and Kahn, R. (1966). *The social psychology of organization.* New York: Wiley.

Kelleher, J. B. (2004, May 6). Investors big and small buy California Economic Recovery Bonds. *Knight Ridder Tribune Business News,* p. 1.

Koven, S. and Lyons, T. (2003). *Economic development: Strategies for state and local practice.* Washington, DC: International City/County Management Association.

Lamb, R., and Rappaport, S. P. (1987). *Municipal bonds.* (2nd ed.). New York, NY: McGraw-Hill Book Company.

Lee, R., Johnson, R., and Joyce, P. (2004). *Public budgeting systems.* (7th ed.). Dudbury, MA: Jones and Bartlett Publishers.

Lessig, H. (2004, March 2). Former governors, Attorney General tackle Virginia budget. *Knight Ridder Tribune Business News,* p. 1.

Lynch, T. (1995). *Public budgeting in America.* (4th ed.). Englewood Cliffs, NJ: Prentice Hall.

Mikesell, J. (2003). *Administration: Analysis and applications for the public sector.* (6th ed.). Belmont, CA: Wadsworth/Thomson.

Moody's cuts bond rating for California. (2003, February 11). *New York Times,* p. A25.

Rosenberg, S. (2002, December 20). S&P lowers ratings on California — State cites a shortfall in revenue as budget gap widens to $34.8 billion. *Wall Street Journal,* p. C12.

Saskal, R. (2004). California's GO deal on tap. *Bond Buyer, 348*(31864), p. 1.

Shear, M., and Jenkins, C. L. (2004, May 8). Va. budget approved, ending marathon: Rise in spending, taxes is major change for state. *Washington Post,* p. A01.

Southwest State University, Regional Data Information Center (n.d.) *General obligation bonds.* Retrieved May 17, 2004, from http://www.southwest.msus.edu/RDIC/gobond.html

Spilberg, P., and Alexander, L. (2003). The California budget crisis: Factors leading to the current budget deficit and a discussion of certain proposed solutions. *National Tax Journal,* *56*(3), 555–566.

Standard & Poor's. (1996). Municipal finance criteria. In J. Rabin, W. B. Hildreth, and G. Miller (eds), *Budgeting formulation and execution,* pp. 341–360. Athens, GA: Carl Vinson Institute of Government.

Sylvester, D. A. (2003, July 31). Budget deal won't boost California's credit rating. *Knight Ridder Tribune Business News,* p. 1.

Temel, J. W. (2001). *The fundamentals of municipal bonds.* (5th ed.). New York, NY: John Wiley & Sons.

Twentieth Century Fund Task Force. (1974). *The rating game.* New York, NY: Twentieth Century Fund, Inc.

Vogt, J. A. (2004). *Capital budgeting and finance: A guide for local governments.* Washington, DC: International City/County Management Association.

Weston II, M. M. (2003, February). *New York's fiscal crisis.* Distinguished Lecture in Urban and Public Policy at School of International and Public Affairs, Columbia University, New York, NY. Retrieved May 19, 2004, from http://www.sipa.columbia.edu/NEWS?Rohatyn%20speech.pdf.

Chapter 12

State Debt Capacity and Debt Limits: Theory and Practice

DWIGHT V. DENISON, Ph.D. and
MERL HACKBART, Ph.D.
Martin School of Public Policy and Administration,
University of Kentucky

12.1   Introduction

The volume of outstanding municipal bonds, particularly those issued by states and state authorities, has increased over recent decades in response to rapidly increasing infrastructure needs and declining federal financial support for domestic programs. As states issue more bonds there is a growing awareness among municipal bond investors, state policy makers and citizens of the potential impact of increased debt on a state's credit worthiness and bond ratings. Realizing the importance of managing their state's debt position, many state's have established debt limits to manage their debt issuance and stabilize or enhance their credit position.

Setting debt limits has been a difficult process for the states as there has been little research focusing on methods for determining and setting appropriate limits. Moreover, there has been limited research regarding the optimal structure of debt limits. For example, if a state decides to set debt limits, it must decide whether to set a single debt limit or if it should establish multiple debt limits based on debt service funding source and type of credit backing.

The policy question of the appropriateness of single or multiple state debt limits has emerged due to a number of factors, including the tendency of states to issue both General Obligation (also referred GO or Full Faith and Credit debt) or "guaranteed" debt as well as un-guaranteed or revenue (project revenue) backed debt. Debate about the appropriateness of single or multiple debt limits has also resulted from the increasing tendency for states to create special funds with earmarked tax and fee resources as a source for bond debt service funding. Earmarked revenues can enhance debt service stability as the earmarking of revenues limits the use of fund revenues to a specific agency or purpose including debt service.

This chapter focuses on the debt limitation policy issues faced by the states as they attempt to meet their infrastructure investment needs by increasing their dependence on bond funding. Among the policy limit issues faced are: (1) should formal debt limits be established, (2) should single or multiple limits be established and (3) if multiple limits are established, what categories of debt should have higher or lower limits. In addressing these issues we consider the theoretical and conceptual issues involved in state debt financing, review state efforts to set debt limits, consider the inter-related issues involved in setting debt limits and review recent research that has focused on these debt policy issues.

12.2 Conventional Wisdom of Debt Finance

The conventional wisdom of state public finance is that current expenditures should be financed by current revenues while capital expenditures may be financed by borrowing funds. The use of debt financing is justified for capital or infrastructure projects by the "benefits received" principle. That is, capital expenditures such as roads and highways, public buildings, and other infrastructure will benefit future taxpayers. Therefore, the cost of such public investments should be borne by future as well as current taxpayers.

One way to ensure that future taxpayers bear their "fair share" of the cost of public facilities is to use a portion of their taxes to amortize the debt needed to finance capital projects (Oats, 1972). Therefore, states often utilize bonds to finance capital projects. In doing so, they attempt to match the projects "benefit stream" with the term of the bond issue issued to finance the project. With such matching the amortization period and the expected lifespan of the "capital" project coincide (Ramsey and Hackbart, 1996).

From a state financing perspective, therefore, state capital budgets have two "appropriate" funding strategies, including: (1) a "pay-as-you-go" strategy or the use of current revenues (current taxes, fees and other source revenues allocated to capital projects), or (2) a debt financing strategy where funds are acquired from bond sales. Revenues that fund a "pay as you go" capital project funding strategy are limited to the revenues allocated to capital expenditures from a state's taxes, fees and other current revenues. Meanwhile, the limit on capital project resources from bond issues is limited by the financial capacity of the state to meet future debt service obligations incurred as a result of issuing bonds.

While it has been established that debt financing is an acceptable option for financing capital projects, the determination of an acceptable maximum level of debt or an appropriate balance between "pay-as-you-go" financing versus debt financing continues to be debated by state policy officials and fiscal policy analysts. As noted by Larkin and Joseph (1996, p. 277), "greater dependence on borrowed funds can have a significant negative impact on a government's credit quality." They further note that "while the issuance of debt is frequently an appropriate method of financing capital projects at the state and local level, it also entails careful monitoring of such issuances to ensure that an erosion of the governments' credit quality does not result" (p. 277).

The ability of a state to meet future debt obligations is, in the strictest sense, limited by the availability of future funds to meet required debt service payments. The availability of debt service funds, while principally determined by economic and tax and revenue factors, is also determined by the willingness of state officials to "trade off" current (current in a future time period) discretionary expenditures to meet previous bond issue debt service commitments. So while, conceptually, there are restrictions on the use of bond financing, states tend to be less restricted, and possibly less disciplined, in the use of debt-financing for capital projects and programs than they are when using the pay-as-you-go capital financing option. Discipline in debt issuance can be further undermined in that debt financing leverages the funds available for current spending and balancing the operating budget. (Rowan and Picur 2000, p. 2).

While pay-as-you-go financing advocates may express concern about the impact that debt financing will have on future budgetary discretion, the stronger incentive for disciplined debt use is probably a state's desire to maintain its credit rating. For the financial markets, a state's credit worthiness is indicated by its bond ratings. Such ratings are determined by a number of factors, including a state's economic and demographic characteristics, its financial position and debt management practices.

Bond ratings provide investors and the financial market with proxy information of a state's credit worthiness, as suggested by Larkin and Joseph (1996, p. 277). The challenge to the states, therefore, is to design and implement debt management policies and bond financing decisions which reflect their capacity to meet debt service obligations. While an admirable goal, techniques for estimating a state's debt affordability or capacity are just beginning to surface.

If a state's debt policy and bond financing record indicates prudent judgment regarding the use of debt financing (including considerations of affordability), ceteris paribus, it is likely that a state's bond rating will be sustained when additional bonds are issued. The challenge for the states, then, is to establish debt financing policies and procedures that ensure that current and future debt issues are affordable and are "perceived" to be affordable by the bond rating agencies and the financial markets.

To manage bond issuance and debt outstanding, states have established a variety of limits and policies. A fairly recent study by Robbins and Dungan found that 24 states have constitutional debt limitations; 5 states have statutory debt limitations, 3 states have debt limit rules of thumb, 3 states have informal limitations and 3 states have other formal limitations (Robbins and Dungan, 2001). As their study focused on analyzing general state debt limit policies, it did not clarify how the various debt limits applied to different categories of state bond issues. For example, many state constitutions establish debt limitations for state General Obligation or GO debt, while the same constitutions are silent regarding revenue or non-guaranteed debt. Some states have established state-wide or "umbrella type" debt limitations by policy or statute for all state debt regardless of type or bond or source of debt service. Meanwhile, other states have established debt limits which cap debt outstanding or new debt issuance by type of debt (GO or revenue) or by debt service source such as General Fund, Agency Funds including the Road Fund, or other specified debt service sources.

The issue of state government debt affordability has been studied by many authors (Robbins and Dungan, 2001; Pogue, 1970; Nice, 1991; and Hackbart and Leigland, 1990). The key consideration of those and other studies (Larkin and Joseph, 1996; Simonson, Robbins, and Brown, 2002; Smith, 1998; Capital Affordability Committee, 1993 and ACIR 1962) has been on assessing the ability of the states to make required debt service payments and to manage debt issuance within a state's "debt capacity." Debt capacity can be conceived of as the level of debt and/or debt service relative to current revenues (or debt ceiling) that an issuing entity could support without creating undue budgetary constraints that might impair the ability of the issuer to repay bonds outstanding or make timely debt service payments (Ramsey and Hackbart 1996).

As observed by Miranda and Picur (2000), the primary approach used by states to assess debt affordability and to set debt limits involves reviewing debt ratios, debt limits and debt burdens of similar governments. By setting state debt policies which reflect national norms or benchmarks regarding debt per capita, debt service as a percent of current revenues or other comparable debt service or debt outstanding standards, the states feel that their debt limit policy reflects national debt capacity or debt affordability standards.

Most of the debt affordability literature has focused on identifying income and wealth variables that are reasonable proxy measures of the fiscal capacity of a state and, consequently, can be used to predict debt capacity or debt affordability levels for states. In some analyses, it is assumed that as a state's income and wealth increases, its capacity to meet debt service or its "debt affordability" proportionately increases. Therefore, as long as debt outstanding or debt service payment commitments expand in proportion to a state's economy and wealth, the rating agencies' concerns about the exhaustion or impending exhaustion of an issuing entities debt capacity should be mitigated and the state's debt rating (ceteris paribus) should be maintained (Hackbart and Ramsey, 1990).

An alternative, more practical, approach to analyzing and managing affordable state debt levels is the use of debt capacity "rules of thumb." These approaches are often based on observations of "industry standards" of appropriate debt ceilings (derived from observations of other state policies) and may or may not be statistically based (Ramsey et al., 1988). Representative rules of thumb include setting ceilings on debt service payments as a percentage of state government expenditures, total debt per capita or other level of debt or debt service ratios.

Examples of this approach include Oregon and Florida. Oregon introduced the practice of setting ranges (represented by "traffic light" signals) of debt affordability or debt capacity utilization (Douglas, 2000). After a review of "best practices," the Oregon State Debt Policy Advisory Commission, established by the 1997 session of the Oregon Legislative Assembly, used the ratio of debt service on net tax-supported debt to General Fund revenues to establish a range of debt capacity utilization categories. The debt service to total General Fund revenues ranged from zero to 10 percent. A range of green (0 to 5%) indicates that Oregon has ample debt capacity, while a debt service to General Fund ratio placing the state's debt capacity in the yellow zone (6 to 7%) suggests that the state is beginning to exceed "prudent" capacity limits. If Oregon's ratio moved in the red zone (8 to 10%), it is assumed that Oregon's debt capacity limit has been reached.

By implication, if Oregon's ratio reaches the yellow stage, the state is nearing it's debt capacity and a review of Oregon's debt issuance policy is in order. It follows that a ratio denoted by red suggests that the state is about to incur the consequences of excessive debt financing and, unless a state modifies its debt financing position, the state could experience reduced bond ratings, increased interest costs and, possibly, reduced access to financial markets (Smith, 1998).

The state of Florida undertook a debt affordability study in 1999 (Douglas, 2000). In evaluating its relative debt position, it relied on Moody's Investors Services 1999 report regarding the relative debt position of the 10 most populous states. Florida ranked second or third in three comparison categories, including net tax supported debt relative to revenues, tax supported per capita debt and tax supported debt as a percent of personal income. The peer group median tax supported debt as a percent of revenues was 3.3 percent and the mean was 3.5 percent, while the ratios varied from 1.3 percent for Texas to 7.4 percent for New York.

After evaluating Moody's comparison data, Florida decided that state debt policy guidelines and estimates of debt capacity were needed. Like Oregon, they based their debt capacity estimates on a ratio of debt service to revenues. They set a target ratio of 6 percent with a cap of 8 percent. The 8 percent cap was selected because a rating agency indicated that a 10 percent ratio was excessive and, therefore, it was assumed that the 8 percent cap provided a "margin of safety." When debt limit or debt capacity "rules of thumb" like those used by Oregon and Florida are employed, the targets or caps provide evidence of state intentions to keep debt levels manageable (Larkin and Joseph, 1996, p. 279).

12.3   Debt Capacity: A Debt Management Perspective

Unfortunately, limited research has been undertaken to determine how state debt limits are set (if they exist) and how debt limits may vary from state to state. With better information regarding policies and actual debt limits, states can make more informed judgments about the reasonableness of their debt management policies and the rating agencies will have better information regarding "industry standards" which are important in making rating determinations.

However, once a state has defined it's debt capacity (whether by national state standards, rules of thumb or more sophisticated methodologies), the next state debt management challenge is the establishment of policies and procedures that will limit debt issuance to the state's established limits. With an established debt limit, the ability of the state to do additional debt financing will depend on it's available or "slack" debt capacity. Slack or available debt capacity can be defined as the value of new debt or bonds that can be issued given the states debt limit and it's inventories of outstanding debt or it's current debt service commitments (depending on the type of debt limit the state has established).

For example, it can be assumed that a state's debt limit in dollar value of outstanding bonds (D_L) or it's debt service limit, for example debt service as a percent of current revenues (D_{DSL}), is set and is applicable to all funds, or separate limits have been set by fund type or by type of bond such as general obligation (GO) or revenue (or non-guaranteed).

Available debt capacity can then be formally expressed as:

$$\mathbf{D_{CA}} = D_L - D_O$$

or

$$\mathbf{D_{DSCA}} = D_{DSL} - D_{CDS}$$

Where:

D_{CA} = Debt capacity available

D_L = Debt limit (maximum debt as defined by policy)

D_O = Debt outstanding (at start of budget and debt authorization process)

and

D_{DSCA} = Debt service capacity available

D_{DSL} = Debt service limit (maximum debt service payment permitted per year which is determined by establishing a maximum percent of current revenues that can be committed to debt service)

D_{CDS} = Current debt service payment (payment required to meet debt service obligation on outstanding bond issues)

When states establish and enforce debt limits, they indicate to the bond rating agencies that they are committed to analyzing and managing their debt capacity. Such efforts also help ensure a state's ability to meet its future debt service obligations.

12.4   Debt Limit Policy Considerations

Effective state debt limit policies should consider more than just the traditional limits on GO bond issues. As illustrated in Table 12.1, we propose that there are at least two considerations in setting debt limits: bond backing (GO or revenue bonds) and the funding structure (General Fund or Special Agency Funds). Most state debt issues are expected to cluster into cells

Table 12.1   State Government Debt Classification Matrix

	Funding Structure	
Bond Backing	*General Fund*	*Special Agency Fund*
General obligation or tax backed debt	A	B
Revenue backed debt	C	D

A and D. The state General Fund is traditionally supported through taxes (cell A), although user fees and other revenue sources like lottery revenues are increasingly important for some states (cell C). In addition, Special Agency Funds, as previously noted, are frequently financed through earmarked revenues or allocations from the general fund (cell D), but in some cases may be granted its own tax authority (cell B).

If state debt was exclusively in classified cells A and D, then debt limits on GO bonds and revenue-backed bonds would be sufficient. However, since some debt clearly falls in cells B and C, it is important to discuss the implications of funding structure on debt capacity and market perceptions of risk.

12.5   Earmarked and Special Agency Funds: Debt Limit Policy Considerations

The proliferation of state earmarked funds and special agency funds pose an additional debt policy issue for state governments. When such "protected" funds are the source of bond issue debt service, they pose different cash flow and risk characteristics than states' General Fund and, therefore, may deserve special debt limit policy consideration. Traditionally a minor component of state revenues, the expanded use of "earmarking" of funds has emerged for three principal reasons:

1. trends by legislatures to increase their reliance on user charges and special fees that facilitate earmarking,
2. efforts by agencies and special interest constituencies to "protect their share of state funds" by switching their funding from the competitive General Fund to a protected Special Agency or Special Revenue Fund, and
3. public demands for greater transparency regarding the source and use of public funds.

In practice, these tendencies reinforce the shift to earmarked funds and are often supported by policy makers who may, coincidentally, wish to reduce agency dependence on the major state fund, the General Fund.

Special Agency Funds tend to have unique cash flow and cash flow variability patterns, due to their unique tax and revenue sources as well as their relative protection from "raids" for other government uses. The degree of protection from such raids during economic downturns is dependent on whether the fund is a constitutional or statutory established fund. Because Special Agency Funds are increasingly becoming the debt service source for state bond issues, debt policy questions are being raised as to whether a state should establish an "across the board" debt-limit or should establish debt limits by fund group or source of debt service. Multiple state debt limits reflect the differential risk and other characteristic differences of dedicated versus state General Funds.

An across the board policy may be appropriate if a state only issues bonds financially supported by a single fund such as it's General Fund. However, with the increasing tendency for states to issue multiple types of bonds and to depend on multiple debt service sources, a more appropriate policy might be to establish debt limits by bond type, by fund or by source of debt service.

Because the expenditure of Special Agency Funds is restricted to certain programs and activities (by constitution or state statute), there is less "expenditure competition" for Special Agency Funds than for their more competitive General Fund counterpart. General Funds are thought to be more "expenditure" competitive than Special Agency Funds as General Funds support multiple government activities and programs. Consequently, appropriation requests for bond debt service (from a state's General Fund) must compete with requests from other programs and departments. Because of General Fund competition, fiscal year appropriation or allocations are subject to changing state priority adjustments and are especially vulnerable during periods of severe state fiscal stress.

Moreover, General Fund monies are principally used to finance current state services and operating programs while some Special Agency Funds, such as a state Road Fund, principally finances capital expenditures such as highway construction and maintenance. Therefore, because the "conventional wisdom" of public finance suggests that debt financing is appropriate for capital expenditures, it might be appropriate to commit a larger share of Road Fund dollars to debt service than for a state's General Fund, which primarily funds current services. It would follow that a different debt limit might be appropriate for a Special Agency Fund such as a Road Fund than might be applied to a state's General Fund.

12.6 State Debt and Debt Limits: An Overview

A study by the National Association of State Treasurers (NAST) provides additional insights into state debt limit policies. NAST (1997) reported that 29 states have constitutional limitations or combinations of constitutional and statutory limitations on General Obligation bonds (somewhat different than the limits reported by Robbins and Dungan); the same report indicated that only 5 states had similar restrictions on revenue or non-guaranteed debt. An additional 24 states had statutory limitations on the total amount of revenue bonds outstanding. The same report indicated that 9 states had "macro" or statewide constitutional or constitutional and statutory limits on all debt outstanding, while 7 states had statewide limits and 29 reported no macro limits (5 states didn't respond to this question). The NAST study did not report on "policy" based debt limits which may not have been codified by statute for either category of bonds or for overall limits.

Because of the rigid constitutional limitations that many states have on the amount of GO debt outstanding that they can hold, they have increasingly turned to revenue or non-guaranteed debt to finance their infrastructure needs. U.S. Census of Governments data indicate that for the 2001–02 fiscal year, state governments had outstanding debt of $1,686 billion of which $1,643 billion was long-term and $43 billion was short-term debt (debt issues with less than one year maturity). Of the long-term debt, $619 billion was General Obligation and $1,024 billion was non-guaranteed or revenue bond debt (U.S. Census Bureau).

12.7 Road Fund Debt Policy: A Dedicated Revenue / Special Agency Example

In most states, highway or "Road Funds" are separate, special funds established by a state's constitution or by statute that restricts the use of fund revenues for the construction and maintenance of a state's highway and road system. Highway or "Road Fund" revenues are principally user fees derived from earmarked motor fuels, sales or usage taxes on vehicles and other special dedicated revenue sources such as registration fees. Therefore, when a state decides to finance highway infrastructure with bonds, the debt service for such bonds involves the commitment of future "earmarked" Road Fund revenues. Because of the uniqueness of Road Fund revenues and the fund's legal standing, it provides a useful example for considering the emerging state debt policy question of whether states should implement statewide debt limits or should develop "fund specific" limits for bonds with different characteristics or debt service sources.

We will use the Road Fund throughout the remainder of this paper as an example of a special or "protected" agency fund for conceptual debt management comparisons with the state General Fund. The comparison of conceptual and theoretical issues, such as revenue volatility, in assessing whether there may be differential risk characteristics of state funds that may warrant specific or tailored limits for some funds that differ from those imposed on general fund issues, regardless of whether they are GO or revenue bonds. The comparison also benefits from a recent study which provided empirical comparisons of debt financing policy and debt limitation information regarding these two state funds.

The Road Fund is a common fund among states that meets the criteria of a fund with large capital expenditure requirements, a dedicated tax or user fee revenue base, and the ability to provide debt service support for bonds independent of financial support from a states' General Fund. By using this example, we do not mean to imply that the Road Fund is the only fund in a state that could meet this criterion or that the Road Fund in a particular state necessarily meets the criteria. The criteria and implications are discussed further later in the paper.

12.8 Restricted Fund Credit Risk: A Conceptual Comparison and Analysis

A successful debt management policy will balance the need to leverage current revenues against the risk of a bond rating downgrade. Without the financial backing of a broad tax base like the General Fund, a major financial objective of the managers of a states' Road Fund supported by limited earmarked revenue sources is the sustainability of the fund. Road Fund financial managers must consider the factors which will impact revenue cash flows, as cash flow variability will impact the Road Fund's financial status and the Fund's debt capacity or ability to meet debt service and other financial commitments. Cash flow variability will, to a great degree, determine the risk of the enterprise (the Road Fund) and greater variability will reduce the manager's ability to assure bond holders that debt service commitments can be made.

Bond rating agencies estimate the credit risk of a government entity by considering the ability and willingness of the government to make debt service payments (Moody, 1991, p. 22). The ability of a government to pay is determined by economic factors such as tax base capacity and stability, community wealth, and current debt outstanding. "Willingness to pay" incorporates the management, community, and politician attitudes toward debt. "Management" also considers factors such as staff expertise and accounting systems.

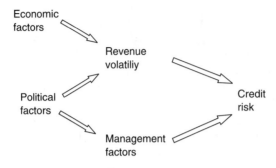

Figure 12.1   Influences on credit risk

Bond rating agencies evaluate credit risk based on their perception of the issuing and supporting entities' ability to meet future obligations. Figure 12.1 illustrates the assessment of credit risk. Fund revenues have some degree of volatility, and the revenue volatility ultimately determines the amount of debt that can be reasonably supported by the fund. Volatility of revenues is driven by both economic and political factors, but the specific factors may vary widely among state fund types depending on the revenue source or sources supporting the fund.

Figure 12.1 also illustrates that there are management factors beyond the revenue volatility that influence credit risk. In the case of government agencies there is often a substantial influence between administration and political factors.

It is helpful to consider these factors in determining whether a macro or fund-based debt policy should be implemented. The state General Fund is likely to benefit from a more diverse tax and fee base and yet a single tax source like the personal income tax or sales tax may comprise the lion's share of the total revenues, making the general fund very elastic to swings in the business cycle. In contrast, the Road Fund may receive the bulk of the revenues from the motor-fuels tax, which could be less volatile if the purchase of motor fuels is less elastic to the business cycle.[1]

The political factors also have interesting implications for the General and Road Fund. Many political factors are unique to the citizens, institutions, and administration of the state, and will similarly influence the credit risk of both funds. However, an earmarked fund like the Road Fund may experience less political tension through the appropriation process, making the resources available for transportation more reliable. By comparison, the General Fund budget process could force competition among competing demands for General Fund resources, increasing vulnerability of appropriations for specific expenditures like debt service.

12.9 State Debt Limits for the General and Road Funds: A Comparative Analysis

The possibility that states might set different debt limits for General Fund debt than for Special Agency Funds such as the state Road Fund is based on two considerations. First, state Road Fund revenues are typically earmarked by state constitutions or state statutes for transportation related expenditures. As a consequence, state officials might conclude that it would be safe or financially prudent to commit a greater portion of "protected" Road Fund revenues to debt service than for the more competitive and unrestricted General Fund.

Second, the majority of highway and road expenditures are capital expenditures that provide public benefits over an extended period of time. Therefore, such expenditures meet the "conventional wisdom" or criterion for the use of public debt financing. By contrast, General Fund revenues are principally used for operating programs rather than for capital investments.

As a result, state financial managers may feel justified in setting less restrictive debt limits for Road Fund bond issues than for General Fund supported issues. Also, the earmark restrictions applied to most state Road Fund revenue sources could make rating agencies more comfortable with less restrictive debt limits for Road Fund issues.

A recent survey of state General Fund debt limit and management policies found that about 84% of the reporting states indicated that they have established debt limits as guides for managing debt levels and bond issuance. The same study surveyed Road Fund administrators and reported that 58% of the reporting states have formal debt polices that guide the debt issuance reliant on the Road Fund (Hackbart et al., 2004).

Table 12.2 summarizes the types and sources of General Fund/State-wide debt limits. The survey data suggest that the states have several types of debt limitation limits and the limits have several sources, including constitutional, statutory, policy and other origins. The most common type of state debt limit is the limit on general obligation (GO) debt, with 12 of the 26 responding states indicating constitutional limits on GO debt, 6 states reporting statutory GO debt limits and 3 states indicated that they had policy based limits on GO debt. Apparently, several states impose duplicate limits on GO debt. For example, a state might have both a statutory as well as a policy limit on GO debt issuance. Meanwhile, 14 respondents have limits on revenue or non-guaranteed debt issuance of statutory and policy origins.

Other types of debt limits include Maine's limit on tax-supported debt service payments by fiscal year on General Fund and highway (Road) fund revenues, Texas's limit on state debt payable from general revenue, and Washington's limit on issuance of new debt if that debt were to raise the

Table 12.2   Origin of General Fund/State-wide Debt Limits

| Debt Limit Category | *Origin of Debt Limits* | | | |
	Constitutional	*Statutory*	*Policy Based*	*Total*
General obligation debt	12	6	3	21
Revenue/non-guaranteed debt	0	9	5	14
All debt outstanding	1	2	5	8
Debt limit by debt service on all funds	1	3	3	7
Debt limit by debt service by fund type	2	5	1	8
Total	16	25	17	58

Note: Twenty-six states responded and reporting states indicated multiple debt limit types. *Source*: University of Kentucky Transportation Center Survey, 2003.

maximum annual debt service over a specified percentage based on a three-year mean. The responding states reported that the debt limits imposed on issuing entities involved 16 constitutional limits, 25 statutory limits and 17 policy limits. In some cases, revenue debt and non-guaranteed debt may overlap as these terms are often used interchangeably. For example, non-guaranteed debt might imply revenue type bonds that are backed by General Fund debt services, while revenue bonds (in their purest form) would be bonds that are supported by a specific cash flow sources (such as toll roads, parking garages, and the like).

As shown in Table 12.3, formal debt limits (constitutional or statutory) are the predominate source of Road Fund related debt limits. Seventeen states report that Road Fund debt issues are limited by constitutional provisions (including specific references to Road Fund debt outstanding, all state debt outstanding and the like) while statutory debt limits of some form were reported by 22 states as well. Similar to the general fund limits, many states apply both constitutional and statutory limits to bond issuance. Meanwhile, 16 states also indicate that their states have "policy" based limitations. The survey results indicate a possible duplication of operative limits (for example, debt policy limits may be established even though "overriding" constitutional limits exist). Such duplicative limits may reflect conscious decisions to establish more rigorous limits in some states.

12.10   Trends in Debt Service Ratios

One measure of debt capacity in the literature is the ratio of debt service to total revenues. Table 12.4 provides a summary of the surveys results regarding the ratio of General Fund debt service payments to total General Fund

Table 12.3   Origin of Road Fund Debt Limitations

Debt limit category	Origin of Road Fund Debt Limits			
	Constitutional	Statutory	Policy Based	Total
Road fund Non-guaranteed/revenue Debt outstanding	4	8	5	17
All state Non-guaranteed/revenue Debt outstanding	2	2	0	4
All state Debt outstanding	3	3	1	7
Road fund Debt payment Per fiscal year	3	4	8	15
All state Debt payment Per fiscal year	4	5	2	11
Total	16	22	16	54

Source: University of Kentucky Transportation Center Survey—2003 40 states responding

revenues for the period 1984 through 2000. In Table 12.4, the first column indicates the number of states with available data, the second column indicates the mean ratios for the reporting states and the final two columns report the minimum and maximum debt service to total General Fund revenues for the states reporting for the various years in the period. The lowest calculated mean ratio value since 1984 occurs in 1989 and 1992 with a debt service ratio of 2.8%. The highest mean debt service as a percent of General Fund revenues (4%) during this time period occurs in 1984. The minimum and maximum ratios reported by individual states included a low ratio of 0.4 percent for several years of the period studied to a high of 11 percent reported by one state in 1984.

The debt service expenditures relative to total General Fund revenues tended to stay in the 3 to 4 percent range for the period. The higher ratios were realized in the mid-1980s when interest rates were higher, while the lower ratios tended to occur during lower interest rate periods. However, additional investigation is required to understand the ratio variances during this period, particularly given the limited number of states with data available for the early eighties.

By comparison, Table 12.5 similarly reports the survey's determined state ratios of debt service to total Road Fund revenues for the period 1980 to

Table 12.4   Debt Service as a Percent of General Fund Revenue: 1984–2000 (Select States)

	Observations	Mean	Minimum	Maximum
1984	4	4.01	0.75	11.00
1985	4	3.83	0.66	10.30
1986	4	3.64	0.61	9.79
1987	4	3.23	0.40	8.74
1988	5	2.89	0.50	7.83
1989	5	2.80	0.50	7.34
1990	8	3.10	0.40	7.00
1991	9	2.94	0.40	6.53
1992	9	2.81	0.40	5.67
1993	11	2.91	0.50	5.01
1994	12	3.28	0.50	5.21
1995	13	3.44	0.50	5.30
1996	14	3.47	0.60	5.31
1997	14	3.55	0.70	5.93
1998	14	3.18	0.70	5.20
1999	15	3.10	0.87	5.07
2000	13	3.19	0.90	5.76

Source: University of Kentucky Transportation Center survey, 2003.

2000 and indicates the number of states with available data, the mean debt service expenditures to total Road Fund revenue ratios per year, and the range of debt service expenditures relative to total Road Fund revenue.

The mean ratio of debt service to total Road Fund revenue for the reporting states ranged from 8.20 percent in 1994 to 13.78 percent in 1983. The range of debt service to total Road Fund revenue ratios varied dramatically, from zero for states that did not issue bonds to support the construction and maintenance of their roads and highways to more than 54 percent for one state in the late 1990s. While the mean ratios of debt service as a percent of total Road revenues fluctuated for the period, the cause of such variation is not clear. The economic downturn of the early 1980s might explain the tendency of states to increase their use of debt financing in that period, but a similar pattern is not observed for the 1991–92 recession. Other possible explanations for the variations over time include a reduction in debt service costs in the early 1990s due to refinancing of bonds issued in the high interest period of the early 1980s, a decline in the demand for infrastructure investment in the early 1990s due to the recession, and an increase in the demand for highway construction and maintenance expenditures in the last half of the 1990s due to the strong economy of that period.

Table 12.5 Road Fund Debt Service as a Percent of Fund Revenue from 1980–2000

	Number of States	Mean	Min.	Max.
1980	11	11.63	0.00	27.94
1981	13	12.37	0.00	27.37
1982	14	13.14	1.35	49.98
1983	15	13.78	3.12	36.58
1984	18	10.55	1.32	28.69
1985	19	11.85	1.43	44.54
1986	20	11.18	1.16	33.08
1987	20	10.39	0.53	33.17
1988	21	11.52	1.77	33.37
1989	21	11.65	1.38	39.05
1990	23	9.50	0.07	22.03
1991	24	9.12	0.22	27.69
1992	24	8.49	0.28	23.25
1993	24	9.32	0.58	35.30
1994	26	8.20	0.46	35.25
1995	26	9.67	0.00	34.90
1996	27	10.26	0.00	52.99
1997	27	10.21	0.00	54.05
1998	27	9.45	0.00	54.22
1999	28	8.93	0.00	37.35
2000	28	8.66	0.00	38.03

Note: 40 states responded to the Road Fund survey. However, the number of states providing expenditure data varied during the 20-year period as indicated in column 1 of this table. *Source*: Calculated from data provided by respondents to University of Kentucky Transportation Center 2003 Survey.

12.11 Comparison of Statewide versus Road Fund Specific Debt Limit Policies

As discussed, Road Fund resources primarily finance capital expenditures for the construction and maintenance of a state's highway and road system. Therefore, it is likely (as suggested by the conventional wisdom of public finance) that debt service payments would constitute a higher percent of that state's Road Fund expenditures than they would for that state's General Fund. This difference would be expected as General Fund expenditures are primarily made for operating programs and activities. Furthermore, the legal structure of the road fund in most states provides more "political" protection.

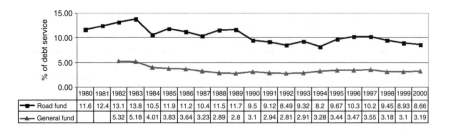

Figure 12.2   Comparison of debt service as a percent of Road and General Fund revenues: 1980–2000. *Source*: Calculated from 2003 University of Kentucky Transportation Center Survey Data.

The survey results indicate a pattern of debt service to total expenditure ratios for the Road and General Funds that is consistent with these assumptions (see Figure 12.2).

As indicated, the General Fund debt service to total revenue ratios were reported to be in the 3 to 4 percent range and the Road Fund debt service to total revenue ratios varied from 7 to 11 percent for the same period. While the Road Fund ratios were higher, they also displayed greater variability for the period. Furthermore, the survey results indicate that state debt financing policies, as revealed by the commitment of Road Fund revenues for debt service varies among the states. In Figure 12.3, the 23 responding states' mean debt service to Road Fund revenue ratios were graphed for the low, middle and high quantiles. The mean ratios of debt service to total Road Fund revenue for the period 1990 to 2000 varied from the 1.6 to 3.2 percent range for the lowest third of the reporting states to approximately 5.8 to 8.1 percent range for the mid-level states.

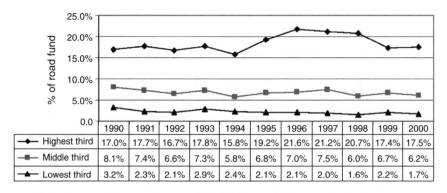

Figure 12.3   State Road Fund debt service as a percent of Road Fund revenues by sub-group: 1990–2000. *Source*: Calculated from University of Kentucky Transportation Center Survey Data.

The highest third of the survey states indicated mean debt service to Road Fund revenue ratios in, approximately, the 16.7 to 21.6 percent range.

An additional comparison of Road Fund and General Fund debt service to total revenue ratios was undertaken for the states, indicating that they had debt limits relative to those states that indicated no debt limits for the 1990 to 2000 period. The results provide an interesting and unexpected result. As shown in Figure 12.4, the states with debt limits reported higher debt service to total Road Fund revenues for the 10-year period. The reason for the ratio divergence is not immediately obvious.

The pattern of higher debt service to total revenue ratios for debt limit states, observed for the Road Fund, was also observed for the General Fund as displayed in Figure 12.5. The debt limit state ratios tended to vary from 2 to 3 percent while the non-debt limit states had ratios in the 4 to 5 percent range. Again, the reason or reasons for this pattern are not obvious. However, the establishment and use of debt limits by the higher ratio states might reflect concern about the potential bond rating impact that could occur if they did not effectively indicate to the bond rating agencies and others that they were managing their debt position by establishing debt limits or other measures. Alternatively, it might indicate that the states that are more aggressively using debt financing are also devoting more attention to the management of their debt issuance and debt outstanding.

Conversely, the lower ratio states might observe that their debt position, relative to their peers, is low and, therefore, the establishment of

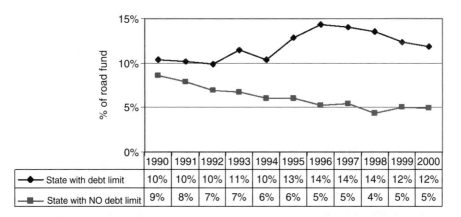

	1990	1991	1992	1993	1994	1995	1996	1997	1998	1999	2000
State with debt limit	10%	10%	10%	11%	10%	13%	14%	14%	14%	12%	12%
State with NO debt limit	9%	8%	7%	7%	6%	6%	5%	5%	4%	5%	5%

Figure 12.4 Comparison of debt service as a percent of Road Fund revenues for states with and without debt limits: 1990–2000. *Source*: Calculated from 2003 University of Kentucky Transportation Center survey data. For this period, eight states with debt limits responded to the survey while fifteen states without debt limits responded.

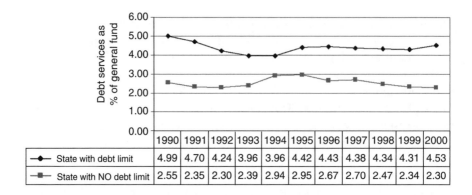

	1990	1991	1992	1993	1994	1995	1996	1997	1998	1999	2000
◆ State with debt limit	4.99	4.70	4.24	3.96	3.96	4.42	4.43	4.38	4.34	4.31	4.53
■ State with NO debt limit	2.55	2.35	2.30	2.39	2.94	2.95	2.67	2.70	2.47	2.34	2.30

Figure 12.5 Comparison of debt service as a percent of General Fund revenues for states with and without debt limits: 1990–2000. *Source*: Calculated from 2003 University of Kentucky Transportation Center survey data. For this period, seven states with debt limits responded to the survey while eight states without debt limits responded.

debt limit policies is not as critical for them as it is for the states that are using debt financing in a more aggressive manner.

12.12 Summary and Conclusions

This chapter has focused on an issue that is gaining greater prominence as states use or consider the use of debt or bond financing as a greater component of their infrastructure financing strategy. The use of debt financing has become more attractive as the states face greater infrastructure investment demand during a period of constrained resources and reduced federal infrastructure financial support. As a result of the increased emphasis on the debt financing option, the states are facing new policy issues such as managing their debt capacity and setting debt limits in order to maintain their credit standing.

Recent studies indicate that states have established, or are more frequently establishing, debt limits to manage their debt capacity and to indicate their commitment to sound debt management practices. Such debt limits have focused on debt issuance, debt outstanding as well as limits on the use of current revenues for debt service payments. The latter limitation also translates into a debt limit on state bond issuance

In this chapter we have reviewed the theoretical and conceptual issues involved in setting state debt limits. However, the main emphasis was directed toward gaining new insights on an emerging debt limit issue — whether states should institute a single or multiple debt limits which reflect differential risk conditions of bond issues resulting from variances in debt service cash flows, opportunities for intended debt service revenue to be diverted to other uses and related factors.

In addition to the theoretical and conceptual issues in setting debt limits, this chapter considered the results of a recent study which compared debt limit policies of states for their General Fund and a fund containing restricted, dedicated tax and revenue funds — the Road Fund. Among other comparisons, the recent study reported on the types of limits the states have imposed on the two funds, along with a comparative analysis of the debt-service as a percent of total revenue ratios for state Road Funds and the General Funds. This empirical summary may indicate that there is an implicit if not an explicit debt limit and management policy. The studies found that debt service to total revenue ratios were greater for the Road Fund than the state General Funds. This finding was not surprising since Road Fund revenues are principally used for capital budget financing and the General Fund principally funds operating budgets. The Road fund revenues are also relatively stable (due to the inelasticity of Road Fund revenue sources) and the earmarked resources also provide some protection against the politics of the state appropriation process.

Surprisingly, the reviewed study indicated that the states with debt limits (both for the Road Fund as well as for the General Fund) had higher debt service to total revenue ratios than the states that did not report debt limits (of any type). While the reason for this result is not clear, it may indicate that the states that use debt financing for their capital budgets may feel it is important that they, simultaneously, possess effective debt management policies if they are to maintain favorable bond ratings. In the same vein, the states with low debt service to total expenditures ratios could be relying more on a pay-as-you-go strategy and therefore do not feel the need to aggressively manage their debt situation, as compared to their peers, since their debt position falls well within their debt capacity.

Note

1. Fuel demand could still deteriorate over the long-term as alternative fuels and more fuel efficient vehicles are developed.

References

The Advisory Commission on Intergovernmental Relations. (1962). *Measures of State and Local Tax Capacity*. Report, M-16. Washington, D.C.: GPO.
Capital Debt Affordability Committee, State of Maryland. (1996). "Understanding and Forecasting Condition or Ability to Repay Debt:

Report of the Capital Debt Affordability Committee on Recommended Debt Authorizations for Fiscal Year 1993." In G. Miller (ed), *Handbook of Debt Management.* New York: Marcel Dekker Inc., pp. 283–322.

Douglas, J.R. (2000). "Best Practices in Debt Management." *Government Finance Review,* 16(2), 23–27.

Hackbart, M., and Liegland, J. (1990). State Debt Management Policy: A National Survey. *Public Budgeting & Finance,* 10(1), 37–54.

Hackbart, M., and Ramsey, J.R. (1990). State Debt Level Management: A Stable Credit Rating Model. *Municipal Finance Journal,* 11(1), 79–96.

Hackbart, M., Sapp, S., and Hur, Y. (2004). *Debt Capacity and Debt Limits: A State Road Fund Perspective.* Lexington, Kentucky. Kentucky Transportation Center, University of Kentucky.

Larkin, R., and Joseph, J.C. (1996). Developing Formal Debt Policies. In G. Miller (ed), *Handbook of Debt Management,* pp. 277–282. New York: Marcel Dekker.

Miranda, R., and Picur, R. (2000). *Benchmarking and Measuring Debt Capacity.* Chicago, IL: Government Finance Officers Association.

Moody's Investors Service. (1991). *Moody's On Municipals.*

National Association of State Treasurers. (1997). *State Treasury Activities & Functions.* Lexington, KY, p. 102.

Nice, D. C. (1991). "The Impact of State Policies to Limit Debt Financing." *Publius: The Journal of Federalism,* 21(1), 69–82.

Oats, W. E. (1972). *Fiscal Federalism.* New York: Harcourt, Brace, and Jovanovich.

Pogue, T. F. (1970). The Effect of Debt Limits: Some New Evidence. *National Tax Journal,* 23(1), 36–49.

Ramsey, J., and Hackbart, M. (1996). State and Local Debt Policy and Management. In G. Miller (ed.), *Handbook of Debt Management,* pp. 255–276. New York: Marcel Dekker.

Ramsey, J.R., Gritz, T. and Hackbart, M. (1988). State Approaches to Debt Capacity Assessment: A Further Evaluation. *International Journal of Public Administration,* 11(2).

Robbins, M.D., and Dungan, C. (2001). Debt Diligence: How States Manage the Borrowing Function. *Public Budgeting & Finance,* 21(2), 88–105.

Simonson, B., Robbins, M.D. and Brown, R. (2002). Debt Affordability. In Jack Rabin (ed), *Encyclopedia of Public Administration and Public Policy.* New York: Marcel Dekker.

Smith, C. (1998). Measuring and Forecasting Debt Capacity: The State of Oregon Experience. *Government Finance Review,* 14(6), 52–55.

U.S. Census Bureau. *State and Local Government Finances — 2002 Census of Governments.* http://www.census.gov/govs/www/estimate02.html accessed July 2004.

U.S. Congressional Budget Office. (1991). How Federal Spending for Infrastructure and Other Public Investments Affects the Economy. Washington, D.C.: GPO.

Chapter 13

Working Capital Management in Government: Basic Concepts and Policy Choices

AMAN KHAN, Ph.D.
Department of Political Science and Administration,
Texas Tech University

Finance managers in government, as in business, spend a considerable amount of their time dealing with problems related to short-term finance. Short-term finance, also known as *working capital*, deals with the portion of balance sheet accounts that arises from routine operations of a government. Although there is no acceptable definition of short-term finance, convention suggests that decisions involving short-term finance usually have a life span of a year or less. For instance, when a government decides to sell a bond issue to finance the construction of a capital project, it is considered a long-term decision, while a decision to invest the proceeds from the bond issue until they are required for construction is a short-term decision.

The point to note here is that normal operations of a government create and liquidate working capital on a regular basis and that time plays an important role in that process.

Good working capital management requires that all financial organizations, including government, use as little resources (money) as possible to run their everyday operations. Obviously, the more working capital an organization uses, the easier it is to run its operations; but it is also more costly, since it will tie up more money in the current accounts. On the other hand, having less working capital, while desirable, puts additional constraints on the organization in running its routine operations. A prudent manager must find a balance between the two. The objective of this chapter is to provide a brief description of these accounts, their underlying structures and, most importantly, to discuss the kinds of decisions that are needed to effectively manage the working capital needs of a government. The latter is known as *working capital management.*

13.1   Elements of Working Capital

The elements of working capital are the accounts in a balance sheet, especially the short-term accounts. A balance sheet consists of three sets of accounts: assets, liabilities, and fund balance (fund equity). An *asset* is something of value owned, a *liability* is something of value owed, and *fund balance* is the difference between assets and liabilities. While the number and size of these accounts vary from government to government, depending on the size of the government and the level of their activities, the structure of the balance sheet remains essentially the same. For working capital, these accounts typically include current assets (such as cash and cash equivalents, marketable securities, taxes receivable, accounts receivable, due from other funds and governments, and inventory), and current liabilities (such as accounts payable, notes payable, due to other funds and governments, and accruals). What distinguishes these assets and liabilities from fixed assets and long-term liabilities is their liquidity. *Liquidity* is the ease with which the current accounts in a balance sheet can be converted to cash and the time it will take to do so. Liquidity plays an extremely important role in working capital management to the extent that it is often referred to as *liquidity management.*

Let us briefly look at some of these elements of working capital before discussing what a government can do, or what measures or strategies it can use, to improve the quality of working capital management. Our discussion focuses on current assets and liabilities, as one would find in a typical balance sheet. As a general rule, these accounts appear on the balance sheet in order of their liquidity. Thus, cash is the most liquid of all assets and accounts payable the most liquid of all liabilities.

13.1.1 Cash and Cash Equivalents

Cash is the first and foremost of the asset accounts. Cash is the money on hand, as well as cash balances in bank accounts. Currency (i.e., the cash a government keeps on hand) is usually a small amount. Governments keep cash balances in bank accounts to pay bills as they become due and as a precaution against unforeseen situations. Cash equivalents, on the other hand, are highly liquid investments that mature usually in less than three months from the day they are acquired.[1]

13.1.2 Marketable Securities

During their normal course of operation governments accumulate cash surplus, resulting from the differences in cash receipts and cash disbursements, which, rather than holding in currency, or in time deposits, they can invest in marketable securities (such as T-bills and commercial paper) to generate non-tax revenue. Marketable securities are short-term investments with a life span of less than a year that pay a modest return and are relatively secure. They are called *marketable securities* because these issues can be sold quickly to generate instant cash. Since they can be easily converted to cash, marketable securities also serve the precautionary needs for cash.[2]

13.1.3 Taxes Receivable

Taxes receivable represent revenue from sales, income, and property taxes that a government has not yet received, but expects to receive within a prescribed time during an accounting period. Receivables are often stated net of an offsetting account called *allowance for delinquency* or *doubtful accounts,* meaning that some accounts are never paid, or will not be paid, within the prescribed time period. They usually are a small percentage of total receivables. For instance, the delinquency rate for property tax, the principal source of revenue for local governments, is hardly more than two or three percent of total tax levy for these governments.

13.1.4 Accounts Receivable

Similar to taxes receivable, accounts receivable represent income or revenue from user fees, charges, fines, forfeitures, as well as from other agencies and governments that a government has not yet received, but expects to receive within a prescribed time during an accounting period. Like property tax, the delinquency rate for user fees, charges, fines, and forfeitures also constitutes a small fraction of the total revenue of a government.[3]

13.1.5 Due from Other Funds and Governments

Very few governments can be defined as self-sufficient. Because of legal and other limits that often impose restrictions on revenues they can generate from their own sources, governments have come to rely on transfers from other funds, as well as from other governments over the years to sustain their routine activities. Although attractive as an important source of non-tax revenue, over-reliance on transfers indicates a weak revenue base for recipient governments and is not generally considered a viable alternative to long-term revenue problems.

13.1.6 Inventory

Governments need to maintain inventories (unused goods, materials, and supplies) to ensure that they are available when needed. Not having enough inventories when needed for a job can create a cost burden for a government from work delay. On the other hand, having too much inventory can also add to the cost of operation due to obsolescence, breakage, theft, and the use up of storage space. At the same time, frequent stockouts when inventories are in short supply can increase the frequency of orders resulting in higher ordering costs. The objective is to maintain an inventory level at which these costs will be minimum, while making sure that the level is sufficient to meet the needs as they arise.[4]

13.1.7 Accounts Payable

Accounts payable are the exact opposite of accounts receivable. Payables generally occur when a buyer buys from a supplier (vendor) on credit. When a credit sale is made, the supplier records a receivable and the purchaser records a payable. For most governments, the bulk of accounts payable arise from the purchase of goods, services, and inventory. Usually there is no security or contractual agreement other than the stipulation that the government will pay the supplier at some future point in time. The length of time allowed for payment for a service, or a purchase, on credit is usually specified in the terms of sale, including the conditions for any penalty for late payment or reward for early payment.[5]

13.1.8 Notes Payable

Governments frequently borrow money by issuing short-term notes to supplement their revenue. Three types of notes are generally issued for this purpose: tax anticipation notes (TAN) issued in anticipation of tax revenue, bond anticipation notes (BAN) issued in anticipation of proceeds from sale of bonds, and revenue anticipation notes (RAN) issued in anticipation of revenue from sale of services such as water, sewer, electricity, etc. The amount that is borrowed against these notes is usually a small fraction of the total tax levy, bond proceeds, or service charges.

13.1.9 Due to Other Funds and Governments

Due to other funds and governments is the exact opposite of due from other funds and governments. It is an obligation, or payment on an obligation to other governments, or to other funds within the same government. Although inter-fund and intergovernmental transfers are quite common, frequent transfers, as noted earlier, can have a negative effect on the operations of a government, as well as of the funds from which the transfers are made by reducing the size of the available resources.

13.1.10 Accruals

Somewhat more complex than most liabilities, accruals are an accounting device that recognizes expenses and liabilities involving transactions that are not entirely complete. The best example of accrual is payroll. As an example, suppose that a government pays its employees every other Friday and that the last day of a particular month falls on a Tuesday and the books are closed for the month at the end of the day, thus producing three days of unpaid labor. If this were to be recognized as a simple payroll expense when the cash is paid on Friday, the three days of labor would go into the second month and there would be no recognition of liability at the end of the month. To correct the problem, the government must have an end of the month accrual entry in the amount of three days of wages and salaries. Assuming the government uses a double-entry accounting system, one side of the entry would show an increase in accrued wages liability on the balance sheet and the other side an increase in wage expense in the closing month.[6]

Other important balance sheet accounts that are not part of working capital, but can have an effect on its performance, include fixed assets (on the assets side), non-current liabilities (on the liabilities side), and fund balance (the difference between assets and liabilities). Fixed assets do not mean they are fixed in location, they simply mean items with longer life spans, usually over a year such as land, building, and equipment. By the same token, the most significant non-current liability is long-term debt consisting primarily of bonds and long-term loans. Finally, fund balance represents the balance, or residue, after adjustments have been made for liabilities from assets.

13.2 Net Working Capital

Although working capital refers to both current assets and current liabilities in a balance sheet account, the term is often associated only with current assets, which are collectively referred to as *gross working capital,* while the difference between current assets and current liabilities is called *net working capital.* In practice, the word "net" is often left out. Net working capital can be positive or negative. A positive working capital occurs when a government's current assets exceed its current liabilities, indicating that it has enough current assets to pay off its obligations. A negative working capital, on the other hand, occurs when a government's current liabilities exceed its current assets, meaning that it does not have enough current assets and, consequently, will need to borrow or liquidate some assets to pay off its obligations. Conceptually, a positive working capital represents the amount of resources (money) a government needs in order to carry out its routine operations. Given a choice, most governments would prefer a positive working capital to a negative working capital. Positive working capital also serves as a measure of safety to government lenders on the assumption that current assets are more likely to maintain a reasonable liquidating value than any other assets of the government.

The relationship between current assets and current liabilities emerges from the fact that current assets are sources of cash inflows and current liabilities are sources of cash outflows. The cash outflows resulting from the payments of current liabilities are relatively easy to predict for most governments with a high degree of accuracy, but what is difficult to predict are the cash inflows because most governments receive their revenues from multiple sources at different times of the year that are not always predictable with accuracy. Thus, the more predictable the cash inflows of a government, the less net working capital it will need to carry out its routine operations. Since cash outflows do not always match cash inflows, governments need to maintain high enough cash inflows (current assets) to cover their cash outflows (current liabilities).

Let us look at a simple example to illustrate this. Suppose that a government has the following amounts in its balance sheet accounts: $1,965,300 in accounts payable, $725,200 in notes payable, $1,234,100

Table 13.1   Current Position of a Hypothetical Government (General Fund Operations)

Current Assets		Current Liabilities	
Cash and cash equivalents	$725,300	Accounts payable	$1,965,300
Marketable securities	1,854,600	Notes payable	765,200
Taxes receivable	2,376,700	Due to other funds	1,234,100
Accounts receivable	1,315,300	Due to other governments	476,200
Due from other funds	351,200	Accruals	2,051,700
Due from other governments	1,526,400	**Total**	**$6,492,500**
Inventory	15,600		
Total	**$8,165,100**		

in due to other funds, $476,200 in due to other governments, and $2,051,700 in accruals — all due at the end of the current period (Table 13.1). The $6,492,500 in outflows is certain. Let us say that the government can be sure that at least $2,579,900 will be available, since it has $725,300 in cash and $1,854,600 in marketable securities, which can easily be converted into cash. The remaining $3,872,600 must come from taxes or accounts receivable, or both, and from other funds and governments. However, the government cannot be sure if all of this amount will be available in time to pay the bills when they become due. Generally, the more receivables (taxes as well as accounts) a government has, the greater the likelihood that it will be able to convert some of these items into cash.[7] Therefore, a certain level of working capital is recommended to ensure the government's ability to pay its bills.

According to the table, the government has $1,672,600 in net working capital ($8,165,100 − $6,492,500), which, more than likely, will be sufficient to cover its bills. It also has a current ratio of 1.26 (current assets/current liabilities), which should provide enough liquidity to meet its financial obligations as long as its receivables and, to some extent, transfers from other funds and governments remain relatively active, although reliance on the latter should be kept to a minimum.

It should be noted, however, that there is a certain amount of risk involved when a government, like any business organization, fails to meet its financial obligations on time. *Risk* is the probability that a government will not be able to pay its bills when they become due. A government that cannot meet its financial obligations is *technically insolvent.* The risk of becoming technically insolvent is measured using one of two things: current ratio or the amount of net working capital. In this chapter we use the latter. In general, the greater the amount of net working capital, the less risk a government has. In other words, the more the net working capital (i.e., the more liquid the government), the less likely it will become technically insolvent.

13.3 Needs for Working Capital

All governments need working capital to carry out their routine operations, but the level of their need varies directly with the level of services they provide and the amount of resources committed to providing them. Obviously, the more services a government provides viz-a-viz the more resources a government commits, the more working capital it will need. However, regardless of the service levels or resource commitments, the working capital needs of a government depend on two basis factors: permanent (permanent needs) and seasonal (seasonal or temporary needs). The *permanent need*, which consists of fixed assets plus the permanent portion of a government's current assets (usually the receivables), is more or less stable, meaning that it does not change much throughout the year. The *seasonal need*, which consists of the temporary portion of a government's current assets, on the other hand, varies during the year (such as during holidays, or winter months, when demand is high for certain services). To a large measure, these variations determine the working capital policy of a government, where the government must decide how much net working capital it will have to maintain relative to its seasonal and permanent needs for the purposes of carrying out its routine operations.

We can graphically illustrate this relationship between current and fixed assets, as well as between permanent and seasonal fund requirements, as shown in Figure 13.1. As the figure shows, the need for fixed assets and permanent working capital will be constant (stable) for a government that

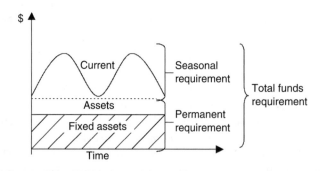

Figure 13.1 Funds requirements: total, seasonal, and permanent (General Fund Operations).

provides more or less the same level of services throughout the year. If the need fluctuates, say, increases rather than decreases, additional investment in current assets will be required to cover the additional increases. In general, these additional amounts are worked off during the downtrend in the fluctuating cycle until the total asset requirement returns to the permanent level.

We can further illustrate this relationship using the information we have for our hypothetical government in Table 13.2. According to the table, the monthly estimates of the government's current, fixed, and total asset requirements are given in columns 1, 2, and 3, respectively. The permanent component, which is the minimum level of funds the government will need for the year is given in column 4, while the seasonal component, which is the difference between the total funds (i.e., total assets) required and the permanent funds required for each month is given in column 5.

A cursory examination of the government's fixed assets (column 2) and permanent funds requirement (column 4) will reveal that permanent funds requirement exceeds the government's level of fixed assets. This is because a portion of the government's current assets is permanent, since they are always being replaced (rolled over). The permanent portion of the current assets for the government is $3,692,000, which represents the base level of current assets that will remain in the government's book

Table 13.2 Fund Requirements for Our Hypothetical Government (General Fund Operations)

Month	Current Assets[1]	Fixed Assets*[2]	Total Assets [3] = [1]+[2]	Permanent Funds Required[4]	Seasonal Funds Required [5] = [3]-[4]
January	$12,234,600	$21,789,500	$34,024,100	$25,481,500	$8,542,600
February	10,645,200	21,789,500	32,443,700	25,481,500	6,962,200
March	9,125,300	21,789,500	30,914,800	25,481,500	5,433,300
April	7,429,800	21,789,500	29,219,300	25,481,500	3,737,800
May	5,876,400	21,789,500	27,665,900	25,481,500	2,184,400
June	3,692,000	21,789,500	25,481,500	25,481,500	0
July	6,571,700	21,789,500	28,361,200	25,481,500	2,879,700
August	8,932,100	21,789,500	30,721,600	25,481,500	5,240,100
September	10,214,300	21,789,500	32,003,800	25,481,500	6,522,300
October	10,976,500	21,789,500	32,766,000	25,481,500	7,284,500
November	11,835,900	21,789,500	33,625,400	25,481,500	8,143,900
December	13,731,500	21,789,500	35,521,000	25,481,500	10,039,500
Average				**$25,481,500**	**$ 5,580,858**

*Assuming no depreciation.

for the entire year. We can also obtain this value by subtracting the level of fixed assets from the permanent funds requirement ($25,481,500 − $21,789,500 = $3,692,000).

13.4   Financing Working Capital Needs

In order to deal with its working capital needs, a government must know how much current liabilities it will require to finance its current assets. For most governments, the amount of current liabilities is restricted by the amount of resources they have committed in accounts payable, notes payable, accruals and, to some extent, in transfers to other funds and governments. Lenders such as banks and other financial institutions that provide short-term loans to governments, do so to allow them to finance temporary or seasonal buildups of receivables and inventory. They usually do not allow these funds to be used to finance long-term needs. What is needed, therefore, is a set of measures that a government can use to adequately finance these needs.

There are four basic measures, or policy choices, available to a government to determine an appropriate mix of short-term and long-term financing: (1) matching policy, (2) aggressive policy, (3) conservative policy, and (4) balanced policy. Understanding these policies are crucial, since they serve as the foundations of working capital management.

13.4.1   Matching Policy

One of the oldest policies in finance, which also applies to government, is based on a principle called the *matching principle*. According to this principle, an organization must finance its short-term needs with short-term sources (such as short-term borrowing) and long-term needs with long-term sources (such as long-term debt). It is called the "matching principle" because the objective is to "match" the maturity of the sources of funds to the length of time the funds are needed.

The underlying logic behind this is quite simple: the matching principle produces lower risk and lower financing cost for an organization in the long run. For instance, if a government finances its long-term needs with short-terms funds (such as short-term borrowing), chances are that it will have to refinance (re-borrow) its short-term debts as they become due. This will add to the total cost of financing from additional transaction costs (such as legal fees, lender fees, etc.) plus a likely cost increase from higher interest rates at which the government will have to re-borrow. On the other hand, if the government finances short-term needs with long-term funds (such as

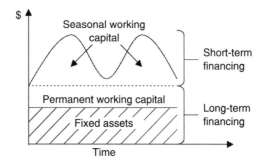

Figure 13.2 Financing working capital: matching policy (General Fund Operations).

long-term debt), it is likely to produce excess funds that it may have to invest in low-yielding securities. The matching principle corrects this problem by making sure that the maturity date of financing (i.e., borrowing) roughly matches the duration of the asset being financed. In other words, funds borrowed to finance an asset should be repayable at roughly the time of the asset's acquisition or construction, which will make the debt-asset combination *self-liquidating*, another term used for matching principle. Figure 13.2 illustrates the essence of this principle.

To give an example, suppose that a government plans to construct a project that would cost $5 million today, but would pay $6.5 million a year from now. Following the maturity matching principle, the government can take out a loan to the amount of $5 million for twelve months (assuming borrowing is the only option available to the government) and use the project's proceeds to pay off the loan. To borrow for a period longer than twelve months would leave unused funds which will continue to draw interest even after the completion of the project. On the other hand, borrowing for a period shorter than twelve months will result in additional borrowings, which will increase the costs of transaction and other costs, thereby adding further to the total cost of borrowing for the government. It makes sense, therefore, to match the duration of short-term projects with the maturity of the finances supporting them and long-term projects with long-term debt that lasts for a long time, usually 15 to 30 years, or more.

13.4.2 Aggressive Policy

Matching policy works as long as an organization finances its short-term needs with short-term resources and long-term needs with long-term sources, but there are circumstances when a management has to pursue a policy that is aggressive. Under an aggressive policy, an organization will

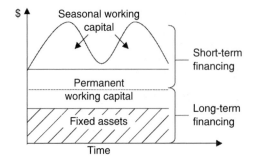

Figure 13.3 Financing working capital: aggressive policy (General Fund Operations).

finance its seasonal needs as well as some of its permanent needs with short-term funds. This is shown in Figure 13.3.

Using short-term funds to finance a government's short-term needs as well as some of its permanent needs is relatively inexpensive, but it is also risky. It is relatively inexpensive because the rates for short-term borrowings are usually lower than long-term rates; therefore, it will cost a government less to use short-term funds to finance its working capital needs. The risk comes from the fact that to finance the portion of permanent needs a government may have to re-borrow, which means that every time a new loan is used the government is likely to face a new set of financial conditions that may be more demanding than the conditions for the initial loans. For instance, the government may have to re-borrow at a higher rate than what it would have paid if it had financed the needs with long-term debt in the first place. In the short-term, however, it reduces costs to the government.

We can look at Table 13.2 to illustrate this. Under the aggressive policy, according to the table, the government will need to borrow an average of $5,580,858 to meet its seasonal needs for funds, and an average of $25,481,500 to meet its permanent needs. Let us say that the annual cost of short-term funds needed by our government is 3.5 percent, and the annual cost of long-term financing is 8.9 percent. The total cost of financing under the aggressive policy, therefore, will be $2,463,183.53; that is,

$$(0.035 \times \$5,580.858) + (0.89 \times \$25,481,500) = \$2,463,183.53)$$

The aggressive policy operates with minimum net working capital, since only the permanent portion of the current assets is financed with long-term funds. For our hypothetical government, the level of net working capital used for this purpose is $3,692,000, which is the amount of permanent current assets, obtained by subtracting the fixed assets for the month of June from the permanent funds requirement for the same month ($25,481,500 − $21,789,500 = $3,692,000). The policy is risky because the amount of net working capital is the lowest and also because the government may need to draw heavily on its short-term funds to meet its seasonal needs.

13.4.3   Conservative Policy

A conservative policy is the exact opposite of an aggressive policy. Under the conservative policy, a government uses long-term funds to finance its permanent needs, as well as a portion of its seasonal needs. This is shown in Figure 13.4. As can be seen from the figure, short-term funds support only the very tip of the seasonal working capital. When long-term funds are used to finance permanent, as well as some seasonal needs, it produces excess funds for governments that can be invested in short-term securities. This ensures that funds are available at all times to meet the working capital needs of a government. Since there is very little possibility of running out of funds, it will produce very little risk for the government; hence the term "conservative" policy.

Although less risky than an aggressive policy option, the conservative policy costs more, since it uses long-term funds which are more costly to start with. To provide an example, let us go back to Table 13.2. Let us say that the annual cost of long-term funds is 8.9 percent, as before. Since the average long-term financing balance under the conservative policy is $35,521,000, which is the month of December when the demand for services is at its peak, the total cost of financing under this policy will be $3,161,369.00 (0.089×$35,521,000). When compared with the figure for the aggressive policy, it clearly indicates that the conservative policy costs more by as much as $698,185.47.

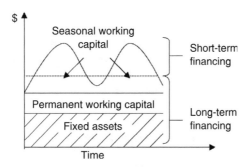

Figure 13.4   Financing working capital: conservative policy (General Fund Operations).

Unlike the aggressive policy, the conservative policy operates with maximum net working capital, since both the permanent and the temporary portion of an organization's current assets are financed with long-term funds. For our hypothetical government, the level of net working capital of $13,731,500 is the highest for the month of December (the peak period), which is obtained by subtracting the fixed assets for the month from the total assets (i.e., long-term financing) for the same period. The $13,731,500 of net working capital also indicates a low level of risk for the government.[8]

13.4.4 Balanced Policy

Both aggressive and conservative policies offer choices that are somewhat extreme. The aggressive policy, while relatively inexpensive, entails a lot of risk. The conservative policy, on the other hand, is safe, but costly. Since most practitioners are risk avoiders,[9] they would prefer a suitable compromise between the matching principle and the conservative policy. If one is willing to accept the conventional wisdom that short-term interest rates are lower than long-term rates and also the expectation that cost advantage of short-term borrowing will not be fully offset by interest income from short-term investment of excess funds into marketable securities, a balanced policy would be most appropriate.

Under the balanced policy, a government is expected to maintain sufficient net working capital and long-term funds to meet permanent as well as seasonal needs. The government should use short-term funds, but not all the credit available to it, to cover part of the peak seasonal needs. As the seasonal needs are reduced, it can pay off its short-term obligations (borrowings) and then invest the excess funds into short-term marketable securities during the period of low seasonal needs. The advantage of this policy is that it provides a safety factor to cover unexpected seasonal needs using short-term funds that have not been planned. If, for instance, the current-asset liquidation (i.e., disposing of current assets) turns out to be less than expected, the government will still be able to pay off its short-term obligations (loans), although less funds will be available for investments. On the other hand, if a credit problem emerges, the government will probably have to pay a higher than expected interest rate on short-term borrowings, but will not run the risk of not having short-term credit available.

13.5 A Digression on Yield Curve

Much of the logic behind the policies discussed above is based on the accepted notion that short-term interest rates are lower than long-term rates.

To a large measure it is true, since historically that has been the case. But what if that were to change, as happened in the early 1980s when the prime rate on bank loans was several percentage points above the interest rate on long-term Aaa bonds. One way to track fluctuations in interest rates and the consequent effect of these fluctuations on an organization's ability to use financing options to meet working capital needs is to use *yield curves.* A yield curve, also known as *term structure of interest rates,* shows the relationship between interest rates on debt securities relative to their maturity.

The yield curve frequently used in the economy is the interest rate-maturity relationship for federal government securities (Figure 13.5) These curves change daily to reflect the conditions in the money and capital market, expected inflation, and changes in general economic conditions. It is important that management understands the information these relationships produce for a government.

The yield curve for federal securities is based on three principal factors: liquidity premium, market segmentation, and expectation on future interest rates. Liquidity premium or *the liquidity premium theory,* as it is called, is based on the notion that long-term rates should be higher than short-term rates. The rationale for this is that since short-term securities have more liquidity than long-term securities, higher rates ought to be offered to potential buyers to entice them to invest in long-term securities.

Market segmentation, also known as *the segmentation theory,* is based on the fact that Treasury securities are often split into several markets by the financial institutions that invest in these securities. For instance, commercial banks prefer short-term securities of one year or less to match their short-term lending strategies. In contrast, savings and loan associations prefer intermediate-term securities of between 5 and 7 years, while pension

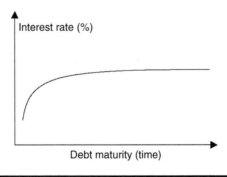

Figure 13.5   A simple interest rate-debt maturity yield curve.

funds and life insurance companies prefer longer-term securities with a life span of 20 to 30 years to match their long-term commitments to their clients. As the needs and strategies of these institutions change over time, they will more than likely have an impact on the nature and relationship of short-term and long-term interest rates.

The third factor, frequently referred to as *the expectations theory*, looks at long-term rates as a function of short-term rates. In its bare bones, the theory states that long-term rates reflect the average of short-term rates expected over the life span of the long-term securities. To give an example, let us say that the expected one-year rates on T-bills at the beginning of each of the next five years are 3, 4, 5, 6, and 7 percent, respectively. If we take the average of these rates for successive years, it will produce the rates for long-term. In other words, a two-year security rate will be the average of the expected rates of two one-year T-bills (i.e., a 2 year security (3% + 4%)/2 = 3.5%), a three-year security rate will be the average of the expected rates of three one-year T-bills (i.e., 3% + 4% + 5%)/3 = 4.0%) and so on, increasing progressively with time.

The expectation comes from the fact that, if long-term rates are higher than short-term rates, the market is said to expect short-term rates to increase. And if the long-term rates are lower than the short-term rates, the market expects the short-term rates to fall. From a policy point of view, the theory should help a government in setting expectations for the cost of financing over time and, in particular, in making decisions as to when to use short-term as opposed to long-term debt, and vice versa. In fact, all three theories have some impact on interest rates, although the level of their impact will not be the same.

To put it in another way, in designing working capital policy, a government should not only focus on the term-structure of interest rates (i.e., the yield curve), but also on the relative unpredictability (i.e., volatility) and the historical level of short-term and long-term rates. This unpredictability is what makes short-term financing strategy challenging. Furthermore, most financial management experts would acknowledge the unpredictability associated with forecasting beyond one-year period, thereby adding further to the problem. The question then is how should a government respond to fluctuations in interest rates and changing term structure? The answer is not complicated: when the interest rate is high and expected to decline, governments should borrow short-term. When rates decline, they should try to lock in the lower rates with long-term debt. With long-term funds available at lower rates, they should try to use some of these funds to reduce short-term debt and the rest for capital expansion and, if required, for working capital.

13.6 Summary and Conclusion

This chapter has provided some basic guidelines for managing working capital in government. Working capital management deals with financing and management of current assets and current liabilities. As with all business organizations, the relationship between current and fixed assets, as well as between permanent and seasonal fund requirements, should determine whether a government should use short-term or long-term financing. To the extent that part of the build-up in current assets is permanent, the government should use long-term financing. By the same token, if the build-up in current assets is seasonal, short-term financing should be used.

In making these trade-offs between short-term and long-term financing, governments face a number of cost-risk decisions. Long-term financing provides a safety margin in availability of funds, but has a higher cost. Short-term financing costs less, but does not assure the safety margin. Therefore, a compromise must be made between the two options. Not only that, each government must tailor its cost-risk tradeoffs to meet its own needs.

Notes

1. Besides holding cash for meeting transaction and precautionary needs, a government also holds cash for speculative (i.e., investment) purposes and to compensate banks for the services they provide. The four objectives are not necessarily additive. For instance, cash available for transactions could also be used for speculative and precautionary purposes, as well as for meeting compensating balance requirements.

2. Investing surplus cash in marketable securities is a specialized function that is usually performed by individuals in government with considerable knowledge about the behavior of the securities market. In the event no such in-house expertise is available, governments should seek professional expertise either through their own primary depository or through other external means.

3. Receivables policy of a government, whether it is for taxes or for accounts, depends on three things: the ability of the taxpayers or consumers to make payments on time, the terms and conditions under which the services are provided, and the collection policy of a government. All three conditions need careful evaluation from time to time to maximize collections with as low costs as possible to the government.

4. As might be expected, the need for inventory varies from government to government. For a government or a government

agency to which inventory is important, it is easier to operate with more inventory than with less. However, carrying additional inventories costs more and, consequently, there should be a trade-off between costs and benefits of maintaining inventories. The idea is to find a level that is optimal or close to optimal in balancing the pluses and minuses for maintaining a given level of inventory.

5. It is important to mention the term "float" when discussing accounts payable or accounts receivable (i.e., when collecting funds or disbursing funds). *Float* is the money tied up in the process of collecting funds or disbursing funds. The former is called *collection float*, and the latter *disbursement float*. In a collection float, the objective is to speed up the collection process, while in a disbursement float the objective is to slow down disbursements as much as possible. To fully avail the advantages of a disbursement float, a government needs to develop strategies to *increase* mail float, processing float, and availability float on the checks it writes. Beyond this, it should develop procedures for minimizing cash held for payment purposes.

6. Accruals occur because governments receive services on an on-going basis, while they pay at fixed intervals. We have discussed payroll accrual already, which is amongst the simplest to understand. However, accruals can be made for any number of services other than labor (i.e., personnel services). Although accruals for labor are generally short term and appear simple, they can be complicated because of market practices and various labor laws, under which all organizations, including government, operate.

7. Receivables can be very high or very low, both of which can signal inefficiency in management operations. Governments must work out an approach that serves their need the best.

8. The level of net working capital is constant throughout the year, since the government has $13,731,5000 in current assets that could be fully financed with long-term funds. Assuming the portion of the $13,731,500 in excess of the schedule level of current assets is to be held in marketable securities, the government's current asset balance will increase to this level.

9. Risk aversion means a low propensity to assume risks. A risk-avoiding manager who tries to avoid risk would require a higher dose of return in order to assume an added increment of risk.

Suggested Readings

Robert Berne and Richard Schramm. *The Financial Analysis of Governments*, Englewood-Cliffs, NJ: Prentice-Hall, 1986.

Charles K. Coe. *Public Financial Management.* Englewood Cliffs, NJ: Prentice Hall, 1989.

Stephen J. Gauthier. Governmental Accounting, Auditing, and Financial Reporting, Chicago, IL: GFOA, 2001.

Leo Herbert, Larry N. Killough, and Alan Walter Steiss. *Governmental Accounting and Control.* Monterey, CA: Brooks/Cole Publishing Company, 1984.

Robert W. Ingram, Russell J. Petersen, and Susan W. Martin, Accounting and Financial Reporting for Governmental and Nonprofit Organizations: Basic Concepts. Boston, MA: McGraw Hill, 1991.

R.S. Kravchuk and W.R. Voorhees. "The New Governmental Financial Reporting Model under GASB Statement No. 34: An Emphasis on Accountability," *Public Budgeting & Finance,* 21, 3(Fall), 2001: 1–30.

Edward S. Lynn and Joan W. Norvelle. *Introduction to Fund Accounting.* Englewood-Cliffs, NJ: Prentice Hall, 1984.

D.M. Mead. "The New Financial Statements: Recommending with the Basics of Public Financial Management," *Journal of Public Affairs Education,* 7, 2(April), 2001: 73–90.

Terry K. Patton and Robert J. Freeman. "Changes for Governmental Financial Reporting" in Aman Khan and W. Bartley Hildreth (eds), *Case Studies in Public Budgeting and Financial Management.* New York, NY: Marcel Dekker, 2003: 425–440.

Terry K. Patton and Aman Khan. "Financial Analysis in the City of Mesquite Falls, TX, using Comprehensive Annual Financial Reports" in Aman Khan and W. Bartley Hildreth (eds), *Case Studies in Public Budgeting and Financial Management.* New York, NY: Marcel Dekker, 2003: 441–468.

Joseph R. Razek, Gordon A. Hosch, and Martin H. Ives. *Introduction to Governmental and Not-for-profit Accounting.* Upper Saddle River, NJ: Prentice Hall, 2000.

Earl R. Wilson, Leon E. Haley, and Susan C. Kattelus, Accounting for Governmental and Nonprofit Entities. Boston, MA: Irwin-McGraw Hill, 2001.

Chapter 14

Fund Balance, Working Capital, and Net Assets

JUSTIN MARLOWE, Ph.D.
Department of Public Administration, University of Kansas

14.1 Introduction

Slack economic resources are an often-cited indicator of financial position. A government that holds assets in excess of its liabilities, the logic suggests, is less likely to increase taxes, change service provision schedules, defer pension obligations, default on debt, or engage in other undesirable behavior in the wake of periodic fiscal stress.[1]Professional associations such as the Government Finance Officers Association (GFOA) have endorsed this logic by recommending that governments and non-profit organizations maintain slack resources totaling some percentage of current annual expenditures, and bond raters, elected officials, state regulators, interest groups, citizens, and other stakeholders are known to monitor adherence to these recommendations (Larkin, 2000). We would therefore expect a certain degree of homogeneity in slack resource management policies and practices.

However, the limited empirical research on these issues suggests this is not the case. For example, average municipal unreserved general fund balance levels have been shown to range from 25–250% of current expenditures (Marlowe, 2004; Schrager, 2003; Tyer, 1993), far in excess of the GFOA's recommended 5–15% for the same indicator (GFOA, 2002). There is also a great deal of divergence in the financial management goals toward which slack resources are directed. Most of the extant literature assumes they are used primarily for fiscal stabilization, but current research has shown they also play a key role in cash flow maintenance, procurement, credit enhancement, and other financial management considerations.[2]

A separate but related body of research finds that decisions regarding the creation and use of slack resources have little to do with a desire to practice good financial management. Many municipal managers and finance directors tell of elected officials who commonly describe fund balance as "the amount we have to satisfy constituents this year." Others characterize slack resource decisions as a "mimetic" process (DiMaggio and Powell, 1991) where levels in one municipality are determined almost entirely by those levels in neighboring communities. Others draw parallels between slack resource debates and the deep ideological conflicts surrounding the scope, timing, and appropriateness of deficit spending (see Kettl, 1992; Buchanan, Rowley, and Tollison, 1989; Poterba and von Hagen; Imbeau, 2004).

These and other observations suggest fund balance, working capital, and net assets are complex and multifaceted phenomena that affect, and are affected by, a broad array of political, economic, and institutional factors. However, our empirical inquiry and practitioner-oriented commentary remains firmly rooted in the assumption that slack resources are merely an indicator of financial condition or a means to achieving other public financial management objectives. While that instrumental conception accurately characterizes some of what is currently happening in slack resources management, it neglects these other important contextual factors. This chapter attempts to bridge this gap in the extant literature by identifying, through a broad overview of current theory, empirical research, and regulatory activity, those areas where actual practice diverges most noticeably from our predominant theoretical assumptions and conventional wisdom surrounding fiscal slack. Identifying this divergence is the necessary first step toward rethinking current theory and recommended practices in this critical area of public financial management.

This discussion proceeds in four parts. It first clarifies the accounting and financial reporting language used to describe key slack resource constructs such as fund balance, net assets, and working capital. It then outlines how recent Governmental Accounting Standards Board (GASB) statements have brought about fundamental changes in slack resource accounting and financial reporting, and how those changes will in turn affect stakeholder perceptions of financial condition and the resulting demand for slack resources. The third section presents an overview of the empirical research into three fundamental financial management questions: (1) What financial management objectives should slack resources be directed towards, and do organizations maintain resources for those or other purposes?, (2) To what extent do slack resources stabilize expenditures during adverse fiscal conditions?, and (3) Given these and other findings, what is the optimal level of slack resources? These three research questions have important implications for slack resource management and oversight. The final section presents a series of research questions and recommendations for future consideration.

14.2   Clarifying Conflicting Concepts

Some delineation of key governmental accounting terms and concepts is necessary to place slack resources in their appropriate conceptual and technical context. This section outlines those key concepts and how the presence of a fund balance might be interpreted within the broader practice of governmental accounting and financial condition analysis.[3]

14.2.1   Fund Accounting and the Combined Balance Sheet

Funds are the conceptual and practical basis of governmental accounting. A fund is an entity within the government that is used to match financial resources to specific uses, goals, and objectives. Funds are also the basis for political and operational decisions about how to allocate current resources in order to meet short-term programmatic objectives. Most governments maintain a variety of "governmental" funds such as a general fund, debt service fund, capital projects fund, special revenue fund, and permanent fund, and each is used to monitor and catalogue a particular type of government activity. For most governments, particularly small municipalities, the general fund is the largest and most inclusive, and therefore the most closely scrutinized by elected officials and other stakeholders.

A "fund balance" is the difference between current assets and current liabilities within a governmental fund. It typically refers to the end of fiscal year balance, although many governments monitor it on a quarterly or even monthly basis. Fund balance also takes on a longitudinal character when retained from one period to the next. Much of the extant literature does not distinguish between "fund balance" and "general fund balance" due to the general fund's central importance. Both the current and the old governmental accounting models allow entities to report fund balance as either "reserved," "designated," or "unreserved" for a variety of general and specific purposes. Each of these fund balance portions is described later in this section.

The fund accounting model is designed to inform short-run financial management decisions. Although it has been widely accepted, this model is far from perfect and has been broadly criticized for its inability to provide users with two critical pieces of information. The first is information about the resources used to execute a government's business or proprietary operations. Most governments maintain utilities, golf courses, swimming pools, and other enterprises that are public in nature and therefore government-controlled. Under the old model, these business-like operations were presented separately from general government operations even though the two interact through debt sharing, interfund transfers, and other financial activity that has a material effect on overall financial condition. But a series of recent changes, most notably those outlined by the Governmental Accounting Standards Board (GASB) in its Statement 34 — *Basic Financial Statements — and Management's Discussion and Analysis — for State and Local Governments*, has taken major steps toward addressing those criticisms. The new reporting model outlined in these reforms provides users a better picture of overall financial condition by requiring governments to integrate their business and current operations into a "combined balance sheet" that illustrates how the interactions between basic services and auxiliary enterprises affect overall financial condition.

The old model was also criticized for not providing enough information about the value of "capital" or "immovable" assets such as roads, bridges, sewers, land, and other public infrastructure, and "intangible" capital assets such as water rights, easements, and right-of-ways. Despite their critical role in providing government services and the enormous costs associated with them, these assets were heretofore largely unrecognized on government financial reports because it is difficult to assess and report their value. The new governmental accounting model recognizes that difficulty, but nonetheless requires entities to determine and report the value of their capital assets in order to provide financial statement users with a more inclusive portrayal of overall financial condition.

These two fundamental changes, incorporating business-like activities and reporting the value of capital assets, impute new meaning to a government's "net assets," or the difference between its long term assets and liabilities. Net assets were reported under the old model but were used almost exclusively in the context of enterprise funds.[4] But under the new model, net assets speak to a government's "net worth" or true overall financial condition. GASB 34 advocates cite these changes as a necessary in the midst of the *Reinventing Government* (Osborne and Gaebler, 1992) paradigm of making government "more like business." This new governmental reporting model provides those who want government to run like a business with the information necessary to compare one to the other. GASB 34 critics wonder whether the costs of implementing these changes justify the benefits received by financial statement users (see, for example, Copley et. al., 1997).

14.2.2   Reserved Fund Balance

Assets considered "current" may actually be subject to a number of restrictions on their immediate use. Current accounting rules therefore allow governments to "reserve" particular portions of their fund balance in order to differentiate between the portion available for immediate appropriation and the portion subject to some sort of legal or technical restriction. A government can legally restrict assets for virtually any purpose. Some of the most common include (1) "Reserved for Debt Service," or resources that will be used to repay debt obligations, (2) "Reserved for Pre-Paid Items" or resources used to procure goods and services in advance of the current fiscal year," and (3) "Reserved for Capital Asset Resale" or revenues to be collected from an expected future capital asset sale.

The reserved portion of a local government's fund balance provides three types of information about current financial condition. First, because the resources included in it reduce the fund balance available for general purposes, reserved fund balance can be considered a reduction in the total fund balance available for immediate appropriation. Second, it illuminates whether a government has formalized certain aspects of its debt management. This formality has been noted as desirable by bond raters because it suggests debt repayment needs are a permanent part of the government's budgeting and planning process (Allen, 1990; Larkin, 2001). And third, many governments use reserved fund balance to report the amount held in a "rainy day fund," "budget stabilization fund," "contingency fund," or some similar mechanism to provide the financial resources needed to prevent service cuts and/or tax increases during periodic economic downturns. It is clear, therefore, that the labels attached to reserved fund balance are almost as important as the amount of resources those labels distinguish.

14.2.3   Designated Fund Balance

Like the reserved balance, certain fund balance portions can also be "designated" for future use. Designations are similar to reservations as both are a "portion of fund balance to indicate tentative plans for future financial resource use" (Gauthier, 2001, 587). Those tentative plans often include anticipated changes in the fiscal environment due to the replacement of equipment, increased wages due to new labor contracts, potential legal settlements or litigation costs, anticipation of new state or federal mandates, or a host of other purposes requiring new financial resources.

Unlike reservations, designations do not carry any legal or formal restriction, but instead represent a managerial commitment or "intent" on their future use. The organizational culture within many governments may imply "managerial intent" is synonymous with "legally binding." But because this is often not the case, the need for a distinction between formal, legal restrictions and intended restrictions is clear. Nonetheless, although they are not legally binding, fund balance designations communicate a great deal of information about the role fund balance will play in executing future plans.

14.2.4 Unreserved Fund Balance

The portion of fund balance not reserved or designated is considered unreserved. It represents financial resources that are available for appropriation during the next budget or fiscal period.

14.3 Fund Balance versus Working Capital[5]

The government fund focus on current assets implies fund balance is synonymous with working capital (Granof, 2001, 33–36). Like many other indicators, such as the current ratio, working capital is viewed as a measure of an organization's capacity to address unforeseen contingencies, and is therefore expressed as a percentage of current expenditures. A typical or target working capital ratio is 1:1, which suggests an organization holds enough liquid assets to cover its current liabilities (Finkler, 2000, 476–477).

Working capital management is a term generally used to describe the process of maximizing the productive use of fund balance resources. There are three unique perspectives on how best to accomplish that objective. The first suggests a sizable working capital reserve is necessary to take advantage of discounts and other short-term procurement opportunities, to prevent fees resulting from late payment of liabilities, and to protect against catastrophic losses resulting from natural disasters and other unforeseeable events. Proponents of this view also suggest working capital provides organizations with a pool of financial resources to meet debt service obligations during tough fiscal times. Credit analysts therefore look favorably upon large working capital reserves, and often award higher ratings to organizations that practice effective working capital management. This perspective suggests organizations ought to keep as much fund balance as possible and manage that balance according to a well-designed working capital strategy.

An opposing perspective suggests working capital is a drag on productivity. Rather than contributing to the production of public goods and services, it instead conceals stale inventory and accounts receivable that may not be realized, unnecessarily quick payment of outstanding liabilities, and other slack resources that detract from overall financial condition. Proponents of this view therefore argue that fund balance should be minimized whenever possible and placed in short-term investments until needed for some specific purpose.

Most public organizations cannot afford wholesale implementation of either strategy due to their uniquely public missions. For example, many entities must tolerate working capital inefficiencies because their missions demand they be prepared for worst-case scenarios such as natural disasters, terrorist attacks, and other situations that require a safety stock of resources. Many public organizations also face severe constraints on the number of available vendors and providers of certain goods and services, which in turn inhibits their ability to manage when and how goods and services will be delivered. These and other considerations suggest a third working capital strategy characterized by the maintenance of working capital for a wide variety of strategic purposes. That strategy was articulated by Shelton and Tyer (2000), who suggest public organizations ought to maintain four different types of working capital reserves:

1. *Transaction balances* — which allow organizations to realize economic gains by paying bills quickly and taking advantage of trade credits.
2. *Compensating balances* — which improve an organization's standing with financial institutions by increasing the amount of money these institutions have available for lending.
3. *Speculative balances* — which allow an organization to take advantage of near-term procurement and other opportunities.
4. *Precautionary balances* — which provide necessary protection against economic downturns and other fiscal shocks.

Public financial managers, according to Shelton and Tyer, are most concerned with speculative and precautionary balances. Speculative balances are often maintained as reserved and designated fund balance, and precautionary balances are often equated to unreserved undesignated fund balance. This application of working capital concepts suggests fund balance is more than simply the difference between current assets and liabilities. It is, according to the working capital management perspective, a pool of strategic resources that can be applied to a variety of financial management concerns.

14.3.1 Net Assets versus Fund Balance

Net assets, or the difference between total assets and total liabilities, are reported in three components. The first is "Invested in Capital Assets Net of Related Debt," or the difference between the value of a government's total assets and debt that was issued to acquire or construct those assets. It is comparable to the equity or residual value derived from capital asset activity. The second is "Restricted Assets," which describes assets other than capital assets that have been restricted for some purpose. Common examples include intergovernmental support for specific services such as public safety or homeland security, grant dollars for a targeted programmatic goal such as community policing or environmental education, and user fees earmarked for service upgrades or expansion of a government enterprise. Restricted net assets are a major portion of many governments' total net assets, and are therefore central to overall financial condition assessment. However, they can also distort the amount of discretionary resources a government appears to have because they are not necessarily available for discretionary spending. It is therefore important to recognize what portion of total net assets is restricted when using those figures as a financial condition indicator. The third category, unrestricted net assets, is the difference between total net assets and the other two net asset components. They have no restrictions on their use, and represent a government's total equity that can be used to meet current or future obligations.

Net assets and fund balance therefore provide financial managers and public organization stakeholders with two different but related pieces of financial information. Fund balance is a good indicator of current financial condition because it illuminates the current or liquid resources a government can bring to bear on immediate demands. Net assets provide a long-term view of the organization's overall economic condition, and are therefore useful in evaluating debt issuance practices, capital infrastructure condition and needs, program creation or expansion, and other decisions that impact the organization's long-term economic prospects. These two indicators ought to be used in tandem to determine a government's overall financial condition.

14.4   Current Issues in Fund Balance and Net Asset Reporting

The GASB has undertaken recent efforts to clarify certain ambiguities inherent to fund balance reporting. The following section outlines one recently adopted GASB statement, two issues currently being considered for GASB action, and how those changes will likely affect public financial management.

14.4.1   How Restricted are Restricted Net Assets?

Some of GASB 34's most notable implementation issues surround the identification and reporting of restricted net assets. Statement 34's language on this issue was designed to establish a consistent method of accounting for assets generated through "enabling legislation," "earmarking," or other legislative action that pairs a specific asset or revenue source with a particular programmatic goal. This is a critical consideration because an entity can overstate its available net assets by understating the restricted portion of those assets, or, by contrast, it can understate its available net assets by applying an aggressively inclusive definition of "restricted." The result in either case is a distorted portrayal of overall financial condition.

The GASB gave government officials the benefit of the doubt by assuming restricted net assets will only be used for their legally specified purposes. However, in light of the ever-present temptation to divert restricted resources to other goals and objectives, GASB 34 limits the definition of restricted net assets to those created by "legally enforceable" enabling legislation. In other words, a net asset is considered restricted only if citizens, the judiciary, another level of government, or some other external party can compel the government to restrict use of that asset to the purpose(s) stated in the enabling legislation.

Many entities, particularly state governments, had difficulty interpreting this language because of the ambiguity surrounding "legal enforceability." On the one hand, it can be argued that the power to enforce the tenets of any legislation, particularly net asset restrictions, rests solely in the hands of citizens. Since citizens in most states have access to the recall, referendum, and other instruments of "direct democracy," the logic suggests all net asset restrictions are truly legally enforceable. But when the discussion shifts from constitutional possibilities to the reality of American political participation, one can claim with equal fervor that only elected officials can enforce the tenets of any legislation. Many state governments were therefore forced to reconsider all their enabling legislation, and some considered reporting no net assets as restricted because of the difficulty in establishing a genuine "legally enforceable" claim. Others pondered whether to declare all earmarking and other enabling legislation unenforceable, and in turn consider non-capital assets to unrestricted. This all or nothing perspective created notable problems for government financial managers, financial statement preparers, and auditors.

The GASB addressed these problems in the recently adopted Statement No. 46 — *Net Assets Restricted by Enabling Legislation*. This statement (1) "confirms that the determination of legal enforceability is a matter of professional judgment, which may entail reviewing the legislation and determinations made for similar legislation, as well as obtaining the advice of legal counsel," and (2) requires governments to disclose in the notes to the financial statements the amount of net assets restricted by enabling legislation during a particular fiscal period. It therefore encourages states and municipalities to (1) determine legal enforceability on a case by case basis by considering the legal, organizational, and political implications of diverting restricted net assets away from their intended use, and (2) improve transparency in this area by disclosing the circumstances surrounding net asset restrictions. This statement is an important step toward ensuring the comparability of net asset figures and overall financial condition across multiple units of government.

14.4.2   Fund Balance Reservations and Designations

At a glance, the differences among the three fund balance portions are apparently clear — reservations are legally established restrictions, designations reflect tentative intentions of either elected or appointed officials, and the unreserved portion is available for immediate spending. But, in practice, these distinctions and their value in understanding financial condition are inherently ambiguous and problematic on three accounts. Each of these three issues may be considered for future GASB statements.

Many local governments outline the parameters of their reserve or contingency funds in intra-organizational working policies, governing board directives to city staff, the budget document preface, notes to the financial statements, or some mechanism other than a municipal ordinance. Although these sorts of "informal reserves" serve the same purpose and are utilized in essentially the same manner as formal reserves, they are not legally binding, per se, and are consequently reported as designated or unreserved fund balance.

The fact that some entities report reserve funds as reserved fund balance, while others report those same reserves in the designated or unreserved portions, raises a number of issues when attempting to evaluate a government's capacity to respond to contingencies. On the one hand, a strategic reserve governed by city ordinance is less likely to have its funds diverted to other purposes. The obvious disadvantage to this strategy is that fiscal crises are difficult to predict (Gold, 1995), and even more difficult to address when a formal reserve fund dictates a particular course of action. By limiting the array of fiscal policy responses, formal reserves may actually do more harm than good.[6] By contrast, the strategy of positing contingency funds in the unreserved designated fund balance allows for greater flexibility in using reserves to address unforeseen contingencies, but leaves open the possibility that funds will be diverted to other purposes. It then follows that further clarification is needed in determining the minimal requirements for establishing and maintaining a local reserve fund, how these funds should be accounted for, and how and where they should be reported.

A second issue is the apparent lack of oversight or understanding surrounding the appropriate use of designated fund balance. Anecdotal evidence suggests designated fund balance is rarely used for its stated purpose because designations are merely "intents" that are not legally binding and can be carried over from one year to the next with little fanfare or protest. Local governments can therefore enjoy the benefits of a large overall fund balance without the potential political pressures that may result from reporting those balances as unreserved. Further clarification is needed to determine how to evaluate whether designated fund balance is used for its stated purpose.

And third, strong empirical evidence suggests unreserved undesignated fund balance levels can be distorted at various points throughout the budget execution process. One notable source of distortion is interfund transfers, or the movement of resources from one fund to another. In some cases, these transfers take the form of interfund loans that will be repaid at some point in the future. In others, transfers are used for one-time interfund support that will not be repaid. Regardless of the normative implications of these sorts of transfers, empirical research has supported the claim that governments transfer excess revenues from electric utilities and other business-type entities to inflate or maintain current fund balance levels (Tyer, 1989). Similar research has found the single most influential factor affecting the size of a local government's unreserved undesignated fund balance is total interfund transfers (Marlowe, 2003). The claim that fund balance represents nothing more than the difference between current fund assets and current fund liabilities may therefore be shortsighted. Further clarification is needed to determine and report this relationship between interfund transfers and fund balance levels.

14.5 Normative Questions and Empirical Answers

This section examines three normative questions that have dominated the slack resource management literature and how those questions have been addressed through empirical research. The first is precisely how local governments manage their slack resources, and whether those actual practices comport with recommended practice. The second is whether slack resources are an effective tool for sub-national fiscal stabilization. The third section takes the first two into account by addressing the question of what comprises an "optimal" fund balance.

14.5.1 Fund Balance Policies and Practices

Under the new reporting model, information about a government's financial condition is intrinsically more useful if that government has clearly stated financial management policies. For example, longitudinal trends in fund balance and net assets are good indicators of financial condition so long as a government has a policy that dictates the conditions under which slack resources will be saved and used. In the absence of such a policy, it is difficult to determine whether trends in fund balance are attributable to managerial discretion, deliberate political action, simple organizational inertia, or something else. The GFOA has actively encouraged governments to promulgate formal reserve fund policies, and a recent analysis indicates that all but 3 states have carried forth on this recommendation by adopting legislation governing their countercyclical reserve or "budget stabilization" funds (Hou, 2003). State-level slack resource management, therefore, clearly comports with these recommended practices.

But the same cannot necessarily be said for municipalities. In a nearly two decades old study, Wolkoff (1987) found most of the 27 largest U.S. cities maintained some sort of countercyclical reserve fund, but less than half had adopted an ordinance or other formal legislative action to govern the use of that fund. The remainder of this section presents findings from a comprehensive analysis (and perhaps the first of its type) of slack resource management practices in small municipalities (Marlowe, 2004) designed to augment the original Wolkoff study. This new analysis was based on data collected from the survey responses of 245 municipalities in Minnesota and Michigan with populations 1000–50,000, and its findings highlight three key areas where municipal fund balance behavior deviates noticeably from both the states and the financial management community's conventional wisdom.[7]

First, less than half the responding municipalities have adopted a general fund balance policy, and less than one quarter maintain a policy regarding the use of unrestricted assets and retained earnings in enterprise/proprietary funds. Moreover, only 42% of cities that have a policy have formalized that policy through an ordinance or other legally binding agreement between the governing board and municipal staff. Instead, fund balance policies are most often characterized as informal, intra-organizational directives from management. While this lack of formalization is not necessary problematic, it calls into question the legal enforceability and political transparency of local fund balance management practices.

A second key finding surrounds the characteristics of the adopted fund balance policies. Figure 14.1 presents a detailed flow chart and relative proportions of fund balance policies that exhibit particular characteristics. The top of the chart shows that 49% of the total respondents, or 115 municipalities, have adopted some sort of fund balance policy. It then flows to the numbers of each type of policy adoption method, then to the measurement basis for the actual fund balance policy, then to the average targeted fund balance amount for each measurement basis. Three main trends in these data are worth noting. First, most policies (42% for the formal agreements between council and staff and 60% of informal, intra-organizational policies) do not specify a particular amount or measurement basis for the expected fund balance level. They instead speak in vague terms such as "fund balance will be kept at a level deemed appropriate by the board and city staff," or "the city administrator will maintain fund balance sufficient to cover fiscal contingencies." An additional 8% of policies (5% of the informal, intra-organizational policies and 3% of the formal agreements between council and staff) specify a target balance but do not specify a basis for that balance. In either case, these policies provide a clear endorsement of management's discretion, but are of limited use to financial statement users.

These data also suggest targeted fund balance levels are for the most part uniformly distributed across the budgeted vs. actual and expenditure vs. revenues bases. There is clearly no single preferred base for fund balance planning, despite the fact that the GFOA recommended practices suggest actual current expenditures. And finally, these findings indicate that every policy, regardless of its basis, includes a targeted balance between 31% and 39%. Therefore, expected balance levels tend to be (1) roughly the same, regardless of their basis, and (2) much higher than the 5–15% range typically cited in the professional literature. Taken as a whole, these trends suggest municipalities have adopted a wide variety of fund balance policies, and that the simple 5–15% rule of thumb does not characterize much of what his happening in actual practice.

And third, these survey results suggest fund balance is used for many purposes beyond fiscal stabilization. The previously mentioned survey included a series of questions asking the CAO of the responding

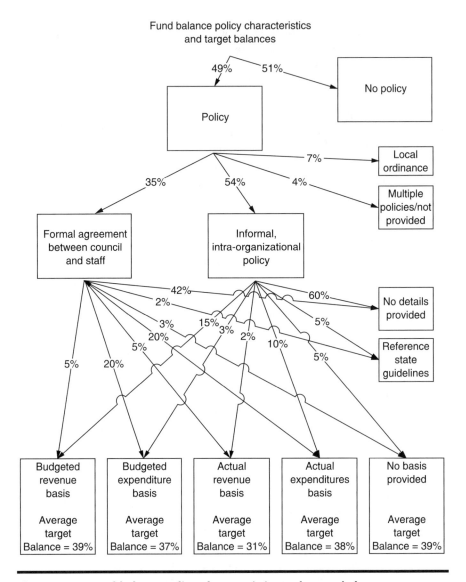

Figure 14.1 Fund balance policy characteristics and target balances.

municipality to rate the importance of 12 different motivations for maintaining fund balance resources. Those reasons were rated along a three point scale where 1 = "not important," 2 = "somewhat important," and 3 = "most important," and the tabulated results are presented in Table 14.1. The highest mean score is for "protection from economic downturns, natural disasters, and other fiscal shocks," which implies fund balance is principally a fiscal stabilization tool. But other reasons, mainly the desire to maintain

Table 14.1   Responses to "Why do you maintain fund balance resources?"

Reason	Mean
Protection from economic downturns, natural disasters, and other fiscal shocks	2.84
Helps maintain consistent cash flow	2.42
Helps maintain consistent tax rates	2.04
Serves as a 'savings' or 'Pay-As-You-Go' account for capital projects	1.80
Improves bond ratings	2.12
Lowers procurement costs	1.48
Good indicator of government's 'bottom line'	1.90
To comply with a state mandate/regulation/law	1.45
Because citizens demand it	1.24
Because neighboring communities do it	1.03
Because the local business community demands it	1.10
Creates flexibility during the budget process	2.20
Facilitates strategic management	2.26

N = 199
Note: Items are scored according to the following scale: 1 = not important, 2 = somewhat important, 3 = most important.

consistent cash flow, the desire to create flexibility during the budget process, and the need to keep fund balance as a tool for strategic management, also received comparatively high scores.

The fact that fund balance is an important cash flow management tool is not surprising, considering many municipalities receive most of their revenues in two main cash infusions — property tax collections and state aid disbursements. Since these infusions happen only once per year (for example, property tax collections in January and state aid disbursements in July) they must keep a pool of resources to meet current obligations during the time between these disbursements. The high mean scores for "creates flexibility in the budget process" and "facilitates strategic management" also support the claim that fund balance is often used for strategic purposes beyond fiscal stabilization.

This section has described, albeit briefly, the state of the practice in municipal fund balance policies. This brief overview highlights a tremendous diversity in the methods, objectives, and operating procedures that municipalities have brought to bear on their fund balance management practices. From a normative perspective, this lack of homogeneity is reassuring as it indicates local governments have crafted a broad array of policy tools to fit their diverse fiscal and management needs. That diversity does, however, complicate the process of evaluating municipal financial condition and the role that slack resources play in maintaining that condition.

14.5.2 Do They Make a Difference? Slack Resources and Fiscal Stabilization

Since Musgrave's (1959) classic treatise, if not before, the federal government has been the exclusive purveyor of fiscal stabilization throughout the American federalist system. But recent macroeconomic changes such as increasingly liquid capital, foreign direct investment, and electronic commerce have rendered local and regional economies increasingly sensitive to global economic conditions (Tannenwald, 1999). These dramatic shifts in the sub-national fiscal context have motivated the first serious inquiry into structure and effects of state and local fiscal stabilization practices (see, for example, Wolkoff, 1999; Mattoon, 2004).

As previously mentioned, nearly all state governments and some local governments maintain "reserve," "contingency," "budget stabilization" or "rainy day" funds designed to mitigate fiscal stress that accompanies economic downturns, fiscal policy shifts, natural disasters, and other exogenous shocks. A number of scholars have examined whether these sorts of funds are in fact able to ensure fiscal stability. Pollock and Suyderhoud (1986) conducted the first systematic inquiry into this question by comparing simulated and actual longitudinal state-level economic behavior. Their findings generally support the claim that reserve funds are an effective stabilization tool, and they interpret those findings in light of the political circumstances that often surround state fiscal policy decisions by stating "If legislators and executives lack the political will to voluntarily support full fiscal stability, an explicit Rainy Day Fund that effectively forces stabilizing behavior may be the only mechanism that can contribute to fiscal stability" (493). Subsequent work by Knight and Levinson (1999) reached essentially the same conclusions, and Hou (2003) found a 1% increase in the size of a state's previous year budget stabilization fund (measured as a percentage of current expenditures) results in a 0.25% decrease in the "expenditure gap," or the difference between projected and actual expenditures (83–84). This collected body of work indicates strong prospects of sub-national fiscal stabilization.

Further studies of stabilization funds have attached two important caveats to these findings. First, many states have formal stabilization funds but do not adequately fund them. Sobel and Holcombe (1996) presented the first analysis of this issue, showing that simply having a rainy day fund does not create any sort of stabilization effect. Their findings do, however, support the claim that formal reserves have a stabilization effect if the fund contains a statutory requirement that resources be added to it during flush economic times. Even today, however, many state BSFs do not carry such a requirement. Douglas and Gaddie (2002) advance and refine this argument by showing how "withdrawal" and "deposit" requirements have their own stabilization effect regardless of the resources contained in the BSF. Their findings suggest BSF action requirements create a "fiscal institution" that forces policymakers to make strategic fiscal decisions.

Another stream of the literature has found that a state's reserve fund characteristics are often unrelated to its level and sources of potential fiscal instability. Joyce (2002) first demonstrated this disconnect by showing state rainy day funds were largely uncorrelated with revenue volatility and other indicators of potential fiscal stress. Wagner (2003) reached a similar finding by showing that increases in formal reserve funds are often accompanied by decreases in unreserved fund balance, a practice which in effect creates "illusory savings." This apparent disconnect between the use of fiscal reserves as a fiscal stabilization tool and past indicators of fiscal stability calls into question the motives that drive actual slack resources management.[8]

Even less is known about fund balance levels and stabilization effects at the local level. One stream of the literature argues convincingly that municipalities should maintain large fund balances governed by formal reserve fund policies (Hembree and Shelton, 1999; Gauthier, 2002). Tyer (1993) further outlines these motivations and provides a series of practitioner-oriented recommendations for how to create and maintain fund balance reserves, even in the midst of political turmoil. But a second group of papers, all grounded in descriptive empirical analysis, suggest actual fund balance behavior deviates considerably from these recommended practices. Hembree and Shelton (1999) found average general fund balances among a sample of small North Carolina and South Carolina municipalities ranged from 25–218% of current general fund expenditures.[9] A similar study commissioned by the Michigan Department of Treasury found that unreserved fund balances among all Michigan municipalities averaged 25% of annual expenditures, and 587 of those governments maintain balances exceeding 100% of total general fund spending (Michigan Department of Treasury 2002). Marlowe's (2003) study of a similar group of Minnesota cities reached essentially the same conclusion. These three analyses suggest the 5–15% indicator has limited applicability in the small government context.

14.5.3 What is the Optimal Fund Balance Level?

Government officials are most concerned with maintaining a pool of slack resources that is large enough to promote fiscal stability without raising opportunity costs and political friction. This delicate balance between the adequacy of reserves and the forces constraining those reserves is perhaps the most important question surrounding fiscal reserves and public financial management. This question of the "optimal" fund balance level has been approached by a number of scholars throughout the past several years.

The extant literature has focused on two main determinants of the optimal fiscal reserve level. The first is revenue structure and macroeconomic conditions. That is, governments relying heavily on personal and corporate income tax, tourism, federal grants, and other elastic revenue sources may experience exacerbated fiscal stress during economic downturns. Entities with non-diversified revenue portfolios also require larger than average reserves because a decline in an important revenue source may have the same detrimental effect. Navin and Navin's (1997) analysis of Ohio's revenue portfolio concluded that a fund balance of 13% was necessary to counteract typical revenue fluctuations. Sjoquist (1998) used a similar methodology to show Georgia would need reserves totaling 27% of own source revenues to mitigate the effects of an an extreme revenue shortfall. Kriz (2002) used the same essential methodology to reach a similar conclusion about the link between local revenue volatility and optimal fund balance at the local level. His analysis, which relies on the value-at-risk methodology common in the finance literature, suggests medium to large cities in Minnesota ought to maintain fund balances of approximately 30% to hedge against typical revenue fluctuations.

Research on national trends in state BSFs has produced similar findings. Lav and Berube's (1999) commentary was perhaps the first to predict the recession of 2001–2003. Their analysis was based on historical trends in revenue fluctuations, and they concluded that most state stabilization funds were not adequate to weather a recession similar to that experienced in the early 1990s. Their analysis suggests an average state ought to maintain a balance of 18.6% of current expenditures, and those states with such a balance at the beginning of the 2001–2002 recession were clearly better prepared than those without. In the aggregate, this literature further supports the claim that, regardless of how revenue volatility is measured, most states do not maintain BSFs large enough to provide fiscal stability during cyclical revenue fluctuations.

However, two recent papers suggest a counterpoint to this claim about underfunding. Cornia and Nelson (2003) provide a different perspective on this relationship between revenue volatility and suggested BSF levels by examining fluctuations in simulated rather than actual revenue trends and economic conditions. Again using a VAR methodology, they establish a predicted range of possible revenue shortfalls based on past variability in key revenue sources, economic conditions, and annual expenditures. Their simulated results for the state of Utah imply there is less than a 5% chance revenue collections would decline by more than $135.75 million in a given year. This $135.75 million figure represents less than 5% of current general fund expenditures, which reinforces the adequacy of the "5% rule."

Gonzalez and Levinson (2003) examined historical trends in all state revenue collections and, similar to Cornia and Nelson, found state rainy day funds more than adequate to weather the fiscal crisis of 2002–2003 had those funds not been diverted to purposes other than countercyclical fiscal relief.

Others have approached the optimal fund balance question from a revenue estimation perspective. States depending heavily on sales taxes, tourism, and other sources that are inherently difficult to estimate, the logic suggests, ought to have higher than average fiscal reserves to buffer against revenue shortfalls resulting from revenue misestimation. Vasche and Williams (1987) examined this issue in California and concluded that a fund balance of 3–10% of current revenues could effectively mitigate the effects of misestimation. However, no study has heretofore incorporated both revenue volatility and estimation difficulty into a single analysis of the optimal fund balance.

The body of literature on these three normative questions suggests actual slack resource management deviates from recommended practice in noticeable and important ways. A typical government keeps reserves far in excess of the current recommended practices. Many governments keep slack resources for purposes other than fiscal stabilization. The most commonly cited fund balance objective among municipal governments was cash flow, which has thus far been considered only a residual purpose surrounding fund balance management. These and other findings suggest slack resources are conceived of very differently and have tremendously differential effects depending on the institutional, political, and organizational context in which they are applied.

14.6 Suggestions for Future Practice and Research

This chapter has attempted to delineate the often-contradictory perspectives and empirical findings on fund balance concepts, policies, and practices, and to show what those divergent perspectives mean for public financial management. In doing so, it has highlighted a series of future research questions that, if explored, could inform key issues of concern to public financial management practitioners and scholars.

14.6.1 Slack Resource Policies and their Determinants

First, what factors account for variations in the patterns of adoption, as well as the content, of local fund balance policies? The discussion in this chapter suggests each of the three fund balance components is designed to convey particular information about different aspects of local government financial position and, perhaps more importantly, about the resources a local government has dedicated to various financial management objectives. Local governments often outline these strategies and desired objectives in policy statements that are said to receive notable attention from policymakers, bond raters, and other local government stakeholders. In spite of their importance, the limited research on these statements has largely ignored their subtle but complex differences and how political, economic, and organizational factors contribute to those differences.

14.6.2 Slack Resource Levels and Management

A second and equally important question is what level of resources do local governments maintain in each of the three fund balance components and, perhaps more importantly, what explains variation in those levels? Again, the existing studies on this issue have used oversimplified measures of fund balance behavior. Utilizing total fund balance, for example, does not account for the fact that each of the three fund balance components provides unique information about different aspects of financial position and divergent financial management objectives. By contrast, only examining one component, such as the undesignated balance targeted in the GFOA standards discounts the possibility local governments use fund balance, working capital, and net assets to convey different types of information to different stakeholders. This is not unlike the "signaling and monitoring" so widely described in the governmental accounting literature (Zimmerman, 1977; Evans and Patton, 1983). This chapter also suggests that, in order to understand slack resource behavior, we must understand how it changes over time. Do total fund balance levels shift dramatically from one period to the next? Does one net asset portion remain stationary while others experience noticeable changes? Do different working capital components experience drastic cross-sectional shifts (Copley and Seay, 1999)? Can we arrive at optimization models for working capital management similar to those proposed for cash management, investment, and other financial management processes (Khan, 2000)? The sheer complexity of slack resources and the reasons for their maintenance begs a far more sophisticated approach to understanding how they are, and how they should, be managed.

14.6.3 State–Local Fiscal Relations

These findings could be particularly useful to state governments, given that of the 15 states known to formally monitor local government financial condition, 14 use some derivative of fund balance as an indicator of financial position (Kloha, Weissert, and Kleine, 2005).

From the perspective of state government officials, the finding that local governments maintain large fund balances for strategic management and cash flow also suggests a complex dilemma. On the one hand, the need for such balances could be alleviated by modifying the state aid disbursement process so aids to localities are distributed in bi-annual, quarterly, or even monthly installments instead of the current single annual payment method used in many states. While this may increase overall intergovernmental efficiency, the costs of doing so are very notable, both in terms of resources and the potential for administrative error. Moreover, such a strategy may bring about a different problem, given that more frequent, yet smaller disbursements may hamper local governments' ability to meet demands for large sums of cash at any given time. This same can also be said for any attempt to modify the local property tax collection process in favor of smaller, more frequent collections. Nonetheless, this chapter reveals that local governments maintain a staggering amount of fund balance resources for the purpose of smoothing out cash flow. At the very least, these findings beg a reconsideration of potential changes to alleviate those cash flow problems.

Notes

1. This discussion focuses almost exclusively on local governments, but many of the concepts are applicable to state governments, health care organizations, non-profit institutions, and other public entities.

2. These assumptions are the subject of some debate within the public financial management community. The current government accounting model was developed by the National Committee on Municipal Accounting (NCMA), an organization that was under the auspices of New York Bureau of Municipal Research (NYBMR) for most of the early 20[th]Century. Historians clearly identify the NYBMR as a driving force behind the widespread diffusion of scientific management in early public administration, so, not surprisingly, the NCMA's accounting model and public financial management as a whole emphasizes parsimony, efficiency, separation of organizational functions, and other values central to the rational comprehensive organization theory espoused by the scientific management school (Golembiewski, 1964). Theorists sensitive to the interpretive, normative, critical, and post-modernist perspectives (Miller, 1992; Orosz, 2001; Gianakis and McCue, 2002) have criticized this approach by arguing that the ambiguity, goal conflict, and uncertainty inherent to local government operations limits

financial managers' ability to arrive at truly comprehensive solutions to organization problems. Instead, their argument suggests, financial managers ought to derive their professional norms and management objectives from an interpretive construction of the conflicting values that act upon their particular environments. Although the traditional, rational perspective continues to serve as the basis for much of the scholarship and practitioner-oriented commentary on fund balance issues, it is nonetheless necessary to recognize this important alternate perspective.

3. Portions of this section are modified from Gauthier (2001, 586–587).

4. Net assets could be determined for enterprise/proprietary funds prior to these changes because these funds use full accrual accounting rather than the modified accrual method used in the governmental funds. Full accrual accounting captures the full, long-term economic implications of assets and liabilities, so the difference between assets and liabilities reported according to a full accrual model can therefore be considered net assets rather than fund balance.

5. Portions of this section were adapted from Marlowe (2005).

6. It should be noted, however, that many states also restrict the size of their stabilization funds to 5% of current expenditures.

7. The sample does not include counties.

8. Wolkoff's (1987) study of municipal rainy day funds reached a similar conclusion.

9. Hembree and Shelton (1999) define fund balance as the total of the reserved, designated, and unreserved portions.

References

Allen, Ian (1990). "Unreserved Fund Balance and Local Government Finance." *Government Finance Officers Association Research Bulletin* (September).

Buchanan, James M., Charles K. Rowley, and Robert D. Tollison (1987). *Deficits* (New York: Basil Blackwell).

Copley, Paul A. and Seay, Sharon S. (1999). "An Analysis of Cross-Sectional Variation in the Financial Ratio Adjustment by City Governments." *Research in Government and Nonprofit Accounting* 10: 111–134.

Copley, Paul A., Rita Hartung Cheng, Jean E. Harris, Rohda C. Icerman, Walter L. Johnson, G. Robert Smith, Kenneth A. Smith, W.T. Wrege, and Robert Yahr (1997). "The New Governmental Reporting Model: Is it a 'Field of Dreams?" *Accounting Horizons* 11(3): 91–101.

Cornia, Gary C. and Nelson, Ray D. (2003). "Rainy Day Funds and Value at Risk." *State Tax Notes* (August 25): 563–567.

DiMaggio, Paul and Powell, William (1991). *The New Institutionalism in Organizational Analysis* (Chicago: University of Chicago Press).

Douglas, James W. and Gaddie, Ronald Keith (2002). "State Rainy Day Funds and Fiscal Crises: Rainy Day Funds and the 1990–1991 Recession Revisited." *Public Budgeting & Finance* 22(1): 19–30.

Evans, John H. III and Patton, James M. (1983). "An Economic Analysis of Participation in the Municipal Finance Officers Association Certificate of Conformance Program." *Journal of Accounting and Economics* 5: 151–175.

Finkler, Steven A. (2000). *Financial Management for Public, Health, and Not-for-Profit Organizations* (New York: Prentice Hall).

Gauthier, Stephen J. (2001). *Governmental Accounting, Auditing, and Financial Reporting* (Chicago: Government Finance Officers Association).

———. (2002). *An Elected Officials Guide to Fund Balance and Net Assets Using the GASB 34 \Model* (Chicago: Government Finance Officers Association).

Gianakis, Gerasimos A. and McCue, Clifford P. (2002). "Budget Theory for Public Administration … and Public Administrators." In Aman Khan and W. Bartley Hildreth, eds. *Budget Theory in the Public Sector* (Westport, CT: Quorum Books).

Gold, Steven D. (1995). *The Fiscal Crisis of the States: Lessons for the Future* (Washington, DC: Georgetown University Press).

Golembiewski, Robert T. (1964). "Accountancy as a Function of Organization Theory." *The Accounting Review* 29(2): 333–341.

Gonzales, Christian and Levinson, Arik (2003). "State Rainy Day Funds and the State Budget Crisis of 2002–?" *State Tax Notes* (August 11): 441–452.

Government Finance Officers Association (2002). *Appropriate Level of Unreserved Fund Balance in the General Fund* (Chicago: GFOA).

Granof, Michael H. (2001). *Government and Non-Profit Accounting: Concepts and Practices* (New York: John Wiley & Sons.

Hembree, Holly and Shelton, Michael (1999). "Benchmarking and Local Government Reserve Funds: Theory Versus Practice." *Public Management* 81(9): 16–22.

Hou, Yilin (2003). "What Stabilizes State General Fund Expenditures in Downturn Years – Budget Stabilization Fund or General Fund Unreserved Undesignated Balance?" *Public Budgeting & Finance* 23(3): 64–91.

Joyce, Phillip G. (2001). "What's So Magical about Five Percent?" *Public Budgeting & Finance* 21(2): 62–87.

Imbeau, Louis (2004). *Politics, Institutions and Fiscal Policy: Deficits and Surpluses in Federated States* (New York: Lexington Books).

Kettl, Donald F. (1992). *Deficit Politics: Public Budgeting in its Institutional and Historical Context* (New York: MacMillan).

Khan, Aman (2000). *Costs and Optimization in Government* (Westport, CT: Quorum Books).

Kloha, Philip, Carol S. Weissert, and Robert Kleine (2005). "Someone to Watch Over Me: State Practices in Monitoring Local Fiscal Conditions." *American Review of Public Administration* 35(3): 236–255.

Knight, Brian and Levinson, Arik (1999)."Rainy Day Funds and State Government Savings." *National Tax Journal* 52(3): 459–472.

Kriz, Kenneth A. (2002). "The Optimal Level of Local Government Fund Balances: A Simulation Approach." *State Tax Notes* (March 10): 887–892.

Larkin, Richard P. (2001). "Impact of Management Practices on Municipal Credit." *Government Finance Review* 17(1): 23–27.

Lav, Iris J. and Berube, Alan (1999). "When it Rains it Pours: A Look at the Adequacy of State Rainy Day Funds and Budget Reserves." *State Tax Notes* (May 17): 1639–1651.

Marlowe, Justin (2003). "The Information Content of the Local Fund Balance: Comparing the Influence of Economics, Organization, and Management." Paper presented at the 2003 Association for Budgeting and Financial Management annual meeting, Washington, DC.

——. (2004). *The Local Fund Balance: Expectations and Implications*, Unpublished Doctoral Dissertation, University of Wisconsin-Milwaukee.

——. (2005). "Working Capital Management." In the *Encyclopedia of Public Administration and Policy*, Jack Rabin, ed. (New York: Marcel Dekker).

Mattoon, Richard (2004). "Creating a National State Rainy Day Fund: A Modest Proposal to Improve Future State Fiscal Performance." *State Tax Notes* (January 26): 271–288.

Michigan Department of Treasury, Office of Revenue and Tax Analysis (2002). "Local Government Fund Balances and Expenditures."

Miller, Gerald J. (1992). *Government Financial Management Theory* (New York: Marcel Dekker).

Musgrave, Richard A. (1959). *The Theory of Public Finance: A Study in Political Economy* (New York: McGraw Hill).

Navin, John C. and Navin, Leo J. (1997). "The Optimal Size of Countercyclical Budget Stabilization Funds: A Case Study of Ohio." *Public Budgeting & Finance* 17(2): 114–127.

Orsoz, Janet Foley (2001). "The Truth is Out There: Is Postmodern Budgeting the Real Deal?" In John Bartle, ed. *Evolving Theories of Public Budgeting* (Oxford: Elsevier Science, Ltd.)

Osborne, David and Gaebler, Ted (1992). *Reinventing Government: How the Entrepreneurial Spirit is Transforming the Public Sector* (New York: Penguin).

Pollock, Richard and Suyderhoud, Jack P. (1986). "The Role of State Rainy Day Funds in Achieving Fiscal Stability." *National Tax Journal* 49(4): 485–497.

Poterba, James M. (1994). "State Responses to Fiscal Crises: The Effects of Budgetary Institutions and Politics." *Journal of Political Economy* 102(4): 799–821.

Schrager, Scott D. (2002). *Cities and Villages at the Crossroads: Fiscal Problems Facing Local Officials* (Ann Arbor: Michigan Municipal League).

Shelton, Michael and Tyer, Charlie (with the assistance of Holly Hembree) (2000). "Local Government Reserve Funds and Fund Balance: Some Applications of Business Concepts." *Municipal Finance Journal* 21(1): 1–18.

Sjoquist, David L. (1998). "Georgia's Revenue Shortfall Reserve: An Analysis of Its Role, Size, and Structure." Fiscal Research Program, Andrew Young School of Policy Studies, Georgia St. University.

Sobel, Russell S. and Holcombe, Randall G. (1996). "The Impact of State Rainy Day Funds in Easing State Fiscal Crises During the 1990–1991 Recession." *Public Budgeting & Finance* 16(3): 28–49.

Sobel, Russell S. and Wagner, Gary A. (2003). "Cyclical Variability in State Government Revenue: Can Tax Reform Reduce It?" *State Tax Notes* (August 25): 569–576.

Tannenwald, Robert (2001). "Are State and Local Revenue Systems Becoming Obsolete?" *New England Economic Review* 4: 28–42.

Tyer, Charlie B. (1989). "Municipal Enterprises and Taxing and Spending Policies: Public Avoidance and Fiscal Illusions." *Public Administration Review* 49(3): 249–256.

———. (1993). "Local Government Reserve Funds: Policy Alternatives and Political Strategies." *Public Budgeting & Finance* 13(2): 75–84.

Vasche, John David and Williams, Brad (1997). "Optimal Governmental Budgeting Contingency Reserve Funds." *Public Budgeting & Finance* 7(1): 66–82.

Wagner, Gary A. (2003). "Are State Budget Stabilization Funds only the Illusion of Savings? Evidence from Stationary Panel Data." *Quarterly Review of Economics and Finance* 43(2): 213–238.

Wolkoff, Michael (1987). "An Evaluation of Municipal Rainy Day Funds." *Public Budgeting & Finance* 7(2): 52–63.

———. (1999). "State and Local Budgeting: Coping with the Business Cycle." In Roy T. Meyers, ed. *Handbook of Government Budgeting* (San Francisco: Jossey Bass).

Zimmerman, Jerrold (1977). "The Municipal Accounting Maze: An Analysis of Political Incentives." *Journal of Accounting Research* 15 (Special Issue): 107–144.

Chapter 15

A Manageable System of Economic Condition Analysis for Governments

DEAN MICHAEL MEAD
Governmental Accounting Standards Board

15.1   Introduction

Over a decade ago, sensing that existing paradigms for assessing financial condition were too complex for most governments to use, a professor from Southwest Missouri State University introduced a relatively simple analytical tool that has become widely popular among finance officers and financial analysts alike. Dr. Ken W. Brown's (1993) "10-point test" employed ten ratios indicative of factors relevant to financial condition. Using the 10-point test, a government would calculate the ratios and would gain or lose points depending on how favorably or unfavorably the ratios compared with the ratios of governments with similarly-sized populations. The resulting sum, when compared with other, similar governments, or with the results of previous years for the same government, could provide a quick read of a government's financial standing (Koloziej, Rogers and Gardner, 1994).

This is an opportune time to review the 10-point test for three reasons. First, the implementation of Governmental Accounting Standards Board (GASB) Statement 34 (1999) has placed new information at a government's fingertips — most notably full accrual, government-wide information — that was not available 10 years ago. This more comprehensive information allows the assessment of a more comprehensive concept of financial health — *economic condition*. Second, some of Brown's ratios could be adjusted to more fully measure certain aspects of economic condition. Third, the ratios should be reviewed in the light of changes in the governmental financial environment during the past decade. For example, forms of debt other than general obligation bonds have grown significantly as a share of total outstanding debt.

This chapter provides an updated 10-point test. It is an attempt to build on and improve upon the original 10-point test by incorporating both short-term and long-term aspects of a government's financial well-being, while maintaining its relative ease of use. The chapter is divided into four parts, beginning with an overview of existing paradigms of financial/economic condition analysis and why they are not appropriate for many government analysts. The following section explains the mechanics of the original 10-point test; this chapter maintains the same, basic structure that Brown originally proposed. The third part is the heart of the chapter, proposing a new set of ratios to replace Brown's and explaining why they are preferable. The chapter concludes by applying the new 10-point test to an illustrative municipality.

15.2 Existing Paradigms of Financial/Economic Condition Analysis

Before looking at the systems for analyzing financial condition, it would be helpful to consider what the term "financial condition" means and how it relates to the more comprehensive concept of "economic condition." The hundreds of articles, books, dissertations, and other documents related to the broad topic of assessing governmental financial health employ a multiplicity of terms to describe financial health. These terms typically combine the words *financial* or *fiscal* with the words *position, condition, capacity, health,* or *status,* and so on. And for each term there is a multitude of definitions. It is not hard to find two or more authors using the same term to mean different concepts, nor two or more authors using different terms to refer to the same concept. The terms financial position and financial condition, in particular, have been used interchangeably. More often than not, however, the meaning is ambiguous or not spelled out at all. Berne (1992) was decidedly understated in concluding that "there is ambiguity over the definition and measurement of financial condition."

Remarkably, despite the variability of terminology applied to the topic of financial health, there is considerable agreement about the key areas of concern that must be considered when assessing financial health. Six areas predominate assessments of government financial health:

1. Fund balances, equity, or net assets
2. Revenues and expenditures/expenses, as well as surpluses and deficits
3. Changes in revenue bases
4. Spending pressures and expenditure needs
5. Outstanding debts, debt service, and postemployment benefits
6. Liquidity.

There was less widespread, though still notable, agreement on several other types of information, including short-term debt, credit ratings, number of employees, condition of the physical plant, output and outcome measures, and management issues such as the quality of financial reporting, planning and budget processes, and accounting practices. Although some definitions of financial condition focus on one or more of the six areas listed above, the concept of "economic condition" employed in this chapter encompasses all of them to present a comprehensive review of governmental financial health.

In the process of developing a conceptual statement on methods of communicating financial information, the GASB considered the variety of definitions applied to the terms *financial position* and *financial condition*. To avoid the general confusion over conflicting meanings, the GASB adopted the term *economic condition* to reflect a broader under-standing of a government's financial well-being. The GASB developed a definition of economic condition as "a composite of its financial health and its ability and willingness to meet its financial obligations and com-mitments to provide services." A government's financial position was identi-fied as a component of economic condition, along with its fiscal capacity and service capacity (GASB, 2004). One reason for updating the 10-point test is to come closer to encompassing this more expansive view of financial health by incorporating the longer-run and more complete information required by GASB Statement 34.

15.2.1   The ICMA Handbook

There are few examples in the literature that set forth a comprehensive model of financial health and attempt to develop an extensive set of indicators for examining the major components of that model. Perhaps the best known of those that do is the International City/County Management Association's (ICMA) *Evaluating Financial Condition: A Handbook for Local Government* (Groves and Valente, 1994). The ICMA model suggests there are four potential meanings to financial condition — cash solvency, budgetary solvency, long-run solvency, and service level solvency (Groves, Godsey and Shulman, 1981). Cash solvency is a government's capacity to generate enough cash or liquidity to pay its bills. Budgetary solvency is a government's ability to generate sufficient revenues over the normal budgetary period to meet expenditure obligations and not incur deficits. Long-run solvency refers to a government's long-run ability to pay all the costs of doing business, including expenditure obligations that normally appear in each annual budget, as well as those that show up only in the years in which they must be paid. Finally, service level solvency relates to whether a government can provide the level and quality of services required for the general health and welfare of a community.

This conception of financial condition is affected by 12 factors. There are six financial factors (revenues, expenditures, operating position, debt structure, unfunded liabilities, and condition of capital plant) that are the results of how five environmental factors (community needs and resources, external economic conditions, intergovernmental constraints, natural disasters and emergencies, and political culture) are responded to by organizational factors (management practices and legislative policies). ICMA suggests three dozen indicators for evaluating the six financial factors and community needs and resources, and calls them "quantifiable indicators of financial condition." However, such an evaluation must take place in light of the other factors — the "environmental and organizational aspects of financial condition" or the context in which the financial activity takes place.

15.2.2   The Florida Auditor General

In Florida, auditors are required under the Local Government Financial Emergencies Act to inform local governments if their financial condition is deteriorating such that a financial emergency may occur. The Auditor General (2001) has developed procedures and a set of financial indicators for auditors to use in making this determination. The methodology employs 14 recognizable indicators and describes how to calculate them using both pre- and post-GASB Statement 34 information, primarily from the fund financial statements. The indicators include typical measures of financial position (such as unreserved fund balance compared to expenditures and revenues) and financial condition (a quick ratio, for instance, and the difference between revenues and expenditures). The methodology also uses a measure of flexibility (intergovernmental revenues divided by total revenues), an indicator of debt affordability (debt service divided by expenditures), and revenue-raising capacity (millage rates compared to legal limits).

15.2.3   Berne and Schramm

Perhaps the only textbook in recent memory entirely devoted to the topic of governmental financial analysis is Berne and Schramm's *The Financial Analysis of Governments* (1986), though it is long out of print. As a textbook, it takes a more theoretical approach to developing a framework and methods for analyzing government finances. Consequently, it is less practical as a ready assessment tool than the documents already discussed. Nonetheless, it is instructive in the factors it emphasizes as important to understanding the financial health of a government and in its thorough consideration of how to examine each.

Berne and Schramm define financial condition simply as "the probability that a government will meet its financial obligations." Financial condition is the product of available resources, on the one hand, and expenditure pressures, on the other. In addition to current expenditure pressures from constituent demands for certain quantities and qualities of service and intergovernmental mandates, governments are subject to expenditure pressures from past decisions and commitments. The resources available to a government are a combination of internal resources that can be converted into cash with varying degrees of difficulty and external resources that can be tapped.

The availability of external resources is ascertained through revenue analysis, which entails an examination of the community's economic base, the government's revenue base, actual revenues, and revenue capacity and reserves. Current expenditure pressures are considered via expenditure analysis, which includes a review of actual expenditures by purpose over time, assessment of the effects of input prices, exploration of the relationship between inputs and service outputs, and comparisons of the foregoing information with community needs in light of production and service conditions. Analyses of outstanding debt and unfunded pensions liabilities provide information about the expenditure pressures of past commitments, and generally involve looking at debt structures, burdens, and affordability, as well as the funding status of pension. Lastly, internal resource analysis involves examinations of liquidity and cash flows, and fund balances and other balance sheet accounts.

Practical applications of Berne and Schramm's paradigm may be found in the financial condition analyses performed for Ambac, a bond insurance company, by Berne and Drennan (1985, 1987a, and 1987b). Their analyses of the fiscal and economic condition of the states of New York, California, and Texas are substantially based on the approach outlined in the textbook. Together, these documents foreshadow Berne's conclusions in a research report written for GASB (1992) and a subsequent book chapter (Berne, 1996).

15.2.4 Systems Incorporating GASB Statement 34

According to another, more recent comprehensive approach authored by Ives and Schanzenbach (2001), financial condition is not merely a state of being that can be assessed at a given point in time. More importantly, it is something to be monitored and managed during the course of the year by a variety of key players, from departmental personnel to the director of finance to the chief executive and governing board, as well as intergovernmental oversight, internal auditors, and rating agencies and insurers.

Ives and Schanzenbach are keenly interested in the influence of economics, demographics, and "managerial adaptation" on financial condition. Their model offers 19 indicators for evaluating four major aspects of financial condition — cash solvency, structural budgetary solvency, long-term solvency, and economics/demographics and other factors. They also put forth 10 indicators of management's ability to adapt, such as accuracy of original budget estimates, management practices such as long-term planning and budgeting and managing for results, political environment and structures, and ability and willingness to influence economic and land use development.

In addition to common-size ratios — percentage distribution and percentage change — for assets, liabilities, revenues, and expenses or expenditures, the GASB's series of user guides (especially Mead 2001a) and subsequent articles by their author (Mead, 2001b, and Chaney, Mead, and Schermann, 2002) identify eight factors to consider in *economic* condition analysis. *Financial position* considers the status of a government's asset, liability, and equity accounts at a given point in time. *Liquidity* examines a government's ability to meet its short-run obligations. *Leverage* and *coverage* are two ways to approach long-run solvency. *Fiscal capacity* or ability-to-pay compares debt and revenue information with economic indicators to assess a government's ability to raise revenues or issue debt when necessary. *Postemployment benefits* information addresses the often expensive long-term obligations governments make to their employees in the form of pensions, health care, and other benefits. *Exposure to risk* ratios measure a government's ability to respond to financial difficulties, such as revenue shortfalls and overspending. A final set of ratios measure the *efficiency* with which a government utilizes its resources. Altogether, 29 ratios are suggested, as well as multiple variations on many of them.

15.2.5 *Shortcomings of These Systems*

The principal problem with the aforementioned paradigms for assessing economic condition is their complexity. Economic condition, when defined as a comprehensive conception of financial health, is complex, so it should not be surprising that an attempt to thoroughly assess economic condition would also be complex. However, one must ask if a complex assessment tool is practical in all situations. For an external analyst with considerable time to focus on a single government, or for a government budget office with the resources to devote to extensive financial self-monitoring, these systems are truly valuable. ICMA's handbook, in particular, is widely used. But for the analyst considering multiple governments that vie for her attention, or the government with scarce resource to spare in its finance office, these systems may be overwhelming.

This may be especially true when one considers the importance of benchmarking to economic condition analysis. It is not sufficient to compute a set of ratios for a single government for a single year. Those ratios alone tell you very little. In order to make them most meaningful, they need the context provided by a comparison with prior years and with other, similar governments. If the task of computing the dozens of ratios in these larger, more expansive systems is immense for just a single government in a given year, then doing so for multiple years and for a comparison group of governments is insurmountable. For many governments and many analysts, a simpler system that trades off some comprehensiveness for ease of use is prescribed. Brown's 10-point test was just such a system.

15.3 How the 10-Point Test Works

The Brown 10-point test begins with the calculation of 10 ratios for the government of interest. Each ratio is then compared with ratios computed for a peer group of similar governments (in terms of population, total revenues, geographic proximity, or other measure). Two points are awarded for each ratio that falls in the top quartile (top 25 percent) of the comparison group. One point is given for each in the second quartile (between

Table 15.1   Interpretation of 10-Point Test Scores

Overall Score	Relative to Other Cities
10 or more	Among the best
5 to 9	Better than most
1 to 4	About average
0 to −4	Worse than most
−5 or less	Among the worst

25 and 50 percent), and no points for a ratio in the third quartile (between 50 and 75 percent). A point is subtracted for a ratio in the lowest quartile.

The points awarded for each of the 10 ratios are then totaled, and can be compared with prior years to track improvements or deteriorations in the government's economic condition. The total score can also be rated against the scores of comparable governments. Brown's suggested interpretation of the summed points is shown in Table 15.1.

15.4   A More Comprehensive 10-Point Test

The original 10-point test addressed four factors relevant to economic condition — revenues, expenditures, operating position, and debt structure (Brown, 1997). If there is a major shortcoming to the 10-point test, it is the fact that it focuses nearly entirely on the short-term finances of governmental activities. One can hardly blame Brown for this; until the issuance of GASB Statement 34, long-run financial information, in the form of accrual-based statements, was not available for the activities accounted for in the governmental funds.

This is not to say that short-run financial information is not valuable. To the contrary, any considered financial analysis should encompass both short- and long-run financial information. Furthermore, one should not only examine the government as a whole, but also the governmental activities separately from business-type activities, and even individual funds, in order to tease out disparate financial results that may be masked when information is aggregated at the government-wide level. Although a major impetus for developing the 10-point test was to give governments a simple analytical tool, the test should nevertheless be responsive to both the short- and long-run factors that affect a government's economic condition. Table 15.2 compares the ratios included in the original 10-point test with a proposed, more encompassing, group of ratios.

Table 15.2   Revisions to the 10-Point Test

Ratios from Brown's 10-Point Test	*Revisions*
(1) Operating position: Unreserved general fund balance ÷ total general fund revenues	(1) Retain as is
(2) Operating position: Total general fund cash and investments ÷ general fund liabilities	(2) Retain as is, but remove deferred revenues from liabilities
(3) Operating position: Total revenues ÷ total expenditures	Replace with (3) change in governmental activities net assets ÷ total governmental activities net assets
(4) Revenues: Total revenues ÷ population	Replace with (4) (primary government operating grants and contributions + unrestricted aid) ÷ total primary government revenues, and
(5) Revenues: Total general fund revenues from own sources ÷ total general fund sources	(5) (Net (expense) revenue for governmental activities ÷ total governmental activities
(6) Revenues: General fund sources from other funds ÷ total general fund sources	expenses) × −1
(7) Debt structure: Direct long-term debt ÷ population	Replace with (6) total outstanding debt for the primary government ÷ population
(8) Debt structure: Debt service ÷ total revenues	Retain, but revise as (7) debt service ÷ noncapital governmental funds expenditures; add (8) (Enterprise funds operating revenue + interest expense) ÷ interest expense
(9) Debt structure: Total general fund liabilities ÷ total general fund revenues	Retain, but revise as (9) (primary government liabilities − deferred revenues) ÷ primary government revenues
(10) Expenditures: Operating expenditures ÷ total expenditures	Replace with (10) (Ending net value of primary government capital assets − beginning net value) ÷ beginning net value

15.4.1   *Financial Position, Financial Performance, Liquidity, and Solvency*

Financial position, roughly defined as a government's financial standing at a given point in time, may be the most frequently mentioned factor in economic condition analysis. Brown's 10-point test included three measures intended to address what he termed "operating position." Two of those measures — *unreserved general fund balance divided by total general fund revenues* and *general fund cash and investments divided by general fund liabilities* — are retained as indicators of short-run financial position and liquidity, respectively. However, the latter ratio is adjusted to remove deferred revenues from the liabilities. Rather than obligations that are awaiting liquidation, deferred revenues are resources that do not yet qualify to be considered revenues, such as taxes receivable that are not expected to be collected within the period of availability to finance current expenditures.

In general, when these ratios are relatively higher, it suggests a better capacity to handle unforeseen resource needs and a greater ability to meet short-term obligations, respectively (see Table 15.3 for a complete list of the ratios in the updated 10-point test and their suggested interpretations).

The third measure Brown employed — total revenues divided by total expenditures — is replaced with *total governmental activities change in net assets divided by total governmental activities net assets* as an indicator of financial performance. Generally, a comparatively high ratio suggests a government is doing a better job of making ends meet each year, though a very high ratio could suggest that a government is raising too much revenue or underspending on needed services.

This change is recommended for several reasons. First, the accrual information for governmental activities eliminates the commingling of capital projects spending in the governmental funds statements. It also avoids concerns about variations among governments regarding other financing sources and uses. Second, using change in net assets, instead of total revenues and expenses, offers a dynamic, rather than static, measure that nonetheless still addresses the same factors, such as whether a government is living within its means. Dividing by net assets puts the measure in a common metric that can be compared across governments, regardless of their size, similar to percentage change and percentage distribution. Finally, the replacement measure also resembles a return-on-net-assets ratio, thereby providing an additional indicator of financial health not previously available in the 10-point test.

A fourth measure adds a long-run dimension: *primary government liabilities (less deferred revenue) divided by total revenues*. This solvency ratio is an indicator of a government's overall capacity for repaying or otherwise satisfying all of its outstanding obligations. A low ratio, other factors being equal, suggests that annual revenues are relatively more sufficient for satisfying the liabilities.

Table 15.3 Suggested Interpretations of the Updated 10-Point Test Ratios

Ratios of the Updated 10-Point Test	Suggested Interpretation
Short-run financial position: Unreserved general fund balance ÷ general fund revenues	A high ratio suggests larger reserves for dealing with unexpected resource needs in the near term.
Liquidity: General fund cash and investments ÷ (general fund liabilities − general fund deferred revenues)	A high ratio suggests a greater capacity for paying off short-run obligations.
Financial performance: Change in governmental activities net assets ÷ total governmental activities net assets	A high ratio suggests that annual costs are being adequately financed and financial position is improving.
Solvency: (Primary government liabilities − deferred revenues) ÷ primary government revenues	A low ratio suggests that outstanding obligations can more easily be met with annual revenues.
Revenues (A): (Primary government operating grants and contributions + unrestricted aid) ÷ total primary government revenues	A low ratio suggests a government is not heavily reliant on intergovernmental aid.
Revenues (B): (Net (expense) revenue for governmental activities ÷ total governmental activities expenses) × −1	A low ratio suggests basic government services are more self-sufficient through charges, fees, and categorical grants, and less reliant on general tax support.
Debt Burden: Total outstanding debt for the primary government ÷ population	A low ratio suggests less burden on taxpayers and greater capacity for additional borrowing.
Coverage (A): Debt service ÷ noncapital governmental funds expenditures	A low ratio suggests general governmental long-term debt can be more easily repaid when it comes due.
Coverage (B): (Enterprise funds operating revenue + interest expense) ÷ interest expense	A high ratio suggests greater resource availability for repaying the debts of enterprise activities as they come due.
Capital Assets: (Ending net value of primary government capital assets − beginning net value) ÷ beginning net value	A high ratio suggests a government is keeping pace, on average, with the aging of its capital assets and replenishing them.

15.4.2 Revenues

The original 10-point test included three measures of a government's revenues. Total revenues per capita was offered as an indication of revenue capacity: a high ratio was suggested to mean greater adequacy of resources. However, in the absence of additional contextual information or a comparison with a relevant economic base, a high ratio could also be interpreted as a comparatively greater burden on taxpayers, and therefore an indicator of *less* capacity to raise revenues if necessary. That ambiguity argues for dropping this measure.

The other two measures of revenues — total general fund revenues from own sources divided by total general fund resources, and general fund resources from other funds divided by total general fund sources — are indicators of the flexibility of a government's revenues. They examine a government's reliance on resources from other governments, which are largely outside of a government's control, and on shifting resources from other funds to finance general governmental functions. The availability of accrual information for governmental activities recommends refocusing from the general fund alone to the government as a whole, replacing the ratio of own-source revenues with *total primary government operating grants and contributions plus unrestricted intergovernmental aid, divided by total revenues*. A low ratio indicates that a government is less reliant on intergovernmental aid to finance services, and therefore less exposed to the potential loss of those resources.

Selecting only 10 ratios for an updated 10-point test requires weighing the relative benefits of each ratio considered. In light of the need to add new ratios that present a long-term and government-wide perspective to the test, the ratio of transfers to the general fund seems less important. A ratio of net transfers to (from) governmental activities might be a useful substitute, but perhaps not useful enough to be one of the 10 ratios. Rather, it could be used as a red flag ratio that highlights potential financial issues that should be investigated further. The presence of special and extraordinary items could be a similarly useful red flag.

The government-wide statement of activities required by Statement 34 presents information about revenue sufficiency and the use of general tax support that has never before been available. The statement subtracts expenses from program revenues to produce net (expense) revenue amounts for each of a government's functions or programs. Governmental activities typically show negative numbers in parentheses, meaning that their expenses generally exceed the revenues they raise through charges, fees, and grants. A ratio of the *total net (expense) revenue of the governmental activities divided by total governmental activities expenses* is an informative measure of the degree to which these functions and programs are self-financing or, on the other hand, the degree to which they depend on financing from general revenues, primarily taxes. To make the calculated ratio easier to interpret, it should be multiplied by negative−1. The lower the resulting ratio, the less reliant the services are on general revenue financing (and, therefore, the more self-supporting they are).

15.4.3 Debt Burden and Coverage

The 10-point test's measure of debt burden — per capita direct long-term debt — could be considered too narrow to accurately reflect present financial reality. The measure is limited to general obligation debt, which is no longer as dominant a financing mechanism as it once was. Governments today are far more likely to utilize revenue-backed bonds, certificates of participation, and tax-increment debt than they once were. Furthermore, debt instruments such as loans and capital leases are conceptually indistinguishable from general obligation bonds and are no less a burden on the finances of the government and the economy of the jurisdiction. Therefore, the ratio is replaced with *total outstanding long-term debt of the primary government divided by population.* All other factors held equal, a lower ratio suggests a lesser debt burden and potentially a greater capacity to borrow if necessary.

The absence of a government-wide cash flows statement means a single coverage ratio cannot be calculated to measure a government's overall ability to repay debt. Separate ratios are necessary to address the outstanding debt of governmental activities and business-type activities. Given the array of revenue streams now used to finance outstanding debt, this may actually be a good thing.

The existing ratio of debt service divided by revenues continues to be useful, though one shortcoming should be remedied. The comparison to total revenues unfortunately mixes in resources intended for capital purposes; ideally this ratio should be a measure of debt service burden relative to total operating costs. The solution is to use *debt service expenditures divided by total noncapital governmental funds expenditures.* This requires subtracting not only capital outlay, but also the capital expenditures reported within the functional expenditure categories on the statement of revenues, expenditures, and changes in fund balances. This total capital expenditure amount can usually be found in the reconciliation appended to the statement. Governments that implement GASB Statement 44 (2004) will be required to present this ratio for a 10-year period in a statistical section schedule of changes in governmental fund balances. In general, a low ratio indicates greater adequacy of revenue to repay outstanding debt as it comes due.

The financial statement information for proprietary funds allows for a more straightforward measure of coverage. A ratio of *enterprise funds operating revenue plus interest expense, divided by interest expense,* indicates the sufficiency of resources to repay debt. Generally, a high ratio suggests greater capacity for repayment.

15.4.4 Capital Assets

An "expenditure" measure in the original 10-point test purported to indicate whether infrastructure was being maintained properly. However, the indicator — operating expenditures divided by total expenditures — could be considered problematic in several ways. For one thing, it considered operating expenditures to be the sum of the general, special revenue, and debt service funds. Yet, those funds often contain capital expenditures, and capital projects funds sometimes contain debt service and other operating expenditures. The revised 10-point test includes instead a measure that utilizes the capital assets information governments now report in the government-wide statements and note disclosures according to Statement 34. *Percentage change of the net value of capital assets* is an indicator of whether a government's investment in purchasing or constructing new assets and refurbishing old assets is keeping pace with the rate of depreciation and disposals of assets. A positive percentage change suggests the capital stock is being replenished; a negative number suggests it is being depleted.

This ratio is not without its own problems of interpretation. For example, because of inflation, the recent replacement of an expensive infrastructure asset could give the appearance that substantial replenishment has taken place, although the vast majority of capital assets have not been improved. One must keep in mind that this is an indicator of overall or average change, rather than a description of the specific condition of individual assets. In that way it is similar to the common usage of accumulated depreciation or net book value divided by historical cost to indicate the general aging of the physical plant.

15.5 Putting the New 10-Point Test to Work

This final section of the chapter walks through the process of utilizing the 10-point test on an illustrative municipal government, the City of Port Hayley. The relevant financial statements and note disclosures are presented in Table 15.A1–15.A8. The information that is needed to calculate the 10 ratios is identified in Table 15.4 and is shaded in Table 15.A1–15.A8.

Table 15.4   Location of Information Needed to Calculate Ratios

Ratio	*Sources*
Short-run financial position: Unreserved general fund balance ÷ general fund revenues	Governmental funds balance sheet; governmental funds statement of revenues, expenditures, and changes in fund balances
Liquidity: General fund cash and investments ÷ (general fund liabilities − general fund deferred revenues)	Governmental funds balance sheet
Financial performance: Change in governmental activities net assets ÷ total governmental activities net assets	Government-wide statement of activities
Solvency: (Primary government liabilities − deferred revenues) ÷ primary government revenues	Government-wide statement of net assets and statement of activities
Revenues (A): (Primary government operating grants and contributions + unrestricted aid) ÷ total primary government revenues	Government-wide statement of activities
Revenues (B): (Net (expense) revenue for governmental activities ÷ total governmental activities expenses) × −1	Government-wide statement of activities
Debt burden: Total outstanding debt for the primary government ÷ population	Long-term liabilities note disclosure and statistical section
Coverage (A): Debt service ÷ noncapital governmental funds expenditures	Governmental funds balance sheet or statistical section
Coverage (B): (Enterprise funds operating revenue + interest expense) ÷ interest expense	Proprietary funds statement of revenues, expenses, and changes in fund net assets
Capital assets: (Ending net value of primary government capital assets − beginning net value) ÷ beginning net value	Capital assets note disclosure

The discussion that follows addresses each of the 10 ratios, what they mean, and how they compare with a peer comparison group of similar cities in the same state. Before proceeding, however, a few words on building peer comparison groups are necessary.

15.5.1 Peer Comparison Groups

The purpose of building a comparison group is to provide some context for understanding the ratios of the government you are interested in. Judgments about whether a ratio is "good" or "bad" or somewhere in between are made easier by comparing a government's results to those of other governments. In a comparative perspective, good becomes "better than other governments" and bad becomes "worse than other governments." Equally as important, you replace the static judgment of good versus bad with a dynamic scale that allows judgments about *the degree to which* a government is better or worse than other governments.

The identification of the peer governments to include depends on several characteristics. First, the group should include the same types of governmental entities; in other words, a general purpose local government should be compared with other general purpose local governments, a school district should be compared with other school districts, and so on. Second, it is preferable to include peer governments from the same geographic region. This can be as small as a county or as large as a state. The benefit to staying local is that the governments are governed by the same regulations, face the same general economic conditions, and are likely to provide similar services. Third, the peer governments should be roughly the same size, in terms of either annual financial activity (revenues or expenses/expenditures) or population or both.

There are a variety of ways to assemble the information necessary to develop a comparison group. Obtaining the relevant information from the financial statements of the peer governments may be the most time consuming approach, but it offers the benefit of being able to see the information first-hand and identify any anomalous circumstances that might adversely affect the comparability of the peers. Alternatively, one may utilize available databases of government financial information. Every state collects financial information from school districts and many states collect financial information from localities as well. The Government Finance Officers Association's (GFOA) financial indicators database includes information drawn from the comprehensive annual financial statements submitted to its certificate of achievement for excellence in financial reporting program. The information can easily be sorted by government size. In fact, Brown's 10-point test draws its comparison groups from GFOA's database.

There are at least two negative factors, however, that weigh against the ease of using such databases. First, they are not timely, taking at least a year, and often several, to be assembled and published. Second, the GFOA database may be skewed toward governments that have better financial management practices and that therefore may perform better financially than the norm for all governments.

15.5.2 Short-run Financial Position

The City of Port Hayley's ratio of short-run financial position is 0.37 (see Table 15.5 for the calculations of Port Hayley's ratios and how they compare with the peer group of cities.) This means that its generally available current financial resources (unreserved general fund balance) are equal to 37 percent of its annual governmental fund revenues. In other words, Port Hayley's unreserved fund balance would be sufficient to keep the city's basic functions running for about 135 days (37 percent times 365 days).

When compared with a peer comparison group of similar cities in the same state, Port Hayley's short-run financial position ratio ranks in the top quartile. Under the 10-point test system, Port Hayley is awarded two points for placing in the top quartile.

15.5.3 Liquidity

Port Hayley's liquidity ratio is 8.9, which means that its resources that are most readily converted to cash amount to nearly nine times more than the obligations that it has to pay off in the next year. This ratio also compares favorably with the peer governments, landing in the second quartile. The city receives one point.

15.5.4 Financial Performance

Port Hayley's financial performance ratio is 0.07. The city's increase in net assets was equal to 7 percent of its total net assets, a result that does not compare well with the peer group. Port Hayley's ratio is in the bottom quartile of the comparison group, and therefore the city loses one point.

15.5.5 Solvency

In order to calculate the solvency ratio, four numbers in the government-wide statement of activities (see Table 15.A2) must be summed — charges for services, operating grants and contributions, capital grants and contributions, and total general revenues. The solvency ratio of 1.14 for Port Hayley means that its liabilities are 14 percent greater than the sum of these annual revenues. In other words, to repay all of its liabilities would take a full year's revenues plus 14 percent of the next year's revenues. This ratio ranks in the third quartile, and no points are awarded.

15.5.6 Revenues

The first revenue ratio requires the addition of operating grants and contributions (which are found in the program revenue section of the statement

Table 15.5 Calculation of Ratios and Assignment of Scores

Ratio	Calculation	Result	Quartile	Score
Short-run financial position	3,903,429 ÷ 10,466,389	0.37	1st	2
Liquidity	4,377,368 ÷ (796,058 − 306,473)	8.94	2nd	1
Financial performance	3,779,620 ÷ 51,504,550	0.07	4th	−1
Solvency	(43,441,261 − 179,857) ÷ (15,877,339 + 1,425,380 + 627,815 + 19,928,578)	1.14	3rd	0
Revenues (A)	(1,425,380 + 2,666,347) ÷ (15,877,339 + 1,425,380 + 627,815 + 19,928,578)	0.09	2nd	1
Revenues (B)	(−15,921,202 ÷ 22,228,063) × −1	0.72	3rd	0
Debt Burden	(22,981,400 + 11,603,300) ÷ 24,907	1,389	2nd	1
Coverage (A)	3,500,823 ÷ (26,518,698 − 4,601,515)	0.16	4th	−1
Coverage (B)	(11,257,893 + 232,908) ÷ 232,908	49.34	1st	2
Capital Assets	[(56,286,652 + 46,993,402) − (54,282,487 + 43,959,679)] ÷ (54,282,487 + 43,959,679)	0.05	3rd	0
			Total	**5**

of activities) and unrestricted intergovernmental aid (located with the general revenues). The ratio of that sum to total revenues is 0.09 for Port Hayley. Port Hayley receives 9 percent of its total revenue in the form of intergovernmental operating support, a comparatively low number that places it in the second quartile of the comparison group. One point is awarded.

The second revenue ratio, which assesses the degree to which general governmental activities are supported by taxes and other general revenues (as opposed to revenues raised by the activities themselves), is 0.72. That means 72 percent of the expenses of Port Hayley's governmental activities was financed with taxes and other general revenues; conversely, 28 percent was self-funded through charges for services, grants, and contributions. This is fairly close to the typical ratio for the peer governments; Port Hayley is in the third quartile, so no points are awarded.

15.5.7 Debt Burden

The calculation of debt burden should include all outstanding debt instruments — not just general obligation debt, but also other types of bonds and notes, loans, capital leases, and so on. The items from the long-term liabilities note disclosure (see Table 15.A8) that should not be included, however, are claims and judgments, compensated absences, postclosure landfill costs, and so on.

Port Hayley's total outstanding debt amounts to $1,389 per resident. This ratio is in the second quartile of the comparison group, garnering one point.

15.5.8 Coverage

The first coverage ratio — comparing debt service to noncapital expenditures — amounts to 0.16 for Port Hayley. That is, general governmental debt service consumes 16 percent of its operating expenditures, a relatively high amount. Consequently, Port Hayley is in the bottom quartile and loses one point.

The coverage ratio for the enterprise funds is a robust 49.34, which means that operating revenues of the business-type activities are more than 49 times their annual interest costs. Port Hayley places in the top quartile with this ratio and receives two points.

15.5.9 Capital Assets

Port Hayley's ratio of 0.05 means that the net value of the capital assets increased 5 percent of the year. In other words, new investment is more than keeping pace with depreciation and the disposal or sale of capital assets. The ratio ranks in the third quartile, for which no points are awarded.

15.5.10 Total Score

The City of Port Hayley's total score of 5 is obtained by summing the points awarded for each of the ratios (refer to Table 15.4). According to Brown's interpretation of the scores (refer to Table 15.1), Port Hayley is just inside the group of governments that are "better than most." Additional meaning can be added to this score by tracking it over time. A score of 5 may be more impressive if Port Hayley had been steadily rising from a score of 2 or 3 several years ago. By contrast, being better than most governments may be less impressive if Port Hayley's score was higher in recent years, say a 7 or 8. In this way, an analyst discovers not only the comparative standing of the government's economic condition, but also whether its economic condition is improving or deteriorating relative to other governments.

15.6 Future Outlook for Economic Condition Assessment

On a conceptual level, most frameworks for evaluating the financial health of governments consider both short-term and long-term factors. Until recently, however, little information was available to inform the long-term aspects of a government's finances. One of the primary motivations for GASB Statement 34 was to round out financial reporting by state and local governments by adding more comprehensive information, covering both the short and long term, to complement the existing short-run, fund-based information the public was already getting.

Now that the basic implementation deadlines for Statement 34 have passed, any government following GAAP — and any analyst examining such a government — has new long-term financial information at its fingertips. This chapter sets forth an example of how this new information can be incorporated into a facile, but thorough, assessment of a government's economic condition. The capital asset, long-term liability, full accrual, and other information needed to calculate the ratios in this chapter's new 10-point test of economic condition is now available, and trends can be constructed with each succeeding year of reporting under the GASB 34 model.

The issuance of GASB Statement 44 in 2004 will also be a beneficial development for the analysis of economic condition. Statement 44 updates and revises the requirements for the statistical section of a government's comprehensive annual financial report (CAFR) for the first time in 25 years. The information in the statistical section is highly valuable to municipal bond analysts and others who make assessments of governmental financial health. The deadline for implementing Statement 44 is fiscal years ending after June 15, 2006.

When a government presents a statistical section with its annual financial statements, it contains schedules of financial, economic, demographic, and operating information for the past ten years. These schedules include all of the basic information necessary to calculate nine of the ten ratios described in this chapter (the exception being the enterprise funds coverage ratio). Analysts examining governments that prepare CAFRs will have readily available trends in long-term financial information extending back to a government's implementation of Statement 34. The final hurdles to comprehensive assessments of governmental economic condition are now being cleared.

Acknowledgment

The opinions expressed in this manuscript are those of the author. Official positions of the GASB are established only after extensive due process.

Appendix

Table 15.A1 City of Port Hayley, Statement of Net Assets, June 30, 200X

	Primary Government		
	Governmental Activities	Business-type Activities	Total
ASSETS			
Cash and investments	$19,600,901	$17,110,793	$36,711,694
Receivables, net	2,328,271	911,057	3,239,328
Internal balances	143,125	(143,125)	-
Due from other governments	1,176,789	179,565	1,356,354
Inventories	150,689	124,822	275,511
Prepaid items and deposits	2,182,444	534	2,182,978
Other assets	-	2,786,819	2,786,819
Restricted cash and investments	20,606	1,789,339	1,809,945
Capital assets, not depreciable	18,347,986	11,715,956	30,063,942
Capital assets, depreciable	37,938,666	35,277,445	73,216,111
Total Assets	$81,889,477	$69,753,205	$151,642,682
LIABILITIES			
Accounts payable	$1,144,939	$787,995	$1,932,934
Accrued interest payable	392,055	-	392,055
Due to other governments	230,052	80,525	310,577
Deferred revenue	179,857	-	179,857
Deposits	2,497,489	34,185	2,531,674
Liabilities payable from restricted assets			
Due to other governments	-	67,213	67,213
Revenue bonds payable due within one year	-	332,115	332,115
Accrued interest	-	229,389	229,389
Noncurrent assets			
Due within one year	2,136,933	318,913	2,455,846
Due in more than one year	23,803,602	11,205,999	35,009,601
Total Liabilities	$30,384,927	$13,056,334	$43,441,261

Table 15.A1 Continued

	Primary Government		
	Governmental Activities	Business-type Activities	Total
NET ASSETS			
Invested in capital assets, net of related debt	$32,965,759	$35,719,964	$68,685,723
Restricted for:			
Encumbrances	61,443	3,350,881	3,412,324
Public works, transportation projects	885,630	-	885,630
Police programs	9,507	-	9,507
Grant funded programs	1,842,618	-	1,842,618
Debt service	542,576	124,520	667,096
Capital projects	-	90,802	90,802
Culture and recreation	38,994	-	38,994
Other purposes	105,927	-	105,927
Unrestricted	15,052,096	17,410,704	32,462,800
Total Net Assets	$51,504,550	$56,696,871	$108,201,421

The accompanying notes are an integral part of these statements.

Table 15.A2 City of Port Hayley, Statement of Activities, June 30, 200X

		Program Revenues			Net (Expense) Revenues		
Functions/Programs	Expenses	Charges for Services	Operating Grants and Contributions	Capital Grants and Contributions	Governmental Activities	Business-type Activities	Total
Governmental activities:							
General government	$2,559,258	$1,672,218	$ 28,043	$ -	$ (858,997)	$ -	$ (858,997)
Community and economic development	2,246,394	77,507	879,648	22,231	(1,267,008)	-	(1,267,008)
Public works	1,428,077	423,776	130,953	151,992	(721,356)	-	(721,356)
Police	6,378,778	416,363	171,732	-	(5,790,683)	-	(5,790,683)
Fire and EMS	3,331,929	991,426	37,179	2,555	(2,300,769)	-	(2,300,769)
Recreation and culture	5,149,158	919,267	165,851	216,121	(3,847,919)	-	(3,847,919)
Interest on long-term debt	1,134,469	-	-	-	(1,134,469)	-	(1,134,469)
Total governmental activities	22,228,063	4,500,557	1,413,406	392,899	(15,921,202)	-	(15,921,202)
Business-type activities:							
Water and wastewater	7,276,199	6,840,671	9,970	169,900	-	(255,658)	(255,658)
Stormwater	820,173	868,273	-	3,053	-	51,153	51,153
Sanitation	3,287,614	3,021,852	2,004	-	-	(263,758)	(263,758)
Port and marina	267,412	268,533	-	61,963	-	63,084	63,084
Golf courses	363,049	336,530	-	-	-	(26,519)	(26,519)

	Expenses	Charges for Services	Operating Grants and Contributions	Capital Grants and Contributions	Governmental Activities	Business-type Activities	Total
Evanston Complex	45,471	40,922	-	-		(4,549)	(4,549)
Total business-type activities	12,059,918	11,376,782	11,974	234,916		(436,246)	(436,246)
Total Primary Government	$34,287,981	$15,877,339	$1,425,380	$627,815	(15,921,202)	(436,246)	(16,357,448)

General Revenues:

Taxes:

					Governmental Activities	Business-type Activities	Total
Property					6,477,373	-	6,477,373
Franchise					1,383,926	-	1,383,926
Utility					3,537,288	-	3,537,288
Sales					1,520,196	-	1,520,196
Other					1,523,224	-	1,523,224
Unrestricted intergovernmental aid					2,666,347	-	2,666,347
Earnings on unrestricted investments					748,524	1,013,673	1,762,197
Rentals					204,794	-	204,794
Miscellaneous					247,697	77,297	324,994
Gain on the sale of capital assets					501,167	27,071	528,238
Transfers					890,286	(890,286)	-
Total General Revenues and Transfers					19,700,822	227,756	19,928,578
Change in Net Assets					3,779,620	(208,490)	3,571,130
Net Assets - Beginning					47,724,930	56,905,361	104,630,291
Net Assets - Ending					$51,504,550	$56,696,871	$108,201,421

The accompanying notes are an integral part of these statements.

Table 15.A3 City of Port Hayley, Balance Sheet, Governmental Funds, June 30, 200X

	General Fund	Neighborhood Improvement	Grants Fund	Nonmajor Governmental Funds	Total Governmental Funds
ASSETS					
Cash and investments	$4,377,368	$3,552,041	$66,250	$6,057,986	$14,053,645
Accounts receivable	52,075	-	-	208,411	260,486
Taxes receivable	5,849	-	-	557,384	563,234
Accrued interest receivable	18,692	25,047	-	14,114	57,853
Notes receivable	145,932	-	889,167	523,704	1,558,803
Due from other funds	74,200	-	-	-	74,200
Due from other governments	113,740	108,352	67,127	931,407	1,220,625
Inventory	26,885	-	-	6,755	33,640
Deposits	7,433	-	1,900,110	19,210	1,926,753
Restricted cash and investments	-	-	-	11,034	11,034
Total Assets	$4,822,176	$3,685,440	$2,922,653	$8,330,004	$19,760,273
LIABILITIES AND FUND BALANCES					
Liabilities:					
Accounts payable	$146,317	$258,249	$8,042	$75,505	$488,113
Salaries payable	284,385	-	1,802	20,968	307,155
Other accrued liabilities	-	136,678	-	4,343	141,021
Due to other governments	324	4	120	151,161	151,609

Due to other funds	–	–	50,000	24,200	74,200
Deposits	58,559	–	1,906,562	39,985	2,005,106
Deferred revenues	306,473	–	889,167	667,741	1,863,380
Total Liabilities	796,058	394,931	2,855,694	983,902	5,030,585
Fund balances:					
Reserved for:					
Encumbrances	88,371	672,894	–	173,465	934,729
Inventories	26,885	–	–	25,803	52,689
Capital improvements	–	–	–	38,944	38,944
Library	–	–	–	29,470	29,470
Arboretum	–	–	–	9,548	9,548
Prepaid items and deposits	7,433	–	–	–	7,433
Unreserved, reported in:					
General fund	3,903,429	–	–	–	3,903,429
Special revenue funds	–	–	66,959	4,202,440	4,269,400
Capital projects funds	–	2,617,615	–	1,179,386	3,797,001
Debt service funds	–	–	–	1,413,127	1,413,127
Permanent funds	–	–	–	273,918	273,918
Total Fund Balances	4,026,118	672,894	66,959	9,963,717	14,729,688
Total Liabilities and Fund Balances	$4,822,176	$1,067,825	$2,922,653	$10,947,619	$19,760,273

The accompanying notes are an integral part of these statements.
Note: The required reconciliation of total governmental fund balance to total governmental activities net assets is not illustrated.

Table 15.A4 City of Port Hayley, Statement of Revenues, Expenditures, and Changes in Fund Balances, Governmental Funds, June 30, 200X

	General Fund	Neighborhood Improvement	Grants Fund	Nonmajor Governmental Funds	Total Governmental Funds
REVENUES					
Taxes	$ 6,816,538	$ -	$ -	$4,870,957	$11,687,496
Licenses and permits	396,776	-	-	-	396,776
Fines and forfeitures	207,103	-	-	127,498	334,602
Charges	1,670,901	-	-	1,473,682	3,144,582
Intergovernmental	580,589	218,938	571,701	5,213,957	6,585,185
Investment earnings	255,385	141,359	5,392	408,726	810,861
Miscellaneous	539,098	130,454	175,274	372,884	1,217,710
Total Revenues	10,466,389	490,752	752,367	12,467,703	24,177,211
EXPENDITURES					
General government	$1,482,256	$ -	$ -	$23,381	$1,505,637
Community and economic development	1,277,207	-	484,562	686,543	2,448,312
Public works	825,638	16,047	-	60,153	901,838
Police	6,031,489	821	-	987,558	7,019,867

Fire and EMS	2,396,349	-	-	-	2,396,349
Recreation and culture	2,966,838	18,115	-	1,160,406	4,145,359
Debt service	-	-	-	3,500,823	3,500,823
Capital outlay	176,769	3,302,475	236,439	884,832	4,600,514
Total Expenditures	15,156,546	3,337,456	721,000	7,303,695	26,518,698
EXCESS (DEFICIENCY) OF REVENUES OVER EXPENDITURES	(4,690,157)	(2,846,705)	31,367	5,164,008	(2,341,487)
OTHER FINANCING SOURCES (USES)					
Transfers in	6,831,073	2,046,139	-	3,951,538	12,828,749
Transfers out	(1,415,643)	(290,400)	-	(10,189,624)	(11,895,666)
Bond proceeds	-	-	-	5,663,464	5,663,464
Payment to escrow agent	-	-	-	(5,416,926)	(5,416,926)
Total Other Financing Sources (Uses)	5,415,430	1,755,739	-	(5,991,548)	1,179,621
NET CHANGE IN FUND BALANCES	725,273	(1,090,966)	31,367	(827,540)	(1,161,866)
FUND BALANCES – BEGINNING	3,300,845	4,381,476	35,592	8,173,642	15,891,555
FUND BALANCES – ENDING	$4,026,118	$3,290,509	$66,959	$7,346,102	$14,729,688

The accompanying notes are an integral part of these statements.

Table 15.A5   City of Port Hayley, Reconciliation of the Statement of Revenues, Expenditures, and Changes in Fund Balances to the Statement of Activities, June 30, 200X

Net change in fund balances, total governmental funds	(1,161,866)
Capital outlay, reported as expenditures in governmental funds, are shown as capital assets in the statement of net assets	4,601,515
Depreciation expenses on governmental capital assets included in the governmental activities in the statement of activities	(2,023,072)
The issuance of long-term debt provides current financial resources to governmental funds, but has no effect on net assets:	
Long-term debt proceeds	(5,663,464)
Long-term debt issuance expense	83,171
Long-term debt refunding payments to escrow agents	6,395,742
Repayment of long-term debt is reported as an expenditure in governmental funds, but is a reduction of long-term liabilities in the statement of net assets	1,507,000
The net revenues of the internal service funds are reported with governmental activities	123,852
Some governmental revenues will not be collected for several months or years after the fiscal year and are deferred in the governmental funds	286,342
Certain items reported in the statement of activities do not require the use of current financial resources and therefore are not reported as expenditures in the governmental funds	(369,599)
Changes in net assets, governmental activities	3,779,620

The accompanying notes are an integral part of these statements.

Table 15.A6 City of Port Hayley, Statement of Revenues, Expenses, and Changes in Fund Net Assets, June 30, 200X

| | Business-type Activities-Enterprises Funds | | | | | Governmental Activities— |
	Water and Wastewater	Stormwater	Sanitation	Nonmajor Enterprise Funds	Total Enterprise Funds	Internal Service Fund
OPERATING REVENUES						
Sales and concessions	$3,129,306	$ -	$ -	$ 54,041	$ 3,183,347	$ 3,206
Service charges and fees	3,588,246	868,273	3,021,852	259,837	7,738,207	5,873,661
Rentals and parking	-	-	-	332,005	332,005	635,459
Other	4,232	-	-	102	4,334	-
Total Revenues	6,721,783	868,273	3,021,852	645,985	11,257,893	6,512,326
OPERATING EXPENSES						
Personal services and benefits	1,748,824	330,217	1,155,854	313,032	3,547,926	1,676,708
Supplies, services and claims	3,931,417	198,373	1,662,201	186,609	5,978,599	4,084,801
General administrative charges	388,800	40,200	204,600	44,801	678,401	-
Depreciation	887,758	214,228	231,758	121,678	1,455,422	837,394
Total Expenses	6,956,799	783,017	3,254,413	666,119	11,660,349	6,598,904
OPERATING INCOME (LOSS)	(235,016)	85,255	(232,561)	(20,134)	(402,456)	(86,577)

(Continued)

Table 15.A6 Continued

	Business-type Activities-Enterprises Funds					Governmental Activities—Internal Service Fund
	Water and Wastewater	Stormwater	Sanitation	Nonmajor Enterprise Funds	Total Enterprise Funds	
NONOPERATING REVENUES (EXPENSES)						
Intergovernmental revenues	15,497	897	2,004	61,963	80,361	-
Pass-through grant	-	-	-	(3,567)	(3,567)	-
Earnings on investments	767,414	124,482	116,978	8,867	1,017,741	188,641
Interest expense	(205,599)	(24,174)	-	(3,135)	(232,908)	(15,316)
Financing fees and premiums	(1,232)	-	-	(2,337)	(3,569)	-
Amortization of bond discount	(4,341)	-	-	(1,585)	(5,926)	-
Gain (loss) on sale of fixed assets	7,061	2,133	17,877	-	27,071	45,244
Miscellaneous revenue	60,353	885	8,955	7,104	77,297	81,040
Total Nonoperating Revenues (Expenses)	639,153	104,224	145,814	67,309	956,500	299,609
INCOME (LOSS) BEFORE CAPITAL CONTRIBUTIONS AND TRANSFERS	404,137	189,479	(86,747)	47,175	554,044	213,032
CAPITAL CONTRIBUTIONS	164,363	2,156	(1,192)	-	165,327	9,840
TRANSFERS IN	-	169,000	-	24,000	193,000	-
TRANSFERS OUT	(668,460)	(123,436)	(233,524)	(56,664)	(1,082,083)	(44,000)
NET CHANGE IN FUND BALANCES	(99,960)	237,200	(321,463)	14,511	(169,712)	178,872
FUND BALANCES - BEGINNING	40,965,394	10,043,607	3,914,593	2,086,113	57,009,708	6,449,450
FUND BALANCES - ENDING	$40,865,434	$10,280,807	$3,593,130	$2,100,624	$56,839,995	$6,628,322

The accompanying notes are an integral part of these statements.

Table 15.A7 City of Port Hayley, Note Disclosure of Changes in Capital Assets

Capital asset activity for the year ended June 30, 200X, was as follows:

	Beginning Balance	Additions	Retirements	Ending Balance
Governmental activities:				
Capital assets not being depreciated:				
Land	$12,260,684	$ 828,246	$ 85,201	$13,003,729
Construction in progress	4,179,128	4,290,673	3,125,544	5,344,257
Total capital assets not being depreciated	16,439,812	5,118,919	3,210,745	18,347,986
Capital assets being depreciated:				
Buildings and systems	29,994,675	351,964	5,875	30,340,764
Improvements and infrastructure	23,061,293	1,668,920	48,867	24,681,346
Machinery and equipment	12,917,677	1,001,161	735,755	13,183,083
Total capital assets being depreciated	65,973,646	3,022,045	790,497	68,205,193
Less accumulated depreciation for:				
Buildings and systems	7,996,958	749,357	5,115	8,741,200
Improvements and infrastructure	12,465,547	811,369	39,000	13,237,916
Machinery and equipment	7,668,466	1,335,535	716,590	8,287,411
Total accumulated depreciation	28,130,971	2,896,261	760,705	30,266,527
Total capital assets being depreciated, net	37,842,675	125,784	29,792	37,938,666
Governmental activities capital assets, net	$54,282,487	$5,244,703	$3,240,537	$56,286,652

(Continued)

Table 15.A7 Continued

Capital asset activity for the year ended June 30, 200X, was as follows:

	Beginning Balance	Additions	Retirements	Ending Balance
Business-type activities:				
Capital assets not being depreciated:				
Land	$1,119,617	$ -	$ -	$ 1,119,617
Construction in progress	6,621,090	5,329,372	1,354,123	10,596,339
Total capital assets not being depreciated	7,740,708	5,329,372	1,354,123	11,715,956
Capital assets being depreciated:				
Buildings and systems	1,514,719	23,577	-	1,538,295
Improvements other than buildings	2,086,817	46,196	2,052	2,130,961
Machinery and equipment	4,047,075	131,675	64,485	4,114,265
Utility systems	49,711,708	1,116,129	909,455	49,918,382
Total capital assets being depreciated	57,360,319	1,317,576	975,992	57,701,903
Less accumulated depreciation for:				
Buildings and systems	521,985	60,522	-	582,507
Improvements other than buildings	1,396,327	72,510	2,052	1,466,785
Machinery and equipment	2,856,784	203,070	44,439	3,015,415
Utility systems	16,366,252	1,037,129	43,629	17,359,752
Total accumulated depreciation	21,141,347	1,373,230	90,119	22,424,458
Total capital assets being depreciated, net	36,218,972	(55,654)	885,872	35,277,445
Business-type activities capital assets, net	$43,959,679	$5,273,718	$2,239,996	$46,993,402

Note: The required explanation of how depreciation was allocated to functional expense categories is not illustrated.

Table 15.A8   City of Port Hayley, Note Disclosure of Changes in Long-term Liabilities

The following is a summary of changes in long-term liabilities of the city for the fiscal year ended June 30, 200X. (dollars in thousands)

	Beginning Balance	Additions	Retirements	Ending Balance	Due Within One Year
Governmental activities:					
Bonds and notes payable:					
General obligations bonds	$ 140	$ -	$ (140)	$ -	$ -
Revenue bonds	19,952	3,464	(5,073)	18,343	1,286
Notes	5,198	1,708	(2,268)	4,638	342
Total bonds and notes payable	25,289	5,172	(7,480)	22,981	1,628
Claims and judgments	1,935	483	(585)	1,833	437
Compensated absences	1,066	130	(70)	1,126	72
Total long-term liabilities, governmental activities	$28,290	$5,786	$(8,135)	$25,941	$2,137
Business-type activities:					
Bonds and notes payable:					
Revenue bonds	$10,145	$ -	$(347)	$ 9,798	$243
Notes	1,500	-	(235)	1,265	53
Total bonds and notes payable	11,645	-	(581)	11,063	296
Compensated absences	458	27	(24)	462	23
Total long-term liabilities, business-type activities	$12,103	$27	$(605)	$11,525	$319

Note: The required explanation of which governmental funds typically have been used to liquidate other long-term liabilities in prior years is not illustrated.

References

Auditor General, State of Florida (2001). Local governmental entity financial condition assessment procedures (draft). Tallahassee: Auditor General.

Berne, R. (1992). *The Relationship between Financial Reporting and the Measurement of Financial Condition.* Norwalk, CT: Governmental Accounting Standards Board.

Berne, Robert. 1996. Measuring and reporting financial condition. In J.L. Perry (ed.), *Handbook of Public Administration,* second edition. San Francisco: Jossey-Bass.

Berne, R. and Drennan, M. (1985). *The Fiscal and Economic Condition of New York.* NY: Ambac.

Berne, R. and Drennan, M. (1987a). *The Fiscal and Economic Condition of Texas.* NY: Ambac.

Berne, R. and Drennan, M. (1987b). *The Fiscal and Economic Condition of California.* NY: Ambac.

Berne, R. and Schramm, R. (1986). *The Financial Analysis of Governments.* Englewood Cliffs, NJ: Prentice-Hall.

Brown, K.W. (1993). The 10-point test of financial condition: toward an easy-to-use assessment tool for smaller cities. *Government Finance Review,* December, pp. 21–26.

Brown, K.W. (1997). *Comparative Ratios for Cities.* Springfield, MO: Solstice Publications.

Chaney, B.A., Mead, D.M., and Schermann, K.R. (2002). The new governmental financial reporting model: what it means for analyzing government financial condition. *Journal of Government Financial Management,* Vol. 51, No. 1, Spring, pp. 26–31.

Governmental Accounting Standards Board (1999). Statement No. 34, *Basic Financial Statements — and Management's Discussion and Analysis — for State and Local Governments.* Norwalk, CT: GASB.

Governmental Accounting Standards Board (2004). Statement No. 44, *Economic Condition Reporting: The Statistical Section.* Norwalk, CT: GASB.

Groves, S.M., Godsey, W.M., and Shulman, M.A. (1981). Financial indicators for local government. *Public Budgeting & Finance,* Vol. 1, No. 2, Summer, pp. 5–19.

Groves, S.M. and Valente, M.G. (1994). *Evaluating Financial Condition: A Handbook for Local Government.* Washington, DC: International City/County Management Association.

Ives, M. and Schanzenbach, K. (2001). *Financial Condition Analysis and Management.* Fort Worth, TX: Sheshunoff Information Services.

Kolodziej, R.L., Rogers, K., and Gardner, L. (1994). Small city use of the 10-point test of financial condition. *Government Finance Review,* December, pp. 29–31.

Mead, D.M. (2001a). *An Analyst's Guide to Government Financial Statements.* Norwalk, CT: Governmental Accounting Standards Board.

Mead, D.M. (2001b). Assessing the financial condition of public school districts: some tools of the trade. In W.J. Fowler, Jr. (ed.), *Selected Papers in School Finance, 2000-01,* pp. 55–76, Washington, DC: U.S. Department of Education, National Center for Education Statistics.

PUBLIC PENSIONS

Chapter 16

The Management of Public Pensions

JERRELL D. COGGBURN, Ph.D. and
CHRISTOPHER G. REDDICK, Ph.D.
Department of Public Administration, University of Texas, San Antonio

16.1 Introduction

Expenditures for human resources typically account for the lion's share of government budgets. As such, sound public financial management requires an emphasis on compensation-related expenditures and obligations. Such compensation-related expenditures go far beyond salary and wages, including merit pay, health benefits, leave benefits, training and development costs, and pensions. As this suggests, public pensions are part and parcel of government's total compensation package: they are an integral component of government's human resources strategy for attracting and retaining valuable employees (Cayer and Volk, 1999). In fact, research suggests public employees receive a larger portion of their compensation in the form of deferred retirement benefits than do private sector employees

(Johnson, 1997), thus making pensions an even more important aspect of government's compensation package.

In financial terms, employer contributions needed to meet pension obligations average between 15 and 16 percent of public sector payroll (Zorn, 1997; Cranford, 1993). These financial costs quickly convey the importance of public pensions, but their importance also is evident in the number of public pension plans, plan participants, and pension fund holdings in the United States. According to data from the United States Census Bureau (2002), there are 2,670 state and local government retirement systems, 219 of which are at the state level and 2,451 at the local level (see Table 16.1). As Table 16.1 shows, these various state and local pension systems cover over 17 million current and former (i.e., retired) public sector employees. Together, in fiscal year 2002 these plans paid out in excess of $110 billion in pension benefits (United States Census Bureau, 2002). As these figures suggest, public pensions in the United States represent a major financial commitment, hence they are a vital part of government finance (Peng, 2004).

Public pensions are not only important from a financial perspective. For government employers, providing for employees' post-employment financial security is also related to employee productivity: "To ensure employees' current commitment and attention on productivity, future security must be guaranteed" (Daley, 1998, 13). Both the financial and performance implications of public pensions are readily seen in the objectives for public pensions identified by the Government Finance Officers Association (GFOA). According to the GFOA's *An Elected Official's Guide to Public Retirement Plans* (Eitelberg, 1997, p. ix), public pension plans seek to:

- Attract and retain a high-quality workforce
- Allow employees to depart from the work force financially secure and maintain the value of benefits throughout retirement
- Provide benefits that are fiscally responsible and financially supportable
- Fund benefits on a contemporary and actuarially sound basis
- Invest assets prudently for the exclusive benefit of plan participants

Despite their size and importance, public pensions have operated, historically, in relative obscurity, typically drawing attention only when stories appeared of investment-related scandal or system underfunding. More recently, however, this relative obscurity has been replaced by increased scrutiny. Indeed, a variety of political, social, and economic developments have served to focus greater attention on public pensions in recent years. Politically, elected officials have shown an alarming propensity for

Table 16.1   Active Membership State and Local Government Pensions

Year	State and Type of Government	Number of Systems	Total Membership	Active Members
2001–2002	United States	2,670	17,246,537	14,123,832
	State	219	15,394,714	12,407,222
	Local	2,451	1,851,823	1,716,610
2000–2001	United States	2,208	16,987,719	13,937,429
	State	220	15,210,686	12,283,791
	Local	1,988	1,777,033	1,653,638
1999–2000	United States	2,209	16,833,698	13,916,706
	State	218	15,077,009	12,281,004
	Local	1,991	1,756,689	1,635,702
1998–1999	United States	2,209	16,195,303	13,472,315
	State	213	14,335,604	11,757,108
	Local	1,996	1,859,699	1,715,207
1997–1998	United States	2,203	16,153,946	13,050,942
	State	214	14,368,496	11,358,499
	Local	1,989	1,785,450	1,692,443
1996–1997	United States	2,276	15,193,756	12,816,685
	State	212	13,502,159	11,210,405
	Local	2,064	1,691,597	1,606,280
1995–1996	United States	2,285	15,155,820	13,017,910
	State	203	13,169,683	11,121,324
	Local	2,082	1,986,137	1,896,586
1994–1995	United States	2,284	14,734,774	12,524,520
	State	200	13,083,119	10,967,868
	Local	2,084	1,651,655	1,556,652
1993–1994	United States	2,233	13,685,330	12,099,212
	State	192	12,055,512	10,545,461
	Local	2,041	1,629,818	1,553,751
1992–1993	United States	2,213	13,272,069	11,768,078
	State	190	11,654,786	10,224,417
	Local	2,023	1,617,283	1,543,661

Source: United States Census Bureau (2002). *2002 State and Local Government Employee-Retirement Systems*. Washington, DC: United States Census Bureau. (See Table 5: Membership by State and Local Government).

sweetening pension benefits for an active political class — public sector employees and retirees — without always fully considering the long-term financial implications of these enhancements for their jurisdictions. Political factors have also played into decisions regarding such things as pension investment policy and pension plan funding. Socially, demographic trends in the United States reveal an aging population. For public pension systems, the prospects of large cohorts of employees becoming retirement eligible, coupled with longer life expectancies, means that pension systems face potential strain. Economically, stock market downturns in the early 2000s, coincident with the bursting of the technology investment bubble, resulted in the handsome returns of the late 1990s giving way to alarming (at least in the short-term) investment losses in the first few years of the 21st century.

Together, these developments have brought public pension management to the forefront of public sector financial management concerns (Daley, 1998). For public officials charged with overseeing and managing these funds, the responsibilities — fiduciary, financial, and managerial — are significant. This chapter examines the management of public pensions. The chapter begins with a consideration of the two major approaches to public pensions, defined benefit and defined contribution plans, and a variety of hybrid plans that have emerged. Next, the chapter turns to specific managerial issues faced by pension systems. This discussion focuses on both the investment side of pensions and the often-neglected benefits side. The chapter concludes with a section on the importance of public pension management to meeting governmental commitments and to ensuring the overall financial health of jurisdictions.

16.2   Types of Pensions

There are two major types of pensions, defined benefit (DB) plans and defined contribution (DC) plans. The DB model has been and continues to be the dominate pension model in the public sector, whereas the private sector has increasingly opted for the DC model. Despite the dominance of DB, the DC approach has garnered substantial interest — and in a few cases, action — in the public sector in recent years. As will be discussed, both plans have positive and negative attributes. In addition, several pension hybrid plans (i.e., pension plans with both DB and DC characteristics) that have emerged in the public sector will be discussed.

In considering pension plans, it is important to bear in mind their underlying financial mechanism. For example, the Kansas Public Employees Retirement System (KPERS, 2002) offers the following simple conceptualization of the financial mechanism behind the operation of both DB and DC plans (see also Findlay, 1997):

$$B = C + I - E$$

Where B stands for benefits paid, C stands for contributions (employee, employer, or both), I stands for income from investments, and E stands for plan administration expenses. As this formula suggests, employee retirement income (*B*) is a product of *C* and *I*, minus the costs of administering the pension system (*E*). Importantly, each variable in this formula applies to — but differs significantly in — all types of pension plans. In other words, "This is an equation that is always and everywhere true and cannot be avoided by changing plan designs" (KPERS, 2002, ii). Given this, reference will be made to the formula in the following discussion which is limited to a description of the various retirement plans and to their respective advantages and disadvantages (Managerial issues like determining benefits and plan funding will be discussed in Section 16.3.).

16.2.1 Defined Benefit (DB) Pension Plans

Defined benefit (DB) pension plans are the dominant pension model in the public sector: approximately 90% of government workers are covered by DB plans. Under a DB plan, an employee's retirement benefit (*B*) is calculated by a predetermined formula which normally includes employees' age, salary, and years of service. In other words, *B* is *defined*: employees who are vested in a DB plan can expect a specific retirement benefit based upon their plan's specific benefit formula. Vesting is a requirement for employees to work for a specified number of years (typically 5 years, but maybe as high as 10 years) before being entitled to pension benefits upon retirement or the funds contributed by the employee if leaving employment before retirement.

In most cases, *C* includes contributions from both employer and employees. *I* is determined by the returns on investment achieved by the plan sponsor who is responsible for investing and managing (either directly with system employees, or indirectly with hired advisors) the plan's assets. *E* is determined by the costs incurred by the plan sponsor in the course of administering the program (i.e., both investment and benefits management costs). Importantly, the *B* an employee is entitled to under a DB plan is not affected by government's contributions (*C*) to the pension fund, the performance of the fund's investments (*I*), nor the expenses (*E*) incurred by the plan sponsor: "The retirement benefit must be paid, either from accumulations in the employee retirement fund (contributions made through the work years plus interest earned on those contributions) or, if they are not sufficient, from current payments into the retirement system" (Mikesell, 2003, 604). As this suggests, DB plans favor the employees' rights to benefits over problems employers may encounter in funding the plan (Cayer, 1995).

There are several advantages to DB plans. From the employee's perspective, DB plans are attractive because they offer the security of a known retirement benefit: *B*s paid to employees do not fluctuate with

C, I, or *E* (Eitelberg, 1997). Second, by considering an employee's years of service and highest salary in calculating benefits, DB plans reward long-term service more than DC plans. Oftentimes, DB plans also grant automatic cost of living adjustments (COLA) or other *ad hoc* benefit enhancements. This is beneficial from the employee's perspective since it helps thwart the effects of inflation on retirement income (Crane, 1995).

From the employer's perspective, DB plans pool assets into reserve funds that are controlled by professional money managers — again, either employed "in house" or externally contracted — which, in turn, can result in greater returns (*I*) on investment (Bill Custer, as cited in Cranford, 1993). This pooling also is advantageous because it creates large plans, thereby enabling plan sponsors to enjoy economies of scale. This is apparent in DB expenses estimated by the National Association of State Retirement Administrators (NASRA) to average around 0.25 percent of plan assets (NASRA, 2003). Finally, DB plans offer an effective human resources tool for attracting and retaining high-quality employees (NASRA, 2003).

Conversely, DB plans are criticized — but not without exception (see Table 16.2) — for a variety of reasons. Perhaps most often cited is the lack of benefit portability for plan members. This can discourage job changes that might be beneficial to the employee and/or the employer (Daley, 1998). Second, since DB plans fix employees' retirement benefits

Table 16.2   Common Myths Regarding Defined Benefit Plans

- The public sector should convert to defined contribution plans, as the private sector has.
- Defined contribution plans are better because they offer greater portability than defined benefit plans.
- Defined contribution plans are better because they allow employees to manage retirement assets themselves.
- An employee must spend his or her entire career with the same employer to benefit from a defined benefit plan.
- Public employees need to worry about politicians mishandling their funds, creating unfunded liabilities, and cutting benefits.
- Defined contribution plans cost less than defined benefit plans.
- Workers want a defined contribution plan as their primary retirement benefit.
- Workers in defined contribution plans will receive substantially higher benefits than those offered by defined benefit plans.

Source: The National Association of State Retirement Administrators (NASRA). (2003). *Myths and Misperceptions of Defined Benefit and Defined Contribution Plans*. Baton Rouge, LA: NASRA. Available at: http://www.nasra.org/resources/myths%20 and%20misperceptions.pdf (Accessed May 27, 2004).

according to formulas, there is no potential for employees to achieve greater retirement income that *might be* gained through individually-controlled retirement accounts. For plan sponsors, the fact that DB plans guarantee certain B levels means that employers assume the risk associated with adequately funding the DB plan so as to meet their pension obligations. This is exacerbated by fluctuating investment returns (I) and changing actuarial assumptions which impact required employer contributions (C) from year to year. Finally, some contend that DB plans are outmoded, "20th-century dinosaurs" that no longer meet the needs of an increasingly mobile workforce (Todd, 1997). Since non-vested employees have no right to the plan sponsor's contributions, the benefits of a DB plan are smaller for non-career employees. This would suggest that a key objective of DB plans (i.e., to attract and reward talented employees) can be undermined (Todd, 1997).

16.2.2   Defined Contribution (DC) Pension Plans

The late 1990s witnessed impressive stock market returns, particularly for those investing in speculative Internet stocks and in the broader technology sector. Many employees covered under the predictable but fixed benefit levels of DB plans found the prospects of large, seemingly limitless returns on investments available under DC plans to be quite alluring. This is not terribly surprising since, as Sostek (2004) suggests, employee interest in DC plans tends to mirror the Dow Jones Index: interest in DC plans waxes as the Dow rises and wanes as the Dow falls (see also Maggs, 2004; Findlay, 1997). So, combined with ongoing efforts to limit government's long-term liabilities and pension-related administrative costs, the returns of the 1990s have focused greater attention on DC plans in the public sector in recent years (Frank, Condon, Dunlop, and Rothman, 2000).

DC plans differ from DB plans in that employees' retirement benefits are variable (undefined) as opposed to fixed (defined). In a DC plan, employers and employees make regular contributions (C) to individual accounts which are held for each employee. Contribution levels vary, but are normally set at a fixed percentage of an employee's salary. As such, C varies with individual employee earnings in DC plans. These contributions then are individually invested by the employees in a variety of investment options which are usually put together by the employer, pension system, or third-party financial services provider (KPERS, 2002). The accumulation of employer and employee contributions (C) in individual employee accounts and the returns realized through the investment of those account assets (I) determine employee retirement benefits (B). Importantly, the effect of administrative expenses (E) under the DC approach *does* have an impact on *B*: the costs (*E*) associated with individually selected investments (e.g., fund management fees) is subtracted from the investment returns, thus affecting *B*. In sum, there is no guaranteed benefit paid by the employer upon an employee's retirement, but neither is there an upward limit on how large the fund can grow or, conversely, how far it can decrease.

There are a number of commonly cited advantages of DC plans. The primary advantage cited for DC over DB plans is portability. Under DB plans, employees who have not yet vested in a system's plan are entitled only to their own plan contributions and earnings should they decide to leave employment of the plan sponsor. For younger and more mobile segments of the workforce who tend to change jobs more often, this can entail significant retirement income losses over the course of a working career (Frank, Condon, Dunlop, and Rothman, 2000). In contrast, DC plans typically have a much shorter vesting period (e.g., a one-year vesting period is most common, and some offer immediate vesting). Assuming that the employee is vested, should he or she decide to change employers, both the employer and employee contributions (*C*) and investment returns (*I*) belong to the employee and can be moved (i.e., "rolled over") into their new employer's DC plan or, if the new employer does not have a DC plan, into an individual retirement account (IRA).

DC plans have other positive characteristics. For example, the plans tend to be easy for employees to comprehend: they know exactly how much retirement savings have been earmarked for them (Sonnanstine, Murphy, and Zorn, 2003). In what may be both an advantage and disadvantage, DC plans offer employees more investment choices for their retirement savings. On the negative side, this can be confusing or overwhelming to employees. On the positive side, this investment flexibility offers the potential for higher retirement benefits based upon high investment performance. Together, proponents of DC plans argue that these DC plan characteristics improve employers' ability to attract and retain qualified workers (Lachance, Mitchell, and Smetters, 2003).

For employers, DC plans are advantageous because they offer funding (*C*) predictability since funding requirements do not change with actuarial assumptions and market performance (Frank, Condon, Dunlop, and Rothman, 2000). This eliminates the prospects of unfunded pension liabilities for the employer since retirement benefits are paid annually. In contrast, when investments (*I*) go South or when fiscal stress prevents regular employer contributions to a DB's pension fund, the employer is still on the hook for providing benefits (*B*) specified by the plan. DC plans also are attractive to governments because they are thought to have lower administrative expenses (*E*) since they do not require actuarial and money management consultants (Petersen, 2002; Frank, Condon, Dunlop, and

Rothman, 2000). Finally, DC plans are attractive from an intergenerational equity perspective. According to Michigan Treasurer Doug Roberts, "Instead of promising new employees a new benefit and amortizing that over 40 years with the next generation's money, this is a way to be honest" (quoted in Lemov, 1997, p. 42).

On the other hand, DC plans have potential downsides. DC plans often are criticized for making employees assume risk: their retirement security is determined by the investment decisions they themselves make. Such a situation can create employee concern and confusion over how to invest retirement funds which, in turn, can lead to anxiety and uncertainty about retirement security. As suggested by Daley (1998), this can have potentially deleterious effects on employee motivation and productivity. DC plans also have no mechanisms like automatic COLAs for retirees or *ad hoc* benefit increases like DB often do. Thus, retirement security under DC plans can be eroded by the effects of inflation. Another important problem with DC plans is that they require relatively unsophisticated public employees (financially speaking) to make important investment decisions. Public employees may have a tendency towards risk aversion which can make them "recklessly conservative" when it comes to making retirement investment decisions (Frank, Condon, Dunlop, and Rothman, 2000). This can have serious consequences on public employees' retirement security.

16.2.3   Pension Hybrids

While public pensions are normally classified as either DB or DC, there are in fact a variety of pension plans available in the public sector. Seldom do governments offer solely DB or DC plans. Instead, a variety of retirement income options are made available by government employers to their employees. These pension "hybrids" include combination plans, cash balance plans, pension balance plans, deferred compensation plans, and deferred retirement option programs (or "DROP" plans).

16.2.3.1   Combination Plans

First, a number of governments have adopted pension plans that include both DB and DC components. These "combination plans" attempt to balance the security and safety of a DB plan with the earnings potential and portability of DC plans. This is accomplished by directing the employer's contribution to a traditional DB plan and the employee's contribution to a DC-type plan.

One example of such a combination plan comes from the state of Oregon. Facing fiscal strain and mounting unfunded pension obligations,

Oregon reformed its state pension plan in 2004. The state's previous DB plan was replaced with a plan combining both DB and DC features: the state's contributions flow into a traditional DB plan with a guaranteed retirement benefit, while employees' contributions flow into a portable, individually-controlled DC plan (Sostek, 2004). Similar plans are in place in other jurisdictions (Crane, 1995), including a plan for teachers in the state of Washington (Lemov, 1998). In general, this approach is attractive because it attempts to offer "the best of both worlds" (Sostek, 2004, 30): the security of DB and the portability and potential for higher yields of DC.

16.2.3.2 Cash Balance Plans

Another approach that has received considerable attention in recent years is the "cash balance" pension plan. While cash balance plans are more common in the private sector, several examples can be found in the public sector, including the state of Nebraska Public Employee Retirement System (Sostek, 2004) and the Texas Municipal Retirement System (Owens, 1999). A cash balance plan is a form of DB plan, but one that takes on certain DC plan characteristics (Owens, 1999). Under a cash balance plan, employees receive benefits credits (i.e., a percentage of pay) based upon years of service or, in some cases, years of service plus age (Green, 2003a). The employer sets up individual employee retirement accounts just like in a DC plan. However, these individual accounts are hypothetical or "phantom" accounts (Crane, 1995) since the employer's actual pension plan contributions are determined actuarially (i.e., sufficient contributions to cover future benefits), pooled into a pension fund, and invested collectively as in a DB plan (Green, 2003a). Thus, employee "accounts" track the hypothetical cash value of an employee's pension benefit. This cash balance is the defined retirement benefit the employee is entitled to.

Normally, employers guarantee a certain return on the funds earmarked for employees' cash balance accounts regardless of actual investment performance. In the public sector, earnings in excess of the guaranteed return are considered profit that flows back to the employer. In the public sector, earnings excess of the guaranteed return can be used to reduce the employer's contributions or, perhaps, to enhance employee benefits.

Employees might prefer the cash balance approach because, like a DC plan, the employee is entitled to take the full "cash balance" (i.e., employer and employee contributions plus earned interest) with them when they leave employment. On the downside, cash balance plans tend to favor younger workers whose cash balances grow larger due to interest earned on contributions made early in their careers (Anonymous, 2003), plus cash balance plans have no multiplier effect like traditional DB plans to reward long-serving employees. In fact, concerns about potential age discrimination effects of cash balance plans have led to legal action. The most visible of these suits was the case of *Cooper versus The IBM Personal Pension Plan* (2003), in which the court ruled that the formulas used in IBM's cash balance plan illegally discriminated against older workers. The court in an earlier cash balance case, *Eaton versus Onan Corporation* (2000) came to the opposite conclusion, ruling that the employer's cash balance plan was legal. Thus, there is some uncertainty about how to ensure that the formulas used in cash balance plans are legal (Barker and O'Brien, 2004), but Weisberg and Vanesse (2003) argue that, on the larger question of plan legality, cash balance plans themselves still should be legal.

16.2.3.3   Pension Equity Plans

Related to the cash balance plans are "pension equity plans." A pension equity plan (sometimes called a life cycle pension plan; see Crane, 1995) is a form of DB plan that expresses an individual employee's pension benefit in terms of lump-sum value payable as either a lump sum or as an annuity (Green, 2003b). Typically, a pension equity plan establishes annual accrual rates (percentages of earnings) that increase with employees' age. When an employee retires or leaves employment, he or she is entitled to a lump sum benefit, calculated by summing the earned accrual rates and multiplying that sum by the employee's final average salary (FAS). So, for example, a plan might specify that employees 30 years of age and younger receive an annual accrual rate of 2.0 percent, employees between 31 and 40 years old receive an accrual rate of 4.0 percent, employees between 41 and 50 years old receive a rate of 6.0 percent, employees 51 to 60 years old receive a rate 8.0 percent, and employees 61 and older receive a rate of 10.0 percent. Assuming that an employee began work at age 26 and retired at age 65, he or she would have earned 245 accrual rates. If the employee's FAS is $50,000, then he or she would be entitled to a lump-sum benefit equal to 245 percent of FAS, or $122,500 (245 percent * $50,000).

Pension equity plans are desirable in that they (like cash balance plans) allow employees to know the current value of their retirement benefits. Also, since pension equity plans' accrual rates typically rise with employee age, there is a built-in adjustment for age and, since the final benefit is calculated using FAS, there is a built-in inflation protection for the employee (Green, 2003b). On the downside, pension equity plans may produce lump-sum benefits that are substantially lower than what would be produced under the lifetime monthly benefits of a traditional DB plan.

16.2.3.4 Deferred Compensation Plans

Many pension systems support plans that allow employees to defer a portion of their current compensation tax-free until retirement. Normally, these deferred compensation or "salary reduction" plans are offered as a voluntary benefit without employer contributions, although there are some important exceptions. Typically, participants' contributions to deferred compensation plans are made automatically through pre-tax payroll deductions.

There are several sections of the United States Tax Code that authorize deferred compensation plans, including 401(k), 403(b), and 457. 401(k) plans allow employees to defer compensation on a pre-tax basis and may also allow employer contributions. State and local governments can no longer establish 401(k) plans, but if such plans were in place prior to 1986 (i.e., before passage of the Tax Reform Act of 1986 prohibited new state and local government 401(k) plans) then they were "grandfathered" and allowed to continue. 403(b) plans, often referred to as "tax sheltered annuities," are available only to certain non-profit organizations (i.e., charitable entities that are tax-exempt under 501(c)(3) of the Tax Code), public schools, colleges, and universities, and public hospitals. These plans operate much like 401(k) plans, with employees deferring portions of their pre-tax compensation. The deferred salary goes into individual accounts in employer-sponsored plans where it grows tax-free until distributed. In some cases the 403(b) plan may be the primary pension benefit for government employees. This is often the case, for example, for higher education employees participating in optional (i.e., non-DB) retirement programs. Finally, 457 plans are the main deferred compensation vehicle used by state and local governments (GAO, 1996). 457 plans allow employees to defer 100% of their gross compensation or an annual dollar limit (e.g., $12,000 in 2003, $13,000 in 2004, $14,000 in 2005, and $15,000 in 2006), whichever is less.

16.2.3.5 Deferred Retirement Option Program (DROP)

A final retirement benefit option is known as the Deferred Retirement Option Program (DROP). DROP plans offer an additional retirement benefit to employees eligible or nearing eligibility for retirement. These plans were initiated in response to concerns over losing experienced employees in critical areas (Daley, 2002). Upon entering a DROP, the employer freezes the employee's retirement benefits formula (in other words, they gain no additional work service credits) at the current rate, but the employee continues working for a specified period of time (e.g., 5 years). The monthly retirement benefit that the employee would be entitled to if he or she had actually retired is deposited (i.e., "dropped") into a DROP account where it earns a guaranteed rate of interest. At the end of the DROP (i.e., when the employee actually retires), the employee receives his or her normal retirement benefit, calculated at the same rate as when they entered the DROP, plus the funds that have accumulated in their DROP account.

In theory, DROP plans represent an attractive human resources strategy for retaining valued employees nearing retirement. In practice, however, DROPs have created a good deal of controversy. Two examples are particularly noteworthy. First, Milwaukee County, Wisconsin, ran into trouble with its DROP plan. The county's personnel director, Gary Dobbert, who designed the city's DROP plan, assured county officials that the DROP plan could be added to the county's pension plan at no additional cost (Walsh, 2004). The lofty guaranteed returns for DROP accounts and the absence of time limits for DROP participation resulted, in some cases, in million-dollar payouts for retirees. In 2004, a criminal investigation into the pension case led to one felony conviction for misconduct in office and two misdemeanor convictions for Dobbert. The second example comes from the city of Houston, Texas. There, city officials had a multi-billion dollar shortfall in their pension system in 2004. While there were several pension design issues that combined to create the shortfall (e.g., investment losses, benefits enhancements, questionable actuarial advice, etc.), a main culprit was the city's DROP (Feldstein, 2004) which, as in Milwaukee, guaranteed high interest returns regardless of actual investment performance. An actuarial study concluded that hundreds of Houston employees would be eligible for million dollar DROP payouts (Walsh, 2004b). Compounding Houston's problems was a newly-passed (2003) state constitutional amendment barring municipalities from lowering pension benefits already earned by employees. In May 2004, however, Houston voters gave city officials a reprieve when a ballot measure, Proposition 1, passed (with 73 percent of the vote) allowing the city to opt out of the state's constitutional amendment. City officials are now working on a plan to put their pension system on a sound footing.

Rather than sounding the death knell for DROP plans, the Milwaukee and Houston cases serve as stark reminders of the importance of sound financial planning and management in the area of pensions.

16.2.4 Defined Benefit versus Defined Contribution: Which is Better? For Whom?

Finally, assuming that pension participants' interests are (or at least should be) the fundamental concern of public pension systems, a fundamental management question is: "How do pension plan members fare under DB versus DC plans?" This question becomes all the more salient as governments consider reforming their pension systems. A report by the United States General Accounting Office (GAO, 1999) shows widespread interest among the states for jettisoning DB plans in favor of DC plans. While it is true that there is interest, wholesale change has occurred in only one state — Michigan. In 1996, Michigan scrapped its DB plan for new state employees (and existing employees who opted to switch) in favor of a DC plan (Lemov, 1997). West Virginia, too, adopted a DC plan in the early 1990s, but its plan is limited to the state's public school teachers.

To date, there is only spotty evidence about how pension members fare under DB versus DC plans, but the evidence that does exist paints a picture of caution for DC plan advocates. Consider the case of Nebraska. According to Sostek (2004), the state opted for a DC program for state and county works in the mid-1960s. In contrast, the state had adopted a DB plan for its teachers and judges decades earlier. In 2000, a study of the state's pension system found that state and county workers covered by the DC plan earned an average return of 6 percent on their investments, while those covered under the DB plan — whose assets were invested by professional money managers — earned a return of 11 percent (Sostek, 2004). Alarmed by the inequity, Nebraska responded by ending the DC plan for all new hires and creating a cash balance plan for them and for existing employees who opted to switch from the old DC plan.

16.3 Managing Public Pensions

Public pension management concerns both investment management (e.g., system oversight, selecting system advisors, determining investment allocations, making actuarial assumptions) and benefits management (e.g., benefits payment, customer service, etc.) (Shen, 1979). While the public administration literature has tended to pay relatively more attention to investment management, benefits management is of no less importance to ensuring a sound pension plan. Since the overwhelming majority of public plans are DB plans, the following discussion will focus primarily (though not exclusively) on managing DB plans.

16.3.1 Managerial Considerations in Pension Fund Investing

Pension systems are responsible for investing billions of dollars annually. The investment policies pension boards develop and pension system staff implement have direct bearing on the health of pension funds.

Miller (1987, 49) offers a concise conceptual framework of the pension investment process:

- An investor's opportunities, constraints, preferences, and capabilities must be identified and specified explicitly in written investment policies.
- Investment opportunities are identified and strategies are formulated and implemented through the purchase of financial securities and related instruments in the marketplace.
- The investor's circumstances, market conditions and relative values of sectors are monitored; results are documented and reported.
- Portfolio adjustments are made in response to new objectives and changing circumstances and results.

While this represents a straightforward conception of investment management, there a number of considerations that affect pension systems' performance.

16.3.1.1 Pension Board Composition

Public pension systems are normally governed by a board or commission. Typically, members of pension boards are a mix of members who are elected by plan participants, appointed by elected officials, and ex-officio members (Zorn, 1997; Coronado, Engen, and Knight, 2003). In some jurisdictions, the pension system may be overseen by an individual such as a state or city treasurer, or by an administrative unit such as the human resources or finance department (Cayer, 1995). Still, the board or commission format is most common. According to Eitelbrg (1997), pension boards normally average in size from to five to nine members. The composition and size of pension boards are important considerations. For example, the long-term interests of plan participants (as represented by their elected board members) may be in conflict with the short-term political interests of politically-appointed board members (Coronado, Engen, and Kinght, 2003). Also, research shows that boards composed of member-trustees (i.e., board members who are themselves participants in the plan) have an impact on funds' actuarial assumptions (Mitchell and Hsin, 1997). As for board size, research suggests that board size is an important consideration: systems with larger boards tend to invest more in equities and international holdings, and they are more likely to have in-house management of fund holdings (Useem and Mitchell, 2000). Smaller boards tend to perform better (Useem and Mitchell, 2000).

Regardless of board size or composition, pension members/trustees have a fiduciary responsibility to represent the interests plan members.

In the private sector, the fiduciary standard is a requirement of federal law, the Employment Retirement Income Security Act of 1974 (ERISA). Since public employers were exempted from ERISA, their fiduciary responsibilities are derived from their respective jurisdiction's laws and regulations (which often use ERISA as a guideline). Basically, serving as a fiduciary means that board members' actions must be made in the interests of plan participants. Nationwide Retirement Solutions (2003, 8), a private provider of public pension services, has identified five basic principles that fiduciaries should follow:

- Act solely in the interest of the plan's participants and beneficiaries
- Maintain the plan and its assets for the exclusive purpose of providing benefits
- Act with care, skill, prudence and diligence as a prudent person would act in a similar circumstance
- Diversify the plan's assets to minimize risk unless it is prudent to do otherwise. For a DC plan, this rule means that you must provide sufficient investment choices to allow participants to diversify their account balance to minimize risk
- Maintain the plan in accordance with governing laws and the plan documentation.

In some cases, however, members of pension boards may lack financial expertise (Miller, 1987). This potentially undermines the capacity of boards to meet their fiduciary obligations. To counter this, jurisdictions may develop required qualifications (e.g., financial management, experience) for their board members. Jurisdictions may also attempt to ensure their boards have the capacity to meet their obligations by ensuring all board members receive a thorough orientation when first appointed or elected and ongoing financial education throughout their tenure on the board. As this suggests, the size of boards and the composition and capacity of members are important considerations.

16.3.1.2 Pension Plan Investment Policy

A major role of boards governing pension systems is setting investment policy for their respective pension plans. Simply put, "an investment policy is the retirement plan board's strategy for developing an asset base to support the plan's current and future benefit commitments" (Eitelberg, 1997, 35). Given differences in past investment performance, assets and liabilities, tolerances for investment risk, pension management capacity, and political circumstances, pension policies can be expected to vary from jurisdiction to jurisdiction and from plan to plan. Generally speaking, though, investment policies perform several important purposes, including (Greifer, 2002, 36):

- To formalize investment goals
- To establish a method for determining and expressing the pension board's investment philosophy and risk tolerance to both staff and third parties
- To clearly demonstrate "due diligence" (that is, that the pension system adheres to a prudent set of procedures)
- To serve as a foundation for internal controls
- To provide guidance to staff and third parties in order to ensure both proper execution of the investment strategy and legal compliance

As this list suggests, pension policies establish the operational framework for pension systems. In fact, so important are pension investment policies that they have been described as being the "linchpin of public pension investment programs" (Greifer, 2002, 36).

A particularly significant component of an investment policy is the asset allocation policy. Asset allocation refers to the broad categories of investments (stocks, bonds, cash, etc.) in which pension funds will invest their assets. Investment policies, which are now ubiquitous in the public pension world (Greifer, 2002), are created by pension boards through an evaluation and development process that varies in terms of analytical rigor (Greifer, 2001; Eitelberg, 1997). In this process, boards examine the resources needed to meet pension plan requirements (e.g., benefits payments, reducing unfunded liabilities, plan expenses) over the near-term (e.g., the next ten years), analyze the risk and return characteristics of various asset classes and asset-class combinations, and adopt an appropriate policy. The importance of asset allocation is evident in research findings that suggest it explains approximately 90 percent of the variation in pension investment performance (Greifer, 2001; Frank, Condon, Dunlop, and Rothman, 2000). It is important to note that the invest policy and its asset allocation policy set the parameters for investing — decisions as to the actual investments made within these asset categories are normally left to pension fund managers (as discussed in more detail below). Also, boards developing investment policies are, in some cases, limited by "legal lists" which are statutory or regulatory restrictions on the types of investments that pension systems are allowed to make. Given the negative effect such restrictions can have on investment returns (e.g., Peng, 2004), most legislative bodies have removed these restrictions in recent years (Petersen, 2002; Lemov, 1998; Peng, 2004).

From a practical standpoint, Greifer (2002) argues that best practice in investment policy includes policies that have breadth, depth, and clarity.

Breadth refers to the comprehensiveness of investment policy, including coverage of the following categories: statement of goal, purpose, and/or mission; identification of decision makers; statement on managing portfolio risk; statement on managing the risk of individual investments; statement of performance measurement; guidelines for money managers; guidelines for other professionals (e.g., investment consultants); legal standards (e.g., the prudent person standard); cost management; and transacting or brokering trades (Greifer, 2002, 37). Depth refers to detailed guidance for these broad categories. Finally, clarity simply means that the investment policy is written and communicated in such a way that it is easily read, understood, and implemented. As this all suggests, investment policies "play a critical role in both developing and executing investment programs of public pension systems" (Greifer, 2002, 40).

16.3.1.3   Investment Strategies: Active versus Passive

Whereas pension boards define investment policy, the actual investment of assets into specific holdings within classes is typically left to professional money managers. These managers may be staff members of the pension system (i.e., "in house" managers) or externally hired money managers. Regardless, pension managers also are bound to adhere to the "prudent person" standard, meaning that investments are made with the care, skill, and diligence of a prudent person (Zorn, 1997; Mikesell, 2003; Petersen, 1993; Eitelberg, 1997). As reported by Mikesell (2003, 608), the GFOA defines "prudent investments" as those meeting tests of creditworthiness (do the investments meet the retirement system's credit standards?), liquidity (are investment maturities matched to the pension system's cash needs?), and market rate of return (are investment yields commensurate with a recognized level of risk?).

Generally speaking, there are two approaches to pension investing: active and passive. An active investment strategy means that pension fund managers focus effort on selecting high-performing sectors of the market and making individual investments (i.e., within the asset allocation limits of their plans' investment policies). The goal of such an approach is to "beat the market," that is to produce investment returns that outstrip measures of overall market return (e.g., Dow Jones, Standard and Poor's 500, and/or Russell 5000 averages). In contrast, proponents of passive investing argue that pension systems are wiser to follow a passive strategy, investing for example in index funds which mirror the overall market or specific sectors (e.g., small- or mid-cap stocks, technology or biomedical sectors, etc.) of the market. The underlying rationale for this approach is the Efficient Market Hypothesis (EMH) which suggests that investors will not be able to systematically outperform the market and that price variations in markets are basically "random walks" (Adrangi and Shank, 1999; Miller, 1987). If this holds, then hiring money mangers, who attempt to bring market analyses to bear upon investment selection, adds little to the information already reflected in equity prices (Adrangi and Shank, 1999). And, as Petersen (1993) notes, research suggests that, on average, actively managed funds have underperformed the market. Given this, it is not surprising that interest among pension systems in shifting to passive investing has grown in recent years.

Whether funds are invested actively or passively, pensions systems have faced increased demands in recent years. As mentioned previously, a variety of political, economic, and demographic forces have strained government's resources. Such fiscal stress often leads to pressure on pension systems to produce greater returns on investments: healthy returns on investment help to hold down contributions required of plan sponsors and participants to fund pension benefits (Zorn, 1997; Petersen, 1993). In contrast, lower returns require greater contributions by plan sponsors if the plans are to remain adequately funded. This, in turn, may force budgetary tradeoffs as legislative bodies appropriate required resources, and/or may require raising taxes in order to meet financial obligations.

The practical implication of this is that pension systems have invested increasingly larger portions of their assets in equities. This marks an important investment change for public pensions systems which have traditionally assumed a less aggressive investment strategy. Indeed, concerns over investment risk once led most pension systems to invest conservatively — to the point of being "cautious to a fault" (Petersen, 1993) — in government bonds. But, being long-term investors, pension systems actually have a high tolerance for risk: "[O]ne should not lose sight of the fact that pension systems are long-term investors, can absorb risk like few others, and that the long-term results favor a very heavy allocating to equities and other high-yielding investments" (Petersen, 1993).

Government's position as a long-term investor, coupled with the need to produce greater returns on investment, has had an impact on pension investments. For example, Table 16.3 juxtaposes the average percentages invested by state and local government pension systems in various investments categories in FY 2002 and FY 1993. As the table shows, pension systems have shifted a larger portion of their investment portfolios to corporate stocks, growing from roughly 33 percent in fiscal year 1993 to roughly 38 percent in fiscal year 2002. What really stands out, however, is the increase in foreign investment from zero percent in 1993 to almost 12 percent in 2002. Once taboo for public pension funds, foreign investments are increasingly viewed as an opportunity for strong returns and a tool for investment diversification. And with such diversification comes a hedge against investment risk: "By investing in multiple asset classes, the plan

Table 16.3   State and Local Government Pension Investments

Investment	2001–2002		1992–1993	
	Receipts	*%*	*Receipts*	*%*
Total securities	$1,875,395,501	86.9	$774,844,444	84.2
Government securities	225,584,917	10.5	203,452,928	22.1
Federal Government	224,762,717	10.4	202,923,476	22.0
United States Treasury	153,870,084	7.1	164,960,892	17.9
Federal agency	70,892,633	3.3	37,962,584	4.1
State and local government	822,200	0.0	529,452	0.1
Nongovernmental	1,649,810,584	76.5	571,391,516	62.1
Corporate bonds	352,193,553	16.3	174,446,987	19.0
Corporate stocks	814,835,143	37.8	301,315,623	32.7
Mortgages	20,765,586	1.0	19,458,912	2.1
Funds held in trust	70,422,530	3.3	0	0.0
Foreign and international	254,662,228	11.8	0	0.0
Other nongovernmental	136,931,544	6.4	76,169,994	8.3
Other investments	172,832,778	8.0	68,813,123	7.5
Real property	42,908,542	2.0	23,635,084	2.6
Miscellaneous investments	129,924,236	6.0	45,178,039	4.9

Source: United States Census Bureau (2002). *2002 State and Local Government Employee-Retirement Systems.* Washington, DC: United States Census Bureau. (See Table 4: Cash and Investments by State & Local Government). Data are in thousands of dollars. Available at: http://www.census.gov/govs/retire02.html (for 2002 data) and http://www.census.gov/govs/retire02.html (for 1993 data). (Accessed June 11, 2004.)

sponsor is attempting to cushion the portfolio from market volatility in any single asset class" (Eitelberg, 1997, 37).

16.3.1.4   Outside Advisers

As mentioned earlier, pension systems often hire external expertise to assist with the administration of their various plans. This might occur in those jurisdictions, particularly small local governments, where pension systems lack the expertise needed to effectively manage pension investments and benefits. Even in the largest pension systems, the advice and expertise of external financial advisors is routinely utilized. When and where external expertise is required, the typical approach is to acquire it through a competitive request for proposal (RFP) process. In a RFP, the jurisdiction publishes an announcement describing the specific financial services needed. The services desired can range from simple advice to full discretionary management of a plan's investment portfolio. The GFOA (2000) has adopted a policy statement on the selection of outside investment advisors. The GFOA statement stresses the need for a merit-based RFP approach in which the responsibilities of the external advisor are clearly articulated, the criteria for evaluating proposals are determined in advance, the appropriate pool of potential candidates is identified, due diligence is performed on all candidates, an appropriate recommendation is made to the pension board regarding selection, and a process for ongoing evaluation of the advisor(s) selected is established.

While the favored approach is the merit-based RFP process, the selection of outside advisors can be marred by political considerations. A good example of the controversy that can be created when political considerations clash with the standards of professional pension administrators comes from the state of Ohio. In 2003, the Ohio state legislature considered a bill, HB 227, that, if passed, would require the state's pension systems to direct 50 to 70 percent of their contracts with investment advisors to Ohio-based companies. The idea, reflecting a local preference as discussed in the next section, was to increase the profits of Ohio-based businesses. HB 227 drew immediate opposition from Ohio pension administrators. The Ohio Retirement Study Council issued a recommendation against HB 227, noting that its requirements "mark a significant departure from well-established legislative principles and past precedents that have guided the investment operations (ORSC, 2003) of the retirement systems over decades" (ORSC, 2003, 12). Ohio administrators were joined in their opposition by the National Association of State Retirement Administrators (NASRA) which issued a letter opposing the proposed changes to Ohio state elected officials.

16.3.1.5   Social and Economically Targeted Investing

While pension system administrators serve as fiduciaries for plan participants, occasions arise when they may be pressured or, in some cases, required to invest funds in ways that promote a government's socioeconomic goals. An abundance of anecdotal evidence exists on socioeconomic investing (e.g., Romano, 1995; Leigland, 1992; Coronado, Engen, and Knight, 2003), suggesting that pressure on pension administrators to engage in this type of investing has increased in recent years (Leigland, 1992).

Socioeconomic investing creates controversy because focus is removed from the total return strategy of investing (Leigland, 1992; Cayer, Martin, and Ifflander, 1986). Given their fiduciary responsibilities, pressure for this type of targeted investing can make pension fund administrators, who are concerned with maximizing returns, "as nervous as a bridegroom at a shotgun wedding" (Eitelberg, 1994, 40).

Socioeconomic or "public purpose" investing takes on a variety of forms. Probably the best known is social investing. Social investing involves making investment decisions according to whether investments promote a social purpose or objective: it attempts to penalize activities investors wish to discourage and support activities they wish to encourage (Cayer, Martin, and Ifflander, 1986). Within this category of investments one can include the well-known prohibitions on investing, or "blacklisting" (Petersen, 1993), in South Africa during the era of apartheid. More recently, the California Public Employees Retirement System (CALPERS) announced that its investment managers had to take into account a country's political stability, financial transparency, record on labor standards, and workers' rights, resulting in a ban on investment in publicly traded companies in China, India, and several emerging markets (i.e., Indonesia, Thailand, Malaysia, and the Philippines) (Shorrock, 2002).

A second approach, economically targeted investing (ETI), can be defined as "investments that are selected for the economic benefits that they create in addition to the investment return to the employee benefit plan investor" (GAO, 1995, p. 5). The idea of ETI is that pension funds should invest funds within their respective states or localities as a tool for state and local economic development (Coronado, Engen, and Knight, 2003). Eitelberg (1994) describes rationales both for and against ETIs. Arguments in favor of ETIs include economic opportunity (allowing investors to take advantage of narrow "niche" investment opportunities), maintaining independence and control (preempting legislative mandates and maintaining pension system control over investments), and general public good (fulfilling the desire to contribute to the community's economic health). Conversely, arguments in opposition to ETIs stress fiduciary duty (perceptions that ETIs conflict with pension funds' fiduciary duties), staff and administrative reasons (concerns over the amount of staff time associated with running an ETI), resistance to external pressures (fears of losing fund independence), and poor performance and notoriety (ETIs are politically risky because of the attention given to ETI failures relative to successes).

In sum, social and economically target investing represent an important managerial consideration for public pension systems. Such investments create tension between public pension fund administrators, whose focus is on serving plan participants, and public officials and interests who seek to pursue substantive policy objectives (e.g., environmental protection, social equity, etc.) through pension investments. And, importantly, research exists suggesting that these types of investments can lead to a sacrifice of plan assets (e.g., Romano, 1995; Coronado, Engen, and Knight, 2003).

16.3.1.6   Pension Funding

As discussed in Section 16.2, pension benefits (B) are a product of contributions (C), plus returns runs on investments (I), minus the expenses (E) of operating the pension system. To this point, much has been said about I, but C is an equally important consideration. As Table 16.4 shows, governments'

Table 16.4   Contributions from State and Local Government Pension Systems

Year/Level	Total Contributions	From Employees	From State Government	From Local Government	Earnings on investments
2001–2002	$38,792,031	$27,544,022	$17,182,861	$21,609,170	-$72,456,581
State	32,059,268	23,006,094	16,795,329	15,263,939	-63,514,230
Local	6,732,763	4,537,928	387,532	6,345,231	-8,942,351
2000–2001	38,844,791	26,437,534	17,594,431	21,250,360	57,940,554
State	32,621,170	21,893,787	17,136,673	15,484,497	39,773,459
Local	6,223,621	4,543,747	457,758	5,765,863	18,167,095
1999–2000	40,155,114	24,994,468	17,546,723	22,608,391	231,900,075
State	33,846,378	20,665,828	17,179,981	16,666,397	192,833,292
Local	6,308,736	4,328,640	366,742	5,941,994	39,066,783
1998–1999	41,733,650	23,565,910	17,147,617	24,586,033	197,865,311
State	33,467,754	19,786,741	16,878,613	16,589,141	166,415,663
Local	8,265,896	3,779,169	269,004	7,996,892	31,449,648
1997–1998	41,850,145	21,834,567	17,957,604	23,892,541	197,631,263
State	34,620,047	18,334,766	17,619,625	17,000,422	159,182,186
Local	7,230,098	3,499,801	337,979	6,892,119	38,449,077
1996–1997	44,901,913	20,930,879	20,588,392	24,313,521	161,223,433
State	36,893,266	17,435,994	20,170,257	16,723,009	133,689,185
Local	8,008,647	3,494,885	418,135	7,590,512	27,534,248
1995–1996	41,522,538	19,372,415	17,294,964	24,227,574	129,561,810
State	32,986,466	16,406,926	16,896,183	16,090,283	106,926,079
Local	8,536,072	2,965,489	398,781	8,137,291	22,635,731
1994–1995	41,011,466	18,599,641	16,607,351	24,404,115	89,231,680
State	31,608,735	15,721,701	16,230,275	15,378,460	75,967,617
Local	9,402,731	2,877,940	377,076	9,025,655	13,264,063
1993–1994	36,772,434	17,341,286	15,874,213	20,898,221	79,180,260
State	29,116,214	14,738,018	15,521,259	13,594,955	66,219,262
Local	7,656,220	2,603,268	352,954	7,303,266	12,960,998
1992–1993	34,991,684	16,137,931	15,186,886	19,804,798	74,812,951
State	27,493,366	13,431,836	14,820,853	12,672,513	62,178,292
Local	7,498,318	2,706,095	366,033	7,132,285	12,634,659

Source: United States Census Bureau (various years). *State and Local Government Employee-Retirement Systems*. Washington, DC: United States Census Bureau. (See Table 2: Contributions by State & Local Government). Data are in thousands of dollars. Available at: http://www.census.gov/govs/retire.html (Accessed June 11, 2004.)

contributions to state and local pension plans totaled roughly $39 billion in fiscal year 2002. This total was paired with an additional $27.5 billion in employee contributions. The table also shows the steady increase in pension contributions over the years.

While these raw numbers convey a sense of the size of annual public pension contributions, a more salient question concerns the health of pension plans. Historically, public DB plans used "pay-as-you-go" funding, meaning that the money needed to pay pension benefits was raised at the time that employees retired and began to receive their benefits (Cayer, 1995). If, on an annual basis, a government was able to use its appropriations process to make the contributions needed to cover pension benefits (i.e., without gutting other government programs or significantly raising taxes), then its plan was considered to be reasonably healthy. And, in fact, the pay-as-you-go approach worked reasonably well for quite some time. But, in the 1970s, government expenditures for retirement spiked while at the same time the public's resistance to new or increased taxes grew (Mikesell, 2003). Private sector companies also faced pension problems at roughly the same time, with some private pension plans being terminated or becoming insolvent. These private sector problems led to the passage of ERISA in 1974. As mentioned above, state and local governments were exempted form ERISA, but their plans did not elude the scrutiny of the federal government. For example, the U.S. House of Representative issued a 1997 report titled *Pension Task Force Report on Public Retirement Systems*, that was critical of state and local pension plan funding (Dulebohn, 1995). The report, along with the general attention on pension plans generated by ERISA, served as stimuli for public entities to get their pension systems in better financial order.

Increased scrutiny on public pension plans' health saw the pay-as-you-go approach fade as more and more governments adopted forward-funding (variously referred to as advanced, actuarial, reserve, and/or full funding). Here, government's required pension contributions are determined by actuarial estimates, calculated by pension system trustees (i.e., by pension system staff or hired actuaries), of the current year's pension costs (referred to as "normal costs") and the costs for paying off past costs that have not yet been funded (referred to as "unfunded accrued actuarial liabilities," or UAAL) relative to pension fund assets (including actuarially estimated investment gains and losses). These actuarial estimates are derived through various assumptions on factors such as inflation, employee salary increases, employee turnover, employee mortality, and anticipated investment returns (Peng, 2004; Mahoney, 2002; Mikesell, 2003). Pension fund health, then, is normally measured by dividing the present value of a plan's actuarial accrued liabilities (AAL) by the value of its assets (Brainard, 2003; Maggs, 2004). The resulting "funding ratio" is the most recognized measure of

public pension fund health (Brainard, 2003). A plan is considered "fully fun–
ded" if its funding ratio equals one (or 100 percent), "overfunded" if its
funding ratio is greater than one (i.e., it exceeds 100 percent), and "under-
funded" if its funding ratio is less than one (i.e., less than 100 percent).
Importantly, research suggests that pension fund health, as measured by
funding ratios, has steadily improved since the 1970s (Zorn, 1997). For
example, Wilshire Associates (2003) reported that the funding ratio for state
pension plans was 91 percent in 2002 (down from 106 percent in 2001),
while the NASRA and NCTR survey estimated the 2002 figure at 92.9 percent
(Brainard, 2003).

Speaking of actuarial assumptions and funding ratios, it is important to
note that assumptions vary widely from plan to plan, and can vary for the
same plan from actuarial evaluation to actuarial evaluation (the GFOA
(1994) recommends plans perform actuarial evaluations at least biennially).
For example, in the NASRA and NCTR survey, assumed investment returns
ranged from a high of 9 percent (for the New Hampshire Retirement System
and the Arizona Public Safety Personnel System) to a low of 6 percent
(for the Minneapolis Employee Retirement Fund), and assumed rates of
inflation ranged from a high of 7.25 percent (for the District of Columbia
Teachers Retirement System) to a low of 2.5 percent (for the New York City
Teachers System and the New York City Employee Retirement System)
(see Brainard, 2003). These differences are important because they have
direct bearing on plans' funding ratios.

Given this, it is not surprising that, in some instances, governments
have manipulated the actuarial assumptions used in determining their
pension funding obligations (Cayer, 1996; Mikesell, 2003; Mitchell and
Smith, 1994; Maggs, 2004). For example, pension plans may adopt
unrealistic actuarial assumptions which, in turn, reduce their legally required
pension contributions (Mitchell and Smith, 1994). This was precisely the
finding of Chaney, Copley and Stone (2002) who reported that fiscally
stressed state governments operating under balanced budget restrictions
tend to have higher discount rates (i.e., higher assumed rates of return on
plan assets), suggesting that these states use the discount rate to obscure
their levels of underfunding. Such practices produce lowered estimates of
required government contribution levels. For example, Mahoney (2002)
cites GAO figures suggesting that a one-percentage point increase
in assumed rates of investment return can result in a 20- to 25-percent
reduction in required annual contributions. These caveats are important
because they suggest the difficulty of ascertaining pension plans' true
health from funding ratios and of making cross-plan comparisons of pension
fund health.

There are other factors that affect governmental funding of public pension plans. Most notably, research suggests that state and local governments

use deferred pension funding as an approach to meeting short-term budgetary shortfalls (Cayer, 1996). For example, Chaney, Copley, and Stone (2002) found that state governments suffering fiscal stress and operating under balanced budget requirements fund their pension systems at significantly lower levels than other states. Similarly, governments that underfund their pension systems may be encouraged to use the "savings" to fund other government services. One empirical investigation found such a relationship, arguing that state governments with higher levels of pension underfunding offer more services than would be possible if their plans were fully funded — a situation referred to as "fiscal illusion" (Sneed and Sneed, 1997; see also Mahoney, 2002). In those cases where the budgetary shortfall is a temporary or cyclical phenomenon, intentional pension underfunding may make some sense; however, where budgetary stress is the result of structural weaknesses the practice only exacerbates government's financial woes (Peng, 2004). For instance, pension underfunding translates into forgone investment earnings that could have been achieved by pensions funds which, in turn, results in the need for even greater future contributions to make up for lost earnings (Mahoney, 2002).

A recent example of a local government purposefully underfunding its pension system comes from the city of San Diego, CA. There, city officials have intentionally underfunded the city's pension system since 1996 and plan to continue to do so until at least 2009 (Mariani, 2004). The city is using the "savings" to help balance the city's budget. The city's decision and other errors in its financial reports have resulted in bond rating downgrade and the initiation of preliminary investigation into the city's pension operations by the Federal Bureau of Investigation and the Securities and Exchange Commission (Mariani, 2004).

While periods of fiscal stress can cause governments to underfund their pension systems, so too can periods of fiscal prosperity. According to Mason (2003), governments can be tempted to take "funding holidays" — in which pension contributions are dramatically reduced or even eliminated — in years when investments show impressive gains. Or, the availability of additional resources might encourage governments to enhance their pension benefit levels (Peng, 2004; Bergsman, 1995). The problem with this, of course, is that when economic conditions tighten and/or investment returns turn sour governments are on the hook for making the contributions required to pay for the enhanced benefits (Peng, 2004).

Finally, an increasing number of state and local governments have turned to another pension funding mechanism — pension obligation bonds (POBs) — to meet their pension funding obligations. Over roughly the last decade, more than 60 local governments have issued POBs (Lemov, 2003). POB activity also has occurred at the state level, with the state of Illinois, New Jersey, and California floating POBs in recent years (Swope, 2003).

In financial terms, POBs are an arbitrage play (Mason, 2003; Maggs, 2004), meaning that government issuers of POBs attempt to take advantage of the difference between the interest payments on the bonds and the investment returns achieved through the investment of the bond sale proceeds. Using the case of a municipality, Warren (1996, 43) describes the process as follows:

> "A municipality issues bonds (federally taxable because of the arbitrage play) and deposits with its retirement system proceeds equal to the municipality's unfunded accrued actuarial liability (UAAL). The debt service on the bonds replaces annual contributions which the municipality had (or, in some cases, had not) been making to amortize its UAAL."

POBs have become an attractive option for governments facing large unfunded pension obligations because of the low interest rate environment experienced in recent years. If, however, government's investments do not produce returns that outstrip the costs of their bonds, then additional unfunded pension liabilities can arise (Petersen, 2003). As this suggests, many consider POBs to be a risky funding strategy for public pensions.

There is no denying the importance of adequate funding to overall pension fund health. Indeed, seriously underfunded pension funds can spell trouble for governments (e.g., lowered bond ratings, budgetary tradeoffs, etc.), taxpayers (e.g., higher taxes), and pension plan participants and retirees (e.g., concern over retirement security). The point should be made, however, that an underfunded pension system does not necessarily mean that retirees or current employees are in jeopardy of not receiving their benefits: "In fact, substantially all underfunded pension plans are able to meet their current obligations" (Brainard, 2003, 1). What is more, according to Mason (2003), a pension plan with a funding ratio of 70 to 80 percent or better is generally considered to be adequately funded, at least from a credit-rating perspective (i.e., assuming that actuarial assumptions are reasonable). Regardless, public pension plan funding represents a major political, economic, and managerial issue for state and local governments (D'Arcy, Dulebohn, and Oh, 1999).

16.3.2 Managerial Considerations in Pension Benefits Administration

In comparison to the investment side of public pensions, the public administration literature has paid short shrift to the benefits side of pension management. This is a curious phenomenon since pension systems exist in the first place to serve pension plan participants. And, it goes without saying that pension systems face considerable challenges in benefits administration. For example, the Association of Public Pension Fund Auditors (APPFA) released a report in 2003 identifying 25 broad categories of operational risk for public pension systems (APPFA, 2003). These broadly defined risk categories include such things as legislation/legal action/court decisions, staffing (e.g., attracting, training, and retaining employees), enrollment of members, collection and maintenance of member data, and communications with members, to name only a few. Given these risks and the importance of the benefits side of pension system management to overall pension effectiveness, this section considers several important managerial issues associated with pension benefit administration.

16.3.2.1 Payout Formulas

Most often, formulas for determining DB plans are determined by legislative bodies. These formulas determine how much employees will receive in retirement benefits. While there are some variations (see Blostin, 2003), the most common approach to determining DB levels is with a formula taking into account: (1) an employee's final average salary (FAS), which is typically the average of an employee's salary over the last three years of employment; (2) years of service; and (3) a retirement multiplier, which is a percentage of salary figure that varies by plan. FAS and years of service are self-explanatory, but the retirement multiplier deserves elaboration. The retirement multiplier "indicates a percentage of FAS that is earned for each year of service" (State of Wisconsin Retirement Research Committee, 2000, 13). The retirement multiplier generally ranges in the area of two to three percent, depending upon plan. The multiplier can be: graduated to reward longer years of service; higher for public safety workers (e.g., police and fire) who have riskier jobs and shorter careers; and/or higher in jurisdictions whose employees are not covered under Social Security (Brainard, 2003). Seemingly small differences in the multiplier can result in substantial differences in retirement benefits. This can be seen in the following example.

Assume that a pension plan's formula includes: (1) FAS over the final three years of employment; (2) length of service; and (3) a two percent retirement multiplier for general/non-uniformed employees and a two and one-half retirement multiplier for police officers. A general employee who earned $32,000, $35,000, and $38,000 over their last three years of employment (for an average of $35,000) and who worked for 25 years would be entitled to an annual retirement benefit of $17,500 (FAS of $35,000 * .02 retirement multiplier * 25 years of service = $17,500). Assuming that the police officer's FAS and years of service are the same, they would be entitled to a retirement benefit of $21,875 (FAS of $35,000 * .025 retirement multiplier * 25 years of service = $21,875). As this demonstrates, the retirement multiplier is an important component of DB formulas.

While legislative bodies may be responsible for determining benefit formulae, it is the responsibility of pension systems to accurately calculate benefits levels for plan participants. Incorrect calculations may mean that retirees are not receiving the benefits they are entitled to, that is they may be receiving too much or too little in retirement income. In order to mitigate these risks, pension systems need to institute controls such as providing retirees with summary data used in calculating their benefits, developing charts and checklists to assist pension system staff in determining benefits, and routinely testing automated benefits calculations for accuracy (APPFA, 2003). As this suggests, ensuring the accuracy of benefits calculations is a fundamental activity for public employee retirement systems.

16.3.2.2 Customer Service

Another primary benefits-administration consideration for public pension systems is customer service. While pension systems have a number of stakeholders (e.g., legislative bodies, taxpayers, financial advisors, etc.), their *key* stakeholders are the current employees and retirees that make up their respective plan memberships. According to the APPFA (2003, 16), pensions systems face three customer-service risks:

- Risk that various forms/methods of communication with members, retirees, and beneficiaries are not coordinated and consistent
- Risk that system communication, processes, and policies are not customer oriented
- Risk that appeals occur because of inadequate communication among members, employers, the pension system, and third party administrators

To mitigate these risks, pension systems can take a number of steps. For example, the APPFA (2003) recommends pension systems hire an information/communications coordinator, hire a manager of quality assurance or establish a quality assurance team, and develop ongoing quality assurance processes. Systems might also evaluate best practices in pension customer service through such venues as the GFOA's Awards for Excellence program which recognizes excellence and innovations in financial management, including pension administration.

Delivering customer service to pension plan participants occurs in a number of media. For example, most pension systems offer one-on-one counseling for plan participants. Similarly, the use of call centers, where plan participants speak with system staff, is a ubiquitous customer-service feature. In addition to personal telecommunications, systems are also developing automated phone systems and integrated voice recognition (IVR) systems, that allow plan participants round-the-clock interactive access to benefits information. As this suggests, pension systems are taking advantage of technological advances to offer improved customer service. Greifer (2000), for example, describes how the New York State Teachers' Retirement System expanded its access to plan participants through the use of video teleconferencing. Such teleconferencing allows for two-way communication between system staff and participants and allows the system to reach participants in remote locations (saving time and money in the process). Pension systems also are developing web-based tools to offer not only pension plan information, but also to allow participants to execute certain transactions via the Internet. The Teacher Retirement System of Texas, for example, has developed a website that allows members to register for benefits presentations on-line, calculate certain benefits estimates (e.g., service credit purchase calculator), and view streaming video of benefits-related information. In all of these cases the goal is for pension systems to offer consistent, reliable, and readily available information on their pension benefits.

The scope and scale of benefits administration service provided by pension systems is impressive. For example, the California Public Employees' Retirement System (CALPERS, 2003) reported in its *2003 Operations Summary* that (among other things) its staff:

- Completed more than 80,000 retirement estimates
- Processed 20,117 new service retirements and paid out nearly $7 billion in retirement, death, and survivors benefits
- Delivered first benefit checks to 97 percent of new retirees within 30 days of their retirement
- Processed 24,774 requests for refunds and processed them all within 30 days
- Completed 3,872 disability retirement determinations
- Processed 45,529 requests for direct deposit of retirement checks
- Provided counseling services to 51,670 visitors in their eight regional offices
- Held 652 retirement sessions at employer sites
- Conducted nearly 1,600 financial planning seminars and retirement planning workshops

Given the importance of customer service, many pension systems have adopted customer service performance standards. For example, a system might establish a goal of ensuring that new retirees receive their first retirement check within 30 days. Or, a pension system call center might establish a performance standard of answering all calls within 60 seconds. Regardless of the specific standards, the point is that many pension systems have recognized plan participants as customers and, as such, have attempted to provide them with the best service possible.

16.3.2.3 Communications

Governments are beginning to recognize the importance of effectively communicating the value of their benefits to prospective employees, current employees, and retirees. For prospective and current employees, such communication may be particularly important from a human resources strategy standpoint since, compared to private sector employees, public employees receive a larger portion of their compensation in the form of pension benefits (Johnson, 1997). Therefore, governments that effectively communicate the relative generosity of their pension plans have a poten-tially potent tool for employee recruitment and retention.

Recognizing the importance of an effective communications strategy, Cost Effectiveness Measurement, Inc., has produced a document chronicling best practices in public pension plan communications (Cost Effectiveness Measurement, 2002). The report suggests a number of specific best practices — complete with illustrations — arranged under three broad headings: *completeness* (e.g., provide benefits publications to members when they join the system; "sell" the value of the benefits); *design* (e.g., make materials inviting; use context-sensitive artwork and pictures; use appropriate paper stock and print quality); and *clarity* (e.g., offering clear understanding of what members will receive when they retire or leave the system before retirement; how members qualify for benefits). There are a number of tools pension systems use to communicate with their plan participants, including posters, payroll stuffers, informational letters, plan brochures and booklets, news-letters, videos, and web-based publications (Eitelberg, 1997).

While there are a number of tools pension systems use for communi-cation, there are certain elements that are necessary for an overall effective communications strategy. According to the GFOA (Eitelberg, 1997, 45), an effective communications strategy requires careful planning and clear goals and objectives, including:

- Creating better understanding of the plan's purpose, how it operates and any participant responsibilities
- Promoting awareness among participants of the plan and issues confronting the plan
- Providing participant access to personalized information

- Education employees about retirement income needs and where plan benefits fit in with overall retirement income resources
- Maintaining contact with all stakeholders, including taxpayers, as well as legislators, employees, retirees, and beneficiaries

As this list of goals suggests, a sound communications strategy is an important aspect of benefits administration. To this point, the focus of this discussion on communications has been geared toward plan participants. But, as suggested in the last goal statement above, pension systems have a number of stakeholders with whom effective communications must be maintained. Consider, for example, legislative bodies. As mentioned in the section on benefits calculations, legislative bodies are normally responsible for determining DB formulas. Moreover, these bodies are responsible for ensuring pension plans are adequately funded. Unfortunately, there can be a disconnect between these two responsibilities, as political decisions to enhance benefits (precipitated, perhaps, by short-term fiscal prosperity) can be made without considering the long-term consequences for pension systems. Such enhancements might be an increase in the retirement multiplier or an early retirement program. In such cases, pension systems need to make decision makers fully aware of the long-term financial effects of those enhancements on the health of pension funds.

Effective communication with stakeholders also is important when pension investments suffer bad years, as was the case in 2001 and 2002. Specifically, pension system administrators have an important role to play in alleviating the fears and concerns of lawmakers, taxpayers, and bond rating companies in addition to plan participants. One way pension systems can do this is by reiterating the long-term health of pension plans. Naturally, poor investment performance — which for larger plans can result in multi-billion dollars dips in plan assets — can be the source of much attention. Such attention can lead to calls for changing asset allocations, investments, and/or external investment advisors. To thwart these short-term reactions, pension trustees and managers must reiterate their investment policy and focus attention on long-term performance. One way pension systems help maintain long-term focus is to smooth (or average) their investment returns over long periods of time (e.g., 5, 10, or even 15 years). Far from being unethical or gimmicky, this common actuarial practice properly focuses attention on the long-term health of the plan's investment returns. Consider the case of CALPERS. CALPERS sent shock waves in 2001 when it announced a $9 billion loss in its investments. Even with those losses, however, CALPERS was able to report in its *2003 Operations Statement* a strong 10-year average return of 8.2 percent, and a 15-year rate of return of 9.6 percent, which exceeded the system's actuarial assumptions (CALPERS, 2003).

As all of this suggests, an important aspect of benefits administration is communications. Whether selling the value of benefits to potential government employees or educating legislative bodies on the long-term consequences of pension benefit changes, pension administrators have an obligation to ensure better awareness, understanding, and appreciation for pension benefits among a diverse group of stakeholders.

16.3.2.4 Educating Employees

Finally, separate treatment should be given to the educative role pension systems play in benefits administration. While education might be properly subsumed under either the customer service or communications categories, the fact that pension systems have a fiduciary duty to ensure their participants receive benefits education (Eitelberg, 1997) justifies brief separate treatment for employee education. In a nutshell, public pension plan sponsors should implement programs designed to educate employees about the importance of retirement savings and the various retirement savings vehicles available to them. This is important for DB plans but even more so for pension systems who sponsor only DC plans. Having employees assume risk for their own retirement security, as is the case with DC plans, does not eliminate a pension plan sponsor from fiduciary duties: employees need to understand asset allocation, diversification, tolerance for risk, what constitutes an acceptable rate of return on investments, and how their employer-sponsored retirement plans fit into their overall retirement income package. Unfortunately, public sector employers have lagged their private sector counterparts in offering financial planning education to employees (Daley, 1998; Sostek, 2004). When coupled with the aforementioned investment conservatism of public employees (Frank, Condon, Dunlop, and Rothman, 2000), the importance of retirement education becomes all the more apparent.

According to the GFOA, "the key to educating participants about investment strategies, plan benefits and retirement planning is to demonstrate the advantages and the pitfalls of inaction" (Eitelberg, 1997, 46). For plan sponsors, this education activity should begin, initially, with a thorough overview of their plan's respective features for new employees and plan participants. Moreover, plan sponsors should provide all participants: asset allocation tools (software, literature, counseling); information on the trade-offs between the probability of high returns and risks of loss; information on risk exposure and historical market returns of various investment choices; periodic statements on the investment performance of participants' accounts; reminders about the need to monitor and rebalance their asset allocations according to their own unique investment strategies; and information on the importance of diversifying their investments (GFOA, 1999). Implementing these educative measures requires a concerted effort, utilizing multiple forums, on the part of pensions systems, as suggested in the above section on communications. Doing so helps to ensure that plan sponsors fulfill their fiduciary duties and that employees are properly positioning themselves for retirement security.

16.4 Conclusion: The Importance of Public Pension Management

Obviously, managing public pensions is major governmental undertaking. Success or failure in pension management has direct bearing on the well-being of governments, taxpayers, and public employees and retirees. Pension systems are responsible for the investment of trillions of dollars in plan assets and for the disbursement of hundreds of billions of dollars in pension benefits annually. Savvy pension administrators, who are able to produce high rates of investment return commensurate with an acceptable amount of risk, can potentially minimize costs to taxpayers and future generations for government's pension commitments. Strong pension fund health also helps to assure the commitment and productivity of current employees and can serve as an important enticement in government's strategic efforts to acquire needed human resources.

In contrast, government decisions to underfund pension plans can have serious consequences. As mentioned above, the city of San Diego, California's unfunded pension liability, which was in excess of $1 billion in 2004, resulted in a downgrade of the city's bond rating by a major bond rating firm. Similar consequences may also obtain for pension systems that make unwise or overly risky investments with pension assets or that use poor assumptions to design flawed retirement plans (e.g., the Houston and Milwaukee DROPs plans mentioned above). As Mahoney (2002) points out, lowered bond ratings increase government's borrowing costs, thus increasing the costs borne by future taxpayers, not only for unfunded pension obligations but also for other government borrowing as well.

Finally, it is important to mention new realities which only accentuate the challenges faced by pension systems. Pension plans have long attended to concerns over plan continuity in the event of a natural disaster (e.g., floods, earthquakes, etc.). Now, in the post-9/11 world, pension systems are in the position of needing to develop and adopt strategies that will ensure the continuity of operations in the event of terrorist activity or other attempts to intentionally interrupt governmental operations. The Louisiana State Employees' Retirement System (LASERS), for example, recently developed a disaster recovery and business continuity plan.

As reported by Hegdal (2003, 6), LASERS' plan suggests the importance of identifying internal and external system risks, prioritizing critical business processes and recovery times, identifying the assets that need to be protected in the event of a disaster, conducting vulnerability assessments (e.g., How will a disaster in one pension system division affect other divisions?), and developing a business continuity plan for each pension system unit.

As this suggests, new workaday realities have direct implications for the effective management of public pensions. Along with the scale and scope of public pensions, shifting demographic trends, and unpredictable political and economic forces, these challenges underscore the importance of effective pension management to government's overall financial management performance. Given this, there is some comfort in knowing that pension fund management has become more professional over the last 10 to 15 years (Walters, 2000). This augers well for the future of both public pension and financial management.

References

Adrangi, B., and Shank, T. (1999). Performance of retirement funds in efficient markets: Case of Oregon Public Employees Retirement Fund. *American Business Review*, *17*(2), 59–69.

Anonymous. (2003). IRS does a u-turn on controversial cash balance plans. *Employee Benefit Plan Review*, *57*(12), 4–5.

Association of Public Pension Fund Auditors (APPFA). (2000). *Public Pension Systems: Statements of Key Investment Risks and Common Practices to Address Those Risks*. Albany, NY: APPFA.

Association of Public Pension Fund Auditors (APPFA). (2003). *Public Pension Systems: Operational Risks of Defined Benefit and Related Plans and Controls to Mitigate Those Risks*. Albany, NY: APPFA.

Barker, R.B., and O'Brien, K.P. (2004). Cash balance emergency preparedness kit: This is not a test. *Benefits Law Journal*, *17*(1), 5–22.

Bergsman, S. (1995). How shaky a foundation? *Pension Management*, *31*(7), 44–47.

Blostin, A.P. (2003). Payment options under retirement plans. *Compensation and Working Conditions Online*. Washington, DC: United States Department of Labor, Bureau of Labor Statistics. Available at: http://www.bls.gov/pub/cwc/print/cm20030409ar01p1.htm (Accessed May 27, 2004).

Brainard, K. (2003). *Public fund survey: Summary of findings*. National Association of State Retirement Administrators and National Council on Teacher Retirement. Available at: http://www.publicfundsurvey.org/ PublicFund Surveyfindings03.pdf (Accessed May 27, 2004).

California Public Employees' Retirement System (CALPERS). (2003). *2003 Operations Summary.* Sacramento, CA: CALPERS.

Cayer, N.J. (1995). Pension fund management. In J. Rabin, T. Vocino, W.B. Hildreth, and G.J. Miller (eds), *Handbook of Public Personnel Administration*, pp. 377–388. New York: Marcel Dekker, Inc.

Cayer, N.J. (1996). Employee benefits: From health care to pensions. In S. Condrey (ed), *Handbook of Human Resource Management in Government*, pp. 658–675. San Francisco, CA: Jossey-Bass Publishers.

Cayer, N.J., Martin, L.J., and Ifflander, A.J. (1986). Public pension plans and social investing. *Public Personnel Management, 15*(1), 75–79.

Cayer, N.J., and Volk, W. (1999). Employee benefits: Creating an environment for excellence. In S.F. Freyss (ed), *Human Resource Management in Local Government: An Essential Guide*, pp. 133–157. Washington, DC: International City/County Management Association.

Chaney, B.A., Copley, P.A., and Stone, M.S. (2002). The effect of fiscal stress and balanced budget requirements on the funding and measurement of state pension obligations. *Journal of Accounting and Public Policy, 21*, 287–313.

Cooper versus The IBM Personal Pension Plan. (2003). WL 21767853 (S.D. Ill., July 31, 2003).

Coronado, J.L., Engen, E.M., and Knight, B. (2003). Public funds and private capital markets: The investment practices and performance of state and local pension funds. *National Tax Journal, 56*(3), 579–594.

Cost Effectiveness Measurement, Inc. (2002). *Benchmarking and Best Practices for Public Pension Plan Member Publications.* Toronto, Ontario: Cost Effectiveness Measurement, Inc. Available at: http://www.nasra.org/resources/cem.pdf (Accessed May 27, 2004).

Crane, R.B. (1995). Defined contribution plans for the public sector. *Government Finance Review, 11*(4), 46–49.

Cranford, J. (1993). Providing cover: A look at public employee benefits. *Governing, 7*(3), 45–50.

Daley, D.M. (1998). An overview of benefits for the public sector: Not on the fringes anymore. *Review of Public Personnel Administration, 18*(3), 5–22.

Daley, D.M. (2002). Compensation. In *Strategic Human Resource Management*, pp. 129–170. Upper Saddle River, NJ: Prentice Hall.

D'Arcy, S.P., Dulebohn, J.H., and Oh, P. (1999). Optimal funding of state employee pension systems. *The Journal of Risk and Insurance, 66*(3), 345–380.

Dulebohn, J.H. (1995). A longitudinal and comparative analysis of the funded status of state and local public pension plans. *Public Budgeting & Finance, 15*(2), 52–72.

Eaton versus Onan Corporation. (2000). 117 F. Supp. 2d 812 (S.D. Ind., 2000).

Eitelberg, C.G. (1994). PERS and ETIs: A marriage made in the DOL? *Government Finance Review, 10*(2), 40–41.

Eitelberg, C.G. (1997). *An Elected Official's Guide to Public Retirement Plans.* Chicago, IL: Government Finance Officers Association.

Feldstein, D. (2004). Confusion surrounds Houston city workers pension vote. *Houston Chronicle,* May 9, 2004.

Findlay, G.W. (1997). In defense of the defined benefit plan. *Government Finance Review, 13*(6), 33–35.

Frank, H.A., Condon, K.M., Dunlop, B.D., and Rothman, M.B. (2000). The retirement planning gap: A view from the public sector. *International Journal of Organizational Theory and Behavior, 3*(1&2), 235–274.

General Accounting Office, United States (GAO). (1995). *Public Pension Plans: Evaluation of Economically Targeted Investment Programs.* Washington, DC: GAO. (GAO/PEMD-95-13).

General Accounting Office, United States (GAO). (1996). *Public Pensions: Section 457 Plans Pose Greater Risk Than Other Supplemental Plans.* Washington, DC: GAO. (GAO/HEHS-96-6).

General Accounting Office, United States (GAO). (1999). *State Pension Plans: Similarities and Differences Between Federal and State Designs.* Washington, DC: GAO. (GAO/GGD-99-45).

Green, L.B. (2003a). Questions and answers on cash balance pension plans.*Compensation and Working Conditions Online.* Washington, DC: United States Department of Labor, Bureau of Labor Statistics. Available at: http://www.bls.gov/opub/cwc/print/cm20030917ar01pl.htm (Accessed May 27, 2004).

Green, L.B. (2003b). What is a pension equity plan? *Compensation and Working Conditions Online.* Washington, DC: United States Department of Labor, Bureau of Labor Statistics. Available at: http://www.bls.gov/opub/cwc/print/cm20031016ar01pl.htm (Accessed May 27, 2004).

Greifer, Nicholas. (2001). Asset allocation practices in the public sector: A primer for finance officers." *Government Finance Review, 17*(4), 28–32.

Greifer, Nicholas. (2002). Pension investment polices: The state of the art." *Government Finance Review, 18*(1), 36–40.

Government Finance Officers Association (GFOA). (1994). *Funding of Public Employee Retirement Systems.* Chicago, IL: Government Finance Officers Association.

Government Finance Officers Association (GFOA). (1999). *Asset Allocation: Guidance for Defined Contribution Plans.* Chicago, IL: Government Finance Officers Association.

Government Finance Officers Association (GFOA). (2000). *Selection of investment advisors for pension fund assets.* Chicago, IL: Government Finance Officers Association.

Hegdal, B. (2003). *Is your system prepared? National Association of State Retirement Administrators News,* Fall(2003), 6–7.

Johnson, R.W. (1997). Pension underfunding and liberal retirement benefits among state and local government workers. *National Tax Journal, 50*(1), 113–139.

Kansas Public Employees Retirement System (KPERS). (2002). Plan Design: A review of Current Pension Issues. Topeka, KS: KPERS.

Lachance, M-E., Mitchell, O.S., and Smetters, K. (2003). Guaranteeing defined contribution pensions: The option to buy back a defined benefit promise." *The Journal of Risk and Insurance, 70*(1), 1–16.

Leigland, J. (1992). Socioeconomic investment practices of state pension funds: The results of a national survey. *Public Budgeting & Finance, 12* (2), 48–58.

Lemov, P. (1997). Michigan's big pension gamble. *Governing, 10*(8), 41–43.

Lemov, P. (1998). Pensions of plenty. *Governing, 11*(12), 64–67.

Lemov, P. (2003). Bad news bear. *Governing, 17*(6), 43–44.

Maggs, A.J. (2004). Everything old is new again: Funding issues in public pensions. *Benefits Law Journal, 17*(1), 115–124.

Mahoney, D.P. (2002). Toward a more ethical system of state and local government retirement funding. *Journal of Public Budgeting, Accounting & Financial Management, 14*(2), 197–224.

Mariani, Michele. (2004). Deferred debt undermines a city's standing. *Governing, 17*(7), 52.

Mason, J.D. (2003). Reversal of fortune: The rising cost of public sector pensions and other post-employment benefits. *FitchRatings.* New York: Fitch, Inc. Available at: http://www.nasra.org/resources/fitchre port0309.pdf (Accessed July 13, 2004.)

Miller, Girard. (1987). The investment of public funds: A research agenda. *Public Budgeting & Finance, 7*(3), 47–56.

Mikesell, J.L. (2003). Managing funds: Cash management and employee retirement funds. In *Fiscal Administration,* 6th ed., pp. 584–621. Belmont, CA: Wadsworth/Thomson Learning.

Mitchell, O.S., and Hsin, P-L. (1997). Public sector pension governance and performance. In

S.V. Prieto (ed), *The Economics of Pensions: Principles, Policies, and International Experience,* pp. 92–126. Cambridge, England: Cambridge University Press.

Mitchell, O.S., and Smith, R.S. (1994). Pension funding in the public sector. *The Review of Economics and Statistics, 76*(2), 278–290.

National Association of State Retirement Administrators (NASRA). (2003). *Myths and Misperceptions of Defined Benefit and Defined Contribution Plans.* Baton Rouge, LA: NASRA. Available at: http://www.nasra.org/resources/myths%20and%20misperceptions.pdf (Accessed 5/27/04).

Nationwide Retirement Solutions. (2003). *Fiduciary Fundamentals for Government Sector Defined Contribution Plans.* Columbus,

OH: Nationwide Retirement Solutions. Available at: http://www.nrsservicecenter.com/nrs/media/images/nrsCommom/fid_brochure.pdf (Accessed June 21, 2004).

Ohio Retirement Study Council (ORSC). (2003). *Analysis: Am. Sub. HB* 227. Columbus, Ohio: ORSC. Available at: http://www.orsc.org/uploadpdf/227AmSubHB.pdf (Accessed 5/27/04)

Owens, Tom. (1999). Cash balance pension plans: Will the public sector follow the private-sector stampede? *Government Finance Review, 15*(4), 65–66.

Peng, J. (2004). Public pension funds and operating budgets: A tale of three states. *Public Budgeting & Finance, 24*(2), 59–73.

Petersen, J.E. (1993). *Governing, 6*(6), 43–49.

Petersen, J.E. (2002). Guide to money management: Searching for security. *Governing, 15*(9), 67–69.

Petersen, J.E. (2003). Guide to public investing: Where did all the money go? *Governing, 16*(9), 46–50.

Romano, R. (1995). The politics of public pension funds. *Public Interest* (119), 42–53.

Shen, Paul. (1979). Cash management of state and municipal pension funds. *The Government Accountants Journal, 28*(2), 53–59.

Sonnanstine, A., Murphy, B., and Zorn, P. (2003). List of advantages and disadvantages for DB and DC plans. GRS Research Memorandum. Gabriel, Roeder, Smith & Company.

Shorrock, T. (2002). CALPERS and Carlyle. *The Nation, 274*(12), 15.

Sneed, C.A., and Sneed, J.E. (1997). Unfunded pension obligations as a source of fiscal illusion for state governments. *Journal of Public Budgeting, Accounting & Financial Management, 9*(1), 5–20.

Sostek, A. (2004). Pension pendulum. *Governing, 17*(6), 28–30.

State of Wisconsin Retirement Research Committee. (2000). *2000 Comparative Study of Major Public Employee Retirement Systems.* Madison, WI: State of Wisconsin Retirement Research Committee.

Swope, C. (2003). Pensions: Payout planning. *Governing, 16*(12), 48–51.

Todd, F.D. (1997). A defined contribution plan is a viable alternative to the traditional defined benefit retirement plan. *Government Finance Review, 13*(6), 32–33.

United States Census Bureau. (2002). *2002 State and Local Government Employee-Retirement System Survey.* Washington, DC: United States Census Bureau. Available at: http://www.census.gov/govs/www/retire02.html (Accessed June 6, 2002).

Useem, M., and Mitchell, O.S. (2000). Holders of the purse strings: Governance and performance of public retirement systems. *Social Science Quarterly, 81*(2), 489–506.

Walsh. M.W. (2004a). Cities enriched pensions, but now struggle to pay. *New York Times,* May 5, 2004, A1.

Walsh, M.W. (2004b). Voters release Houston from pension law. *New York Times,* May 5, 2004.

Walters, J. (2000). Pension fund follies. *Governing, 13*(11), 54–55.

Warren, D.P. (1996). Pension obligation bonds: practices and perspectives. *Government Finance Review, 12*(6), 42–44.

Weisberg, M.S., and Vanesse, M. (2003). Are cash balance plans really unlawful? *Benefits Law Journal, 16*(4), 86–92.

Wilshire Associates. (2003). *2003 Wilshire Report on State Retirement Systems: Funding Levels and Asset Allocation*. Santa Monica, CA: Wilshire Associates.

Zorn, P. (1997). Public pensions. *Public Administration Review, 57*(4), 361–362.

Chapter 17

An Econometric Assessment of State and Local Government Retirement System Governance Practices, Investment Strategies, and Financial Performance

WILLIAM G. ALBRECHT, Ph.D.
Department of Political Science and Public Administration, University of North Carolina, Pembroke

THOMAS D. LYNCH
Department of Public Administration, Louisiana State University

17.1 Introduction

Issues involving the administration of state and local government pension funds are currently on their way to the apex of the current domestic policy agenda. This statement is not to suggest that these variants on retirement security have not been on such a track before. In fact, various questions concerning their management and overall purpose have waxed and waned, at least since Israel Rafkind generally acknowledged the renewed interest in public sector retirement systems due to the "new" social security program in 1939. Ever since that publication the concerns of state and local government retirement systems have focused on a number of topics ranging from the mundane notion of an actuarially sound pension plan to hot button issues such as the collective potential of economically targeted investments and the ethical standards of socially responsible investing. Of course the rise and fall of any particular discussion or debate largely depends on the underlying economic and political climates of a specific era. Retrospectively speaking, these factors always appear to serve as an impetus for an administrative idea whose time has come.

The relevant question now is what makes the contemporary ascension by public pensions to the top of the domestic policy agenda any different from the past? A complete and honest answer must first acknowledge that not all fundamental aspects surrounding the present situation are completely dissimilar in a historical sense. The moral and communal aspects surrounding the management of public monies in any climate are always of interest to a civil society and will inevitably provide a bridge between the past, present, and future. However, there is one concern that is of immense practical consequence which separates the modern condition from earlier periods; the imminent retirement of the baby boom generation[1].

This cohort of seventy six million Americans, born between 1946 and 1964, has long attracted the attention of demographers, politicians, marketers, and other social scientists. Typically regarded as a positive but distant and discounted constant in terms of age related calculations, the defining feature of the baby boom issue is the proximity of the retirement event to a forecasted starting date. For example, according to the Economic Report of the President (1999) by 2029, when the youngest baby boomers retire, 20% of Americans will be 65 or older, approximately 2.5 times the proportion of the elderly in 1950.

The sheer magnitude of this segment of the citizenry and the immediacy of the issue are inevitably moderating traditional discussions in favor of those that focus on either strengthening existing retirement security options or the sharing of risks and rewards in unconventional ways. Considering recent global variability in the social, economic, and political spheres, an argument might be made that dialogues concentrating on the latter topic are dominant or perhaps more relevant. Either way, potential financial and budgeting implications, commencing with a massive and voluntary exit of labor from the available pool, are prompting researchers to focus on the generation of useable knowledge that can be used by financial managers, public administrators, policymakers, and other stakeholders to address this impending issue.

Given the above, the overall purpose of this chapter is to provide an econometric assessment of state and local government pension fund governance practices, investment strategies, and financial performance at the system level. This task is primarily accomplished through the statistical pursuit of three separate but cumulative and interdependent questions. Specifically, we ask:

1. What are the most recent trends in state and local government pension fund governance practices, investment strategies, and financial performance?
2. Are there associations between (a) governance practices and financial performance, (b) investment strategies and financial performance, and (c) governance practices and investment strategies?
3. Do investment strategies mediate the relationship between governance practices and financial performance?

The overall intent is to delineate and document the factors underlying the data generating process of the inherently valued outcome defined as "financial performance." To some extent we also seek to clarify the meaning of financial performance with multiple measures that arguably address different administrative and/or policy relevant questions.

For example, a number of authors, including Useem and Hess (2001) and Useem and Mitchell (2000), suggest that state and local government retirement systems are the best units of analysis for studying the potential stewardship of funds should Social Security assets ever be invested in financial markets. We seek to contribute to this discussion by directly linking to these prior investigations and extending the work with new data, a variation in methodology, and a potentially relevant but less used measure of financial performance in tandem with that which is traditionally used to assess this outcome. Our findings suggest that governance practices are important determinants of both investment strategies and financial performance. However, complete interpretations of the data generation process are dependent upon the type of criterion being considered.

The remainder of the chapter proceeds as follows. Section two discusses the economics of public pension funds from both a theoretical and practical perspective. The definitions of governance practices and investment strategies are also given in this segment. Section three reviews the most recent econometric literature investigating this subject. The fourth section pertains to the methods of this study while section five presents the results. A discussion of the findings and general conclusions and comments are given in the sixth and final section of this chapter.

17.2 The Economics of Public Pension Funds

According to the latest figures from the US Census Bureau, retirement funds for public sector employees are distributed across some 2,670 retirement systems in the United States.[2] Of these systems 2,451 are administered by local governments with more than 70 percent being supervised by municipalities. In terms of membership approximately 90 percent of all participants are covered by state systems which paid benefits to more than 6 million beneficiaries in Fiscal Year 2001–2002. By comparison, more than 1 million beneficiaries received periodic benefit payments from local government pensions during this same period.

Unlike the US Social Security system, Public Employee Retirement Systems (PERS) are not pay-as-you go schemes and are jointly funded by contributions from employers and employees as well as returns on assets that are invested in financial markets. Most systems house Defined Benefit plans (DB), meaning that (a) capital along with any accumulation is later distributed according to a predetermined formula and (b) benefits, in the event of unfunded liabilities resulting from contribution and/or investment shortfalls, are essentially guaranteed by the ability of governments to raise contribution rates or to tax and borrow as needed.[3] The tremendous size of these institutional investors (currently estimated to be in excess of $2 trillion), in combination with the fact that most are overseen by a board of trustees, in a public setting, have resulted in a stream of administrative and policy related econometric research that examines PERS governance practices, investment decisions, and financial performance.

17.2.1 *Governance Practices*

To some extent public pension researchers face inherent ambiguity when trying to provide an explicit definition of governance. This "fact" within the broader realm of social science inquiries confronts other scholars in public policy and administration as well (Lynn et al., 2000, 1–2). However, when the term is used for retirement system research at the system level, "governance" typically refers to the structure of a pension plan board in combination with the complex of rules and practices that guide the oversight of fund assets (Useem and Mitchell, 2000, 490). Given the nature of the field this rather broad definition appears to be necessary if not sufficient for two interrelated reasons.

First, while trustees typically have a fiduciary responsibility to represent the interests of plan participants there is no federal law requiring them to do so. Instead PERS fiduciary responsibility is usually left to state or local laws that vary across jurisdictions (Coronado et al., 2003, 580). And, as noted by Useem and Hess (2001), the trustees of public retirement systems, as well as the legislative bodies overseeing them, have interpreted their duties in varying fashions (133–134). By comparison, private sector pension representatives are obliged to conduct themselves in accordance with the Employee Retirement Security Act of 1974 (ERISA) which requires trustees to act with the care, skill, prudence and diligence of a prudent person acting in the interests of participants and beneficiaries (Miller, 1987, 8).[4] This variation in fiduciary interpretations (within the public realm) and responsibility (across the sectors) has prompted researchers to examine questions concerning this particular aspect of governance and whether or not there is any deterministic impact on investment decisions and/or financial performance. Historical conclusions regarding superiority along these dimensions appear to favor the private sector. However, recent evidence suggests that this disparity may be diminishing.[5]

The second reason for proclaiming the definition as appropriate is that the characterization intrinsically acknowledges that those pursuing such inquiries also confront the theoretical and/or practical economics of public organizations.[6] For example, researchers focusing on theoretical issues surrounding publicly managed retirement schemes have often sought to determine whether agency costs are associated with how PERS are governed. Agency costs are economic inefficiencies that exist when the decision rights over an organization's assets and cash flows are improperly aligned with the organization's residual claimants (Nofsinger, 1998, 89). Since the majority of public pension systems house DB plans the residual claimants are generally deemed to be taxpayers who ultimately benefit/suffer from good/bad pension fund performance.[7] The potential for an agency problem arises because PERS boards of trustees are often comprised of members who are appointed or elected by plan participants or officials with little or perhaps no fiduciary responsibility towards the larger public.

On the other hand practically oriented research has tended to focus on the competence of trustees and the potential for administrative costs via governance practices. To illustrate, research on both the private and public sectors indicates that the size of boards, operating in any capacity, can matter in terms of operating efficiency and performance. In terms of pension funds, Useem and Hess (2001) note that having too few members denies a board experience, expertise, and wisdom, while too many members can undermine communication, consensus, etc. (p. 137).[8]

Beyond this aspect, PERS representatives are usually not professional money managers and may be unfamiliar with the intimate technicalities surrounding financial markets and investment decisions (Useem and Mitchell, 2000, 47).[9] Again, in terms of comparison, an important point to note is that these types of board structures do not exist in the private sector, which are usually overseen by financial professionals or officers of the sponsoring corporations. Hypotheses concerning the competence of PERS trustees tend to posit that the lack of expertise impacts both investment decisions and financial performance in the public sector. The latter of course is arguably an administrative cost from an economic perspective.

17.2.2 Investment Decisions

The examination of investment decisions by PERS can be classified as one of two types. The first is best described as investment policy decisions. These types of decisions often involve choices concerning general system approaches, overall goals, or even authoritative controls. To illustrate, in addition to constitutional provisions or statutory limitations, many systems have internal policies placing ceilings on the percentage of assets that can be invested in stocks, the bonds of any single issuer, or foreign investments. Some funds may even prohibit investing in specific types of companies, such as those selling tobacco or doing business with Northern Ireland.[10] Others might require that some portion of a system's assets be invested in a home state for economic development purposes. Investments of this variety are commonly referred to as Economically Targeted Investments (ETIs).

The second type of decision is more specific in that the particular use or allocation of a pension's funds are involved with the specific intent of generating a rate of return on existing assets. Therefore, compared to investment policy decisions, these types of choices are typically referred to as investment strategy decisions.[11] Some important examples include determining (a) the distribution of available funds among asset classes such as stocks, bonds, cash, etc., (b) whether or not to invest in foreign investments, (c) whether or not to invest "tactically" based on prevailing economic conditions or "passively" in broader indexes that track particular markets, and (d) the fraction of funds that should be managed internally by PERS representatives or externally by professional money managers.

The analysis of investment decisions is important because at this juncture researchers studying PERS not only face the economics of public organizations but the economics of financial markets. Within this realm time and uncertainty are dominating features and the empirical financial literature indicates that investment choices can have a very substantive impact on financial performance. This has shown to be most true for asset allocation decisions which are often cited as the most important determinants of financial performance. For example, in two widely cited studies Brinson et al. (1991) and Brinson et al. (1986) demonstrate that 90 percent of an investing fund's financial performance over time can be explained by asset allocation decisions. In an extension of these investigations Ibbotson and Kaplan (2000) go on to show that asset allocation choices explain 40 percent of the variation in financial performance among investing funds.[12]

In addition, the analysis of investment decisions is valuable because choices reflect prevailing PERS views regarding overall financial and social goals and the efficiency of financial markets to allocate financial resources. PERS concerned with social issues may very well have policies prohibiting or limiting the placement of funds in specific investments, while attempting to enhance local economies with the infusion of financial resources.[13] Other funds may not believe that markets are truly efficient in terms of asset pricing and seek to employ tactical investment strategies.[14] Concomitantly, trusts that do believe in relatively efficient markets might pursue longer term investment choices. Conservative pensions could opt for the safety of principle over the extent of income (Donner, 1939, p. 10). Finally, decisions to place a fund's assets under external management might reflect the sentiments of PERS trustees or representatives about their own investment abilities, net of cost. The real question, of course, is how any one of these decisions affects the most inherently valued outcome of financial performance.

17.3 The Econometrics of Public Pension Funds

Compared to other types of institutional investors the econometric analysis of subnational PERS governance practices, investment decisions and financial performance is a relatively recent phenomenon.[15] And, somewhat predictably, the majority of these studies ultimately involve the use of multivariate regression techniques on similar variables of interest which are derived from identical sources of data.[16] The defining feature of any specific investigation is the research question that is being asked and the definition of financial performance.

17.3.1 Governance Practices and Investment Decisions: The Impact on Financial Performance

The results of five contemporary and well known studies concerning the impacts of public pension fund governance practices and investment decisions on financial performance are summarized below in Table 17.1.

Table 17.1 Five Econometric Studies Concerning the Effects of Governance and Investment Decisions on PERS Financial Performance*

	Mitchell and Hsin (1997)	Nofsinger (1998)	Useem and Mitchell (2000)	Munnell and Sunden (2001)	Coronado and et al. (2003)
Sample periods	90	90–92	92	90, 92, 94, 96	98
Measure(s) of performance	90 total ROR[a]	Abnormal ROR (bench–total)	93 Total ROR	Total ROR[a]	98 total ROR
ROR = Rate of Return	5 yr. avg. ROR			5 yr. avg. ROR	5 yr. avg. ROR
Governance policies					
Constitutional restrictions		−, insignificant	−, insignificant	−, insignificant	
Prudent standard	+, insignificant				+, insignificant
Performance evaluation	−, insignificant		+, insignificant	−, significant[a]	
Board purview					
Board sets callocation			−, insignificant		
Board directly Invests			+, insignificant		
Board composition					
Total board members			−, significant		
Percent elected	−, significant[a]	−, insignificant		+, insignificant	+, insignificant
Investment decisions					
ETI policy	−, significant[a]	−, significant	+, significant	+, insignificant	−, insignificant
Percent equities strategy		+, insignificant	+, significant	+, significant	+, significant
Foreign investment strategy			+, insignificant		
Tactical investing strategy			+, insignificant		
External mgt. strategy			+, insignificant		
Other control					
System size		−, significant	+, insignificant	+, significant	+, significant

*Conclusions based on final regressions in Mitchell & Hsin's Table 4.6, Nofsinger's Table 3, Useem and Mitchell's Table 3, Munnell and Sunden's Table 3, and Coronado et al.'s (2003) Table 5.

[a]Significant for total return only. Technical differences between Total Return and Abnormal Return are noted later in this chapter.

To clarify, the table organizes specific measures under four broad categories: governance policies, board purview over investment decisions, board composition, and actual investment decisions.[17] Specifically, governance policies and board purview variables consist of whether or not (a) investment restrictions are specified in a fund's state constitution, (b) a system is formally subject to prudent standards when making investment decisions, (c) a system obtains independent investment performance evaluations, (d) board members are involved with asset allocation decisions, and (e) the pension fund board is responsible for the investment of system assets. Investment decision variables include the investment policy of investing in ETIs and the investment strategy variables concerning the fraction of a fund's assets placed in equity investments, and whether or not a fund invests tactically or in foreign investments, and whether or not a fund externally manages all of the system assets. System size (measured as the value of total assets) is also listed as a control variable. A subjective assessment of the literature suggests that these measures are among the most commonly used in terms of modern econometric research concerning this subject.

Referencing Table 17.1, the most consistent finding in terms of governance practices is that few of the variables examined appear to exhibit any independent effect as defined by statistical significance. The intermittent effects that do exist seem to be reflected in the studies by Mitchell and Hsin (1997) and Munnell and Sunden (2001). During the course of these investigations the authors find some evidence supporting negative impacts on the total return associated with the percentage of a board which is elected and the obtainment of independent investment performance evaluations, respectively. However, even these results are not duplicated by earlier/later investigations.[18] In contrast, the latest reports do appear to find a positive impact on financial performance when controlling for the size of a system. The typical conclusion here is that there are economies of scale in investing and that larger systems are more able to capitalize on these factors.

By comparison investment decisions do appear to exert more of a consistent effect on financial performance. For example, both Mitchell and Hsin (1997) and Nofsinger (1998) find evidence of a negative association in relation to ETI policies. In terms of investment strategies, the fraction of a fund's assets invested in equities is reported to have a positive and statistically significant effect by Useem and Mitchell (2000), Munnell and Sunden (2001), and Coronado et al. (2003). The positive coefficient on Useem and Mitchell's (2000) measure of foreign investments appears to corroborate the assertion that asset allocation decisions are the most important of all investment strategies when financial performance is defined as the total rate of return on existing assets.

17.3.2 Governance Practices: The Impact on Investment Decisions

The results of two well known studies concerning public pension fund governance practices and investment decisions are summarized in Table 17.2.[19] Referencing the earliest of these investigations, Nofsinger (1998) reports negative and statistically significant effects on decisions to implement ETI investment policies in relation to the use of prudent standards in investment decisions. To interpret, this result suggests that public pension funds which adhere to prudent standards are less likely to implement ETI policies.

In terms of investment strategy decisions Table 17.2 shows that Useem and Hess (2001) report positive and mostly statistically significant relationships (excluding tactical investing) between all of the investment strategy decisions and the obtainment of independent investment performance evaluations. Constitutional investment restrictions are also found to be negatively related to every investment strategy listed. However, the coefficient on foreign investment is not statistically significant. Positive and statistically significant associations are also noted to be present for (a) board responsibility for investments and decisions to index equity investments, (b) the total number of board members and percent equities and the decision to place some funds in foreign investments, and (c) the percentage of a board's trustees who are elected and tactical investing strategies.

17.3.3 The Data Generating Process and Financial Performance

Collectively speaking the econometric studies discussed above portray a compelling and consistent view of a data generating process underlying the "production" of financial performance. Specifically, the investigations suggest that the ways in which PERS are governed have a direct bearing on investment decisions and these investment decisions in turn affect the financial performance of public pension funds with little direct impact from governance practices.[20] Figure 17.1 visually portrays this proposition. Ignoring path c for the moment, investment decisions are depicted as mediating (accounting for) the relationship between governance practices and financial performance. Again, referencing Tables 17.1 and 17.2, this acknowledgment appears to be particularly true for ETI policy and asset allocation decisions with respect to total rate of return; the most frequently used variant of financial performance. Yet, a central question emerges as to how this overall conclusion should be interpreted given that there are both theoretical and practical issues to consider.

Table 17.2 Two Econometric Studies Concerning the Effects of Governance Practices on PERS Investment Decisions, 1992*

Investment Decision	Nofsinger (1998)			Useem and Hess (2001)	
	ETI Policy	Percent Equities	Foreign Investment	Tactical Investing	Equity Indexing
Governance policies					
Constitutional restrictions		−, significant	−, insignificant	−, significant	−, significant
Prudent standard	−, significant				
Performance evaluation		+, significant	+, significant	+, insignificant	+, significant
Board purview					
Board sets allocation		+, insignificant	−, insignificant	−, insignificant	+, insignificant
Board directly invests		+, insignificant	+, insignificant	−, insignificant	+, significant
Board composition					
Total board members		+, significant	+, significant	+, insignificant	−, insignificant
Percent elected	−, insignificant	−, insignificant	−, insignificant	+, significant	+, insignificant

*Conclusions based on final regressions in Nofsinger's Table 4 and Useem and Hess' Table 7 and Table 8.

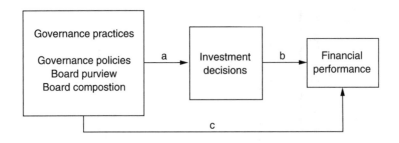

Figure 17.1 Conceptual framework relating governance practices and invest-ment decisions to financial performance.

Theoretically, modern investment theory asserts that meaningful dis-criminations between superior and inferior financial performance across units of analysis (e.g., individual investors, institutions, etc.) require the use of risk adjusted performance measures (Haugen, 1997). The reason for this is that total rates of return are more likely to depend on targeted levels of risk and the performance of markets than on "other" characteris-tics (e.g., superior/deficient skills, knowledge, governance practices, etc.). To illustrate, PERS with fewer near term liabilities may be in a position to try and capture higher returns associated with a bullish equity market while those with pending liabilities may not. Somewhat paradoxically, the financial investment literature is replete with theoretically acceptable measures of risk adjusted financial performance such as the Jensen or Treynor Indexes.[21] However, the lack of appropriate data in all likelihood hinders their employment for the foreseeable future.[22]

Given these inherent limitations on available information, pension fund researchers have tried to account for risk in a number of ways. Fre-quently the allocation of a system's portfolio to equities is cited as a con-trol variable for risk (e.g., given that stocks are generally more risky than bonds, cash, etc.). While not shown in Table 17.1, Useem and Mitchell (2000) do include the standard deviation of a system's annual rate of return over five years (1988–1992) as a risk control. They find a positive yet statistically insignificant coefficient for this variable.

While these exogenous measures are certainly useful and creative econometric constructs a couple of other practical and substantive issues remain. For example, since asset allocation strategy decisions appear to correlate highly with total returns there is a possibility that raw total fund returns may be too noisy for comparative measurement purposes. Indeed, this was part of Ambachtsheer's (1994) thesis in his analysis of the char-acteristics of 184 public and corporate pension plans during 1990–1993. If his assertion continues to be correct then the possibility exists that any direct governance practice effects, and/or their statistical significance, may essentially be hindered by noise. Therefore, the econometric assessment of path c in Figure 17.1 may be problematic.

Beyond this aspect there is also the chance that total return and risk adjusted measures of financial performance, should the latter be calculable, could lead to different findings and subsequent recommendations in terms of public policy and administration. For example, while Table 17.2 indicates that independent investment performance evaluations tend to result in public pensions placing higher percentages of assets in equity investments, and Table 17.1 indicates that marginal increases in equity investments result in positive changes for total rates of returns, neither table indicates that independent performance evaluations result in superior financial performance on a risk adjusted basis.[23]

So the question becomes "How can these possibilities be examined with the information that is currently available?" The best answer to this question appears to reside with Ambachshteer (1994) and Nofsinger (1998), who both perform an analysis that compares a pension's total rate of return against a simple benchmark return that attempts to account for retirement system portfolios with lower, similar, and higher levels of risk. Again, referencing Table 17.1, this result is what Nofsinger (1998) refers to as Abnormal Return.[24] Note that the absence of results in the third column of the table hints that the relationships between the previously unexamined predictors (listed in the first column) and the abnormal rate of return measure of financial performance are a logical next step in terms of econometrically oriented pension fund investment research.

17.4 Methodology

17.4.1 Target Population, Data Sources, and Sample Selection

The study population may be broadly defined as all large state and local government pension systems in the United States and corresponding territories. Systems responding to the Public Pension Coordinating Council's (PPCC) 1997, 2000, and 2001 *Surveys of State and Local Government Employee Retirement Systems* were selected for a purposive sample. The Public Pension Coordinating Council (PPCC) conducted the investigations between January and August of 1997, January and October of 1999, and during the Summer of 2001, respectively.

The information is publicly available in a variety of electronic formats.[25] The data files are extensive and include similar or identical items pertaining to a system's governance practices, assets, investment strategies, and financial performance for Fiscal and Calendar Years ending 1996, 1998, and 2000.[26] In discussing an earlier PPCC survey, Mitchell and Hsin (1997) state that " ... there is no larger, more up-to-date, and more representative survey of state and local pension plans in the country; the federal government collects no centralized information of this type (though many have suggested it should)" (p. 104).

17.4.1.1 Qualifications

Before continuing, a few of qualifications are in order. First, the data sources for this study are the most recent available and are from the same source as those discussed in Tables 17.1 and 17.2 above. Second, information from the 2000 survey was used by Albrecht and Hingorani (2004) in a companion analysis that limited the sample to those systems (a) offering DB plans only, (b) reporting the existence of a board of trustees, and (c) not allocating all assets to cash. We note in passing that sample definition appears to have little substantive impact on findings. However, this adjustment, in combination with the examination of different variables, does change the number of observations from that of the prior study. Third, the analyses that follow concentrate on investment strategy variables, only. Investment policies such as ETIs are left to future research.

17.4.2 Measures

Variable selection is based primarily on the review of econometric studies given above. Specifically, judgments regarding the inclusion of a particular governance practice, investment strategy decision, or measure of financial performance, in all or part of the analyses that follow is based on the works of Mitchell and Hsin (1997), Nofsinger (1998), Useem and Mitchell (2000), Useem and Hess (2001), Munnell and Sunden (2001), and Coronado et al. (2003). A notable exception exists in relation to trustee composition as Albrecht and Hingorani (2004) find some evidence of a negative effect for the percentage of a board that is appointed. Since this is deemed to be a policy relevant variable, the measure is also included in this investigation.

Table 17.3 presents the variables of interest and their derivation from each of the three surveys. The type of allowable response is also given in the second column. An important point to note is that several measures are constructed from existing survey items. This includes the percentage of a pension's membership which is elected or appointed and the actual allocation of a fund's portfolio to equity and fixed income investments.

Table 17.3 Survey Questions, Variable Constructions, and Possible Responses*

Survey Question or Variable Construction	Possible Responses
Governance policies	
Are investment restrictions specified in your state's constitution?	Yes or No
Does the system obtain independent investment performance evaluations?	Yes or No
Under what investment restrictions do you operate?(Prudent person or expert rule)	Yes or No
Board purview	
Who sets your asset allocation?	Yes or No
(Retirement Board/Trustees)	
Are the trustees of the system directly responsible for the investment of system assets?	Yes or No
Board composition and system size	
What is the Board's Composition?	Discrete
(Total number of board members)	numbers
What percentage of the board is elected or appointed?[a]	
(Total elected or appointed/ total number of Board members) × 100	
Investments (at fair value, in $ millions)	Continuous number
Investment strategies	
Percent equity	Continuous
(Domestic + Foreign + Real Estate + Other)	number
Percent fixed income	Continuous
(Domestic + Foreign + Other)	number
Some international investment of system assets[a]	Yes or No
(International equities + fixed income) > 0 = 1: 0 Otherwise	
Some indexing of stocks and bonds[a]	Yes or No
(Stock index funds + Bond index funds) > 0 = 1: 0 Otherwise	
Is your asset allocation long term?	Yes or No
(Not often changed with varying economic conditions)	
Financial performance	
Time weighted market rate of return (gross of investment fees) in calendar year	Continuous number
Abnormal return = Time weighted market rate of return (gross of investment fees) in calendar year − benchmark return[a]	Continuous number

*Questions are from the PPCC's Database User's Guides for 2001, 2000, and 1997 by Zorn, GFOA, and Zorn, respectively.
[a]Variable constructed from existing items but some existing forms are also used.

Originally, two investment strategy variables (some international investing and some indexing of system assets) were continuous in nature.
However, the dichotomy used here is consistent with prior studies.

17.4.3   Data Management and Screening

Prior to analysis all of the variables in each of the three surveys were
examined for accuracy of data, missing values, and fit between their
individual distributions and the assumptions of multivariate analysis.
Consistency checks revealed several reporting errors which were most
concentrated among portfolio distribution responses for the 1997 and
2000 surveys. Missing values were largely associated with the total return
measure of financial performance. To the extent possible corrections were
made for the 2000 survey during the companion investigation mentioned
earlier. A number of methods were pursued for remedy including examination of audited financial reports, website searches, cross checks with the
existing surveys, and personal contact of PERS representatives.[27]

As expected the system size variable, measured by the fair market value
of assets, was found to be extremely skewed in a positive direction.
Therefore, in order to mitigate this occurrence and to improve pairwise
linearity, the variable was logarithmically transformed. The transformation
reduced skewness from 4.33 to −0.12 for the 1997 survey, 4.30 to −0.12
for the 2000 survey, and 3.99 to −0.45 for the 2001 survey. Scatterplots
of each measure of financial performance against the transformations
indicate significant bivariate improvements for all three years.

17.4.4   Description of Procedure

Referencing the research questions in the introduction section of this
chapter, the approach taken here involves three primary stages. First, an
assessment of the trends in public pension governance practices, investment strategies, and financial performance is conducted with univariate
statistics over time. Second, bivariate associations between specific governance practices and investment strategies, and each measure of financial
performance is analyzed by the calculation of correlation coefficients. Third,
we consider the potential of a mediating role for investment strategies
through a series of multivariate regressions and a procedure proposed by
Baron and Kenny (1986).[28]

Given that the evidence concerning direction and statistical significance
in Tables 17.1 and 17.2 is generally mixed, two tailed tests of significance are reported below. However, our a priori expectations are that
governance   policies   entailing   constitutional   investment   restrictions

negatively impact financial performance while the implementation of prudent standards and independent performance evaluations exert a positive influence. Similarly, systems indicating board purview over asset allocation and investment decisions are anticipated to have a negative association with financial performance, as are marginal increases on both measures of board composition. Following Nofsinger (1998) and Coronado et al. (2003) findings are considered to be statistically significant provided that $p < 0.10$.

17.4.5 Sample Characteristics

Table 17.4 displays the number of state and local government retirement systems participating in the three surveys along with summary statistics of their wealth and other factors of interest. Signifying the significant positive skew of system assets the mean value of investments at fair market value is in excess of 9 times the median value for any given year. Reflecting a vibrant economy and stock market, the median value of pension fund assets increased by more than 76 percent between 1996 and 1998 and nearly 56 percent between 1998 and 2000. Overall, median assets increased by approximately 174 percent during the latter half of the 20th century while the mean value essentially doubled during the same time period.

Table 17.4 Summary Information of State and Local Government Pension Survey Respondents, 1996–2000*

	1996	1998	2000
Number of systems			
Responding to survey	261	246	153
Reporting value of assets	261	240	152
Fair value of system assets ($ millions)			
Mean	$5,026	$7,355	$10,351
Median	418	737	1,146
Maximum	100,700	143,300	172,200
Minimum	0.00	0.00	0.05
Total	1,311,739	1,765,276	1,573,278
Other summary information			
Number of plans	379	371	263
% of active plan members covered	81	85	67
% of assets reported by federal reserve	81	77	68

*Source: Authors' calculations except for "Other Summary Information" which is from individual GFOA Survey Reports that correspond to each year.

Collectively, total public pension wealth for the respondents increased by approximately 20 percent.

Table 17.4 also shows that the amount of assets reported by survey respondents constitutes a substantial proportion of all public pension assets as reported by the Federal Reserve. Even though representation was higher in the earlier accounts more than two-thirds of all wealth was held by those PERS continuing to participate in the 2000 survey. The same can be said for the number of active members covered by participants of the survey relative to that reported by the US Bureau of the Census. These figures underscore the extensive representation of monies and membership within this purposive sample.

17.5 Results

17.5.1 Univariate Statistics

17.5.1.1 Trends in PERS Governance Practices

To reiterate, the focus of this study is on three sets of key characteristics comprising PERS governance practices: (1) Governance Policies, (2) Board Purview over Investment Strategy Decisions, and (3) the Composition of Governing Boards. Focusing on these aspects the evidence shown in Table 17.5 reveals some changes in terms of governance policies against

Table 17.5 PERS Governance Characteristics, 1996–2000*

Governance Practices Mean (standard error)	1996	1998	2000
Governance policies (% using)			
Constitutional restrictions	19.11 (2.63)	20.35 (2.65)	20.27 (3.32)
Prudent standard	88.14 (2.11)	90.87 (1.90)	95.07 (1.82)
Performance evaluation	86.15 (2.28)	87.34 (2.16)	89.93 (2.47)
Board purview (% using)			
Board sets allocation	84.21 (2.42)	84.14 (2.43)	n.a.
Board directly invests	55.60 (3.27)	55.79 (3.26)	n.a.
Trustee composition			
Total board members	8.60 (0.23)	8.40 (0.21)	8.92 (0.28)
Percent appointed[a]	46.36 (1.98)	47.16 (2.10)	48.51 (2.50)
Percent elected[a]	35.22 (1.66)	35.67 (1.74)	34.30 (2.21)

Source: Authors' calculations.
* The number of retirement systems providing responses for each item ranges from 225 to 245 in 1996, 219 to 239 in 1998, and 142 to 149 in 2000.
[a]*Note*: Percentage is based on boards with a positive number of members only.

more persistent levels of board structures and measures of board authority over investment decisions. According to the table eight to nine trustees served on the typical board during all three years with more than one-third of them being elected to their positions. By comparison, more than 45 percent of members were appointed in both 1996 and 1998. However, by 2000 nearly half of PERS trustees were appointed with a 95 percent confidence interval, ranging from roughly 44 to 53 percent for survey respondents.

The trend evidence seems to favor the appointment form of member ship relative to that of elections. However, the data available for board purview in relation to investment decisions indicates that their authority is not necessarily increasing. Approximately 84 percent of PERS trustees were involved with asset allocation in both 1996 and 1998, the years for which data is available. And nearly 56 percent of trustees were directly responsible for investment decisions during these same time periods.

In terms of governance policies, nearly 20 percent of respondents reported the existence of investment restrictions in state constitutions for all three surveys. However, the implementation of prudent standards and independent investment performance evaluations continued to trend upward, with nearly 95 and 90 percent indicating affirmative responses for these queries by the year 2000, respectively.

17.5.1.1.1   Comparison to Earlier Findings

In some ways the results here are similar to that reported in a prior study by Useem and Hess (2001) and in other ways there are differences. In terms of corresponding parallels, the earlier investigators found the same overall persistent structure in terms of an average governing board's composition for the years 1990–1996. As shown in Figure 17.2, the mean estimates for the average number of trustees and the percentage of a board elected are also very comparable with this study in terms of magnitude.[29]

The major diversions relate more to changes in system policies and board purview over investment decisions. While the previous authors conclude (correctly) that changes in these characteristics were widespread during the period considered during their investigation, the results here are different. Figure 17.3 presents evidence in support of this statement.

To illustrate, Useem and Hess (2001) report that investment restrictions and board responsibility for investment decisions decreased during 1990–1996, from 26.2 to 19.1 percent and from 60.4 to 55.6 percent, respectively. They also show that board involvement with asset allocation decisions and the use of independent performance evaluations increased between 1992 and 1996 from 72.7 to 84.2 percent and from 70.6 to 86.2 percent, respectively.[30] These results lead the authors to state that

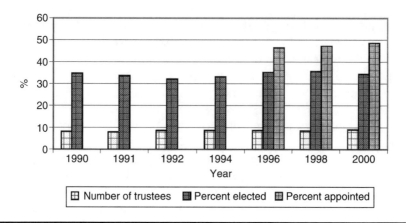

Figure 17.2 Public pension governing boards, 1990–2000.
Source: 1990–1996, Useem and Hess (2001): 1998–2000 authors' calculations.

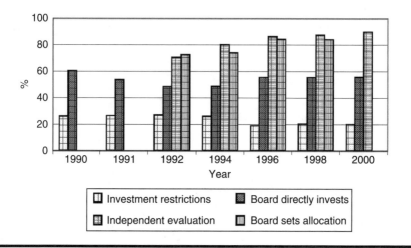

Figure 17.3 Public pension policies and purview, 1990–2000.
Source: 1990–1996, Useem and Hess (2001): 1998–2000 authors' calculations.

"if past trends are predictive of future movements, the recent past suggests that state prohibitions will diminish further, more boards will fix allocations, and outside appraisals will become the standard" (Useem and Hess, 2001, 136). However, referencing the last three columns of Table 17.5, a general result emerges that, other than an increase in the use of independent investment performance evaluations, which currently appears to be on the path to unanimous adoptions by PERS, little has changed in any

Table 17.6 PERS Investment Strategies, 1996–2000*

Allocation Strategies Mean (standard error)	1996	1998	2000
Domestic equity	42.73 (0.97)	45.22 (0.89)	44.25 (0.94)
International equity	6.85 (0.42)	8.31 (0.44)	10.78 (0.64)
Total equity	52.37 (1.17)	56.31 (1.05)	57.99 (1.19)
Domestic bonds	38.18 (1.19)	35.65 (1.06)	32.42 (1.25)
International fixed income	1.72 (0.26)	1.73 (0.20)	1.50 (0.21)
Total fixed income	41.17 (1.11)	38.82 (1.01)	33.91 (1.22)
Other strategies (% using)			
Long term	90.00 (1.90)	91.30 (1.86)	n.a.
Some indexing (stocks or bonds)	44.29 (3.44)	54.72 (3.43)	n.a.

Source: Authors' calculations.
*Number of systems responding ranges from 210 to 249 for the 1997 survey , 212 to 230 for the 2000 survey, and 148 for the 2001 survey.

substantive way. This indicates that these particular governance practices may have reached a point of equilibrium sometime during the mid 1990s.[31]

17.5.1.2   Trends in PERS Investment Strategy Decisions

Considering investment strategy decisions, Table 17.6 reveals that the percentage allocated to total equity investments continued to increase during the latter half of the 20th century to a mean value of nearly 58%. The standard error indicates that the 95 percent confidence interval for the year 2000 ranges from approximately 56 to 60 percent.

An interesting finding is that the positive change appears to be primarily from an increasing allotment towards international equities against a more persistent level of domestic stock. By comparison, the amount targeted towards international fixed income investments during the same time period remained relatively small but stable against a declining level of total and domestic fixed income investments. The 95 percent confidence interval indicates that PERS placed between 32 and 36 percent of funds into this latter asset class.

Considering choices in relation to other tactics, the information that is available suggests that PERS continued to invest more long term. The data also suggest that substantially more funds placed at least some of their assets in index funds in 1998 than in 1996. Collectively, these results at least hint at the prospect that those charged with the oversight of state and local government investment activities are increasingly favoring the notion of efficient markets.

17.5.1.2.1   Comparison to Earlier Findings

Figure 17.4 compares selected aspects of these recent findings against Useem and Hess's (2001) earlier account. Obviously PERS have continued to place more of their funds in equity investments over that of fixed income investments. They have also continued the trend of investing more in international stock. By comparison, the evidence in the figure indicates that allotments towards foreign fixed income may very well have climaxed in the mid to late 1990s and began somewhat of a downturn. Decisions to invest long term also show some evidence of continuing to trend upward, at least for the years in which data is available.

17.5.1.3   Trends in PERS Financial Performance

Prior to considering the trend in PERS financial performance the abnormal return measure was calculated by first creating a benchmark return for each system and then subtracting the benchmark return from a system's total return for the calendar year. The benchmark return was constructed by weighting returns to various indexes according to the reported asset allocation of each system. For example, the total return of a fund with reported allocations of 60 percent in domestic equities, 30 percent domestic bonds, and 10 percent cash is measured against a benchmark portfolio of 60 percent in domestic equities, 30 percent domestic bonds, and 10 percent cash. Equation (1) below is a general formula for this risk

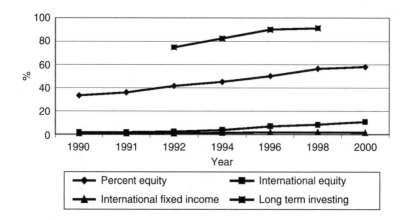

Figure 17.4   Select PERS investment strategies, 1990–2000.
Source: 1990–1996, Useem and Hess (2001): 1998–2000 authors' calculations.

adjusted measure of financial performance, using the year 2000 as an example:

$$2000 \text{ Abnormal Return} = 2000 \text{ Total Return} - 2000 \text{ Benchmark Return} \quad (1)$$

The asset classes and benchmark indexes are as follows: (a) domestic equities indexed by the S&P 500, (b) international fixed income indexed by the MSCI EAFE, (c) domestic fixed income and real estate mortgages indexed by the Lehman Aggregate, (d) international fixed income indexed by the Salomon World Government Index, (e) real estate equities indexed by the Dow Jones Wilshire REIT Index, (f) cash and short term securities indexed by the US Treasury Bill, (g) alternative and other investments indexed by the NCREIF Property Index.[32]

Table 17.7 lists the indexes along with their values for each year. The table also presents averages for each measure of financial performance. As shown, total return ranged from a high of 14.41 percent in 1998 to a low of 6.37 percent in 2000. This reflects the performance of the stock market during these periods (Harris, 2002, 7). By comparison, abnormal return ranges from a high of 1.32 percent in 2000 to a low of −3.96 percent during 1998.[33] Noting that average 1996 abnormal return is slightly positive, the years which would appear to be inferior on a total return basis are in fact superior on this measure of financial performance.

Table 17.7   Financial Performance for Public Pensions and Various Indexes, 1996–2000

Financial Performance Mean (standard error)	1996	1998	2000
Total ROR	13.66 (0.26)	14.41 (0.35)	6.37 (0.54)
Abnormal ROR	0.34 (0.20)	−3.96 (0.32)	1.32 (0.57)
Index[a]			
Benchmarks			
S & P 500	23.07	28.75	−9.10
MSCI EAFE	6.36	20.33	−13.96
Lehman aggregate	3.61	8.67	11.63
Salomon World Gov't.	3.63	15.29	1.60
Dow Jones Wilshire REIT	37.05	−17.01	31.04
U.S. treasury bills	5.30	5.02	6.21
NCREIF property	10.31	16.24	12.24

[a] All Index data are from page 43 of the Illinois Municipal Retirement Fund 2000 Comprehensive Financial Report except for the Dow Jones Wilshire REIT Index and the NCREIF Property Index which are from www.wilshire.com last accessed 7/15/04, and www.ncreif.com last accessed 7/15/04, respectively.

17.5.2 Bivariate Results[34]

17.5.2.1 Governance Practices and Financial Performance

In order to determine whether or not an association exists between PERS governance practices and either measure of financial performance a bivariate analysis is conducted using the 2000 survey data; the latest year for which all data is available. Due to the restricted range of the prudent standard variable as shown in Table 17.5, this measure is dropped from further consideration. In addition, the insignificant findings of elected membership, as shown in Tables 17.1 and 17.2, support the elimination of this variable in order to concentrate on appointed membership.

The results are presented in Table 17.8.[35] The reader should note that, in order to facilitate a comparison, the correlation coefficients corresponding to total return are located to the left (Southwest) of the principal diagonal in column 1, while correlation coefficients corresponding to abnormal return are located to the right (Northeast) of the principal diagonal in row 1. Naturally, the rest of the values are symmetric.

Referencing the first column and the first row of the table, the most important result appears to be that the correlation coefficients differ both in terms of magnitude and direction. For example, while the calculated coefficients for constitutional investment restrictions in relation to both measures of financial performance are negative, the coefficient corresponding to total return is stronger. By comparison, the positive association between total return and independent performance evaluations does not hold when considering abnormal return. Interestingly, the coefficients between the board purview variables and abnormal return are slightly more substantive than when considering total return. In addition, the percentage of board members who are appointed appears to have a negative relationship with both measures of financial performance.

The central point here is that the evidence indicates that there are statistically significant associations between individual governance practices and either measure of financial performance. In addition, the direction for like measures are identical to that shown in Table 17.1. This suggests that path c in Figure 17.1, the direct path between governance practices and financial performance, may be relevant prior to multivariate examinations that allow for other factors to be held constant.

17.5.2.2 Investment Strategies and Financial Performance

In order to determine whether or not an association exists between PERS investment strategies and either measure of financial performance another

Table 17.8 Correlation Coefficients of Governance Practice Variables and Financial Performance (1998)*

	Financial Performance	Constitutional Restrictions	Performance Evaluation	Board Allocates	Board Invests	Percent Appointed	Total Members	System Size
Financial performance	1.00	-0.061	-0.045	-0.220[c]	0.103	-0.127	-0.071	0.212[c]
Constitutional restrictions	-0.116[a]	1.00	-0.067	-0.050	-0.106	-0.027	-0.178[c]	-0.173[c]
Performance evaluation	0.153[b]	-0.067	1.00	0.122[a]	0.025	0.004	0.078	0.367[c]
Board allocates	-0.183[c]	-0.050	0.122[a]	1.00	0.123[a]	0.029	0.091	-0.012
Board invests	0.070	-0.106	0.025	0.123[a]	1.00	0.03	0.055	0.111[a]
Percent appointed	-0.174[b]	-0.027	0.004	0.029	0.030	1.00	-0.025	-0.054
Total members	0.034	-0.178[c]	0.078	0.091	0.055	-0.025	1.00	0.387[c]
System size	0.319[c]	-0.173[c]	0.367[c]	-0.012	0.111[a]	-0.054	0.387[c]	1.00

Source: Authors' calculations.

*Note: Southwest = 1998 Total return and Northeast = 1998 Abnormal return.

Only those systems with acceptable reports on portfolio distribution are utilized when considering abnormal return.

[a] $p < 0.10$, [b] $p < 0.05$, [c] $p < 0.01$.

Table 17.9   Correlation Coefficients of Investment Strategies and Financial Performance (1998)*

	Financial Performance	Percent Equity	Fixed Income	Foreign Investment	Long Term Investing	Some Indexing
Financial performance	1.00	−0.180[b]	0.168[b]	−0.092	0.169[b]	−0.004
Percent equity	0.363[c]	1.00	−0.857[c]	0.497[c]	0.084	0.209[c]
Fixed income	−0.330[c]	−0.857[c]	1.00	−0.467[c]	0.008	−0.204[c]
Foreign investment	0.104	0.497[c]	−0.467[c]	1.00	0.008	0.150[b]
Long term investing	0.231[c]	0.084	0.008	0.008	1.00	−061
Some indexing	0.020	0.209[c]	−0.204[c]	0.150[b]	−0.061	1.00

Source: Authors' calculations.
* Note: Southwest = 1998 Total return and Northeast = 1998 Abnormal return.
Only those systems with acceptable reports on portfolio distribution are utilized when considering abnormal return. Number of systems ranges from 184–212.
[a] $p < 0.10$, [b] $p < 0.05$, [c] $p < 0.01$.

bivariate analysis is conducted using the 2000 survey data. The results are presented in Table 17.9.

Again, referencing the first column and the first row of the table, indexing tactics do not appear to correlate strongly with either measure of performance. By comparison, decisions to invest long term tactics correlate positively with both measures. However, the most important result that emerges is the opposing relationships for each measure of financial performance in relation to asset allocation decisions. The next section begins to decipher these complex relationships through the use of multivariate techniques.

17.5.3   Multivariate Results

17.5.3.1   The Impact of Governance Practices on Investment Strategies

To examine the extent to which governance practices determine investment strategy decisions, each strategy is regressed on the governance practices that remain of interest for the 2000 survey. The results are reported in Table 17.10.

Table 17.10 Regressions of 1998 Investment Strategies on Governance Practices (standard error)

Variable	Percent Equity	Fixed Income	Foreign Investment	Long Term	Indexing Portfolio
Constant	40.059^c (4.638)	51.362^c (4.428)	−0.678 (0.769)	0.930 (1.05)	−0.529 (0.739)
Governance policies					
Constitutional restrictions	−4.968^a (2.568)	2.064 (2.391)	−0.843^b (0.399)	0.475 (0.724)	−0.494 (0.383)
Performance evaluation	16.278^c (3.077)	−13.161^c (2.888)	1.209^b (0.476)	1.178^a (0.626)	1.109^b (0.526)
Board purview					
Board sets allocation	−0.258 (2.706)	3.793 (2.537)	−0.501 (0.495)	1.125^b (0.559)	0.219 (0.422)
Board directly invests	−1.448 (2.023)	3.613^a (1.892)	0.038 (0.353)	0.945^a (0.547)	0.383 (0.304)
Board composition					
Percent appointed	−0.029 (0.032)	0.037 (0.030)	−0.006 (0.005)	−0.001 (0.008)	−0.005 (0.005)
Total board members	0.688^b (0.299)	−1.064^c (0.285)	0.212^c (0.067)	−0.093 (0.064)	−0.036 (0.045)
R^2	0.173^c	0.180^c	0.121	0.067	0.053
n	210	212	212	212	194

Source: Authors' calculations.

[a] $p < 0.10$, [b] $p < 0.05$, [c] $p < 0.01$; linear regressions for percent equity and fixed income; logistic regressions for other criterion variables; Cox and Snell R2 for logistic regressions.

As shown, the configuration of PERS governance practices has a substantive impact on investment strategy decisions. Focusing on those variables with statistically significant coefficients, public pensions operating in states with constitutional investment restrictions allocate less of their assets to equities and foreign investments. On the other hand, systems obtaining independent investment performance evaluations place more of their monies within both of these measure while decreasing their allocations to fixed income investments. In addition, systems with this form of governance policy are more likely to invest long term and to index some portion of their stock and bond investments. Boards with purview over asset allocation decisions and direct responsibility for investing system assets also tend to invest long term while placing more assets with fixed income investments. While the latter measure is not statistically significant for fixed income decisions the substantive magnitude is worth mentioning.

When considering the composition of pension fund boards, the results indicate that the addition of a trustee enhances the likelihood that a fund places at least some assets in foreign investments and also increases the percentage allotted towards equity investments by nearly seventy basis points. Conversely, this same marginal change in membership appears to decrease the percentage allocated to fixed income investment by slightly more than a full percentage point, holding all other factors constant.

17.5.3.2 The Impact of Governance and Investment Strategies on Financial Performance

In order to examine PERS performance another series of multivariate regressions are conducted, with both outcomes as criterion variables on governance practices that continue to be of interest and the investment strategy variables. Referencing Table 17.9, the highly collinear relation between percent equities and percent fixed income ($r = -0.86$, $p < 0.01$), suggests that only one of these strategies should be included. Since fixed income investments remains a largely unexamined aspect of PERS research, a decision is made to include this measure along with the foreign investments tactic and another previously unexamined investment strategy variable; some indexing of stock and bond investments. Referencing Table 17.6, the poor dichotomous split associated with long term investing tactics restricts the sample range and is subsequently dropped from further analysis.[36]

The results of these regressions are portrayed in Table 17.11. Some significant and general findings include the fact that the measures for board and system size remain statistically significant for all regressions, albeit in different directions. In addition, while the indexing strategy coefficient is

Table 17.11 1998 Financial Performance on Governance and Investment Strategies (standard error)

Variable	Total Return	Total Return	Abnormal Return	Abnormal Return
Constant	14.751^c (1.593)	20.721^c (2.308)	-1.773 (1.471)	-4.864^b (2.210)
Governance policies				
Constitutional restrictions	-1.053 (0.814)	-1.341 (0.831)	-0.443 (0.754)	-1.051 (0.789)
Performance evaluation	0.114 (1.071)	-0.193 (1.173)	-1.825^a (0.980)	-0.760 (1.118)
Board purview				
Board sets allocation	-1.436^a (0.864)	-0.750 (0.930)	-1.590^b (0.806)	-1.662^a (0.882)
Board directly invests	0.228 (0.629)	0.254 (0.643)	0.673 (0.576)	0.512 (0.606)
Board composition				
Percent appointed	-0.022^b (0.010)	-0.015 (0.010)	-0.015^a (0.009)	-0.016^a (0.010)
Total board members	-0.187^a (0.098)	-0.256^b (0.102)	-0.235^c (0.090)	-0.216^b (0.096)
Other control				
System size	0.517^c (0.145)	0.548^c (0.162)	0.463^c (0.135)	0.620^c (0.153)
Investment strategy				
Fixed income		-0.112^c (0.028)		0.061^b (0.026)
Foreign investments		-1.328 (0.900)		-0.908 (0.879)
Indexing portfolio		-1.744^b (0.686)		-0.693 (0.648)
R^2	0.145^c	0.209^c	0.140^c	0.212^c
n	202	179	196	171

Source: Authors' Calculations.

[a] $p < 0.10$, [b] $p < 0.05$, [c] $p < 0.01$

Note: The definition and construction of Abnormal Return requires accurate portfolio data and only those systems within tolerance are included in the regressions for this measure of financial performance (see note 27). This explains why the fourth column here mirrors the top portion of Table 17.3.

negative for both measures of financial performance, the coefficient is more substantive and statistically significant only when considering total return. Somewhat more interesting results appear in relation to independent investment performance evaluations, board involvement with asset allocation decisions, the appointed membership of trustees, and the percentage of funds in fixed income investments.

Specifically, the coefficient on independent investment performance evaluations, while never statistically significant, changes direction after controlling for investment strategies when considering total return criterion. At the same time, the magnitude of "negativity" and statistical significance are both reduced on this measure when considering abnormal return. This same occurrence of events happens when taking into consideration the effects of percent appointed and board purview over asset allocation decisions on total return. By comparison both of these measures remain negative and statistically significant when considering the abnormal return measure of financial performance, even after controlling for investment strategies. And, apparently fixed income investments appear to continue exhibiting different types of impacts on each measure of financial performance.

Finally, an important point to note is that most of the associations (for total return) which are statistically significant in Table 17.8 virtually disappear in the multivariate analysis. A notable exception applies to the total board members variable which is not statistically significant in Table 17.8. By comparison, more governance practices are significant predictors of abnormal return in Table 17.11 than in Table 17.8.

17.5.3.3 Testing Mediation

Given that the fixed income investment strategy remains a statistically significant predictor for both measures of financial performance, a decision was made to more comprehensively test the potential for a mediating role (Figure 17.1) of this variable in the data generating process. Following a statistical procedure outlined by Baron and Kenny (1986) the following series of regressions were run:

1. First, each measure of financial performance was regressed on all governance practice variables while controlling for system size. This step essentially tests "path c" in Figure 17.1 within a multivariate framework.[37]
2. Second, the fixed income investment strategy was regressed on all governance practice variables while controlling for system size. This step essentially tests "path a" in Figure 17.1 within a multivariate framework.

3. Third, each measure of financial performance was regressed on all governance practice variables and the fixed income investment strategy variable while controlling for system size. This step essentially tests "path b" in Figure 17.1 within a multivariate framework.

Some important points to note are that the first step essentially calculates the total effect of a particular governance practice on financial performance holding other factors constant. Concomitantly, the product (multiplication) of any particular governance practice coefficient calculated in step 2 and the coefficient on the fixed income investment strategy variable calculated in step 3 reveals the indirect effect for any particular governance practice on financial performance holding other factors constant. In order to assess the statistical significance of indirect effects the following Z score was calculated:[38]

$$Z = ab/(S_a^2 S_b^2 + b^2 S_a^2 + a^2 S_b^2)^{1/2}$$

Where:
S_a = Standard error of path a in Figure 17.1
S_b = Standard error of path b in Figure 17.1
a = Path coefficient of a in Figure 17.1
b = Path coefficient of b in Figure 17.1

Findings were then analyzed for the presence of three types of mediating relationships.

1. *Weak mediation:* This form requires only that the coefficient for a particular governance practice be statistically significant in the second regression and that the fixed income investment strategy coefficient be significant in the third regression.[39]
2. *Partial mediation:* This form requires that the coefficient for a particular governance practice be statistically significant in the first, second, and third regressions. In addition, the fixed income investment strategy coefficient must be statistically significant in the third regression while the absolute value of a governance practice coefficient must necessarily be less in the third regression than in the first regression.
3. *Complete mediation:* This form requires the same conditions as partial mediation with the exception that a particular governance practice is not statistically significant in the third regression.[40]

The results in relation to total return are presented in Table 17.12 while parallel findings relative to abnormal return are given in Table 17.13.

Table 17.12 Beta Coefficients for 1998 Total Rate of Return (n = 191)

Variable	B	SE	p
W/out fixed income			
Constitutional restrictions	−0.841	0.846	0.321
Performance evaluation*	0.223[c]	1.099	0.840
Board sets allocation	− 1.538	0.904	0.090
Board directly invests*	− 0.024	0.647	0.971
Percent appointed	− 0.022	0.010	0.033
Total board members*	− 0.136	0.101	0.181
System size	0.414	0.152	0.007
	$R^2 = 0.110$		0.003
With fixed income			
Constitutional restrictions	− 0.638	0.817	0.435
Performance evaluation*	− 0.810[c]	1.092	0.459
Board sets allocation	− 1.344	0.872	0.125
Board directly invests*	0.264	0.627	0.674
Percent appointed	− 0.017	0.010	0.096
Total board members*	− 0.209	0.099	0.037
System size	0.358	0.147	0.016
Fixed income	−0.093	0.024	0.000
	$R^2 = 0.179$		0.000

*Indicates a statistically significant impact on fixed income investment strategy.
[a]Difference between B values in equations with and without Total Fixed Income: $p < 0.10$
[b]Difference between B values in equations with and without Total Fixed Income: $p < 0.05$
[c]Difference between B values in equations with and without Total Fixed Income: $p < 0.01$

Due to the fact that the procedure outlined by Baron and Kenny (1986) requires complete information only those systems without any missing observations are included in the analysis.[41]

Considering the total return measure of financial performance, the most significant finding is that there is a reduction in the original value for all governance practice coefficients, except for the total number of board members variable which increases from −0.136 to −0.209. Excluding this variable, the general interpretation of these results are that fixed income strategies, which is negatively associated with total return, weakly mediate the relationship between some governance practices and this measure of financial performance. This determination is based on the fact that, while three governance practice variables (obtainment of independent investment performance evaluations, percentage of the board appointed, and total number of board members) are found to have a statistically

Table 17.13 Beta Coefficients for 1998 Abnormal Rate of Return (n = 191)

Variable	B	SE	p
W/out fixed income			
Constitutional restrictions	−0.443	0.754	0.557
Performance evaluation*	−1.825^c	0.980	0.064
Board sets allocation	−1.590	0.806	0.050
Board directly invests*	0.673	0.576	0.244
Percent appointed	−0.015	0.009	0.094
Total board members*	−0.235^b	0.090	0.010
System size	0.463	0.135	0.001
	$R^2 = 0.140$		0.00
With fixed income			
Constitutional restrictions	−0.587	0.739	0.428
Performance evaluation*	−1.096^c	0.988	0.269
Board sets allocation	−1.727	0.789	0.030
Board directly invests*	0.470	0.568	0.409
Percent appointed	−0.019	0.009	0.036
Total board members	−0.183^b	0.090	0.043
System size	0.503	0.133	0.000
Fixed income	0.066	0.022	0.003
	$R^2 = 0.181$		0.00

*Indicates a statistically significant impact on fixed income investment strategy.
[a]Difference between B values in equations with and without Total Fixed Income: $p < 0.10$
[b]Difference between B values in equations with and without Total Fixed Income: $p < 0.05$
[c]Difference between B values in equations with and without Total Fixed Income: $p < 0.01$

significant impact on the fixed income investment strategy variable, only one of them meets the more strict requirements for partial or complete mediation at the 10 percent level of significance.

Focusing on Table 17.13 a somewhat different picture emerges. For example, the inflation and deflation of governance practice coefficients indicates a varying role for the fixed income investment strategy in relation to abnormal return, which is positive and statistically significant. In addition, the reduction in the absolute value of the coefficients and corresponding significance tests for two variables, obtainment of independent investment performance evaluations and the total number of board members, indicates complete and partial mediation for these measures, respectively. However, in both of these cases, the indirect effects (which can be calculated by subtracting the governance practice coefficient reported in the lower half of the table from the governance practice coefficient reported in the upper half of the table) are relatively less substantive than the direct effects that are reported in the lower half of the table.

17.6 Discussion and Conclusion

As noted in the introduction, the primary purpose of this chapter was to generate useable knowledge that can be used by financial managers, public administrators, policymakers, and other stakeholders to address issues surrounding the impending retirement of the baby boom generation. This was accomplished by seeking answers to the following three research questions:

1. What are the most recent trends in state and local government pension fund governance practices, investment strategies, and financial performance?
2. Are there associations between (a) governance practices and financial performance, (b) investment strategies and financial performance, and (c) governance practices and investment strategies?
3. Do investment strategies mediate the relationship between governance practices and financial performance?

Regarding the first question, the univariate time series analysis suggests that PERS are relatively heterogeneous institutions in some ways and increasingly less so in others. For example, the formal use of prudent standards in relation to investment activities is now nearly unanimous for all state and local government retirement systems. Given this result, a likely explanation for the lack of historical statistical significance when considering the relationship between prudent standards and financial performance (e.g., Table 17.1) is that PERS may have always operated "prudently," whether such a policy was officially in place or not. In addition, the obtainment of independent investment performance evaluations also appears to be on the way to implementation by all public pension funds. Therefore, if a governance equilibrium was indeed reached the during the latter portion of the 1990s the remaining measures of governance used here are likely to be the source of most variation. In any respect, the results reported here suggest that the average state and local government retirement system currently:

- is relatively unrestrained by constitutional investment restrictions;
- uses the prudent standard when making investment decisions;
- obtains independent investment performance evaluations;
- gives trustees purview over asset allocation and investment decisions;

- is composed of eight to nine members, half of whom are appointed, a third of whom are elected.

Should a national governing board be established according to subnational governance practices, the configuration of a governing board might be expected to be the same.

In terms of investment strategies, the great majority of funds now claim to invest long term. By comparison PERS asset allocation tactics are quite varied among funds and an increasing percentage of these monies appear to be placed in indexes. Coincidentally, increases in the placement of funds with index investments is consistent with the notion of long term investing. Interestingly, state and local government retirement systems do seem to be increasingly interested in what is going on financially oversees. To summarize, the evidence presented here suggests that the average state and local government retirement system currently:

- chooses long term investment strategies over tactical investing techniques;
- indexes some portion of stock and fixed income investments;
- places nearly 11 percent of funds in foreign equity investments;
- allocates nearly 60 percent of assets to equity investments and more than a third to fixed income investments.

Again, should a national governing board be established according to subnational governance practices the investment decisions of trustees might be anticipated to be similar.

Considering these simple observations of what appears to actually be in terms of PERS governance practices and investment strategy decisions, a natural question is whether or not this is what "should be" in terms of financial performance. On this question the results are somewhat mixed. Referencing Table 17.7, while average total return is strictly positive for PERS during all three years, average abnormal return is positive for 2000, negative for 1998, and nearly 0 for 1996, with a 95 percent confidence interval ranging from −0.05 percent to 0.73 percent. Therefore, while the typical fund did increase system assets during these periods, the question of whether or not the return was commensurate with the risk entailed is not completely clear.

Considering the bivariate analysis in Table 17.8, all of the substantive and statistically significant associations between either measure of financial performance and governance practices are negative except for one specific relationship: total return and the obtainment of independent investment performance evaluations. Table 17.9 indicates opposing relationships for asset allocations to equity and fixed income investments which concomitantly depend on the definition of financial performance. By and large these results are fairly persistent even during multivariate analyses of (a) investment strategy criterion variables on governance practices (Table 17.10), and (b) financial performance criterion variables on governance practices and investment decisions (Table 17.11). However, governance practices continue to exhibit more direct and substantive effects on abnormal return when examining the mediating potential of the fixed income strategy (Table 17.12).

Therefore, compared to the examination of "what is" the statistical and substantive results reported here suggest that PERS should:

- continue to be relatively free of constitutional investment restrictions;
- re-evaluate the implementation of independent investment performance evaluations;
- reconsider the involvement of trustees in asset allocation decisions;
- reduce the percentage of appointed membership;
- re-evaluate the actual investments within asset classes, especially equity investments, in order to not only achieve higher total returns but risk adjusted returns as well.

A rather important point to note when considering the second and fourth bullets above is that there appears to be a contradiction in the literature concerning the proper role of performance evaluations in pension fund investment management. For example, in discussing positive theory, Bailey suggests that when properly implemented "performance evaluation operates as a feedback-and-control mechanism carried out within the context of investment policy ... and can not be used to judge the appropriateness of investment policy" (p. 31). The author also cites a number of questions appropriate for performance evaluations, including "what did the policy allocations to asset classes and individual managers contribute to investment results" (p. 32).

By comparison, Useem and Mitchell note that, despite an increase in risk, external evaluators may often push retirement systems to invest more heavily in equities so as to increase total returns (p. 33). This suggestion is at odds with the discussion presented by Bailey and may indicate an inappropriate use of performance evaluations by systems in assessing investment policies rather than focusing on performance attribution. This may explain why the coefficient for this measure is completely mediated in a negative direction when considering abnormal return. In any respect, these are issues that should be considered if a national governing board is to be established according to subnational governance practices and investment decisions.

17.6.1 *Additional Considerations*

Despite the decomposition and statistical testing of effects, one interesting and pertinent question remains as to whether or not the results and subsequent conclusions would still apply after accounting for expenses. For example, international strategies are likely to entail more investment expenses than fixed income investments and post investment performance is a relevant consideration.

While not examined here, we note that in the companion analysis to this investigation an investment expense ratio was calculated by dividing 1998 investment activity expense by 1998 total system assets.[42] Even though the average investment expense ratio was more than 3.5%, the figure declined with system size ($r = -0.34$, $p < 0.001$). There was no statistical or substantive evidence that the ratio was correlated with either of the investment strategies. Therefore, net asset returns should be similar to those given above.

17.6.2 *Limitations and Suggestions for Future Research*

The findings must be interpreted in light of several limitations. First, the data are cross sectional: assessing the effects of governance practices and investment strategies on financial performance with longitudinal data is critical. Second, the choice of index is likely to be somewhat of a determining factor in the construction of abnormal returns. Risk adjusted financial performance, as a key construct, could be stronger if better measures were available. Third, investment strategies examined here are not the only tactics used by public pension funds. These decisions should be examined in conjunction with other strategies such as hedging. Finally, structural equation modeling would be beneficial in assessing the simultaneous effects of multiple factors.

Nonetheless, we hope that this econometric study of state and local government retirement systems during the last decade of the 20th century has contributed in some positive way. And, we look forward to the advances of the future.

Notes

1.   According to the American Association of Retired Persons (1999, p. 1) "Baby Boomers represent the largest single sustained growth of the population in the history of the United States … this generation has reinterpreted each successive stage of life … they are again poised to redefine the next stage, retirement."

2. The following figures are available from http://www.census.gov/govs/www/index.html. Last Accessed 08/02/04.

3. In public defined benefit plans, participants are promised a benefit depending on factors such as salary, length of employment, inflation, etc. (Nofsinger, 1998, 89). By comparison, defined contribution plans do not guarantee such a benefit and essentially shift decision making and risk towards plan participants. This chapter limits the discussion to defined benefit schemes which currently dominate state and local government retirement systems (GFOA, 2000, 29).

4. Most states and localities hold each member of a retirement board to fiduciary standards of conduct known as the prudent-person rule. This concept, grounded in English common law, requires each board member to perform his or her duties as a prudent person would when acting in a like capacity and in a similar situation (Eitelberg, 1997, 9).

5. For a discussion of this topic see Coronado et al. (2003), pages 581–582.

6. A strictly theoretical or practical administrative dichotomy does not exist within the literature as some researchers investigate both aspects at the same time. However, the dissection is useful for the purpose of discussion.

7. The definitions of agency costs and residual claimants as given above can generally be attributed to Fama and Jensen (1983). However, the demarcation seems very apposite from a political economy perspective. See Bickers and Williams (2001), pages 22–24 for a discussion on delimiting the relevant public.

8. Useem and Hess (2001) also note the theoretical possibility of a curvilinear relationship between the number of board members and performance. However, empirical verifications of this prospect do not appear to exist in the PERS econometric literature at this time.

9. To illustrate, in the public sector there would be nothing unusual about having a county retirement system largely staffed by members whose primary occupations are that of high school educators.

10. As noted by Coronado et al. (2003) during the 1980s, many public plans restricted investment in South Africa in protest of the government's apartheid policy. While these restrictions no longer exist today, many states require investment managers to invest only in companies following the MacBride principles, which restrict religious discrimination in employment in Northern Ireland (584).

11. An argument could be made that ETIs are investment strategy decisions. However, they are not considered as such in this chapter.

12. Interestingly, a theme underlying the work of Ibbotson and Kaplan (2000) was that the overall conclusion of the Brinson et al. studies was not being interpreted correctly by financial researchers. Their extension of the earlier investigations really amounted to a very informative demonstration of this observation and a correction in interpretations.

13. Presumably funds that do this believe that capital gaps exist and that the market is inefficient in not channeling resources to these projects.

14. There are variations on the theory of efficient markets. But the important point here is the view of PERS concerning whether or not asset prices reflect all available information.

15. In the authors' opinions national schemes have received far more attention.

16. Most of the data for these studies comes from the Government Finance Officers Association's periodic surveys of state and local government retirement systems.

17. These classifications follow that used by Useem and Hess (2001) and Useem and Mitchell (2000).

18. To be clear, percentage elected is not defined (measured) exactly the same way for each of these studies. To facilitate discussion we simply mean this to be a general category for this variable.

19. The sample period for both studies is 1992.

20. This statement is a variation on that given by Useem and Mitchell (2000) on pages 489 and 502. However, in their study the authors are referring only to investment strategy decisions.

21. As noted by Gallagher (2003), risk-adjusted performance metrics commonly employed in the published literature rely heavily on the theoretical Capital Asset Pricing Model (CAPM). Readers interested in an accessible discussion of this subject may wish to consult Haugen (1997), pages 305–340.

22. Nofsinger (1998) acknowledges the lack of appropriate data on page 91.

23. One way around this might be to simply interpret equities as a proxy for risk. But this potentially confounds a meaningful interpretation of equities as a strategy variable.

24. Ambachtsheer (1994) refers to this measure as "implementation return".

25. Specifically, the data for the 1997 and 2000 surveys may be purchased from the Government Finance Officers Association (GFOA), along with accompanying software packages which are collectively known as the PENDAT 1997 and 2000 databases. The data for the 2001 survey can be downloaded free of charge as a Microsoft Access 2000 database from the PPCC's web site at www.ppcc.grsnet.com.

26. While not a major concern of this study one might wish to note that the PENDAT FILES and the Microsoft Access 2000 database include other information concerning a system's auditing and accounting, funding practices, benefit mixes, etc. There are some time series items associated with the PENDAT databases as well.

27. Missing data and reporting errors are certainly not confined to this investigation. For example, Nofsinger (1998) and Mitchell and Hsin (1997) report the existence of similar problems in their studies using earlier PENDAT surveys. For a more detailed discussion of remedies in relation to the 2000 survey see Albrecht and Hingorani (2004) and Albrecht (2001). We note in passing that portfolios distributions summing to 100± 3 percent were considered acceptable for this study.

28. An important point to note is that in order to directly connect to earlier studies we do not employ any of the remedies listed above during the univariate portions of this study. Therefore, the data remains as is. However, to improve sample size we do import missing information for the total rate of return variable from the 2001 survey to use during the bivariate analysis relative to abnormal return and all multivariate procedures.

29. The authors did not examine appointed membership.

30. These were the years for which data was available.

31. The authors did not examine the prudent standard.

32. The indexes here are not completely identical to that used in the companion analysis by Albrecht and Hingorani (2004). However, all indexes are common in the financial literature.

33. This figure is comparable with the -4 percentage points Albrecht and Hingorani (2004) find when analyzing the more restrictive sample.

34. Beginning with the bivariate analysis, we import reported values for the 1998 total return from the 2001 survey for those which are missing in the 2000 survey.

35. Pearson's r is the reported coefficient unless both variables are dichotomous. Under these conditions Phi is the statistic that is reported.

36. Tabachnick and Fidell (2001) discuss the problems associated with "deflated correlations" on pages 57–58.

37. This step is noticeably absent in the econometric literature discussed earlier.

38. The Z score above is given in Kenny, Kashy, and Bolger (1998) on page 260. Their derivation of the statistic is based on the work of Sobel (1982).

39. This form of mediation is essentially that discussed by Useem and Mitchell (2000).

40. Partial and complete mediation are the terms used by Baron and Kenny (1986).

41. To facilitate comparison, only those systems with both measures of financial performance are included. Otherwise the number analyzed for total return would be higher than that for abnormal return.

42. This procedure replicated that of Useem and Mitchell (2000).

References

Albrecht, W.G. (2001). Effects of governance and investment strategies on public pension outcomes. Unpublished Ph.D. dissertation, Southern University, Baton Rouge, LA.

Albrecht, W.G., and Hingorani V.L. (2004). Effects of governance practices and investment strategies on state and local government pension fund financial performance. *International Journal of Public Administration,* 27 (nos. 8 & 9), 673–700.

Ambachtsheer, K.P. (1994). The economics of pension fund management. *Financial analysts Journal* Nov/Dec, 21–31.

American Association of Retired Persons (1999). Retirement Research. http://research.aarp.org/index.html Last Accessed 11-00.

Bailey, J.V. (1997). Investment policy: the missing ink. In F.J. Fabozzi (ed), *Pension Fund Investment Management,* pp. 17–34. New Hope: Frank J. Fabozzi Associates.

Baron, R.M., & Kenny, D.A. (1986). The moderator-mediator variable distinction in social psychological research: conceptual, strategic, and statistical considerations. *Journal of Personality and Social Psychology,* 51 (no. 6), 1173–1182.

Bickers, K.N., and Williams, J.T. (2001). Public Policy Analysis: A Political Economy Approach. Boston, MA: Houghton Mifflin Company.

Brinson, G.P., Singer, B.D., and Beebower, G.L. (1991). Determinants of portfolio peformance II: an Update. *Financial Analysts Journal,* May/June, 40–48.

Brinson, G.P., Hood, L.R., & Beebower, G.L. (1986). Determinants of portfolio performance. *Financial Analysts Journal,* July/August, 39–44.

Coronado, J.L., Engen, E.M., and Knight, B. (2003). Public funds and private capital markets: the investment practices and performance of state and local pension funds. *National Tax Journal,* 56 (no. 3), 579–594.

Donner, J. (1939). Investment of pension and other trust funds. *Municipal Finance,* 12 (no. 2), 10–16.

Economic Report of the President (February, 1999). United State Government Printing Office. Washington 2000. http://accessgpo.gov/eop. Last Accessed 11-00.

Eitelberg, C.G. (1997). An elected official's guide to public retirement plans. Chicago, IL: Government Finance Officers Association of the United States and Canada.

Fama, E.F., and Jensen, M.C. (1983). Separation of ownership and control. *Journal of Law and Economics,* 301–325.

Gallagher, D.R. (2003). Investment manager characteristics. *Accounting and Finance,* 43, 283–309.

Government Finance Officers Association (2000, April). 2000 survey of state and local government employee retirement systems survey report. Chicago, IL: Public Pension Coordinating Council.

Government Finance Officers Association (2000, April). 2000 survey of state and local government employee retirement systems pendat database user's guide. Chicago, IL: Public Pension Coordinating Council.

Harris, J.D. (March 2002). 2001 survey of state and local government employee retirement systems survey report. Available online *www.ppcc.grsnet.com.* Last Accessed 03/30/04.

Haugen, R.A. (1997). *Modern Investment Theory,* 4th ed. Upper Saddle River, NJ: Prentice Hall.

Kenny, D.A., Kashy, D.A., and Bolger, N. (1998). Data analysis in social psychology. In D. Gilbert, S.T. Fiske, and G. Lindsey (eds), *The Handbook of Social Psychology,* 4th ed. Vol. 2, pp. 233–265.

Ibbotson, R.G., and Kaplan, P.D. (2000). Does asset allocation policy explain 40, 90, or 100 percent of performance? *Financial Analysts Journal,* 26–33.

Lynn, L.E., Jr., Heinrich, C.J., and Hill, C.J. (2000). Studying governance and public management. In C.J. Heinrich and L.E. Lynn, Jr.(eds), *Governance and Performance: New Perspectives,* pp. 1–33. Washington, D.C.: Georgetown University Press.

Miller, G. (1987). Pension Fund Investing. Chicago, IL: Government Finance Officers Association.

Mitchell, O.S. and Hsin, P.L. (1997). Public pension governance and performance. In S.V. Prieto (ed), *The Economics of Pensions: Principles, Policies, and International Experience,* pp. 92–123. New York: Cambridge University Press.

Munnell, A.H., and Sunden, A. (2001). Investment practices of state and local pension funds: implications for social security reform. In O.S. Mitchell and E.C. Hustead (eds), *Pensions in the Public Sector,* pp. 153–194. Philadelphia: University of Pennsylvania Press.

Nofsinger, J.R. (1998). Why targeted investing does not make sense! *Financial Management,* 27 (no. 3), 87–96.

Rafkind, I. (1939). Public employee retirement in the United States. *Municipal Finance,* 11 (no. 3), 10–13.

Sobel, M.E. (1982). Asymptotic Confidence intervals for indirect effects in structural equation models. In S. Leinhardt (ed), *Sociological Methodology,* 1982, pp. 290–312. San Francisco: Jossey Bass.

Tabachnick, B.G. and Fidell, L. S. (2001). *Using Multivariate Statistics,* 4th ed. Needham Heights, MA: Allyn and Bacon.

Useem, M., and Hess, D. (2001). Governance and investments of public pensions. In O.S. Mitchell and E.C. Hustead (eds), *Pensions in the Public Sector,* pp. 132–152. Philadelphia: University of Pennsylvania Press.

Useem, M., and Mitchell, O.S. (2000). Holders of the purse strings: governance and performance of public retirement systems. *Social Science Quarterly,* 81 (no. 2), 489-506.

Zorn, P. (2001). 2001 survey of state and local government employee retirement systems database user's guide. Chicago, IL: Public Pension Coordinating Council.

Zorn, P. (1998). 1997 survey of state and local government employee retirement systems database user's guide. Chicago, IL: Public Pension Coordinating Council.

Zorn, P. (1997). 1997 survey of state and local government employee retirement systems survey report. Chicago, IL: Public Pension Coordinating Council.

PERFORMANCE BUDGETING AND MANAGEMENT

Chapter 18

Toward Financial Freedom: Budgetary Reform in the U.S. Courts

J. EDWARD GIBSON
Department of Public Administration, Virginia Polytechnic and State University

The record of budgetary reform has demonstrated results, especially in the ability of states and municipalities to function with constrained revenues, but thus far has generated a plethora of locally specific rationales rather than a compelling theoretical foundation. Though anomalous in its structure, governance, and constitutional position, the federal Judiciary may provide analytical leverage in buttressing the theoretical underpinnings of the study of budgetary reform through the example of its budget decentralization initiative. Moving in relatively short order from the constraint of an archaic requisition system to the flexibility of a virtually automatic allotment system and broad budget execution authority, managers responsible for court budgets were freed to reprogram virtually at will. Coupled with a parallel reorganization of the agency's appropriation development process, the budget decentralization initiative improved financial accountability internally, as well as externally — between the Judiciary and Congress. The key organizational elements of this reform are examined descriptively and theoretically to determine their applicability for other agencies.

The relevance of institutional norms in promoting the adoption of new methods and principles occupies a central focus, particularly in contrast to the emphasis often placed on explicit incentives by agency theory.

18.1 Introduction

The federal Judiciary needed only a decade to make dramatic changes in how its budgets were developed and executed, transforming in relatively short order from laggard to leader in the practice of federal budgeting and financial management. After removal of the constraints of an archaic requisition structure, introduction of a virtually automatic allotment system, and adoption of broad budget execution authority, court administrators could plan on anticipated amounts with confidence and reprogram virtually at will. Centralization of the appropriation development process and Congress' willingness to cooperate with the Judiciary in relaxing the restrictions of the appropriation language complete the narrative of these reforms. The speed and apparent impact of these changes, as well as their uniqueness — distinct from government-wide efforts — recommend the U.S. Courts' experience for study.

The record of budgetary reform has demonstrated results, especially in the ability of states and municipalities to function with constrained revenues (Rubin, 1998; Willoughby, 2004). Research on budgetary reforms has often utilized a case study methodology (e.g., studies by Douglas (1999) and Lauth (1985) of Georgia and by Grizzle and Pettijohn (2002) of Florida). Generalizing the Georgia case to search for common themes that contribute to the success of reform efforts, Douglas (2000) sets an example to be emulated for the work at hand. The specific factors that enabled Georgia's redirection effort to accomplish the goals of prioritizing functions within agencies and reducing the proportions of requested increases — principally the power of a determined, constitutionally strong governor coupled with the willingness of the legislature to defer somewhat to the executive's priorities — will not apply in this case. Beyond the special position of the courts, treated at length below, the differences between state and national constitutional structures account for considerable divergence between what may be achieved at the state level and what should be expected of a federal government initiative. Recognizing the sensitivity of budgetary mechanisms and techniques to the structural and political peculiarities of specific jurisdictions, this research will focus on establishing an organizational context for reform and targeting those factors that create the requisite climate for reforms to take hold, rather than emphasizing particular forms or processes. This approach follows the recommendation of Forrester and Adams (1997), who proposed a normative approach to improve budgeting by incorporating organizational culture and learning. Notwithstanding the implicit challenge of augmenting the literature on budgetary theory by employing an exceptional instance, the Judiciary's fundamental alteration of how its budgets are produced and executed can illuminate underlying factors that transcend the particular environmental considerations of other agencies.

18.1.1 Distinctive Attributes of the Federal Judiciary

The example of the U.S. Courts, because of its distinct constitutional role and political independence, should be labeled "handle with care" to avoid uncritical application to the rest of the federal government. Whereas the presidency and Congress carry the inevitable imprimatur of the administration and majority party, the federal Judiciary follows its own cycle. Chief Justice William Rehnquist, appointed to the Supreme Court by Richard Nixon, has served in his present capacity during four administrations. Moreover, the Judicial Branch accounts for roughly two percent of the federal budget (Office of Management and Budget, 2003, p. 100) — a trifle compared to the outlays of the Executive Branch, which has been the subject of virtually all analyses of federal budgeting and financial management. Scale aside, the courts' constitutional insulation suggests separation of powers as the salient analytic feature, spawning much of the scholarship that has concerned judicial budgeting. Examples include Douglas and Hartley's (2001) study of state judiciaries under different budgetary structures, pursuing judicial independence as the outcome of interest. Glaser's (1994) treatment of the stand-off between New York's governor and chief justice considered the judicial branch's inherent power to fund its own activities. Notwithstanding its distinctiveness, the Judiciary's experience may apply more broadly through a focus on administration rather than separation of powers. Yarwood and Canon (1980) described the isolation of adjudicative issues from the budgetary ones in the justices' presentation of the Supreme Court's request to Congress. This separation is even more distinct in the remainder of the budget — the Supreme Court represents only a small portion of the Judiciary's funding requirement — because of the numerous (approximately 200) courts of appeals, district courts, and bankruptcy courts, which tackle diverse legal issues, include judges appointed by both parties, and constitute a major part of the nation's on-going system of justice: an integral component of the legal and regulatory structure that undergird the economy and, as such, not to be unduly manipulated. Though "inferior courts" constitutionally, their financial management has been the prime target of reform under the present "administration," marked by the tenures of Chief Justice Rehnquist and

Administrative Office of the U.S. Courts (AO) Director L. Ralph Mecham, appointed by Rehnquist's predecessor.

The continuity of such longstanding leadership marks one of the noteworthy elements of this anomalous case; the other is relative freedom from recent trends that couched budgetary issues in performance-based terms through strategic plans, including goals, objectives, and derivative metrics. Passage of the Government Performance and Results Act (GPRA) during the Clinton Administration and its successor's introduction of the Program Assessment and Rating Tool as an instrument of further control by the Office of Management and Budget (OMB) over agency budgets (Gibson, 2003) tie budgetary issues ever closer to those of performance. The budgetary manifestations of this array of objectives and metrics are complex and arcane, as the technocratic tone of a recent analysis (McNab and Melese, 2003) of the prospects for successful adoption conveys:

> [T]hree potential solutions exist to the multiprincipal, multi-dimensional bargaining game. First, one may restrict the principals' incentive schemes ... . Second, it may be possible to group principals whose interests are closely aligned ... . Finally, more agents can be created by reassigning activities and programs (p. 92).

Small wonder that "the future of GPRA is not bright" (p. 94), given such daunting complexity and the acknowledged past failures of performance budgeting attributed to the usual suspects: "administrative complexities, lack of investment in managerial, accounting, and information systems, and the absence of institutional incentives to promote gains in economic efficiency" (p. 73). Distinguishing the Judiciary's simpler approach from the recent tendency toward nominally results-based orientation should not be interpreted to convey that performance is foreign to or estranged from budgeting, only that performance has a more traditional derivation than the recent, highly technical variety advanced through heightened scrutiny from program analysts, particularly within OMB. Nor is the Judiciary subject to the President's Management Agenda, whereby the George W. Bush Administration enlists agency efforts behind its operational priorities, such as "competitive sourcing" intended to increase contracting-out (Gibson, 2004). Attending these developments, the hiatus (LeLoup, 2002, p. 5) that followed the heralded demise of incrementalism as a theory (pp. 1–5) — awaiting its successor — promises to usher in a thoroughgoing revision of practice at the federal level (pp. 12–13). Given this development in budgeting and financial management, the Judiciary's example represents an alternative perspective: sacrificing technical sophistication for pragmatic judgment, while promoting local autonomy rather than overhead direction and scorekeeping.

The anomalous nature of the Judiciary's approach has a clear heritage. For much of the previous century, the U.S. Courts followed a budgetary course manifestly out of phase with the rest of government. While the burgeoning expenditures (Schick, 1990, pp. 17–20) that emerged from the New Deal, Second World War, and Cold War expansions filled Washington with a public sector that was truly national in scale, the Judiciary still retained its traditional form and size in 1960 (Posner, 1995). As a "late-blooming" claimant to significant federal dollars, the Judiciary's growth coincided with a period when the size of government was first questioned, then attacked (LeLoup, 2002, pp. 6–8). The Judiciary appeared similarly out of step in its budgetary strategy: "unable to get Congress' attention" (Walker and Barrow, 1985) because of the small size of its request and the lack of electoral advantage from funding it. Douglas and Hartley (2001, pp. 57–58) concisely summarized the prevailing view of this strategy: personal and conservative.

Yet, the conclusion that bolder, policy-centric appeals by executive agencies place the Judiciary at a disadvantage requires a second look. Perhaps advocacy by judges — respected and well-connected within their states — has proven resilient in comparison with the political constituencies of prominent programs, increasingly vulnerable to partisan threats. Or the parsimonious fiscal climate of the mid-1980s through the end of the 1990s could have favored conservatism. For whatever reason, the Judiciary's success in sustaining steady, and sometimes dramatic, increases in funding during a generally unfavorable climate for non-defense-related expenditures demonstrates noteworthy fiscal success. Observing the role of competition in garnering budget increases, Irene Rubin (2000) tabbed the Department of Justice as the clear winner within the Commerce, State, and Justice appropriations subcommittee. But that appropriations bill also funds the Judiciary, which, overlooked by Rubin, enjoyed a slightly larger proportional increase during the same period (1980–97) than the Justice Department.[1] Potential explanations abound for this performance — foremost on its face the increase in caseload, which is treated below. Another straightforward rationale for favoring the Judiciary's and Justice's budget requests above those of State and Commerce is bipartisan support for law enforcement. That explanation ignores the Judiciary's programmatic breadth, which encompasses civil litigation (including product liability torts) and bankruptcy adjudication, as well as indigent defendants' legal representation, hardly prone to unqualified support from the law-and-order constituency. Nonetheless, connections with the criminal justice system form a central thrust of the judiciary's presentation of its budget request (Arnold, 1996). Whether owing to presentation, programmatic appeal, or other factor(s), the Judiciary's recent budgetary prowess reflects an enviable relationship with congressional appropriators.

18.1.2 Autonomy and Accountability

Chief Justice Rehnquist (1998) characterized the Judiciary's change as an "archetype" for "devolution of management authority." Notwithstanding the profound increase in authority and responsibility granted to court administrators, such latitude depends on courts' management of more flexible funding: a bargain with Congress as fiscal custodian. The reciprocal power of newly integrated budget processes, equally forceful if less obvious than the devolutionary impetus toward local control, also merits our attention. Accordingly, the parallel developments of greater local autonomy and improved accountability to Congress are treated together, as "part and parcel" of a sustainable reform initiative. I examine the reasons why budgetary changes took hold in the Judiciary, how centralization complemented decentralization, and whether any broader significance should be attached to this case. This inquiry encompasses the aims of these budgetary reforms, the ways and means, and the reasons for their apparent inculcation within the Judiciary's culture. I also inquire what recent fiscal straits may portend for sustaining autonomy.

18.1.3 Methodology

Befitting a case study, the initial thrust of this research is descriptive. The authoritative account of the Judiciary's budget decentralization initiative was authored by Joseph Bobek (2004), former assistant director of the AO for finance and budget and the Judiciary's chief financial officer, who was retained under contract to write the history of the changes he had overseen. This history complemented a study of the effects of budget decentralization conducted by KPMG, LLP (2004). The author was granted access to final proof drafts of these studies, which are intended to remain internal AO documents. To augment these sources, the author interviewed court participants in the initiative, whose acquaintance was made while working on related efforts as a contractor during 1997–98 to develop approaches to fund lawbook purchases and local automation infrastructure. Because these court participants constitute commentators rather than a sample, their insights should not be construed as representative of court administrators' views generally. Nevertheless, they are informed by their roles within advisory groups that played a central role, as described below, in the budget decentralization initiative. Interviews with Bobek and a current senior budget manager contributed further insights into how the budget decentralization was conceived and sustained, and how recent funding constraints may impact it. Another crucial interview was conducted with Judge Richard S. Arnold, who presided over budget decentralization as chairman of an oversight committee. The variety of assembled vantages — administering a court, directing an initiative, seeking a consensus among judges, and coordinating with a congressional committee — contribute to the "thick" description appropriate for analyzing a complex organizational change (Brady and Collier, 2004; Eckstein, 1975; Yin, 2003).

18.2   Decentralization of Budget Execution

A straightforward account of budget decentralization begins, as Chief Justice Rehnquist proclaimed, with "devolution" to the individual courts, situated in 94 judicial districts and 12 geographic circuits nationwide, as well as other courts of special jurisdiction (but not the Supreme Court, which has always maintained a separate budget from the district courts and courts of appeals). Devolution has a certain irony in the Judiciary — "a decentralized entity by nature" according to Judge Arnold (2003) — considering the freedom of the "[original] 16 district judges, who were wholly independent to do whatever they wanted administratively." But the system evolved administratively in the modern Judiciary to a level of coordination and oversight almost certainly unrecognizable to those first judges.

18.2.1   Preexisting Constraints on Court Autonomy

The AO, established in 1939 as a central entity supporting finance, personnel, statistical reporting, and related management functions, curbed courts' budgetary autonomy. Limits on administrative independence arose repeatedly in Arthur Hellman's (1990) study of the Ninth Circuit, which coincided with the advent of decentralization: the result of the AO's influence through

> decisions about budgeting, equipment, and, above all, personnel ... [A Ninth Circuit] judge has gone so far as to say, "Until the circuit councils and the court of appeals are given some autonomy in resource allocation, it is probably a benign form of fraud to label courts as carrying policy-making authority" (p. 222).

In the same study, Doris Provine (1990) found that "[s]pending for courts traditionally has been handled almost entirely from Washington. ... Thus judges contact the Administrative Office if they need extra office supplies or new furniture," which some found "advantageous" (p. 271). Dispensing funds in this fashion, the AO presented the appearance to several judges Provine interviewed of "a sugar daddy who dispenses money from an unseen pocket of unknown depth" (p. 271–72).

Courts submitted requests under "an old requisition system" (Bobek, 2003) that were then reviewed, decided on, and executed, once approved, by the AO. Kay Guillot (2003), circuit librarian of the Fifth Circuit, described the process thus:

> If you wanted a photocopier, you would have to request it. They'd ask: 'How many copies do you need? How old is the current one?' Then, months went by; you might have to call on the status. Sometimes you never found out anything until it came.

John Shope, district executive of the Northern District of Georgia, joined the U.S. Courts just before budget decentralization began after managing a large municipal court. He reported being "disillusioned" at finding a "Mother-may-I?" system that required him to "ask Washington for funds to print; ask Washington for a copier" (Shope, 2003).

Budgeting prior to decentralization was burdensome and highly procedural, exemplified by the staffing review process (KPMG, 2004):

> The AO scrutinized these [staffing] requirements using workload formulas and other projections to determine the number of staff that a court should need. The AO would not approve any additional staffing requests by a court unless the court was able to satisfactorily justify its additional needs (p. 7).

Other financial requirements met comparable obstacles, to wit, forms such as the "AO 19" for most non-personnel expenditures and the "AO 20" for travel. Program divisions, which held most of the allotments, were routinely involved with court operations, requiring court administrators to deal with an estimated 40 different AO officials in the course of their work (p. 8). In addition to the burden of added paperwork, the courts labored under the impression it was "*who you knew*" that mattered. The top financial manager (prior to the Chief Financial Officer Act) in the AO was known as the ultimate arbiter of courts' requests, according to Judge Arnold (2003): "If he thought you ought to have it, then you got it." Hardly an uncommon circumstance in government agencies; nonetheless, the "role of professional administrators in the distribution process" was controversial in the Judiciary, flying in the face of the dogma: "Decisions about who gets what . . . should be made by judges" (Provine, 1990, p. 272).

18.2.2 The Origins of Decentralization

With due regard for judges' dispositive role, both in and out of the courtroom, the central figure in budget decentralization — "decentralized financial management" as he prefers to think of it — was an administrator: Joseph Bobek, who joined the AO two decades ago as chief of the Budget Branch ("Bobek to Head AO Office of Finance and Budget," 1996). Although Bobek (2003) conceived the simplified structure "brainstorming" with his staff on weekends spent developing pre-reform budgets, the vision he broadcast — "to push a button and do the allotments" — was pursued by opportunistic increments, rather than a grand design. When the Circuit Executive Committee on Budget Decentralization convened, Bobek advised the group, helping to advance the concept against the parochial interests of his organization and his superior, who "lost power because it had been a 'good old boy' system." The committee endorsed the following goals (Bobek, 2004, p. 19):

- Reduce operating costs by five percent.
- Create the ability to prioritize expenditures.
- Provide a means to respond to local needs.
- Offer incentives for good management at the local level.
- Provide a better capability for planning at all levels.
- Allow more flexibility to absorb reductions in funding caused by Gramm-Rudman-Hollings or other legislative actions.
- Reduce paperwork at all levels.
- Allow for better monitoring of expenditure patterns by the AO.
- Create a greater capacity to avoid excessive year-end spending.
- Delegate responsibility for Financial Management to the operational level.

A decentralization initiative followed the circuit executives' recommendations, beginning with pilot courts, which were allotted funds based on prior year amounts plus an increment or justified by budget calls for zero-based categories such as equipment (Bobek, 2003). A concurrent pilot, the "Personal Computer Purchases with Personnel Lapses Program" (Judicial Conference of the United States, 1988), recognized the need for automation, crediting positions not filled toward the purchase of computers:

> Courts could elect to keep a position vacant for the time required to accumulate sufficient salary savings to purchase personal computers . . . . The program also required that 25 percent of the savings be used as a contingency fund (Bobek, 2004, p. 25).

Another program considered at this time was formulated under the auspices of the Eleventh Circuit Court of Appeals, which liberalized budget execution, but "also provided a mechanism to allow savings from district courts' allotments to be reprogrammed to the circuit for application to the highest priority in the circuit" (p. 25). Ultimately, these programs were discontinued after the pilot decentralization program was expanded.

The initial success of pilot courts' financial management resulted in the return of $4 million in unused funds in the first year (Mecham, 1990, p. 72). Nonetheless, the pilot had to run its three-year course before nationwide implementation proceeded, ultimately awaiting the conclusions of a National Academy of Public Administration (NAPA) report, which set prerequisites for the national roll-out: additional pilots to prove the concept in smaller courts and standardization of local financial accounting procedures, delays that Bobek fought. He prevailed: courts were allowed to volunteer for decentralization; virtually all did within three years (Bobek, 2003). A liberalized personnel system structure followed, which freed managers from requesting positions or promotions from the AO, but required a mechanism to ensure the new system would be "cost neutral" (Bobek, 2004, p. 44). As John Shope (2003) explained, the flexibility presented opportunities for abuse because positions could be upgraded at the discretion of court managers. He collaborated with Bobek to develop the concept that became the Cost Control Monitoring System (CCMS), which "produced the controls necessary to insure the cost neutrality of the new [Court Personnel System] CPS ... [and] moved the courts from a salary control system based on end-of-year employment ceilings to a dollar-driven system" (Bobek, 2004, p. 44). The incentive for court managers was the virtual elimination of funds retained by the AO to meet personnel-related requests, no longer necessary because clerks and other budget holders were held to monetary rather than personnel-based limits. Reserving less funding for contingencies freed up approximately four percent of salaries — gained in the annual allotment to the courts (Shope, 2003).

18.3 Decentralization Takes Root

Nothing demonstrates the Judiciary's commitment to budget decentralization as clearly as the investment in training. More than one thousand court managers were trained for each of the budget decentralization and CCMS implementations (Bobek, 2004, p. 77). Guillot (2003) identifies the initial training in 1991–93 as "the biggest thing that made budget decentralization successful." Court managers were immersed through both temporary separation from their operational responsibilities — emphasized by the venues, such as "the Meridian in Newport Beach, the

Ritz-Carlton in Buckhead [Atlanta], and a resort in Arizona" — and the comprehensive curriculum: "morning theory, afternoon scenarios ... [on] developing budgets, submitting requests, appeals, prioritization." Students were "kept prisoner." Instructors included AO budget staff, advisors (e.g., Guillot), and representatives of the pilot courts. The courses not only covered mechanics, but principles: "you want to get heads going up and down." Guillot concludes "we could never afford to do it again."

Institutionalization of new financial management principles was tested by the next evolution in decentralization. Whereas CCMS had been a "day-forward" system that assumed the personnel allotments to each court, based on their prior requests to the AO for positions and promotions, were correct, the allotment simplification initiative provided, for the first time, common criteria by which courts' resource needs could be determined (Shope, 2003). This final stage of decentralization enhanced the key concept of equity by applying statistical analysis to the spending patterns of the courts. Chief Justice Rehnquist (1998) summarized in his 1997 end of year message:

> Funds previously allocated in 40 separate expense categories were combined in one aggregate amount based on formulas developed by teams of statisticians, financial analysts, program experts, and court staff. As a result, the paperwork burden for preparing each court's budget requests was substantially reduced or eliminated, and the courts were assured of an equitable distribution of these operating funds.

Dependence on variable inputs meant that allotments could fluctuate from year to year — discontinuously rather than incrementally. To ease the transition to simplified allotments for those whose expenditures were higher than the formula predicted, no court experienced more than a five percent reduction in the first year and ten percent in the second year. Everyone was expected to be "lean and mean" (Shope, 2003) by the third year, which required clerks and other unit executives to anticipate that a change in the formulas' inputs, such as their district's or circuit's caseload, meant a proportional change in their budget. Participants in the formula development emphasized that fiscal conservatism guided the actions of successful unit executives. Those who staffed too aggressively faced reductions when local caseload trends reversed. Barry Polsky (2003), chief probation officer for the Eastern District of Pennsylvania, averred such trends were evident to careful administrators in time to take appropriate action — "good managers know how to take care of that stuff"; his fiscal conservatism made possible significant transfers from his unit's funds to cover shortfalls within the district. Not all unit executives welcomed the new responsibility: "courts that wanted to keep the AO in the middle and just tell the judges they can't get a decision from the AO' or 'the AO won't approve this. Some courts were afraid of the additional responsibility" (Bobek, 2003). Decentralization advocates consider the exodus of managers unequal to their new responsibilities a necessary development (Wynne, 2003; Guillot, 2003; Polsky, 2003).

18.3.1 Factors in the Institutionalization of Reform

Among the themes recurring in both personal and official accounts of budget decentralization was the crucial role of courts' involvement. Bobek trumpeted the central message that "it would be a fair and equitable system," taking every opportunity to get the message across: "at any forum, all over the country, for example, a group of probation chiefs at a circuit conference." He "made a lot of friends in the courts, and was probably better known in the courts than anyone from the AO except for the director" (Bobek, 2003). One unit executive involved in decentralization underscored this claim, relaying a colleague's tribute: "they ought to erect a monument to Joe Bobek and put it in the lobby of the AO" (Wynne, 2003).

In turn, Bobek (2003) credits Director Mecham's strong support as a key element of the reform's success, including travel and training funds, but not dedicated staff — only four were assigned from the Budget Division. Besides "all the dollars that he needed," Bobek had staff detailed part-time from the AO program divisions, which oversaw courts' administration and policy. But the bulk of the effort relied on court volunteers, who staffed standing committees that produced "deliverables," from training plans and materials to recommendations of courts to be implemented first — courts meeting stringent criteria, such as clean audits. For the volunteers Bobek (2003) provided whatever resources were necessary: "They could meet as often as they wanted," which required travel budgets, usually subject to severe scrutiny in any agency. His aim was to "take away any excuse for failure," relying on "peer pressure" from court colleagues to provide an incentive for timeliness. He "hand-picked" court members of an executive steering committee, which had two crucial decision points: the first to approve his concept; and the second "to ensure that the stamp of the courts" was on the work being done by the standing committees.

Unit executives found a national advocate of local control. Polsky (2003) gave Bobek credit not only for shrewd politics, but also for instincts that "there were good people in the field, every district was unique, every unit was unique," enabling the courts to establish national rules that secured independent local action. Shope (2003) confirms that the development of key elements "by the courts was important to their being accepted. The courts are usually suspect of ideas that are generated centrally without their involvement." Guillot (2003) characterized their suspicion vividly: "the first reaction is — how will they get me on this one?" while emphasizing the Budget Division's outreach:

> of all the divisions in the AO, Budget was the only one that had a working advisory group that came to Washington twice a year .... Not only did they get good advice, but you get advocates. It's our message, too. We're shills for them, carry their water. But it's good because it's communication — Budget used the group, used newsletters, used the Web to communicate.

Courts' engagement grew during the final phase of decentralization. Court managers formed a working group to review the statistical analysis and evaluate how well alternative sets of variables fit expenditures, approving separate budget formulas to govern the allotment to each court type and administrative unit (probation, pretrial services, and libraries). Anticipating the inevitable controversy associated with formulaic budgets that were insensitive to special circumstances, or in some cases caused funding to drop, court representatives were recruited for another crucial role: appeals of the calculated amounts were controlled by a board composed of the court managers who had participated in the construction of the formulas. Shope served on the board, which exacted a compelling need before additional funding was provided: "When you go before your peers, they know where the skeletons are hidden" (Shope, 2003). The number of special circumstances appealed constituted the formulas' true test. Appeals decreased steadily from 1996 to 2001, with the exception of 2000 ("Appendix 21," 2004).

18.4   Centralization of Budget Development

Although the collaboration of administrators and court executives created the impetus for decentralization as described above, they alone could not have implemented the policy because "everything that goes on in the Judiciary is determined by judges" (Arnold, 2003). At each stage of decentralization, the Judicial Conference Committee on the Budget (Budget Committee) accepted the policies and recommended that the Judicial Conference approve them, although not without reservations. For example, the Budget Committee weighed its judgment on the necessity for better responsiveness to local requirements and improved fiduciary performance more heavily than promises of realized savings, deciding nonetheless to proceed with pilot decentralization (Bobek, 2004, p. 19). Policymaking did not stop with Judicial Conference approval, however, as budgetary policy seldom lies solely within the province of an agency, even when the agency in question constitutes a branch of government. Congressional acquiescence constituted an essential facet of both decentralization and broader changes in the budgeting and financial management that occurred during the same time. Greater responsibility granted internally to allotment holders advanced hand-in-hand with better coordination with Congress on appropriation requests, a seemingly "virtuous cycle" of authority and accountability that warrants closer inspection.

18.4.1 Reform of the Appropriation Process

As Budget Committee chairman, Judge Arnold (2003) also assumed responsibility for an open-ended appropriation process, which in his first year as chairman of the Budget Committee produced a request for a 30 percent annual increase, termed "an outrage" by a Republican on the Senate appropriation subcommittee staff. The obvious question: How could such a large increase be submitted given even a rudimentary process of review and approval within the Judiciary? To appreciate the answer requires a basic understanding of its policymaking process. The most remarkable aspect is that the Third Branch of government is literally "run by committee." The "supreme" governing body is not the court of that name, although its chief justice serves as the administrative as well as legal head of the courts through his role as chairman of the Judicial Conference. All policy-related and administrative decisions — everything that must be decided for the whole court system outside of specific cases — are formally made by this body, comprising the chief justice of the Supreme Court, two representatives from each circuit, one of whom is the chief judge of that circuit, and representatives of special courts (Fish, 1973 pp. 254–57). The Judicial Conference meets semiannually, operating in the meantime through delegation to committees and to the AO, which is responsible for the staff work supporting the Conference and its committees, as well as the day-to-day administration. In their account of the former Fifth Circuit Court of Appeals' division into the current Fifth and Eleventh Circuits, Walker and Barrow (1985) pose a model of judicial governance that incorporates many elements that may be unfamiliar, even to those quite familiar with the operation of the other two branches of the federal government. Figure 18.1 depicts a model of budgetary decision-making, adapting Walker and Barrow's structure.

The Judicial Conference and its committees oversee the Judiciary's administration: the budgetary, personnel, and other policy areas that are

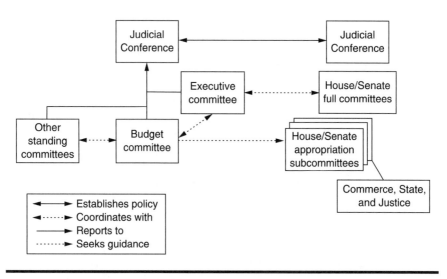

Figure 18.1   Judiciary policymaking entities and relationships.

the purview of the political appointees in executive agencies (Fish, 1973, pp. 444–45). Approval of the Judiciary's budget request occurs during semi-annual Conference meetings, which is the forum for other policy matters such as proposed changes to procedural rules. Because judges are primarily responsible for deciding cases and have quite limited availability for administrative duties, the considerable staff work associated with policy development and promulgation falls largely on the AO. Judicial Conference committees, meeting in the intervals between the Judicial Conference sessions, guide and approve this staff work. Foremost among these committees is the Executive Committee, which stands in for the Judicial Conference on matters that require interim actions, establishes its agenda, and bounds the responsibilities of the other committees. Within the network of committees that accomplish the work of the Judicial Conference between its formal meetings, responsibility does not imply control. Witness the significant budgetary roles played by other committees, for instance establishing resource requirements for personnel, facilities, and information technology, circumscribing the Budget Committee's role to coordination and consolidation, a role described in the Annual Report of the Director (Mecham, 1990) thus:

> to determine the maximum attainable level when formulating the budget. This level is based on past experience and discussion with appropriation committee staff ... . Instead of simply collecting the requirements of the courts and incorporating them

in a budget submission, the Chairmen of the substantive committees of the Conference met with the Budget Committee to arrive at a reduced number (p. 73).

In the first year, the result was a 25 percent reduction in the size of the increase (p. 73). Seizing on the most obvious feature of this change, *centralization*, I follow Rubin (2000) in examining

> two related concepts: (1) the degree to which the budget process is bottom-up or top-down, and (2) the degree to which power is scattered among independent committees, commissions, and elected officials without an effective coordinating device (p. 85).

Bobek (2003) felt that the Budget Committee's evolving role — "coming up with a number that would be politically acceptable to Congress" — elevated their responsibility, thus countering the dispersion of power and its consequence (Rubin, 2000, p. 85): "When power is widely shared, the effect may be to immobilize decision making." Yet, the process cannot be necessarily described as "top-down" because of the large number of committees with input into the product; hardly "ignored" as Rubin (2000, p. 85) finds typical of those outside the central core in hierarchical organizations. Indeed, the policymaking structure depicted above confounds the basic notion of "bottom-up or top-down" by its highly networked topology.

Given its non-traditional governance, the second concept, coordination, yields stronger relevance for the Judiciary's experience. Barrow and Walker (1988) found the dispute over splitting the Fifth Circuit exemplified the Judiciary's "strong norms of decentralization and accommodation," which tend toward dispersion and limit coordination, especially given the expectation that "unanimity needed for such change will not be present . . . [so that] the policy is likely to reflect agreement on the least common denominator" (p. 263). Nevertheless, during his first years Judge Arnold (2003) and the members of his committee

> told these committee chairmen: "The increase will be [for example] 12 percent; we don't care how you do it." And we'd leave them in a room, until they got the matter decided among them.

The process later became formalized (Arnold, 2003), fortifying the norm of economy through an additional structure: "the Efficiency Subcommittee: their job was to go over the requests of those committees responsible for the budget items and get them reduced or made more efficient." Yet, this central role in the budgeting process did not involve direction *per se*. Arnold (2003) recalled the chairman of the committee responsible for automation asking "to be turned loose" to pursue donation of equipment by vendors. His response was: "'you are loose,' in effect because … his role was not to tell other committee chairmen what they could and could not do.'" Although the proposal was ultimately abandoned, its treatment illustrates the crucial but constrained role of the Budget Committee under Judge Arnold (2003): "to make it possible to get whatever the judges needed once it was clear what was needed."

18.4.2 Flexibility in Financial Management

Sought after as a key element of federal financial management reform proposals for many years, budgetary flexibility in federal agencies has nonetheless received lukewarm support from Congress. Rubin (2000) cited two examples of failure to achieve the benefits of greater flexibility. Advanced billings in Defense capital revolving funds raised congressional concerns of "reprogramming without official notification" (p. 237). Indeed, the recent trend has been toward more oversight due to "the history of prior abuse of discretion that made some members of Congress suspicious about new sources of discretion as unofficial reprogramming" (p. 237). Not only abuse of discretion, but inability to take advantage also discourages its broader use, as the example of the Forest Service shows. Rubin reported that the agency — despite relaxed reprogramming requirements and broader construction of budget line items — "seldom requested changes between line items, either before the reforms or afterward," concluding that "the changes seemed to have made little difference to agency management" (p. 236). Notwithstanding the apparent flexibility of courts to reprogram at will, the Judiciary has not been granted special waivers. Its extensive reprogramming works within the appropriation rules because of broadly structured, programmatic line items, such as district, bankruptcy, and appellate courts, which Congress established at the Judiciary's request to make decentralization possible. The former structure, in which salaries for support personnel across all court types constituted a single line item, would have stymied decentralization (Bobek, 2004, p. 36). Previously, actions that court managers needed to take — spending personnel funds for automation for instance — triggered reprogramming restrictions whenever they exceeded $500,000, which would have rendered decentralization impractical due to continuous AO monitoring and congressional involvement being required (KPMG, 2004a, p. 10).

Unlike the Forest Service, flexibility garnered results in the Judiciary, which reciprocated Congress' accommodation by returning funds from an annual appeal from the AO to the courts back to the Treasury, accumulating

Table 18.1 Allotted Funds Voluntarily Returned by Courts (in thousands of dollars)

FY1994	FY1995	FY1996	FY1997	FY1998
$7,103	$30,525	$22,727	$39,886	$43,428

FY1999	FY2000	FY2001	FY2002	**Total**
$31,178	$15,751	$56,150	$46,289	$293,037

the totals contained in Table 18.1 over the course of the budget decentralization initiative ("Appendix 1," 2004):

In addition to the nearly $300 million in returned allotments, the Judiciary reported over $1 billion saved over the same period from centralized programs (ibid.), although it is uncertain which of these programs returned funds formally allotted to them, as was the case for the individual courts.

New appropriation language crafted by Bobek (2003) made possible the use of these returned funds, directing expenditure of appropriated funds first, then fee receipts, which "essentially made everything no-year funding." Even though the individual courts returned the funds unconditionally, the Judiciary as a whole suffered no penalty; its base unaffected: "the appropriation committees just ask how much is in the fee accounts and reduce the appropriation by that amount" (Bobek, 2003). During the budget stalemate between the Clinton Administration and the 104th Congress that shut down approximately half of the government, it was this flexibility that, "[r]ecognizing the need for the federal courts to continue operations, ... allowed the Judiciary to function through limited fee income and a small amount of carry-over funds" ("Judiciary Secures FY 96 Funding," 1996). When these funding sources neared depletion, "personal phone calls to two key Senate leaders" by Chief Justice Rehnquist and contacts between judges and "pivotal members of the Congress" enabled the Judiciary's appropriation and programs within the Department of Justice to be passed separately from the larger appropriation bill (ibid.).

It remains to be seen whether the Judiciary will emerge from the latest belt-tightening unscathed. In any case, the trend toward tighter coordination of budgetary decision-making has continued into a new era of fiscal stringency. The Executive Committee has taken a prominent role in establishing the parameters of the fiscal year 2006 appropriation development by underscoring the dire impact of potential budget targets on discretionary expenditures — exclusive of judicial salaries, those of direct staff, and related expenses, as well as other budget categories outside of unit executive control, which are classified as mandatory — and tasking committees with budgetary impacts to identify immediate economies to reduce pressure on the impending budget crunch (King, 2004). A senior budget manager expressed the hope that a revised framework for courts' budgetary responsibilities would emerge from this review, reconfiguring their decision parameters — excluding, for example, some of the administrative functions more properly handled centrally — while sustaining the level of discretion achieved by the decentralization initiative.

18.4.3   Challenges to Local Autonomy

Increasing budgetary constraints prompted several of the court managers who played key roles in budget decentralization to express concern that the exigency of current fiscal pressure may weaken the commitment to local autonomy. The Judicial Conference favored the personnel category in recent (2003) cuts to court operating budgets (personnel categories reduced by six percent, but other operating costs by thirty-two percent), protecting positions, but, according to Guillot (2003), "causing a little disgruntlement" by precluding an across-the-board cut that "hits every court the same." Implicit in shielding personnel-related categories from deeper cuts that would accompany across-the-board reductions was the necessity of a new baseline or "snapshot," the first since 1995 (Bobek, 2004, p. 44). This reallocation, according to Shope (2003), disadvantaged "conservative" court managers who had maintained lower average salary structures because disproportionately more of their budgets were subject to the higher level of cuts. He says that those whom he taught to think in terms of dollars rather than positions were ill-served. His court's use of contracted training services rather than an on-staff trainer is an example of a practice that the new "snapshot" disfavors. Departure from the rules appears to renege on decentralization's promised equity, even committing the cardinal breach: "messing with my court" (Shope, 2003). The tension between institutional commitment to its people and adherence to the principle of local accountability, while "not a death knell," captures the challenge to the "integrity" of the process "when there's not enough money nationally," according to Guillot (2003). Shope (2003) predicted a diminished response to the AOs annual appeal to return unused funds.

Another development is the increased acceptance of appeals — now judged by the AO program divisions rather than court peers — blamed by some former appeals board members for undermining the principles of local responsibility and accountability by rescuing failed management practices. Shope (2003) is unsure whether the impetus for re-imposition of the central oversight on courts' finances reflects a heightened sense of compassion for those whose jobs are threatened, or a response to the courts' recent strides toward financial autonomy by Washington staff who had increasingly lost control. Bobek (2003) did not raise this issue, but did note that courts who used to talk to their program divisions every day, now go months without calling. While concerned, court veterans of decentralization remain advocates: Shope (2003) calls decentralization "salvageable"; Polsky (2003), "the best system around."

18.5   General Applicability of Budgetary Reforms

The Judiciary's experience is not offered as a template — reproducible in other federal agencies — because important differences complicate the application of these lessons. Issues that are crucial for other federal agencies, such as the role of the President's Budget and by extension OMB's function (e.g., White, 1991), lack relevance because the Budget and Accounting Act of 1921 requires the Judiciary's request to be submitted to Congress unchanged, circumventing OMB's involvement. Conversely, recommendations aimed at research on municipal budgeting by Gianakis and McCue (2002) appear apt enough in the case of this highly decentralized agency. In particular, their characterization of a "weakly integrated organization ... highly permeable to the political environment, and ... subject to enormous centrifugal forces" (2002, p. 160) applies equally well to the Judiciary as to the local governments for which that description is intended. The impact of "centrifugal forces" is quite evident in the description of the initiative's progress: spawned by local agitation for greater financial authority, tested in a handful of courts, and approved *on a voluntary basis* for national adoption by the responsible committee and governing conference of judges. Thus, the prerogatives of individual judges count heavily and shared policy objectives rest tenuously on hard-won consensus.

The challenge of integrating policy in a decentralized environment forms the core of the descriptive theory-building focus, one of four distinct dimensions of budgetary theory that Gianakis and McCue (2002) identify, discussion of which immediately follows. Assumptive and normative theory dimensions will next be treated in turn. The fourth vantage on budgetary theory, an instrumental dimension, will not be addressed explicitly in order to deemphasize the specific methods the Judiciary used and in keeping with the organizationally sensitive approach of Forrester and Adams (1997), which informs the discussion of normative theory. Other agencies must exercise their own judgment on which, if any, of the Judiciary's specific budgetary processes may be suitable.

18.5.1 Connection with Descriptive Theory-Building

Gianakis and McCue (2002) establish descriptive analysis as the prerequisite for establishing further dimensions of budgeting. But in the wake of incrementalism, what descriptions apply? Whether incrementalism was a descriptive theory or merely a description, nothing has replaced it as shorthand for the predominant budgetary practice. Performance budgeting appears a strong candidate, prevalent in the literature (e.g., Gianakis, 1996; Willoughby, 2004), legislated through GPRA, and enforced by the National Performance Review and President's Management Agenda of the last two administrations. The issues for performance budgeting are well known, for example, the technical complexity of relating funding to performance (Gianakis and McCue, 1999, pp. 25–26), but the Judiciary's ability to allot funds to each court based on workload and other parameters exhibits considerable technical prowess.

Unlike many agencies, for which GPRA introduced formal measurement, Judge Posner's (1995) study of how methods have changed in response to caseload shows that metrics mattered in the Judiciary for decades. He measured the evolution of the adjudicative function by the steadily declining cost per case (pp. 185–89) — just the kind of "objective" success that the performance movement in government has sought. Even though the Judiciary does not submit a performance plan to OMB as executive agencies do, publications such as the *Annual Report of the Director* (Mecham, 2001) include dozens of statistical tables focused on input, throughput, and results of the judicial process. Acute issues, such as the explosion of bankruptcies filed and the associated impact on required resource levels (p. 3), receive special attention. The nominal connections with performance-based budgeting extend further, encompassing the linkage of inputs and outputs.

Bobek (2003) highlighted the prominence of statistical workload analysis, calling it the "springboard for decentralization." Workload analysis involves a specialized team who apply the "statistical method of work measurement known as operational audit" to randomly selected courts ("AO Staff Measures the Needs of the Courts," 1999). The resultant system of measurement has been in use for approximately twenty years and, according to the judge overseeing their use, "reflects the Judiciary's commitment to requesting only those resources required to fulfill our core mission of handling cases in a just, timely, and efficient manner" (Gibbons, 1999). Yet, on closer inspection, the expression of the resource levels required in terms of expected workload does not represent performance-based appropriation.

Abandoning its insistence on full funding of the caseload-based requirement — as the Judicial Conference (1989) decided in 1988 by adopting the alternate request recommended by the Budget Committee — in favor of an increase closer to the level requested by executive agencies, notwithstanding the array of workload measurement data backing up the full request, represents a break with the metric-based budget. Judge Arnold's successful establishment of a new role for the Budget Committee — determining the level of increase over the prior year that represented a politically reasonable opening position — marked a clear preference for negotiation of "base" and "fair share," recalling Wildavsky's (1984) description of classical budgeting. Budget requests for fiscal years 2000 and 2001 lagged behind the rate of caseload growth, which provided another example of the Judiciary conforming its request to the budgetary environment (Mecham, 2000; 2001). Workload formula recalibration in 2001 (Mecham, 2001) may represent an attempt to reestablish the importance of metrics as dispositive, rather than decorative.

Individual courts, by contrast, are subject to tight linkage between budget and workload, but because cases flow into the courts at litigants' instigation, the impacts are beyond the courts' control. Acutely sensitive to caseload fluctuations, unit executives nonetheless cannot influence but merely react to the factors on which future budgets depend. For this reason, caseload and the other variables of the allotment formulas serve not as incentives but as courts' due: determining their share of the appropriation, demanding concern but resisting control. Lacking influence over their workload, unit executives respond to other cues, ultimately confounding the governance by metric that performance-based budgeting promotes.

Despite failing to meet the rhetorical threshold of "outcomes rather than outputs," of the Service Efforts and Accomplishments project (Gianakis, 1996) and performance-based budgeting generally (Martin, 2002), the dissemination of workload through publications such as the *Annual Report of the Director* and use of common funding formulas create the prospect of comparisons across districts and establish a mechanism for reputational dynamics. Judges are susceptible to performance issues, according to Judge Posner (1995, 222–23), as evidenced by the potential for "shaming" those who lag behind recognized norms. Perhaps financial management will also generate normative dynamics — judges after all are ultimately in charge of administration as well as adjudication — that may sensitize courts to financial outcomes. But any incentives for financial management will remain indirect: judges' direct support, including salaries, space, and staff, are inviolable due to classification as mandatory expenditures (King, 2004). Notwithstanding routinized metrics in the Judiciary, the motivational complexity described above belies the straight-line connection between strategic direction and management behavior underlying performance-based budgeting. The foundation of this performance turn will be revisited in the context of court governance, while discussing assumptive theory below. Yet, the essential point is that, despite tantalizing parallels, the Judiciary's decentralization initiative lacks key elements that would characterize a performance-based case.

If performance-based budgeting represents an ill-fitting template to describe the experience of the Judiciary, target budgeting (Rubin, 1998) promises a closer match. Target budgeting couples central constraint (the target) with considerable latitude for autonomous organizational components to determine their priorities and budget and spend accordingly. Target budgeting serves to make budgetary units accountable at a macro level, while discarding micro-level controls, which is the mechanism at work in the individual courts as a result of budget decentralization. Courts are free to prioritize. Because the main factors impelling the Judiciary were the ability to meet local priorities more quickly and to overcome the appearance of favoritism given by an AO-dominated process (Bobek, 2004), the target budget's chief attribute of proportional sacrifice or gain and its decentralized planning and execution correspond well with the Judiciary's experience. For example, the study found widespread reprogramming into automation (KPMG, 2004, p. 36), which was perceived as an unmet need (Arnold, 2003). Targeted budgeting also helps to explain the changes in appropriation development that the Budget Committee wrought by imposing a ceiling on annual increases to bind the committees with budgetary responsibility, but not dictating how it would be maintained. To the extent that apparently evenhanded treatment of budget-holders is of significant concern, then target budgeting by its straightforward sharing of largesse or hardship achieves the appearance of equal treatment, which is an important attribute in an enterprise with many co-equal constituents.

18.5.2 Connection with Assumptive Theory-Building

Locating a theoretical vantage that accounts for the above-described processes is the task Gianakis and McCue assign to *assumptive* budgetary theory. Whereas affixing a descriptive label to the Judiciary's experience poses the challenge of selecting among abundant alternatives, establishing an explanatory foundation begs simple classification. Nonetheless, I follow Forrester (2002) by investigating whether agency theory can shore up weaknesses in the theoretical underpinnings of budgetary scholarship.

Agential tenets are not fundamentally different from those underlying the "default" (Gianakis and McCue, 2002, p. 165) model of self-interested administrator as budget maximizer or wastrel because they explain objectives and motivations instrumentally: derived from calculation of the likelihood and consequences of alternative courses of action. At base, the foundations of instrumentality are deductive, nomothetic, and utilitarian: deductive in the stepwise progression from ends to means; nomothetic in its reference to absolutes, manifest rather than negotiable; and utilitarian in its reduction of choices to trade-offs based on welfare economics, as computed through cost-benefit analysis or other rational mechanisms. Agency theory merely adds a second entity, the principal, whose interests and expectations counteract, reinforce, or simply coexist with the agent's, as well as a structure for executing agreements such as a contract.

The contractual basis of principal-agent relationships provides a template for instrumental development and execution of budgets. Budget development proceeds from requests, winnowed and refined through intra-agency prioritization, conformed to administration priorities and aggregated by OMB to produce the President's Budget, thence to congressional disposition. At each stage, those who claim are accountable to those who conserve, using Schick's (1990, pp. 64–65) terms, for sound foundation and reasonable presentation underlying the requests. Hardly powerless, claimants influence the disposition of their requests by selectively informing decision makers, whose relative ignorance renders them subject to nominal subordinates. The tension between knowledge and authority, which contend rather than cohere, at least in theory, results in budgetary compromise between official objectives and local, even personal, prerogatives.

Accountability for budget execution flows from Congress — notwithstanding the presidential veto power — to the Executive and Judicial Branches: traceable through successive agential dyads, from apportionments and allocations that allow agency heads to execute their financial plans to allotments whereby accountable executives authorize specific expenditures. As in budget development, contending asymmetries of authority and information influence and constrain individual actors at each stage, as they weigh personal, official, and organizational incentives. Termed "moral hazard," the issue of abrogating official responsibilities hinges on expectations of likely outcomes and associated rewards or penalties. Observance of official duties is reduced to a balance struck between proprietary knowledge, which, kept from principals, permits agents' independent action, and incentive structures calibrated to discourage misbehavior.

The crisp theoretical model resulting from the expectation-driven behavior attributed to principals and agents seems promising, but encounters obstacles in simulating how agential incentives should have worked in the Judiciary's case. Figure 18.2 models the implications of the decentralization initiative from the vantage of tactical use of information to attain control by the principal, designated as the "central approving authority," or to resist control by the agent, the court in this depiction. The initial phase, which models the pre-existing system, reveals many apertures — budget calls, requisitions, and reprogramming requests — affording the principal regular and multifaceted visibility into the local situation. Such knowledge gives the principal increased leverage to exert effective control, while constraining

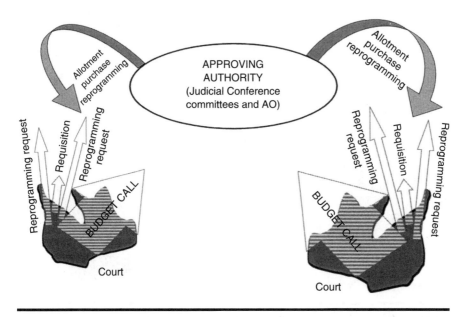

Figure 18.2   Simulation of principal-agent dynamics in budget decentralization.

the agent's latitude for independent action and ultimately denying the agent control.

Figure 18.3 depicts the interim phase, corresponding to the pilot decentralization, which reduces the occasions for information exchange to more narrowly focused budget calls, stripped of historically based cost categories. With local information more closely held and fewer opportunities to breach the proprietary "membrane" bounding discrete organizations, principal and agent each exercise limited control. The demarcation of agential control coincided with the limit on reprogramming, set at $5,000 or 10 percent, whichever was greater, during the pilot program (Bobek, 2004, p. 31).

The ultimately decentralized budgetary process, depicted in Figure 18.4, disengages the principal and agent through the mechanism of the "court attributes" — the collection of court data whereby formulas compute budgets for allotment of funds. Nominal control exercised by the principal in this case is based on management of the budgetary policies, amendable in response to new *general* information; for example, the new "snapshot" for compensation. The crucial distinction is between control and impact, which remains the province of the central authority — even disproportionate impact, as from the "snapshot" that John Shope maintained

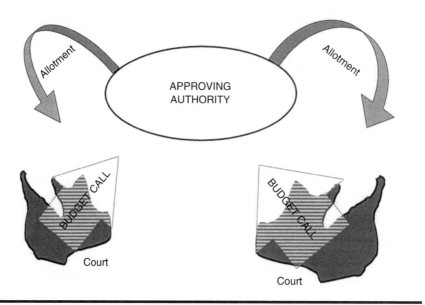

Figure 18.3   Simulation of principal-agent dynamics in interim budgetary reform.

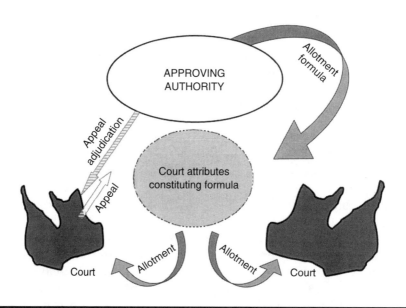

Figure 18.4   Simulation of principal-agent dynamics in mature budget decentralization.

disadvantaged fiscally conservative courts. But control is illusory without the ability to set differentiated policies or take targeted actions that apply to particular courts based on specific knowledge of the consequences. The appeal does represent such an opportunity for direct intervention, but the limited number and specific circumstances of appeals preclude systematic control by the principal.

The mechanisms of agency theory simulated above appear unable to account for the concerted efforts applied toward reforming financial management given the lack of explicit incentives in the Judiciary. To illustrate that application of agency theory would yield a starkly different result, I contrast the relaxation of hierarchical management systems shown above with the prominent role of intricate measurement schemes in the idealized behavioral description of GPRA by McNab and Melese (2003, pp. 92–93), in which carefully calibrated incentive systems serve to "discipline" agencies as a substitute for the market-based discipline meted out in the private sector.

Confounding such formulations, budgeting and financial management in the Judiciary proceeded more simply. Unaccountably (at least by agency theory), change occurred without the control mechanisms, relinquished by the AO, and without the chain of command exerted by the political leadership found in an executive agency. Leadership operates, of course, but in a form peculiar to the Judiciary: district-by-district and circuit-by-circuit direction established by judges, who defer to other judges within and across jurisdictions. They maintain collegial relationships partly by strict separation of duties and space (each federal judge occupies a separate courtroom) and long established protocols and rules (for example, a district's chief judge is the longest serving judge who is less than sixty-five years old). The connection from the "center," represented by the Judicial Conference and the AO, to the individual courts defies explicit delineation. The intermediate level ostensibly occupied by the circuit councils (chaired by the chief judge of the respective circuit courts of appeals) imposes slight to moderate constraint on the administration of the district courts within the circuit, but in no case displaces local control (Fish, 1973, pp. 404–9). For staff, who are not appointed for life, personnel actions and professional advancement derive from local factors, not from central authority. So, allegiance to their courts governs unit executives' responsiveness to local needs and establishes the tenor of the courts' operation. (It is worth noting in this regard that three unit executives serve at the pleasure of the district court judges through the chief judge; four in the circuit courts.)

Yet, it was precisely such parochial attention to local interests that the stewardship emphasis of decentralization training targeted. To the extent courts practiced strict financial management that deferred local spending, they demonstrated institutional concern for the Judiciary extending beyond local jurisdictions. Courts revealed this concern by responding to the request each summer for unused funds that courts could defer spending, which Director Mecham (2001) characterized as follows:

> This was not done without sacrifice ... courts had to delay or defer hiring needed staff, training, automation projects, and other important activities.

Courts' willingness to "sacrifice" counters the agential assumption of direct responsiveness to personal incentives because unit executives could expect no benefits from this corporate stewardship, given locally determined career prospects.

Assumption of greater accountability also confounds predictions limited to incentives of aggrandizement or self-preservation. Court managers' reliance on the AO's review, prior to decentralization, to excuse failure to provide staff, equipment, or other resources is an example of exploiting information asymmetries for personal advantage, i.e., job security without performance. Decentralization forced active resource management; its absence became readily apparent, forcing the departures noted above. Voluntarily undertaking greater responsibility and risk runs counter to the presumed tendency reported by Forrester and Adams (1997 p. 476) for "bureaucrats and administrators to protect themselves, whether by obscuring information ... or by putting budgetary requests in the best light." Thus, accepting a broader definition of their responsibility, encompassing the Judiciary as a whole, and greater accountability for managerial results signaled institutional rather than agential orientation. Juxtaposition of agential and institutional assumptions is, of course, an oversimplification, characterized by Scott (2001) as the

> tension between those theorists who emphasize structural and cultural constraints on action and those who emphasize the ability of individual actors to "make a difference" in the flow of events (pp. 74–75).

Scott sought sufficient leeway in institutional constraints to permit "attention to the ways in which individual actors take action to create, maintain, and transform institutions" (ibid.). The roles of Bobek, Arnold, and the court managers who supported decentralization demonstrate the importance of strong individual responsibility for advancing institutional aims. Despite the prominence of "change agents," the course of budgetary reform in the courts underscores that empowering court managers represents an improvised but institutionally appropriate step, rather than rote application of a theoretical notion: an important caveat for agencies who seek to follow the Judiciary's example. While efficiency was a real as well as a public rationale for decentralization, Judge Arnold attributes important institutional causes — "unit heads felt disrespected" under the old system — in addition to the economic ones. Contrary arguments were also less rational than institutional, for example,

> the fear that the change might create a scandal: a clerk or unit head or employee would use funds in a way that would bring disrepute on the Judiciary. If you do 99 things right and one thing wrong, and the one thing is sufficiently attention-getting, then it reflects badly on the institution. Their [the courts'] image influenced their standing with the public and with Congress (Arnold, 2003).

Concern above all else for the Judiciary's perceived propriety represents not only organizational loyalty, but institutional commitment to the legal system as well. Public regard for the reputation of the courts contributes to their standing as a manifestly co-equal branch of government, a reputation at least partially dependent on financial stewardship, as Glaser (1994) found true for the New York state courts. The political independence and wide discretion of the American courts, so remarkable to de Tocqueville (1956, p. 76), represent values that permeate the legal system, providing institutional values that permeate the legal system, providing fertile ground in which budgetary reforms may take root.

18.5.3   *Connection with Normative Theory-Building*

From the normative vantage, Forrester and Adams (1997) advocated the study of budgetary processes for organizational improvement, which follows closely on the discussion above of the assumptive basis of institutional factors versus agential ones. The premise that budgetary theory building had sought better theories rather than better functioning organizations provided their explanation for why budget reforms so frequently failed (pp. 467–71). I submit that the Judiciary's budget decentralization initiative aptly illustrates the practically oriented and organizationally sensitive reform from which Forrester and Adams promised results. The prime distinction of the organizational view of budgetary reform is that its purpose derives from intrinsic need, rather than prescription of curative technology.

Despite the apparent connection to performance-based budgeting, nothing points to budgetary reform having been conceived as an abstract ideal, rather as a practical response to exigency. Bobek (2003) points to his chief motivation as the "inability to respond to the requirements of the courts" during a period of sustained growth. By tracing the initiative's source to an inability by the Judiciary to meet the demands of rapid growth, Bobek established budget decentralization's organizational bona fides. When NAPA's recommendation to predicate further decentralization on standardized accounting procedures provided a pretext for adding technological sophistication, he resisted it in favor of sustained momentum toward simpler but internally sanctioned methods.

Just as the "why" of budget reform was couched in organizational context, so the "how" of the Judiciary's initiative arose from within, exuding sensitivity to March and Olsen's (1989) logic of appropriateness. Budget decentralization's vanguard — working groups who developed the approach and the steering committee that ratified their products — heralded practicality while Judicial Conference sanction accorded propriety.

The joint imprimatur of court managers and judges signified an initiative of, for, and by the courts, establishing an authentic impetus for reform. While budget decentralization issued from the panoply of official organizational commitment, the hands-on engagement of court managers such as Guillot, Polsky, and Shope spanned the decade-long implementation of decentralization, for some continuing to the present day. Judge Arnold's tenure as Budget Committee chairman also coincided with the period of major changes, providing continuity of policy. Finally, AO executive direction under Bobek and Mecham ensured consistent administration of budget reforms, at least until Bobek's retirement. Pursuit of decentralization — piloted with allotments replacing requisitions, expanded to personnel flexibility, and streamlined and systemized by allotment simplifications — proceeded apace, but not beyond courts' readiness to absorb change. Bobek (2003) identified a number of key steps integrating the organizational and technical aspects of these reforms: the careful selection by a committee of peer managers of volunteer courts to follow the pilot five; the intensive training — not only about means, but ends and principles as well; supervision of the specialists developing statistical formulae by veterans of the initiative; and oversight of the formulae's implementation as an appeals board. These organizationally appropriate safeguards over the technical mechanisms epitomize the self-paced, self-directed budget reform management promoted by Forrester and Adams (1997, pp. 472–73).

Gianakis and McCue (1999) assert that budget development activities can serve as an organizational development process in local government to counteract the "centrifugal forces" of distributed operations serving separate clienteles. They suggest the forms of budgeting may provide a cohering factor, of which there is some evidence in the Judiciary's case. For example, common budgetary process manifested itself in easier access to budget projections, through the "Infoweb" computer program (Bobek, 2004, p. 48). This provides access Judiciary-wide to the funding amounts for the coming year, based on caseload and other parameters. The process of simply looking up the planned funding, computed simultaneously for all courts, reinforces the impression that the resulting amount is the court's due, not dependent on the largesse of central administrators. Another common form is the Electronic Status of Funds reporting mechanism, through which courts report their spending to date and provide estimates for the balance of the year (Bobek, 2004, p. 50). The combined effect of these forms — funds provided as a matter of course that are accounted for by the unit executives responsible for prudent expenditure — represents trust conferred on the individual courts, their judges and managers, which reinforces the tradition of autonomy, and introduces a new norm, that of stewardship.

18.6   Lessons for Other Agencies from the Judiciary's Experience

Convincing appropriators while instituting financial management reforms to ensure funds were well spent, the Judiciary's apparent success depended on a tricky combination of top-down program planning and local autonomy in budget execution. Before too much is made of the significance of these achievements beyond the Third Branch, however, it would be well to consider crucial differences that many limit broad applicability.

Crucial differences attend the constitutional prerogatives of a co-equal branch of government: foremost, the unique posture before congressional appropriators, befitting special considerations denied to agencies generally. Notwithstanding scholars' dubious assessments of a co-equal branch's special status, Judge Arnold (2003) observes, "the Department of Agriculture ... does not appear in the Constitution" and Congress is "respectful" of this distinction. The essence of the Judiciary's successful collaboration with Congress is trust, as Judge Arnold (2003) identifies: "We are always very frank; our greatest asset is our candor." The Judiciary's rapport with Congress issues partly from budgetary law — the budget's direct submission bypassing OMB — but clearly redounds to the significance of constitutional structure and the institutional significance of a politically independent judiciary. Finally, Bobek (2003) credits the "stability of executive direction in the Judiciary," with its current head, Director Mecham, approaching two decades of service, and Judicial Conference committees led by long-serving judges. Accordingly, he is skeptical of the ability of executive agencies — with typical tenures of assistant secretaries for administration under two years — to sustain the attention necessary for completing such an initiative (Bobek, 2003).

Studying the Judiciary's budget decentralization initiative illuminates distinct vantages vying to explain the mechanisms that impel and sustain organizational change. The theoretical tension between institutional and agential frameworks permeates the account of changes wrought in the Judiciary's budgetary process. The norms that underlie institutionalism impacted this evolution significantly; so too a the formal accountability of designated agents for outcomes. Clearly, institutional norms and structures played a great role in gathering the impetus and sustaining the direction for decentralization in budget execution. The most basic norm is that of autonomy: courts have been self-administered throughout their history. Regard for the reputation of the Judiciary and the need to show respect for court managers are institutional considerations that weighed heavily, along with the economic rationale, in the decision to proceed with decentralization. Their role in crafting the rules and the perceived fairness of the rules were keys to the court managers' acceptance of the initiative. Continued scrutiny of the evenhandedness of new developments occasioned by recent fiscal straits introduces the new role of observer: gauging the relative austerity of their budgets and judging the equity of the system accordingly. Despite the appearance of outcome-based budgeting, fair share is manifested by the sensitivity of the Judiciary's principal negotiators to what executive agencies request, and the willingness to reset, suspend, and recalibrate its workload-based requirements mark a negotiated rather than engineered budgetary approach.

But, above all, the Judiciary's case demonstrates how overriding necessity inspired ingenuity and opportunistic action — reform molded around organizational contours as Forrester and Adams have urged rather than forced to fit. Whether similar results are obtainable by cultivation of a comparable culture to nurture change through shared belief systems, or through selection and empowerment of change agents, remains indeterminate. Although there are clearly lessons to be drawn by other agencies observing the Judiciary's budgetary reform, they must be drawn from the underlying motives — institutional commitment, stewardship, and managerial accountability and risk tolerance — rather than skimmed from the surface.

Note

1. Outlays by the Department of Justice grew from $2,538 million in 1979 (Office of Management and Budget, 1998, p. 67) to $14,310 million in 1997 (p. 69), accounting for the 463% increase cited by Rubin (2000, p. 128). During the same period, outlays for the Judiciary grew from $481 million to $3,259 million, a 577% increase.

References

AO Staff Measures the Needs of the Courts. 1999. *The Third Branch*, 31(8). Washington: Administrative Office of the U.S. Courts. On Internet at www.uscourts.gov/ttb/aug99ttb/measure.html.

Appendix 1: Cumulative Savings in the Salaries and Expenses Appropriation by Activity, Fiscal Years 1994–2002 (2004). In Joseph Bobek, (ed.), *Assessment of the Judiciary Budget Decentralization Program — Part 4* (p. 1). Washington, DC: Administrative Office of the U.S. Courts.

Appendix 21: Number of Court Budget Appeals Processed by Fiscal Year and Amounts Requested, Approved, and Denied (2004). In Joseph Bobek, (ed.), *Assessment of the Judiciary Budget Decentralization Program—Part 4* (p. 35). Washington, DC: Administrative Office of the U.S. Courts.

Arnold, Honorable Richard S. 1996. Cited in "Judiciary Presents FY 97 Funding Request." *The Third Branch*, 28(5). Washington: Administrative Office of the U.S. Courts. On Internet at www.uscourts.gov/ttb/may96/97fund.htm.

—— 2003, August 20. Telephone interview by author.

Barrow, Deborah J. and Walker, Thomas G. 1988. *A Court Divided: The Fifth Circuit Court of Appeals and the Politics of Judicial Reform.* New Haven, Connecticut: Yale University Press, p. 263.

Bobek, Josesph. 2003, July 16. Interview by author. Washington, DC.

——. 2004. Assessment of the Judiciary Budget Decentralization Program — Part 3: History and Current Status. Washington, DC: Administrative Office of the U.S. Courts.

"Bobek to Head AO Office of Finance and Budget." 1996. *The Third Branch*, 28(6). Washington: Administrative Office of the U.S. Courts. On Internet at www.uscourts.gov/ttb/jun96ttb/bobek.htm.

Brady, Henry E. and Collier, David, eds. (2004). *Rethinking Social Inquiry: Diverse Tools, Shared Standards.* Lanham, Maryland: Rowman & Littlefield.

de Tocqueville, Alexis. 1956. Democracy in America (R.D. Heffner, Ed). New York: Mentor Books (originally published in 1835).

Douglas, James W. 1999. "Redirection in Georgia: A New Type of Budget Reform." *American Review of Public Administration*, 29(3), 269–289.

—— 2000. "Budget Reform Theory: A Guideline for Successful Budget Reform." *International Journal of Public Administration*, 23(11), 1967–1996.

Douglas, James W. and Hartley, Roger E. 2001. "The Politics of Court Budgeting in the States: Is Judicial Independence Threatened?" *Public Administration Review*, 33(1), 54–78.

Eckstein, Harry (1975). "Case Study and Theory in Political Science." In Fred I. Greenstein and Nelson Polsby (eds.) *Handbook of Political Science: Strategies of Inquiry*, vol. 7. Reading, Massachusetts: Addison-Wesley, pp. 79–136.

Fish, Peter Graham. 1973. *The Politics of Federal Judicial Administration.* Princeton, New Jersey: Princeton University Press, pp. 444–45.

Forrester, John. 2002. "The Principal-Agent Model and Budget Theory." In Aman Khan and W. Bartley Hildreth (eds.), *Budget Theory in the Public Sector.* Westport, Connecticut: Quorum, pp. 123–138).

Forrester, John P. and Adams, Guy B. 1997. "Budgetary Reform through Organizational Learning: Toward an Organizational Theory of Budgeting." *Administration & Society,* 28(4), 466–488.

Gianakis, Gerasimos A. 1996. "Integrating Performance Measurement and Budgeting." In Arie Halachmi and Geert Bouckaert (eds.), *Organizational Performance and Measurement in the Public Sector,* Westport, Connecticut: Quorom.

Gianakis, Gerasimos A. and McCue, Clifford P. (1999). *Local Government Budgeting.* Westport, Connecticut: Quorum.

—— 2002. "Budget Theory for Public Administration ... and Public Administrators." In Aman Khan and W. Bartley Hildreth (eds.), *Budget Theory in the Public Sector.* Westport, Connecticut: Quorum, pp. 158–71.

Gibbons, Honorable Julia Smith. 1999. Cited in "AO Staff Measures the Needs of the Courts."

Gibson, Ed. 2003. "Program Assessment Rating Tool (PART): The Bush Administration's Hierarchical Management Tool?" Presented to the Fall Meeting of the Association for Public Policy Analysis and Management. Washington, DC.

Gibson, Ed. 2004. "Admitting a Bad Influence: Contracting the Public Service." *International Journal of Public Administration,* 27(7), 481–490.

Grizzle, Gloria A. and Pettijohn, Carole D. 2002. "Implementing Performance-Based Program Budgeting: A System-Dynamics Perspective." *Public Administration Review,* 62(1), 51–62.

Glaser, Howard B. 1994. "Wachtler v. Cuomo: The Limits of Inherent Power." *Judicature,* 78(1), 12–24.

Guillot, Kay. 2003, July 24. Telephone interview by author.

Hellman, Arthur D. 1990. "Governance and Administration: Introduction." In Arthur D. Hellman (ed.), *Restructuring Justice: The Innovations of the Ninth Circuit and the Future of the Federal Courts.* Ithaca, New York: Cornell University Press, pp. 221–25.

Judicial Conference of the United States. 1988. *1988 Reports of the Proceedings of the Judicial Conference of the United States.* Washington: Administrative Office of the U.S. Courts.

Judicial Conference of the United States. 1989. *1989 Reports of the Proceedings of the Judicial Conference of the United States.* Washington: Administrative Office of the U.S. Courts.

Judicial Conference of the United States. 1994. *1994 Reports of the Proceedings of the Judicial Conference of the United States.* Washington: Administrative Office of the U.S. Courts.

Judiciary Secures FY 96 Funding. 1996. *The Third Branch,* 28(1). Washington: Administrative Office of the U.S. Courts. On Internet at www.uscourts.gov/ttb/jan96ttb/96fund.htm.

King, Honorable Carolyn Dineen, to Honorable Sim Lake (2004, April 29).

KPMG, LLP. 2004. *Assessment of the Judiciary Budget Decentralization Program — Part 2.* Washington, DC: Administrative Office of the U.S. Courts.

Lauth, Thomas P. 1985. "Performance Evaluation In the Georgia Budgetary Process." *Public Budgeting and Finance* 5(1), 67–82.

LeLoup, Lance T. 2002. "Budget Theory for a New Century." In Aman Khan and W. Bartley Hildreth (eds.), *Budget Theory in the Public Sector.* Westport, Connecticut: Quorum, pp. 1–21.

March, James G. and Olsen, Johan P. 1989. *Rediscovering Institutions: The Organizational Basis of Politics.* New York: Free Press.

Martin, Lawrence L. 2002. "Budgeting for Outcomes." In Aman Khan and W. Bartley Hildreth (eds.), *Budget Theory in the Public Sector.* Westport, Connecticut: Quorum, pp. 246–260.

McNab, Robert M. and Melese, Francois. 2003. "Implementing the GPRA: Examining the Prospects for Performance Budgeting in the Federal Government." *Public Budgeting & Finance* 23(2), 73–95.

Mecham, Leonidas Ralph. 1990. Annual Report of the Director of the Administrative Office of the U.S. Court: Fiscal Year 1989. Washington: Administrative Office of the U.S. Courts.

———. 2001. Fiscal Year 2000 Report to Congress on the Optimal Utilization of Judicial Resources. Washington: Administrative Office of the U.S. Courts.

———. 2001. Annual Report of the Director of the Administrative Office of the U.S. Court: Fiscal Year 2000. Washington: Administrative Office of the U.S. Courts.

———. 2002. Fiscal Year 2001 Report to Congress on the Optimal Utilization of Judicial Resources. Washington: Administrative Office of the U.S. Courts.

Office of Management and Budget. 1998. " Table 4.1—Outlays by Agency: 1962–2003." In *The Budget for Fiscal Year 1999: Historical Tables.* Washington: Government Printing Office, pp. 70–75.

———. 2003. " Table 5.3—Percentage Distribution of Budget Authority by Agency: 1976–2008." In *The Budget for Fiscal Year 2004: Historical Tables.* Washington: Government Printing Office, pp. 97–100.

Polsky, Barry. 2003, August 12. Telephone interview with author.

Posner, Honorable Richard A. 1985. *The Federal Courts: Crisis and Reform.* Cambridge, Massachusetts: Harvard University Press.

Posner, Honorable Richard A. 1995. *The Federal Courts: Challenge and Reform.* Cambridge, Massachusetts: Harvard University Press.

Provine, Doris Marie. 1990. "Governing the Ungovernable: The Theory and Practice of Governance in the Ninth Circuit." In Arthur D. Hellman (ed.), *Restructuring Justice: The Innovations of the Ninth Circuit and the Future of the Federal Courts.* Ithaca, New York: Cornell University Press, pp. 247–80, p. 271.

Rehnquist, The Honorable William H. 1998. "The 1997 Year-End Report on the Federal Judiciary." *The Third Branch*, 30(1). Washington: Administrative Office of the U.S. Courts. On Internet at www.uscourts.gov/ttb/jan98ttb/january.htm.

Rubin, Irene S. 1998. *Class, Tax, and Power: Municipal Budgeting in the United States*. Chatham, New Jersey: Chatham House.

———. 2000. *The Politics of Public Budgeting: Getting and Spending, Borrowing and Balancing (4th ed.)*. Chatham House Publishers: New York.

———. 2003. *Balancing the Federal Budget: Trimming the Herd or Eating the Seed Corn*. Chatham House Publishers: New York.

Schick, Allen. 1966. "The Road to PPB: The Stages of Budget Reform." *Public Administration Review*, 26(6), 234–58.

———. 1988. "An Inquiry into the Possibility of a Budgetary Theory." In Irene Rubin (ed.), *New Directions in Budget Theory*. Albany, New York: State University of New York Press, pp. 59–69.

———. 1990. *The Capacity to Budget*. Washington: Urban Institute Press.

Scott, Richard W. 2001. *Institutions and Organizations* (2nd edition). Thousand Oaks, California: Sage.

Shope, John. 2003, September 10. Telephone interview by author.

Walker, Thomas G. and Barrow, Deborah J. 1985. "Funding the Federal Judiciary: The Congressional Connection." *Judicature*, 69(1), 43–50.

White, Joseph. 1991. "Presidential Power and the Budget." In Thomas D. Lynch (ed.), *Federal Budget and Financial Management Reform*. New York: Quorum, pp. 1–29.

Wildavsky, Aaron. 1984. *The Politics of the Budgetary Process*. Boston, Massachusetts: Little, Brown, revised 4th ed.

Willoughby, Katherine G. 2004. "Performance Measurement and Budget Balancing: State Government Perspective." *Public Budgeting & Finance*, 24(2), 21–39.

Wynne, William. 2003, August 6. Interview by author. Washington, DC.

Yarwood, Dean L. and Canon, Bradley C. 1980. "On the Supreme Court's Annual Trek to the Capitol." *Judicature*, 63(7), 322–27.

Yin, Robert K. 2003. *Case Study Research: Design and Methods*. Thousand Oaks, California: Sage.

Chapter 19

Public Participation in Local Performance Measurement and Budgeting

ALFRED HO, Ph.D.
Department of Public Administration, Indiana Universtiry

PAUL COATES, Ph.D.
Department of Political Science, Iowa State University

19.1   Introduction

Public budgeting is a political process in which scarce resources in society are extracted from the private economy and allocated to public service providers to accomplish the social, economic, and political goals desired by the public (Mikesell, 2002). Since there are diverse and often conflicting interests and priorities in society, policymakers and budgeters in a democratic society have to articulate these preferences carefully and try to reach policy compromises in spending and revenue decisions. The decision about who gets what and when is often not purely a question of allocative and technical efficiency, but an issue of who controls the agenda and information flow and who has enough political leverage in the decision-making process within a specific social and ideological environment (Jacoby, 2000; Lee, Johnson, and Joyce, 2004). Thurmaier and Willoughby (2001) argue that budgeting is built on multiple rationalities. Economic rationality, social norms and beliefs, political feasibility, and legal constraints all play an important role in influencing budgetary decisions.

For the past few decades, however, many budgetary and managerial reforms have tried to downplay this political reality and focused primarily on the technical rationality of the process. Influenced by the paradigm of scientific management and the discipline of cost accounting and economic analysis, many reformers believed that the government should run more like a business and should operate with greater economic and technical rationality. At the turn of the 20th century, the idea of performance measurement was introduced to give decision-makers more tangible information for budgetary decision-making, such as cost and output data (Bureau of Municipal Research of New York, 1915; Williams, 2003). Since then, various professional organizations, including the International City Management Association (which later became the International City/County Management Association) and the Urban Institute, have invested significant effort to disseminate this concept and provide technical assistance to encourage state and local officials to adopt the practice in program management and budgeting (Ridley and Simon, 1938; the Urban Institute and ICMA, 1974). Performance measurement also caught the attention of federal reformers. From the introduction of program-planning-budgeting system in the late 1960s, zero-base budgeting in the 1970s, management-by-objectives in the 1980s, to recent legislative and executive initiatives such as the Government Performance and Results Act in 1993 and Performance Assessment Rating Tools under the George W. Bush administration, federal policymakers have tried to change how budgeting works by building a more rational and coherent structure between policy goals, delivery mechanisms, program performance, and budgeting decisions (U.S. GAO, 1997).

Unfortunately, past studies have suggested that most of these reforms have had very little direct impact on appropriation outcomes. Legislators often pay little attention to the performance information submitted with budget requests, and continue to budget in the same way that they have been doing for decades (Larkey and Devereux, 1999; Jordan and Hackbart, 1999; Joyce, 1993; Wang, 2000; Willoughby and Melkers, 2000). Even though these rational budget reforms may have made a significant impact on the executive process of public budgeting, they often hit a wall when budgetary and performance information leaves the budget office and reaches elected representatives.

One of the reasons for the difficulty in implementing performance budgeting is because of an inherent weakness in many of the past budgetary reforms — many of them were initiated by the executive branch without much participation by the legislative branch and core constituencies. As a result, the process and outcomes of these reforms often lacked the political credibility and buy-ins needed to make a substantial impact in the political process.

This history is a primary motivation for the new paradigm of performance measurement introduced in this paper — the "citizen-initiated performance assessment" (CIPA) model for local governments. In CIPA, local officials engage citizens and elected officials to jointly develop performance measures so that the performance information can incorporate the citizens' perspective and have greater political credibility in the political decision-making process. In the following discussion, this paper first presents the rationales and conceptual framework of CIPA. It then examines how nine Iowa cities implemented the model in 2001–2004 and analyzes the impact of the project from the perspective of city officials and citizens. The paper concludes by drawing from this analysis, to discuss the future of performance budgeting reforms and suggest what should be done to enhance the public accountability and technical rationality of the budgetary process within the political constraints of a democratic system.

19.2 The Concept of "Citizen-Initiated Performance Assessment"

The "Citizen-Initiated Performance Assessment" model is built upon the premise that citizens are not only the customers but also the owners, issue framers, co-producers, and evaluators of government (Epstein et al., 2000; King and Stivers, 1998; Schachter, 1997; Thomas, 1995). Customers select and pay for the services that they want, but do not have any direct authority over the service provider except for their indirect influence through market forces. In a democratic society, citizens are more than customers because they have the right as well as the responsibility to influence the decision-making process of the government and can hold public officials accountable for their budgetary and policy actions. Through their elected representatives, citizens indirectly determine what government should and should not do and how it should tax and spend taxpayers' money. Citizens also influence government policies directly through their participation in citizen surveys, citizen committees and commissions, public meetings, and interactions with public officials, and indirectly through various civic organizations and special interest groups (Ebdon, 2002). They can also have direct influence on the delivery of public services by volunteering in government programs and working with community organizations that co-produce public services with the government.

Despite these participatory channels, there has been a growing public distrust toward the institution of government for the past two decades (Ebdon and Franklin, 2005). Many citizens still do not feel that they understand how the government operates and what their tax money is used for. Many citizen groups also argue that the government is wasteful and inefficient, is bankrupted by special interest politics, and has lost the voice of the general citizenry. This trend has emerged despite the decades-long effort by managers and budgeters to measure the performance of government to "enhance public accountability".

This problem reflects a clear gap between what public officials try to measure and communicate to the public about their service efforts and accomplishment, and what citizens perceive through the mass media and personal experience. The problem cannot be attributed to lack of performance data, as past studies have found that many governments, big or small, have been collecting all kinds of output and outcome performance measures for internal purposes (Ho, 2003, 2005). What public officials need is a viable mechanism to connect the exercise of performance measurement with what the stakeholders and constituencies look for in terms of government performance. This is why citizens' and other stakeholders' input, especially at the local level, is important in performance measurement.

Figure 19.1 illustrates the conceptual framework and process of the "citizen-initiated performance assessment" model, in which citizens are a major contributor to the development of performance measures. Its core component is the formation of a "citizen performance team" comprised of city council members, administrators, and citizen representatives. These citizen representatives can be recruited from a variety of sources, such as the current membership of various citizen advisory boards and the leadership of neighborhood organizations, or by open public recruitment. If a city does a citywide survey regularly, it may also include a question in the survey asking for volunteer help and use this method to recruit new members into the team. It is essential to have a council representative and at least a staff representative on the team to build the tie with the city council and with various departments.

Once the initial citizen performance team is constituted, they should receive some orientation about the concept of performance measurement and the basics of city operations and the major responsibilities of different departments. The team then identifies specific services that they wish to

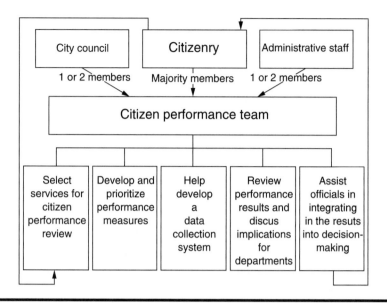

Figure 19.1   The conceptual framework of CIPA.

focus on to develop performance measures. To help the team become more familiar with the process first, it is recommended that they should only select one or two service areas initially and expand to other service areas later. This incremental approach also allows the performance team to re-examine their demographic composition and recruit other citizens and community representatives when they expand to other service areas and want a different representation of stakeholder interests in the CIPA process.

A two-step approach is recommended for developing performance measures for a specific service. First, in a meeting of about two hours, members of a citizen performance team are asked to identify the "critical elements" of a public service. For example, in a discussion about the police department, citizens may suggest that officers' legal knowledge and compliance, the adequacy of their training, response time, and their professionalism in interacting with citizens, are critically important. In a discussion of street services, citizens may be more concerned about traffic flow, road safety, timeliness of repairs, accessibility of emergency services when needed, and clarity of signs and road marks.

These "critical elements" become the basis for developing performance measures. In the process of generating performance measures it is recommended that a facilitator be used to organize the discussion, ensure fair opportunities for all members to participate, and provide technical assistance if needed. A facilitator is especially helpful in the initial brainstorming process and the follow-up discussion to select specific performance measures. In this process, the facilitator and the performance team may use the following criteria to guide the discussion:

- Are the measures helpful to citizens in evaluating the performance of the service? Can ordinary citizens understand the measures?
- Are the measures quantifiable and clearly defined?
- Is there data available? Will it be too costly and time-consuming to collect it? Is the value of the information worth the time investment and cost?

A worksheet can be used to help citizens think through these criteria and ensure that performance measures truly reflect the concerns and priorities of citizens, rather than city officials (see Table 19.1 for an example). Also, the worksheet offers an opportunity to compare the value of different measures, eliminate duplication, and prioritize data collection tasks for city staff.

After performance measures are developed, the third stage of CIPA focuses on data collection, review of measures based on quality of data, and the dissemination of information to the public. While departmental staff bear the primary responsibility for data collection, citizens can contribute to the process by reviewing data collection instruments, such as citizen or user surveys, and by sharing some data collection tasks, such as volunteering to hand out user surveys in a public library or recreation center.

After the performance data is collected, the fourth and the fifth stages of the CIPA process involve the transfer of the measures and data to the city council. Usually, a meeting between the CIPA performance team and the entire council should be held to allow the CIPA team to discuss

Table 19.1 Worksheet for Evaluating Performance Measures

	Service		
	Rating from 1 to 4 *(1 = least useful, 4 = most useful)*		
Performance Measures brain-stormed by citizens	*Useful to citizens?*	*Understandable and clear to citizens?*	*Useful to department?*
1.			
2.			
3.			
etc.			

their assessment of the data and formally ask the city council to take into consideration the citizens' perspective. This step is critically important to the success of CIPA. By having an opportunity to look at the data and performance results together, citizens and elected officials can have a constructive dialog about how public services should be improved, what constraints the government faces, and what the public can do to help. This also creates a landmark showing the results of the hard work by citizen representatives, and further enhances the legitimacy and political buy-ins of the measures for elected and departmental officials.

Once this is completed, it is important to integrate CIPA into the decision-making process of the city council. Work sessions for city council members can be organized to help them understand possible applications of the measures and data. This activity is especially important to cities that do not have a history of using performance measurement. A facilitator may be used to provide technical support and coordinate the discussion to see how the citizen-initiated performance measures can be used in strategic planning, budgeting, program evaluation, and policy development.

It should be noted that the citizen performance team is only a bridge to the larger public in evaluating the quality of public services. While the size of the performance team cannot be too big for efficiency purposes, other mechanisms of public input, such as general citizen surveys, user group surveys, customer service hotlines, and complaint statistics, should be used to ensure that the performance of public services is not evaluated by a small group of citizens who may not be representative of the population or the user group. The choice of these methods depends on the nature of the service and public concerns, the target audience, the structural character-istics of a community, and the administrative capacity of the government (Ebdon, 2000; Thomas, 1993; Walters et al., 2000). What is important here is to develop a portfolio of these mechanisms so that the results of CIPA can reflect the diverse perspectives of a community and its service users.

19.3   The Experience of Implementing CIPA in Iowa

Between 2001 and 2004 nine Iowa cities decided to experiment with this CIPA model (see Table 19.2 for a brief profile of these cities). After the initial orientation, the performance teams in each of these nine cities organized a series of meetings to understand the operation of city governments, select the service areas for the CIPA program, identify the critical elements of these services, and develop performance measures. Some cities also provided departmental tours to citizens to give them some hands-on experience about the operations of the selected services. During the discussion of perfor-mance measures, city staff assistance was often needed to provide technical

Table 19.2   Profile of the Iowa Cities in the CIPA Experiment

City Name	Brief Description of the City	Sources of Citizen Performance Team	Public Services Selected for CIPA
Burlington	Burlington has a population of about 27,000. It is an industrial town located in the eastern part of Iowa.	Citizen budget committee members, and open invitation to the public.	The police and fire departments
Carroll	Carroll has a population of 10,106. It is an economic center of the rural areas in Central Iowa.	Open invitation to the public, and citizen representatives from different citizen committees.	The recreational center, snow removal, public works, water
Clive	Clive has a population of 12,855. It is one of the booming suburbs in the Des Moines metropolitan area.	Citizen budget committee and other committee members.	Police, fire, and emergency medical services
Des Moines	Des Moines is the state capital of Iowa and has a population of about 200,000.	Representatives from Des Moines Neighbors Association, and recruited members from neighborhood surveys and public announcement.	Neighborhood community development and nuisance control (which covers multiple departments, including police, public works, and community development)
Indianola	Indianola has a population of 13,000. It is one of the bedroom communities in the Des Moines metropolitan area	Open invitation to the public, members from various citizen committees, and members of "Friends of the Library."	Library and public works (street repairs and snow removal)

Johnston	Johnston is one of the fastest growing suburbs in the Des Moines metro-politan area, with a population of about 10,000.	Open invitation to the public, and members from various citizen committees.	Street services and fire protection
Marion	Marion is a suburb outside the metro-politan center in Cedar Rapids, with a population of 26,294.	Open invitation to the public, and members from various citizen committees.	Public works and solid waste management
Marshall-town	Marshalltown has a population of 26,009. It is one of the industrial towns in Iowa. In recent years, it has had an influx of Hispanic immigrants, who work primarily in manufacturing and meat processing industries.	Open invitation to the public, and members from various citizen committees.	Snow removal, street services, and public transit
Urbandale	Urbandale has a population of 29,072. It is also one of the booming suburbs in the Des Moines metropolitan area.	Open invitation to the public, and members from various citizen committees.	Almost all municipal services

information, such as professional standards, state mandates, and the availability of existing data to measure some of the citizen-initiated performance measures.

Since the performance teams of the nine cities operated independently, they showed very diverse progress in implementing CIPA. In a few cities, the performance teams adapted to the process quickly and became very comfortable with the idea of performance measurement. Over a period of three years, these cities expanded the process to cover many of the essential municipal services, such as fire, police, road maintenance and construction, traffic control, snow removal, and garbage collection. In other cities, citizens demanded more detailed information and needed more time to go over each service. Also, some performance teams had more schedule conflicts than others and had to meet more sparingly. As a result, these cities could only cover a few services.

Regardless of the pace of progress, all performance teams had open and constructive discussion about city services. Most city staff were genuinely interested in how citizens perceived their work and what concerns they had. When comments and suggestions about specific services were made by citizens, departmental representatives usually responded by explaining some of the legal, fiscal, and managerial constraints they needed to face but would accept any innovative solutions suggested by citizens. Over time, citizens showed greater understanding of the complexities of city operations and respected city officials for what they were trying to accomplish. Some of the citizen participants who had been cynical about city bureaucracy in the beginning of the process even began to understand how much the city government could do and how citizens themselves might take greater responsibility for some of the community problems and concerns.

The performance measures recommended by CIPA were generally well received by departments. Most city officials tried to collect all the data based on these measures and report the results back to performance teams. The data collection tasks were demanding but not overwhelming because many of the citizen-initiated measures were not significantly different from some of the existing measures collected by the departments or suggested by professional organizations, such as the ICMA and the Urban Institute (ICMA, 1979; Hatry, 1980). For example, in evaluating police services, many citizens agreed that crime rates are useful and important information. Also, they were interested in the response time in police, fire, and emergency medical services, as well as the response time for other departments to respond to citizens' complaints or requests for services. Many also asked for citizen satisfaction or user survey results to evaluate the effectiveness of programs.

A major contribution of CIPA to the practice of performance measurement is the "citizen perspective" on some of the professional measures

(Ho and Coates, 2004a). First, citizens were generally less interested in "input measures", such as the number of city staff employed and the amount of raw materials needed, and were more interested in outcomes, such as whether the job was done well and how satisfied users were with the quality of services. The only input measures that attracted the interest of many performance teams were the training and qualifications of emergency response officials, such as how many hours and what types of training police and fire officers received annually. These input measures were important to citizens because they were interested in the quality of the officers. Knowing that these officers were well-trained gave citizens a better sense of security, even though solid training does not necessarily guarantee the actual outcomes of crime and fire protection.

The CIPA experience also showed that citizens want performance measures that they could relate to. In library, park, and recreation programs, for example, measuring the number of users and the extent of user satisfaction through surveys are the standard ways to measure the effectiveness of program delivery. In CIPA meetings, most citizens also accepted these measures as valid and useful, but they demanded that these measures should be broken down by age groups and gender, so that citizens and officials could use the measures to evaluate service effectiveness by user types.

Similarly, citizens wanted to "localize" performance measures so that the measures meant something to them. In police and emergency-medical services, for example, several performance teams recommended that the crime rates and response time measures should be sub-categorized by geographical divisions of a city. In many other services, the number of complaints, citizen service requests, and the efficiency measures of service delivery, should also be reported by geographical areas of a city so that citizens could see whether there was any concern of inequity in service delivery and whether a specific neighborhood had more serious problems that should be addressed.

19.4 The Impact of CIPA on City Governments

Past studies of federal, state, and local governments have found that performance measurement can help enhance the communication among departments and between the budget office and other departments. It also provides useful information to the budgetary discussion between the executive and legislative branches, even though performance results cannot be linked linearly and significantly with appropriation outcomes (Broom and McGuire, 1995; Lee, 1997; Willoughby and Melkers, 2000; Willoughby and Melkers, 2001; Willoughby, 2002). Furthermore, performance measurement can contribute to the practice of strategic planning and the culture of public accountability (U.S. GAO, 2000; GASB, 2001).

Since it may take years to change organizational culture and practices to integrate performance measurement into the decision-making process of government, it may be premature to make any conclusive statement about the impact of CIPA. However, we expect that CIPA should have an effect similar to what previous studies of performance measurement have shown. Through field observations, interviews with citizens and city officials, and survey studies, we have found that CIPA helps strengthen the customer-orientation of many city officials and challenges them to re-think the operations and delivery mechanisms of city governments.[1] In the daily operations of many departments, many city managers tend to focus only on the technical details of getting the job done. They are also concerned about the bottom line — how much a task costs and how many people they need to finish it. Citizens, on the other hand, are more concerned about the ultimate results and their relationship and interaction with city officials in service delivery. The "performance" of government is often not determined by objective measures of cost-effectiveness, but by personal experiences and perceptions of the city government. For example, in the discussion of police, fire, and emergency medical services, many citizens wanted the city governments to measure not only the response time and successes of these services in resolving cases, but also the officers' professional outlook and their manner in interacting with citizens. External appearance and the "perception" of professionalism in citizen-official inter-actions were important aspects of "performance" to citizens, especially those in cities with volunteer officers, even though these factors might not contribute directly to the efficiency and outcomes of these services. Similarly, in the areas of planning and zoning, neighborhood development, and public works, several performance teams wanted to measure the performance of departments in communication with citizens. These citizens expected public officials not only to work on a case request diligently and cost-effectively, but also to communicate what actions had been taken or would be taken within a specific time frame after a request had been made. In the course of the discussion, citizens explained that they could under-stand why a request might need a lot of time to be resolved because of legal constraints and other technical difficulties. However, they had the greatest frustration with city governments when city officials did not explain what was going on after a request was made and left citizens in the dark about the status of a request after weeks or months.

Discussion like this in the CIPA project helped many city officials realize the differences between the citizen's perspective and the internal, manage-rial perspective on "performance". Many officials realized that they often focused only on the technical details of performance measurement and overlooked the importance of customer relationships and public communication. In response to this problem, several cities in the CIPA project began to introduce innovative reforms. For example, one city decided to give notification cards to citizens after a public work request is finished and to survey them about their satisfaction with the quality of work. Another city decided to track all citizen requests and complaints in their computer system and allow citizens to browse case status online.

Besides strengthening the customer orientation of government, CIPA also reinforces the culture of performance measurement, contributes to the practice of strategic planning, and enhances communication between elected officials and departmental staff. Based on the results of CIPA, several cities held special work sessions between the city council members and the CIPA performance teams to discuss the performance data and the implications for service delivery and departmental management. City council members and departmental staff in these cities also held separate meetings to discuss how they could use the information to establish strategic goals, budget and personnel policies, and changes in program management. A survey distributed to Iowa elected officials in city governments with populations above 10,000 toward the end of the CIPA project in 2004 shows that officials in CIPA cities were more likely to discuss performance results in meetings than officials not in the CIPA program (see Table 19.3).[2] In addition, departments in CIPA cities were more likely to present performance targets to the city council annually or biennially than departments not in the program (see Table 19.4). Hence, CIPA has also shown some preliminary positive effects on internal management and has reinforced the results orientation of city governments.

At the time of this writing, it is not yet clear how CIPA might impact the budgetary decision-making of the participating cities because most of the cities have just begun to integrate the performance measurement results into their strategic planning and council decision-making mechanisms.

Table 19.3 Frequency of Discussion about Performance Measurement Results

	Number of respondents	No performance measures collected	Once a year	Occasionally during a year	Frequently during a year
CIPA cities	24	3 (12.5%)	8 (33.3%)	6. (25.0%)	7 (29.2%)
Non-CIPA cities	78	23 (29.5%)	16 (20.5%)	24 (30.8%)	15 (19.2%)

Note: Six officials did not respond to this question.

Table 19.4   Presentation of Performance Targets to the Council

	Number of respondents	*Do departments present performance targets (i.e., what they will do in the future) to you annually or biennially?*			
		No	*Only a few departments*	*All or almost all departments*	*Don't know*
CIPA cities	25	4 (16.0%)	6 (24.0%)	14 (56.0%)	1 (4.0%)
Non-CIPA cities	79	24 (32.9%)	13 (16.5%)	36 (45.6%)	6 (7.6%)

Note: Four officials did not respond to the question.

Based on field observations and interviews with officials, we expect that the results of citizen-initiated performance measures will be used and discussed in budgetary decision-making. Several budget officials and city council members have expressed strong commitment in using the information in the budgetary process, and several city managers have also expressed interest in reporting the results in their budget and policy documents to communicate more effectively with the public about what the government has accomplished with taxpayers' money. However, it is already apparent that CIPA information is only part of the input in the budgetary process. Other factors, such as the pressure to stimulate economic development, the political influence of constituency groups, federal and state mandates, and rising health care and pension costs, will continue to dominate the agenda of local budget discussions and influence how tax money is used. Hence, how much influence CIPA may have on local budgeting is likely to vary significantly, depending on the dynamics of these political, economic, and organizational factors.

19.5   Lessons Learned Through the CIPA Project

The three-year project in Iowa shows that citizen input can add a lot to the exercise of performance measurement that has been driven primarily by managers and budgeters for decades. Citizen input increases the political credibility of the performance measures and helps increase the likelihood that the information is used by elected officials in decision-making. However, these successes do come at a cost. Through the experience in the Iowa project, we have identified the following challenges:

1. Attracting and sustaining citizen interest in a somewhat technical process and the ability to develop representative performance teams.
2. Building the comfort level for city officials to participate with citizens.

3. Building a viable and lively process of developing and prioritizing performance measures.
4. Identifying data collection methods, including the exploration of how citizens could play a role in the generation of data.
5. The ability to transfer the measures and data on the measures to the decision making processes.

19.5.1 Creating Citizen Interest in the CIPA Process

As previously mentioned, there are diverse mechanisms to recruit citizens to participate in CIPA. From the experience of the Iowa project, it does not appear as if one method is more successful than others in getting citizens to participate. However, when examining the ability to sustain members, it seems that cities using existing advisory committees as the recruitment base are more likely to sustain a higher level of participation over time. For example, cities such as Clive, Marion and Urbandale adopted this method and generally held the interest of a higher percentage of the original participants. Des Moines also fared well as it relied on the existing neighborhood umbrella organization known as Des Moines Neighbors to play an active role in appointing citizens in the CIPA process.

Another challenge in sustaining citizen participants' interest is to balance the time invested in orientation and the time spent in substantive discussion about performance measures. An obvious failure in the initial phase of the project was that too much time was spent on orienting the team about city operations, performance measurement, and discussion about the representativeness of the team. As a result, some participants felt that the meetings did not go into the substance of the program and dropped out after a few meetings. Hence, how to organize a meeting meaningfully has a direct impact on citizen participation. Based on this experience, a facilitator should manage the discussion process so that a particular service area can be handled within two or three meetings, each lasting about 90 minutes.

19.5.2 Building the Comfort Level for City Officials to Participate

This area is another challenge faced by the CIPA process, which emphasizes partnership among citizens, elected officials, and city staff. For elected officials, the CIPA process was more natural because engaging with citizens is central to their job nature. Working directly with citizens is a greater challenge for many departmental staff. Initially, departmental representatives seemed to be more reluctant to become actively engaged. This could be somewhat attributed to the uncertainty about the process and their role in that process, and they did not want to be perceived by citizens as capturing the process. Some of the staff therefore played a passive role as "experts" on the service by only offering answers to questions, rather than serving as contributors or as equal partners with citizens in identifying critical elements or measures. The situation, however, changed in all performance teams once there was a strong trust built between citizens and city staff, and citizens welcomed staff representatives to contribute ideas. The realization by city staff that CIPA was not an individual personnel evaluation, but rather a process aimed at identifying performance measures for programs and services, also helped them become more open in the discussion.

Based on the Iowa experience we believe that it is feasible to build a partnership among citizens, city staff and elected officials in developing performance measures. However, the atmosphere of meetings has to be maintained as cordial, constructive, and open, the content of the discussion has to focus on the performance measures of programs and services rather than on city policies and personnel evaluation, and there has to be a certain degree of trust among the three participating parties. An external facilitator from a university or a non-profit organization may be helpful to build these environmental factors.

19.5.3 *Building a Viable and Lively Process of Developing and Prioritizing Performance Measures*

The "critical element" approach as a way to help citizens think about what is important to them in a service area is extremely helpful to the CIPA process. The Iowa experience shows that this is an excellent link between citizens' general concerns and performance measures, because it allows citizens and city staff who are not familiar with performance measures to first express the idea of performance in their own words. The process takes time, but it certainly facilitates the later process of identifying performance measures.

There are also challenges in the process of writing up the performance measures. In most of the Iowa cities, the performance teams worked with their facilitators to write their own performance measures and then asked the project staff to review and make suggestions. In a couple of cities, however, the performance teams asked the project staff to show them existing performance measures used by other cities in the country after they developed the critical elements, and then chose the performance measures that best matched their critical elements. The experience suggests that there is more than one approach to identifying performance measures, depending on the familiarity of citizens with the idea of performance measures and their willingness to invest time and thought in the process.

19.5.4 Identification of Data Collection Methods

Once the process moves into data collection, the challenge of CIPA is primarily loaded on the administrative staff. Most cities actually collect a lot of performance data through their operating and reporting routines, but they often ignore them after the data are collected and do not spend time to organize, analyze, and report the data to help program and policy decision-making. The CIPA process provides new incentives for staff to re-think what and how data should be collected, and how managers may use them meaningfully. This often requires managers and staff to have some basic statistical training. Also, many need orientation about survey designs and analysis because this is a common tool for performance measurement. In addition, many need to work more closely with their information technology staff to find out how they can retrieve and re-organize many existing data to produce meaningful analyses. These challenges can be serious in smaller cities that have greater personnel and technological capacity constraints. External assistance from universities or private consultants may be necessary to train the staff to overcome these problems.

19.5.5 Transferring Performance Measures and Data to Decision Makers

The final set of challenges is to transfer the measures and data to the decision makers. This may be the most critical step in guaranteeing the long-run success of CIPA. Failure of the decision makers to appreciate the value of performance measures can undermine the credibility of the entire process in the eyes of citizens and makes them question the need to participate in the process. To overcome this challenge, the performance teams themselves, not the city staff, should report their meeting results before their city councils regularly. City officials and citizens should also engage the mass media, such as local newspapers, to report about the process and results. It is important to publicize the effort and results of CIPA, so that performance measurement is not just an internal managerial exercise, but also a communicative platform and policy planning tool for decision-makers.

19.6 Conclusion

Performance measurement of government has been practiced in city governments for many decades and has shown some positive impact on inter-organizational communication and program management. However, many stakeholders, such as the city council and citizens, are seldom involved, and the practice remains primarily an internal, executive tool and demonstrating limited impact on the legislative decision-making process. This chapter therefore presents a model of "citizen-initiated performance assessment," which emphasizes collaboration among citizens, elected officials, and city staff in developing performance measures. It also summarizes the implementation experiences in nine Iowa cities between 2001 and 2004. The results show that CIPA helps communicate the citizens' perspective to elected and departmental officials, challenges the conventional focus of city management, and helps officials direct their attention more to outcomes and the critical concerns of citizens in performance measurement. It offers a potential tool to decision-makers, not only in the process of internal program management, but also in public communication, strategic planning, and budgetary decision-making.

These successes, however, do have a price, because citizen engagement requires a lot of time and effort by city officials in recruiting citizens, organizing meetings, and communicating the results of citizen participation to the public. City staff also needs to pay extra attention and effort to integrate performance measurement into the city council's decision-making process because this is the most important payoff for citizens who participate in the process (Ho and Coates, 2004b). This is why, to sustain the practice of CIPA in the long run, a local government has to build a strong culture in civic engagement, customer focus, and results-oriented management, and the support for the practice has to come not only from the top executives but also from the operating staff in individual departments. Otherwise, it is difficult to break the long-standing culture that views performance measurement merely as an internal managerial exercise.

Notes

1. In March and April, 2003, a semi-structured phone survey was conducted by a university staff person who was not a team member of the CIPA project. All respondents from the 9 cities were identified only as "city managerial staff," "elected officials", or "departmental staff" to protect their anonymity and encourage openness in discussion about the CIPA results. Out of a total of 37 officials, 28 officials (76%) were reached and responded to the survey.
2. The survey was sent in April 2004 to mayors and council members in 34 Iowa cities with populations above 10,000. The group included

officials from both CIPA cities and non-CIPA cities, thus allowing the researchers to compare and contrast how officials in both groups used and practiced performance measurement, and whether CIPA has made a significant impact. Out of a total of 241 sent out, 108 surveys were received. The response rate was 44.8 percent.

Acknowledgment

The Iowa "Citizen-Initiated Performance Assessment" project and this study were made possible by a grant from the Program of Performance Assessment of Municipal Governments, the Alfred P. Sloan Foundation.

References

Bowornwathana, B. (Fall 1997). Transforming Bureaucracies for the 21st Century: the New Democratic Governance Paradigm. *Public Administration Quarterly*, 21(3), 294–308.

Box, R. (1998). *Citizen Governance.* Thousand Oaks, CA: Sage.

Callahan, Kathe (2000). Citizen Participation Run Amok. *Public Productivity and Management Review*, 23(3), 394–398.

Broom, Cheryle A., and Lynne A. McGuire (1995). "Performance-Based Government Models: Building a Track Record." *Public Budgeting & Finance*, 15(4), 3–17.

Bureau of Municipal Research of New York. (1915). "The Citizen and the Government. A Statement of Policy and Method," *Municipal Research*, 57, 1–4.

deLancer Julnes, Patria (2001). Does Participation Increase Perceptions of Usefulness? An Evaluation of a Participatory Approach to the Development of Performance Measures. *Public Performance and Management Review*, 24(4), 403–418.

Durant, Robert F. (1999). Missing Links? Civic Trust, Civic Capital, and Public Administration. *Journal of Public Administration Education*, 5(2), 135–144.

Ebdon, Carol (2000). The Relationship between Citizen Involvement in the Budget Process and City Structure and Culture. *Public Productivity and Management Review*, 23(3), 383–393.

Ebdon, C. (2002). "Beyond the Public Hearing: Citizen Participation in the Local Government Budget Process," *Journal of Public Budgeting, Accounting and Financial Management*, 14(2).

Ebdon, C. and Franklin, A. (2005). "Citizen Participation in Budgeting Theory," *Public Administration Review*.

Epstein, P., Solomon, R., and Grifel, S. (July 2000). High Value Performance Measurement: For Sustainable Results that Matter to Citizens. *Bottom Line*, 18, 5–14.

Epstein, P. (1992). Measuring the Performance of Public Services. In M. Holzer (Ed.) *Public Productivity Handbook* (pp. 161–193). New York, NY: Marcel Dekker.

Fountain, J. R., Jr. (1991). Service Efforts and Accomplishments Reporting. *Public Productivity and Management Review*, 15(2), 191–198.

Friedman, L. (1979). Performance Budgeting in American Cities. *Public Productivity Review*, 3(4), 50–51.

Frisby M. and Bowman, M. (1996). What We Have Here is a Failure to Communicate. *Public Management*, 78(2), A17–A5.

Government Accounting Standards Board (GASB) (1997). Survey of the Use and Reporting of Performance Measures. [On-line] Available: http://www.gasb.org.

Government Accounting Standards Board (GASB) (2001). *Performance Measurement at the State and Local Levels: A Summary of Survey Results.* [On-line] Available: http://www.gasb.org.

Hatry, H. P., and Fisk, D.M. (1972). *The Challenge of Productivity Diversity*. Washington, D.C.: The Urban Institute and the International City Management Association.

Hatry, H. P., Blair, L.H., Fisk, D. M., Greiner, J. H., Hall Jr., J. R., and Schaenman, P. S. (1977). *How Effective are Your Community Services? Procedures for Monitoring the Effectiveness of Municipal Services.* Washington, D.C.: The Urban Institute and the International City Management Association.

Hatry, H. P. (1980). "Performance Measurement Principles and Techniques. An Overview for Local Government." *Public Productivity Review*, 4(2), 312–339.

Ho, Alfred Tat-Kei (2003). "Perceptions of Performance Measurement and the Practice of Performance Reporting by Small Cities." *State and Local Government Review*, 35(3), 161–173.

Ho, Alfred Tat-Kei (2005). "Accounting for the Value of Performance Measurement from the Perspective of Midwestern Mayors." *Journal of Public Administration Research and Theory.*

Ho, Alfred Tat-kei, and Paul Coates (2004a). "Citizen-Initiated Performance Assessment — the Initial Iowa Experience." *Public Performance & Management Review*, 27(3), 29–50.

Ho, Alfred Tat-Kei, and Paul Coates (2004b). "Citizen involvement in performance measurement—Experience from the Iowa citizen-initiated performance assessment project." Paper presentation at the annual conference of the European Group of Public Administration, Ljubljana, Slovenia, September 1–4.

International City Management Association. (1979). *Using Productivity Measurement: A Manager's Guide to More Effective Services.* Washington, D.C.: International City Management Association.

Jacoby, William G. (2000). "Issue Framing and Public Opinion on Government Spending," *American Journal of Political Science*, 44(4), 750–767.

Jordan, Meagan, and Merl Hackbart. (1999). "Performance Budgeting and Performance Funding in the States: A Status Assessment," *Public Budgeting & Finance* 19(1), 68–88.

Joyce, P. (1993). Using Performance Measures for Federal Budgeting: Proposals and Prospects. *Public Budgeting & Finance,* 13(4), 3–17.

King, C. S., and Stivers, C. (1998). Government is us. Public administration in an anti-government era. Thousand Oaks, CA: Sage.

Larkey, Patrick D. and Erik A. Devereux (1999). "Good Budgetary Decision Processes," *Public Management Reform and Innovation: Research, Theory, and Applications,* edited by H. George Frederickson and Jocelyn M. Johnston. Tuscaloosa: University of Alabama Press.

Lee, Robert. (1997). "A Quarter Century of State Budgeting Practices," *Public Administration Review*, 57(2): 133–140.

Lee, Robert, Ronald W. Johnson, and Phil Joyce. (2004). Public Budgeting Systems, 7th edition. Jones and Bartlett Publishers.

Mathews, David (1999). *Politics for People*, 2nd edition. Urbana, IL: University of Illinois Press.

Mikesell, John (2002). Fiscal Administration: Analysis and Applications for the Public Sector, 6th edition. Thomson Wadsworth.

Poister, T. H. and Streib, G. (1999). Performance Measurement in Municipal Government: Assessing the State of the Practice. *Public Administration Review*, 59(4), 325–335.

Richards, C. E., and Shujaa, M. (1990). School Performance Incentives. In P. Reyes (Ed.), *Teachers and their Workplace* (pp. 115–140. Newbury Park, CA: Sage Publications.

Ridley, C. E., and Simon, H. A. (1938). Measuring Municipal Activities. A Survey of Suggested Criteria and Reporting Forms for Appraising Administration. Chicago: The International City Managers' Association.

Sample, V. A. (1992). Resource Planning and Budgeting for National Forest Management. *Public Administration Review*, 52(4), 339–346.

Schachter, H. L. (1997). Reinventing Government or Reinventing Ourselves. The Role of Citizen Owners in Making a Better Government. Albany, NY: State University of New York Press.

Stanley, H. W., and Niemi, R. G. (1998). *Vital Statistics on American Politics: 1997–1998*. Washington, D.C.: Congressional Quarterly.

Theurer, J. (1998). Seven Pitfalls to Avoid When Establishing Performance Measures. *Public Management,* 80(7), 21–24.

Thomas, J. C. (1993). Public Involvement and Governmental Effectiveness. A Decision-Making Model for Public Managers. *Administration and Society,* 24(4), 444–469.

Thomas, J. C. (1995). *Public Participation in Public Decisions*. San Francisco, CA: Jossey-Bass.

Thurmaier, Kurt, and Katherine Willoughby (2001). *Policy and Politics in State Budgeting*. Armonk, NY: M.E. Shape.

Tracy, R., and Jean, E. P. (December 1993). Measuring Government Performance: Experimenting with Service Efforts and Accomplishments Reporting in Portland, Oregon. *Government Finance Review*, 11–14.

U.S. General Accounting Office (1997). *Performance Budgeting: Past Initiatives Offer Insights for GPRA Implementation.* GAO/AIMD-97-46. Washington, D.C.: U.S. General Accounting Office.

U.S. General Accounting Office (2000). *Managing for Results. Emerging Benefits from Selected Agencies' Use of Performance Agreements.* GAO report GAO-01-115. Washington, D.C.: U.S. General Accounting Office.

Urban Institute, and the International City Management Association. (1974). *Measuring the Effectiveness of Basic Municipal Services: Initial Report.* Washington, D.C.: The Urban Institute and the International City Management Association.

Walters, L. C., J. Aydelotte, and Miller, J. (2000). Putting More Public in Policy Analysis. *Public Administration Review*, 60(4), 349–359.

Wang, Xiaohu. (2000). "Performance Measurement in Budgeting: A Study of County Governments." *Public Budgeting & Finance* 20, no. 3, 102–118.

Wang, Xiahou. (2001). Assessing Public Participation in U.S. Cities. *Public Performance & Management Review*, 24(4), 322–336.

Williams, Daniel W. (2003). "Measuring Government in the Early Twentieth Century," *Public Administration Review,* 63(6), 643–659.

Willoughby, Katherine G., and Julia E. Melkers. (2000). "Implementing PBB: Conflicting Views of Success," *Public Budgeting & Finance,* 20(1), 105–120.

Willoughby, Katherine, and Julia E. Melkers. (2001). "Assessing the Impact of Performance Budgeting: A Survey of American States," *Government Finance Review* (April), 25–30.

Willoughby, Katherine. (2002). "Performance Measurement Utility in Public Budgeting: Application in State and Local Governments." Paper presented at the 2002 Annual Conference of the Association for Budgeting and Financial Management, Kansas City, MO, October 10–12.

U.S. General Accounting Office. (2000). *Managing for Results. Emerging Benefits from Selected Agencies' Use of Performance Agreements.* GAO report GAO-01-115. Washington, D.C.: U.S. General Accounting Office.

Chapter 20

Enhancing the Utilization of Performance Measures in Local Government: Lessons from Practice

MILAN J. DLUHY, Ph.D.
Department of Political Science, University of North Carolina

20.1   Introduction

Although the Government Performance and Results Act of 1993 required federal agencies to develop strategic plans and to tie them to budgets and performance measures, local governments, especially municipal governments, have been slower to adopt a "results-oriented management" approach (Broom, 1995; Aristigueta, 1999). However, there has been more evidence in the last ten years that Performance Measurement (PM) at the municipal government level is now finally taking hold. Poister and Streib (2005) reported in a survey of municipalities over 25,000 that 44% of these municipalities had either completed or were underway with the development of strategic plans. They also reported that 28% of these municipalities indicated that their jurisdiction also used performance measures to track outcome conditions targeted in the strategic plan (Poister and Streib, 2005).

Earlier studies in the 1990s like the one conducted by GASB (Government and Accounting Standards Board) and NAPA (National Academy of Public Administration) indicated that 44% of the responding cities reported that performance measures had been developed for a number of their programs and that 37% reported that these measures had been used in decision making processes like budgeting, performance evaluation, and strategic planning (GASB and NAPA, 1997). The Poister and Streib (2005) survey showed a lower percentage (28%) of utilization than the studies in the 1990s because the question asked in 2005 required more of a commitment to and integration of PM into the management system of the local government — that is the measures had to be used to track outcomes for/in the strategic plan. Thus, the studies in the last decade show that somewhere between 25% and 44% of the municipalities over 25,000 are using PMs to one degree or another. This also means that somewhere between 56% and 75% of the municipalities have not as yet integrated strategic planning and PM into their management systems. Accordingly, there is a major opportunity in the field of public administration to find out better ways to fully implement PM in the future in local governments. There are still plenty of jurisdictions that could commit themselves to the integration of PM and strategic planning into their management systems.

Earlier, Poister and Streib (1999) looked at municipalities over 25,000 and found that 46% of the municipalities had trouble getting managers to support performance measurement systems, while 28% indicated that they had trouble getting city councils to support these systems. In addition, 61% of lower level employees did not support these systems and 45% reported that staff lacked the analytical skills to develop and analyze PMs. So the rough 50-50% split between those using and those not using or resisting PMs appear consistent across the surveys in the last decade.

Berman and Wang (2000) focused on counties over 50,000 and they found that about one third of the counties use PMs but only one fifth of these jurisdictions had a high level of use. More telling is the fact that in this same survey only one third had an adequate level of capacity to support this kind of management system. Capacity requires jurisdictions to relate outputs to operations, to collect timely data, have staff capable of analyzing the performance data, have adequate information technology, and have support from department heads and elected officials (Berman and Wang, 2000). Thus counties appear to be even further behind in adopting these systems than cities. And, of course, without survey data for municipalities under 25,000 and counties under 50,000, there is no way of knowing whether PMs and strategic planning have had any impact on smaller jurisdictions. My guess from experience is that the utilization figures for these small jurisdictions would be very low, perhaps well under 20% (Dluhy et al., 2000).

Therefore, an important observation about the literature on utilization is that, while there are an ever-growing number of local jurisdictions using PMs, there is still a long way to go before widespread utilization of "results-oriented management" can be claimed at the local level. Now is the time to take stock about what we know about utilization over the last two decades and attempt to abstract some lessons from practice that can be applied to the large number of remaining jurisdictions who are currently not using PMs. Developing these lessons about utilization is the purpose of this Chapter.

In the context of lessons, the idea is to find a number of supporting sources for a "lesson learned" and to make that evidence as rigorous as possible. Patton urges the triangulation of supporting sources of evidence for the lesson (Patton, 2001). In this Chapter, the " lessons learned" are derived from the recent literature on utilization of PMs and a south Florida survey (Dluhy et al., 2000). The south Florida survey included the results from 125 practitioners from Miami-Dade, Broward, and Palm Beach counties who attended a series of seminars on performance measurement sponsored by the Institute of Government at Florida International University. All together the participants represented 30 cities and all 3 counties or 38% of the total number of jurisdictions in the region. Although an availability sample, the participants filling out the survey were very well educated (i.e., 38% had BAs; 30% had Master's Degrees) and very experienced (i.e., mean years of employment 21.7 years). This elite group of government employees provided us with practice insight into what they had learned about the implementation of PMs (Dluhy et al., 2000). In the rest of this discussion, the results will be referred to as "lessons" from the south Florida survey.

20.2   Performance Measurement Nomenclature

For clarity, this discussion uses the following definition for Performance Measures (PM):

> "A quantifiable, enduring measure of outcomes, outputs efficiency, or cost-effectiveness. In general, measures should be related to an agency's mission and programs, and they should not merely measure one-time or short-term activities" (Newcomer, K. et al., 2002)

PMs have a variety of uses in local government and Poister and Streib (2005) have reported that PMs have been used to:

- Track projects in the strategic plan
- Track accomplishments of goals and objectives in the strategic plan
- Track outcome conditions targeted in the strategic plan
- Report measures associated with the strategic plan to elected officials and the public
- Perform more intensive evaluations of programs included in strategic plan
- Benchmark PMs with other jurisdictions to gauge effectiveness
- Track performance over time to determine trends and progress

What emerges from surveys like this is that once PM and strategic planning have been adopted by local governments, the measures collected have a wide variety of uses and most governments using this management approach rate it as successful and useful. For example, Poister and Streib (2005) indicated that 79% of the municipalities over 25,000 reported very positive benefits for PMs when it came to promoting improved external relations with the community and elected political leaders. The communication of the PM results has provided local governments with another tool to help them to evaluate the past policy and program efforts as well as to develop new directions.

Some PM experts, however, warn us that while the popularity and utility of PM is increasing, we also need to make sure that the measures used are ones that are relevant to what government is actually doing (Perrin, 1998). Perrin's advice is to avoid the use of meaningless and irrelevant measures and to keep a focus on what counts in the long run. For example, in a recent discussion with local officials from law enforcement, there was a heated debate about whether average response time or the clearance rate for the year was a better indicator of performance in law enforcement (Dluhy et al., 2000). Skeptics indicated that unless the police arrived in two or three minutes after a crime was committed, there was almost no chance of apprehending the criminal(s). Why argue about lowering the response time from an average of eight minutes to seven or six minutes. It would not do much good and it would cost a great deal in resources to make this reduction. On the other hand, the clearance rate is a better indicator of long-term success since it shows how effective law enforcement is in the long run, i.e., they can clear 50% of the cases. Using this reasoning, it may be nice to get the squad car to a home robbery quicker but in the long run that may have nothing to do with solving the case or tracking down the criminal.

As the next section of this paper will illustrate, investment of time with expert and political stakeholders in the construction of PM is absolutely essential to the long-term success and utilization of PM management systems. The message is to always keep the eye on relevant measures and ones that will have pay off in the future. The guiding principle is not to collect what is easy and on the face valid but to focus on the best and most valid/reliable long run measures.

20.3   Lessons from Practice That Will Enhance Utilization

Harry Hatry, one of the best known experts on PM, indicates that a performance measurement system can be said to be fully implemented when it is taken for granted and its data are used regularly to help make program and policy changes that lead to improved services (Hatry, 1999). In short, the policy and management system relies on good PM data to make a wide variety of decisions, a ranging from resource allocation to program and policy evaluation. What follows is a short list of the most critical "lessons learned" about how to successfully implement a PM system. They are derived from the literature and the south Florida survey.

20.3.1   *Picking the Right PM Requires the Active Involvement of Stakeholders in the Development, Reviewing, and Revision of Measures*

This also means that the stakeholders need to also be actively involved in the interpretation of findings and the identification of implications. Poister and Steib (2005) found the most support and involvement for strategic planning and PM (i.e., in communities who had completed strategic plans or their development was underway) from the following stakeholders:

- City Managers or Chief Administrative Officers — 97%
- Department Heads — 93%
- City Councils — 80%
- Mayors — 78%
- Citizens and citizen groups — 62%
- Lower Level Government Employees — 46%

The south Florida survey asked a somewhat different question but the rank order of support and involvement of stakeholders paralleled the 2005 survey; that is, top administrators were the most supportive, then came elective officials and citizen groups, and finally lower level government employees. Therein lies the dilemma for leadership in the development of PM — measures will be needed that satisfy different kinds of audiences. Also it is natural that the top administrators will be more committed and that more effort will need to be devoted to external stakeholders and elected officials. A variety of stakeholders will have to "buy into" the development and use of PM.

Another way of stating the dilemma faced in the development of feasible PM is to think about how to build collaborations around outcomes. How can successful collaborations be built across organizations and sectors so that a selected number of PMs can reflect the consensus of the community (Newcomer, K. et al., 2002). An example will demonstrate the challenge to building collaborations around outcomes. Let's take the law enforcement field again. As indicated earlier, citizens are often enamored with response time because they feel comfort when police cars come quickly and are visible at the scene of the crime, regardless of whether response time has any impact on whether the case is solved. Professionals in the police department, however, prefer clearance rates. They feel that actually closing cases is the bottom line in crime fighting. Of course, budget and fiscal people will most certainly ask for the cost of a call for service. We also know that most elective officials like the reduction in crime rates as a measure (Dluhy et al., 2000).

So what can be done? The answer is to design a decision making process to develop the PMs from the beginning which includes representatives from all relevant audiences. You cannot simply rely on top-level management to develop and implement indicators, you will need to design a collaborative development process. One popular approach is to use a Community Advisory Task Force made up of citizens, community groups, elective officials, top-level administrators, and rank and file employees. This Task Force should hold community forums, run focus groups, seek community input, encourage input from the bureaucracy, and allow elective officials to participate as well as to endorse the measures adopted. The Asheville-Buncombe Community in North Carolina about ten years ago began developing and is now using indicators which were developed and then sanctioned by a cross cutting Community Advisory Board (Asheville-Buncombe Vision, 2005).

While there are certainly other collaborative approaches that can be used, the main "lesson learned" about stakeholder involvement is that the development of performance measures are not to be left to expert consultants or professional staff as a bureaucratic exercise. Real "results-oriented management" requires widespread stakeholder involvement and the building of consensus around a small set of outcome measures. In the example above, it may be necessary to include response time, clearance rates, crime rates, and the cost of calls for service in the final measurement paradigm adopted. Consensus in the use of outcome measures may simply mean having enough measures to satisfy different constituencies but the critical message is — do not exclude the outcome preferences of important stakeholders. PM is not a narrow bureaucratic responsibility, it is a community based effort where important stakeholders each have their expectations included in the group of final measures used, even if that means that 5–10 measures per service area ultimately get adopted and used. Enhancing utilization means involving key stakeholders and expanding the "by in" process across the community and the bureaucracy.

20.3.2 Long-term Success for PM Requires That the Concepts of PM be Fully Integrated into the Organizational Culture and the Community. PM Needs to be Institutionalized in Government and the Community

Long-term success also means penetrating all levels of the organization, not just the upper levels and spreading the concepts into different sectors of the community. Accordingly, here is a list of activities, which will support the integration of PM into the bureaucracy:

- Require the use of PM in budget proposal justifications
- Provide training in PM for all levels of the organization
- Use PM in contracts for service
- Use PM in annual performance appraisals for employees
- Connect pay to performance
- Use PM in program evaluations
- Incorporate PMs into the Strategic Planning or other planning processes

In addition, the following activities will support the integration of PM into the community:

- Annual or quarterly reports to the public on the results of performance measures
- Community forums discussing PM
- Maintenance of interactive government web-sites where the measures are posted
- Press releases and news conferences where results are presented and discussed
- Sponsor PM conferences and seminars for community leaders and citizens
- More generally keep the data in front of the media using a comprehensive public relations strategy

This type of comprehensive integration of PM into the bureaucracy and the community requires what Carter calls the need for a Champion (Wholey, 1994). Champions are leaders inside or outside of government who take on a single mission like the development and implementation of PMs in government and the community. From the south Florida survey, participants agreed that it usually takes around three years to develop and fully implement a performance measurement system and that a champion with visibility and credibility is absolutely essential. PM needs leadership and people need to see and hear about the vision of where the government and the community will be after a PM system is fully implemented (Dluhy et al., 2000).

20.3.3 Successful Utilization of PM also Requires Clear and Persuasive Presentations of Results to Different Audiences

Harry Hatry (1999) devotes more than half of his popular book on PM to how practitioners can specifically present PM in a way that varied audiences can understand the data. It is also important for PM advocates to provide the public and other audiences with the reasons or explanations for changes or trends in the data. When presenting the numbers, advocates of PM need to make sure to also include brief but succinct explanations for changes and trends in the data. Some of the other important tips on data presentation are (Hatry, 1999):

- Use simple line graphs and trend lines to portray data changes over time
- Use bar graphs and pie charts to show differences in percentages and proportions
- Use color coded GIS (government information systems) maps and breakouts for neighborhoods, jurisdictions, and regions to dramatize differences in service measures
- When comparing oneself to other jurisdictions or communities normalize or standardize the data wherever possible
- Use average performance levels when comparing a large number of jurisdictions and then indicate how close to the average your jurisdiction is (or is not)

Another aspect of good data presentation is to make sure the data used is credible and of the highest quality. One suggestion here is to regularly involve experts from a local or regional university, think tank, or well-respected consulting firm to join in the development and reporting of the information. These research oriented experts can be part of the larger Community Advisory Task Force mentioned earlier or they can be assembled regularly to provide technical advice on the measures used and their reporting. Working with these type of expert organizations also allows the government and the community to supplement census and other government-collected data with other data, since larger universities and expert organizations are very likely to have other applied research capabilities like survey research. Involvement of experts will give further legitimacy to PM and enhance the use of it in the community.

Finally, with data presentation, it is important to be extremely cautious when using PM data to benchmark your government or community with another government or community. In this context, benchmarking means looking at others providing the same service and comparing you with them. That is, how are you doing compared to your peers ? The trick, of course, is to be able to select the appropriate peers for comparison and to make sure the service measures used are indeed comparable. A number of years ago, a colleague and myself were engaged in research comparing fiscal stress and economic development strategies between Miami and other cities around the country (Dluhy and Frank, 2002). Some colleagues argued that Miami should be compared to other large cities in Florida, others said the comparison should be made with cities around the country and still others said cities in Latin America since Miami's population is so heavily Hispanic.

After much debate, a decision was made to compare Miami with other cities in the U.S. that were about the same population size since the size factor allowed many of the peer differences to wash out. Miami wound up being compared to places like Newark, St. Louis, and Cleveland rather than N.Y., Los Angeles, or Chicago or to much smaller cities in Florida. When the analysis was finally completed, it was interesting that cities of about the same size only differed slightly on things like poverty, educational levels, and spending and service levels and Miami did not look too bad at all. However, had Miami been compared to Florida cities, it would have looked very troubled using almost any indicator. The lesson is to carefully and cautiously pick peers when comparisons are being made. You could make a big political mistake if you compare an apple with an orange.

20.3.4 Successful Implementation of PM Requires Leadership to Build Trust and Credibility in the Community

Building trust and credibility in any government enterprise is a necessity.

Whether it is the PM champion or a group of top administrators, or the City or County Manager or an elective official who is leading the effort for institutionalizing PM, the broader community will demand that those leading the efforts are *not using PM for personal or political reasons*. Many in the community want to trust the data, accept the interpretation of the trends taking place, and support the efforts aimed at improving or at least maintaining the desirable outcomes. With this as a back-drop, when measuring an outcome you should not avoid measuring the hard ones or choosing measures that have long term meaning. It would be easy, for example, to measure easy things with no meaning like response time in law enforcement, the number of re-zoning applications approved in planning, or the number of homeless people in shelters on the coldest day of the year. It would be more difficult to identify the intended or preferred outcome of interest that a consensus of stakeholders believe makes a real, long term difference. So, to build credibility and trust we need to work hard at getting at the right thing. In the examples above, clearance rates for criminal cases, the impact of the re-zoning application on traffic flows and infra-structure, and the percentage of homeless who return to the labor force are a lot better indicators to use.

Trust and credibility are also hurt when we misuse data, exaggerate its importance, or select measures that make the government service look good. To avoid these kind of pitfalls, expert stakeholders must be teamed with more political and organizational stakeholders when the measures are developed. It is human nature for department heads, CEOs, and elective officials to look for the easy way out, which in this case means selecting measures that they know in advance will give a positive spin on the service in question. We may not want to hear that response to burglar alarms are expensive to respond to and that 95% of them are false. Many citizens would rather hear that the average response time to the alarm is 8 minutes. In the long run, you have to pick the best measure not the expedient one.

Another dimension of this discussion of choosing the most appropriate measures involves whether you select indicators that are the easiest to influence. For example, a look at the federal mandates under the " No Child Left Behind" Legislation is revealing. As we know, students in certain grades are regularly tested to see if their test scores in reading, science, and math are improving. Of course, as a result of the legislation, the teachers are now teaching to the tests so that the school is not penalized in the budgetary process for slumping scores. What is being avoided is measuring the longer-term effects of instruction and types of instruction on employment, wages, career development, addiction, violence and incarceration, etc. The test scores are easier to measure and influence than the other outcomes mentioned above but the longer-term measures are more revealing and salient.

PM systems can provide the best benchmarks for how things have progressed over time, how a service or government compares to other services and jurisdictions in other communities, and how expectations for performance can be developed for the future. Without an open and credible process for developing a set of indicators, citizens will eventually increase their cynicism and lower their levels of trust in "results-oriented management". Political trust in the U.S. has suffered over the last few decades but now the "results-oriented management" approach offers an alternative to this historical lack of trust and cynicism in government and government processes.

20.4 Conclusion

Cities and counties are making progress in the development and utilization of PM and strategic planning. Although a majority of local jurisdictions still do not have such systems in place or are not now developing them, there are signs that many communities are moving forward. The literature demonstrates that stakeholder support and involvement in the development and implementation of PM varies considerably and that lower level employees and citizens and citizen groups are the least likely to have "bought into" the PM system. Yet the advice given in this Chapter is that a wider variety of stakeholders need to be included and that PM or "results-oriented management" should not become dominated by upper level, elite bureaucrats. That would be shortsighted. The process of PM development should be inclusive when it comes to stakeholders.

Utilization of PM will be enhanced by stakeholder involvement in the design and implementation process but utilization will also be enhanced only after the concepts have been fully integrated into the organizational and community culture. A substantial amount of emphasis by leaders and champions of PM should be placed on tailoring and presenting clear and persuasive performance measures to different audiences. Dissemination of accurate and compelling data that people trust and that people will use is critical to the whole debate around PM. Think of where we would be today had we not supported the measurement of poverty, unemployment, or the incidence of heart disease. Measures over time become our guides to how well we are doing and what policies and programs we should support. Good data helps to develop good policy. At the local level, the quest for better policy is now a goal and the use of PM is one important way of moving toward better governance. To minimize cynicism and lack of trust in the use of PM, leaders and champions need to pick the right measures and then stand by them. "Results-oriented management" is one tool for substantially improving governance at the local level and the field of public administration now has a wonderful opportunity to provide a lot of the training in PM for lower level government employees, elective officials, and citizens who currently are less likely than other stakeholders to "buy into" a new management system (Newcomer, K. et al., 2002).

References

Aristigueta, M., 1999. Managing for Results in State Government. Westport, CT: Quorum Books.

Asheville-Buncombe Vision, 2005. www.asheville.com

Berman, E. and Wang, X., 2000, "Performance Measurement in U.S. Counties: Capacity for Reform," *Public Administration Review*, volume 60, no. 5, 409–420.

Broom, C., 1995. "Performance Based Government Models: Building a Track Record," *Public Administration Review*, volume 15, no. 4, 3–17.

Broom, C. 2000. *Performance Measurement: Concepts and Techniques.* Washington, D.C.: American Society for Public Administration.

Dluhy, M. and Frank, H., 2002. *The Miami Fiscal Crisis: Can A Poor City Regain Prosperity?* Westport, Conn.: Praeger.

Dluhy, M., Frank, H. A., Guerra, C., Newell, A. L. and Topinka, J. 2000. *Handbook on Performance Measurement for Cities in Florida.* Miami: Florida Institute of Government at Florida International University.

Government Accounting Standards Board ad National Academy of Public Administration, 1997. *Report on Survey of State and Local Government Use and Reporting of Performance Measures.* Washington, D.C.: GASB.

Hatry, H., 1999. *Performance Measurement.* Washington, D.C.: The Urban Institute Press.

Newcomer, K., Jennings, E. T. Jr., Broom, C. and Lomax, A. 2002. *Meeting the Challenges of Performance-Oriented Government.* Washington, D.C.: American Society for Public Administration.

Patton, M., 2001. "Evaluation, Knowledge Management, Best Practices, and High Quality Lessons Learned," *American Journal of Evaluation*, volume 22, issue 3, 329–337.

Perrin, B. 1998. "Effective Use and Misuse of Performance Measurement," *American Journal of Evaluation*, volume 19, issue 3, 367–380.

Poister, T. and Streib, G., 2005. " Elements of Strategic Planning and Management in Municipal Government: Status after Two Decades," *Public Administration Review,* volume 65, no. 1, 45–56.

Poister, T. and Streib, G., 1999. " Performance Measurement in Municipal Government: Assessing the State of Practice," *Public Administration Review,* volume 58, no. 4, 325–335.

Wholey, J., Hatry, H. and Newcomer, K. 1994. *Handbook of Practical Program Evaluation.* San Francisco: Jossey-Bass Publishers.

Chapter 21

The Intersection of Accounting and Local Government Performance Measurement

KEN SMITH, Ph.D.
Atkinson Graduate School of Management, Willamette University

LEE SCHIFFEL, Ph.D.
Jones School of Business, State University of New York

"Even (this) brief survey ... make(s) apparent the fragmenting nature of the results obtained and the confusion in objectives and terminology — a natural result when a problem is attacked from such diverse points of view."

—(*Measuring Municipal Activities* by Ridley and Simon 1938, p. 9)

"(Accounting) is simply too important to be left to accountants."

—(*Relevance Lost* by Johnson and Kaplan 1987, p. 262)

"The professional associations should develop a standard portfolio of terminology standards, training and presentation so that seventy years from now we are still not having this conversation."

—(Annual Meeting Comments by O'Neill 2004 Executive Director of the ICMA)

Measuring the performance of governmental organizations is one of the oldest and most perplexing issues faced by a civilized society. Societies from the beginning of recorded history have struggled both to delineate the appropriate roles of the government and to evaluate how effectively or efficiently the government has accomplished whatever roles it attempts, regardless of the appropriateness of those roles.

For financial matters, accounting is the most developed profession and academic discipline concerned with measuring and reporting the past results of an organization's performance. The primary question addressed in this chapter is the extent to which accounting, or any of the accounting specialties, is relevant to measuring the non-financial performance of governmental entities. A secondary question is the extent to which accounting is relevant to determining the roles or policies of government, due to the opposition to the GASB and accounting in mandating performance reporting (GFOA, 1993, 2002; Olson et al., 1998; Burke, 2004).

Our general conclusion is that performance measurement is an extremely broad topic that suffers from the lack of a single academic, conceptual or professional home discipline (Behn, 2003; Rivenbark, 2004). Accounting is in some ways similar to performance measurement in that it is extremely broad, encompassing numerous specialties; however, in accounting there is general clarity about those specialties, the types of problems they are well-suited to address and the boundaries beyond which the specialty does not have expertise.

A common theme in cost accounting is the need to use "different costs for different purposes" (Horngren et al., 2003) which is very similar to Behn's (2003) prescription to use "different performance measures for different purposes". We identify five distinct specialties within the broad field of performance measurement and examine problems from each specialty for which accounting provides insight. We also observe that much of the professional and academic literature on performance measurement does not incorporate accounting specialties to the degree that these specialties appear beneficial (Kloby and Kim, 2004). We suggest that the manner in which accountants and public managers are educated and trained is an important reason for these omissions. The chapter is organized into five sections:

1. Brief history of performance measurement problems
2. Specialties within performance measurement
3. Accounting concepts and specialties
4. Examples of comparable performance measurement
5. Summary and conclusions

21.1   A Brief History of Performance Measurement Problems

This section discusses performance measurement in three time periods: the 1930s, the 1970s and 2003–2004. The selection of these time periods is somewhat arbitrary as this is not intended to be a complete history. Rather, the choice of these time periods reflects times of significant energies directed toward improving the state of the art, discussions of which are relatively easy to locate in published works. It is suggested, but by no means proven, that the themes regarding performance measurement are quite enduring, with very few new concepts or problems introduced in each era (O'Neill, 2004). We do argue, however, that the accounting profession was largely absent from the discussion in the first two eras. Two other items absent in the first two eras were low cost information processing and extensive virtual networks. Any inferences regarding management reforms in the last decade must consider the new environment created as a result of advances in information technology.

21.1.1   Performance Measurement in the 1930s

Our history begins in 1938[1] with a publication of the International City Manager's Association (ICMA) titled *Measuring Municipal Activities: A Survey of Suggested Criteria and Reporting Forms for Appraising Administration* (Ridley and Simon, 1938). The author team included the Executive Director of the ICMA, Clarence Ridley, and a promising graduate student named Herbert A. Simon, the recipient of the Nobel Prize in 1978 for his subsequent work on bounded rationality. Ridley and Simon spend only the first nine pages covering definitions, theory and basic problems. The next 58 pages examine specific issues and measures for eleven service areas (see Table 21.1) and the last 25 pages provide illustrations of actual reporting forms for all but the city planning service area. Some of the measures, such as Crime and Fire statistics, are still used today. Ridley and Simon use a dichotomy of "legislative problems" and "administrative problems," which are synonymous with our use of the "role" and "performance" of government. Problems or issues they identify include:

- need for more than one measure with examples of "innumerable" problems with tax rate (p. 2)
- lack of profit as a measure of overall performance (p. 1)
- need for the legislator to determine the goals (p. 2)
- need for the legislator to evaluate the relative importance of different goals (p. 2)
- need for a consistent record-keeping system — especially one that can withstand employee turnover (p. iii)
- efficiency can not be measured by dollars and cents alone (p. iii)
- aims and objectives of each activity need to be clearly recognized and defined (p. iii)
- need for specifying the level of efficiency from a choice of six levels (p. 3)
- need to determine the circumstances beyond administrative control (p. 3)
- can the administrator allocate funds to various functions without encroaching on legislative role (p. 5)
- how to reconcile the different information needs of citizens, legislators and administrators (p. 6)
- as quoted in the beginning, how to attack the problems from a unitary (or less diverse) point of view (p. 9).

In spite of this litany of problems, Ridley and Simon are generally optimistic about the opportunities to use well-defined performance measures to assess achievement of well-defined objectives. The lack of considerable published activity during the next 40 years suggests that the "time had not come" for widespread adoption of their ideas.

21.1.2 Productivity Symposia in the 1970s

Moving forward to the 1970s, *Public Administration Review* had two Symposia on the topic of "Productivity."[2] While the terminology of "Productivity" is not the same as the performance measurement language from Ridley and Simon, the concepts are very similar. Harry Hatry (1972) defines productivity measurement as "essentially ... relating the amounts of input of a service or product to the amount of outputs. Traditionally this has been expressed as ... the number of units produced per man hour." (p. 777)

Hatry states that the "current state of productivity measurement is poor" with few governments systematically keeping measurement data and even fewer examining that data on a regular basis. He believes productivity measures will be particularly useful if they are compared in any of three ways: (1) over time, (2) among similar jurisdictions, or (3) among similar operational units within a jurisdiction (i.e. police precincts against each other, or solid waste crews or social service offices). Similar to Ridley and Simon, Hatry provides a list of service areas and some representative measures (see Table 21.1). He also notes that crime statistics are the only area where consistent comparable measures are available and this is due to the federal government having reporting requirements.

Hatry acknowledges that it is much more difficult for local governments to measure productivity because they do not produce tangible "products", but produce "services". Thus, the "quality of service" becomes an essential, but difficult to measure, ingredient of output. Hatry states that even the private sector has "failed to measure services adequately". Performance measurement problems noted by Hatry (1972) include:

- defining output (p. 777)
- measuring output (p. 777)
- measuring "quality of service" (p. 777)
- perverse measurement incentives when measures are used in compensation plans (p. 777)
- need for a multiple set of measures (p. 778)
- need to include explanatory factors (p. 778)
- need to include all costs such as fringe benefits or additional support personnel (p. 780)
- need to consider trade-offs in inputs such as using different factors of production like machines versus labor (p. 778)[3]
- need to consider inflation in costs (p. 778)
- need to understand the decision, different measures for different decisions (780)
- lack of comparable, meaningful data on other cities (p. 781)
- difficulty in separating costs when a person works on two objectives at the same time (p. 782)
- need to find comparative cities most likely to form groups of similar size or demographic characteristics (p. 781).

Table 21.1 Service Areas with Lists of Performance Measures

ICMA	NCBP	MPMP	Ridley/Simon 1938	Hatry 1972	GASB 1990
Fire	Fire	Fire	Fire	Fire	Fire
Police	Police	Police	Police	Police	Police
Refuse	Refuse	Garbage		Solid waste collection	Sanitation collection
Highways/road	Asphalt maint. and repair	Transportation		Street maintenance	Road maintenance
Code enforcement	Building inspections				
Housing		Land use planning	City planning		
Recycling	Household recycling				
	Yard waste/leaf collection				
Fleet maintenance	Fleet maintenance				
Purchasing		Administration	Municipal finance		
Information technology					
Risk management					

Human resources

Personnel

Public works
Public health

Health and hospital
Courts

Colleges and universities
Economic development
Elementary and secondary education
Health care
Mass transit
Waste and water treatment

Public assistance

Primary and secondary education

Water

Liquid waste

Water

Sewer
Social services

Public welfare

Emergency communications

Public libraries
Recreation

Recreation

Libraries
Parks and recreation
Facilities management

He concludes that "effort by the federal government seems vital if adequate comparative data ... is to be provided. A set of common definitions and, to the extent possible, common data collection practices need to be provided ..." (p. 783).

The 1978 Symposium is introduced by Walter Balk as "one of the most compelling and complex issues in the field of public administration" (1978, p. 1). The general tone of the articles is "somber and guarded" and expresses concern that "progress seems retarded by the plodding nature of bureaucracies and the apathy of politicians and citizens alike". Burkhead and Hennigan (1978, p. 34) attempt to provide conceptual clarity to the subject as they find productivity "related to or defined by the following terms: efficiency, effectiveness, cost savings, program evaluation, work measurement, employee incentives, management effectiveness, input-output analysis, work standards, and the political/social environment."[4]

Burkhead and Hennigan's focus is on a result measure — total value produced by the government — perhaps something beyond the scope of measurement techniques. They describe a system-analysis approach to productivity that requires analyzing a minimum of five vectors (E–Environmental, I–Input, A–Activities, O–Output and C–Consequences). Two additional considerations for spatial distribution and neighborhood participation would need to be added for a social-states analysis. They are critical of the methods used by Harry Hatry and the Urban Institute on theoretical grounds. They then suggest five groups of efforts: (1) activity-output measurement, (2) employee-incentive approaches, (3) organizational behavior, (4) productivity bargaining, and (5) technology transfer. Together these form a large part of the accounting specialty of management controls (see Section 21.3.3).

Quinn (1978) produces a typology of three different individuals interested in productivity: Economist, Industrial Engineer and Administrator (p. 42). The bottom line is that the economist and engineer desire measures that are precise; the administrator desires measures that are ambiguous. He believes productivity "has come to mean many things ... it may be useful to replace the term with several other terms that are more precise" (pp. 45–6).

Hatry (1978) comments, once again, on the fairly low number of local governments that collect, report or use productivity measures. He finds that 15 out of 25 state budget offices rank their efficiency measures as barely adequate or inadequate and all 29 out of 29 rank their effectiveness measures as inadequate. He notes that the time to collect and analyze data is likely prohibitive. On the positive side, universities were training MPA students to use a wide variety of quantitative tools so future managers will be familiar with these new techniques. He foreshadows the GASB approach in his conclusion, "there is likely to be a considerable amount of experimentation in future years. If help is forthcoming, including training by universities and others ... substantial albeit slow progress seems likely to occur over the forthcoming decade" (p. 33).

21.1.3   Performance Measurement in 2003–2004

Recent reviews (Kelly and Rivenbark, 2003; Melkers and Willoughby, 2004) indicate that many governments are now engaged in the process of performance measurement and performance budgeting, especially at the state level where performance budgeting has been required since the late 1990s (Melkers and Willoughby, 1998). Behn (2003) attempts to address the confusion about performance management in that he identifies eight different managerial purposes for which performance measures can be used. Frank and D'Souza (2004) discuss a lack of clarity in doing research on implementing performance measurement and find a lack of definitional clarity. They also note the tendency to use survey research methods when other methods may be more appropriate to the question at hand (different methods for different purposes once again). Rivenbark (2004) addresses confusions about performance budgeting terminology. Themes that repeat in all three time periods we examined include:

1. Consistent understanding of basic measurement terms (input, output, outcome, efficiency, effectiveness, and the need for explanatory "text").
2. The recognition of cross-disciplinary issues involving technical measurement and managerial discretion.
3. Difficulty in creating precise terms to delineate the different purposes for which the basic measures will be applied.
4. A sense of optimism in the power of reliable and relevant measures — that we are just a few steps away from some great accomplishment. This optimism is tempered by the history of slow or nonexistent progress and the fear that it is a "fad" that will disappear with the next administration.
5. Relative lack of clarity regarding the importance of "roles" and "policies" (Simon's legislative problems) versus the "administration" issues of executing those roles or policies when they are reasonably clearly communicated in the form of goals or objectives.

21.2   Specialties Within Performance Measurement

We believe there are five distinct specialties[5] within the broad field of performance measurement: (1) Performance Measures (technical measurement issues); (2) Performance Reporting; (3) Performance Benchmarking;

(4) Performance Management; and (5) Performance Budgeting. Many others have noted the lack of agreement on the boundaries of these different areas (Frank and D'Souza, 2004; Rivenbark, 2004; Behn, 2003). Our purpose here is to provide brief definitions of each and identify at least one current issue or problem for which an accounting specialty provides insight.

Performance Measurement in our framework involves the creation and refinement of the measures and is really the foundation for the other specialties, since reliable and relevant measures must be developed before they can be used in reporting, benchmarking, management, and budgeting. Issues in this arena include what should be measured and how to measure it. Practitioners and researchers alike have added to the current state of the art in performance measurement for state and local governments, starting with Ridley and Simon in 1938 and continuing with Harry Hatry (1999) and the Urban Institute, the GASB, the ICMA, various state and local governments, and many others. Throughout our discussion we will highlight some of these advancements and Table 21.1 provides the reader with an overview of service areas which have been measured.

Performance Reporting encompasses the communication of the measures once the measures have been defined and once the data has been collected and appropriately aggregated. Reporting can take many forms, dictated in large part by the intended audience. One sub-classification scheme distinguishes between reports that are intended for internal uses (management and budgeting) and reports that are intended for external users (citizens/taxpayers, creditors, bond rating analysts, regulators, etc.). The appropriate format for the report (and concerns regarding the relevance, timeliness, and credibility of the reports) is driven by the intended audience. The internal use of performance measures for one purpose or another (Behn, 2003) appears to be widely accepted at this point. As discussed later, there is still much controversy over whether performance measures should be reported externally. The dichotomy here is similar to the split in accounting between financial and managerial accounting, where the information needs of managers are met through non-regulated internal reporting while the needs of external users are met through highly regulated and audited external reports.

Performance Benchmarking is similar to Performance Reporting, but there are a few subtle, but important differences. Ammons (1999) provides a summary of theory and practical guidance. Burke (2004) discusses the benchmarking program in Ontario, Canada (discussed in detail in Section 21.4; see also PSBS (2004) for an effort in the United Kingdom). One key difference is the tendency to share results privately with other benchmarkers, but not with the public. Another difference is that external reporting is usually motivated by accountability concerns, while benchmarking is motivated by the desire to improve services. Benchmarking is also seen as more collaborative, while comparable external reporting often is competitive. Benchmarking operates on a voluntary basis whereas reporting is generally governed by some regulatory body (i.e., GASB or FASAB). Current benchmarking efforts are sponsored by several organizations, including the University of North Carolina, ICMA, the United Kingdom, and Ontario. One of the concerns with current benchmarking efforts is the cost/benefit trade-off since several participants have dropped out of the ICMA project (Section 21.1) and the counties have dropped out of the NCBP (Section 21.2). The process of setting accounting standards with precisely defined and agreed upon terminology is a useful framework that is emulated by those doing benchmarking.

Performance Management is perhaps the broadest specialty. We believe performance management encompasses all of the tools that leaders[6] use in order to accomplish the goals of the organization. Consistent with Ridley and Simon, we do not believe performance measures can assist in the determination of objectives and values, these are policy or legislative problems. However, whenever reasonably clear objectives have been stated, performance-oriented managers must evaluate all of the tools at their disposal to execute a strategy to accomplish these goals. We agree with Behn (2005) that there is no magic "system" that can be created and then managers push the start button. Rather, performance management requires the skills of a human leader similar to the viewpoint of the accounting specialty of management controls (Anthony and Govindarajan, 2004; Anthony and Young, 2003; Steiss, 1982).

Performance Budgeting is defined by Rivenbark (2004, p. 28) as "a process for budget preparation and adoption that emphasizes performance management, allowing decisions to be made *in part* on the efficiency and effectiveness of service delivery" (italics in original). Kelly and Rivenbark (2003) argue against the use of an Outcomes view of budgeting reform, where the reform is successful only if the amounts allocated change as a result of the reform. Smith and Cheng (2004) concur that the Process view of budgeting reform is superior to the Outcomes view and suggest that the theories of Signaling and Monitoring in government accounting reform (Zimmerman, 1977; Evans and Patton, 1987) are also candidates for determining the success of budgeting reforms.

Budgeting in government has traditionally been much more important than accounting (Martin et al., 1995). When viewed as a political process (Wildavsky, 1964), there is little that accounting can provide other than assistance in the four other specialties. Ridley and Simon note that there are a few "administrative problems" (1938, p. 60) in budgeting such as the accuracy of revenue estimates, the flexibility of expenditures, timeliness and accuracy; however, it appears that budgeting receives the majority of attention from academics and practitioners, with perhaps too little attention in the other four areas.

21.3 Accounting Concepts and Specialties

This first part of this section reviews the development of accounting concepts related to performance measurement and, to some extent, summarizes the intersection of accounting with state and local government performance measurement to date. The genesis for many of the ideas espoused by the GASB appears to come from Harry Hatry at the Urban Institute (1972, 1978, 1999). We begin with GASB's Concepts Statement No. 1 issued in 1987 and conclude with the recently issued Special Report (2003).

The second part of this section lists ten specialties within the discipline of accounting. For each specialty, performance measurement problems are identified in conjunction with the insight and/or skills the specialty might offer in addressing the problem, i.e., the potential for future intersections between accounting and state and local government performance measurement. We believe that Accounting is similar to Medicine in that both have a large number of specialties. Care must be taken to use the appropriate specialty. We believe that not enough attention has been paid to which accounting specialty might be relevant to the particular performance measurement specialty (Benchmarking, Management, External Reporting, etc.).

21.3.1 Accounting Concepts for Performance Measurement

Parry et al. (1994) note that, while some scholars question the ability of the accounting profession to play a meaningful role in performance measurement and reporting, other scholars point to the accounting discipline as a model for the type of structure necessary for the long-term success of the practice. The proponents identify the accounting profession's track record in setting performance goals, the use of common terminology, and the development of data collection techniques and reporting models. From its inception in 1984 the Governmental Accounting Standards Board (GASB), the standard setting body for governmental accounting, has signaled a strong interest in performance measurement and reporting under the name Service Efforts and Accomplishments (SEA).[7]

In its 1987 Concepts Statement No. 1, "Objectives of Financial Reporting" the GASB identifies **accountability**, the obligation to explain one's actions, as the cornerstone of all governmental financial reporting:

> Governmental accountability is based on the belief that the citizenry has a "right to know", a right to receive openly declared

facts that may lead to public debate by the citizens and their elected representatives. Financial reporting plays a major role in fulfilling government's duty to be publicly accountable in a democratic society.

Four purposes for local and state financial reports are delineated in the Concepts statement: (1) to compare actual financial results with the legally adopted budget, (2) to assess financial condition and the results of operations, (3) to assist in determining compliance with finance-related laws, rules, and regulations, and (4) to assist in evaluating efficiency and effectiveness. While in 1987 the GASB only explicitly mentions the role of financial reporting in fulfilling government's responsibility of account-ability, it should be noted that the GASB champions the citizen's "right to know." It is in the assessment of operations and the evaluation of efficiency and effectiveness of the governmental entity that traditional financial statements fall short and there is a need for non-financial performance measures. In fact, the GASB *Codification* Section 100.177c states, "Financial reporting should provide information to assist users in assessing the service efforts, costs, and accomplishments of the governmental entity."

Smith (2004) and Burke (2004) note the ongoing controversy regarding the public reporting of performance measures. Consistent with Concepts Statement No. 1, the GASB continues to argue in favor of publicly reporting performance measures as a necessity for governmental accountability to the citizenry. On the other side of the debate is the Government Finance Officers Association (GFOA), perhaps the most vocal critic of the GASB's efforts toward public reporting. In 1993, and again in 2002, the GFOA issued statements emphatically objecting to the GASB's involvement in the development of performance measurement and reporting in the public sector (GFOA, 2002). The GFOA believes that performance measures are a management and budgetary tool and, as such, are designed for internal purposes only.

Undaunted by its critics the GASB forged ahead, albeit slowly, with its performance measurement agenda. A number of academic researchers responded to the GASB's call for research on SEA reporting (see Smith, 2004). This body of research consists mainly of case studies and surveys, with an emphasis on the types of measures currently in use and the uses (internal or external) of the measures. Surveys to assess what is being measured, the uses for those measures, and current reporting practices have been used throughout the GASB's SEA project (see www.seagov.org for more details on these surveys). Under the auspices of the GASB, researchers closely examined the use of performance measures in twelve service areas, including fire departments, police departments, public health, hospitals, mass transit, road maintenance, sanitation, water and wastewater treatment, and elementary, secondary, and higher education (see Table 21.1). These studies, summarized by Hatry et al. (1990) provide an assessment of the performance measures being collected and reported by municipalities in either budgetary documents or financial reports and of the verifiability of those measures.

In a discussion of one of the service areas, Parry et al. (1991) note a general consensus among fire departments as to the most useful performance measures for fire suppression, fire protection and explanatory factors. However, they also note a great disparity among the measures for fire prevention. Parry et al. posit that, due to the nature of the measurement — attempting to measure the ability to prevent an event or that which does not happen — this may be inherently more difficult. Osborne and Gaebler (1992, 18) seem to support this hypothesis when they note that the low level of agreement on preventive measures may be exacerbated by the predominance of a reactive approach by many fire departments. For each service area researchers recommended a set of measures for consideration by governments implementing performance measurement. Many municipalities and state governments have experimented with performance measurement and reporting, some quite successfully. Section 21.4 highlights the experiences of some of these endeavors.

21.3.2 Concepts Statement No. 2 — 1994

After extensive research, GASB's Concepts Statement No. 2 was issued in 1994. This concepts statement reaffirms the GASB's conviction that performance measures are necessary for government to fulfill its accountability role and the GASB's goal to include performance measures in general purpose external financial reporting. Three broad categories of SEA measures are enumerated: (1) measures of service efforts, (2) measures of service accomplishments, and (3) measures that associate efforts with accomplishments. Service efforts focus on the resources or **inputs**, both financial and non-financial, to the provision of goods or services. Financial measures include the costs incurred in the provision of the goods or services, such as fire department expenditures per fire; non-financial measures are frequently stated in terms of man-hours or equipment-hours, such as total man-hours devoted to fire suppression. The measurement and reporting of these inputs may assist in eliminating waste in internal processes.

Indicators of service accomplishments are divided into two components: outputs and outcomes. **Outputs** are measures of the volume of activity with no regard for the success or failure of the activity. Outputs may reflect either the quantity of a service provided, such as the number of fires hydrants inspected, or the quantity of a service provided that meets some specified quality requirement, such as the number of fire-fighters certified to a given level of training. Outputs are useful in assessing the entity's workload or activity level over a given period of time. **Outcomes** represent financial and non-financial measures of the social benefits provided by the good or service, such as time to control the spread of a fire or the number of lives or dollar amount of loss from a fire. Outcomes are indicators of the quality of the services provided.

Efficiency measures relate the quantity, or cost, of resources used to the unit of output. Efficiency measures are essential in assessing the efficiency and effectiveness of an entity. Finally, users of performance measures should be aware that each entity is unique and many outside factors can impact its performance. The use of **explanatory factors** allows the entity an opportunity to help users fully assess its performance. Echoing a theme since the 1930s, Parry et al. (1994) caution that a common set of performance measures cannot be compared between entities without careful analysis of these explanatory factors.

While the GASB concluded that SEA reporting was both desirable and necessary, it also recognized that performance measurement expertise and ability had not been developed to the point that mandated reporting was feasible. Therefore, Concepts Statement No. 2 does not require SEA reporting. Rather, it lays out a broad framework and issues a call for "extensive research and experimentation" (1994, 32).

21.3.2.1 Sloan Foundation Grants

One of the proponents of external reporting of government performance measures, the Sloan Foundation, awarded the GASB with a grant in 1996 to further SEA research, to address developmental needs for performance measurement, and to encourage reporting of performance information to citizens. This grant was renewed in 2000 for an additional three years. The GASB's intent was to use these funds towards consideration of whether performance measurement has developed enough to consider mandated reporting for state and local governments as part of general purpose external financial reporting. The GASB website for performance measurement (item 1 below) summarizes the six-phase project resulting from this grant, including:

1. Establish an internet based clearinghouse for performance measurement. Completed in 1998, the clearinghouse can be accessed at www.seagov.org.
2. Analysis and evaluation of the uses and effect of using performance measures for budgeting, management and reporting.

3. Analysis and evaluation of users' responses to performance measures.
4. Development of a set of suggested criteria to assist governments in effectively reporting and communicating performance information.
5. Encourage experimentation with the suggested criteria for external reporting.
6. Evaluation of the effectiveness of the suggested criteria for reporting performance information and assessment of whether they have developed enough to warrant further consideration by the GASB.

As of this writing, the GASB reports completion of phases two through four and the inception of phase five (note that Sloan Foundation funding for the project was to be exhausted in June 2004). **Phase two** utilized in-depth interviews as researchers visited twenty-six state and local governments to determine:

- why and how performance measures were being used
- how widely the performance measures were being reported to citizens and other external users
- the effects of using performance measures
- the methods being employed to ensure the relevance and reliability of the measures being used.

Fifteen to twenty interviews were conducted at each of the twenty-six sites with researchers attempting to get many different perspectives, including that of budget and planning officers, the comptroller, human resources, legislators, auditors, and taxpayers. Twelve individual case studies examining six states and six cities were published in 2000 and the findings of an additional six case studies were released in 2003. Interested readers can find these case studies at the SEA clearinghouse website. Wang (2002) reviews these case studies.

To assess users' responses to performance measures, **phase three** employed the use of nineteen focus groups held at various locations around the country. These discussion groups, held between November 2000 and July 2001, found that citizens were interested in access to performance information and that they felt this information would be most helpful if citizen groups were involved in the selection of the measures reported, specifically participants indicating an interest in outcomes measures. Perceived benefits of performance reporting included an increase in government accountability and an increase in citizen participation, an increased ability for citizens to analyze and evaluate government's performance, and an increase in citizen confidence about their government's performance.

In August 2003 **phase four** culminated in the release of a special report entitled *Reporting Performance Information: Suggested Criteria for Effective Communication* (GASB, 2003). This report, which is known as the Green Book for its green ink, is intended to provide a basis for further experimentation in external reporting of performance measures. The GASB proposes sixteen criteria that state and local governments can use to assist them in reporting "relevant, reliable information about the results of government programs and services to elected officials, citizens, and others." The criteria delineated in this report represent the lessons learned from the earlier phases of the SEA project.

Chapters one through five of the Green Book set the stage for the GASB's recommendations: chapter one introduces the external performance measure report, including a statement of the report's purpose and an overview of its contents. Chapters two and three provide an historical perspective of performance reporting and the concept of managing for results. Chapter four presents the GASB's focus on accountability and the role of performance measures within that concept. Chapter five provides an explanation of how the criteria were developed and in chapter six the reader will find a detailed discussion of the sixteen suggested criteria. See Table 21.2 for a listing of the criteria. An additional eleven "best practices," which were not deemed to be sufficiently developed and tested to warrant inclusion among the suggested criteria, are discussed in Chapter 7. GASB's continuing cautionary approach is found in Chapter 8 where it calls for additional experimentation as a way of advancing the state of the art in performance reporting.

21.3.2.2 The Green Book Criteria

The sixteen criteria are organized into three general categories: (1) the external report, (2) what performance information to include, and (3) communicating the information. For each of the sixteen criteria, along with a statement of the criterion, the purpose, and a description, the reader is presented with the rationale for each of the criterion, how it can be applied, and appropriate examples.

The first category of criteria sets out the format and general tone of **the external performance report**. Criteria #1 advocates a statement of the purpose and scope of the report both to inform the user and to protect the preparer. GASB defines the purpose of the external report on performance information as "providing a basis for understanding the extent to which an organization has accomplished its mission, goals, and objectives ... " Given this definition, it becomes obvious that the reporting entity should include a statement of major goals and objectives

Table 21.2 GASB's Suggested Criteria for Effective Communication of Performance Information (2003)

Criteria Category	Criteria
External performance report	#1 Statement of the purpose and scope
	#2 Statement of major goals and objectives
	#3 List parties involved in establishing goals and objectives
	#4 Use of multiple levels of reporting
	#5 Analysis of results and challenges
	#6 Focus on key measures
	#7 Reliability of the information
Information to be included	#8 Performance measures included should be relevant in assessing the organization's success in meeting its objectives
	#9 Information regarding the resources expended (inputs) and perhaps information that relates those costs to outputs and outcomes (efficiency measures)
	#10 Citizen and customer perceptions
	#11 Comparative information from other periods or benchmarks
	#12 Discussion of explanatory factors affecting results
	#13 Use of aggregated and disaggregated data
	#14 Consistency (comparability across time) where possible and an explanation of changes where changes are warranted
Communication of the performance information	#15 Performance report is easy to find, access, and understand
	#16 Reporting is regular and timely

(criteria #2) and who was involved in establishing those goals and objectives (criteria #3). Additional criteria in this category include:

- use of multiple levels of reporting (#4)
- provision of an analysis of results and challenges (#5)
- a focus on key measures (#6)
- ensuring reliability of the information (#7)

The focus of the criteria regarding **information to be included** is on communicating the degree to which the entity and the programs it operates contribute to meeting the stated goals and objectives. Performance measures chosen for inclusion should be relevant in assessing the organization's success in meeting its objectives (criteria #8). Criteria #9 recommends that these measures include information regarding the resources expended (inputs) and perhaps information that relates those costs to outputs and outcomes (efficiency measures). To further assist the user, the inclusion of citizen and customer perceptions is encouraged (criteria #10), as is the inclusion of comparative information from other periods or benchmarks (criteria #11) and a discussion of explanatory factors affecting results (criteria #12). The use of aggregated and disaggregated data, geared towards the anticipated needs of the report's users (criteria #13), is advocated as a means of reporting information that is relevant and does not obscure the true performance of the reporting entity. Finally, the GASB advocates consistency (comparability across time) where possible and an explanation of changes where changes are warranted (criteria #14).

Criteria for the **communication of the performance information** are predicated on the premise that a reasonably well informed user should be able to find and use the information. This category contains only two criteria: (a) that the performance report be easy to find, access, and understand (criteria #15) and (b) that reporting be both regular and timely (criteria #16). Those familiar with the tenets of the financial accounting reporting system for the private sector will recognize many of the same ideals encompassed in the sixteen criteria — relevance and reliability, conciseness and timeliness, comparability and consistency.

Due in part to the efforts of the GASB, our knowledge regarding the types of performance measures that may be appropriate and the current uses of those measures has advanced considerably. Highly qualified public managers and increased information technology capabilities now facilitate the sophisticated performance measurement and reporting systems necessary to move forward with this endeavor. Increasing public demand for government accountability mandates increased public reporting. Savvy public administrators can use publicly reported performance measures to demonstrate results and win public support.

We believe that some form of performance reporting should be and eventually will be mandated as part of governmental accounting. However, the controversy over mandated reporting continues. Even among those in favor of mandated reporting there is not yet consensus as to what kinds of measures should be reported or the extent or required auditing on those measures and reports.

21.3.2.3 AGA

Based on their Certificate of Excellence in Accountability Reporting (CEAR) program for reviewing federal agency performance and accountability reports, the Association of Government Accountants[8] (AGA) instituted a similar program for state and local governments. The Certificate of Excellence in Service Efforts and Accomplishments Reporting, created with funding from the Sloan Foundation, completed its pilot phase in 2004 (Fountain, et al., 2004). The program collects SEA reports from participating governments and reviews those reports. The review process has three major components: (1) a review team composed of three individuals with knowledge and experience in state and local government performance reporting, (2) the GASB's 16 criteria are used as guidelines for the review, and (3) communication, to include whether the certificate was awarded and detailed recommendations for improvement, from the AGA back to the participating government.

During this pilot phase 68 reviewers were recruited and trained. A team of reviewers then reviewed the SEA reports of 20 state, county, and local governments. A follow-up survey provides evidence that the reviewer comments were helpful and that the review process provided a valuable learning experience for the participating governments (AGA 2004). The implementation phase reviews are underway; reviewers have been identified and trained and the AGA has begun to receive fiscal year 2004 SEA reports from participating organizations. This program will serve to recognize the hard work and successes of those governments voluntarily issuing performance reports and to encourage other state and local governments to engage in performance reporting.

21.3.3 Specialties in Accounting

Table 21.3 lists ten specialties within the accounting profession. The important point is that the term "accounting" by itself is not descriptive, we need more precision and clarity in our definitions. Each of these specialties provides solutions to a fairly known set of problems. The current discipline of double entry bookkeeping has been around for a long time (most trace its roots to the 1400s). The development of cost and managerial accounting occurred in the 1800s and the modern era of financial accounting and auditing begins in the 1930s, following the stock market crash of 1929. Prior to the creation of the Securities and Exchange Commission in 1933, audits of financial statements were not required and the financial statements were often difficult to compare across companies due to differences in reporting style and definitions of basic terms. In comparison to local government performance measurement, the discipline of financial accounting has progressed much farther in terms of professional standards and clarity, notwithstanding the recent setbacks due to the bankruptcies of Enron and the Andersen CPA firm.

Many individuals that are not accountants or familiar with the discipline may believe that accounting is not relevant to their performance measurement issues. In many ways, these individuals are probably correct *IF*

Table 21.3 Accounting Specialties and the Intersection with Performance Measurement Specialties

Specialty	Focus	Typical Employers	Professional Designation	Lessons/Concepts for Performance Measurement	Intersects with/Performance Specialties
Financial	Focus on preparation of financial statements and related footnotes sent to external parties	Corporations, Small business, Government, Non-profit	CPA	External standard setting: (a) phase in, b) due process, (c) alternatives, (d) ignore if not reliable	Benchmark, Report, Measurement
Managerial	Focus on internal decision-makers. "Different costs for different purposes"	Corporations, Small business, Government, Non-profit	CMA, CPA	Non-financial measures "linked" to strategy (BSC), Marginal decision-making, ABC, CVP, Flex budgeting	Management, Budgeting, Measurement
Cost	Focus on the costs of products and services. Allocating fixed costs is major problem	Corporations, Small business, Government, Non-profit	CPA, CMA	Different measures for different purposes, allocations matter, fixed versus variable-beware of unit costs	Benchmark, Management, Budgeting, Measurement
Auditing	Focus on giving opinion on financial statements (or other report). Must understand evidence gathering in addition to underlying report (i.e., GAAP)	CPA firm, Government, Corporations (internal audit)	CPA, CIA	Systems approach more efficient than substantive, Assurance requires professional judgement	Benchmark, Report, Measurement

(Continued)

Table 21.3 Continued

Specialty	Focus	Typical Employers	Professional Designation	Lessons/Concepts for Performance Measurement	Intersects with/ Performance Specialties
Taxation	Focus on differences between GAAP and tax rules. Many tax accountants take an "advocate" role in trying to find most deductions	CPA firm, Tax prep firm (HR Block), Government, Corporations	CPA, Lawyer, Enrolled agent	N/A	N/A
International	Focus on GAAP rules in various countries. Growing trend towards harmonization to reduce number of differences	CPA firm, International Corporations	CPA (US), Chartered Accountant (worldwide)	N/A	N/A
Management controls	Focus on the overall operation of the organization from strategic planning to task control. Concerned with budgeting, responsibility centers, transfer pricing, non-financial performance measures (BSC), asset performance (ROI, EVA, NPV)	CPA firm, Corporations, Consulting firms	CPA, CMA	Responsibility centers, Integrate strategic planning and budget	Management, Budgeting, Benchmark-ing
Information systems	Focus on the manner in which information is captured and processed, especially important with the increase in the number of transactions that are completed digitally without paper documents	CPA firm, Consulting firms, Corporations, small business, Government, Non-profit	CPA, CISA	Single database, contains all data-not just financial	Management, Budgeting, Benchmark, Reporting, Measurement

Governmental	Focus on the preparation of external accounting reports for governmental entities. The GAAP is determined by GASB for state and local and the FASAB (not FASB) for federal	Federal, state and local, CPA firms	CPA, CGFM	Government account-ing textbooks focus on budgetary and legal compliance. Little attention to manage-ment or non-financial measurement	Reporting, Budgeting
Nonprofit	Focus on the preparation of external accounting reports for non-profit entities. The GAAP is determined by FASB for most, but non-profits related to a government use GASB	Nonprofits	CPA	Texts include perform-ance measures, enhance fundraising, management techni-que and controls	Management, Benchmark, Reporting, Budgeting

the person is considering one of the accounting specialties that is not designed or suited to their problem. The concern we have is that another one of the accounting specialties might be extremely well-suited to assisting with their performance measurement issue. Thus, this section provides a brief overview of specialties that we believe are relevant to the performance measurement problems of both yesterday and today. Consistent with our view that performance measurement is also a field with specialties, Table 21.3 identifies the performance specialties for which each accounting specialty appears to be useful. We will primarily discuss just the first three specialties, Financial, Managerial and Cost accounting, but we believe there are useful intersections with Auditing, Information Systems and Management Controls.

Financial accountants prepare financial statements according to GAAP (Generally Accepted Accounting Principles) as well as the footnotes or written support as required by GAAP or regulatory bodies such as the SEC (Securities and Exchange Commission). As a result of the needs of reliable and comparable external reports, the external reporting specialty has developed a system of creating accounting principles that everyone can read and understand. The standard-setting bodies (FASB, GASB and FASAB) all follow a "due process" that encourages all affected parties to comment on how they view a possible standard even before it is voted on by the Board (see Harris 1995 for an analysis of the comments sent to GASB related to Concepts Statement No. 2). Accountants who pass a professional examination and meet other education, experience and ethical requirements, can become licensed to practice "public" accounting with the title Certified Public Accountant or CPA.

Management accountants focus on preparing information to assist decision-makers within an organization. The GAAP numbers are often times NOT appropriate for internal management decisions, so managerial accountants are very sensitive to understanding the decision-making process of a wide variety of internal users. The managerial accountants often use non-financial information in addition to financial information (Johnson and Kaplan, 1987; Kaplan and Norton, 1996a, 1996b; Horngren et al., 2003). Due in part to the nature of managerial accounting being much less rules-focused and much more decision-focused, management accountants developed a certification called the CMA (Certified Management Accountant) that parallels the difficulty of the CPA designation, but focuses on the unique and varied tasks of management accounting. The CMA designation is not a license issued by state governments; rather, it is a designation given by a professional association, the Institute of Management Accountants.

Cost accountants focus on determining how much cost should be assigned to various products or services. Cost accounting is used by both financial and managerial accountants. Financial accountants need cost measures that conform to GAAP while managerial accountants need cost information that relates to the decision at hand.

Two books in management accounting appeared that captured the difficulty accounting experienced with the movement to more difficult to measure organizational performance. The first, *Relevance Lost* (Johnson and Kaplan, 1987), argues that management accounting is no longer relevant. This was a time where most businesses in the United States were moving from a manufacturing focus to a service or information focus. As noted by Hatry, back in 1972, it is difficult for business organizations to measure services just as it is for governments. Manufacturing organizations could largely be managed and controlled via the financial statements. Profits were a good sign and losses required managerial attention. In the mid-1980s, it became clear that a manager could not wait until the financial results were poor to determine managerial actions. The financial results were "lagging" indicators and insufficient to guide the strategy and decisions faced in an uncertain and fast-paced environment.

The formula for relevance and success was predicted to be in the area of non-financial performance measures. They conclude the book with a quote in our introduction "the task (of accounting) is way too important to be left to accountants" (p. 262). They mean that accounting for services and difficult to measure environments requires the collaboration of many parts of the organization. The accountants are still the ones with the expertise in collecting, summarizing, auditing and reporting the information about organizational performance, but the accountants must collaborate with other parts of the organization and vice versa. We believe a similar collaboration is needed in government with accountants becoming more in tune with organizational processes and non-financial data. Additionally, non-accountants could benefit from a willingness to listen and follow the suggestions of those trying to collect, summarize, audit and report the data on the performance of their agency.

After the publication of *Relevance Lost*, Robert Kaplan joined with David Norton to develop a conceptual framework for linking these non-financial measures to the financial results. The framework is called the Balanced Scorecard (BSC) and has received enormous attention from academics and practitioners. Kaplan and Norton published two articles in the *Harvard Business Review* on the BSC in 1992 and 1993 and then a book and an article in 1996 (1996a, 1996b) that expanded the BSC as a way to translate an organizations' strategy into action. More recently (2001), Kaplan and Norton published an article on the BSC in nonprofit organizations with a specific reference to the city of Charlotte, one of the standard-bearers of good performance measurement practices.

To modify the BSC for governments, Kaplan and Norton (2001) removed the financial focus on profit at the top of the scorecard and identify two basic customers: resource providers and resource beneficiaries. For the governmental sector, Kaplan and Norton recommend the use of three "higher-level" perspectives: Cost, Value/Benefit, and Legitimizing support (i.e. legislative funding). In the GASB's terminology, the Cost perspective is similar to Outputs, the Value/Benefit is similar to Outcomes and the Legitimizing is similar to Inputs. Numerous resources abound online, including www.balancedscorecard.org which focuses primarily on government applications. President George W. Bush's "Management Agenda" is based on the principles of the BSC.

A critical observation about the BSC is that it is generally seen as an internal and organization-specific tool, rather than an external and comparable tool. Thus, accountants would classify the BSC as "managerial" accounting rather than financial accounting. As such, the rules are not as precise and the information is not typically "audited," although organizations will probably perform quality control procedures on key measures. A major leap of faith must be taken in order to support the use of an inherently individualistic tool such as the BSC for external reporting.

The primary concern in external reporting is typically the **reliability** of the measures, whereas **relevance** is the chief concern of internal or managerial reporting. Perhaps the biggest debate regarding the appropriate uses or disciplinary "location" of the performance measurement revolution is centered on the debate over non-financial performance measures reliability; however, the true concern when reading opposition statement's like the GFOA's[9] (1993; 2002) or Olson et al. (1998) is that the reported measures will not be relevant to the user if standard measures are required across all jurisdictions. If BSC principles apply, this argument appears reasonable. If, on the other hand, the non-financial performance measures are simply surrogates of activities or results that are more universal, then the opposition seems unwarranted.

21.4 Examples of Comparable Performance Measurement

In this section we describe four projects of comparable performance measurement. The current ICMA Center for Performance Measurement has been around since 1994; however, the ICMA sponsored the Ridley and Simon (1938) book, so it arguably has been working in the area for seven decades. The North Carolina project has the most developed program that reports results to the public, tracing its beginnings to 1995. The province of Ontario, Canada is a very interesting "laboratory" because it has two programs going concurrently: the mandatory MPMP and the voluntary

OMBI. The Ontario programs did not issue reports until 2001, but they are based upon a significant study of the lessons and pitfalls from the ICMA and NCBP programs as well as the many negative reactions of local governments to the GASB's efforts over the past decade. These are by no means the only projects currently underway in the U.S. (Morley et al., 2001) or overseas (U.K. and New Zealand), but they are well-documented and are the closest approximations to an external reporting system consistent with GASB Concepts No. 2 (1994) and Green Report (2003).

21.4.1 ICMA Center for Performance Measurement (CPM)

The ICMA's Center for Performance Measurement (CPM) is a fairly traditional performance benchmarking initiative. The CPM is open to any organization that is willing to pay the annual membership fee of $5,000. On-site training is also provided to first-year participants at an additional cost of $3,900. The ICMA project does not share results publicly, but results are shared among members. The ICMA program puts out publications such as What Works (2001; 2002) that highlight programs that have been successful. The level of cost accounting and definition agreement do not appear to be as deep as in the NCBP.

According to the participant list on the ICMA website, the number of participants has remained fairly stable over a recent 18 month period, but the turnover was high (http://www.icma.org/CPMParticipants/index.cfm?hsid = 1&ssid1 = 50&ssid2 = 220&ssid3 = 300). The turnover was much greater for the smaller jurisdictions, with a total of 65% of the small governments leaving the project compared to only 39% of the large governments (see Table 21.4). It is unclear why so many organizations have come and gone, but the cost is certainly one aspect (see also Barrett and Greene, 2005,

Table 21.4 ICMA Participant Turnover

	# @ 7/29/03	Drop	Remain	New	#@ 1/29/05
Large	70	27	43	20	63
Medium	25	11	14	10	24
Small	26	17	9	17	26
Total	121	55	66	47	113
Large	100%*	39%	61%	29%	90%
Medium	100%	44%	56%	40%	96%
Small	100%	65%	35%	65%	100%
Total	100%	45%	55%	39%	93%

*All percentages based on number at July 29, 2003.

for cuts of management analysts). Certainly, the benefits from such a program may be greater at the outset as obvious discrepancies can be located fairly quickly. Ongoing commitment to the project may not justify the cost. While no direct estimates of cost are available, several case studies have indicated the significant number of hours to both begin and maintain a benchmarking program. Perhaps the organizations learn "how to" collect and report performance measures and then no longer need the services of the ICMA.

The types of measures being reported is another topic of interest. The measures are ones for which definitions and processes appear to be relatively consistent across organizations. As with all of the documented measures, the service areas appear to be ones that are inherently easier to measure (see Table 21.1).

21.4.2 North Carolina Benchmarking Project (NCBP)

The NCBP was initiated in 1995 as a joint venture that has included cities and counties within North Carolina and several supporting organizations: (a) School of Government at the University of North Carolina at Chapel Hill, (b) North Carolina Local Government Budget Association, (c) North Carolina Association of County Commissioners, (d) North Carolina League of Munici-palities, and (e) The North Carolina Government Finance Officers Associ-ation. This is an impressive list of organizations and the broad support from these various viewpoints undoubtedly assisted the project in maintaining a trajectory of improvement. Interestingly, there are no groups directly representing the profession of accounting.

The project website (www.sog.unc.edu/programs/perfmeas/index.html) provides history and current results. The pilot stage of the project involved three phases, as noted in Table 21.5. After the pilot stage, 14 cities agreed to continue with the project and are included in the annual reports that are issued each February for the Fiscal Years ending the prior June 30. As of February 2004, the sixth annual report was issued for Fiscal Years 2002–2003 (Rivenbark and Dutton, 2004).

We believe the format of the "Final Report" is very similar to external financial statements. Thus, in many ways the successful performance measurement programs have already intersected with accounting funda-mentals. The "Final Report" provides two pages of information for each city for each service area. One page has bar graphs of 6–10 measures within the service area. Each bar graph has the city's score beside the average for all cities that reported this measure. Three years of data are provided for most measures. The bar graphs are similar to the quantitative financial statements. The second page has a column for the city profile and several paragraphs of

Table 21.5 Phases of North Carolina Benchmarking Project

Phase I	Phase II	Phase III/IV
7 cities	7 counties	14 medium/small cities and counties
Began 1995	Began 1995	Began 1997
Report issued October 1997	Report issued August 1998	City report — March 1999 County report — April 1999
Performance and Cost Data Reports issued February 1999, 2000, 2001, 2002, 2003, 2004	Performance and Cost Data Reports issued February 2000, 2001	

explanatory information. Each city can add comments under the heading "Conditions Affecting Service, Performance, and Costs." The second page of explanatory information is very similar to the footnotes required by the accounting standard-setting bodies. Also, Rivenbark (2000) explains the importance of Cost Accounting in both the external reporting and internal benchmarking exercises. Rivenbark is one of the few to acknowledge the important intersection of accounting and performance measurement.

For example, three of the fourteen cities in the Fiscal Year 2002–2003 report provide residential refuse collection service in the backyard, while the other 14 provide curbside service. The explanation at one of the backyard cities, Raleigh, notes this fact and adds "This is a relatively labor intensive process and represents a high level of service" (p. 29). This information is very useful in that it allows readers to see if the costs are higher than average (which they are), that this is due in part to the trade-off of higher service. In fact, Raleigh is the only city that collects refuse 2 times per week.

On the flip side, Raleigh has the lowest complaints per collection point, suggesting that the increased cost is being realized in higher value. Another interesting comment is from the city of Wilson that "considers all complaints to be valid complaints." Since the project reports both "complaints" and "valid complaints" it appears that there is a disagreement among the cities as to this definition. The project appears to have found ways to deal with these kinds of differences and yet still report useful data.

The analogy to corporate reporting and footnotes appears strong, every public corporation is expected to follow the same rules, but they sometimes report alternative information (such as "pro-forma" earnings). This other information is useful, and acceptable, as long as the descriptions are complete. Some decision-makers rely more on the GAAP- (or Project-) defined measures, while others use the alternate information. The trade-offs from having more than one number, but the number being clearly marked as not following the general rules, is a trade-off that appears to work in the corporate reporting world and for the NCBP.

21.4.3 Ontario Examples: Mandatory MPMP and Voluntary OMBI

Ontario is perhaps the most interesting example of performance measurement due to its two concurrent programs (Burke, 2004). The MPMP (Municipal Performance Measurement Project) requires all 448 municipalities to report measures publicly while the OMBI members forbid the public sharing of data about member governments. Burke describes how the mandatory nature of the MPMP project appears to be contrary to the prescriptions of benchmarking practices. While this may be true, the end result is something that looks very close to the ideals envisioned by the GASB over a decade ago.

21.4.4 Discussion of Examples

Based upon the above analysis as well as our broader readings, we see several themes that seem to exist in the four different projects. These themes include:

- Outside funding and support to offset high costs to start
- Commitment from political leaders
- Appropriate balance of both collaboration and competition
- MUST take time to get agreement on definitions and measurement — BUT agreement comes if the time is taken (Hatry, Fountain and other proponents recognize this)
- Negative reporting from media is a large concern for those involved in benchmark (No great response even today — so the press effort to increase accountability may actually be diminishing it)
- Participation rates fluctuate when it is voluntary (NCBP kept the cities but lost the counties; OMBI steady; ICMA-high turnover). Is this due to alleged "performance paradox" or more to perceived cost/benefit (high cost from time — benefits could be too slow in coming, or the "best" may not have much to learn)
- Omission of the difficult to measure (social services in MPMP and NCBP)
- IMPLICATIONS for accounting:
  - Need someone to define measures
  - Need a standard reporting format

– Need trade-offs (omit difficult to measure — for now)
- Absent some innovation that impacts the frontier[10] (typically from a combination of factors, rather than getting people to work "harder" — Newland 1972), the benefits appear to be greatest in the early stages when those most inefficient organizations (i.e. furthest from the frontier) learn about and implement better methods
- Insufficient time has passed to assess whether an ongoing system of widely available external reporting would tend to atrophy and have costs exceeding the benefits — OR, if the ongoing use of the system would lead to frontier-pushing innovations that would generate aggregate benefits exceeding aggregate costs
- The assessment of individual organization benefits and costs is likely to result in some that are net losers — perhaps those closest to the frontier (expending lots of time innovating and reporting — receiving fairly modest gains) — and some net winners — typically the most inefficient at time zero.

21.5 Summary and Conclusion

We have tried to show that the term "accounting" has very little meaning by itself due to the number and variety of specialties within accounting. Similarly, the term "performance measurement" also suffers from multiple meanings and specialties. We do not assert that accounting should become the home discipline for performance measurement, largely due to the lack of adequate educators, trainers and professional associations.[11]

In Section 21.2 we attempted to clarify the terminology surrounding performance measurement as it relates to its intersection with accounting. The terminology is not new, but we do advocate careful use of each term to more concisely convey the tool being discussed. We further assert that the conceptual clarity of discussing performance measurement would improve with appropriate references to the tools and concepts of at least six of the accounting specialties (financial/external reporting, cost, managerial, auditing, information systems and management controls). Along with this improved conceptual clarity, we believe that the practice of performance measurement can improve as public managers become better skilled at choosing "the right measurement (or specialty) for the right issue."

Our primary focus in this treatise was to determine the intersection of accounting and performance measurement. Through our analysis of the state of the art in performance measurement we identified several areas where accounting and performance measurement appear to intersect and yet there does not appear to be much discussion across the disciplines, except the North Carolina Benchmarking Project (Rivenbark, 2000). We then examined the accounting discipline to identify those skills and areas of expertise that accountants might possess as we attempt to move the combined disciplines forward (those areas of intersection). As we began to more fully understand this intersection, the disconnect or lack of intersection between the primary disciplines involved in moving performance measurement forward became painfully obvious and appears to haunt us across time from the 1930s to present.

The three quotations used as an introduction to our discussion were chosen very carefully to indicate this concern throughout the decades — from Ridley and Simon in 1938 to O'Neill in very recent times (2004) the lack of connection between the professions has been noted as a stumbling block. We concur with Kaplan and Johnson — accounting is too important to be left to the accountants. This is not an abandonment of our discipline nor its unique expertise; rather it is a recognition that in the area of performance measurement we must utilize the expertise of the other disciplines that have their own unique set of skills to apply to the remaining problems. We join O'Neill in his conviction that we MUST "develop a standard portfolio of terminology standards, training and presentation so that seventy years from now we are still not having this conversation."

Finally, we believe the answer to our secondary question, "is accounting relevant to determine roles or policies of government?" is no. We have seen nothing from the history of accounting or its specialties to indicate that accounting can or should serve a "line" function of determining or executing strategy. Accounting is best as a staff or support function. While it is clearly evident that some have feared such an effort was the intention of the GASB or accountants (GFOA, 1993, 2002; Olson et al., 1998; Burke, 2004), we find no indication of this motive nor the ability to execute it even if it was a motive. It is inconsistent with the professional ideals and norms of the profession.

Notes

1. For a history of performance reporting prior to 1930, see Williams (2004).
2. While the majority of the articles in both Symposia were generally in favor of the ideals of the productivity movement, Thayer (1972) provides a dissenting view that examines the similarities with the current efforts and Taylor's Scientific Management approach that was seen as dehumanizing and outlawed in government in the early 1900s.
3. Newland (1972), writing about personnel concerns with the Productivity movement notes that, "Experience in both private enterprise and in government demonstrates that economic growth now

results more from technological efficiency in combining factor inputs of people capital and natural resources than from any one of those separate factors. Thus, both Hatry and Newland acknowledge the need for managerial innovation and creativity in the use of all resources rather than a mechanical and dehumanizing use of performance measures — see footnote 2.

4. Burkhead and Hennigan adopt a quantitative economics approach and appear to be adding a large amount of complexity to the basic observations from Ridley and Simon, that it is difficult to measure output and that the goals or objectives are often not clearly stated, without adding much clarity to those basic observations.

5. Other possible specialties include performance contracting and pay-for-performance. We consider these as part of performance management, although they are certainly candidates for specialty status.

6. Typical leadership titles include governor, mayor, legislator, city council member and agency director. We make no distinction about the title, rather, any one of these titleholders may be able to provide clear and legitimately accepted goals and objectives.

7. A complete timeline of the SEA project and the associated research projects, including case studies, surveys, and focus groups can be found at www.seagov.org.

8. The AGA changed its name to Advancing Government Accountability around the same time the GAO changed its name from General Accounting Office to Government Accountability Office.

9. Another explanation of the opposition or fear of the GASB requiring particular measures may stem from the "evangelical" style of two of it early proponents — Harry Hatry and Jay Fountain. While both of them understood the need for due process, they also felt like the "time had come" by 1990 to get busier in reporting. Unfortunately, their passion may have delayed the opportunity to mandate reporting. As seen in the Ontario example in section 21.4.3, a form of mandated benchmarking, as Burke (2004) calls it, may be just the type of reporting format the GASB and local government can live with.

10. By "frontier" we invoke the concept of a production frontier curve that incorporates all possible variables and relates them to the level of output or outcome.

11. During our analysis of both accounting and performance measurement literatures, we were struck by the question of how government managers and accountants are trained in new concepts such as performance measurement and accounting. We recognize that performance measurement has been a significant part of many Masters in Public Administration (MPA) programs, and yet we believe there are very few accounting academics on the faculty in MPA

programs. Similarly, most accountants are trained in a business school and there are very few accounting faculty that specialize in government accounting. In fact, most universities do not teach a separate accounting course in governmental accounting. Even if the topic is taught as a part of another accounting class, it is rarely taught by someone with a deep understanding of governmental entities and government management reforms. Thus, in order for our proposed intersections to be improved, there may be a significant difficulty in conveying the message to the relevant educators.

References

AGA (Association of Government Accountants). 2004. Pilot Phase report.

Ammons, David N. 1999. A proper mentality for benchmarking, *Public Administration Review*, 59(3), 105–109.

Anthony, Robert N. and Govindarajan Vijay. 2004. *Management Control Systems, 11th ed.* Irwin-McGraw Hill, New York, NY.

Anthony, Robert N. and Young, David W. 2003. *Management Control in Nonprofit Organizations, 7th ed.* McGraw-Hill, New York, NY.

Balk, Walter L. 1978. A Symposium: Productivity in government, *Public Administration Review*, 38(1), 1.

Barrett, Katherine and Greene, Richard. 2005. Grading the states 2005: A management report card, *Governing Magazine*, February, 2005.

Behn, Robert D. 2002. The psychological barriers to performance management: Or why isn't everyone jumping on the performance-management bandwagon? *Public Performance & Management Review*, 26(1), 5–25.

———. 2003. Why measure performance? Different purposes require different measures, *Public Administration Review*, 63(5), 586–606.

———. 2005 quoted in article in *Washington Post* by Stephan Barr titled "Expert sees problems in the search for a perfect system", January 12, 2005.

Burke, Brendan F. 2004. State-ordered benchmarking: A comparison of voluntary and mandated performance measurement in Ontario. Paper presented at Association for Budgeting and Financial Management conference, October 9, 2004, Chicago, IL.

Burkhead, Jesse and Hennigan, Patrick J. 1978. Productivity analysis: A search for definition and order, *Public Administration Review*, 38(1), 34–40.

Evans, John H. and Patton, James M. 1987. Signaling and monitoring in public sector accounting, *Journal of Accounting Research*, 25(Supplement), 130–158.

Fountain, James R., Patton, Terry K. and Steinberg, Harold I. 2004. Improving performance reporting for government: New guidance and resources, *Journal of Government Financial Management*, 53(1), 60–66.

Frank, Howard and D'Souza, Jayesh. 2004. Twelve years into the performance measurement revolution: Where we need to go in implementation research, *International Journal of Public Administration*, 27(8/9), 701–719.

GFOA (Government Finance Officers Association). 1993. Service efforts and accomplishments reporting: Public policy statement. Available at http://www.gfoa.org/services/policy/gfoapp1.shtml.

———. 2002. Performance measurement and the Government Accounting Standards Board: Public Policy Statement. Available at http://www. gfoa.org/services/policy/gfoapp1.shtml.

Governmental Accounting Standards Board. 1987. *Concepts Statement No. 1: Objectives of Financial Reporting*. GASB, Norwalk, CT.

———. 1994. *Concepts Statement No. 2: Service Efforts and Accomplishments Reporting*. GASB, Norwalk, CT.

———. 2000. *State and Local Government Case Studies on Use and Effects of Using Performance Measures for Budgeting, Management, and Reporting*. GASB, Norwalk, CT.

———. 2003. *Reporting Performance Information: Suggested Criteria for Effective Communication*. GASB Norwalk, CT.

Harris, Jean. 1995. Service efforts and accomplishment standards: Fundamental question of an emerging concept, *Public Budgeting and Finance*, 15(4), 18–37.

Hatry, Harry P. 1972. Issues in productivity measurement for local governments, *Public Administration Review*, 32(6) 776–784.

———. 1978. The status of productivity measurement in the public sector, *Public Administration Review*, 38(1), 28–33.

———. 1999. *Performance Measurement*. Urban Institute Press, Washington, DC.

Hatry, H., Fountain J., Sullivan, J., and Kremer, L. eds. 1990. *Service Efforts and Accomplishments Reporting: Its Time Has Come*. GASB Research Report, Norwalk, CT.

Horngren, Charles T., Datar, Srikant M., and Foster, George. 2003. *Cost Accounting: A managerial emphasis, 11th ed*. Prentice Hall, Upper Saddle River, NJ.

ICMA. 2001. *What Works: Management applications of performance measurement in local government*. International City/County Management Association, Washington, DC.

ICMA. 2002. *What Works 2002 Case Studies: Management applications of performance measurement in local government*. International City/County Management Association, Washington, DC.

Johnson, H. Thomas and Kaplan, Robert S. 1987. *Relevance Lost: The rise and fall of management accounting*. Harvard Business School Press, Boston, MA.

Kaplan, Robert S. and Norton, David P. 1996a. *Balanced Scorecard*. Harvard Business School Press, Boston, MA.

———. 1996b. Using the Balanced Scorecard as a strategic management system, *Harvard Business Review*, 74(1), 75–85.

———. 2001. Balance without profit. *Financial Management* (CIMA), January 2001, 23–26.

Kelly, Janet M, and Rivenbark, William C. 2003. *Performance Budgeting for State and Local Government*, M.E. Sharpe, Armonk, NY.

Kloby, Kathryn and Kim, Younhee. 2004. Performance measurement: Recent publications, *Public Performance & Management Review*, 28(2), 281–289.

Martin, Bernard H., Wholey, Joseph S. and Meyers, Roy T. 1995. The new equation at OMB: M + B = RMO. *Public Budgeting and Finance*, 15(4), 86–96.

Melkers, Julia and Willoughby, Katherine. 1998. The state of the states: Performance–budgeting requirements in 47 out of 50, *Public Administration Review*, 58(1), 66–73.

———. 2004. Staying the Course: The use of performance measurement in state governments, IBM Center for the Business of Government. Available at www.business of government.org.

Morley, Elaine, Bryant, Scott P. and Hatry, Harry P. 2001. *Comparative Performance Measurement*. Urban Institute Press, Washington, DC.

Newland, Chester A. 1972. Personnel concerns in government productivity improvement, *Public Administration Review*, 32(6), 807–815.

Olson, Olov, Guthrie, James and Humphrey, Christopher. 1998. *Global Warning: Debating International Developments in New Public Financial Management*. Cappelen Akademisk Forlag, Oslo, Norway.

O'Neill, Robert J. 2004. The performance dividend: High performing organizations and performance management. Presentation at ICMA 90th Annual Conference, San Diego, CA. Viewed January 31, 2005 http://www.icma.org/upload/news/attach/{0521A93B-AB19-48B8-A364-16452CF4680E}.pdf.

Osborne, David and Gaebler, Ted. 1992. Reinventing Governement: How the entrepreneurial spirit is transforming the public sector. Addison-Wesley, Reading MA.

Parry, R. W., Sharp, F. C., Vreeland, J., Wallace, W. A. 1991. *Service Efforts and Accomplishments Reporting: Its Time Has Come—Fire Department Programs*. GASB Research Report, Norwalk, CT.

Parry, R. W., Sharp, F., Wallace, W. A., and Vreeland, J. 1994. The Role of Service Efforts and Accomplishments in Reporting Total Quality Management: Implications for Accountants, *Accounting Horizons* (June) 25–43.

PSBS (Public Sector Benchmarking Service). 2004. About Benchmarking. Site visited at July 12, 2004 at www.benchmarking.gov.uk/default1.asp

Quinn, Robert E. 1978. Productivity and the process of organizational improvement: Why we cannot talk to each other, *Public Administration Review*, 38(1), 41–45.

Ridley, Clarence E. and Simon, Herbert A. 1938. *Measuring Municipal Activities: A survey of suggested criteria and reporting forms for appraising administration.* International City Managers' Association. Chicago, IL.

Rivenbark, William C. 2000. The role of capital cost in performance measurement and benchmarking. *Public Performance & Management Review,* 24(1), 22–29.

———. 2004. Defining performance budgeting for local government, *Popular Government,* Winter 2004, 27–36.

Rivenbark, William C. and Dutton, Matthew H. 2004. Final Report on City Services for Fiscal Year 2002–2003: Performance and cost data, UNC School of Government, University of North Carolina at Chapel Hill.

Smith, Kenneth A. 2004. Voluntarily reporting performance measures to the public: A test of accounting reports from U.S. cities, *International Public Management Journal,* 7(1), 19–48.

Smith, Kenneth A. and Cheng, Rita H. 2004. Assessing reforms of accounting budgeting and reporting. Paper presented at Association for Budgeting and Financial Management conference, October 9, 2004, Chicago, IL.

Steiss, Alan W. 1982. *Management Control in Government.* Lexington Books, Lexington, MA.

Thayer, Frederick, C. 1972. Productivity: Taylorism revisited (round three), *Public Administration Review,* 32(6), 833–840.

Wang, Xiao Hu. (2002). Assessing performance measurement impact: A study of U.S. local government, *Public Performance & Management Review,* 26(1), 26–43.

Wildavsky, Aaron B. 1964. *The Politics of the Budgetary Process.* Little Brown Publishing, Boston, MA.

Williams, Daniel W. 2004. Evolution of performance measurement until 1930, *Administration & Society,* 36(2), 131–165.

Zimmerman, Jerold L. (1977). The municipal accounting maze: An analysis of political incentives, *Journal of Accounting Research,* 15(Supplement), 107–144.

Chapter 22

Reformed County Government and Service Delivery Performance: An Integrated Study of Florida Counties

ALEJANDRO RODRIGUEZ, Ph.D.
School of Urban and Public Affairs, University of Texas, Arlington

This study tested the proposition that reformed government positively correlates with cost-efficient service delivery. A county government reform index developed for this study is composed of form of government, home-rule status, method of election, number of government jurisdictions, and number of elected officials. The government reform index was used to assess the impact of reform on two measures of service output, (1) mean county road pavement conditions and, (2) per capita county road improvement and maintenance expenditures. Data were collected from semi-structured interviews of county officials, secondary archival sources, and a survey of 544 elected and appointed officials from Florida's 67 counties. The results converged in finding that reformed Florida counties are more likely than unreformed counties to provide better road service and to spend less on road expenditures. Because the county government reform index was operationalized acknowledging the reform theory as well as the public-choice model the results help explain contradicting findings in the urban service research.

22.1 Introduction

The central issue in public service delivery within the local sector is whether or not smaller, competing jurisdictions within a metropolitan area are more cost-efficient and effective providers than regional or centralized entities (Barlow, 1991; DeSantis and Renner, 1994; Ostrom, 1976; Schneider and Park, 1989; Svara, 1994). Adherents of the "New Political Economy" or public choice believe that small and frequently overlapping jurisdictions are "closer to the people" and more flexible; hence they can offer higher quality, lower cost service, and will suffer outflow of people and businesses if they fail to do so. Contrariwise, for the past century mainstream public administration has advocated for more centralized administration organized along the lines of the Weberian monocracy, with particular emphasis on professional managers rather than elected officials serving in key adminis-trative posts (DeSantis and Renner, 2002; Osborne and Plastrik, 2000). Implicit in the mainstream argument is an inherent belief that clarity of organizational structure, coupled with operational economies of scale, will ultimately result in lower cost, and higher quality service delivery.

Empirical evidence on this fundamental question is mixed. Early work by Lineberry and Fowler supports the reform framework (Lineberry and Fowler, 1967). Dye and Garcia (1978) and Liebert (1974) found that functional responsibility rather than community structure per se, was the primary determinant of service efficiency. Lyons (1978) found that reformed municipalities had lower service delivery cost, findings supported by Stumm (1998). Morgan and Pelissero (1980) and, more recently, Morgan and Kickham (1999) found no difference in taxes or spending among the reformed or non-reformed communities. In essence, the jury is out on whether the public choice or reformed worldview of urban service delivery has a clear-cut advantage in service cost or quality, with the very real possibility that the "truth" lies in a hybrid or two-tier approach that assigns certain functions to metropolitan-wide service delivery and others to the local- or neighborhood-level (Bish and Ostrom, 1979).

This study returns to the public choice versus mainstream service delivery question. It does so with several key components:

1. It focuses on the county as a unit of analysis. While there is growing agreement that the county is becoming an increasingly important service provider (Benton and Menzel, 1993; DeSantis and Renner, 1994; Marando and Thomas, 1977; Marando and Reeves, 1991). This level of government remains under-researched in terms of empirical analysis linking structure to policy outcome, with the underlying assumption being that municipally-based findings readily apply to counties (DeSantis and Renner, 1994).

2. It focuses on a single county service as a measure of performance. A single county service was used to better control for variations in functional responsibility across variables as well as to better account for the effects of intermediate variables. The selection of an appropriate county service was driven by the following criteria: (a) the scope and quality of the service was clearly mandated and specified as a condition for funding; (b) it was a high service priority for Florida counties; (c) the service was entirely provided by a county government and not by cities or any other overlapping local jurisdictions within county boundaries; and (d) the service was measurable in quantitative terms. Based on these criteria, county road services were selected to measure county service performance. Specifically, this study used two dimensions of county road services: (i) pavement condition ratings; and (ii) per capita road expenditures.

3. This research is methodologically triangulated to enhance internal and external validity. The study's findings are based on quantitative analysis of survey data, interviews with key informants, and assessment of archival data related to cost and quality of road maintenance in Florida's 67 counties. This mix of quantitative, qualitative, and historical research approaches yields a more robust and valid set of findings than could be derived from a single research approach (Kidd, Smith and Kidder, 1991; Yin, 1994).

4. The study's findings are generalizable to other counties outside of Florida. Florida counties are representative of both urban and rural counties in the U.S., large and small counties (population and geography), rich and poor, form of government (commission vs. commission-manager), and size of governing board. Nationally, the average number of counties per state is 63. Florida closely represents the national average with 67 counties.

5. The operationalization of key constructs in the study draws on frameworks established by adherents of both the public choice and reformed schools. From the author's vantage, this obviates biases

(either advertent or inadvertent) that may have contributed to prior findings. This work is eclectic in its operationalization and draws upon the best insights of both camps in its design.

22.2   Problem Definition

This study assesses the relative strengths and weaknesses of the public choice versus reformed perspectives of urban service delivery by focusing on a quintessential county function: road improvement and maintenance. Berman (1993) found that road expenditures is one of the top county service expenditures. One finding of Berman's study is that transportation is one of the highest priorities for fast growing counties, and that Florida counties outpace U.S. counties or urban counties nationally in the level of commitment to transportation expenditures. This fact is not surprising when one considers that all Florida counties are statutorily mandated to provide road construction and maintenance. Based on data from a national survey of 1,026 counties, Marando and Thomas (1977) found that road construction and maintenance was ranked the sixth most frequently performed function out of 44 different county functions, and that this service is the number one concern for both urban and non-urban counties. This is remarkable because, in all other functional areas, urban and non-urban counties differ significantly in their priorities. Finally, Marando and Thomas' survey of Florida and Georgia county commissioners determined that roads were a severe problem area, second only to county financing concerns.

The county government reform index developed for this study is composed of form of government, home-rule status, method of election, number of government jurisdictions, and number of elected officials to assess reformism impact on mean county road pavement conditions and alternatively county per capita road expenditures. The use of a reform index variable goes back to early attempts to research political structure linkages to policy output. The main assumption of researchers, political activists and concerned citizens of the Progressive Era was the belief that reformed structures of local government positively correlated to its performance (Lyons, 1978; Park, 1994). Reformers sought to reverse the stronghold of the party machine politics, which operated by securing votes in exchange for favors. In their view, city government had to be democratized and rationalized by substituting politics of the party machine with leadership focused on the public interest (Lineberry and Fowler, 1967). Government responsiveness was believed to be better achieved by at-large and non-partisan elections, and the commission form of government (Lyons, 1978). The commission form of government was later abandoned for the council-manager model seeking to maximize professionalism and administrative efficiency. Moreover, the executive role played by a manager was argued to promote coordination and cohesiveness while rejecting factional politics (Lyons, 1978). Both non-partisan and at-large elections were advanced to minimize the effects of divisive political forces and to prevent their interference with local decision-making. It was argued that national and state party issues were in most cases irrelevant to local needs and were better kept away from local politics. Moreover, at-large elections were believed to reduce the negative effects that ethnic minorities or 'socio-economic cleavages' could impose on the general community by voting for their particular preferences. In sum, the reformers sought to establish profession-alized political structures that valued efficiency and represented the interest of the public at large as opposed to special interest groups.

22.3   Research Design, Variables, and Implementation

22.3.1   *Triangulated Research Design*

This study relies on the joint strength of three research methods — a four-county case study, secondary data analysis, and a survey study. This method seeks to corroborate or triangulate the results of different research meth-ods and data analysis to strengthen internal and external validity of the study. First, as part of a four-county case study (Brevard, Hardee, Madison, and Miami-Dade counties), 15 county officials were interviewed (three to five per county) to help clarify propositions about county reform and to pretest the questionnaire instrument to be used later in the study. Next, secondary data related to county government and road maintenance performance variables for all 67 Florida counties were collected and analyzed to test the study's hypotheses, using mostly regression analyses. Finally, data collected through questionnaires mailed to 544 county officials, complemented by socioeconomic data, were used to retest the study's hypotheses. Correlation and regression analyses were used to model the interactions between the independent and dependent variables while controlling for county level of resources, population size, and paved road mileage. The combined findings of both the four-county case study and the secondary data regression analysis were compared to the conclusions drawn from the survey data analysis.

22.3.2   *Variables*

This study's main independent variable is a measure of the political and organizational reform of county government in Florida, which includes: (1) form of government; (2) number of county elected officials; (3) number of local government jurisdictions; (4) home-rule status; and (5) method of elections. Counties were scored from 0 to 5 depending on the presence of the reform components in their political structures. The reform components were not multiplied by some arbitrary constant and instead equal weights for all components were used, primarily because reformism is considered to be a continuous, summative, and nearly unidimensional variable (Lineberry and Fowler, 1967; Clark, 1968; Sharp, 1986). Also, unequal weights were not used because a theoretical or empirical sound basis for such scoring method is not agreed upon or even appropriately discussed in the literature. See Table 22.1 for a full discussion of the county government reform index and its instrumentation.

The main dependent variable used in this study is a measure of county road pavement conditions — an outcome indicator. County road pavement condition ratings are measures of road surface conditions and the type of surface put on the roadway (Florida Department of Transportation, 1998). Personnel from the Florida Department of Transportation State Materials Office collect annual road pavement condition data for all Florida counties. Conditions are rated to the nearest tenth within the applicable range of a 1 to 5 scale developed by the Florida Department of Transportation. On this scale 1 equals "very poor" and 5 represents "very good" pavement conditions. While a single scale is used there is great variability in the number of road segments measured for each county. For instance, Flagler and Calhoun counties had a single road segment measured while Miami-Dade County measured 213 road segments and Pinellas County (one of the smallest counties) had 207 road segments measured. For this reason, mean pavement condition ratings for each county were used in the regression model as the dependent variable.

As an alternative independent variable, a measure of relative government fragmentation was used. Relative fragmentation is comprised of three components of the county government reform index. These are form of government, number of elected officials, and number of local government jurisdictions within a county. These three components were included in the index to account for the full range of the fragmentation variable; that is, political and territorial fragmentation. To construct the relative fragmentation variable for each county the scoring scheme was reversed. Accordingly, one point was assigned to counties governed by commission,[1] one point was assigned to those counties with a large number of elected officials relative to their population size, and one point was assigned to counties with a large number of local government jurisdictions relative to their population size. Thus, a high score represents a higher level of fragmentation.

Per capita county road expenditures was used as an alternative dependent variable to test the level of association between reformed structures of county government and policy output. Government expenditures can

Table 22.1   Independent Variable: County Government Reform Index

The main independent variable used in this research is a measure of the political and organizational reform of county government in Florida, which includes, in addition to form of government, home-rule status, method of elections, number of local government jurisdictions, and number of county elected officials. Counties are scored from zero to five, where five indicates that all reform components were present for a particular county. Operationalization of the five reform index components follows.

- *Form of government* — The commission form of government is inherently more functionally fragmented than either the administrator or the executive mayor forms of government. That is due to the fact that commission forms of county government govern by plurality. No single person is responsible and accountable for policy implementation and decision-making. One point is assigned to the elected executive or appointed administrator forms of government; no point is assigned to the commission form of government.
- *Home-rule status* — Home rule is used in this research as an indicator of the functional, organizational, and fiscal autonomy of counties. By definition, home-rule promotes the reform of local governments in three related dimensions: structural, functional, and fiscal capacity. Home rule empowers local governments to strengthen fiscal capacity primarily through (1) the power to levy local taxes; (2) the ability to create special taxing districts and alternative revenue sources, such as franchise and utility fees; (3) the authority to determine the level of debt most appropriate to its particular needs; and, (4) the control on elected county officials' salaries to fit local needs and in accordance with available resources. Home-rule counties are assigned one point; no point is assigned to constitutional or non-home rule counties.
- *Method of election* — This reform component should help to account for the decision-making and legislative dynamics of county government. At-large elections are believed to enhance representative politics, as opposed to district elections that arguably serve special interests. At-large election methods are assigned one point. Counties that use the single-member district election method are not assigned any points. However, counties that use a mixed method of election single-district and at-large are assigned one point.
- *Number of elected officials* — Florida counties are constitutionally mandated to elect five or seven members to boards of county commissioners plus five constitutional officers. In addition to county commissioners and constitutional officers, counties might elect officers to independent special districts. In the county government reform index, one point is assigned to small counties (population less than 50,000) that elect five special district officers in addition to the constitutionally mandated officials. That is, a small county may be considered reformed (in terms of the number of elected officials) if voters elect up to seven commissioners, five constitutional officers, and five special district officials for a maximum of 17 elected officials. One additional elected

(Continued)

Table 22.1 Continued

official is permitted for each additional 100,000 population. This population factor controls for population size differences, but a large metropolitan county might still be considered functionally fragmented if its number of elected officials exceeds its assigned population factor. Finally, while most small counties comparatively elect few officials, some choose to establish a large number of independent special districts and end up being considered fragmented.

- *Number of local government jurisdictions* — For the purpose of building a reform index, this research assigned one point to counties with a comparatively "small" number of jurisdictions within their boundaries. Defining comparative "small" number of jurisdictions within a county is guided by the following method: (1) Add the number of cities and independent special districts within a county to get the total number of jurisdictions within a county; (2) divide the number of jurisdictions by 699, which is the statewide number of counties, cities and independent special districts in Florida to get the jurisdiction ratio; (3) divide a county's population by the total population in Florida to get the population ratio: (4) if a county's population ratio is greater than its jurisdiction ratio, one point is assigned to the county's reform index value. To sum up, a county is considered functionally fragmented if its relative fragmentation level (number of county jurisdictions divided by statewide jurisdictions) is greater than its relative population level (county population divided by statewide population).

Control variables

The control variables used in this study fall into three general areas: Urbanization (including population size and growth), functional scope, and relative fiscal capacity or community wealth. The following variables were used in this study:

Urbanization

Population (97). The impact of jurisdictional size (assuming that bigger counties need more services) was measured by the size of the official estimated 1997 county population.

Population growth (90–97). The jurisdiction's rate of growth was controlled by including in the analysis model the percentage change in population between 1990 and 1997.

Population change (90–97). Defined as change in population between 1990 and 1997 and used in the analysis as an alternative measure of jurisdictional growth.

Functional scope

Unincorporated population growth (90–97). The percentage rate of unincorporated population was included as a measure of the impact of suburbanization on the county's functional scope and the added demand for services. Greater expenditures and added responsibilities are assumed for counties with larger unincorporated populations.

Table 22.1   Continued

Paved road mileage/ unpaved road mileage. These two logically opposite variables were alternatively tried in the analysis model to sort out their impact on county road maintenance expenditures. The variables were also used as an alternative measure of the county's functional scope. It is assumed that counties that have a high mileage of paved roads have relatively greater functional responsibilities and are more committed to road improvements than counties with a low mileage of paved roads. Counties with higher mileages of paved roads would necessarily incur greater maintenance expenditures.

Fiscal capacity and community wealth

Per capita county taxable value. The per capita county taxable value was included to provide a measure of the fiscal capacity of counties. It is defined as the per capita county assessed value of property minus the amount of any exemption approved by the county property appraiser.

Per capita transportation revenues. Per capita transportation-related revenues are included as an additional measure of and control for fiscal capacity. Transportation revenues come from transfers of fuel taxes imposed by the State of Florida and from local fuel taxes imposed by counties.

---

be analytically conceptualized as both inputs and outputs (Lewis, 1982). As outputs resulting from budgetary policy or organizational decision-making, expenditures can be considered dependent variables. The log (base 10) of the per capita road expenditures was used to control for population differences and to transform the data to approximate a normal distribution.

The use of general government expenditures as a dependent variable has been used to measure service performance or output (Clark, 1968; Cole, 1971; Lineberry and Fowler, 1967; Morgan and Kickham, 1999; Morgan and Pelissero, 1980; Park, 1994; Schneider and Park, 1989; Sharp, 1986; Stumm, 1998). The assumption is that lower expenditures are an indication of greater cost-efficiency. The methodological problem with this assumption is that differences in general government expenditures may be unrelated to cost-efficiency and, in fact, the result of many other confounding variables. To name a few, these could include service cuts, or dramatic increases in social service demands, natural emergencies, geographic and topographic differences, different levels of intergovernmental funding and, in general, different scopes of functional responsibility (Liebert, 1974; Dye and Garcia, 1978). To control for these intervening variables, this study used expenditures specifically incurred in the improvement and maintenance of county roads wholly within the jurisdiction of counties as opposed to using general government expenditures.

Control variables used fall into three general areas. These are measures of urbanization (including population size and growth rate), functional scope, and relative fiscal capacity or community wealth.[2] See Table 22.1 for a full discussion and instrumentation of all control variables used in this study. Furthermore, the study focused on a single state (Florida) to control for regional differences and widely dissimilar state laws mandating county government policy-making, and service delivery. A focus on a single state also controlled for varying population growth rates, different measures of county wealth and sources of revenue, government structural differences, different functional scopes and service demands, varying effects of regional political culture, climate differences (Florida is one of the states with the most constant mean temperatures across regions) and other variables relevant to service delivery research.[3]

22.3.3 Implementation

Weighted least-squares (WLS), as opposed to ordinary least-squares (OLS) regression analysis, was the statistical technique used since the dependent variable (mean pavement conditions) was calculated from a remarkably varying number of pavement condition measurements taken for each county. For instance, Flagler and Calhoun counties had a single road segment measured while Miami-Dade County measured 213 road segments and Pinellas County (one of the smallest counties) had 207 road segments measured. This variability in the number of measurements results in very unequal variances and thus inefficient parameter estimates if OLS were used.

Data transformation was a possible remedy, but a readily available solution is weighted regression when the dependent variable is in the form of means. The difficult part about weighted regression is finding the appropriate weighting constant because it should be proportional to the inverse of the variance of the observation or measurement ($1/s^2$). However, since the variance of a mean is the inverse of the number of observations (n) used to calculate that mean, the number of observations is the correct weighting constant (s^2/n) (Littell, Freund and Spector, 1991). In sum, finding the appropriate weight constant for weighted regression was facilitated because the mean of the pavement condition measurements was used in the analysis. Most importantly, the use of WLS ensured that observations with large variances received less weight than observations with smaller variances (counties with fewer road segments measured).

OLS was used to model the regression equations when per capita road expenditures were included as the alternate dependent variable. The log base 10 of per capita road expenditures was used to facilitate the interpretation of the relative importance of all regression coefficients and to maximize the linearity of the per capita road expenditures variable. All regression analyses were done following the hierarchical method to better discern the extent of the contribution of the research variable of interest beyond the combined effect of all other variables. The order in which predictor variables are entered in a regression equation have been found to make a great deal of difference in terms of the amount of the dependent variable's variance explained (Stevens, 1992). This is especially true when the predictors are correlated. Thus, to truly assess the contribution of the main independent variable it is important to first enter all control variables and then enter the independent variable. The resulting change in R^2 (if any) is the contribution of the independent variable above and beyond the combined contribution of the control variables.

The study limited the number of controlling variables to three for several reasons. The first is that these three variables were identified by the multi-county case study as important in determining road improvement performance. Second, a limited number of variables is recommended, given that the number of counties in the study is relatively small (67). The "general rule is to find the best solution with the fewest variables possible" (Tabachnick and Fidell, 1989, 13); another general rule to improve the model's reliability is to allow one variable for each 15 subjects in social science research (Stevens, 1992). Too many variables relative to sample size may provide a good model fit and perhaps a moderate increase in the R^2 coefficient, but such an "overfitted" model diminishes the value of the findings. Finally, the regression analysis was limited to three variables to reduce the threat of multicollinearity. Several potential variables were dropped from further analysis after finding that they were highly correlated with each other. Their inclusion in the regression model would have limited the ability to determine the relative importance of a given variable because high intercorrelation confounds the variables' effects.

22.4   Hypotheses

The review of the two prevailing approaches to solving the service-delivery problem helped with the conceptual definition of reformed government. However, how government political structures might be linked to policy output differences would benefit from the development of a causal model. Figure 22.1 illustrates a model developed by Lineberry and Fowler (1967) and adapted by DeSantis and Renner (1996). The model relates county socioeconomic characteristics, political culture, and political structure, to public policy outputs.

As noted by DeSantis and Renner "there is certainly ample evidence that the socioeconomic characteristics of a county influence both political

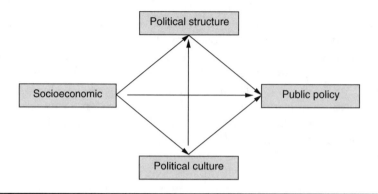

Figure 22.1 A causal model of county government political structure, socio-economic characteristics, political culture, and policy output.

culture and political structure, which are also likely to be correlated" (DeSantis and Renner, 1996, 84). Using Elazar's (1966) well-known political cultures, DeSantis and Renner connect traditionalist cultures to commission form of government (unreformed), moralist cultures to modern (reformed) county government, and individualist cultures to forms of government somewhere in the middle. The connection between political culture and political structure is thus theoretically explained. Not explained in the causal model is the linkage between political structure and public policy outputs. That linkage is the focus of this study.

The theoretical framework and causal model informed the development of four hypotheses used in this research. Of the four hypotheses, the first two relate county government reform to either road pavement conditions or to road expenditures. Thus, the following associations are expected:

- Hypothesis 1: All other factors being equal, more reformed county governments are likely to have higher pavement condition ratings than less reformed county governments.
- Hypothesis 2: All other factors being equal, more reformed county governments are likely to have lower expenditures in the main-tenance and construction of county roads than less reformed county governments.

Hypotheses 3 and 4 were used to test whether the level of government fragmentation affects road pavement conditions or alternatively per capita road expenditures.

- Hypothesis 3: All other factors being equal, less fragmented county governments are likely to have higher pavement condition ratings than more fragmented county governments.

- Hypothesis 4: All other factors being equal, more fragmented county governments are likely to have higher per capita road expenditures than less fragmented county governments.

As an alternative measure of county government service performance, hypotheses 3 and 4 were estimated using per capita county road expenditures as the dependent variable. The use of government expenditures as a dependent variable was used cautiously in this study because of its well-known methodological limitations. The validity of this variable was strengthened by using expenditures specifically incurred in the improvement and maintenance of county roads wholly within the jurisdiction of counties. Furthermore, this variable was only used as an alternative measure and for the purpose of strengthening the overall empirical validity of the study's findings.

22.5   Findings

22.5.1   Multi-County Case Study

The analysis of the data collected through the one-on-one interviews of the 15 appointed and elected county officials generally agreed with the research propositions. The commissioners did not agree that form of government, number of government units, number of elected officials, or home-rule status affect how cost-efficiently counties provide road services. By contrast, public works directors and county administrators were mostly inclined to respond that these structural factors do make a difference on performance. A public works director, responding to whether form of government affect service delivery remarked, "Yes, it does make a significant difference; the type of political subdivision and the structure of that subdivision has a significant bearing ... " Finance directors were mostly uncertain as to whether any of these government characteristics makes a difference in road maintenance performance. The county size or level of urbanization was not found to have an effect on how participants responded to the questions on county reform.

An early consideration was to limit the survey to commissioners and county administrators. However, the data resulting from the interviews showed that the opinions on county government reform held by public works and finance directors were significantly different than the opinions of commissioners and county administrators. Based on this finding, both the public works and finance directors were included in the survey to get a more balanced and complete understanding of the issues. Furthermore, the interviews helped to identify three important factors contributing to the cost-efficient delivery of county road services: county fiscal resources, percentage of paved roads, and county population. These three factors were included as controlling variables in the regression model developed for this research. The county officials were also instrumental in pre-testing the questionnaire subsequently used in the study. They were asked to complete a draft of the questionnaire and comment on the wording and ordering of the questions and whether they believed the questions were relevant to the research topic. As expected, the interviews helped to further define the research propositions and the questionnaire design. Some questions were eliminated, others added, and many were reworded.

22.5.2 Regression Analysis

Table 22.2 shows the four models used to test hypotheses 1 through 4. Models 1 and 2 tested the effect of county government reform (reform

Table 22.2 Regression Analysis Results of the Effect of County Government Reform and Fragmentation Level on Road Pavement Conditions and Per Capita County Road Expenditures

	Dependent Variables			
Controlling for	Pavement Conditions Model 1	Road Expenditures Model 2	Pavement Conditions Model 3	Road Expenditures Model 4
Per capita county taxable value	0.197 (1.93)*	0.316 (3.01)**	0.227 (2.19)*	0.292 (2.81)**
Population change (90–97)	0.426 (3.04)**		0.450 (3.21)**	
Population (97)		−0.642 (−4.28)***		−0.641 (−4.33)***
Paved roads	−0.273 (−2.02)**	0.475 (3.15)**	−0.238 (−1.76)*	0.445 (3.05)**
Independent variables	Reform index	Reform index	Fragment Level	Fragment Level
	0.402 (3.58)***	−0.229 (−1.84)*	−0.360 (−3.36)***	0.232 (2.07)*
R^2	0.295 F = 8.77	0.314 F = 9.62	0.295 F = 8.77	0.314 F = 9.62
Total R^2	0.415	0.350	0.403	0.358

Note: Figures in parenthesis are t values corresponding to the standardized regression coefficients shown for each of the variables.
*$p<0.10$. **$p<0.01$. ***$p<0.001$. N = 67.

index) on road pavement conditions and per capita road expenditures (road expenditures) respectively. Models 3 and 4 tested the effect of the level of fragmentation on road pavement conditions as well as per capita road expenditures. Models 1 and 3 were significant at the 0.001 level while Models 2 and 4 were significant at the 0.10 level. Table 22.2 also shows the standardized beta coefficients for all control variables and both independent variables (t values and corresponding significance levels are shown below the beta coefficients in parentheses). The beta weights provide an indication of the relative importance and contribution of each respective variable in comparison to the total variation in a particular model. For example, population change has the greatest influence in Model 1 (0.426) followed closely by the county government reform variable with a beta weight of 0.402. Furthermore, the reform variable beta coefficient reveals that there is a positive linear relationship between county government reform and pavement condition (a measure of performance in maintaining county roads). As expected for Model 2, there is a negative relationship between the reform variable and road expenditures, meaning that less reformed counties spend more in road maintenance. Likewise, as shown for Models 3 and 4, more fragmented counties have lower pavement conditions and spend more in road maintenance respectively.

The magnitude of the Models' R^2 coefficients further supports all four hypotheses. Model 1 with a R^2 of 0.415 suggests that about 42% of the variance in county pavement condition is explained by the set of the independent and controlling variables used in the equation. These findings support hypothesis 1: more reformed counties, as measured by the county government reform index, are more likely to perform better in terms of county pavement conditions than are unreformed counties. Similar arguments can be made for all remaining models. The proportion of variance in the dependent variable explained by the combination of variables in the equations range from approximately 35% of the variance for Model 2 to 40% for Model 4. These findings support hypotheses 2 through 4: more reformed counties are likely to have lower county road expenditures than unreformed counties and more fragmented counties are likely to have lower county pavement condition ratings, as well as higher county road expenditures, than unfragmented counties.

22.5.3 Survey Data Analysis

Table 22.3 shows the four models used to retest hypotheses 1 through 4 using survey data (see Table 22.4 for a list of selected survey questions). In general, the results of the regression analysis support all four hypotheses and provide added validity to the findings of the secondary data

Table 22.3 Regression Analysis Results of the Effect of County Government Reform and Fragmentation Level on Pavement Conditions, Efficiency Rate, and Per Capita County Road Expenditures

	Dependent Variables			
Controlling for	*Pavement Conditions Model 1*	*Efficiency Rate Model 2*	*Pavement Conditions Model 3*	*Road Expenditures Model 4*
Fiscal capacity	0.385 (6.99)***	0.210 (3.71)***	0.420 (7.59)***	
Per capita transport revenues				0.291 (4.89)***
Per capita county taxable value				0.373 (6.99)***
Population change (90–97)	0.105 (1.76)*			
Unincorporated population growth		0.131 (2.18)*		
Population growth			0.006 (0.10)	0.196 (3.31)***
Unpaved roads	−0.146 (−2.62)**	0−0.087 (−1.51)*	−0.163 (−2.91)***	
Paved roads				0.158 (2.75)**
Independent variables	Reform Index 0.085 (1.62)***	Reform Index 0.273 (4.78)***	Fragment Level −0.116 (−2.06)*	Fragment Level 0.195 (3.68)***
R^2	0.260 F = 33.76	0.066 F = 6.86	0.246 F = 27.96	0.264 F = 24.56
Total R^2	0.267	0.133	0.258	0.299

Note: Figures in parenthesis are t values corresponding to the standardized regression coefficients shown for each of the variables.
*p<0.10. **p<0.01. ***p<0.001. N = 335.

analysis. Models 1 and 2 tested the effect of county government reform on either road pavement conditions or efficiency level. Models 3 and 4 tested the level of fragmentation effect on either pavement conditions or road expenditures. Mirroring the secondary data findings, Models 1, 2, and 4 were significant at the 0.001 level, while Model 3 was significant at the 0.10 level.

As expected and corroborating secondary data findings, the standardized coefficients reveal that there is a positive linear relationship between

Table 22.4   List of Selected Survey Questions Used in the Study

- Questions 4 and 5 asked respondents to assess the number of elected county officials in their counties as either "too few," "too many," or "adequate." The responses to both questions were added into a composite measure of political fragmentation.
- Question 11 asked respondents to rate the service-delivery efficiency of their counties. The item was scaled from 1 to 10, with 1 representing "very low' and 10 "very high" efficiency level.
- Question 18 asked respondents to rate the level of reform of their respective counties using a Likert type scale where 1 represented "very unreformed" and 5 "very reformed."
- Question 19 of the questionnaire asked respondents to rate their county road pavement conditions on a 5-point scale. The question was adapted from a scale developed by the Florida Department of Transportation's Materials Research Office to measure pavement conditions for all Florida counties, which rate pavement conditions with 1 representing "very poor" and 5 "very good."
- Question 20 collected data on fiscal capacity using a 10-point scale, with 1 representing "very low" and 10 representing "very high" fiscal capacity.

county government reform and pavement condition as well as government reform and efficiency rate (a measure of performance in maintaining county roads). In addition, as shown in Models 3 and 4, more fragmented counties have lower pavement conditions and spend more in road maintenance respectively.

While the magnitude of the coefficients of determination (R^2) of each of the models is not as high as those for the secondary data, the significance of the regression coefficients and the R^2 values are still high enough to corroborate and add validity to the findings of this study. As shown in Table 22.3, the models' coefficients of determination range from 0.133 for Model 2 to 0.299 for Model 4. That is to say that, for Model 4, approximately 30% of the differences in the road expenditures is explained by the combined variance of the set of independent variables used in the model.

22.6   Discussion

One important finding of this study is that reformed county governments showed lower expenditures in road maintenance and improvement. This finding is consistent with one of the most frequently cited tenets of the reform theory; that is, reformed governments are more cost-efficient. This proposition has been supported by findings from many city studies, which concluded that government structure was related to lower expenditures and property taxes (Cole, 1971; Dye and Garcia, 1978; Lineberry and

Fowler, 1967; Lyons, 1978; Stumm, 1998). However, previous research on counties appears to contradict this study's findings and the reform theory. For example, DeSantis and Renner (1994) and Schneider and Park (1989) found that reformed counties spend more.

This apparent contradiction seems to result from inherent differences between cities and counties. Reform advocates promoted changing cities' form of government to control runaway expenditures resulting from patronage, nepotism, and other corrupt practices (Marando and Reeves, 1993). County government changes, however, are believed to follow added demands for service resulting from urbanization and growth. Hence, county government structural changes focus on improving professional capacity to best manage increasing demands. Thus, the appointment of a professional administrator may not decrease expenditures in absolute terms but instead focus on the best use of committed resources (DeSantis and Renner, 1994; Schneider and Park, 1989).

This study's findings shed further resolve into this seeming contradiction by carefully controlling for variation in functional responsibility. Controlling for this variation is critical in thorough and systematic comparative analysis of local governments (Clark, 1968; Dye and Garcia, 1978; Liebert, 1974). This study's careful structural operationalization was buttressed by utilizing mean county road pavements as opposed to aggregate expenditures, a careful reckoning of both maintenance and improvement funds and, lastly, eliminating other general fund expenditure subsidies of human services and welfare functions that differ greatly among Florida's 67 counties.

It was also found that reformed counties tend to have better road pavement conditions. This corroborates the findings related to lower road expenditures. These findings are congruent with the reformed tradition theory that reformed governments are more cost-efficient than unreformed governments — in this case, better roads at a lower cost. Nonetheless, it is important to note that both the traditional reform movement and the public choice perspective were assumed as commingling conceptually to define reformed government. That is, reformed government is not at either extreme of the consolidated-public choice spectrum. On the contrary, reformed government is a measure of the best fit between forms of government on the one hand, and political, functional, and fiscal components of government reform on the other. That "best-fit" or ideal number of government units, number of elected officials, and form of government depends on population and other contextual metropolitan factors. Since some components of the county government reform index and the fragmentation level variable were operationalized based on such relative terms and not on absolute values, the connection to one theory or the other is not mutually exclusive. For instance, the county government reform index and the fragmentation variable take into account the number of government units but relative to the county's population and to the number of local governments statewide. Likewise, the number of elected officials also used in the definition of the variables is a value that depends on the county's population — this assumes that greater population demands greater numbers of elected officials to be responsive.

As such, neither the public-choice arguments for a greater number of smaller local governments, nor the traditional reform calls for fewer elected officials and consolidated government, are absolute truths. The traditional reform theory brings to mind a single highly centralized and consolidated large unit of government, whereas the public-choice model evokes a multi-layered myriad of local government units with overlapping functions and boundaries. Neither is a true picture. However, these mental constructs are the source of definitions used by researchers who may have focused on the rival explanations of the urban governance problem, resulting in "selective perception" (Dooley, 1990). This prevents the appropriate for-mulation and operationalization of critical constructs, resulting in conflict-ing results. It is hoped that the balanced methodology deployed here sheds critical light on the ongoing reform-public choice debate, drawing on insights from both sides to support its findings.

Notes

1. The commission form of government is inherently more function-ally fragmented than either the administrator or the executive mayor forms of government. This is due to the fact that commission form of government governs by plurality. No single person is responsible and accountable for policy implementation and decision making.
2. Urbanization is also used as a proxy for varying volumes and classification of traffic over county roads. It is assumed that more urbanized counties would also generate more commercial and industrial traffic in addition to larger traffic volumes (including residential traffic). Instead of adding more variables to the models and also increasing the multicollinearity threat, we opted for the urbanization variables.
3. Service delivery patterns have more to do with the state in which the county is located than urbanization or county population size. Some factors mentioned in the literature that are believed to influence county service delivery include: differing state laws regulating public debt and debt service; different state laws regarding county government deficits; varying levels of revenue-sharing and other funding transfers; varying uses of local property taxes; different levels of fiscal and administrative capacity; and diverse nature and level of unfunded mandates.

References

Barlow, I. *Metropolitan Government.* Routledge: New York, 1991.

Benton, J. and Menzel, D. County Services: The Emergence of Full-Service Government. In *County Governments in an Era of Change,* Berman, D., Ed.; Greenwood Press: Westport, Connecticut, 1993, 53–70.

Berman, D., Ed. *County Governments in an Era of Change.* Greenwood Press: Westport, Connecticut, 1993.

Bish, L. and Ostrom, V. *Understanding Urban Government: Metropolitan Reform Reconsidered.* American Enterprise for Public Policy Research: Washington, D.C., 1979.

Clark, T. "Community Structure, Decision-Making, Budget Expenditures, and Urban Renewal in 51 American Communities." *American Sociological Review* 3(4), 1968, 576–593.

Cole, R. "The Urban Policy Process: A Note on Structural and Regional Influences." *Social Science Quarterly 52,* 1971, 645–655.

DeSantis, V. "County Government: A Century of Change." In *The Municipal Yearbook 1989.* International City Management Association: Washington, D.C., 1989, 55–65.

DeSantis, V. and Renner, T. "Structure and Policy Expenditures in American Counties." In D.C. Menzel (ed), *The American Country: Frontiers of Knowledge* (pp. 80-91). Tuscaloosa, Alabama: The University of Alabama Press: Tuscaloosa, Alabama, 1996.

DeSantis, V. and Renner, T. "City Government Structures: An Attempt at Clarification." *State and Local Government Review* 34(2), 2002, 95–104.

Dooley, D. *Social Research Methods,* 2nd Ed. Prentice Hall: Englewood Cliffs, New Jersey, 1990.

Dye, T. and Garcia, J. "Structure, Function, and Policy in American Cities." *Urban Affairs Quarterly* 14 (September), 1978, 103–122.

Elazar, D. *American Federalism: A View from the States.* Thomas Y. Crowell: New York, 1966.

Florida Department of Transportation. *Roadway Characteristics Inventory Handbook.* Transportation Statistics Office: Tallahassee, Florida, 1998.

Kidd, C., Smith, E. and Kidder, L. *Research Methods in Social Relations.* Rinehart, and Winston: Orlando, Florida, 1991.

Lewis, C. "Interpreting Municipal Expenditures." In *Analyzing Urban-Service Distributions,* Rich, R., Ed.; D.C. Heath: Lexington, Massachusetts, 1982; 203–218.

Liebert, R. "Municipal Functions, Structure, and Expenditures: A Reanalysis of Recent Research." *Social Science Quarterly* 54 (March), 1974, 765–83.

Lineberry, R. and Fowler, E. "Reformism and Public Policies in American Cities." *American Political Science Review* 61, 1967, 701–717.

Littell, R., Freund, R. and Spector, P. *SAS System for Linear Models,* 3rd Ed. SAS Institute: Cary, North Carolina, 1991.

Lyons, W. "Reform and Response in American Cities: Structure and Policy Reconsidered." *Social Science Quarterly* 59(1), 1978, 118–132.

Marando, V. and Reeves, M. "Counties as Local Governments: Research Issues and Questions." *Journal of Urban Affairs* 13, 1991, 45–53.

Marando, V. and Reeves, M. "County Government Structural Reform: Influence of State, Region, and Urbanization." *Publius: The Journal of Federalism* 23 (Winter), 1993, 41–52.

Marando, V. and Thomas, R. *The Forgotten Governments: County Commissioners as Policy Makers.* University Presses of Florida: Gainesville, 1977.

Menzel, D. Ed. *The American County: Frontiers of Knowledge.* The University of Alabama Press: Tuscaloosa, Alabama, 1996.

Morgan, D. and Kickham, K. "Changing the Form of County Government: Effects on Revenue and Expenditure Policy." *Public Administration Review* 59 (July/August), 1999, 315–324.

Morgan, D. and Pelissero, J. "Urban Policy: Does Political Structure Matter?" *American Political Science Review* 74, 1980, 999–1006.

Osborne, D. and Plastrik, P. *The Reinventor's Handbook: Tools for Transforming Your Government.* Josey-Bass: San Francisco, 2000.

Ostrom, E. *The Delivery of Urban Services: Outcomes of Change.* Sage Publications: Beverly Hills, 1976.

Park, K. "Expenditure Patterns and Interactions among Local Governments in Metropolitan Areas." *Urban Affairs Quarterly* 29(4), 1994, 535–564.

Park, Y. *The Impacts of Reformed County Political Structures on County Policy Outcomes.* Ph.D. Dissertation, University of Southern California, 1995.

Schneider, M. and Park, K. "Metropolitan Counties as Service Delivery Agents: The Still Forgotten Governments." *Public Administration Review,* 1989, 345–352.

Sharp, E. "The Politics and Economics of the New City Debt." *American Political Science Review* 80(4), 1986, 1271–1288.

Stevens, J. *Applied Multivariate Statistics for the Social Sciences,* 2nd ed. Lawrence Erlbaum Associates Publishers: Hillsdale, New Jersey, 1992.

Stumm, T. "City Managers: Do They Promote Fiscal Efficiency?" *Journal of Urban Affairs* 20 (Summer), 1998, 343–349.

Svara, J. "The Structural Reform Impulse in Local Government: Its Past and Relevance to the Future." *National Civic Review* 83 (Summer-Fall), 1994, 323–346.

Tabachnick, B. and Fidell, L. *Using Multivariate Statistics,* 2nd ed. Harper & Row Publishers, Inc.: New York, New York, 1989.

Yin, R. *Case Study Research: Design and Methods,* 2nd ed. Sage Publications, Inc.: Thousand Oaks, California, 1994.

Chapter 23

Federal Performance Reporting Requirements: From Financial Management to E-Government

PATRICK R. MULLEN, Ph.D.
U.S. Government Accountability Office, Washington DC

In order for federal agencies to better manage and budget for their operations, Congress has enacted laws meant to address certain deficiencies. These laws require agencies to report on their progress in improving performance management, financial management, and information technology. Taken together, the laws require numerous reports, some of which are not as useful as they could be. In response to this problem, Congress has recently allowed agencies to consolidate their reports. An agency can now offer an integrated picture of performance in one report. Consolidated reporting can lead to better information for decision-makers in Congress, the executive branch, and the public. The opinions in this chapter are solely the author's and do not represent those of the U.S. General Accounting Office. He can be reached at mullenp@gao.gov.

23.1 Introduction

Complaints by federal managers about the number of congressional reporting requirements imposed on agencies have existed for a long time. For example, in a 1989 news conference, then Secretary of Defense Dick Cheney stood beside two ceiling-high stacks of reports and complained that congressional reporting requirements, while not all bad, were nevertheless excessive and impaired Pentagon efficiency. A little more than a decade later, Vice President Al Gore held a similar news conference, with even more stacks of reports, to make the same point (on a governmentwide basis) for the National Performance Review (NPR). As a result of an NPR recommendation, the Federal Reports Elimination and Sunset Act of 1995 (Public Law 104-66) was passed. Hundreds of reports were subsequently eliminated. But the need to consolidate reporting requirements, as well as reports, persists.

These reporting requirements are intended to promote a results-oriented management and decision-making process within Congress and the executive branch, as well as accountability to the American public. The requirements are included in laws in three broad categories:

- performance management, the Government Performance and Results Act of 1993 (GPRA);
- financial management, such as the Chief Financial Officers Act of 1990 (CFO Act); and
- information technology (IT), such as the Clinger-Cohen Act of 1996 (CCA).

The laws provide a framework for reports by federal agencies and programs. These reports help Members of Congress, who face a broad range of decisions as members of committees, including budget, authorization, oversight, and appropriations. They also help departmental and agency leadership, budget and planning analysts, the Office of Management and Budget (OMB), the General Accounting Office (GAO), and inspectors general (IGs) to carry out their management and oversight responsibilities. Because of the importance of these laws to reporting, it is essential that Congress and agency management understand both the difficulty in meeting requirements for reporting and the usefulness of moving toward consolidated reports.

23.2 Agencies Have Difficulty Meeting Reporting Requirements

The goals of requirements for agency reporting are (1) to provide Congress, as well as departmental and agency leadership, with useful information in carrying out effective oversight of programs and in making budgetary decisions and (2) to promote government accountability to the American public. But these reports have not been as successful at informing their intended audience as they could be. This is because lengthy and numerous reports — without clear, concise, and focused messages — are not likely to be read by busy congressional decision-makers or the American public. In addition, effectively implementing agency reporting requirements is difficult because of four issues:

- the complexities of the federal government's decision-making process,
- skepticism about lasting management reform,
- problems in developing realistic performance management goals and measures, and
- too many requirements create a "crowded management space."

The first three issues are discussed briefly. The last issue — "crowded management space" — the primary focus of this chapter, is developed extensively.

23.2.1 Complexities of the Decision-Making Process

The federal government's decision-making process is complex, and congressional reporting requirements add another layer of complexity with which federal managers have to cope. These requirements primarily relate to the laws for periodic reports from agencies to Congress to explain what programs are accomplishing. For example, the GPRA law draws on and even transplants concepts from private sector management models. In particular, GPRA establishes a system in which market like disciplines can be used to improve management of the federal government, including setting performance goals and holding agencies accountable for program results. The focus on program results is made more complex, however, by the lack of good performance measures to use in reports. As Donald F. Kettl (1977) commented: "Successful performance management systems hinge on careful integration of politics and management. Elected officials are the ultimate audience for agency performance measures. The measures offer great potential for improving legislative oversight; it is easier to ask good questions about results if results-based information is readily available."

This observation meshes with a principle of public administration propounded by Ronald C. Moe and Robert S. Gilmore (1995): "Policy and program objectives specifically agreed to and incorporated into enabling legislation, subject to reasonable standards of measurement and compliance, facilitate effective implementation." For example, passing and implementing GPRA necessitated extensive discussions between OMB, GAO, executive agencies, and congressional committees to determine answers to these two questions: What should the laws require? What constitutes good performance-based reports? The answers, however, are complicated by the structure of government. As Beryl A. Radin (1998) notes in a section aptly named "The Context of Fragmentation, Decentralization, and Devolution," although the aims of management reporting suggest that the information produced will support more rational decision-making, the structure of the government makes this extremely difficult. Factors such as the need for increased management capacity at OMB, political hostilities, divided government, and fragmented congressional power compound the problems.

Fragmentation exists in Congress, Radin (1999) also notes, in its role as receiver — through the various reports that go to different committees (e.g., authorizing, appropriations, and budget committees in the House and Senate) — of management information for review. Therefore, agencies are asked for different responses from these different committees. Anticipating congressional responses to reporting is a challenge for agency managers, according to Kathryn E. Newcomer and Aaron A. Otto (1999–2000); this challenge is made even more so, given the polemical and politically charged rhetoric that sometimes comes from the Congress in press releases on GPRA reports from agencies.

23.2.2 Skepticism about Lasting Management Reform

Some observers (Radin, 1998) of management laws initially raised questions as to whether laws like GPRA may become another flavor-of-the-month reform, which could go the way of so many others. Examples of past management initiatives — which have attempted reform, but did not last — include applying planning-programming-budgeting systems (PPBS) in non-defense agencies, management by objectives (MBO), and zero-base budgeting (ZBB). Generally, however, most experts in the field currently view GPRA and similar management laws as reflecting a trend to try to increase (1) public confidence in government and (2) government effectiveness and accountability. To realize this trend increased responsibility is delegated to managers. They are required to report to Congress and the public on the results of program accomplishments in relation to goals. Success in carrying out these requirements is difficult, with many problems, as discussed below. Lack of success — in developing or meeting management goals, whether for GPRA or other management laws — can potentially generate skepticism about whether these reform laws are accomplishing their intended effects.

23.2.3 *Problems Developing Realistic Performance Management Goals and Measures*

There are significant problems in developing realistic performance goals and measures, as required by GPRA, for many government programs. In addition, these goals and measures should include consideration of financial management and IT. But creating yet another set of reporting requirements without an understanding of the complexity involved "runs the risk of poisoning an otherwise promising effort," as Philip G. Joyce (1993) cautions. For example, each of the performance measurement systems the Congressional Budget Office analyzed, he points out, required a great deal of data in order to survive, and much of the data produced was never used. This suggests that before setting out reporting requirements for goals and measures, it is necessary to think through how information will be used and how performance management reporting will be put into effect. Ultimately, Joyce concludes, the budget process is not likely to change substantially until, and unless, decision-makers use information from required reports when making budget-allocation decisions for programs.

The problems in developing realistic performance goals and measures are also illustrated in critiques of agency performance by congressional leaders. For example, for fiscal year 1999 performance reports, Senator Fred Thompson, Chairman of the Senate Committee on Governmental Affairs, on Oct. 31, 2000 released "grades" for 24 of the largest federal agencies. Senator Thompson based the grades he gave on analyses — by GAO, the Congressional Research Service, and George Mason University's Mercatus Center — of the agencies' performance reports, including initial plans, as well as related IG reports. While the performance reports were required to inform Congress and the public about what agencies are doing and how well they are doing it, the Senator stated, the reports were not meeting that requirement. In particular, agencies failed to identify the goals they had established to accomplish their primary missions. Seven different agencies, he noted, identified "reducing the availability of illegal drugs" as part of their missions, yet "none of them had a specific performance target for actually doing that." Senator Thompson praised three agencies — Transportation, the Social Security Administration, and the Veterans Administration — for demonstrating "a commitment to results-oriented performance and accountability." The performance management in these three agencies therefore can serve as models for other agencies, so they can improve the usefulness of their performance reports to Congress.

Factors that influence the quality of performance goals and measures, as well as the subsequent utilization of agency reports, include the credibility of the office preparing the report, political circumstances, relevance to stakeholder information needs, continued stakeholder involvement in the performance management process, the report timeliness, and clarity of the message (Wholey and Hatry, 1992; Newcomer and Otto, 1999–2000). As discussed later, Congress has made it possible for agencies to improve their performance reporting by (1) providing positive feedback to agencies and (2) taking legislative actions.

23.2.4 Too Many Requirements Create "Crowded Management Space"

The term "crowded management space," used by Beryl Radin (1998), means that, at the same time agencies are responsible for implementing GPRA, they are also responsible for implementing numerous other management requirements established by law, executive orders, and OMB directives. Each of these requirements, she notes, has a unique internal logic, but this logic is sometimes incompatible with that in other requirements. This incompatibility can lead to differing decisions about appropriate policy objectives. In addition, these requirements, which are supposed to reinforce one another, are often given to different staff units, each with their own perspectives on what needs to be done to accomplish each requirement's objectives. Thus, within a department or agency, the budget office, planning office, financial office, evaluation office, or other units are responsible for satisfying the various requirements of differing reporting laws.

The term crowded management space also applies to the number of reports that Congress has to deal with. Because each management law has many requirements, several reports may be required for each one and sometimes by different agencies. The number of reporting requirements has occasionally been reviewed and assessed by Congress, to determine whether (1) the executive branch is adequately responding to the requirements and (2) the reporting requirements are still meeting their intended purposes or are an unreasonable burden. For example, in 1982, Congress passed the Congressional Reports Elimination Act and, in 1995, the Federal Reports Elimination and Sunset Act. The Reports Consolidation Act, passed in 2000, discussed in more detail below, continues the goal of report elimination by encouraging agencies, OMB, and congressional committees to examine how reports can be consolidated to better utilize government resources. In addition, the crowded management space can be seen in the relationship of the reports to the congressional budget schedule, set by the Congressional Budget Act of 1974 (2 U.S.C. 601-661), as shown in Figure 23.1. While this act created a timetable for the budget process, in reality the schedule is often modified.

Finally, the crowded management space refers to the crowded statutory framework, which includes several laws, with different reporting requirements, that agencies must follow. These laws can be grouped into the three broad categories mentioned earlier — performance management, financial management, and IT. Each of the laws contains different reporting requirements, due at a specified time during the fiscal year. All of the laws require reports to provide information to Congress, and some require additional reports to or from agency heads, OMB, GAO, or IGs. The congressional reporting laws that require reports to be submitted to Congress are summarized in Table 23.1.

As illustrated in Table 23.1, laws with reporting requirements can be grouped into performance management, financial management, and IT. For each of these categories the major reporting requirements are discussed below.

23.2.4.1 Performance Management: The Government Performance and Results Act (GPRA)

Perhaps the best known performance management law is GPRA, or the "Results Act," as it is referred to by many in Congress. As required by the Act, all major agencies must submit strategic plans to Congress by September 30th each year, starting in 1997. Each agency's strategic plan, as well as the congressional consultation process, has started to provide an important opportunity to establish the foundation for making improvements in federal management. These strategic plans should eventually prove useful to Congress in undertaking the full range of its responsibilities — appropriation, budget, authorization, and oversight — and to agencies in setting a general direction for their efforts. So far, the plans appear to provide a workable foundation for the next phase of GPRA's implementation, discussed below. This implementation means submission of annual performance planning reports, including goals and measures, to Congress. Nonetheless, the agencies' strategic planning efforts and, more generally, overall implementation of GPRA itself, most observers agree, are still very much a work in progress. The strategic plans that agencies provided to Congress and OMB are only the starting point for the broad transformation

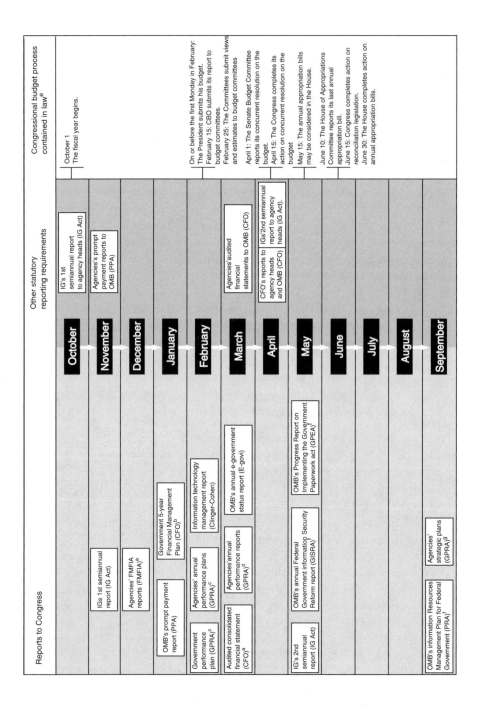

Figure 23.1   Time line for reporting requirements of selected laws.

Legend

CFO Act	Chief Financial Officers Act, 1993
CCA	Clinger-Cohen Act, 1996
E-gov	Electronic Government Act, 2002
FMFIA	Federal Manager's Financial Integrity Act, 1982
GISRA	Government Information Security Reform Act, 1982
GPES	Government Paperwork Elimination Act, 1998
GPRA	Government Performance and Results Act, 1993
IG Act	Inspector General Act, 1978
PPA	Prompt Payment Act, 1982
PRA	Paperwork Reduction Act, 1995

[a]The law requires the submission of these reports to the President at the same time that they are submitted to Congress.

[b]In practice, these reports are generally issued in June and include OMB's prompt payment report, as well as the status report on credit mangement and debt collection required by the Debt Collection Act of 1982 (DCA), as amended.

[c]GPRA requires these performance plans, beginning with fiscal year 1999.

[d]The first of an angency's reports, on program performance for fiscal year 1999, was due to Congress and the President by March 31, 1999.

[e]Congressional Budget Act of 1974, 2 U.S.C. 631; this schedule is often modified.

[f]PRA, GISRA, and GPEA each require an annual report from OMB, but do not specify when they are due. OMB submitted the last PRA report in September and the GISRA and GPEA reports in May.

[g]GPRA required agencies' first strategic plans by Septem 30, 1997. They are to be update at least every three years and submitted to OMB and Congress.

Source: Analysis of laws cited above, examination of required reports to Congress, and the congressional budget schedule as established in the Congressional Budget and Impoundment Control Act of 1974.

Table 23.1 Laws With Congressional Reporting Requirements

Law by category	Purpose
Performance management	
Government Performance and Results Act of 1993 (GPRA)	• Hold federal agencies accountable for program results • Require federal agencies to clarify their missions • Set program goals and measure performance toward achieving those goals
Financial management	
The Inspector General Act of 1978 (IG Act)	• Combat waste, fraud and abuse by establishing IG offices in federal departments and agencies
Prompt Payment Act of 1982 (PPA)	• Encourage government managers to improve their bill- paying procedures
Federal Managers' Financial Integrity Act of 1982 (FMFIA)	• Establish a framework for ongoing evaluations of agency systems for internal accounting and administrative control
Debt Collection Act of 1982 (DCA) and Debt Collection Improvement Act of 1996 (DCIA)	• Require the heads of agencies to collect debts owed the federal government • Authorize the compromise of some debts and suspension of collection actions in particular circumstances • Authorize federal agencies to use certain collection tools
Chief Financial Officers Act of 1993 (CFO Act)	• Improve and strengthen federal financial management and accountability
Government Management Reform Act of 1994 (GMRA)	• Preparation and audit of 24 agencywide financial statements • Preparation and audit of consolidated financial statements for the federal government
Federal Financial Management Improvement Act of 1996 (FFMIA)	• Ensure that agency financial management systems comply with requirements of federal financial management system • Provide uniform, reliable, and useful financial information
Information technology (IT)	
Computer Security Act of 1987 (CSA)	• Improve the security and privacy of sensitive information in federal computer systems
Paperwork Reduction Act of 1995 (PRA)	• Minimize the public's paperwork burdens • Coordinate federal information resources management

Table 23.1   Continued

Law by category	Purpose
	• Improve dissemination of public information • Ensure the integrity of the federal statistical system
Clinger-Cohen Act of 1996 (CCA)	• Improve federal programs through improved acquisition, use, and disposal of information technology resources
Government Paperwork Elimination Act of 1998 (GPEA)	• Require federal agencies to provide the public, when practicable, the option of submitting, maintaining, and disclosing required information electronically
Government Information Security Reform Act of 2001 (GISRA)	• Directs federal agencies to conduct annual IT security reviews • Inspectors general (IGs) to perform annual independent evaluations of agency programs and systems and report results to OMB • OMB to (1) report annually to Congress on governmentwide progress and (2) issue guidance to agencies on reporting instructions and quantitative performance measures
E-Government Act of 2002 (E-Gov)	• Promote the use of the Internet and other IT to provide government services electronically • Strengthen agency information security • Define how to manage the federal government's growing IT human capital needs • Establish an Office of Electronic Government, within OMB, to provide strong central leadership and full-time commitment to promoting and implementing e-government

that is needed to successfully implement performance management, and difficult implementation issues still remain.

In addition to strategic planning reports, GPRA requires agencies to submit annual performance reports to the President and Congress (beginning March 31, 2000), covering performance for the previous fiscal year. Reports beginning in fiscal year 2002 must include actual results for the three preceding fiscal years. The performance reports must cover the following:

- Review how successfully performance goals were achieved.
- Evaluate the performance plan for the current year, relative to the performance goals achieved during the fiscal year(s) covered.

- Explain and describe, where goals are not met, (1) why the goals were not met, (2) plans and schedules for achieving the goals, and (3) if the goals are impractical or infeasible, why that is the case and what action is recommended.
- Describe the use and assess the effectiveness in achieving performance goals of any waiver under 31 U.S.C. 9703.
- Include the summary findings of program evaluations completed during the fiscal year.

Several challenges to effective implementation of GPRA include overlapping and fragmented crosscutting program efforts, the often limited or indirect influence that the federal government has in determining whether a desired result is achieved, and the lack of results-oriented performance information. Instilling an organizational culture that focuses on results remains a work in progress: linking agencies' performance plans directly to the budget process has not yet taken place and has faced difficulties within both the agencies and Congress. Addressing some of these challenges will raise significant policy issues for Congress and the administration to consider and will most likely be difficult to resolve.

23.2.4.2 Financial Management: The Chief Financial Officers (CFO) Act

The CFO Act is the legislative basis for the federal government's providing reliable financial information, through audited financial statements, to taxpayers, the nation's leaders, and agency program managers. The Act is also the basis for improving the federal government's financial systems, providing a focus on reporting program results to Congress, in particular the Senate Governmental Affairs and House Government Reform Committees. The Act centralizes the establishment and oversight of federal financial management policies and practices within OMB, primarily through the deputy director for management and the OMB Office of Federal Financial Management.

The Act requires 24 agencies to have chief financial officers and deputy chief financial officers and specifies their authority and functions. The Act also sets up a series of pilot audits, requiring certain agencies to prepare agencywide financial statements and subject them to audit by the agencies' IGs. For each of these agencies, the first of these statements was due in March 1997; beginning in 1997, the Treasury Department started to report to Congress on a consolidated financial statement for the federal government. The Government Management Reform Act (GMRA), discussed below, also requires GAO to audit this financial statement annually, with the first audit required in early 1998. In addition, the CFO Act requires OMB to prepare a congressional report on a five-year governmentwide financial management plan. This report is to describe what OMB and agency CFOs plan to do over the next five years to improve the financial management of the federal government. OMB is also required to submit to Congress, by January 31 each year, an updated five-year financial management plan, to cover the succeeding five fiscal years, and an annual financial management status report. The annual report is to provide the following information:

- A description and analysis of the status of financial management in the executive branch.
- A summary of the most recently completed agency financial statements, financial statement audits, and reports.
- A summary of reports on agency internal accounting and administrative control systems, submitted to the President and Congress under the Federal Managers' Financial Integrity Act (FMFIA).
- Any other information OMB considers appropriate to fully inform Congress about financial management of the federal government.

In addition, the Act requires agencies to prepare and annually revise their plans to implement OMB's 5-year financial management plan. Other requirements address the need for the systematic process of reform; the development of cost information; and the integration of program, financial, and budget systems.

23.2.4.3 Financial Management: The Government Management Reform Act (GMRA)

GMRA expands the requirements relating to fully auditing financial statements under the CFO Act. GMRA requirements affect the 24 agencies already covered by the CFO Act, and allow for federal entities other than agencies, to be designated by OMB, to be covered.[1] Beginning with fiscal year 1997, auditors for each of the 24 major departments and agencies must report, as part of their annual audits of the financial statements, whether the financial management systems comply substantially with

- federal financial management systems requirements,
- applicable federal accounting standards, and
- the standard general ledger (SGL).

GMRA also requires GAO to report on implementation of the Act, starting in 1997, and by the beginning of each fiscal year thereafter.

Of particular note in relation to congressional reporting requirements is the Act's enhancement of OMB's authority to manage agency submissions of reports to Congress, the President, and OMB. This enhancement of authority resulted in OMB's pilot accountability report, which consolidated reporting

requirements under GPRA and CFO acts, as well as FMFIA, the Prompt
Payment Act (PPA), and the Debt Collection Act (DCA).

23.2.4.4 Financial Management: The Inspector General (IG) Act

The IG Act identifies 26 federal agencies that are required to have an IG who
is appointed by the President and confirmed by the Senate. The act also
designates 30 federal entities other than agencies, each of which is to have
an IG appointed by the appropriate head official. Each IG must prepare
semiannual reports, no later than April 30 and October 31 of each year, that
summarize the IG's activities. The head of each agency transmits these
reports, unaltered, to Congress and subsequently makes them available to
the public.

Since passage of the IG Act, IGs have been combating fraud, waste,
and abuse and promoting economy, efficiency, and effectiveness by
(1) strengthening federal internal audit and investigative activities and
(2) improving operations within the federal government. However, during
the 1990s, legislation — such as GPRA, the CFO Act, and GMRA — has
dramatically changed the management and accountability of the federal
government and, in turn, has demanded shifts in the IGs' focus and
contributions. It is critical for IGs to keep pace with such changes, various
chairmen of House and Senate oversight committees have observed, and
ensure that IG work continues to provide meaningful insight for evaluating
and measuring the government's effectiveness.

23.2.4.5 Information Technology (IT): The Clinger-Cohen Act (CCA)

The CCA, like the Acts discussed above, imposes rather detailed reporting
requirements on federal agencies (Mullen, 2004 and forthcoming). The CCA
requires OMB to do the following:

- Issue directives to executive agencies concerning capital planning
  and investment control, revisions to mission-related and administrative processes, and information security.
- Promote and improve the acquisition and use of IT through performance management.
- Use the budget process to (1) analyze, track, and evaluate the risks
  and results of major agency capital investments in IT and information csystems and (2) enforce accountability of agency heads.
- Report to Congress on the agencies' progress and accomplishments.

CCA also requires additional reports to Congress from OMB, agency
heads, and GAO.

23.2.4.6   Information Technology (IT): The Government Paperwork Elimination Act (GPEA)

GPEA authorizes OMB to provide for acquisition and use of alternative IT by federal agencies. Alternative IT includes (1) electronic submission, maintenance, or disclosure of information as a substitute for paper and (2) electronic signatures in conducting government business through e-government transactions. The law calls for the Director of OMB, in conjunction with the National Telecommunications and Information Administration, to study the use of electronic signatures in e-government transactions and periodically report to Congress on the results of the study.

23.2.4.7   Information Technology (IT): Government Information Security Reform Act (GISRA)

GISRA is intended to do the following:

1. To provide a comprehensive framework for establishing and ensuring the effectiveness of controls over information resources that support federal operations and assets.
2. To recognize the highly networked nature of the federal-computing environment, including the need for federal government interoperability and, in the implementation of improved security management measures, ensure that opportunities for interoperability are not adversely affected.
3. To provide effective governmentwide management and oversight of related security risks, including coordination of information security efforts throughout the civilian, national security, and law enforcement communities.
4. To provide for development and maintenance of the minimum controls required to protect federal information and information systems.
5. To provide a mechanism for improved oversight of information security programs in federal agencies.

23.2.4.8   Information technology (IT): The E-Government Act (E-Gov)

E-Gov[2] was passed to enhance the management and promotion of e-government services and processes. To increase citizen access to government information and services, the law established a federal Chief Information Officer (CIO) in an Office of E-Government within OMB — which oversees information resources management (IRM), including development and application in the federal government — and established a broad framework of measures that require the use of Internet-based IT. The act also authorizes $45 million for an e-government fund in the U.S. Treasury to pay for IT projects aimed at linking agencies and facilitating information sharing.

The act is designed to streamline the government's information resources, close security gaps, and create more public-centered Web sites. In addition, E-Gov does the following:

- Directs OMB to establish an interagency committee on government information and to issue guidelines for agency Web sites.
- Requires federal courts to establish Web sites with information about the court and cases being presented.
- Requires federal agencies to adhere to uniform security standards for information.
- Creates an IT interchange program between the private and public sectors.
- Authorizes governmentwide use of share-in-savings contracts, which permit agencies to pay contractors using savings realized through technological improvements.
- Requires federal agencies and OMB to submit reports to Congress.

As shown in this section, there are many reporting requirements affecting federal IT and e-government. The next section discusses what these reports tell Congress about the current state of IT and e-government activities.

23.3 Agencies Moving Toward Consolidated Reports

On November 22, 2000, President Bill Clinton signed the Reports Consolidation Act of 2000 (RCA) (P.L. 106–531), which authorizes each federal agency to consolidate, into one annual report, several different performance management, financial management, and IT reports required by law. The consolidated report would present, in one document, a comprehensive and integrated picture of each agency's performance. Such an integrated picture would be more useful to Congress, the executive branch, and the public. As noted above, OMB had authority to consolidate reports on a pilot basis, but that authority expired in April 2000. The RCA restores that consolidation authority to OMB, making it permanent; the act also contains several enhancements designed to make the reports more useful. The reasons Congress passed this law mirror some of the concerns about numerous reporting requirements discussed earlier. The reasons are summarized in the legislation:

> (a) FINDINGS. Congress finds that:
> > (1) existing law imposes numerous financial and per-formance management reporting requirements on agencies;
> > (2) these separate requirements can cause duplication of effort on the part of agencies and result in uncoordi-nated reports containing information in a form that is not completely useful to Congress; and
> > (3) pilot projects conducted by agencies under the direction of the Office of Management and Budget demonstrate that single consolidated reports providing an analysis of verifiable financial and performance management information produce more useful reports with greater efficiency.[3]

In remarks introducing the legislation on the House floor, Congressmen Steve Horn (R-Ca.) and Jim Turner (D-Tx.) discussed the benefits of con-solidating reporting requirements into one document that would be more useful to recipients:

> [Mr. Horn]: The consolidated reports would present in one document an integrated picture of an agency's performance. As such, they will be more useful to Congress, to the executive branch, and to the public ... Congress has attempted to instill the principles of performance-based management throughout the Federal Government. The report authorized by this bill would give Congress and the American people a single source of information about the management of each Federal agency. This information is critically important if Congress is to hold agencies accountable for the resources it spends to do the people's business.
> [Mr. Turner]: This is a good government piece of legislation that would allow all of our Federal agencies to consolidate into a single annual report a whole variety of different financial and performance reports that they are required by law to submit. This will go a long way toward reducing administrative burdens within the agencies and avoid unnecessary duplication. It is a provision that will allow the public and the Congress and the agencies themselves to see in one document a variety of various reports that need to be in one place in order to adequately review

them and to make them more useful to this Congress in pursuing our goal of trying to improve the efficiency and the effectiveness of the Federal agencies.[4]

Each agency can submit a consolidated report within 180 days from the end of fiscal year 2000 and fiscal year 2001 and within 150 days from the end of every fiscal year thereafter. The Act requires that each consolidated report has two assessments: (1) by the agency head, which describes the reliability of the agency's performance data, and (2) by the agency IG, which addresses the agency's most serious management challenges.

Report consolidation has been a long-standing discussion topic among agencies producing the many reports called for by the various congressional reporting requirements of the 1990s. FFMIA was passed to address the need for consolidated reports, which would be useful in efficiently and effectively managing the day-to-day operations of the federal government and provide accountability to taxpayers. The central challenge in producing such reports has been seen as one of (1) overhauling inadequate and outdated systems relating to financial management and (2) upgrading IT capability. For example, GAO reported that 21 of 24 agencies covered by the CFO Act did not comply substantially with FFMIA's requirements.[5]

Now that agencies will be allowed to consolidate reports into one annual report, the challenge will be how to do so successfully. There are a number of sources of guidance on how reports can be successfully consolidated. For example, GAO has issued much guidance on how to improve agency reporting.[6] In addition, in 2000, OMB issued instructions (Circular A-11) and letters to agencies on requirements for report content and OMB's review procedures. Nongovernmental sources of guidance about producing useful agency reports are also available, for example, from George Mason University's Mercatus Center (McTigue, Ellig, and Richardson, 2001) and the PricewaterhouseCoopers Endowment for the Business of Government (Newcomer and Shirer, 2001).

To help Congress assess each year's reports and help agencies improve the quality of their next year's reports, a Mercatus Center research team evaluates the reports produced by the 24 agencies covered under the CFO Act. The Mercatus team uses 12 criteria to answer three questions:

- Does the agency report its accomplishments in a transparent fashion?
- Does the report focus on documenting tangible public benefits the agency produced?
- Does the report show evidence of forward-looking leadership that uses performance information to devise strategies for improvement?

The Mercatus Center said the three requirements that many agencies met best were (1) improving the readability of the reports, (2) clearly articulating results-based goals, and (3) discussing major management challenges. The three requirements that many agencies had the greatest difficulty meeting were (1) making reports accessible to the public (for example, posting reports on agency Web sites), (2) demonstrating a cause-and-effect relationship between the agency's actions and observed outcomes, and (3) linking performance data to costs. However, a few agencies did these well.

Congress and the new Bush administration have taken additional steps to reinforce the need for improving reports and incorporating performance information into congressional decision-making. The Rules Committee, U.S. House of Representatives, adopted the following rule change, on January 3, 2001, for the 107th Congress:

> Performance Goals and Objectives. The requirement that committee reports include a summary of oversight findings and recommendations by the Committee on Government Reform, if timely submitted, is repealed and replaced with a new requirement that committee reports include a statement of general performance goals and objectives, including outcome-related goals and objectives, for which the measure authorizes funding.[7]

This means that every piece of authorizing legislation coming out of the House will be required to have a performance goal associated with it and will increase congressional scrutiny of agency reports.[8] In addition, President George W. Bush spelled out his core proposals for government reform in his President's Management Agenda. One proposal is to enforce GPRA by recommending higher levels of funding for programs that work, as demonstrated by meeting performance goals. Agency IGs are also being called upon to enforce the accuracy of GPRA reports. For example, OMB is to factor the results — the information on performance — into its budget decisions. As Joseph Wholey (1999) noted, "GPRA is beginning to change the dialogue with Congress and in the OMB, that is, the way in which people talk about policy choice." The recent emphasis on carrying out GPRA and other related laws should continue to provide more useful information to congressional decision-makers and improve the quality of the policy dialog.

23.4 Conclusions

The purpose of reporting requirements is to strengthen management controls and processes to increase agency accountability. The information required in reports to Congress is intended to be a valuable resource for Congress. It can use this information in carrying out program authorization, oversight, and appropriations responsibilities, as well as to ensure the public a more accountable and responsive government. An excessive number of reports on different issues within an agency are not likely to get the attention of busy congressional decision-makers or the public. One consolidated report — containing useful and understandable information dealing with an agency's performance management, financial management, and IT issues — is more likely to fulfill the intent of laws with reporting requirements: to produce useful information that had not previously been available. The information in a user-friendly, one-volume report is much more likely to be read and acted upon. To be most useful, each report should be readable (include an executive summary and be as brief as possible) and easily available on agency Web sites (Mullen, 2003).

Notes

1.   OMB has designated the military services, the Health Care Financing Administration, and the Internal Revenue Service as entities that must prepare audited financial statements.

2.   U.S. Congress. *E-Government Act of 2002*, P.L. 107-347. Title III of the E-Government Act is also referred to as the *Federal Information Security Management Act* (FISMA). FISMA lays out a framework for annual IT security reviews, reporting, and remediation planning.

3.   Reports Consolidation Act of 2000, sec. 2(a).

4.   See *Congressional Record.* 106th Cong., 2d sess., Oct. 26, 2000: H11349-51.

5.   This includes requirements for federal financial management systems; applicable federal accounting standards; and the U.S. Government standard general ledger, which provides a chart of standard accounts and transactions that agencies are to use in all financial systems. See U.S. General Accounting Office, *Financial Management: Federal Financial Management Improvement Act Results for Fiscal Year 1999* GAO/AIMD-00-307 (Washington, D.C.: GAO, Sept. 2000).

6.   See, for example, U.S. General Accounting Office, Managing for Results: Critical Issues for Improving Federal Agencies' Strategic Plans GAO/GGD-97-180 (Washington, D.C.: GAO, Sept. 1997) and Agencies' Annual Performance Plans Under the Results Act: An Assessment Guide to Facilitate Congressional Decisionmaking GAO/GGD/AIMD-10.1.18 (Washington, D.C.: GAO, Feb. 1998). This and other related guidance are available on GAO's Web site at www.gao.gov.

7. Rule XIII, clause 3[c]; rule X, clause 4[c][2].
8. It is too early to assess the impact of this requirement.

References

Joyce, Philip, "Using Performance Measures for Federal Budgeting: Proposals and Prospects." *Public Budgeting and Finance* 13 (Winter 1993): 3–17.

Kettl, Donald, "The Global Revolution in Public Management Systems: Driving Themes and Missing Links." *Journal of Policy Analysis and Management* 16 (1997): 446–462.

McTigue, Maurice, Ellig, Jerry, and Richardson, Steve, "2nd Annual Performance Report Scorecard: Which Federal Agencies Inform the Public?" Arlington, Va.: Mercatus Center, George Mason University, 2001.

Moe, Ronald, and Gilmore, Robert, "Rediscovering Principles of Public Administration." *Public Administration Review* 55 (1995): 135–146.

Mullen, Patrick, "The Need For Government-wide Information Capacity." *Social Science Computer Review,* edited by David Garson. Idea Group Publishing, Hershey, PA. (2003).

Mullen, Patrick, "Information Technology and E-Government Performance Reporting Requirements." *Handbook of Public Information,* 2nd ed., edited by David Garson. Idea Group Publishing, Hershey, PA. (2004).

Mullen, Patrick, "U.S. Performance-Based Laws: Information Technology and E-Government Reporting Requirements." *International Journal of Public Administration,* edited by David Garson. Marcel Dekker, Inc., New York (Forthcoming).

Newcomer, Kathryn, and Otto, Aaron, "Are We Improving the Performance of the Government Through GPRA?" *The Public Manager* 28 (Winter 1999–2000): 21.

Newcomer, Kathryn, and Scheirer, Mary Ann, *Using Evaluation to Support Performance Management: A Guide for Federal Executives.* Washington, D.C.: PricewaterhouseCoopers Endowment for the Business of Government, 2001.

Radin, Beryl, "The Government Performance and Results Act (GPRA): Hydra-headed Monster or Flexible Management Tool?" *Public Administration Review* 58 (July–Aug. 1998): 307–316.

Radin, Beryl, "The Government Performance and Results Act (GPRA) and the Tradition of Federal Management Reform: Square Pegs in Round Holes?" (Paper presented at the National Public Management Conference, Texas A and M University, Dec. 3–4, 1999).

U.S. Congress, Chief Financial Officers Act of 1990 (CFO), P.L. 101–576.

U.S. Congress, Clinger-Cohen Act of 1996 (CCA), P.L. 104–208. (Note: The Omnibus Consolidated Appropriations Act of 1996 (P.L. 104–208) included provisions for both FFMIA and CCA.)

U.S. Congress, Computer Security Act of 1987 (CSA), as amended, P.L. 100–235.

U.S. Congress, Debt Collection Act of 1982 (DCA), as amended, P.L. 97–365, and Debt Collection Improvement Act of 1996 (DCIA), P.L. 104–134.

U.S. Congress, E-Government Act of 2002 (E-Gov), P.L. 107–347.

U.S. Congress, Federal Financial Management Improvement Act of 1996 (FFMIA), P.L. 104–208.

U.S. Congress, Federal Managers' Financial Integrity Act of 1982 (FMFIA), P.L. 97–255.

U.S. Congress, Federal Reports Elimination and Sunset Act of 1995, P.L. 104–66.

U.S. Congress, Government Information Security Reform Act of 2001 (GISRA), P.L. 106–39.

U.S. Congress, Government Management Reform Act of 1994 (GMRA), P.L. 103–356.

U.S. Congress, Government Paperwork Elimination Act of 1998 (GPEA), P.L. 105–277.

U.S. Congress, Government Performance and Results Act of 1993 (GPRA), P.L. 103–62.

U.S. Congress, Inspector General Act of 1978 (IG Act), as amended, P.L. 95–452.

U.S. Congress, Paperwork Reduction Act of 1995 (PRA), P.L. 104–13.

U.S. Congress, Prompt Payment Act of 1982 (PPA), P.L. 97–177.

U.S. Congress, Reports Consolidation Act of 2000, P.L. 106–531.

U.S. Congress, *Congressional Record*. 106th Cong., 2d sess., Oct. 26, 2000: H11349–51.

U.S. Congressional Budget Office, Using Performance Measures in the Federal Budget Process (July 1993).

U.S. General Accounting Office, Agencies' Annual Performance Plans Under the Results Act: An Assessment Guide to Facilitate Congressional Decisionmaking GAO/GGD/AIMD-10.1.18 (Washington, D.C.: GAO, Feb. 1998).

U.S. General Accounting Office, Financial Management: Federal Financial Management Improvement Act Results for Fiscal Year 1999 GAO/AIMD-00-307 (Washington, D.C.: GAO, Sept. 2000).

U.S. General Accounting Office, *Managing for Results: Critical Issues for Improving Federal Agencies' Strategic Plans* GAO/GGD-97-180 (Washington, D.C.: GAO, Sept. 1997).

Wholey, Joseph S., "Performance-Based Management: Responding to the Challenges." *Public Productivity and Management Review* 22 (1999): 288–307.

Wholey, Joseph S., and Hatry, Harry P., "The Case for Performance Monitoring." *Public Administration Review* 52 (Nov–Dec. 1992): 604–610.

INTERNATIONAL
PERSPECTIVES

Chapter 24

Public Finance Reform in Selected British Commonwealth Countries

JAYESH D'SOUZA
Public Administration Program and Metropolitan Center,
Florida International University

24.1 Introduction

It is a good bet to predict that the number of public financial systems vary with the number of countries that exist globally. Broadly speaking, some countries have designed their public financial systems in accordance with the British model while others, the American. There are still some countries whose systems display similarities with the old Soviet model of central planning. Yet other financial systems exhibit nuances of the Dutch, French and Portuguese colonialist models. Accordingly, the features of these systems differ widely from each other. Take budget timetables as an example. Premchand explains that budgetary timetables that follow the British system are generally short "in that it takes about sixteen months before the start of the fiscal year for the budget to be prepared ... supplementary budgets are also traditionally submitted thrice during the year. In the US-based systems, the long lead time contributes to unrealistic budget estimates." (Premchand, 1999).

No matter what the differences among public financial systems around the world, they have been impacted by common factors. Poor public sector performance and fiscal crises caused by large budget deficits have forced governments to pay particular attention on the way they function. 'Value-for-money' is the new buzzword in public finance used to describe the re-alignment of government's fiscal priorities. This has involved the re-allocation of program expenditures and enhanced cost-effectiveness in their delivery. As Campos and Pradhan put it, "Leaner budgets have meant that some program expenditures have to be cut and improved efficiency could help offset some of the cuts. Which expenditures to cut and how they can be achieved have indeed become equally pressing problems." (Campos and Pradhan, 1997). This gave impetus to works like Osborne and Gaebler's *Reinventing Government: How The Entrepreneurial Spirit is Transforming the Public Sector* (1993) and governmental programs such as the United Kingdom's Next Steps program. (Campos and Pradhan, 1997).

Addressing these problems has required substantial reform in financial management and budgetary processes. Current reform initiatives, commonly discussed under the rubric of New Public Management (NPM), "describe a management culture that emphasizes the centrality of the citizen or customer, as well as accountability for results. They also suggest structural or organizational choices that promote decentralized control through a wide variety of alternative service delivery mechanisms, including quasi-markets with public and private service providers competing for resources from policymakers and donors. NPM does *not* claim that government should stop performing certain tasks. Although it often is associated with this policy perspective, NPM is *not* about whether tasks should be undertaken or not. It is about getting things done better." (Manning, 2000).

In short, modern-day governments are out to achieve fiscal responsibility. For the purpose of our research, we define fiscal responsibility "in terms of two dimensions:

- first, it implies that government budget setting — outlays, revenues, and balances — are determined so that they promote strong, sustainable growth in economic activity and employment. In addition, it implies that government budgets are themselves sustainable, and do not store up problems for future generations, including by racking up high public debts; and
- second, being fiscally responsible implies that government operates efficiently and effectively — in raising revenue and in spending taxpayers' money. This aspect of fiscal responsibility can help to bolster the first." (French, 1997).

In consideration of the above, this chapter sheds light on the changes in financial management frameworks implemented by governments at the forefront of the reform movement — the United Kingdom, New Zealand, Australia and Canada. We begin with the nation that is home to the Crown — the United Kingdom — and document its attempt to achieve fiscal responsibility.

24.2   Principles of the Budgetary Framework in the United Kingdom

The Government of the United Kingdom (UK) used past experience "in the design and implementation of the new public spending framework, which is based on the following principles:

- The new macroeconomic framework is based on a clear set of principles and rules designed to embed policy credibility and economic stability. A platform of low inflation and sound public finances means affordable public spending plans can be set on a firm basis for the longer-term.
- Estimates of cyclically-adjusted fiscal balances and trend growth are published regularly, allowing proper scrutiny of policy decisions.
- Cautious and prudent assumptions help ensure the Government's fiscal rules are met and significantly reduce the chances of spending plans being derailed by unexpected events.
- This prudent approach means that public service priorities can now enjoy sustained high growth without the fear of sudden retrenchments.
- Capital spending is protected so that necessary investment in public infrastructure is not cut for short term reasons.
- Published performance targets in the Public Service Agreements focus planning on the end results which funding is supposed to deliver, and which taxpayers expect." (HMT, Planning Sustainable Public Spending).

These key principles "are reflected in reforms to the planning and control regime which were implemented in the 1998 Comprehensive Spending Review and in successive spending reviews. The 1998 Comprehensive Spending Review (CSR), published in July 1998, was a review of departmental aims and objectives alongside a zero-based analysis of each spending program to determine the best way of delivering the government's objectives. It allocated substantial additional resources to the government's key priorities, particularly education and health, for the three-year period from 1999–2000 to 2001–02." (HMT, Public Expenditure and Planning Control in the UK).

While the 1998 CSR laid the foundation for the UK's reform agenda, the 2000 Spending Review helped advance it by introducing "new features to the public expenditure planning and control framework including service delivery agreements, the implementation of the first stage of a resource budgeting system, departmental investment strategies[2], and a wide range of cross-cutting reviews.[3] This spending review also developed public service agreements (PSA) set out in the 1998 CSR by reducing the number of targets (from around 300 to 160) and including at least one target in each departmental PSA about improving efficiency or value for money. Service delivery agreements and technical notes were introduced setting out lower level input targets and milestones and explaining how performance against each PSA target will be measured." (HMT, Public Expenditure and Planning Control in the UK).

The 2002 Spending Review consolidated the UK's public finance reform program and "was the first spending review to be conducted on a full resource-budgeting basis. It allocated resources to the government's key priorities of raising productivity, extending opportunity, building strong and secure communities, and securing Britain and British interests in the world. PSAs were further refined from 160 to 130 by, for example, introducing a new cross-departmental PSA for child development programs such as Sure Start, Childcare and Early Years." (HMT, Public Expenditure and Planning Control in the UK). Further details of the changes to the UK's public financial management framework are explained below.

24.2.1 Fiscal Rules

The fiscal rules established by the Government of the UK are "based on its fiscal policy objectives of:

- over the medium-term, ensuring sound public finances and that spending and taxation impact fairly both within and across generations. In practice this requires that:
  - the Government meets its key taxation and spending priorities while avoiding an unsustainable and damaging rise in the burden of public debt; and
  - those generations who benefit from public spending also meet, as far as possible, the costs of the services they consume; and

- over the short-term, supporting monetary policy, where possible, by:
  - allowing the automatic stabilizers to play their role in smoothing the path of the economy in the face of variations in demand; and

- where prudent and sensible, providing further support to monetary policy through changes in the fiscal stance. (HMT, Analysing UK Fiscal Policy).

Under the new public financial management order, budgets are set every two years for a three-year period. A three-year period was thought best to give departments a sufficient timeframe for future planning. Secondly, more accurate forecasts are obtained over three years than over a longer time period. Finally, departments have a fair amount of flexibility in planning strategically over a three-year period than a shorter one. Within this horizon, "it has been possible to remove unnecessary lower level controls on spending, operating instead through overall spending limits and performance targets rather than on micro-management through a detailed system of approvals.

The framework for public expenditure, then, is divided between:

- Departmental Expenditure Limit (DEL) spending which is planned and controlled on a three-year basis in biennial spending reviews; and
- Annually Managed Expenditure (AME) which is expenditure which cannot reasonably be subject to firm, multi-year limits in the same way as DEL. AME includes social security benefits, local authority self-financed expenditure, payments under the Common Agricultural Policy, debt interest, and net payments to EU institutions. AME is reviewed twice a year as part of the budget and pre-budget report process. " (HMT, Public Expenditure and Planning Control in the UK)

In the spending reviews, firm DEL plans are set for departments for three years. To encourage departments to plan over the medium-term and avoid wasteful year-end surges in spending, departments may carry forward unspent DEL provision from one year into the next.

The other category of public expenditure, AME, is "not subject to the same three-year expenditure limit as DEL but is still part of the overall envelope for public expenditure. Affordability is taken into account when policy decisions affecting AME are made. The government has committed not to take policy measures which are likely to have the effect of increasing social security or other elements of AME, without taking steps to ensure that the effects of those decisions can be accommodated prudently within the government's fiscal rules. These are:

- the Golden Rule which states that over the economic cycle, the government will borrow only to invest and not to fund current spending; and

- the Sustainable Investment Rule which states that net public debt as a proportion of GDP will be held over the economic cycle at a stable and prudent level. Other things being equal, net debt will be maintained below 40 percent of GDP over the economic cycle.

Given an overall envelope for public spending, forecasts of AME affect the level of resources available for DEL spending. Cautious estimates and an AME reserve, the AME margin, are built into these AME forecasts and reduce the risk of overspending on AME." (HMT, Spending Review 2002, p. 4).

A final point of note with regard to the nexus between the fiscal rules and the public expenditure framework is that "the budget preceding a spending review sets an overall envelope for public spending that is consistent with the fiscal rules for the period covered by the spending review. In the spending review, the budget AME forecast for Year 1 of the spending review period is updated and AME forecasts are made for Years 2 and 3 of the spending review period. Longer term budgets have been set: five years for health (in the 2002 Budget) and ten years for transport, recognizing the need for longer term planning and stable growth in these areas. Together, DEL and AME sum to Total Managed Expenditure, the broadest measure of total public spending." (HMT, Public Expenditure and Planning Control in the UK).

The question often asked is, "How effective are the new fiscal rules in the new budgetary framework?" As stated earlier, the government is on track to meet both its fiscal rules in the near future if what has been forecast is accurate. However, "there is nothing sacrosanct about these two rules, nor are they necessarily optimal. While it is true that meeting them would mean that the public finances were kept in relatively good shape, a failure to do so would not automatically render the public finances unsustainable, and meeting them does not even necessarily imply generational fairness .... Conversely, government policy can impose costs on future generations that are not reflected in current spending, the most obvious example being future pension liabilities." (Emmerson, Frayne and Love, 2001, p. 2). In order to better account for liabilities such as pension, the UK Government adopted a new reporting system, resource accounting and budgeting (RAB).

24.2.2 Resource Accounting and Budgeting

A key reform to the UK's public expenditure planning and control regime has been the introduction of resource accounting and budgeting (RAB). This was necessary because the "central government [had] failed to keep pace with improvements in basic financial management in the rest of the economy. The system for authorizing, controlling and accounting for public money had changed little since the middle of the 19th century. This system, based almost solely on cash, gave a distorted picture of the cost of providing services, building in perverse incentives and in particular a bias against essential long-term investment. Because of these weaknesses, the Government actively and vigorously pursued the introduction of RAB. Resource accounting applies best practice from commercial accounting to government finance, and resource budgeting uses this as the basis for planning and controlling expenditure." (HMT, Better Management of Public Services, 2001).

The new system "addresses the limitations of a solely cash-based regime and builds on the other significant reforms in public spending in recent years, which have been designed to foster better long term planning, a focus on outcomes rather than inputs, and an emphasis on investment for the future, underpinned by long term fiscal stability. Internationally, RAB and other changes to the management of public spending have placed the United Kingdom at the forefront of public sector reform." (HMT, Better Management of Public Services, 2001). The process, which includes "the move to resource-based financial management from 2001–02, involved:

- Conducting the first resource-based public expenditure survey in the 2000 Spending Review and moving to full resource budgeting in the 2002 Spending Review.
- Presenting the first full set of resource-based Estimates for 2001–02 to Parliament in April 2001.
- Resource accounts replacing cash-based appropriation accounts in respect of 2001–02. A full set of resource accounts for 1999–00 and 2000–01 was also produced and published alongside the appropriation accounts for those financial years." (HMT, Implementing Resource Based Financial Management, 2002).

Efficiency in resource utilization is one of the benefits of RAB; to elaborate further, RAB "supports the Government's agenda by delivering:

- new incentives for the management of assets and investment, supporting the Government's plans for increased investment, to reverse the decline in the nation's infrastructure;
- a long term planning framework removing distortions and perverse incentives intrinsic in the old system, and building in new incentives to reward good management;

- better information for managers on the costs of providing public services on which to base decisions and better information for Parliament and the public with which to scrutinize the Government's performance; and
- higher quality financial management throughout Government.

The move to full resource budgeting in the 2002 Spending Review was intended to further help the Government to get the most from its assets and new investment. Under RAB, departments' accounts and budgets reflect the full cost of holding and using capital. This means a charge for depreciation — using up an asset — counts as part of the budget, as does a cost of capital charge, reflecting the fact that the Government has borrowed to fund investment and has tied up resources in assets which could have been used elsewhere. As a result of the inclusion of the costs of holding and using capital in departmental budgets, there were new incentives to drive down capital costs, to improve the quality of maintenance, to extend the useful lives of assets where it is cost-effective to do so, and to dispose of assets no longer required." (HMT, Better Management of Public Services, 2001).

Besides improved asset management, RAB offers other advantages. For example, "because of the increased sophistication of the financial data available under RAB, decision-takers have information available to allow them to view the long term consequences of their actions, not just the immediate cash consequences. And the resource budgeting system has incentives built in to reward good decision-taking, allowing resources to be redeployed into priority areas. Some examples of the other benefits for the management of public services brought about by the full introduction of resource budgeting include:

- improvements in the management of public liabilities — including early retirement costs for public servants and a range of compensation liabilities;
- better management of working capital — debtors, creditors, stock and cash;
- a new framework for managing some of the remaining publicly-owned companies, providing them with greater commercial freedoms; and
- significant improvements in the level of financial expertise within government departments." (HMT, Better Management of Public Services, 2001).

To illustrate the impact of RAB, we use the example of the Ministry of Defense (MoD) "where the numbers have changed significantly under

Table 24.1 Comparing Cash and Resource Based DELs for MoD

£ million	2001–02 cash	2001–02 resource
Current/resource DEL	21,441	18,072
Capital DEL	1,550	5,105
Total DEL	22,991	23,177

Source: HM Treasury Public Expenditure Statistical Analysis 2002.

resource budgeting. Table 24.1 shows the cash numbers for MoD for 2001–02, the baseline year for the review and compares these numbers with their treatment under resource budgeting.

The conversion process from cash to resource, for both current and capital expenditure, is explained in Tables 24.1a (current side) and 24.1b (capital budget side)." (HMT, Resource Budgeting and the 2000 Spending Review, 2000).

To sum it up, resources accounting and budgeting is tremendously advantageous because "intergenerational fairness is important in fiscal policy. It reflects the degree to which the government today is paying the costs of services today, as opposed to shifting costs to other periods. [RAB] provides a longer term perspective for judging the impact of policies. For example, without [RAB], decisions on pensions that create pension liabilities may not fully consider the impact of the liabilities on future budgets." (Ball, Dale, Eggers and Sacco, 1999). Needless to say, the adequacy of any accounting system would be evaluated based on the performance of the overall budgetary framework. The UK Government's effort to improve performance is discussed in the following section.

24.2.3 Public Service Agreements

A critical innovation introduced in the 1998 CSR was the Public Service Agreements (PSAs) which "set out the aim and objectives of every main government department together with measurable targets. The new spending regime places a strong emphasis on setting outcome targets, for example, better health and higher educational standards or service standards. The government monitors progress of departments against their respective PSA targets and reports this, in detail, in annual departmental reports (published in spring). [Departments also report publicly against their targets in autumn performance reports (introduced to enhance accountability in 2002)]. This provides Parliament and the public the opportunity to

Table 24.1a Current DEL Cash to Resource DEL

Note	£ million	2001–02
	Current DEL - cash starting point	21,441
A	+/− timing adjustments	134
B	+/− changes in current/capital classification	−3,467
C	+ capital charges on the civil estate	0
D	+/− full resource consumption of arms length bodies (NDPBs)	0
E	+/− full resource consumption of public corporations	−35
	= Resource DEL	18,072

Notes

A. This reflects overall movements in the level of debtors, creditors and stock consumption in the year in question.

B. National accounts treat spending on fighting equipment as current spending on the grounds that this spending does not represent an addition to the capital base. But, under resource budgeting, this expenditure is treated as capital expenditure, which is a better way of ensuring that what the Department spends on current expenditure, and what it spends on equipment are kept separate. The change represents a switch of some £3.5 billion from the resource to the capital budget in 2001–02.

C. The MoD does not have civil estate holdings. However, for most departments this line will lead to a small increase in Resource DEL.

D. As with many departments, the net effect of this line is zero. This can happen for one of two reasons. If a Non-Departmental Public Body (NDPB) is entirely grant funded, measuring total resource consumption does not change the number. Or, as in the case of MoD NDPBs, the organizations are too small to affect the overall total. However, some NDPBs will fund consumption from cash reserves or from other sources — in this event, the Resource DEL will increase to reflect the full consumption of the body, not what has been paid to it in grants by the department.

E. Profits of public corporations score as a credit in the resource budget, and losses as a cost. Previously, the interest and dividends paid by the body scored in the department's budget. So a higher profit than was due to be paid in dividends scores as a credit, as in this case, while a loss would hit the budget.

Source: HM Treasury Public Expenditure Statistical Analysis 2002.

monitor the progress of the departments in meeting their targets." (HMT, Spending Review 2000).

The UK Government distinguishes between performance measurement and performance management. It conducts performance measurement by periodically measuring progress against goals, against target levels of intended accomplishment and against third parties. Measures change as progress is made. Performance measures are generally based on a set of principles (Specific, Measurable, Attainable, Relevant, Timely) that departments are encouraged to keep in mind in setting targets. There are around

Table 24.1b   Capital DEL Cash to Capital DEL Resource

Note	£ million	2001–02
	Capital DEL – cash starting point	1,550
F	+/– changes in current/capital classification	3,467
G	+/– full capital expenditure of public corporations	98
	= Capital DEL in resource terms	5,105

F.   This line represents the switch from the resource to the current budget of fighting equipment, that is, the reverse of Note b.

G.   This reflects the addition to the MoD budget of capital expenditure by their public corporations financed from trading or other sources of income rather than simply loans and grants from the department. Previously, this expenditure scored in the accounting adjustments in AME.

Source: HM Treasury Public Expenditure Statistical Analysis 2002.

130 PSA targets, an average of fewer than seven per department; departments are trained in their usage through a series of workshops. Departments are set their own targets but some targets are set to be achieved collaboratively between departments. The targets reflect what the Government wants from the public service which, in turn, reflects what the citizenry wants from the Government.

The actual metrics used for measuring progress against the targets are agreed upon and set out in Technical Notes for each target (which are published on departmental websites, in order to make clear exactly how the targets will be assessed). Specifically, "each PSA target is underpinned by a technical note, which sets out how the target is measured, how success is defined, the sources of the relevant data, and any other relevant information such as geographical or demographical coverage. In order to properly assess progress towards targets, a department's performance data should be examined in conjunction with the technical notes." (HMT, Public Services Performance Index).

Finally, the UK Government undertakes performance management to set direction using performance information to manage better, demonstrate what has been accomplished and set actions to improve. FABRIC (Focused, Appropriate, Balanced, Robust, Integrated, and Cost-effective) is a set of principles of good performance management that serve as a guide for departments to have more effective systems.

PSAs are complemented by Service Delivery Agreements (SDAs) introduced in the 2000 Spending Review which "set out lower level input targets and milestones underpinning delivery of the headline PSA performance targets." (HMT, Public Expenditure and Planning Control in the UK). The SDA "starts with a clear accountability statement of who is responsible for delivering the agreement and:

- how in broad terms the department's high level objectives will be achieved;
- how performance will be improved within the department and the bodies responsible to it;
- how the department will focus more closely on the needs of consumers of its services;
- how the department's human and IT resources will be managed to achieve change; and
- the steps in hand to improve policy-making in line with the underpinning policy in particular." (HMT, A Guide To The Service Delivery Agreements).

So how does this new focus on performance stack up? Some experts contend that "when the New Labor government of Tony Blair was elected in 1997, it embarked on a seemingly radical reform of the way in which public spending was to be decided and managed. It was almost like a revolution — government departments breaking free of the shackles of annularity for most of their spending programs and held to account by tough contract-like performance targets. Departmental managers would be able to engage in real strategic planning and management focused on delivery." (Talbot, 2001). Others explain that "there has never been a history of differentiation between performance measurement at policy, program, and operational levels. Early attempts at measurement were mainly financially based, with managers tending to produce and publish statistics as an end in itself. A much wider range of measures now exists, and there is more thought in their application." (Mawhood, 1997, pp. 136). The hard part, one gathers, is conveying to the various departments within the Government that these are changes for the better and convincing them to accept these changes.

24.3 Principles of the Budgetary Framework in New Zealand

Besides the UK, "New Zealand is another country that has adopted a very proactive and open approach to managing its public finances. The *Public Finance Act 1989* and the *Fiscal Responsibility Act 1994* provide an elaborate structure for setting and implementing fiscal policy. Rather than fixed rules, the framework allows 'fiscal provisions' to evolve over time. They are determined at the start of each parliamentary cycle that sets, inter alia, fiscal limits for the coming period." (Simes, 2003). Of the two, the *Public Finance Act 1989* is considered revolutionary in New Zealand public financial management in stipulating the following:

"An Act to amend the law governing the use of public financial resources and to that end to:

(a) Provide a framework for Parliamentary scrutiny of the Government's management of the Crown's assets and liabilities, including expenditure proposals; and

(b) Establish lines of responsibility for the use of public financial resources; and

(c) Establish financial management incentives to encourage effective and efficient use of financial resources in departments and Crown entities; and

(d) Specify the minimum financial reporting obligations of the Crown, departments and Crown entities; and

(e) Safeguard public assets by providing statutory authority and control for the raising of loans, issuing of securities, giving of guarantees, operation of bank accounts, and investment of funds." (New Zealand State Services Commission, 1998).

The *Financial Management Act 1994*, on the other hand, is seen as one of the final, major pieces of legislation in the reform movement that was passed after the *State Owned Enterprises Act 1986*, the *State Sector Act 1988*, the *Public Finance Act 1989*, and the *Financial Reporting Act 1993*. It forms the basis of New Zealand's present governmental operations by "requiring the Government to:

• follow a legislated set of principles of responsible fiscal management, and publicly assess their fiscal policies against these principles. Governments may temporarily depart from the principles but must do so publicly, explain why they have departed, and reveal how and when they intend to conform to the principles.

• publish a 'Budget Policy Statement' well before the annual Budget containing their strategic priorities for the upcoming Budget, their short term fiscal intentions, and long term fiscal objectives. A 'Fiscal Strategy Report' that compares Budget intentions and objectives with those published in the most recent Budget Policy Statement is to be published in conjunction with the Budget.

• fully disclose the impact of their fiscal decisions over a three-year forecasting period in regular 'Economic and Fiscal Updates'.

- present all financial information under Generally Agreed Accounting Practice.
- require the Treasury to prepare forecasts based on its best professional judgment about the impact of policy, rather than relying on the judgment of the Government. It also requires the Minister to communicate all of the Government's policy decisions to the Treasury so that the forecasts are comprehensive.
- refer all reports required under the Act to a parliamentary select committee." (NZ Treasury, 2003).

Based on the groundwork established mainly by these Acts, the Government of New Zealand was able to advance its fiscal reform agenda through the establishment of fiscal principles, accounting reform and accountability requirements. These are discussed next.

24.3.1 Fiscal Principles

The *Financial Management Act 1994* advocates a number of principles that serve as general fiscal rules governing New Zealand's financial management framework:

- "Reduction of total Crown debt to prudent levels – to provide a buffer against factors that may impact on the level of debt in the future. To achieve this, Government must keep total operating expenses of the Crown in each financial year less than its total operating revenue until these are achieved.
- Maintaining prudent levels of debt once these have been achieved – by ensuring that total operating expenses do not exceed total operating revenue. There is some leeway allowed for here, as the levels are expected to be maintained on average through time.
- Achieving and maintaining levels of Crown net worth – so as to provide a buffer against factors that may impact adversely on the Crown's net worth in the future.
- Managing prudently the fiscal risks facing the Crown.
- Pursuing consistent policies – with a reasonable degree of predictability about the level and stability of tax rates for future years." (New Zealand State Services Commission, 1998).

The specifics of these are provided in Table 24.2.

The Government's fiscal modus operandi has also been revised "to reflect the change to the presentation of the Crown financial statements introduced from 1 July 2002. This involved a move from the modified

Table 24.2   Long-Term Fiscal Objectives

Long-term fiscal objectives	To achieve the objectives of fiscal policy, the Government's high level focus is on:
Operating balance	
Operating surplus on average over the economic cycle sufficient to meet the requirements for contribution to the New Zealand Superannuation Fund (NZS) and ensure consistency with the long term debt objective	Rising surpluses (1) during the transition and build up phase of the NZS Fund, with a focus on core Crown revenue and expenses, including: • Tax-to-GDP around current levels. • Core Crown expenses (plus the net payment/withdrawal to the NZS Fund) averaging around 35% of GDP over the horizon used to calculate NZS Fund contributions
Revenue	
Ensure sufficient revenue to meet the operating balance objective	• A robust, broad-based tax system that raises revenue in a fair and efficient way • SOEs and Crown entities contributing to surpluses consistent with their enabling legislation and Government policy
Expenses	
Ensure expenses are consistent with the operating balance objective	Focus on building the NZS Fund assets rather than reducing debt. Increasing net worth consistent with the operating balance objective is projected to see net worth at around 30% of GDP by 2011
Net worth	
Increase net worth consistent with the operating balance objective	Consistent with the net worth objective, there will also be a focus on quality investment SOEs will have debt structures that reflect best commercial practice. Changes in the level of debt will reflect specific circumstances
Debt	
Manage total debt at prudent levels. In the longer term, gross sovereign-issued debt below 30% of GDP on average over the economic cycle (2)	Net debt will be at levels that are consistent with the gross debt objective and the Government policy of holding financial assets. Net debt, including NZS Fund assets, is expected to fall below 0% of GDP by the end of the decade

Source: NZ Treasury New Zealand Economic and Financial Overview 2003.
(1)   The surplus includes the net (after tax) return on the NZS Fund, which the NZS Fund will retain. Effectively the Government is targeting operating surpluses excluding the NZS Fund's retained investment returns.
(2)   Sovereign-issued debt is debt issued by the New Zealand Debt Management Office (NZDMO) and the Reserve Bank; it excludes debt issued by SOEs and Crown entities and the sovereign-guaranteed debt of SOEs and Crown entities. Gross sovereign-issued debt includes any New Zealand government stock held by the NZS Fund.

equity accounting method for accounting for the Government's investment in state-owned enterprises (SOEs) and Crown entities to full line-by-line consolidation of the entities. There is no change to the Government's fiscal policy approach as a result of the change to the basis of preparing Crown Financial Statements." (NZ Treasury, 2003).

24.3.2 Accounting Reform

Accounting reform adopted by the New Zealand government took place in two stages. First, "an amendment was made to the *Public Finance Act 1989* to provide that the financial reporting requirements of the Crown, departments and Crown entities would be established through the same processes existing under the *Financial Reporting Act 1993*.[5] In essence, the various reports required to be prepared under both the *Public Finance Act* and the *Fiscal Responsibility Act* must be prepared in accordance with generally accepted accounting practice.

The term *generally accepted accounting practice* (GAAP) means:

- approved financial reporting standards (determined in accordance with the *Financial Reporting Act 1993*) so far as those standards apply to the Crown or the particular entity; and
- in relation to matters for which no provision is made in approved financial reporting standards and which are not subject to any applicable rule of law, accounting policies that are *appropriate* in relation to the Crown or the relevant entity *and* have *authoritative support* within the accounting profession in New Zealand." (Simpkins, 1998).

Second was the adoption of accrual accounting practices. This was gradual but the results were impressive as "legislation requiring departments to develop accrual accounting systems was passed in early July 1989. It gave departments two years to move from their existing situation to the new full accrual basis: all but three of approximately 45 departments effected the change successfully within one year. The entire government moved its financial reporting to an accrual basis in December 1991, as required by the *Public Finance Act*, but it was not until 1994 that the budget was on this basis. Since 1994, the government's entire financial-management system has been on a full accrual basis. While the whole process, from initial policy development to implementation, took seven years, one major change, moving departments onto an accrual basis, effectively took less than two years." (Ball, Dale, Eggers and Sacco, 2000).

These accounting changes could be considered successful based on "a survey of government managers [which] revealed that of the many public-sector management reforms that have occurred in New Zealand, the accrual reforms received the highest grade ... and the reforms appear to have improved the ability to identify inefficiencies in the costing and provision of public services and enhanced accountability." (Ball, Dale, Eggers and Sacco, 2000).

24.3.3 Accountability Requirements

Besides the adoption of accrual accounting methods, the Government of New Zealand has adopted other measures to enhance accountability of the public service. Similar to the reformed system in the United Kingdom, "accountability revolves around the ex ante specification of both financial conditions and outputs and the ex post reporting of results. Ministers and managers must agree in advance on financial performance and the outputs to be produced, the money to be spent on the agreed outputs, and the quality and timeliness of the work to be performed. This advance specification of performance enables Ministers and managers to compare the volume, cost, and quality of the outputs actually produced to planned levels. This is the essence of managerial accountability – doing what was contracted at the agreed price and explaining any variance between planned and actual performance." (New Zealand State Services Commission, 1996).

Another measure of accountability adopted by the Government is the imposition of a charge for the use of capital which is benchmarked to that used by the private sector. Specifically, "in keeping with the overriding framework of the reforms, managers are given more freedom to manage but are also held more accountable for results. On one hand, chief executives are given the authority to buy and sell assets without a specific appropriation from Parliament, enabling them to choose the right mix of capital. On the other hand, they are subject to a capital charge that forces them to prioritize asset purchases and gives them an incentive to sell surplus assets. The capital charge essentially applies an interest rate to all capital, creating an actual cost for using capital. The charge creates an incentive to balance a capital expenditure against its usefulness in achieving the agency's goals." (Ball, Dale, Eggers and Sacco, 1999).

These and other reforms "have improved [New Zealand's] fiscal position dramatically. Surpluses have been recorded since 1994, following two decades of deficits. In 1995/96 the operating surplus was 3.7 percent of GDP; net worth turned positive, reaching 3.7 percent of GDP; and net public debt declined to 31 percent of GDP. State-owned enterprises, and the government itself, abide by the same set of rules and regulations (including taxation), disclosure requirements, and accounting practices that apply to the private sector. And the results, in terms of efficiency gains and the dramatic turnaround in the country's fiscal position, are impressive", according to an assessment by the International Monetary Fund (IMF). (Cangiano, 1996).

24.4 Principles of the Budgetary Framework in Australia

Australia followed New Zealand's lead by establishing a similar set of financial principles and adopting an accrual accounting system. In order to avoid repetition, we will cover these briefly. We begin with the foundation of Australia's fiscal framework which was laid by the *Charter of Budget Honesty 1998*. Its aim was "to improve the discipline, transparency and accountability applying to the conduct of fiscal policy. The Charter comprises three elements, namely fiscal policy formulation, fiscal reporting and the costing of election promises. Each year, the Charter requires a 'Fiscal Strategy Statement' which should:

(a)   specify the Government's long term fiscal objectives within which shorter term fiscal policy will be framed;

(b)   explain the broad strategic priorities on which the budget is or will be based;

(c)   specify the key fiscal measures that the Government considers important and against which fiscal policy will be set and assessed; and

(d)   specify, for the budget year and the following 3 financial years:
  (i)   the Government's fiscal objectives and targets; and
  (ii)   the expected outcomes for the specified key fiscal measures;

(e)   explain how the fiscal objectives and strategic priorities specified and explained as required by paragraphs (a), (b) and (d) relate to the principles of sound fiscal management;

(f)   specify fiscal policy actions taken or to be taken by the Government that are temporary in nature, adopted for the purpose of moderating cyclical fluctuations in economic activity, and indicate the process for their reversal; and

(g)   explain broadly the reporting basis on which subsequent Government fiscal reports will be prepared."

Arising out of Australia's new fiscal framework is a set of fiscal principles and financial risks, which are discussed next.

24.4.1 Fiscal Principles

Australia's fiscal framework is supported by principles which "focus attention on a range of issues that must be addressed. The principles require the Government to:

- manage financial risks faced by the Australian Government prudently, having regard to economic circumstances, including by maintaining general government debt at prudent levels;
- ensure that its fiscal policy contributes to achieving adequate national saving and to moderating cyclical fluctuations in economic activity, as appropriate, taking account of the economic risks facing the nation and the impact of those risks on the Government's fiscal position;
- pursue spending and taxing policies that are consistent with a reasonable degree of stability and predictability in the level of the tax burden;
- maintain the integrity of the tax system; and
- ensure that its policy decisions have regard to their financial effects on future generations.

The financial risks identified by the Charter include:

- risks arising from excessive net debt;
- commercial risks arising from ownership of public trading enterprises and public financial enterprises;
- risks arising from erosion of the tax base; and
- risks arising from the management of assets and liabilities." (Finance and Administration, 2003).

One of the attempts made to control these risks was through the introduction of accrual accounting. This is discussed next.

24.4.2 Accrual Accounting

In addition to the newly designed fiscal principles by the Australian Government, "financial management was modernized through three pieces of legislation designed to improve the quality and clarity of understanding of the Commonwealth's financial management framework. These were the *Financial Management and Accountability Act 1997*, the *Commonwealth Authorities and Companies Act 1997* and the *Auditor-General Act 1997*. The legislation sharpens accountability and emphasizes performance and propriety. It also facilitated the subsequent, separate decisions to replace cash accounting with accrual-based budgeting and output and outcomes reporting. Together, with the full adoption of accrual-based budgeting in 1999, the current arrangements have aimed at achieving:

- improved accountability;
- improved outcomes- and outputs-based budgeting and reporting; and
- better understanding of the true cost of government." (Australian Public Service Commission, 2003).

The context for Australian governmental agencies' reporting system is the outcomes and output framework.

24.4.3   Outcomes and Output Framework

Introduced with the 1999–2000 federal budget, the outcomes and output framework has two basic objectives: to improve agencies' corporate governance and enhance public accountability. Managing through outcomes and outputs helps improve decision-making and performance by "focusing attention on the fundamental questions:

  i.   What does government want to achieve? (outcomes)
 ii.   How does it achieve this? (outputs and administered items)
iii.   How does it know if it is succeeding? (performance reporting)

It is intended to improve the understanding and knowledge of those outside the agency who have an interest in its performance, including ministers, parliament and external accountability bodies such as the Auditor General."

A significant feature of the outcomes and output framework is that "agencies are responsible for developing a series of outputs which, in conjunction with administered items, work directly towards the delivery of the relevant outcome. Outputs are the actual deliverables (i.e., goods and services) agencies produce which, together with administered items, generate the desired outcomes specified by government. All departmental outputs must contribute to the realization of a specified outcome. This also applies to purchaser/provider arrangements where the provider is delivering services to contribute to the purchaser's outcomes." (Kristensen, Groszky and Buhler, 2002).

An emphasis of the framework is on performance and "the main vehicles for agencies to externally report on planned and actual performance against outcomes and outputs are:

- Portfolio Budget Statements; and
- Annual Reports.

Portfolio Budget Statements identify each agency's plans for the coming budget year, while Annual Reports detail the degree to which those plans have been realized and the efficiency of agency outputs and administered items used to achieve this. In preparing the two documents, agencies are required to enable a clear read between planning information and actual performance" (Chan, Nizette, La Rance, Broughton, and Russell, 2002).

In order to monitor performance, the Australian government uses performance indicators as a tool and these "fall into two categories — indicators of effectiveness and indicators of efficiency. Effectiveness indicators should be designed to identify as clearly as possible the causal relationship between the outcome and the outputs and administered items in place to achieve it. Efficiency indicators provide information on the productivity of a given output in terms of the combined and interdependent effects of its quality, quantity and price" (Kristensen, Groszky and Buhler, 2002).

24.5 Principles of the Budgetary Framework in Canada

Canada's experience with public finance reform was much the same as that of the other countries covered in this study and also "provides a good example of the difficulty of 'reading' budget reforms. In the early 1980s, the federal government introduced a range of budget-modernizing measures — a Policy and Expenditure Management System (PEMS), a Multi-Year Operational Plan (MYOP) and an Operational Framework Plan (OFP). On paper, this system sounded highly rational. In practice, however, under the Mulroney administration from 1983, the PEMS system singularly failed to persuade or enable ministers to achieve their expenditure targets. It was partially replaced in 1989 and then in 1995 completely superseded by a new Expenditure Management System (EMS). EMS managed to deliver the first balanced budget for more than a decade, but even then the relationship between budget allocations and performance was debatable" (Pollitt and Bouckaert, 2000).

Like the other countries, Canada's new fiscal framework emphasized performance and, with the Program Review of 1994, Canada increased its efforts to implement outcome-focused management. The Program Review aimed at ensuring that the federal government's resources were directed to the highest priority requirements and to those areas where the federal government was best placed to serve citizens. Following this review, departments and agencies began to plan and report on medium and longer term results, called "Key Results Commitments." All government departments now plan and report against their Key Results Commitments and present this information to Parliament and the public (Kristensen, Groszky and Buhler, 2002).

24.6 The American Comparison

Fiscal management and budgetary reform within the British Commonwealth countries compared to that in the United States provides for an interesting study. In the US, "traditional budgeting as it evolved in the twentieth century has been characterized as focused upon a single year, relying upon line-items or objects of expenditure to provide control over appropriations, using incremental decision techniques that dealt with inputs and emphasized a concept of budget base that preserved past decisions without subjecting them to re-examination. V. O. Key, in 1940, decried the 'lack of a budgetary theory' which over-emphasized the mechanics of the budget process rather than confront how to decide how to allocate 'X dollars to activity A instead of activity B?' As governmental involvement in society grew during the New Deal and following World War II, choices became even more important ... In the 1990s, considerable attention has been refocused upon performance budgeting ... " (Tyler and Willand, 1997). Kamensky (2001). traces the commencement of this endeavor, in the US, to the *Chief Financial Officers Act 1990* which "required the development and reporting of systematic measures of performance for twenty-three of the larger federal agencies [and the *Government Performance and Results Act 1993* (GPRA) which linked performance plans to budgets]" (Kamensky, 2001).

Within the realm of GPRA, "the United States Government established a performance management framework which consisted of Strategic Plans, Annual Performance Plans and Annual Performance Reports. In *Strategic Plans*, which cover a period of at least six years, agencies present their mission statements and define a set of long-term goals. These long-term goals are mainly outcome goals and describe how an agency will carry out its mission. The *Annual Performance Plan* translates the goals of the Strategic Plan into Annual Performance Goals that will be achieved during a particular fiscal year. These performance goals are usually a combination of outcome and output goals. The Annual Performance Plan also includes information on how much money will be spent to achieve a set of performance goals. *Annual Performance Reports* compare actual performance with planned outcomes and outputs in the Annual Performance Plan. If some goals haven't been achieved, there will be an explanation of the reasons, and a schedule and steps for meeting the goal in the future. The Annual Performance Reports also include a summary of the findings and recommendations of any program evaluation completed during the fiscal year" (Kristensen, Groszky and Buhler, 2002, pp. 28–29).

However, only recently did the budgetary reform effort in the U.S. gather impetus. Kamensky notes that "in August 2001, President (George W.) Bush released his management agenda in which one of the five key priorities described was to better integrate budget and performance. That same year, the director of the Office of Management and Budget (OMB), Mitch Daniels, met individually with key agency heads and asked them to develop performance-based budgets for fiscal year 2003 for at least two of their programs. As a result, as agencies submitted their draft budgets to OMB, nearly 100 programs were judged on a totally different basis than in the past" (Kamensky, 2001). In spite of the prolonged initiation of performance-based budgeting in the U.S., the practice has broadly permeated throughout U.S. government agencies. A study conducted in 2002 by the U.S. General Accounting Office of the first four years of agency efforts to implement the GPRA found "that agencies continue to tighten the required linkage between their performance plans and budget requests. Of the agencies reviewed over this period, all but three met the basic requirement of the act to define a linkage between their performance plans and the program activities in their budget requests, and most of the agencies in [the GAO's] review had moved beyond this basic requirement to indicate some level of funding associated with expected performance described in the plan" (GAO, 2002).

It must be noted that progress of performance-based initiatives within government could be marred by potential pitfalls. Tyer and Willand (1997) expound these by citing a 1993 study of the U.S. Congressional Budget Office (CBO) *Using Performance Measures in the Federal Budget Process* which "concluded that performance measurement 'is limited in its ability to bring about substantial change'. It noted, however, that some of these limitations had nothing to do with commitment but rather with the diffi-culty of measuring government performance itself, and particularly that of the national government. The greatest obstacle it found was the identifica-tion of the measures, in large part because at the national level 'so many programs [are] influenced by other actors, including state and local governments, private businesses, and individuals.' In so far as performance budgeting itself is concerned, the CBO, after studying state and local government experience, concluded that performance measures did not appear to significantly influence the allocation of budgetary resources. Rather, they were used more to carry out budgets than to make decisions" (Tyer and Willand, 1997).

With all the emphasis on performance, has the reform movement in public financial management actually been worth the effort? While the performance of some public systems have shown signs of enhanced viability, it is hard to isolate the impact of other reform efforts such as structural reforms (e.g., increased privatization) from that of public finance reforms. Nonetheless, it spurs a debate on key issues that is the focus of the concluding section.

24.7 Conclusion

The effectiveness of financial management practices instituted under New Public Management leaves a lot of unanswered questions. Let us begin with fiscal rules and principles formulated by the various jurisdictions under study. There is no guarantee that these nations will stick to these principles especially under conditions of economic or financial burden. For example, countries might not adhere to debt limit stipulations when there is a downturn in the economy during a recession. The U.S. is one jurisdiction where its House of Representatives (Congress) recently voted to raise its debt ceiling substantially. Faced with billions of dollars of spending on war and domestic priorities like health care, and a government with a strong belief in tax cuts, the U.S. would have been well served with spending and tax caps to maintain its level of debt. Instead, its fiscal policy included generous tax cuts with no limit on dollars flowing out of the government coffers which resulted in the need to raise the debt ceiling set earlier. It would not be wrong to assume, then, that if its key allies in "the war on terror", Great Britain and Australia, face similar fiscal pressures, they too will fold and compromise their fiscal rules/principles. This immediately raises the question, "Why would government establish a set of fiscal rules only to break them?"

A second question of doubt that public financial reform raises is, "Will accounting practices adopted from the private sector result in misuse as experienced by some private sector entities?" It is true that accrual accounting has several advantages over cash accounting but its inheritance from the private sector could possibly vilify the public sector's reputation and prestige. The energy company, Enron Corporation, is the perfect example. Accused of skullduggery, mainly manipulative accounting practices, this corporate giant fell from being one of the most respected corporations in the United States to one of the least. By following accounting procedures used by the tainted private sector, citizens' trust in government is bound to erode. The Canadian government has reeled from a "sponsorship scandal" involving the misuse of public funds. Although this has little to do with manipulative accounting practices, it demonstrates the importance of sustaining public faith in government. The Liberal government, at the center of the scandal in Canada, lost its majority hold of Parliament as a result of the controversy and faces a difficult road ahead in regaining the confidence of the Canadian citizenry. The burning issue now that governments have adopted private sector accounting practices is, what will they do to prevent Enron-style manipulative accounting corruption from occurring within their respective jurisdictions? The response is a slew of disincentives and safeguards, besides current audit procedures, but a detailed discussion of these would fill up a whole other chapter.

Performance measure utilization creates its own set of questions which I addressed in an article co-authored with Dr. Howard Frank. These include: "Whom is performance measurement for — the public, bureaucracy or elected officials?"; "Can performance systems realistically be integrated with operational functions such as strategic planning, individual performance appraisals, and budgetary resource allocations?"; and "Is external bench-marking imperative for performance measurement to be effective?". Government needs to answer these fundamental questions before it conceptualizes and designs its performance management system. A number of jurisdictions have jumped on the performance measurement bandwagon and one can't help but wonder if this is simply a result of "follow the leader" or if these jurisdictions have done so as a result of a preliminary benefit-cost analysis. Anecdotal evidence suggests that "the most important prerequisite [to performance management implementation] may be a commitment to matching analytic method to the problem at hand." (Frank and D'Souza, 2004). In other words, understanding the causatum is a prerequisite for government action. While this might not be that easy for some jurisdictions due to organizational and monetary constraints, it certainly is a starting point that will set nations on the road to fiscal prosperity.

Notes

1. This section has been directly referenced from material provided by the Government of the United Kingdom and interviews with United Kingdom government officials with the permission of the Government of the United Kingdom.

2. Departmental Investment Strategies set out each department's plans to deliver the scale and quality of capital stock needed to underpin its objectives. The DIS includes information about the department's existing capital stock and future plans for that stock, as well as plans for new investment. It also sets out the systems that the department has in place to ensure that it delivers its capital programs effectively.

3. The 2000 Spending Review recognized the importance of the integrated development of government policy by incorporating fifteen full cross-departmental reviews. These covered a wide range of areas including the criminal justice system, nuclear safety, crime reduction

and conflict prevention in sub-Saharan Africa. These reviews resulted in a wide variety of new working arrangements including the refocusing of departmental programs and the creation of pooled budgets and management structures.

4.   After this chapter was written, the British Government concluded Spending Review 2004 and now have a set of 110 PSA targets (though departments remain accountable for targets set in Spending Review 2002 while they remain live, in most cases to 2006).

5.   This put in place mechanisms for a statutory accounting standard setting process to apply in New Zealand (Simpkins, 1998).

Acknowledgment

The author would like to thank the Government of the United Kingdom for information provided through interviews and publications. The author would also like to thank University Graduate School at Florida International University for partial financial support for this study.

References

Australian Department of Finance and Administration. Charter of Budget Honesty. Retrieved on January 16, 2005 from the web site http://www.finance.gov.au/budgetgroup/other_guidance_notes/charter_of_budget_honesty.html. Updated on October 21, 2003.

Australian Public Service. (2003). The Australian Experience of Public Sector Reform, June 2003.

Ball, I., Dale, T., Eggers, W., and Sacco, J. (1999). Reforming Financial Management in the Public Sector: Lessons U.S. Officials Can Learn from New Zealand. Policy Study No. 258. Reason Public Policy Institute.

Ball, I., Dale, T., Eggers, W., and Sacco, J. (2000). Reforming Financial Management in the Public Sector: Lessons Canada Can Learn from New Zealand. Policy Study No. 6. Frontier Center For Public Policy.

Campos, J. and Pradhan, S. (1997). Evaluating Public Expenditure Management Systems: An Experimental Methodology with an application to the Australia and New Zealand Reforms. Asian Development Bank: page. 2.

Cangiano, M. (1996). Accountability and Transparency in the Public Sector: The New Zealand Experience, IMF Working Paper 96/122, December 16, 1996.

Chan, M., Nizette, M., La Rance, L., Broughton, C., and Russell, D. (2002). Australia, *OECD Journal of Budgeting*, Vol. 1, No. 4, page 53.

Emerson, C., Frayne, C., and Love, S. (2001). *The Government's Fiscal Rules*, The Institute of Fiscal Studies, Briefing Note No. 16, Updated August 2004.

Frank, H. and D'Souza, J. (2004). Twelve Years into the Performance Measurement Revolution: Where We Need To Go In Implementation Research. *International Journal of Public Administration*, 27:8 and 9.

French, S. (1997). Being Fiscally Responsible in Policy Development, Speech given by Mr Steve French, Assistant Secretary, Budget Policy Branch, Fiscal Policy Division, Treasury to the fifth annual Government Policy Conference, held in Sydney on 4–5 August 1997.

GAO. (2002). Managing For Results: Agency Progress In Linking Performance Plans With Budgets And Financial Statements. United States General Accounting Office Report to the Ranking Minority Member, Committee on Governmental Affairs, U.S. Senate. GAO-02-236.

HM Treasury. (2000). Resource Budgeting and the 2000 Spending Review, July 2000.

HM Treasury (2000). Spending Review 2000. Prudent for a purpose: Building Opportunity and Security for all.

HM Treasury. (2001). Better Management of Public Services: Resource Budgeting and the 2002 Spending Review, November 2001.

HM Treasury. (2002). 2002 Spending Review: Opportunity and Security for All: Investing in an Enterprising, Fairer Britain.

HM Treasury. (2002). Managing Resources. Implementing Resource Based Financial Management, September 2002.

HM Treasury. Public Expenditure Planning and Control in the UK — A Brief Introduction. Retrieved on January 16, 2005 from the web site http://www.hm-treasury.gov.uk/spending_review/spend_plancontrol.cfm.

HM Treasury. Planning Sustainable Public Spending: Lessons From Previous Policy Experience. Retrieved on January 16, 2005 from the web site http://www.hm-treasury.gov.uk/media/83D/66/86.pdf.

HM Treasury. Analysing UK Fiscal Policy. Retrieved on January 16, 2005 from the web site http://www.hm-treasury.gov.uk./media/7AD/F6/90.pdf.

HM Treasury. Public Services Performance Index. Retrieved on January 16, 2005 from the web site http://www.hm-treasury.gov.uk/performance/#Public.

HM Treasury. A Guide To The Service Delivery Agreements. Retrieved on January 16, 2005 from the web site http://www.hm-treasury.gov.uk/spending_review/spending_review_2000/service_delivery_agreements/spend_sr00_sda_whiteguide.cfm.

Kamensky, J. (2001). Performance Budgeting – American Style, *American Society for Public Administration Online Column*, Page Available At ASPA Online Column Archive.

Kristensen, J., Groszky, W., and Buhler, B. (2002). Outcome-focused Management and Budgeting, *OECD Journal of Budgeting*, Vol. 1, No. 4, page 18–20.

Manning, N. (2000). The New Public Management and its Legacy. Retrieved on January 16, 2005 from the web site http://www1.worldbank.org/publicsector/civilservice/debate1.htm.

Mawhood, C. (1997). Performance Management in the United Kingdom (1985–1995). In Evaluation For The 21st Century. Eds. Eleanor Clelimsky and William Shadish. Thousand Oaks: Sage Publications, pp. 136.

National Audit Office, UK. (2003). Managing Resources to Deliver Better Public Services, December 12, 2003.

New Zealand State Services Commission. (1996). The Spirit of Reform: Managing The New Zealand State Sector In A Time Of Change.

New Zealand State Services Commission. (1998). New Zealand State Sector Reform: A Decade of Change.

New Zealand Treasury. (2003). New Zealand Economic and Financial Overview 2003. Retrieved on January 16, 2005 from the web site http://www.treasury.govt.nz/nzefo/2003/publicfinance.asp.

Osborne, D. and Gaebler, T. (1992). *Reinventing Government: How the Entrepreneunial Spirit is Transforming the Public Sector.* Reading, Mass: Addison-Wesley Publishing.

Pollitt, C. and Bouckaert, G. (2000). Public management reform: a comparative analysis. Oxford ; New York: Oxford University Press, 2000.

Premchand, A. (1999). *Public Financial Management: Getting the Basics Right.* ed. Governance, Corruption and Public Financial Management. Asian Development Bank: pp. 50, 55.

Simes, R. (2003). Fiscal Policy Rules in Australia, A Paper Prepared for the Chifley Research Center, September 2003.

Simpkins, K. (1998). Budgeting and Accounting Issues – New Zealand, Presentation to the International Federation of Accountants Public Sector Committee, Executive Forum, Washington DC, Thursday, April 30, 1998.

Talbot, C. (2001). Government by Performance Based Budgeting. American Society for Public Administration Online Column, Page Available At ASPA Online Column Archive.

Tyer, C. and Willand, J. (1997). Public Budgeting in America: A Twentieth Century Retrospective. *Journal of Public Budgeting, Accounting and Financial Management* in Vol. 9, no. 2 (Summer 1997).

Chapter 25

Modernizing Public Budgeting and Financial Management in China

YUN MA, Ph.D.
College of Politics and Public Affairs, Zhongshan University,
People's Republic of China

MEILI NIU
Department of Public Administration, University of Nebraska

25.1   Introduction

Since the founding of the People's Republic of China in 1949, China's budgeting system has experienced three major stages that reflect the evolution of public budgeting in China. Before 1978,[1] China's budgeting system was plan-dominated. Under a planned economy, public budgeting was insignificant since budgetary revenues were allocated by plans responding to significant public polices. From 1978 to 1999, China's budgeting system was in transition. During this period, although the traditional budgeting system was de-integrated, a new and effective budgeting system was not developed because fiscal reforms during this period were centered on the revenue side (Wang, 2001).

The need to establish a modern budgeting system has become obvious since the 1990s. In 1994 China passed the first law on budgeting, the *Budget Law*, providing a legislative foundation for a new budgeting system. Moreover, as early as 1993, several local governments in China started adopting zero-based budgeting (ZBB) in compiling governmental budgets. The number of local governments conducting ZBB has increased in the past several years. Since 1999 the evolution of China's budgeting system has entered the third stage. Under the lead of the central government, China has initiated a new stage of fiscal reform, focusing on expenditure management to restructure budget compilation and budget execution. First, a system of departmental budgeting is created, in which every governmental department is required to compile its own annual budget, including all revenues and expenditure items. Moreover, the central government recommended using ZBB as a basic format to compile departmental budgets. Second, upon a single accounting system, a centralized treasury management system is created to replace the old treasury management system that is fragmented and decentralized in nature. Third, a governmental procurement reform is carried out to improve expenditure efficiency and transparency. Fourth, the recent budget reform has witnessed an increase of legislative involvement in the budgetary process, which reflects various efforts by China to democratize its budgeting system. All these efforts indicate that China is aimed to increasing allocation efficiency, enhancing fiscal control, and improving public accountability in the field of public budgeting.

This study examines the major efforts that China has made to modernize its budgeting system and financial management since 1999. The questions addressed in this study include: (1) What are the reasons driving China to conduct a series of budget reforms? (2) How does China reform its budgeting and financial management system? (3) To what extent have these reforms changed and improved China's budgeting and financial management? And (4) What are the problems that China's budget reform is facing now? The data employed in this study is from accessible official documents and published secondary data, as well as first-hand data from our fieldwork in three provinces (Hebei, Hubei, and Guangdong) and two special cities (Shenzhen and Dalian).[2]

25.2 Pre-Reform System

To understand the forces driving China to reform its budgeting and financial management system, it is necessary to examine pre-reform budgeting system. This section focuses on three aspects of the pre-reform system: how did it work? what were its basic features, and what kind of problems did it face?

25.2.1 Budgeting and Financial Management in the Planned Economy

China's economic system before 1978 was plan-dominated. The conventional fiscal system established in the early 1950s was a Stalinist style system in which the budget was secondary to the economic plan. Under this system, the economic plan was the only basis for compiling the governmental budgets. That is to say, resource allocation was determined by the national economic plan. After the plan had been set, there was little that the budget could change except for responding to the plan. Therefore, departmental budgeting was not necessary because the budgetary process was top-down in nature. Furthermore, in the traditional system, the principle of comprehensive budgeting was required to be observed, i.e., "with the exception of special funds and minor locally raised funds, all receipts and expenditures of all government agencies should be listed in the national budget" (Ko, 1959, p. 174). In order to keep the planned control, budgetary balance was required to be strictly observed (Ko, 1959, p. 174).

Under the traditional budgeting system, state-owned enterprises (SOEs) were dominant in the national economy and were tightly controlled by various levels of governments. As a result, SOEs' budgets were a major part of the governmental budget. Moreover, the governmental budget was closely related to the credit loan policy of the central bank. Finally, local governments were also institutions for implementing the central economic plans, although in the late 1970s some SOEs had been devolved to local governments. Consequently, a unified budget system was used to frame the relationships of various levels of governments, i.e., local governments were required to remit all of their fiscal revenues to the central government, which then redistributed allocations to cover the expenditures of local governments. All financial plans and accounts of the central and sub-national governments were jointly presented, and local budgets had to meet the targets laid down by higher levels of government (Ko, 1959, p. 174; World Bank, 1990, p. 83, 247). Under this system, sub-national governments had not been treated as autonomous budgetary units.

The above analysis suggests that the pre-reform budgeting system was highly centralized. First, the fiscal relationships between the higher and the lower levels of governments were very centralized. The higher governments' fiscal policy greatly shaped the lower level of governments decision-makings with regard to expenditures. Second, at each level, the allocation decision was centralized in the hand of the Plan Commission rather than the Ministry of Finance (MOF) at the central level or local finance bureaus.

However, financial management operating under such a centralized system was highly decentralized (Wang, 2003). First, there was no single account system. As a result, cash management was decentralized, in which cash balance was scattered among various accounts opened by spending departments in the state-owned banks. Second, corresponding to the decentralization of cash management, payment for products and services used by the government was made by spending departments through state-owned banks where spending departments opened accounts. Third, the accounting system — which was also decentralized and fragmented — was inadequate to effectively record and supervise fiscal transactions that occurred in the expenditure cycle. The traditional governmental accounting system, called budgetary accounting in China, was composed of three separate accounts: the administrative unit account, the institutional unit account, and the general budgetary account, which were responsible for recording fiscal transactions that occurred in different areas and were controlled by different organizations. Administrative unit accounts were used by administrative organizations to record fiscal transactions that occurred within their organizations, while institutional unit accounts were used by institutional organizations to record fiscal transactions within their organizations. The general budgetary account, which represented the government as a whole, was used to record fiscal transactions that occurred at the point of appropriation. Therefore, under this system, information about fiscal transactions that occurred at administrative and institutional organizations was scattered in all spending departments and beyond the general budgetary account and hence was beyond the control of the finance bureaus at all levels of governments. Consequently, after budgetary revenues were appropriated to spending departments' accounts, it was impossible for the finance bureau to monitor spending behaviors of spending departments (Wang, 2003).

25.2.2 Budgeting and Financial Management from 1978 to 1999

In 1978 China initiated its market-oriented economic reform, bringing about significant impacts not only on macroeconomic system but also on governmental finance management. SOEs' budgets were gradually disconnected from the governmental budget and monetary policy was separated from government budgets. Meanwhile, the principle of budget balance was abandoned at the central government. Furthermore, intergovernmental fiscal relationship was no longer operated in the traditional sense.

Fiscal decentralization between 1978 and 1994 greatly increased the autonomy of local governments. Theoretically, the national budget would consolidate the budgets of all levels of governments, and each provincial government would also consolidate all its lower level government budgets. However, in the 1980s, provincial government budgets were not fully developed to provide such detailed budgetary information of sub-national governments, which made it difficult to conduct revenue and expenditure forecasts in certain areas (World Bank, 1990, p. 83). The fiscal decentralization also resulted in the decline of the ratios of budgetary revenue to GDP and the central government revenue to total government budgetary revenue. To arrest the fall of the two ratios, since 1994 a tax sharing system has been implemented, aiming at centralizing a large amount of revenues into the coffer of the central government (Teng, 2003, p. 43).

However, before 1999, the fiscal reform mainly concentrated on the revenue side, including re-constructing taxation system, creating a new revenue sharing system between the central and local governments, and modifying the relationship between the government and SOEs (Wang, 2001). On the expenditure side, only several minor reforms were witnessed. First, China reformed its public investment system. Before the reform, public investment expenditure (construction investment), which was the largest type of investment, was allocated to SOEs for free. A system of *bo gai dai* (change appropriation to loan) was first applied in 1979 and then formally established in 1985. Under this system, a certain interest rate was charged for all investment expenditures. Further, in 1989, the central government adopted a national basic construction investment budget system. By doing so, the investment fund was divided into two parts: budgetary appropriation, applied to non-business-like basic construction investments, and a loan system, applied to business-like basic construction investments. In 1993, together with the accounting system reform, an enterprise capital fund was created for all SOEs. Since then, SOEs' budgets have been disconnected from the governmental budget (Wang, 2001).

Second, China reformed its budgetary management system for public institutions, such as government owned universities, research institutes, theaters, hotels, etc. Before 1996, China applied three different types of funding systems to three kinds of public institutions. For the first group of the institutions, all revenues came from budgetary appropriation. For the second group of the institutions, the government only provided revenues to cover the gap between their expenditures and their own revenues. For the remaining part, the government required that they use their own revenues to pay for all of their expenditures. In 1996 the government relinquished this system and implemented a new system, in which the government may provide a certain amount of grants but stipulated that the government would not provide appropriation for any over-spending (Wang, 2001).

Third, in 1994, China passed the first law on government budgeting, the *Budget Law*. The main goal of the 1994 *Budget Law* was to transform public budgeting from central planning to indirect macroeconomic management and it also set basic rules on budgetary procedures and expenditure management. Under this law, the local budget is to be formulated first and then fed into the central budget. Thus, the state budget can be formulated in a coherent framework. Moreover, local governments are required to run balanced budgets. Local governments are not allowed to finance their deficits with bond issues or bank borrowing. If they cannot maintain balanced budgets with their budgetary revenue, they must use accumulated budgetary surpluses or extra-budgetary funds to finance the deficits. The central government is no longer allowed to borrow from the central bank and has to finance its deficits by issuing bonds (Tseng et al., 1994, p. 35).

Fourth, as early as 1993, several provincial governments started experimenting with zero-based budgeting (ZBB) in compiling governmental budgets, including Hubei, Anhui, Hainan, Shengzhen, etc. The number of local governments conducting the ZBB experiment has increased in the past decade (MOF, 1997).

However, these reforms are not aimed at establishing a foundation for a new budgeting system. During the period between 1978 and 1999, although the role of the plan as the tool of resource allocation began to decline as a result of the market-oriented economic reform, a new and effective budgeting system was not developed to fill the vacuum. Consequently, both budgeting compilation and execution were problematic.

25.2.2.1 Budgeting Compilation

Budgeting compilation employed during this period was problematic in the following aspects. First, the budgeting authority was fragmented at all levels of government. The power of allocating fiscal resources formerly controlled by the Plan Committee was gradually grabbed by a variety of functional departments. At provincial level, besides the finance bureau, several other departments also had the authority over certain types of governmental expenditures, including the Development and Reform Committee (the former Plan Committee, mainly in charge of basic construction expenditures), Science and Technology Department (in charge of three science and technology improvement funds), Economy and Trade Commission (in charges of state-owned enterprises technology improvement funds), and Health Department (in charge of public healthcare funds) (Ma, 2003).

The fragmentation of budgeting power was exacerbated by the expansion of off-budgeting finance since the 1978 economic reform, in which each department held its own off-budgetary revenues and had the authority of spending them. The fragmentation of budgetary power reduced the allocation efficiency because (1) different organizations tended to adopt different methods of making allocation decisions, reducing the competition among departments and programs in public money; and (2) under which it made it impossible to pool all fiscal revenues together in order to achieve allocation efficiency at the governmental level (Li and Liu, 2003, p. 33; Ma, 2003).

Second, the budget report itself was too coarse to provide detailed information for fiscal control either by the finance bureau or by the legislature. During this period, despite a decline of the planned economy system, its budget format was comfortably inherited. As a result, governmental expenditures continued to be compiled in terms of the functions that expenditure items play in the economy rather than on the departmental basis. This budget method failed to provide sufficient budgetary information based on activities of each spending department. Actually, it was the finance bureau rather than spending departments that were responsible for compiling budgets. Moreover, the budget contained only very sketchy information of revenues and expenditures due to the simple classification of revenues and expenditures and the existence of off-budget finance not being included in the governmental budget (Li and Liu, 2003, p.12). Therefore, it was almost impossible for the finance bureau and the People's Congresses at all levels to effectively examine and supervise governmental budgets (Xiang, 2001, pp. 90–91).

Third, during this period, within the finance bureau, the process of examining budget requests was decentralized, in which each specialized division within the finance bureau allocated certain types of expenditures to various spending departments, while each spending department went to almost all divisions of the finance bureau to ask for money in terms of the types of expenditures. One of the problems under this system was that there was not any division able to have a complete budget for each spending department. From the perspective of the spending departments, efficiency was lost with the increase of transaction costs since they had to negotiate with various divisions for budget requests.

Fourth, for many years, budgeting decisions had been made upon previous budget appropriation plus an increase (*ji shu jia zeng zhang*), similar to the so-called incremental budgeting. However, under China's incremental budgeting, the budgetary base was decided very arbitrarily. For example, at the provincial level, a variety of *previous* central laws and policies, provincial policies, and spending needs of powerful politicians were three major factors to shape budgeting decisions. In many cases, although certain central and provincial policies were no longer solid and reasonable for revenue and expenditure forecasting, they continued to be used to justify budgetary requests. Besides the influence of those policies, powerful politicians, mainly the Standing Committee members of Chinese Communist Party (CCP) governors or vice governors, had *informal* power to ask the finance bureau to allocate money to certain departments or programs that they favored.[3] Consequently, the departments tended to bypass the finance bureau and directly lobbied key politicians for budgetary appropriation at any time during one budgetary year. If the politician thought that a department's request was reasonable from his/her personal judgement, he/she would write a note to endorse this budgetary request, called as *pi tiao zi* (writing a note) in Chinese budgeting practice. With this note in hand, the department could get budget appropriation easily, barely refuted by the finance bureau (Ma, 2003).

China's incremental budgeting also resulted in an unequal budgetary appropriation among spending departments and failed to reflect the changes in both the economic environment and department demands (PPRCSUFE, 2003). It created a stable allotment among departments, thus leading to an inefficient allocation of public resources because it encouraged some departments to overspend (Wang, 2001) and made re-allocation almost impossible. As a result, budget allocation became less efficient.

25.2.2.2 Budgetary Execution

Budgetary execution under pre-reform budgeting system was also problematic, largely because of the decentralized treasury management developed during the planned economy period. First, in the process of budgeting execution, spending departments never took the budget seriously. They frequently went to the finance bureau whenever they ran out of expenditures allocated to them, or they wanted to increase revenues for existing programs or carry out a new program. Therefore, supplemental appropriation and budget adjustments were very prevalent in China's budgeting system. Moreover, the policy-making and budgetary process were separated. Key political figures (members of the Standing Committee of the CCP, governors, and vice governors) could make policies at any time during budget execution,[4] demanding additional funds to support these policies. In this situation, the current budget had to be adjusted or reserved fund had to be put into use.

Second, revenue management was low in efficiency. The departments that had authority to collect revenues did not directly submit the collected revenues to the governmental treasury. Instead, they opened a variety of transitional accounts in commercial banks where those departments deposited the revenues before they were submitted to the treasury. And the management of transitional accounts was beyond the supervision of the finance bureau. These practices not only decreased revenue collection efficiency but also increased the risk of corruption (Wang, 2002).

Third, expenditure management was underdeveloped. There was no single account system. Besides the accounts under the finance bureau, spending departments also opened their expenditure accounts in commercial banks, and almost all spending departments opened several accounts in one or more banks. After budgetary appropriations were approved, they were transferred to the spending departments' accounts and spent at the discretion of spending departments with no intervention of the finance bureau. Therefore, there was not such a system of the fiscal direct payment as that in Western countries, in which the treasury directly pays providers of products and services from a single account. Instead, before the payment finally reached the receivers, the payment always involved multiple-levels of accounts. This system reduced the efficiency of cash management and fund using, and increased the risk of misuse, misappropriation, and corruption (Wang, 2002; Xiang, 2001, pp. 136–137).

Meanwhile, procurement was decentralized in nature, in which each spending department procured its own products and services and paid for them. This system was problematic in the following aspects: (1) the procurement was beyond the control of the finance bureau, (2) it did not take the price advantage on large-scale purchases to save governmental expenditures, and (3) it lacked competition and transparency (Xiang, 2001, p. 145).

25.2.3   The Recent Budget Reforms

The necessity of establishing a modern budgeting system became obvious in the late 1990s. Since 1999, under the lead of the central government, China has initiated a new stage of fiscal reforms to restructure budget compilation and execution. As Vice-Finance Minister Jiwei Lou (2002) summarized, the current budget reforms were composed of three basic elements. The first reform is the budgeting compilation reform, aiming at improving the process and the method of compiling governmental budgets. It emphasizes establishing a departmental budgeting system, in which the governmental budget is compiled on a departmental basis, and every governmental department is required to submit its own budget, including all of its revenues and expenditures, including off-budgetary revenues and expenditures. The second reform is the treasury management reform. The central theme of this reform is to create a centralized system of financial management to replace the old fragmented and decentralized treasury management system. The foundation of this reform is the creation of a single account system for revenue collection and expenditure payment. Upon this, a fiscal direct payment system will be created, in which governmental expenditures are paid directly from the treasury's single account to product and service providers. The goal of this reform is to enable the finance bureau to control spending behaviors and monitor daily fiscal transactions during the whole expenditure cycle. The third reform is the expenditure management reform. It is centered on reforming public procurement. The aim of governmental procurement reform is to create a centralized governmental procurement system to replace the decentralized governmental procurement system.

Without any doubt, these efforts are trying to reinforce fiscal control on the budgeting system. That is, it is aimed to create a control-oriented budgeting system. First, departmental budgeting reform will enable the finance bureau to centralize budgeting power into its own hand. Second, treasury management reform and public procurement reform will enable the finance bureau to control spending departments' spending behaviors. Third, by introducing ZBB into the budgetary process; the reform also seeks to incorporate the budgeting rationality into the budgetary process, that is, to allocate fiscal revenues in terms of priority rather than previous policies and politicians' willing. Finally, the budget reform will contribute to democratize the budgetary process in China, because the establishment of a departmental budgeting system will make it much easier for the legislature to effectively examine the governmental budget.

25.3   Departmental Budgeting Reform

In the departmental budgeting system, the governmental budget is compiled on the basis of spending departments. Each spending department is required to formulate its own budget, projecting all of its revenues and expenditures, and putting all of its revenues and expenditures into a single departmental budget. The departmental budget is then submitted to and examined by the finance bureau. The latter is responsible for preparing the budget proposal that incorporates all departments' budgets and submitting the proposal to the People's Congresses for legislative review.

25.3.1   Reorganizing the Budgeting Office

The departmental budgeting reform is aimed to centralize budgeting power into the hands of the finance bureau in order to impose fiscal control over the spending departments. To effectively examine the departments' budgetary requests, the finance bureaus at all levels of governments have been reorganized.

During this process, local governments mainly followed the reorganization strategies developed by the central government. At the beginning of the departmental budgeting reform, the internal organizational structure of the central government's budgeting office (i.e., the MOF) remained intact, proving to be a hindrance to the budget reform (Li and Liu, 2003, p.144). Therefore, in June 2001, the MOF was reorganized. Within the MOF, two new divisions were established to separate the budgetary compilation from the budgetary execution: the Budgeting Division, which is responsible for examining budgetary requests of spending departments, and the Treasury Division, which is responsible for daily financial management. Moreover, to improve the process of budgetary examination, the MOF adopted a system called *gui kou guan li*, which changed each specialized division's (e.g., the Division of Education, Science, Culture, and Health) function from being in charge of specific types of fiscal expenditures for all departments to being in charge of all expenditures of specific departments (Li and Liu, 2003, p. 145). This creates a centralized budgetary examination process, in which each department's budget request is now examined only by one specialized division and then submitted to the Budgeting Division for further examination based on a macro analysis incorporating all spending departments' requests. It is expected that this restructuring will significantly improve MOF's fiscal control over the departments' requests because it enables MOF (with the assistance of its specialized divisions and Budgeting Division) to hold a complete picture of each department's revenue and expenditure activities. It also saves transaction costs occurring in the bargains between the finance bureau and the departments.

Such reorganization has been adopted by most of the provincial governments. However, at the local level, there are certain variations. For example, Hebei province, the first local government to adopt departmental budgeting reform, emphasizes not only the separation between budget compilation and execution but also a further separation between budget compilation, execution, and supervision. The power to compile a budget is centralized from various specialized divisions to the Budgeting Division. The specialized divisions are responsible for examining budget requests and monitoring the use of budget appropriations. The Budgetary Examination and Review Service Center was established to provide assistance to the Budgeting Division for examining departments' budget requests and compiling budget proposals. In addition, the General Office of Budget Execution was established to combine the general budget accounting management of the provincial finance bureau with the accounting management conducted by the departments. Finally, the Supervision

Division was created to supervise both budgeting compilation and execution (Wang, 2000, p. 202). However, several provincial governments such as Guangdong and Dalian have not applied *gui kuo guan li*, although they have also created the Budgeting Division and Treasury Division.

25.3.2 Restructuring the Budgetary Process

In the new system, the budgetary process has been fundamentally restructured. A so-called *liang shang liang xia* (two-ups and two-downs) procedure is carried out by the central government and most of local governments. Under this procedure, the spending departments formulate and submit their budget requests to the finance bureau with a variety of evidence (laws and policies) supporting their requests (the first up); then, the finance bureau examines the departments' budget requests and makes a comprehensive analysis by combining those requests and other budget appropriations approved by other bureaus (e.g., the Science and Technology Bureau) holding partial budgeting allocation authority. After that, the finance bureau sets a budgetary quota or a ceiling for each spending department (the first down). The latter then adjusts its budget request under this ceiling and resubmits a modified budget request to the finance bureau (the second up). After reviewing the spending departments' revised budget requests, the finance bureau works out a governmental budget proposal including all spending departments' budgets and submits it to legislative review. Once the budget proposal is approved, the finance bureau instructs spending departments to begin execution (the second down) (MOF, 2003).

However, according to our interviews, at the provincial level there are certain variations in the budgetary process. For example, in Dalian, although the finance bureau stated the use of *two-ups and two-downs*, the budgetary process still follows the conventional one-up and one-down (*yi shang yi xia*) procedure, in which the finance bureau gives departments a ceiling first (first down), and then the spending departments submit their budget requests based on the ceiling (the first up). Additionally, since there will be no major changes after the legislative review, the second down existing in other places is not very meaningful for Dalian.

In Tianjin the budgetary process is more complex because Tianjin carries out a three-downs and three-ups procedure (*san xia san shang*). First, the finance bureau issues guidance to all departments, specifying each department's budgetary goals and the size of expenditures (first down). Next, each department compiles its budget and submits it to the respective specialized division of the finance bureau (the first up); the division then examines the department's request and submits it with the division's suggested adjustments to the Budgeting Division for further examination and approval. The Budgeting Division submits the departmental budget and its examination to chief executive meeting of the finance bureau and the metropolitan government meeting (the second up). Then, the Budgeting Division sends back its budgetary examination to specialized divisions and spending departments to ask for their opinions (the second down). The spending departments will re-compile their budgets according to the finance bureau's suggestions and re-submit them to respective specialized divisions of the finance bureau. The divisions examine modified budget requests and combine them with other sources of budget appropriation; upon this, the divisions re-submit the departments' new budget to the Budgeting Division. Then, all the departments' budgets are combined into one governmental budget proposal and submitted to the chief executive meeting of the finance bureau, the metropolitan government, and then the legislature for examination (the third up). After the governmental budget has been approved by the legislature, the Budgeting Division, with the assistance of specialized divisions, authorizes the budgets to all spending departments (the third down) (Li and Liu, 2003, p. 175).

25.3.3   Budget Format: ZBB or TBB?

ZBB has not been systematically implemented until the recent departmental budgeting reform, though early in 1993 several provincial governments had begun to adopt it. First, before the departmental budgeting reform, governmental budgets were not compiled on the departmental basis. Actually, it was the finance bureau that was responsible for compiling the budgets for the departments. Therefore, before the recent budgeting reform, ZBB during this period was mainly employed by the finance bureau to make budgetary decisions with no involvement of the departments. Second, before the departmental budgeting reform, ZBB had few influences on most of the departments' expenditure decisions because of the fragmentation of budgetary power as mentioned before, in which a large amount of the departments' expenditures was beyond the control of the finance bureau. The recent departmental budgeting reform provides an opportunity for ZBB to be systematically applied. First, it emphasizes consolidating off-budgeting revenues and expenditures into the budget, thus putting them under the control of the finance bureau. Second, as the governmental budget is compiled on the departmental basis, ZBB is therefore employed not only by the finance bureau to make budgetary decisions but also by the departments to formulate their budget requests (Ma, 2003).

However, our investigations reveal, at least at the provincial level, it is Target-Based Budgeting (TBB) rather than ZBB that has been put in place.

At this point, Hubei's experience is much informative. At the outset, ZBB was created as an alternative of the incremental budget format. In 2001, when the departmental budgeting reform was initiated in Hubei, spending departments were required to use ZBB to formulate all their requests. The budgetary process then was bottom-up, starting with the formulation of fund requests by agencies within the departments. Each agency formulated its requests according to its work goals and submitted them to the department's financial office. The latter examined these requests in terms of program priority and then ranked them. Ranked expenditures were then submitted to the departmental director and the Chinese Communist Party (CCP) group (*dang zu*) within the department for examining and adjustment. Finally, the approved and ranked expenditure list was compiled into the departmental budget and submitted to the finance bureau (Ma, 2003).

However, at that time, as there was no ceiling set for the departments' initial requests, requests made by the departments were much higher than available revenues estimated by the finance bureau. With no choice, the finance bureau had to refuse all departments' requests and set a ceiling for each department, and then the departments were required to revise their requests under their ceilings. For instance, according to the Hubei case, the original budget the Social Security Department formulated according to the logic of ZBB came up to RMB 1.5 billion yuan. After the ceiling control system was put in place the department was required to re-formulate its request under the ceiling of RMB 87 million yuan, which was a dramatic cut. Since then the ceiling control system has been institutionalized and manifests itself in the *two-ups* and *two-downs* budgetary procedure — a firm ceiling is given for each department at the first down (Ma, 2003).[5]

The ceiling control system is much similar to TBB, viewed as a modification of ZBB in USA,[6] though there was not any respondent of this study ever mentioned in the terms of TBB. For instance, in Hubei, many budgetary officials from spending departments called the whole system "control budgeting" right after the compilation of 2001 budget.[7] The finance bureau in local China heavily relies on the ceiling to constrain the departments' requests while leaving certain flexibility to spending departments in budgetary trade-off under the ceiling.

25.3.4 A Discriminated Alignment in China's Budgeting System

However, the Chinese style TBB is not exactly same as the TBB practiced in U.S. local governments. As our investigation shows, the installation of TBB has not brought an end of ZBB. Instead, ZBB is largely applied on one type of expenditures, i.e., program expenditures. The departmental budgeting reform re-clarifies and unifies the scope, category, and composition of the departmental budget. The departmental budget is composed of three major categories: personnel, operating, and program expenditures. Personnel expenditures include wages and welfare expenditures of civil servants. Operating expenditures refer to expenditures spent on administrative operation of the departments, such as printing, meeting, traveling, vehicle maintenance, and electricity. Program expenditures are expenditures for the departments to achieve certain specific administrative missions or goals (Ma, 2003).

As mentioned above, at the provincial level, ZBB is mainly applied to program expenditures. For example, in Hubei, only in the section of program expenditures does the name of ZBB appear in the *Notification of Compiling 2004 Provincial Departmental Budgets* issued by the finance bureau. Moreover, in our interviews, respondents tend to describe their budgeting methods as "personnel expenditures according to real need, operating expenditures according to the standard, and program expenditures according to the rank," suggesting that ZBB is just applied to program expenditures rather than all types of expenditures. It seems that basic expenditures (personnel and operating expenditures) and program expenditures are viewed as different in nature, and hence, they are budgeted differently, which suggests a kind of discriminate alignment (Patashnik, 1996, p. 200) may exist in the provincial budgetary process. Lastly, as one respondent in Hubei stated, "[s]ince personnel and operating expenditures are fixed, ZBB mainly fall in program expenditures" (Ma, 2003). Due to the same reason, the control of the budget ceiling also mainly falls in program expenditures. Figure 25.1 presents the budgeting methods applied to different types of expenditures in the budgetary process.

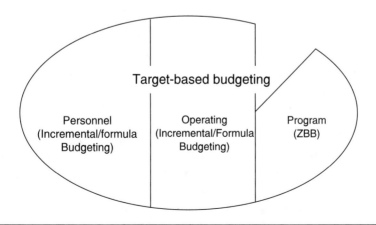

Figure 25.1   The nature of the departmental budget reform.

25.3.4.1 Personnel Expenditure and Operating Expenditure

Personnel and operating expenditures are termed basic expenditures in China. According to our investigation, both of them are determined by a combination of formula budgeting with incremental budgeting. In China four organizations involve the decision of personnel expenditure: the spending departments, the staff size authorizing committee (SSAC), the personnel bureau, and the finance bureau. The SSAC determines how many employees each spending department can hire. According to the wage policy issued by the State Council, the personnel bureau calculates the total wages and an average personnel expenditure standard (e.g., RMB 20,000 yuan per person each year), which is then submitted to the finance bureau. The finance bureau will review this standard according to its estimation of available revenues, a comparison with the salary level of non-government employees, and local living level. Since personnel expenditure enjoys high priority in the budgetary process, usually, the finance bureau will accept this expenditure standard (Ma, 2003).

Theoretically, spending departments could make their own budgetary requests for personnel expenditure. Actually, they have no discretion to make their own recommendation on personnel expenditures because both the staff size and expenditure standards are beyond their authority. For them, the determination of personnel expenditure is a straight calculation according to formula. Spending departments must follow the staff quota set by the SSAC and the average personnel expenditure standard decided by the personnel bureau and finance bureau. However, when the personnel bureau and finance bureau make their decisions on the standard, the budgetary appropriation of last year still plays an important role in defining the standard. Therefore, the determination of this part of the budget requests indicates a combination of incremental budgeting and formula budgeting (Ma, 2003).

The determination of operating expenditure involves a more complicated calculation. In the budgetary decision on operating expenditures, the finance bureau calculates an operating expenditure standard for every department based on their activities, e.g., RMB 20,000 yuan per capita each year for the education department, and 30,000 per capita each year for the police department. At the earliest stage of the reform, most local governments carried out departmental budgeting reform in some spending departments rather than all departments. For the departments being included into the departmental budgeting reform, operating expenditure standards are determined item by item according to the average expenditure of the selected representative departments during the past several years.[8] For example, the printing expenditure standard can be set as RMB 60 yuan per capita annually based upon the average printing expenditure of the representative departments during the past several years. After all items have been measured as such, a total operating expenditure standard is computed. Next, these standards will be slightly adjusted according to the departments' function, workload, and previous budget appropriation of each department (Ma, 2003). Usually, a higher standard is given to important departments such as the police departments and the judicial system, while a lower standard is given to less important departments such as the associations of women. Also, the operating expenditure standards vary among regions and levels of government due to their fiscal situation. At the central government, the average standard was RMB 40,000 yuan per capita in 2003. In Guangdong, the richest province in terms of both local economy and fiscal revenue, the standard was RMB 50,000 yuan per capita in 2003. In Hubei province, which faced serious fiscal stringency during these years, the standard was RMB 20,000 yuan per capita in 2003.[9]

No matter how big regional distinctions are, the determination of the average standard of operating expenditures is under the control of the finance bureau. Multiplying the average standard by the number of employees, the spending department then gets its budget request for operating expenditures. Therefore, for spending departments, the budgetary decision on operating expenditures is also carried out according to certain formulas. Nevertheless, as the above analysis suggests, the previous appropriation of operating expenditures is still one key element to decide the average operating expenditures, suggesting the budgetary base matters as well.

For other departments not being included in the departmental budgeting reform, budgetary decision-making is still a kind of incrementalism. As a budgetary official in Hubei said, "operating expenditures will be decided on the basis of last year's budgetary expenditure, and then we will take into account this year's change" (Ma, 2003). However, these departments' budget requests are constrained by the available revenues, and a low expenditure standard is applied to these departments. For example, in Hubei province, the standard was around only RMB 6,000–7,000 yuan per capita in 2003.

The problems with the basic expenditures are largely related to operating expenditures. First, in provinces facing fiscal stringency, the operating expenditure standard has been set too low to cover actual operating expenditures. Therefore, during these years, all spending departments have been misappropriating expenditure from program appropriations or even extra-budgetary revenues to compensate operating expenditures in order to support their daily operations. Second, although adjustment of operating expenditure standards among departments is expected, usually, the operating expenditure standard is applied to most departments with no consideration of the real need of different departments, largely due to the difficulty of measurement.

25.3.4.2 Program Expenditure

Program expenditure is required to be decided within the framework of ZBB. In the interviews, as far as the program expenditure was concerned, budgetary officials would use terms of ZBB to describe their budgetary processes, including program priority, rank, and zero-base. Our investigation shows that, to a large extent, ZBB in China is regarded as a budget preparation technique designed to improve fiscal control over department requests, similar to the practice of ZBB in Georgia that Professor Lauth (1978) found twenty-six years ago.

Nevertheless, since ZBB over program expenditures is operated under the Chinese style TBB, its implementation has something unique. While ZBB in theory follows a bottom-up process, ZBB implementation in China is both bottom-up and top-down. It is bottom-up because, given the ceiling, the directors of the departments are given the option of putting important programs into their requests and taking other less important programs out of current budgetary year's requests. However, it is also a top-down process because the ceiling control mainly falls on the program expenditures, as has been mentioned. Moreover, in the provincial governments, the finance bureau actively directs the departments' budgetary trade-off through the implementation of program inventory system (*xiang mu ku*).

Although the departments and their subordinate agencies are responsible for decision-unit analysis — the first step of ZBB (Pyhrr, 1973), the Hubei case shows that the finance bureau actively intervenes in such analysis. For program expenditures the decision units are the programs. Some departments really conducted decision units analysis, reexamining the purposes, activities, and operation of the decision unit, and asking whether certain programs can be terminated. However, the finance bureau actively involved the departments' decision unit analysis by stipulating which program must be terminated or partly cut (Ma, 2003).

Further, with the establishment of the program inventory system, the finance bureau actually involves in not only the departments' decision unit analysis but also their ranking process. In creating the program inventory system, the finance bureau first asks all departments to develop their own program inventories by analyzing and ranking their programs according to the importance of programs, based on the consideration of their functions and the central and provincial policies. After that the finance bureau will construct its own program inventory system, in which all departments' programs are ranked in terms of priority. To be honest, the inventory system is created to reflect the need of the departments. However, once the program inventory system has been put in use, especially when the finance bureau's program inventory system is decided, it will impose certain constraints on the departments' requests over program expenditures (Ma, 2003).

However, the impacts of ZBB in China should not be overstated. Not all program expenditures are determined within the framework of ZBB because the finance bureau is still not the only department having the authority to allocate budgetary revenues, and several other departments continue to hold the authority to allocate certain types of budgetary expenditures outside the departmental budgeting system. For example, the Three Funds for Science and Technology Improvement (*ke ji san xiang*) is controlled and allocated by the Science and Technology Department (Ma, 2003).

Moreover, according to a recent investigation of ZBB in Hubei provincial government (Ma, 2003), even in the field of program expenditures where ZBB is practiced, ZBB has not produced fundamental changes in the budgetary process and outcomes. The implementation of ZBB in China, especially in local governments, is severely beset with three structural elements. First, revenue stringency has greatly impeded the implementation of ZBB in some provinces facing fiscal stringency. In fiscal stress, budgetary revenues must first be allocated to personnel and operating expenditures. But, after this, remaining revenues are relatively small in amount, making it difficult to apply ZBB to program expenditures. This is because, in this situation, if ZBB had been exactly carried out, that is revenues had been allocated according to the priority until all available revenues were exhausted, most programs planned by the departments would not receive any money even if they were desirable and had strong and reasonable policy rationale. Worse, there would be many departments receiving no funds for their programs. The finance bureau trapped in such a budgetary environment would find it is difficult or impossible to exactly implement ZBB because of the resistance from the departments (Ma, 2003).

Second, the practice of "biting program expenditures" (*chi zhuan xiang*), stealing program appropriation to compensate operating expenditures, is a common practice in China's local budgeting system, which further impeded ZBB implementation. Compared with personnel and operating expenditures, spending departments have more discretion in the formulation and execution of program budget. Meanwhile, since the low operating expenditure standard set by the finance bureau is far from satisfying the real operating demand of spending departments, departments tend to use part of program budget to meet their operating needs (Ma, 2003).

Third, certain political elements have produced negative impacts on ZBB implementation. For instance, the practice of "writing a note" by powerful politicians to support certain budget requests persists into the new budgetary process. Excessive intervention of politicians in the budgetary process of ZBB greatly impaired the ranking process, makes it completely meaningless (Ma, 2003).

25.3.5   Summary

It is clear that the departmental budgeting reform is a control-oriented budgeting reform. It centralizes budgeting powers from the departments to the hands of the finance bureau by gradually consolidating off-budgetary revenues into the departmental budgets. Moreover, with the establishment of the departmental budgeting system, the finance bureau now examines budget requests on a departmental basis rather than on the types of expenditures as it did before, indicating the finance bureau is now able to examine the budget requests in detail. Upon these, it is possible for the finance bureau to impose fiscal control over the departments. The fiscal control is materialized by two mechanisms: ZBB and the ceiling control system. To improve allocating efficiency, the departmental budgeting reform is also oriented to incorporate budgeting rationality into the budgetary process by experimenting with budgeting techniques such as ZBB. Lastly, to enhance its capacity to supervise the departments' budget activities, the internal organizational structure of the finance bureau has been restructured. All this suggests that the finance bureau will be created as a real "central budgeting office," powerful and capable in its bargaining with the departments.

However, to fully realize the goals of the departmental budgeting reform, that is to achieve fiscal control and allocation efficiency, China needs to make more efforts to solve problems now besetting its budgeting reform. The first of the problems is to firmly constrain politicians' arbitrarily intervening in budgetary decisions, that is to say to further formalize the budgetary structure and process and reduce the role of informal budgetary process. Second, it is necessary to further centralize the budgeting authority from other departments still holding certain budgeting authority to the hands of the finance bureau. Lastly, it is important to further improve the organizational capacity of the finance bureau in budgeting examination. In our interviews, many budgetary officials openly question the finance bureau's capacity in budgetary examination.

25.4   Treasury Management Reform

While the departmental budgeting reform mainly focuses on restructuring the budgetary process and improving the allocation efficiency and fiscal control in budgetary compilation, treasury management reform concentrates on establishing a centralized treasury management system to enhance management efficiency and external control in budgetary execution.

Local governments are credited with moving ahead toward treasury management reform. In 1995, Jingzhou City Government in the Hubei province experimented with a so-called *ling hu ti xi* (Single Account System) in one of its districts as an alternative to the old accounting system. By doing this, spending departments opened a single account under the finance bureau's supervision, thus centralizing the account reporting system (Zhang, Yuan and Wang, 2001, p. 295–296). In June 1998 Yichang County Government in Hubei province installed a system called *ling hu tong guan* (Unified Management by Single Account) to improve financial management in several township governments and then extended the system to all township governments in September 1998. The reform aimed at centralizing the accounting system in township governments and tightening financial management. Yichang's experiments have been proved to be very successful, abolishing 728 departmental accounts and centralizing fiscal specific funds as much as RMB 15 million yuan. Based on Yichang's success, in December 1998, the finance bureau of the provincial government recommended all township governments adopt the single account system. In 2000 Hubei provincial government further endorsed this reform, deciding to carry it out in all township governments (Tong, 2001, p. 4–5). In 1999 many county governments in Zhejiang province began to move toward a centralized financial management system, similar to the new system recently adopted by the central government, which is discussed next (ZPAPF, 2002).

In 2001 the treasury management reform entered into a new stage as the central government adopted a new system and required subnational governments to follow. The new system is called Treasury Direct Collection and Payment System (TDCPS), imposing an external control over revenue and expenditure activities of the departments. The central government first installed TDCPS in six ministries, including the Ministry of Finance, Ministry of Science and Technology, National Natural Science Funds, China Academy of Science, and Law Office of the State Council. In 2002 this new system was extended to seventeen ministries at the central level. Meanwhile, local governments also began a similar reform. The TDCPS is composed of three elements: (1) establishing a single account system, (2) centralizing revenue management, and (3) centralizing expenditure management. Moreover, to provide support for TDCPS, other related efforts were carried out, such as modifying the accounting system of the administrative units and institutional units, reforming the public procurement system, establishing new organizations responsible for treasury management, i.e., the Treasury Division and Public Procurement Center (Zhang and Teng, 2002; Xu, 2003). Compared to the pre-reform system, this is a highly centralized system because all revenue and expenditure transactions occurring in spending departments must be reflected in TDCPS under the finance bureau's supervision and management.

25.4.1 The Single Account System

In the former system, the finance bureau opened a treasury account for budgetary revenues and a special account for extra-budgetary revenues in the central bank and commercial banks. Also, spending departments opened their own accounts in commercial banks. Now, TDCPS establishes a Treasury Single Account (TSA) system in which governmental departments no longer open their own revenue and expenditure accounts in commercial banks; instead, the finance bureau opens five types of accounts in the central bank and commercial banks (Xiang, 2001; Zhang and Teng, 2002; PPRCSUFE, 2003):

1. The finance bureau opens a *treasury single account* (TSA) in the central bank, which is used to record all financial transactions related to governmental revenue and expenditure activities, and liquidate with zero-balance accounts that the finance bureau opens at commercial banks.

2. The finance bureau opens *zero-balance accounts* (ZBAs) for both itself and spending departments in commercial banks. The finance bureau's ZBA is used for direct fiscal payment in which the finance bureau directly transfers fiscal revenues from this account to providers of goods and services to the government. Spending departments' ZBA is used for delegated fiscal payment in which the finance bureau allows spending departments to spend without the permission of the finance bureau. Both accounts are required to liquidate with the TSA. The two ZBAs and the TSA construct the basic account system for the TDCPS.

3. To tighten the management of extra-budgetary funds, the finance bureau opens a *special account for extra-budgetary funds* in commercial banks to record and monitor financial transactions related to extra-budgetary activities.

4. To record and monitor financial transactions related to expenditures in small amounts, the finance bureau opens a *small amount cash account* for spending departments in commercial banks.

5. The finance bureau opens a *special account* to record and monitor financial transactions related to some special revenues and expenditures of various budgetary units.

The TSA system is presented in Figure 25.2.

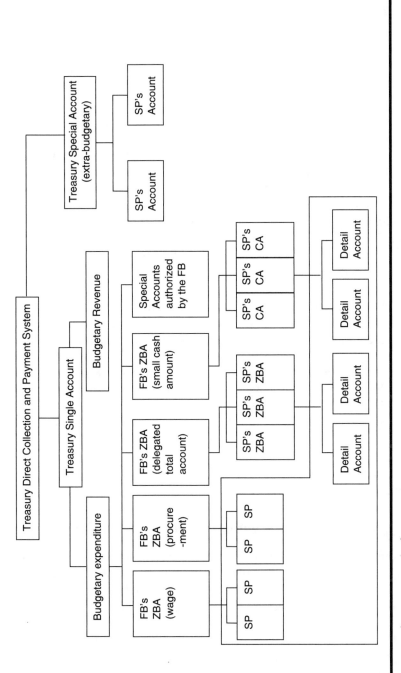

Figure 25.2 The treasury single account system.
Source: Zheng (2003, p. 86).
Note: SP refers to spending departments.

25.4.2   The Centralized Revenue Collection Procedure

In the new treasury management system the revenue collection and submitting procedure is centralized. Various transitional accounts existing in the pre-reform system have been abolished. Usually, revenue-collecting departments are required to submit revenues directly to the treasury. The new system uses two methods to submit revenues to the treasury: direct submission and pooled submission (Lou, 2002; PPRCSUFE, 2003; Xiang, 2001; Zhang and Teng, 2002; Zheng, 2003).

In direct submission, taxpayers first present their submission application to the tax bureau. Then, the tax bureau will give taxpayers a submission certificate after it examines the applications. Taxpayers will transfer the certificates to the commercial bank(s) where they opened accounts. Then the taxpayers' bank(s) will transfer money from their accounts to the TSA, and the bank(s) will liquidate between those two accounts. The treasury's bank will report this transaction to both the collecting bureau and finance bureau. Meanwhile, the submission of extra-budgetary revenues follows a similar procedure, except the money is submitted by payers to the treasury's delegated bank rather than regular commercial banks, and then it is transferred to the treasury's extra-budgetary special account. Moreover, the procedure requires that a clearing be conducted between the TSA and the treasury's delegated bank.

The pooled submission is applied to small amount taxes and other extra-budgetary revenues submitted in cash. In this method, taxpayers submit taxes to the tax bureau. Next, the tax bureau will pool all taxes submitted by taxpayers and submit them to the TSA. The bank holding the account for the treasury will then report this transaction to the tax bureau and finance bureau. Extra-budgetary revenues falling in this procedure are submitted in a similar procedure except that revenues are submitted by the collecting agency to the treasury's extra-budgetary special account.

25.4.3   The Centralized Spending Payment Procedure

The spending payment procedure is also centralized in the new system. According to differences of payment units and types of expenditures (purchase or transfer expenditure), two types of payment methods are installed: fiscal direct payment and fiscal delegated payment. For the former, the finance bureau writes a payment command, and then directly transfers fiscal funds to receivers by the TSA. For the latter, spending departments with the finance bureau's delegation write a payment command to transfer the funds from the TSA to receivers. Most payments are required to be conducted through fiscal direct payment (Lou, 2002; Zhang and Teng, 2002; Xiang, 2001; Zheng, 2003, pp. 87–90).

The following expenditures are required to adopt fiscal direct payment: (1) wage expenditures, governmental purchase expenditures, special transfers from the central to sub-national governments, and appropriations to enterprises' construction programs or large facilities procurements, (2) transfer expenditures (except the central special transfer), including the tax return, subsidies retained from the old system, transitional transfers, subsidies to enterprises, and special expenditures without assigned use requirements (Xiang, 2001). As an illustration, Figure 25.3 presents the procedure of fiscal direct payment in the Sichuan province.

The fiscal delegated payment is applied to occasional expenditures and purchase expenditures whose procurement decisions are made by the spending departments. Under the finance bureau's delegation, spending departments can ask for payment from the treasury account without the finance bureau's permission. Therefore, more authority is given to spending departments in their spending activities. Of course, spending departments are not free from external control. First, the finance bureau controls the spending departments through the control of the authorized payment amount. Usually, in the early stage of budgeting execution, the spending department will submit its spending plan to the finance bureau, which divides the department's budgetary appropriation into several periods (usually first by quarterly and then by monthly). The finance bureau will examine this plan in terms of the approved departmental budget and cash flow of the treasury, and then it makes certain changes and authorizes the spending plan, which determines the available amount during a certain period for the department. Second, the finance bureau is able to monitor the spending activities of the

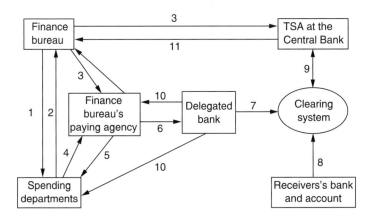

Figure 25.3 The fiscal direct payment procedure.
Source: Wang, L., Zhang, S. Z., Chen, Q. Y., and Huang, Y. X. (2003, pp. 24–25), with certain modifications.

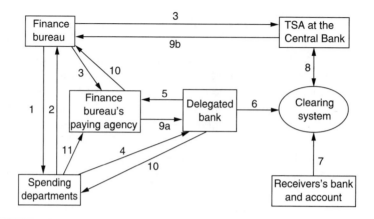

Figure 25.4 The fiscal delegated payment procedure.
Source: Wang, L., Zhang, S. Z., Chen, Q. Y., and Huang, Y. X. (2003, pp. 24–25), with certain modifications.

department because, although it is now the department that issues the payment order to the delegated bank, the payment actually goes through the ZBA that the finance bureau opens for the department, which is part of the TSA. Moreover, fiscal revenues are directly transferred from the ZBA to individuals and organizations providing products and services to the government. Again, as an illustration, Figure 25.4 presents the fiscal delegated payment procedure in Sichuan province.

25.4.4 *Achievements and Problems*

Although the treasury management reform is far from completion at this point, it has already produced several positive impacts on China's governmental financial management. First, with the implementation of the new system, the finance bureau's control of unspent expenditures is enhanced because the unspent revenues are now retained at the treasury of the finance bureau rather than "sleep" at a variety of accounts of spending departments in commercial banks. This provides a foundation for China to conduct cash management in the future (Zhang and Teng, 2002). For example, in Panzhihua City Government of Sichuan province, there was RMB 4.48 million yuan unspent expenditure that had been saved after adopting the new system for half a year in 2003 (Panzhihua Finance Bureau, 2003).

Second, with the assistance of the TSA system, treasury management reform enables the finance bureau to implement external control over spending departments' expenditure activities, i.e., all expenditure activities of spending departments during the expenditure cycle are now under the daily control of the finance bureau.

Third, the new system greatly improves the efficiency of revenue collection and expenditure payment. For example, in the central government, after the 2001 experiment, it takes only one day for the fiscal fund to be transferred from the treasury account to receivers, while the payment process tended to take weeks to be completed in the previous system (Zhang and Teng, 2002).

Finally, as many government officials identify, to some extent the new system will help to curb corruption because under this system the spending departments can only see the "numbers" in their budgets instead of the real "money," since the money is paid directly from the treasury account to receivers providing services and goods to the government or the public employees' personal accounts in commercial banks.

However, treasury management reform faces some problems that need to be solved in further implementation. First, although the new system pools all extra-budgetary revenues into a special account to improve the finance bureau's monitoring of financial transactions, extra-budgetary revenues and expenditures are actually outside the TSA system. Moreover, information about extra-budgetary revenues and expenditures is managed by commercial banks instead of the central bank. To some degree, this weakens both the finance bureau and the central bank's control over extra-budget items. It also makes it more difficult for the central bank to integrate monetary policy with fiscal policy (Xu, 2003).

Second, not all sub-national governments opened their TSA at the central bank. Instead, some established their TSA at commercial banks, which may produce certain fiscal risks in the future since commercial banks may transfer the fiscal revenues into their investment accounts for a higher return, putting the fiscal account in risk. Moreover, it weakens the central bank's ability to monitor financial transactions related to these revenues and to effectively implement monetary policy (Xu, 2003).

Third, the selection of commercial banks for finance bureaus and spending departments to open ZBAs lacks a standardized procedure and objective criteria to follow, which has resulted in certain disorderly competition among commercial banks as well as corruption (Xu, 2003).

Lastly, the account reporting systems used by the central and sub-national government are different. At the local level, the pattern is to abolish spending departments' accounts opened in commercial banks, and then create an "account reporting center," "fiscal reporting center," "fund clearing center," or "treasury centralized payment center" to centralize the accounting and reporting activities. However, at the central government, although it also centralizes revenues and expenditures into the hands of the MOF, the accounting and reporting system is kept in the spending ministries (Xu, 2003).

The local pattern enhanced the finance bureau's ability to control spending activities but reduced spending departments' ability to carry out internal control. Meanwhile, the central pattern assisted spending departments in carrying out internal control but reduced the finance bureau's ability to impose external control. For a better financial management it seems that China needs to find a certain balance between these two methods.

25.5   Governmental Procurement Reform

Before the recent budgeting reform, together with the pre-reform treasury management system that was decentralized in nature, governmental procurement was also decentralized, as has been mentioned before. Governmental procurement reform therefore aims to create a centralized governmental procurement system in the hope of incorporating competition, transparency, and economy into governmental procurement.

In 1995 the central government authorized several sub-national governments such as Shanghai, Guangdong, and Jiangshu to establish a new governmental procurement system. In 1996 the finance bureau of Shanghai, together with the health bureau, first applied the method of "open bidding and centralized procurement" to the purchase of hospital facilities. In 1998, under the guidance of the State Council, a procurement reform leading team was established. The MOF created a governmental procurement branch under its Budgeting Division, proclaiming the start of procurement reform in China. In the same year twenty-nine provincial governments and metropolitan governments began to experiment with governmental procurement. In 1999 the MOF formulated a series of regulations to define the scope of the procurement and management agency to improve procurement methods, bidding procedures, contracting process, procurement budgeting, payment for procurement, and the supervision of procurement. In 2000 the MOF shifted the governmental procurement branch from the Budgeting Division to the Treasury Division. In the same year, in all provinces, independent procurement branches were established within finance bureaus.

With the inception of departmental budgeting reform in 1999, spending departments were required to work out a procurement budget as a part of their departmental budgets. In 2001 the MOF explicitly required a separation of procurement management from the purchase process to create a check and balance mechanism in the procurement system. Meanwhile, all levels of governments conducted specific staff training for the implementation of governmental procurement. On January 1, 2003, the *Governmental Procurement Law* began to be executed, creating a legislative base for the separation of supervision from procurement (Anonym, 2003a, p. 14; Chu, 2003, p. 243; Xiang, 2001, p. 145).

There are several basic themes of the governmental procurement reform in China. First, the reform aims to create a centralized governmental procurement system to replace the pre-reform decentralized system (PPRCSUFE, 2003). The new system will put all spending departments' procurement under the management and control of the finance bureau. By doing so, spending departments will not purchase goods or services from the market by themselves. Therefore, the new system requires the establishment of a governmental procurement center at each level of government except at the township government. Moreover, a governmental procurement management division is established within the finance bureau to supervise the governmental procurement and to arrange payment whenever the procurement involves the fiscal direct payment. Of course, partially constrained by the fact that the fiscal direct payment system has not been completed, decentralized governmental procurements are allowed for certain areas. Therefore, the current reform is a combination of both centralized and decentralized procurement. Second, to increase the transparency of the governmental procurement process, open and competitive bidding is required to be used in the procurement. Meanwhile, other procurement strategies, such as competitive negotiation of procurement, are also used (Lou, 2003, pp. 243–247; MOF, 2003; Xiang, 2001, p. 145).

During the past several years, the basic framework of the governmental procurement system has been founded and great achievements have been witnessed. The amount of procurement expenditure within the new system has increased rapidly. The fiscal fund spent by the governmental procurement system was 3.1 billion in 1998. However, it was over 100 billion in 2002 (Anonym, 2003a, p.14; MOF, 2003). Moreover, the scope of governmental procurement has been extended. At the beginning, it covered only a few products, but, since 2000, services and big construction projects in addition to limited number of products have been purchased through the governmental procurement system (MOF, 2003). Figure 25.5, which presents the items purchased since 2000, further illustrates this change.

Moreover, pooled procurement has been the main method of governmental procurement. In 2001 66% of RMB 65.32 billion yuan procurement expenditure employed pooled procurement. In 2002 this percentage increased to 73% (MOF, 2002, 2003). Additionally, open bidding and competitive negotiation came to be the main rules used in the purchasing process. In 2001 53% of procurement used open bidding (MOF, 2002). Largely due to the use of pooled procurement and open bidding, procurement reform has resulted in saving public money. In 2001 the total

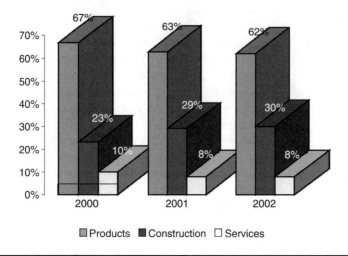

■ Products ■ Construction □ Services

Figure 25.5 Percentages of item expenditures in the total procurement budgetary expenditures. *Source*: MOF (2003, Table 1).

procurement budget was RMB 73.16 billion yuan. But the actual procurement expenditure was RMB 65.32 billion yuan, with a 10.7% saving rate. In 2002 the saving rate was 11.8%. At local level the saving rate is much more attractive. For instance, in Qingdao City Government, the saving rate was 15.3% in 2003, an increase of 30% compared to 2002. In Shengzhen City Government, the saving rate was 12.5% from January to November in 2003. During the past five years the average saving rate of Shijiazhuang City Government was 14.33% (Zhou and Huo, 2004; http://www.ccgp.gov.cn).

As Table 25.1 indicates, local governments have made more progress in governmental procurement reform than the central government has in terms of using pooled procurement and open bidding. As many officials interviewed state, the success of procurement reform in local governments is mainly due to two reasons. First, local governments started this reform earlier than the central government. Second, and more important, since the 1994 fiscal reform centralized a large amount of revenues in the central government while leaving most of the spending responsibilities at the local levels, local governments during these years have been facing severe fiscal difficulties. They therefore have a strong interest in governmental procurement reform, which has proved to be an effective way to save public money.

Although an increasing application of pooled procurement and open bidding is expected, there are several problems that China needs to solve before the goals of the reform can be completely realized. First, supervision

Table 25.1 Governmental Procurement in 2002 (Unit: RMB 1,000 yuan)

		Procure Budget	Procured Amount	Saving	Saving Rate (%)	Fiscal Direct Payment (%)	Pooled/Decentralized Procurement		Open Bidding(%)
							Pooled (%)	Decentral-ized (%)	
Total		11,354,167	10,096,000	1,258,166	11.08	-	73.00	27.00	48.04
Local	Total	8,954,632	7,880,121	1,074,510	12.00	49.74	82.64	17.36	48.88
	Products	5,491,480	4,909,404	582,076	10.06	53.32	85.84	14.16	41.94
	Construction	2,637,932	2,275,367	362,564	13.74	45.03	75.58	24.42	64.84
	Services	825,220	695,350	129,870	15.74	39.87	83.09	16.91	45.69
Central	Total	2,399,535	2,215,879	183,656	7.65	-	37.94	62.06	45.03
	Product	1,496,209	1,352,573	143,636	9.60	-	35.73	64.27	34.36
	Construct	822,207	786,194	36,013	4.38	-	42.66	57.34	65.93
	Service	81,120	77,113	4,007	4.94	-	28.74	71.26	18.89

Source: MOF (2003, Table 1).

over governmental procurement is still weak. As many budgetary officials point out, after the establishment of the pooled procurement, an effective internal control within the governmental procurement has become necessary. Without such control there will be a new kind of corruption that they term *ji zhong fu bai* (pooled corruption) since pooled procurement accumulates a large amount of procurement expenditure under the control of only one agency, meaning centralized decision-making. The weak internal control within the procurement system leaves rooms for corruption (Zhang and Hu, 2003). To prevent pooled corruption from happening, the reform requires creating an internal control mechanism by separating procurement management from the purchasing process within the finance bureau. However, it is questionable whether such mechanism is able to impose sufficient constraints on misbehaviors. It seems that a special and independent supervision agency is desirable.

Second, although the reform has largely improved the transparency of governmental procurement, there are still more steps China needs to take before achieving the goal of transparency. For instance, although open bidding is emphasized in procurement reform, its percentage to total procurement is still low. It was 53% in 2001, and dropped to 48% in 2002. At the local level there has been violation of the requirement of open bidding. For example, in the Jiangxi province, an investigation found that, among 951 projects required using open bidding, only 78% of them actually used open bidding in governmental procurement (Zhang and Hu, 2003). In the Sichuan province, in 2003, 24% projects violated the rules of opening bidding by not using, and 45.9% of them only partially used, open bidding although they were required to do so (Ma, 2004).

Third, it has also been found that the implementation of governmental procurement reform has been greatly constrained by the incompletion of the departmental budgeting reform and treasury management reform. For example, many spending departments do not seriously prepare their procurement budget while compiling their departmental budgets. As a result, during budgeting execution, spending departments usually have many additional procurement requirements for meeting the demands of their daily operations and for the provision of public services. Furthermore, since the treasury management reform is far from complete, only a small amount of procurement expenditures was paid through the fiscal direct payment system. That is to say, most procurement expenditure is beyond the monitoring of the treasury system. As Table 25.1 shows, in 2002, at the local level, only 49.74% of procurement expenditures were paid through the fiscal direct payment system. In some local governments the percentage was even lower. For example, in Jiangxi province, only 3% of procurement expenditures were paid by this system (Zhang and Hu, 2003).

25.6 Budgeting Democratization: The Rise of the Legislature

The rise of the legislature in the budgetary process has been conducted step by step. The 1982 Constitution stipulated that the congresses at all levels of governments were in charge of the supervision and approval of budget reports and budget execution of respective levels of governments. The *Budget Law* issued in 1994 provided a more detailed explanation of the legislature's power in supervising and authorizing budget compilation and execution (Liu, 1999). However, practices are very far from the institutional design. For many years, the legislature has been an insignificant participant in the budgetary process. The recent budgeting reform provides an opportunity for the legislature to play a more important role in the budgetary process. The legislature has been gradually transformed from a rubber stamp into an influential participant in budgeting decision-making. To some extent, the rise of the legislature in China's budgetary process would lead to budgeting democratization in China, which would contribute to political democratization in the long run.

25.6.1 The Rise of the Legislature in the Central Budgeting System

During the past more than two decades, China has witnessed the rise of the legislature in the political area. The rubber stamp image of the National People's Congress (NPC) has been shaken off accompanied with the growth of the NPC as a possible counter-balance to the party and executives. The rise of Chinese parliamentary power was due to the following reasons: (1) the development of economic reform enhanced understanding of the role of the legislature in providing laws and statutes to normalize and constrain both the government's and enterprise's behavior, and (2) the strong leadership of several chairmen of the NPC greatly improved the influence of the legislature, including Zhen Peng, Li Wan, Shi Qiao, and Peng Li (O'Brien, 1994; Tanner, 1994).

However, the legislature's power grabbing in the field of public budgeting was not as successful as expected before the late 1990s. For example, the first draft of the Budget Law contained the specifications that all levels of congresses had the right to supervise how their governments compiled and implemented their budgets. The representatives of congresses were empowered to ask all ministries for explaining their expenditure decisions. However, the final version of the Budget Law only granted local congresses some powers of supervision. While at the central level, only the general principles, such as the judicious use of funds, were endorsed to the NPC without any additional power on budgeting approval, execution, and supervision.

At the end of the 1990s, a breakthrough change was witnessed in the development of budgeting democratization accompanying the proceeding of the departmental budgeting reform which has provided detailed budgeting information of governmental departments to the legislature for examination. To improve its supervision over the governmental budgets, in 1998 the NPC established a Budgeting Committee (BC) as an assistant agency for the NPC's Standing Committee. The responsibility of the committee is to assist the NPC's Fiscal and Economic Committee (FEC) to supervise budget compilation, execution, and adjustment. In the following several years the BC became one of the two most important divisions within the Standing Committee of the NPC.

In June 1999 the NPC proposed to further reform the budgeting system, requiring the government to provide budgetary information in detail and emphasizing the importance of promoting budgetary transparency. Specifically, the NPC stated that the budgetary draft submitted should include expenditures of all the central government's ministries, expenditures for major programs, and the central subsides to local governments. It indicates that the NPC has been one of the driving forces of adopting departmental budgeting reform. In July 1999 the MOF formally proposed for creating a departmental budgeting system. In August 1999 the MOF discussed the departmental budgeting reform twice with other ministries with budgeting authority. Then the departmental budgeting reform proposal was submitted to and approved by the State Council. On September 17 the Central Political Politburo Standing Committee of the CCP agreed on the budgeting reform proposal submitted by the State Council. On September 20 the MOF issued the notification of departmental budgeting reform, requiring an adoption of the departmental budgeting reform at the central level. In December the NPC Standing Committee issued a "decision," proclaiming to stress legislative supervision of the governmental budget, clarifying the requirement of a department-based budget, and stating the time of submitting budget to the NPC, the contents of the budget submitted, and supervision methods. This year the NPC's FEC, with the assistance of the Budgeting Committee, became the budgeting supervision committee. The FEC required that the central government submit its budget, including 29 ministries, and that the departments' budgeting execution must be audited by the Ministry of Audit (Li and Liu, 2003, pp. 3–4; Yan, 2001).

Under the NPC's promotion, in 2000, departmental budgeting reform was experimented with in four central departments: the Ministry of Education, Ministry of Agriculture, Ministry of Science and Technology, and Ministry of Social Security. Moreover, in August 2000, for the first time, the State Council submitted two budgetary bills to the NPC's Standing Committee for legislative approval. One was to issue additional RMB 50 billion yuan national debt to invest in fixed asset. The other one was to ask for an adjustment of the 2000 central budget. In 2001, except for the Ministry of Defense, the Ministry of Security, and the central bank, all other twenty-six central ministries' budgets were included in the central governmental budget and were submitted to the NPC (Lou, 2002; Yan, 2001; Zheng, 2003, p. 68).

25.6.2 The Rise of the Legislature in Local Budgeting

At the local level, the rise of the legislature in the budgetary process was much more impressive. To fulfill the budgetary power that the 1982 Constitution granted to the legislature, local legislatures have passed many local statutes defining the legislature's supervision of governmental budgets. In 1988 the Anhui Provincial People's Congress (PPC) passed a statute defining the legislative supervision over the governmental budget. In the early 1990s more than ten provincial legislatures passed similar local statutes, such as Sichuan, Hebei, Sanxi, etc. At present almost all provincial legislatures have passed supervision statutes. Meanwhile, in the 1990s, to facilitate the legislative supervision of the use of extra-budgetary funds, some PPCs passed statutes over extra-budgetary funds (Liu, 1999; Yu and Chen, 2003).

Moreover, in the 1990s, especially after the passage of the 1994 Budget Law, there was an increasing trend for local legislatures to become a possible counter-balance to the government in the budgetary process. In Raoyang, Hebei Province, when the county legislature examined the 1995 governmental budget, it twice vetoed the county governmental budget because the budget failed to guarantee public school teachers' wages and had a fiscal deficit. As a result, it took more than three months for the governmental budget to be approved. This is an unusual phenomenon in Chinese polity (Liu, 1999). On May 25, 1998, when the Standing Committee of Hunan PPC received the audit report of budget execution of the 1997 budget, it found that the provincial Immigration Department had embezzled immigration funds to build an immigrant training center. The committee members were shocked by this change. After some investigations, twenty congress members proposed a bill concerning this event. In November the provincial government reported its investigation and specific solutions to the legislature's standing committee. The investigation revealed that the department illegally transferred RMB 43.23 million yuan to build luxury offices, hotels, and even entertainment facilitates (Xu, 2002). In 1999, in the second session of the Ninth Term of Henan PPC, twenty PPC representatives proposed a bill questioning the construction department's illegal use of housing procurement funds for public housing reform. After examining the response provided by the construction department, the representatives were dissatisfied with the department's explanation and required further reasonable justification. As a result the construction department had to promise to return the funds it had misused (Xu, 2002).

However, until the recent departmental budgeting reform, these legislative efforts were sporadic. Additionally, the legislatures in general did not effectively supervise the governmental budgets. The departmental budgeting reform makes it possible that the legislature can effectively supervise the governmental budgets, because the budgeting reform not only requires the government to submit its budget to the legislature for examination and approval, but also to provide budgetary information about each spending department. Local legislatures fully recognize the opportunity that the budgeting reform provides them and are actively involved in the reform. Now, almost all of the provincial legislatures have established budgeting branches to examine and supervise the governmental budget. Several provincial legislatures established a Special Budgeting Committee under the PPC, while most of them established a Budgeting Committee under the legislature's standing committee (mainly The Fiscal and Economic Committee). The distinction between a Special Budgeting Committee under the PPC and a Budgeting Committee under the PPC Standing Committee is that the former has the power of drafting and inspecting besides the power of supervising that the latter has. The creation of budgeting branch within the legislature, especially the creation of the Special Budgeting Committees, greatly increases legislative capacity in the budgetary process.

Among all local governments, Guangdong and Shenzhen might be the most impressive cases demonstrating legislative efforts in democratizing public budgeting in China. Before the departmental budgeting reform, Guangdong provincial government provided only a very simple and sketchy budget draft to the PPC for examination. Usually, the draft was one page in length. In 2001, for the first time, the governmental budget proposal submitted to the PPC included the information of seven departments' expenditures and revenues. In 2002 the departmental budgeting reform was extended to twenty-seven departments. In January 2003 Guangdong provincial government made a large stride in submitting to the PPC a budget draft as thick as 602 pages, including information on all departments' budgets (102 departments), and covering 97% of budgetary expenditures. Moreover, when the legislature examined the 2003 budget, some representatives of the PPC showed increasing interest in budgeting examination. For example, some of them openly questioned and attacked an expenditure program of a department's budget, which allotted more than RMB 10 million yuan to build a day care center for the department's employees. Other representatives, led by Ms. Xiaoyun Liao, a representative from a business company, proposed a revision bill to the budget draft, asking for inclusion of a basic health care insurance fund in the governmental fund budget. This is the first case in China's budgeting history that representatives proposed a revision bill to the governmental budget. The PPC gave serious consideration to this revision bill and had a special meeting to address this requirement. Finally, the legislature meeting concluded that the legislative was unable to include this bill in the agenda because the provincial legislature does not have the legal power to establish a new type of social insurance fund, which is under the authority of the central government (Anonym, 2003b).

The experience of Shenzhen in improving the legislature's role in the budgetary process has been more successful than that of the Guangdong provincial legislature. In 1995 the PPC's Standing Committee established a Planning and Budgeting Supervision Committee (PBSC), responsible for examining and supervising the governmental budget. In 2000 the PBSC was promoted as an independent committee, called the Special Committee for Planning, Budgeting, and Supervision (SCPBS). In Shenzhen, early in 1997, the legislature viewed the departmental budgeting reform as the "breakthrough point" to improve the legislature's role in the budgetary process. Therefore, during the past seven years, the legislature has been a driving force to implement and improve the departmental budgeting reform. To make the legislature's supervision effective, the legislature has made the following innovations.

First, it attempts to normalize the structure, format, and contents of the budget, and to promote budgetary transparency. For example, to improve the allocation efficiency and budgeting transparency, it requires the implementation of comprehensive budgeting principles, combining the budgetary revenues and extra-budgetary revenues together in the budgeting decisions. The SCPBS also emphasizes the link between the budget appropriations and the work the department has to accomplish. To facilitate the examination of the budget by the representatives, the legislature requires that when government compiles budget proposals, it must make the budget easy for the representatives to understand, for example, including written description of the programs and the expenditure objections (GDPPCBSO, 2003).

Second, due to the limitation of staff size in the SCPBS, the legislature invented two methods to conduct the examination of the governmental budget during the process of budget formulation: (1) *Selective Supervision.* In the process of budget formulation, before the budget is submitted to the PPC, the budget is submitted to the PPC's Standing Committee for preliminary examination. However, since the legislative representatives serve the legislature part time and the legislature's full time staff is limited, it is impossible for the legislature to conduct a comprehensive and in-depth budgetary examination in the preliminary examination. To solve this problem and to conduct an effective budgetary supervision, Shenzhen's legislature has decided to adopt a strategy of selective supervision; that is, during the preliminary examination stage, several departments that citizens are most concerned with (such as the Police Department, the Environment Department, and the Education Department) will be selected as the targeted departments whose budgets will be examined comprehensively and in depth by SCPBS. (2) *Specific Topic Supervision.* During the annual People's Congress Meeting, to conduct an effective budgetary examination, the PBSC organizes the representatives by important topics and issues that might have great impacts on citizens' lives and social welfare. Usually, the representatives who hold fiscal expertise and are familiar with the operations of these relevant departments are selected to have a face-to-face discourse with the heads of the government's finance bureau and relevant departments (GDPPCBSO, 2003).

Third, Shenzhen's legislature is also actively involved in the budgetary execution. For many years, a persistent problem in budgetary execution in China has been the delay in authorizing approved budgetary appropriation to the departments. To solve this problem, the legislature in Shenzhen requires that the governmental finance bureau authorize the budget approved by the legislature to spending departments within one month after the annual congress and then report the authorization to the legislature.

Besides this, the legislature has succeeded in solving two persistent problems in Chinese budgetary execution. The two problems are: (1) The allocation of revenues over the revenue forecast is always beyond the control of the legislature. The government tends to report to the legislature after these revenues have been appropriated to spending departments. In certain cases, the government even chooses not to report to the legislature; and (2) The budgetary adjustment is frequent and arbitrary. And, more seriously, the government tends to make adjustments to the approved budget without asking for the permission of the legislature in advance.

During the past few years, Shenzhen's legislature has made great efforts to strengthen the legislature's supervision in these two areas. The legislature requires the government to ask the legislature's permission before it makes any budgetary adjustment and budgeting decision on over-collected revenues. During the past five years, the legislature have vetoed and changed some of the government's budgeting decisions in these two areas, which is quite seldom in Chinese budgeting history. For instance, during the past several years, for the over-collected revenues, the legislature discovered RMB 8.16 billion yuan illegal expenditures and vetoed and changed eight governmental programs involving revenues as much as RMB 1.9 billion yuan. The legislature also established rules on the use of the over-collected revenues, for example, setting in advance their expenditure objections.

In the budgetary execution, the legislature also adopts the strategy of selective supervision to oversee the budget execution of important departments with a large amount of public expenditure and important public programs. The legislature requires that the government's investment programs be submitted to the legislature for examination, and only programs approved by the PPC to be included in the governmental budget. Moreover, the legislature asks the audit department to conduct a performance audit of important programs that citizens most concern with or that involve a large amount of expenditures, and then report the audit results to the legislature (GDPPCBSO, 2003). Because China uses internal government audits,[10] the effectiveness of such an auditing strategy has been questioned. However, in the Shenzhen case, with the legislative efforts, the audit department has proved to be an effective and cooperative agency in overseeing the budget execution. For example, on December 22, 2003, according to the audit report of the 2003 budget execution, there were four large programs involved in fiscal losses, misappropriation, and waste. This resulted in an "audit storm" in Shenzhen (Lei, 2004), also making the government feel it is going through a tough period. It is quite an unusual phenomenon in Chinese polity.

25.6.3   Impediments Ahead

Despite these promising progresses in budgeting democratization, many impediments are on the way for the legislature to become a capable and autonomous actor in the budgetary process. The first impediment is related to the attitude and support of the CCP. It should be noted that these budget reforms related to the legislature are carried out in a Party-State where the CCP is the most powerful political actor in the polity. To transform the legislature into an autonomous budgetary actor means that the legislature will be an autonomous political actor as well. Therefore, as our interviews reveal, certain conservative CCP politicians are reluctant to go further in moving toward the direction of budgeting democratization, for example, giving more power to the legislature and opening the governmental budget to citizens. Budgeting democratization within the Party-State polity has unavoidable limitations.

Second, because of the CCP's reservation in granting budgetary autonomy to the legislature, the legislature's capacity has been limited. Although budget reforms have increased the legislature's organizational capacity in budgeting supervision, the legislature is still far from transforming itself into a capable budgeting participant in examining and overseeing the governmental budget because the legislature's personnel, budget, and organizational structure are tightly controlled by the CCP. Although the recent reforms contributed to the establishment of an independent division within the legislature responsible for examining the budget requests of the government and overseeing the budgetary execution, the staff size of such an agency is still very small in most provinces, usually around five. As many officials in the legislature have complained, it is impossible to conduct effective budgetary supervisions with such a small number of employees. Moreover, the legislature does not have its own audit agency; thus, it has to rely on the government's audit department to conduct auditing. Even though the experience of Shenzhen suggests this may workable, it does not appear to be true in other local governments.

25.7 Conclusion

It seems unusual that it is not until the late 1990s that China started to modernize its public budgeting and financial management; twenty years after its economic reform. However, this is not hard to understand considering that the reform of budgetary process requires a spontaneous change of political system. Fundamentally, although China is being transformed from an "owner-state" (Campbell, 1996) into a "tax-state" (Schumpeter, 1918) in terms of revenue extraction since the 1978 economic reform, that is, the state is now spending the money of "others" (taxpayers), the political system has not been reformed to reflect taxpayers' wills. Therefore, China's politicians and bureaucrats have been free from the pressure that they must efficiently spend taxpayers' money and spend with public accountability.

To some extent, the recent budgeting reform can be viewed as efforts to create a modern budgeting system with three main goals, i.e., allocation efficiency, operation efficiency, and public accountability. It is expected that allocation efficiency will be realized by the implementation of the departmental budgeting reform, operation efficiency by the treasury management reform and governmental procurement reform, and public accountability by budgeting democratization. Putting it differently, to achieve these goals, the budgeting reform aims at establishing a new budgeting system that is control-oriented, emphasizing two kinds of budgeting control: administrative control within the executive budgeting and legislative control over the government. The former is realized by (1) centralizing the power to allocate fiscal resources in the hands of the finance bureau, that is, to transform it to be a real "central budgeting office"; and (2) creating an external control over the departments' spending behaviors, that is, to putting the departments' spending behaviors under the fiscal and administrative control of the finance bureau. The latter is realized by increasing the legislature's power in the budgetary process. It is therefore reasonable to conclude that, basically, China is moving toward the "Budgeting Era" using Caiden's (1978) terms,[11] as western countries were during the 19th and early 20th centuries.

However, the attempts on those two types of budgeting controls have not been equally emphasized. The recent budgeting reform in China concentrates more on enhancing the administrative control within the executive budgeting than the legislative control over the government. Therefore, witnessed accomplishments of the reform mainly lie in the improvement of administrative control. To the students of China's political and budgeting systems, this shall not be a surprising finding, because to improve the legislative control requires a fundamental change of China's political process and a redistribution of the political power, which is still not an attractive road for the CCP holding the paramount power in Chinese polity so far.

Lastly, China's budgeting reform also greatly benefits from contemporary budgeting reforms of other countries, especially western countries. Besides its control-orientation, the recent budgeting reform also exports budgeting innovations appearing in the past several decades. ZBB is one of such budgeting innovations. Recently, as our interviews suggest, budgeting reformers in China are discussing the possibility of introducing performance budgeting, public hearing system, and even accrual accounting into China's budgeting system.

Notes

1. The year of 1978 is the starting point of China's overall economic reform, the so-called Reform and Opening (RAO). The purpose of RAO was to establish a socialist market economy. By doing so, budgeting and financial management in China made some significant adjustments to serve the transition from a planned economy to a market economy.

2. Shenzhen and Dalian are not provincial units in the Chinese administrative system. However, they are two of the sixteen cities granted with special financial and panning authority (*jihua danlie*) and hence with fiscal and planning authority as other provincial governments. The date of interviews was as follows: Hubei (August 2003), Guangdong (September, December 2003; April 2004), Shenzhen (January 2004), Hebei (January 2004), Dalian (December 2003).

3. Actually, in a province, there are around seven such political officials.

4. Based on our interviews.

5. From interviews conducted in Hubei in August 12–20, 2003.

6. In TBB, to resolve the game playing and antagonism between the budgeting office and spending departments, the budgeting office gives a firm ceiling to the departments for their budget requests at

the beginning of the budgetary process. Spending departments are then required to keep their requests under this ceiling. If the departments' requests are above this ceiling, the budgeting office will return the requests to the departments and ask them to revise. The revisions are accepted only if they come under the ceiling. Of course, as early as the 1920s, TBB had appeared, much earlier than ZBB (Rubin, 1998, p. 2206).

7. From interviews conducted in Hubei in August 12–20, 2003.

8. The representative departments are selected based on the types of public services that they provide since the attitudes of their businesses and workload are the key factors to decide the demand for operating expenditure. Further, their expenditure will be calculated at quota standards and will become an important reference in deciding other departments' operating expenditures with similar functions.

9. Based on our interviews in these provinces.

10. In China, the audit department belongs to the executive branch, rather than working under the legislature's delegation.

11. According to Caiden (1978), the moving from Pre-budget Era to Budget Era is characteristic with enhancing administrative control and accountability.

References

Anonym. (2003a). Major events of governmental procurement reform. *China Logistics & Procurement, 3*, 14.

Anonym. (2003b). *Yang Cheng Wan Bao*. Guangzhou, P. R. China, January 21, 2003.

Caiden, N. (1978). The pattern of budgeting. *Public Administrative Review, 38*, 539–543.

Campbell, J. L. (1996). An institutional analysis of fiscal reform in post-communist Europe. In John L. Campbell and Ove K. Pedersen (eds), *Legacies of Change*, pp. 137–176. New York: Aldine De Gruyter.

Chen, W. Y., Chen, H., Zhang, X. H., Chen, D. Z., Lin, C., and Yu, B. L. (2002). A research on reforming expenditure management institution. In Zhejiang Province Association of Public Finance (eds), *Exploring on Hot Topics of Fiscal Reform*, pp. 100–116. Beijing, P.R. China: Economic Science Press.

Chu, M. (2003). Governmental budgetary execution in China. In Lou Jiwei (eds), *Government Budget in China: Institution, Management, and Cases*, pp. 207–254. Beijing, P.R. China: China Financial & Economic Publishing House.

GDPPCBSO (Guangdong Provincial People's Congress's Budgetary Supervision Office). (2003). An investigation report of Shenzhen metropolitan's budgetary examination and supervision. *Budgetary Supervision Information*, *5*, 1–14.

Ko, C. (1959). China's Budget during the Transition Period. New York: U.S. Joint Publications.

Lei, J.Q. (2004). The story of audit storm in Shenzhe. *South Weekend* (Guangzhou, P.R. China, January 15, 2004).

Li, N. (2000). Financial minister on financial spots. *Beijing Review*. Beijing, P. R. China, March 15, 2000.

Li, P., and Liu, S. (2003). *Theories & Practices in Departmental Budgeting*. Beijing, P. R. China: China Financial & Economic Publishing House.

Liu, L. (1999). A retrospection and prediction of local People's Congress budgetary supervision. *People's Congress Study*, *10*, 6–10.

Liu, Y. (2000). Looking for budgetary reform in Hebei. In Chinese Association of Fiscal Study (eds), *Creating a New System for Budgeting Management*, pp. 135–150. Beijing, P. R. China: Economic and Science Press.

Lou, J. (2002). Reforms of government budgeting management system and accounting in China. In Xiaorui Chen and James Chan (eds), *Government Budgeting and Accounting Reform*, pp. 41–66. Beijing, P. R. China: CITIC Publishing House.

Ma, J. (2003). Zero-based budgeting in China: Experiences of Hubei province. Paper presented at The 13th Association of Budgeting & Financial Management, September 16–20, 2003, Washington, D.C.

Ma, X. (2004). Seven phenomena of violating regulations in large construction projects in Sichuan province. *Construction Daily*. Beijing, P. R. China, January 13, 2004.

MOF (Ministry of Finance, P.R. China). (1997). *Zero-based Budgeting*: Economic Science Press.

MOF (Ministry of Finance, P. R. China). (2002). Governmental procurement expenditure reaches RMB 65.3 billion yuan in 2001. *Information Report* (6).

MOF (Ministry of Finance, P. R. China). (2003). Governmental procurement expenditure is over RMB 100 billion yuan in 2002. *Information Report* (5).

O'Brien, K. (1994). Chinese People's Congresses and legislative embeddedness: Understanding early organizational development. *Comparative Political Studies*, *27*, 1, 80–107.

Panzhihua Finance Bureau. (2003). The preliminary achievement of Panzhihua treasury direct payment reform. *Sichuan Finance* (Chengdu, P. R. China), *5*, 55.

Patashnik, E. M. (1996). The contractual nature of budgeting: A transaction cost perspective on the design of budgeting institutions. *Policy Science*, *29*, 189–212.

PPRCSUFE (Public Policy Research Center of Shanghai University of Finance and Economics). (2003). *A Report of China's Fiscal Development*. Shanghai, P. R. China: Shanghai University of Finance and Economics Press.

Pyhrr, P. A. (1973). *Zero-base budgeting: A practical management tool for evaluation expense*. New York: John Wiley and Sons, Inc.

Rubin, I. (1998) Target-based budgeting. In Shafritz, J. M. (ed), *International Encyclopedia of Public Policy and Administration*, pp. 2203–2208. Colorado: Westview Press.

Schumpeter, J. A. (1918/1991). The crisis of tax state. In Richard Swedberg (ed), *Joseph A. Schumpeter: The Economics and Sociology of Capitalism*, pp. 99–140. Princeton: Princeton University Press.

Tanner, M. S. (1994). The erosion of Communist Party control over lawmaking in China. *China Quarterly, 138*, 381–403.

Teng, X. G. (2003). *The Fee for Tax Reform and Local Fiscal Institution Building*. Beijing, P. R. China: Economic Science Press.

Tong, D. Y. (ed). (2001). *Unified Management by Single Account*. Beijing: Chinese Finance & Economy Press.

Tseng, W., Khor, H. E., Kochhar, K., Mihaljek, D., and Burton, D. (1994). *Economic Reform in China*. Washington, D.C.: International Monetary Fund.

Wang, J. (2000). Constructing new mechanism for budgetary management. In Chinese Association of Fiscal Study (eds), *Creating a New System for Budgetary Management*, pp. 199–207. Beijing, P. R. China: Economic and Science Press.

Wang, J. (2001). The history and future of fiscal expenditure reform. In General Office, Ministry of Finance of P. R. China (eds), *Optimization of Fiscal Expenditure Structure and Expenditure Efficiency*, pp. 19-29. Beijing, P. R. China: Economic Science Press.

Wang, L., Zhang, S. Z., Chen, Q. Y., and Huang, Y. X. (2003). *Fiscal Treasury Collection and Payment Management*. Chengdu, P. R. China: Southwest Fiscal & Economic Press.

Wang, Y. J (2002). Treasury system restructuring and public financial management reforming. *Fiscal Studies, 4*, 11–14. Beijing, P. R. China.

World Bank. (1990). *China: Revenue Mobilization and Tax Policy*. Washington, D. C.: World Bank.

Xiang, H. (2001). *China's Fiscal Management*. Beijing, P. R. China: China Financial & Economic Publishing House.

Xu, S. (2002). Local People's Congresses adopted question power for twenty years. The Center of People's Congress and Legislature at College of Law of Beijing University. Retrieved from http://www.ecpcs .org/zxcx_d.asp?id=136.

Xu. S. N. (2003). A Study on China's centralized collection and payment treasury system. Journal of Shanghai Finance & Economy University, 5, 2:10-18.

Yan, J. (2001). A memorandum of the management of budget by law in Chinese National People's Congress. *Law Rule Daily*. Beijing, P. R. China, March 15, 2001.

Yu, G., and Peng, Chen. (2003). The status of provincial People's Congresses made budgetary supervision statutes. *Chinese People's Congress*. Beijing, P. R. China, *9,* 12–14.

Zhang, Q., and Hu, Y. (2003). The operation situation and reforming ideas of Jiangxi provincial governmental procurement. *Enterprise Economy.* Beijing, P. R. China, 8, 70–72.

Zhang, T., and Teng, X. (2002). Causes, achievements, and future of reforming China's fiscal treasury management system. *Fiscal Studies, 9,* 2–9.

Zhang, X., Yuan, X., and Wang, W. (2001). *A Study of Departmental Budget Reform.* Beijing, P. R. China: Economic Science Press.

Zheng, J. (2003). *A Study on Chinese Government's Reform of Budgetary Institution.* Beijing, P. R. China: Chinese Fiscal and Economic Press.

Zhou, L., and Huo, Q. (2004). The improvement of the governmental procurement system in Shijiazhuang city government. *Hebei Daily.* Shijiazhuang, P. R. China, January 30, 2004.

ZPAPF (Zhejiang Province Association of Public Finance). (2002). *Exploring on Hot Topics of Fiscal Reform.* Beijing, P. R. China: Economic Science Press.

Index